I0121823

Diasporic Constructions of Home and Belonging

Diasporic Constructions of Home and Belonging

Edited by
Florian Kläger and Klaus Stierstorfer

DE GRUYTER

ISBN 978-3-11-057781-5
e-ISBN (PDF) 978-3-11-040861-4
e-ISBN (EPUB) 978-3-11-040869-0

Library of Congress Cataloging-in-Publication Data
A CIP catalog record for this book has been applied for at the Library of Congress.

Bibliographic information published by the Deutsche Nationalbibliothek
The Deutsche Nationalbibliothek lists this publication in the Deutsche Nationalbibliografie;
detailed bibliographic data are available on the Internet at http://dnb.dnb.de.

© 2015 Walter de Gruyter GmbH, Berlin/Boston

This volume is text- and page-identical with the hardback published in 2015.
Printing and binding: CPI books GmbH, Leck
∞ Printed on acid-free paper
Printed in Germany

www.degruyter.com

Table of Contents

Home-Making: Space, Virtuality, Ideology

Narratives of Belonging: (Hi-)stories, Boundaries, Trajectories

Florian Kläger and Klaus Stierstorfer
Introduction

Diaspora studies has developed in recent years from disparate enquiries into diasporic phenomena in political science, anthropology, history, geography, and
literary and cultural studies. Its emergence as a full-fledged transdisciplinary research field has been predicated to a large degree on an interest in questions of
dispersal and mobility. As Robin Cohen has shown, the field is currently in a
state of consolidation: while complex phenomena such as deterritorialization
and globalization cannot be neglected, notions of home and the inflection of
homeland remain important discourses.[1] This volume shares the focus on phenomena of home-making and the articulation of a sense of belonging in diasporic contexts. Contributors from a broad range of disciplines discuss a variety of
historical and geographical instances of diasporas, exploring the methodological
and theoretical challenges posed by the subjects of 'home' and 'belonging.' All
contributions acknowledge that our globalised world is inescapably shaped by
international migration, with large numbers of individuals, groups or even nations on the move for a wide variety of reasons. This phenomenon creates massive challenges to nation states and civil societies, culturally, economically and
politically, but it also creates opportunities and new perspectives to an unprecedented extent. The impetus behind this volume has been the desire to spell out
some of the historical, cultural, political, sociological and legal dimensions of
this predicament, and to assist in theorizing the ramifications of a transdisciplinary approach to diaspora. While truly transdisciplinary, rather than interdisciplinary diaspora studies are a desideratum and perhaps will remain so for some
time to come, the present volume suggests ways in which students of diaspora
from various disciplines can engage in a dialogue over specific issues. Hence,
the scope of this volume narrows the traditional focus of diaspora studies by
zooming in on the diasporic meaning(s) of home and diasporic constructions
of belonging.

Current academic discourse offers at least two major ways of conceptualizing diaspora, both providing intriguing perspectives on home and belonging.
The first, centrally influenced by the historical experience of the Jewish people,
is based on a number of criteria suggested by scholars such as William Safran.

---

1 Robin Cohen, *Global Diasporas: An Introduction*, second ed. (New York: Routledge, 2008): 2.

His essay "Diasporas in Modern Societies: Myths of Homeland and Return"[2] is widely accepted as a seminal text marking, as Robin Cohen emphasizes in what has itself become another classic text in the field, "the beginning of contemporary diaspora studies."[3] According to Safran, diasporas are groups of people dispersed from a place of origin to different locations. Shaped by experiences of alienation in the new environment, these scattered individuals are linked by the hope of returning to an (idealized) homeland ('myth of return'). Arguably, Safran's static conceptualization is a model of victimization that regards members of diaspora groups as uprooted individuals bereft of their identities and "oppressed by an alien ruling class."[4]

The work of James Clifford, Paul Gilroy, Stuart Hall, and Homi K. Bhabha is representative of a paradigm shift within this diaspora discourse. What emerges from such texts as James Clifford's "Diasporas,"[5] Paul Gilroy's *The Black Atlantic*[6] or Stuart Hall's "Cultural Identity and Diaspora"[7] is a dynamic concept that no longer focuses on the idea of a return to a concrete geographical place called home. According to Clifford, it is a common history of dispossession and the fight for social and political equality that binds together individuals within the diaspora.[8] Engaged in an ongoing process of negotiation, diasporic identities are no longer constituted as subjects of nation states but as powerful agents in various cultural exchanges. Thus, the diasporic experience, as Stuart Hall puts it, is not defined "by essence or purity, but by the recognition of a necessary heterogeneity and diversity; by a conception of 'identity' which lives with and through, not despite, difference; by *hybridity*."[9] In *The Location of Culture*, Homi K. Bhabha likewise asks the reader to "think beyond narratives of originary and initial subjectivities,"[10] discarding the idea of pure authentic cultural identities and focusing our attention on statements, forms and systems created at the intersection of cultures. *The Location of Culture* explicitly refers to the role of post-colonial subjects and migrants who live "in-between" different nations.

---

2 William Safran, "Diasporas in Modern Societies: Myths of Homeland and Return," *Diaspora* 1.1 (1991): 83–99.
3 Cohen, *Global Diasporas*, 4.
4 Robin Cohen, "Diasporas and the Nation-State: From Victims to Challengers," *International Affairs* 72:3 (1996): 507–520, 508.
5 James Clifford, "Diasporas," *Cultural Anthropology* 9.3 (1994): 302–338.
6 Paul Gilroy, *The Black Atlantic: Modernity and Double Consciousness* (London: Verso, 1993).
7 Stuart Hall, "Cultural Identity and Diaspora" [1990], in *Theorizing Diaspora: A Reader*, ed. Jana E. Braziel, Anita Mannur (Malden, MA, Oxford et al.: Blackwell, 2003): 233–246.
8 Clifford, "Diasporas," 306.
9 Hall, "Cultural Identity and Diaspora," 244.
10 Homi K. Bhabha, *The Location of Culture* (London: Routledge, 1994): 2.

Standing at the border, those individuals are perceived as agents of change who are involved in the transmission of cultural traditions and able to transform well-established ideas.

One could argue that the dynamic interpretation of diaspora is part of a new conceptualization of space that the humanities and social sciences have embraced since the end of the 1980s. In the globalized world, space is no longer seen as an unchanging factor that determines cultural behavior but as a product of social exchange. The so-called spatial turn in diaspora studies manifests itself in a number of different concepts of space, for instance in Avtar Brah's 'diaspora space' as well as in Arjun Appadurai's 'global ethnoscapes.' Appadurai's model helps us understand how members of a diaspora create a feeling of home that is no longer bound to a geographically fixed territory. In *Modernity at Large*, Appadurai focuses on the cultural dynamics of a phenomenon called deterritorialization – the dissolution of borders and boundaries.[11]

According to Appadurai, the term deterritorialization not only refers to obvious examples such as international money markets, but also to diaspora groups transcending the borders of specific territories and fixed identities. Appadurai creates the neologism 'ethnoscapes' in order to capture this idea of "the changing social, territorial, and cultural reproduction of group identity."[12] The term 'ethnoscape' refers to the amalgamation of different peoples from various locations and social, cultural, and political backgrounds, alluding to the flexibility of those border-crossing movements. In addition, for Appadurai the local level is of utmost importance because it is not just a place in which global developments are reflected or have effects. Rather, the idea is that global interconnectedness is achieved through face-to-face contact and with the help of local actors.[13]

In *Cartographies of Diaspora*, Avtar Brah focuses on the diasporic construction of home both in its geographical and its metaphorical sense. Like Clifford, Gilroy and Hall, she unfolds a diaspora concept that is not grounded on the desire to return to an authentic origin. At the same time, however, she argues that members of diaspora groups are characterized by a craving for home as a "mythic place." In Brah's view, home is "a place of no return, even if it is possible to visit the geographical territory that is seen as the place of origin."[14] Her theory of

11 Arjun Appadurai, *Modernity at Large: Cultural Dimensions of Globalization* (Minneapolis: U of Minnesota P, 1996): 48–65. See also Waltraud Kokot, "Culture and Space: Anthropological Approaches," *Ethnoscripts* 9.1 (2007): 15–18.
12 Appadurai, *Modernity at Large*, 48.
13 Daniel A. Yon, *Elusive Culture: Schooling, Race, and Identity in Global Times* (Albany: State U of New York, 2000): 150.
14 Avtar Brah, *Cartographies of Diaspora: Contesting Identities* (London: Routledge, 1996): 180.

diaspora is no longer based on the dichotomy of majority/minority, as she repudiates the historical and ideological implications of the terms. Instead, she embeds her concept of diaspora in a multi-axial understanding of power. Furthermore, her focus is not so much on the initial dispersion of any diasporic group but on their later arrival and settlement, their negotiating the concept of 'home' within their new host community. She introduces the idea of a 'diaspora space' based on "the intersectionality of diaspora, border, and dis/location as a point of confluence of economic, political, cultural, and psychic processes."[15] In contrast to a diaspora, the diaspora space is composed of both migrants and the "indigenous" population, who are closely intertwined and in constant negotiation of "boundaries of inclusion and exclusion, of belonging and otherness, of 'us' and 'them'."[16] Thus, any analysis of the construct of diasporic home and belonging inevitably has to take into account this close relationship between the different groups that inhabit the diaspora space and the practices generated within these groups.

Informed by Appadurai's important suggestion that the concept of home is no longer necessarily linked to a geographically fixed territory, this volume offers analyses of various forms of constructing home and belonging in different diaspora spaces. In their various ways, and across a wide interdisciplinary range, a number of contributions to this volume study diaspora spaces 'bottom-up' on micro-levels (be they specific social groups, individual texts, or other material formations) in order to examine the interrelatedness of 'local' realities and global and deterritorialized structures. As Khachig Tölölyan has stressed, practitioners of diaspora studies must always be mindful of the dual movement of diasporic identity, "that amazing complexity, which is the product of diasporic efforts to construct, represent and discuss the quotidian life of local diaspora communities while also attending to the demands of engagement with other diaspora communities and the homeland":

> The paradoxical combination of localism and transnationalism, the fierce aspiration to achieve economic and social success and the willingness to sacrifice for the community and the homeland, indeed the oscillation between loyalty and skeptical detachment that characterizes the performance of diasporic lives, is in my view an example of the way everyone, including nationals, will have to live in an increasingly heterogeneous and plural world.[17]

---

15 Brah, *Cartographies of Diaspora*, 208.
16 Brah, *Cartographies of Diaspora*, 209.
17 Khachig Tölölyan, "Diaspora Studies: Past, Present and Promise," *International Migration Institute Working Papers* 55 (2012) <http://www.migration.ox.ac.uk/odp/pdfs/WP55%20Diaspora%20studies.pdf> (acc. 22 June, 2014): 12–13.

Overall, then, contributors to the volume are united by a transnational approach to diaspora studies that is attentive to the dynamic interdependence between rooted subjectivity (on a local level) and global identity.[18] In keeping with dynamic conceptualizations of diaspora such as these, contributors to this volume examine the ways in which diasporics come up with new concepts of home and belonging, enter into a constructive dialogue with host societies, (attempt to) participate in political discourses as equal partners, and produce innovative cultural artefacts that challenge static concepts of race, national identity, citizenship, gender, age, and other categories of collective identification.

Theory has been an abiding inspiration for diaspora studies, and we believe that it constitutes the prime means for carving out a truly transdisciplinary approach to the field. Explorations of key concepts and issues, and the varied responses they have elicited from a range of disciplines thus structure the present volume, rather than an approach guided by geographical, historical, or national contingencies. Hence, the volume opens with a section offering reflections on the meanings of its central terms by eminent and in more than one case, indeed, inaugural practitioners of the field, sketching their suggestions on directions that diaspora studies might take in the future.

The second section focuses on diasporic self-fashioning. How, contributors ask, have identities been 'made' and 'performed' through practices of commemoration across a range of historical and geographical instances? From early modern Catholic Englishwomen on the European continent to UN peace-keeping forces in present-day Africa, chapters in this section explore the significance and articulation of a shared memory and the resulting exercise of agency for identity fashioning, both on an individual and collective level. They pursue questions after the ways in which diasporics commemorate and identify with their homeland and maintain contact with it, but also after the ways in which the category of 'home' is transcended and re-conceptualized in various diaspora spaces. As individuals and collectives construct 'homes' in the past, and as they variously attempt to act on these constructions, they encounter challenges and opportunities for self-making that offer instructive insights into the dynamics of diaspora.

With regard to the ideological ramifications of diaspora's spatial conceptualization, contributions to the third section examine the geography and topology of 'home' and 'belonging'. How are 'home spaces' turned 'homely', how is dia-

---

18 Janet Wilson, "Introduction," *Rerouting the Postcolonial: New Directions for the New Millennium,* ed. Janet Wilson, Cristina Sandru, Sarah Lawson Welsh (London: Routledge, 2010): 17–21, 18.

sporic identity expressed through such spaces, and how is it impressed through the ideological regulation of space? Ranging from explorations of architectural design and the legal definition of citizenship to the rhetorical and literary construction of home spaces, these chapters track the ways in which space comes to be charged with ideas and meanings.

The narrative construction and re-construction of home and belonging in a diasporic context is the focus of the fourth section. Analyses of storytelling across media – from medieval poetry to contemporary novels and films – investigate how identities are made, unmade, and remade by means of fictionalizing. Often with a focus on the translation of biographical experience into fiction, these chapters consider the role of literary practice, but also literary theory for diaspora studies. However, we also believe that it is not enough to focus only on the creative possibilities of diasporic spaces. A number of contributions also acknowledge, in various ways, what Brent Hayes Edwards would call moments of *décalage* within diasporic communities: certain points of misunderstanding, certain gaps that cannot be bridged, certain differences that cannot be translated, among diasporic communities throughout the world.[19] An account of diasporic constructions of home and belonging concerned only with celebrating their creative potential would be as flawed as one exclusively attacking the suffering and wrongs they are often prompted by, or entail. The ways in which identities are constructed and performed, through narrative, as based on gender, faith, age, culture, among others, is conceptualized in these case studies as a contribution to the literary study of diaspora.

In sum, this research agenda reflects a procedural approach that acknowledges diasporas as global phenomena embedded in a complex web of relations and economic conditions. One main objective is to investigate how the concept of diaspora is constituted by diasporics' cultural agency and social relations, expressed in everyday life through terms such as identity, culture and mobility. The aim of the volume is, then, to suggest the dynamics of concepts of home and belonging in diaspora studies by identifying, mapping, categorizing and quantifying their practices, relations and social structures that emerge and are reproduced within the transnational diaspora space.

The volume, as it is, has multiple origins and many trajectories of development and growth. At its core, it is an outcome of the Marie Skłodowska-Curie Initial Training Programme on "Diasporic Constructions of Home and Belonging" (CoHaB), in which fourteen researchers and numerous academics at the partner institutions of the University of Oxford (Faculty of English and COMPAS), SOAS

---

19 Brent Hayes Edwards, "The Uses of Diaspora," *Social Text* 19.1 (2001): 45–73, 64–66.

at the University of London, the University of Northampton, the University of Stockholm and the University of Mumbai with the associate partners of CASII (Centre for Advanced Studies in India), the Migration Policy Group in Brussels and members of the European Immigration Lawyers' Network (EILN) were coordinated at the Chair of British Studies in Münster to collaborate in the field of diaspora studies with a specific interest in the concepts of home and belonging. Several of the chapters included here had their early test run as papers within the network or at one of its events, notably its international conference in Münster in September 2013. Much has been added and developed since, and all members of CoHaB have put in their share, strengthened by an advisory board as select as committed, consisting of Homi K. Bhabha, Avtar Brah, Ceri Peach and Khachig Tölölyan. The volume only came to fruition with the aid of an indefatigable team of support to which the editors feel deeply grateful: most notably Markus Nehl, M.A., to whose conceptual prowess and knowledgeable input many of the more felicitous turns of phrase in this project are indebted; to Annika Merk, M.A. and Marlena Tronicke, M.A., who not only provided valuable academic input but helped to shape the progress of the project at large by facing all administrative challenges (of whom there were many) with outstanding professionalism; to Svenja Pauly, Laura Schmitz-Justen, and Lea Vogtt for help with the formatting; and to Chris Wahlig, who has supported everyone throughout on the secretarial side. All shortcomings in the setup of this volume remain, of course, the responsibility of the editors.

Münster, July 2015

'Home' and 'Belonging' in Diaspora Studies Now

Homi K. Bhabha in Interview with Klaus Stierstorfer on "Diaspora and Home"[1]

K.St.: Professor Bhabha, you have spent the greater part of your life in research on people on the move between and beyond the confines of cultures, nations and all those other contexts that traditionally are thought to generate a feeling of home and belonging. In a sense, you are thus a specialist on cultural "misfits," those who do not fit into the readily available categories of civil societies. Your special area is not so much the home as the "unhomely" or even the "uncanny," as Freud's famous term of *das Unheimliche* is generally translated.[2] In fact, you have yourself been referred to as "Mister In-Between,"[3] and I may therefore start this interview on a personal note in consideration of the fact that you have just arrived here in Münster, Germany, not as originally planned, from Cambridge, Massachusetts, where you hold a famous Chair at Harvard University, but from Mumbai, your place of birth, where a family emergency had taken you at short notice: how much have you perceived yourself as being such a 'misfit' and in what ways has this aspect of your biography influenced your research?

H.Bh.: This is a very interesting, rather reflective question. So let me start with what you say at the very head of the question, as my being a specialist on cultural "misfits." I think I would phrase it somewhat differently. I think what is interesting about culture itself is that it is often in its most interesting manifestations in a state of the "misfit"; to fit the different bits or parts of a particular cultural apparatus or experience together always creates a problem because the parts do not necessarily form a whole. And people regret that (*e pluribus unum*). Wouldn't it be great if everybody, whatever cultures, all fit together in one big whole. But it seems to me that the most interesting and most important ethical and political problems have emerged precisely because cultures are not a seamless whole. There are discordant elements; there are divisive elements; there are divergent elements. Let me be, on the one hand, a little more precise about this, in political terms, and then let me give you a sense of how I think one can

---

1 The interview was originally conducted at Schloss Wilkinghege, Münster, Germany, on September 22, 2013.
2 Homi K. Bhabha, "The World and the Home," *Social Text* 31/32 (1992): 141–153, 141.
3 Interview, Christian Höller and Homi K. Bhabha, "Don't Mess With Mister In-Between," qtd. in Karen Struve, *Zur Aktualität von Homi K. Bhabha: Einleitung in sein Werk* (Wiesbaden: Springer VS, 2013): 193.

theoretically look at the problem. In political terms the "misfit" is often the minority. And yes I have been very interested in processes and practices of minoritization. What I mean to say by this is that it's not that I'm only interested in national minorities or religious minorities or political minorities; I am interested in those. But more than that, or as interested as I am in specific minority situations, I am interested in the whole process by which cultures, groups, societies produce a structure of minoritization. Sometimes it is a structure of alterity; sometimes it is a structure of stereotopy; sometimes it is the reflection of a hegemony; sometimes it is the promise of heterogeneity. So, this whole process of minoritization as part of the very nature of cultural ethics, cultural politics, and cultural semiosis is the ill-fitting nature of the cultural, if you like, the culture as a misfitting apparatus. If that is the more direct, political aspect of this problem of culture as a misfitting apparatus, the philosophical or conceptual metaphor I would use is the famous image of the broken vessel which Walter Benjamin uses in his essay on translation: he says that the pieces of a broken vessel fit together not because they are the same as each other but they fit into each other in all their differences.[4] It is that which gives the vessel its strength, and therefore I would say to you that what you have described as the cultural "misfit" is always the problem of cultural translation. So culture is a translational reality, and to that extent it depends upon its moving parts, its often contradictory, asymmetrical moving parts, its tensile strength. After all, to put it very simply, the question "What is your cultural identity?" is unanswerable. However, if somebody asks you about a particular cultural practice with which you're in line, you can answer that question. It's almost as if the very nature of the cultural is metonymic in that sense.

Now, you want me to answer this in terms of my own particular history, but I feel I need to lay the grounds conceptually before I do this. It's very interesting because Parsis were amongst the most prominent creators of urban modernity in India. Nowadays they have a very small public profile. It is forgotten, however, that amongst the early political leaders emerging in British times to represent Indians as a whole, if you like, Parsis were very prominent. So Parsis are themselves part of this asymmetric, interstitial group. A very small minority, neither Muslim nor Hindu, nor Christian – the three major faiths in India – yet Parsis

---

4 "Fragments of a vessel which are to be glued together must match one another in the smallest details, although they need not be like one another. In the same way a translation, instead of resembling the meaning of the original, must lovingly and in detail incorporate the original's mode of signification, thus making both the original and the translation recognizable as fragments of a greater language, just as fragments are part of a vessel" (Walter Benjamin, *Illuminations: Essays and Reflections* [New York: Schocken, 1969]: 78).

were able to play in the interstices; they were able to bridge those differences to their advantage, sometimes in a creditable way, and sometimes less creditably, as they became the middle man in India. But Parsis as a culture have various missing parts. At the heart of the faith-based culture, there is tremendous orthodoxy. As part of the life experience or the "life world," to use a Habermasian term, the life world of the Parsis is hugely cosmopolitan. Parsis are a minority and yet they've made a disproportionate contribution, particularly in Delhi and Bombay, to urbanity in India and to modernity. Some of the leading businessmen, the leading merchants, the leading professionals – doctors, solicitors, accountants – were Parsis. So if you like, my own experience of the misfitting nature, and yet the efficacy of that misfitting dissymmetry or asymmetry is that it's not a paralyzing condition. It can be a condition of various, varied contingencies and interventions. That's the whole experience, I think, that comes from my own, from the Parsi community.

K.St.: To put it provocatively, Parsis in a sense of being or seeing themselves as a diasporic group could still be seen as one of the diasporic groups who have taken on almost a sort of national representative function.

H.Bh.: Well I wouldn't quite say they are. Yes and no. I mean, in the political field they are not at all. Now they have no national profile; they haven't had that for a long time. In the business world, yes they do have a certain kind of national profile. In terms of institutions, they don't particularly, in terms of the academic world, they used to, but now they don't. You know, it's a very mixed picture.

K.St.: And their Parsi affiliation is not particularly highlighted, is it? Famous Parsi authors would not immediately be marked as Parsi writers. They would be writers in Indian English, theorists in Indian English, and it is only then when the Parsi background may come in. They certainly don't seem to me like a particularly 'fundamentalist' group.

H.Bh.: No. Absolutely not. However, there is a small but growing body of Parsi literary production, you know, which states the Parsi experience. It's a very fascinating experience, and a very powerful one. It's not a very representative experience in the context of India or the world, but it is to me a very intriguing experience because it is really so much about interstitial negotiations, and today just after I've seen some of your own postdoctoral fellows and students, who referred to themselves as a network, what is more important in a network than the interstitial relations? What Hannah Arendt called human "inter-est,"[5] that which is between people and brings them together. So it's not that the group is larger than its parts, it actually is its parts. It's partiality that creates that network. And I think Parsis are part of this. I mean, they have always been a kind of networking society. And now of course, if you read a journal like the main organ for Parsi life, it's called *Parsiana*, published in Bombay, you turn the pages to find it is such a network. The Parsi community in diaspora sees itself as an effective network, bringing together all the continents – the Parsis in Australia, Canada, of course Toronto very prominently, the United States; Africa. So really I think Parsis are a network, and the Parsi community is about the contingent and interstitial nature of the contemporary world.

K.St.: That almost begins to sort of broach on the next question I was going to ask you about more the sense of belonging, less the sort of diasporic dispersion part. When you talk about a sense of belonging, a sense of home, and you add that kind of your own itinerary, you know, from India to England to the US, and now the world, how much change do you think a person can take, in that sort of leaving home, rebuilding home, leaving home? Is there a point when the "not being home" becomes a part of the institution of home? You know that becomes a sort of diverse sort of floating buzzwords, like nomadism, and you know you begin to feel having a cosmopolitan existence. Is there a point when that switches over from, you know, making home here, making home there, and doing the same over and over again, to sort of switching around on a mental level and beginning to have a different kind of existence, almost, in terms of making home?

H.Bh.: I particularly like this question when it is formulated as you did a moment ago; you said, "you know, how much displacement can an individual take, or a group take?" Let me try and answer it from my own experience. I think the very term "home" has two aspects of it, just as a concept. One – something to do with the normalized, the naturalized, the inevitable, the original. It's there – the "thereness" of your existence, even more than the "hereness" of your existence. It is always there; this is my home. I understand this landscape. I know these people. I know the language, and so on. So that's one important concept. And the other, it seems to me, is the kind of Conradian idea that home is what you return to. So, there are these two moments of temporality, these two narrative moments – coming out of the home and somehow allowing yourself to imagine,

---

5 See Hannah Arendt, *The Human Condition* [1958] (Chicago: U of Chicago P, 1998): 57–58.

whether you can or you can't, that you can go back: so emergence and return are complicit with the concept of home.

Now it seems to me that those of us who move homes often, though not always, follow a certain kind of narrative pattern. By that I don't mean that everyone who moves on follows a certain narrative structure. All I mean is that in my movements, there is a narrative. There are reasons why I move; there are the losses of it, of where I moved from, and the gains of where I move to. So, it is part of a process of choice and judgment. And that sense of choice and judgment is lost very often with generalized terms like cosmopolitan or the other one you mentioned – planetary – or nomadism. [**K.St.:** Gilroy talks about "conviviality."] Or conviviality. You know, I think what is lost is the fact there are certain times in which you make a decision, you make it for certain purposes; there are pluses and minuses. So there is a narrative plotting, and it is not just an endless back-and-forth. Once you have got that narrative, and I think most people do, then you can move back into the nodal points. And you know why you're doing that.

I know I go to India regularly, because primarily my family is there. If my family were not there, I don't know whether I would. But my family *is* there. I have major intellectual interests. Out of that I have a body of people that I go to see. And my life now is lived: other than my work commitments, my lecturing commitments send me all over the place, but generally it's lived between Bombay and Boston. Those are the markers of home. Now, there was a time when it was much more triangulated, having spent many years in England, owning a home I love in London; I would move between there and Boston, or Chicago. I love being in America; my work, I find, is most productively supported there. That's part of the narrative. I moved there because my work is productive, I have many colleagues. Now I have many close friends. I have family connections. But initially it was a decision made for a certain purpose. And out of that came a "homeyness," if I might put it. So it's not as if you go and think, "I want to make my home in America." You go for certain specific reasons. These reasons, these choices are difficult to make, these reasons have been deliberated, and then you go. And I used to go at the end of the academic term. We would always go to England for a while, and then we would go to India. Circumstances change. Now I go to England more for specific events that I'm invited to do. But because my mother is in her late 80s and she's alone, we no longer go and spend a long time in London, which we always did because we've got very old and close friends there; I've got family there. Now London is not as it had been the primary home; I spent more years in England than I had in either the States certainly, or in India. Now I no longer go there in that "homey" way. I go there to give lectures, for work, to meet people. Does it mean then, that in my existential sense of belonging, London has ceased to exist as a home? No! It has not ceased to exist, but because of certain decisions, and because of certain circumstances, it is not the same kind of destination.

So I'm suggesting that we tend to talk theoretically about diaspora, about cosmopolitanism. We tend to use these general terms which have encrypted in them a kind of ceaseless notion of movement, of nomadism. But in fact that's not the way life works. I'm saying there are very distinct forms of narrativity, choices, judgments, which evaluate certain locations, which create a home around certain locations. My natal home is in Bombay. My home that came out of my work is in the United States. London used to be an in-between space of a certain home. But that changes. So I think there is a continual trans-valuation, or a changing. That depends very much on decisions you make.

K.St.: So, your idea would not be so much that, to take your metaphor or your concept of a narrative of relocations, a sheer iteration in that narrative could actually cause a breakdown in that narrative that entirely changes the quality of what you feel home is, the quality of the home concept so much. But it remains, as you describe it, a dynamic process all along.

H.Bh.: Yes, because what is being iterated or articulated around the concept of home are certain needs, certain interests, certain passions and affects, which actually then create that life-world, that existential comfort that you associate with home. But it seems to me that we have, to use a word I very rarely use, "essentialized" iteration, in terms like diaspora, or movement, or migration. You know, it seems as if everybody were migrating now. That is exaggerated. There are life worlds that are made for specific reasons, and they have many geographical and temporal locations. And that, I think, is both the trajectory of home, and the continual tension of home.

K.St.: I'd like to take this biographical approach a little bit further towards your work and your thinking, as it sort of runs through your very substantial and impressive life's work now. Much of the postcolonial thinking, specifically, you have become famous for originally drew on the kind of Theory with a capital 'T' which became prevalent throughout the 1980s and has been losing ground perhaps again from the 1990s onwards. In fact, in *The Location of Culture*, you put up an eloquent defense of the uses of Theory in your essay "The Commitment to Theory."[6] From hindsight today, as literary and cultural studies are leav-

---

6 Homi K. Bhabha, *The Location of Culture* [1994] (London: Routledge, 2008): 28–56.

ing the so-called Theory Wars at least behind, would you re-define or re-adjust the place of Theory in your readings, especially where they address postcolonial or diasporic concerns? Has that changed?

H.Bh.: I think I'm happier answering this as a more general question about the place of the theoretical. My own turn to theory came not because I had available to me a whole lot of theoretical possibilities when I was at university. When I went to university, when I was at Oxford, in the mid- to late-70s it wasn't at all like that as an undergraduate. Not at all! All the exciting courses were on feminism and psychoanalysis. But I think my attraction to theory, then and now, is not that different. My attraction to the theoretical is primarily the possibility of being able to confront what is for me, at first, a problem whose parameters I am uncertain about. I am uncertain about the epistemological notion of the parameters; I am uncertain about the historical notion of the parameters; I am uncertain about the philosophical notion. When I confront a problem, whatever nature it is, and I absolutely can put it in no frame, or it has shattered the frames that I have brought, that's when I turn to theory. People have always looked at my work as being extraordinarily difficult to read, and they think that I have a *penchant* for difficulty. My passion for difficulty is expressed in my love for poetry, not in my attraction to theory. If you really want something difficult, read poetry; read Rilke, if you really want something problematic. But for me the theoretical is a way of understanding how to at least make a representation of, or put a frame around, a problem, which breaks down your notion of scholarly propriety, competence, disciplinary determination and so on. To that extent I was always criticized for not having affiliations to any one particular theorist. I told them for me the creative move was to see a problem and then to take what I needed from a particular theory – syncretic, hybrid, call it what you like – to take it and transform it in a conversation with other theoretical assumptions or theoretical traditions. So in a way, I'm not even sure that what I was doing was simply a theoretical enterprise, although it is often represented as such. The question you posed makes me think that what I do, and what I did, is much more to establish a protocol for dealing with some problematic, neglected area, some problem that people had not confronted or had marginalized. It was much more to bring things, in the Hegelian phrase, into "a regime of recognition."[7] That's what I was trying to do. Which is why I've been attracted not sim-

---

7 Charles Taylor, "The Politics of Recognition," in *Multiculturalism: Examining the Politics of Recognition*, ed. Amy Gutmann (Princeton: Princeton UP, 1994): 50; see also Bhabha, *Location of Culture*, 157.

ply by theoretical elaborations, or theoretical exemplification which doesn't attract me at all. What I have been attracted by is to somehow put a frame on something that could have been missed, left invisible. And somehow by putting a frame around it, that thing gains importance. Therefore, for me, theory is about a kind of empowerment, rather than exemplification. The question came up again today, and comes up again and again: in your class amongst your CoHaB-cohort somebody said,[8] "you know, we were working with your theory, and then we looked at a book, an example, and it somehow didn't fit." And I said, "Well exactly! How boring would it be if it did?!" I've been asked again and again to write histories of theory, to do anthologies of postcolonialism, and I've always resisted that because I am not interested in codifying what has already been named. I am interested in trying to name what has *not* been named!

K.St.: I really like your phrase of theories functioning as to bring things into recognition. Would that also apply to texts? Is that how texts become literature, possibly with a capital "L," when you apply theory? They become literature?

H.Bh.: Well, you need that: the bringing to recognition. And when you say "the bringing to recognition" you blur the distinction between the object of analysis, or the object of attention, and the constituting conditions of intelligibility. So the theory/practice distinction, as far as I'm concerned and to put it bluntly – never really existed.

K.St.: You've begun to think about the legal aspects of diasporic situations in your recent work. Your Harvard Website announces a forthcoming book of yours with Columbia University Press under the title "The Right to Narrate," and you have given a keynote lecture at a conference in Hanover "On Writing and Rights."[9] Do you expect lawyers and legal scholars to play a more prominent part in defining and negotiating the place of diasporic groups vis-à-vis majority cultures and traditions? And does law have things to learn from literature (or vice

---

8 The interview was held immediately after a colloquium with doctoral students of the Marie Curie Initial Training Network "Diasporic Constructions of Home and Belonging" (CoHaB), funded by the European Commission as part of the Marie Curie Actions under the Seventh Framework Programme FP7 – People. For information on the network, see <itn-cohab.eu>.
9 *Our Common Future, The interdiscipliniary congress for a cross-generational dialogue about issues of our common future* (Hanover/Essen, November 2–6, 2010) <http://www.ourcommonfu ture.de/en/> (acc. October 17, 2014).

versa) in tackling these complicated issues? Hence, do we need a law and literature movement in diaspora studies?

H.Bh.: Yes, very much so. You know people always think that I only do theory, but no history; the sessions with your students in Muenster brought this up a great deal, and we talked about various formations of what a diasporic legal aspect or perspective would be. We talked about the fact that there are these bodies of international civil society, the Rome Declaration,[10] the criminal courts, the truth and reconciliation commissions. We might see these in many ways as being postcolonial or postnational, as bodies of knowledge, as archives, as well as institutions. It absolutely surprises me that we don't have a more vivid and a more vital movement in this direction because there is no body of people whose very internal souls have been marked by the law as refugees, migrants – economic or political –, those who are documented or undocumented. The very soul-making of these groups becomes a legal issue.

One of the things that also interests me is the way in which the diasporic impacts on the concept of citizenship – and here you have the legal, the cultural aspect, and a social or political aspect. Very significantly for those of us interested in diasporic studies, the notion of cultural citizenship as a form of political agency is extraordinarily important, and yet an area that is still often only descriptively presented and not conceptually, historically and theoretically laid out, which is one of the things I am trying to do. You know, the approach of analyzing law as if it were literature and using the hermeneutic methods of literary analysis to read the law is, frankly, somewhat passé and not very interesting. I think what is much more exciting is to begin to see how some of the concepts, some of the materials with which we are involved as literary scholars, scholars of culture – the issue of time, the issue of temporality, on the one hand, the issue of civility, the issue of ethicality on the other – how these issues play out in the particular political personae that get created through migration and diaspora. And what do I mean by this? For instance, it seems to me that, although there is so much discussion these days about global citizenship, or national citizenship,

---

10 "On September 23, 2013, representatives of seventeen EU states met in Rome to condemn racist insults against Cécile Kyenge, the Italian Minister for Integration [...]. After the meeting, the EU representatives signed the Rome Declaration urging more commitment and European action to promote diversity" ("Rome Declaration," <http://www.integration.ie/Website/omi/omi webv6.nsf/page/Racism-eudevelopmentsRomeDeclaration-en> [acc. August 4, 2015]). See "Sub-Committee alarmed at the spreading of racism and intolerance in Europe" (October 1, 2013), *Parliamentary Assembly* <http://www.assembly.coe.int/nw/xml/News/News-View-EN. asp?newsid=4664&lang=2&cat=135> (acc. June 7, 2015).

transnational citizenship, those ways of thinking about belonging still participate in a discourse of permanence: whether it's between two nations, whether it's across the world – the notion of citizenship is, in a sense, about the possibilities of establishing yourself; it's the politics of recognition. And I'm beginning to think that maybe the most important way we can rethink how we belong in the world is to take, ironically, the short temporal span of the refugee.

When you see "refuge," or "taking refuge," at the heart of what it would be to construct a polity of citizenship, you see that moment which militates against citizenship as a long-term element of community building. But if you take the concept of the refugee and see that as the central political practice, then, I think, you really begin to understand that we need to generate these terms of global subjectivity, transnational citizen, and so on. Maybe it's not the permanence, but the impermanence of the status of the refugee that will be most helpful to us. Because the refugee condition makes the most stringent and severe demands on the national community or the "world community" to recognize the global *right of hospitality* which is at the heart of human survival itself. It is 'survival' rather than 'sovereignty' that should frame the ethical and political values that provide us with a workable concept of the good life lives with others – side by side solidarity with conditions of alterity.

K.St.: What you see sounds much more radical than Seyla Benhabib's position as presented in her 2004 monograph *Rights of Others*.

H.Bh.: Benhabib's book, I think, is really about the philosophical problem of alterity. For me, the contrast is not primarily citizenship versus alienage; the other side of citizenship really is the refugee. The former is about long-term, the latter is about short-term perspectives. We need to conceive citizenship in a more open, more liberal, more diverse, more empathetic way. I think we need to change the very value-based time scale to create and think of the refugee, in that short moment, as the one who does not belong and who maybe provides the representative time frame for re-thinking this problem. The refugee thus becomes the model and the basis on which we should think about belonging.

Ihab Hassan

Extraterritorial: Exile, Diaspora, and the Ground under Your Feet

Abstract: The following offers autobiographical reflections on the materiality of home in the body and the idea of language as an extraterritorial home, with particular reference to the events of the so-called 'Arab Spring' and its aftermath. In dialogue with his past and possible self, Hassan considers how poverty and violence fuel diaspora and exile. He concludes that for him personally, the focus of his diasporic identity has been and continues to be, "not on the sorrows of departure but on the challenges of arrival."

We all live in an age of diasporas, are part of their perplexity and pain. Wave after human wave breaks over continents and recedes, leaving friends stranded in faraway places, leaving relatives in rock-pools of time. This, at the very moment that the Internet is creating diasporas of its own while undermining the diasporas of old. Let's follow the ironies and paradoxes of this turbulent subject, where history and autobiography tangle, and none can foresee the outcome.

Consider a playful etymology of key words in the title of this volume. 'Diaspora' originally meant 'scattering' and 'dispersal', but also 'sowing', and from seeds things may grow. 'Home', like its stronger sister-word, *Heimat*, alludes to settling in – say pitching your tent after a long trek across the steppes of Asia – and suggests as well haunting a place. As to the term 'construction', which I always disliked because of its mechanical ring, well, its origins hint strain in piling up things. (We can understand this strain; it's not easy to build a home of immaterial bricks or stone; ask the bombing brothers who blew up the Boston Marathon.)

Now vault over millennia, from the roots of natural languages to the algorithms of the digital age. What can diaspora and exile mean in a time of virtual borders, multiple identities, and global states? From Tokyo to Timbuktu, people roam in cyberspace. From the favela of Rio to the slums of Calcutta, people can project their plight on the entire world. Hence the talk in China about cyber-visas to cross the Great Firewall. It seems, then, that we all live in two worlds at once, one physical, the other virtual, as Eric Schmidt and Jared Cohen say in *The New Digital Age*.[1] Yet, such is the obduracy of the human element that the virtual world now mimes the real world with all its greed, passions, and strife. Alas, no utopias await us in Web 2.0.

---

1 Eric Schmidt and Jared Cohen, *The New Digital Age. Transforming Nations, Businesses, and Our Lives* (London: Vintage, 2014).

I touch on these extremes of the subject because the discourse of diaspora, which abounds with conflicting tendencies, is also charged with grief, anger, nostalgia, and fraught with prejudices, including my own. It's a bum rap. Can you wonder that I often fall back on personal experience in order to ground my discourse, or at least lay its assumptions bare? But let's be candid: What convincing personal experience can I claim? I never wandered in the Texas or Arizona night, looking for a shallow crossing or a breach in the iron fence; I haven't bobbed like human jetsam in the Indian Ocean while sharks circle around; and I've never suffered from the torturer's red hand. Yet I feel that the topic of this volume is closer to all of us than we realize, close to our body, our very skin. This includes billionaires who belong to the 'business diaspora' – as it's called – and nabobs who buy up citizenships at whim.

Let me now explain why I say 'body', why I say 'skin.' Some years ago, responding to the agonies of migrations around the world, the Louvre Museum sponsored an ambitious, multi-disciplinary event, called "The Foreigner's Home." Toni Morrison served as its presiding spirit. She chose Géricault's painting of 1819, "The Raft of the Medusa," as an icon of the program. For her, the distraught sailors struggling to stay afloat provided a haunting – perhaps also melodramatic – image of the millions who wandered the earth "like nomads between despair and hope, breath and death."[2]

Imagine for a moment the tempestuous sea, seething with monsters; imagine the splintered, overloaded raft and shredded sails, tossed about, without destination or aim; imagine them symbolizing our collective destiny. What kind of politics or ethics can sustain such wrecked lives? What kind of art or faith? Morrison's answer is startling: look to the individual human body, she says, the choreography of feelings and bones. In a sea of distress, she said, "you have the body in motion and you have the obligation of seeing the body as the real and final home."[3]

As it happens, I visited Paris again, a few months ago. In the Jeux de Paume Museum, a stone's throw from the Louvre, I witnessed a droll and deeply unsettling exhibition of the Albanian-born artist, Adrian Paci. One series of photographs, covering an entire wall, is entitled "Home to Go." The catalogue reads:

---

2 Toni Morrison, quoted in Alan Riding, "Rap and Film at the Louvre? What's Up With That?", *New York Times* (November 21, 2006) <http://www.nytimes.com/2006/11/21/books/21morr.html> (acc. March 3, 2015).
3 Qtd. in Riding, "Rap and Film".

In this series of photographs taken from a performance, the artist appears in his underwear, carrying on his back a fragment of a rooftop whose V-shaped form brings to mind the wings of a bird. A poignant metaphor for his personal experience as a migrant, "Home to Go" also conveys its oppressive weight. These images also evoke pictorial tradition by reviving the themes of the Carrying of the Cross and the fallen angel.[4]

Such bland words, of course, fail to convey the pain and humor of the work, its grimaces and contortions, its ethos of clownish despair, rendered in details of knotted rope and hairy flesh. But the most poignant detail is visible only in a video, displaying the image of the artist's two children, permanently tattooed on his chest, as he wandered, back and forth, from continent to continent before finally settling in Italy, where he now lives.

The video concerns my present argument less than the tattoo because the latter recalls Morrison's resonant phrase, "the body as the real and final home." The body, that is, not only as a social or economic entity, and not only as the refuge of exiles who sew their lips and of artists who mutilate themselves – including their genitals – but also as the ground of both intimate and historical experience. The body as the substance of exilic memory and recreated identity, of silent autobiography if you wish, as it feels the dry or muddy ground under the migrant's feet. *Of course, the body!* Do we not think of physical features, textures of hair and colors of skin, when we think of migrants of the world?

Now, despite my references to art, I speak of the body somewhat abstractly. As Proust says, "What intellect restores to us under the name of the past, is not our past. In reality, as soon as each hour of one's life has died, it embodies itself in some material object, as do the souls of the dead in certain folk-stories..."[5] In Proust's case, it was the famous madeleine (actually "some slices of dry toast"); in my more prosaic case, it may have been the smell of soot and grease emanating from the smokestack of a departing ship.

In truth, my exilic – really self-exilic – story is banal. A year after the Second World War ended, I boarded a Liberty Ship in Port Said called the *Abraham Lincoln*. (That augured well.) As I waved goodbye to my father from the boat deck, I felt the capstans grind, the engines rumble, and soot from the smokestack flecking my nostrils. *Old Abe*, as my shipmates called her, pushed off the pier and

4 "Adrian Paci, Lives in Transit, 26 February – 12 May 2013," *Jeu de Paume Concorde* 101 (Paris: Jeu de Paume, 2013) <http://www.jeudepaume.org/pdf/PetitJournal_AdrianPaci-GB. pdf> (acc. March 3, 2015).
5 Marcel Proust, "Contre Sainte-Beuve," in *Marcel Proust on Art and Literature: 1896–1919*, trans. Sylvia Townsend Warner, 2nd ed. (New York: Carroll & Graf, 1997): 17.

glided past the imperial statue of de Lesseps, bound for New York. But a long-shoreman's strike diverted the ship to New Orleans. Weeks of rolling and pitching, of boredom, anxiety, and hope ensued. Then, on a damp September day, I found myself slipping into the underside of the American Dream through bayou channels infested with alligators and poisonous snakes.

I never returned to Egypt. People ask why, why not for even a short visit, but all my answers seem to me chatter and chaff. Obviously, I had no wish to return. Yes, yes, but why? My childhood was no more happy or unhappy than the average childhood – I can swear to this on a stack of Korans – yet my later constructions of it instilled in me some indelible aversion. Again, why? Families everywhere are battlefields – recall Greek tragedies, if you please – and family reunions often prove to be occasions for subtle payback more than full-throated celebration – think of all those Christmas and Thanksgiving dinners, turning sour. Anyway, I walked away from family and native ground. Is this so unnatural, so freakish?

True, small, ominous signs of alienation hovered about me in Egypt. For instance, the only subject I failed in school was Arabic. Beggars on the streets of Cairo often addressed me as *Khawaga* (Mr Foreigner). And to this day, I can't tell you the colors of the present Egyptian flag, only of the royal standard of my childhood, green with a white crescent cradling three stars. But why this perverse aversion of mine when fellow Americans flock every winter to the temples or beaches of Egypt, in search of ancient glory and the unblinking sun? What black construction had I made of Egypt in the caverns of my mind, my heart? To this day, the answers seem to me haphazard and dubious. For instance, I could say that I was romantic in my youth, inebriate of horizons. Or that I became fixed in a childish fantasy of changelings. Or that I saw no future for myself in Egypt as the son of a land-owning civil servant. Or that I sought my 'identity' – a concept more porous than a sponge – and found it out of Egypt, in a foreign language, in English, to be exact. Would such answers satisfy you?

Well, it's no big deal, really: human beings have been always addicted to self-creation – we are all rattletrap fantasy machines.

But I want to shift now from partial memoir to insecure theory. I want to dwell on an idea crucial to this paper: the idea of language as an extraterritorial home. Theodor Adorno once said: "The fluency and clarity which Heine appropriated from current speech is the very opposite of native 'at-homeness' (*Geborgenheit*) in a language. Only he who is not truly inside a language uses it as an instrument."[6] Only he who is not truly inside a language uses it as an instrument. This is the quality George Steiner, in his work titled *Extraterritorial*, adduces to Beckett and Nabokov.[7] (He could have adduced it to himself.)

I shudder at the thought of inviting a comparison with two titans of literature. Yet the point stands: legions have found a provisional home in English, the digitized lingua franca of the world. But I don't allude only to the weary phenomenon of globalization. I refer, rather, to the uncanny power of a particular language to penetrate the human psyche, to inform values and invade dreams. Indeed, the Eros of Language is no less cunning than his raunchy sibling, the Bowman of Love. Here's autobiographical proof. (Yes, I must switch hats again.)

Though I speak every language with an indefinite accent, I won my first prize – a lacquered note pad – in English. I was seven or eight. Since then, I've read more books in English than in any other language, and I've felt viscerally closer to Shakespeare than to the great Arab poets of the *Mu'allaquat* (or Suspended Odes), their lofty verses presumed to have hung from the walls of the holy K'aba since pre-Islamic times. Un-riddle that: an Egyptian boy enamored of the language of Kitchener and Cromer! The example, by no means unique, applies to many writers of different kinds. Whether they recall a happy childhood – like Salman Rushdie – or an edgy one – like Doris Lessing – they often end by making their home in a world elsewhere. As Lessing put it: "I am always half somewhere else. I have just been to Zimbabwe for five weeks and I am certainly not Zimbabwian. But more people in the world are like this now."[8] More people – not just writers – recognize themselves as hybrid, yet many more adhere to an idea of ethnic purity – the most dangerous idea in the world, as Rushdie said.[9] Many more still cling to an Edenic vision of their birthplaces. It's no use reminding them of the facts of their past, of the wretchedness and oppression they endured in their native lands, since nostalgia can skew memory and trump facts. This is understandable: Human beings will always seek to transcend the pain and insecurities of the present in an imagined future (called Paradise) or a fictive past (named Eden).

But there's another aspect to language, an aspect less verbal than evolutionary. I refer to the primal adhesive instinct, once so crucial to human survival,

---

6 Theodor W. Adorno, "K" [1963], in *Language and Silence*, ed. George Steiner (New York: Athenaeum, 1967): 175–187, 185.
7 George Steiner, *Extraterritorial. Papers on Literature and the Language Revolution* (London: Faber and Faber, 1968).
8 Doris Lessing, *African Laughter. Four Visits to Zimbabwe* (London: HarperCollins, 1992).
9 Colin MacCabe and Jeff Adams, "Interview. Salman Rushdie Talks to the London Consortium About *The Satanic Verses*," *Critical Quarterly* 38.2 (1996): 51–70, 65.

now a collective menace. The "mass-soul," as Elias Canetti called it, perpetrates atrocities around the globe.[10] It defines in black, never in white, the Other, that same Other who is part of ourselves, and without whom we do not know who we are. I mean the Other who also lives in the pronouns of language, especially that dread pronoun, Them. Call it the beast in the prison house of language, call it the mother tongue – the adhesive instinct abides.

Alterity, however, can assume strange forms. As Arjun Appadurai has argued persuasively in his book, *Fear of Small Numbers: An Essay on the Geography of Anger*, the Other may express itself in an irrational antagonism to small minorities – like the Copts in Egypt – groups that would seem unthreatening to an impartial eye. For in the age of fractured globalization, where rhizomes prevail instead of roots, and where nations are less defining than ethnic, religious, or civic communities, the monopoly of violence slips out of the grip of the state. (I hear Max Weber turning in his grave.) The result is a "surplus of rage." This new brutality, Appadurai maintains, is not about old hatreds and primordial fears, really; rather, it "is an effort to exorcise the new, the emergent, and the uncertain, one name for which is globalization."[11]

In view of these obscure anxieties, how can immigrants, strangers, expect civility from their hosts? How can Arabs, for instance, who are inclined to a quick and shallow pride, feel at home in foreign places, even without suicide bombers on the ground and fiery planes in the sky? It's all too easy for them to become defensive, resentful, hostile, as their hosts give them the cold shoulder or look at them askance – if not worse. It's all too easy for everyone to recover the brute in oneself.

I can testify to my own rudeness in a ludicrous incident that betrays my reconstruction of the country I left behind. It happened this way. For decades after I left Egypt, I avoided my former compatriots. One day, however, shortly after the spectral Arab Spring, the phone rang in my study in America's Dairyland. When I picked up the receiver, I heard a garbled voice speaking Arabic. I explained that I did not understand Arabic (which is 83 percent true). The voice rose a few decibels and said: "Consulate of the Arab Republic of Egypt. Just a minute, sir, just a minute." Hurried whispers in the background; the voice faded and returned: "Just a minute, sir. We find the Consul General." More minutes passed and I began to wonder why I still held that phone. I had no rela-

---

10 Elias Canetti, *Auto Da Fé* [1935] (New York: Random House, 2011): 411.
11 Arjun Appadurai, *Fear of Small Numbers: An Essay on the Geography of Anger* (Durham, London: Duke UP, 2006): 47–48.

tives in Egypt; I wanted nothing from the Consulate; and I had learned that the world holds you by the throat of your needs. Before I could hang up, though, I heard a plummy voice, the Consul General himself: "*Sabah el khair*, Mr. Ihab. We call to ask for a small favor." Pausing for effect, he added: "We want proof that you are alive." "I beg your pardon?" I said incredulously. "A bank in Cairo wants proof positive that you're still alive. They don't tell us why." "You're talking to me, aren't you?" "Yes, but how do we know you are you and not someone else?" The Consul said this pleasantly, chuckling, a joke between friends. I hung up, instantly regretting my boorishness. Why couldn't I bring myself to laugh with the Consul? Obviously, I was considered effectively dead in Egypt, and this did not please me. I laughed mirthlessly: the joke had been on me. By hanging up on the Consul, I had expressed not only my rejection of Egypt but also my anger at Egypt's rejection of me. Thus in exile we both construct and are constructed by our former homes.

Again, I looked irritably at the silent phone in the room. Did something else lurk in that object? Could it be disappointment at the consequences of Tahrir Square, a slow-burning despair of change in the Arab world, with its long history of affliction and civic abuse? Or was that "disappointment" merely a mask of some unknown specter in my past? The questions regressed endlessly, each smirking within the other like Matryoshka Dolls.

But forget the dolls now and forget the specters, and cast an objective glance on the Middle East. For exile is not merely a distance in space-time or a warp in the individual heart; exile also unravels the strands of history even as it weaves them into present and future lives.

When I heard the media phrase, "Arab Spring," I said to myself, how many centuries then did the Arab Winter last? Or is that so-called spring merely an interlude, heralding yet another ice age? Ah, I rebuked myself, give hope its due. A Tunisian street vendor called Mohamed Bouazizi torched himself and the Middle East blazed. When the smoke cleared, the world saw green shoots of freedom, sprouting between desert rocks and spreading over sand dunes. Isn't that a bright page in the somber book of Middle Eastern history?

But was it democracy really that we saw sprouting or does the word mean what every despot wants it to mean? Who empowered all those tyrants, in the first place? And what about those jihadists who keep outraging our nice Western sensibilities? Have we become inured to extremists as we have to global warming or Wall Street greed? These true believers could be broken-mirror images of the tyrants themselves; for they all share a certain mind-set in an obsessively male culture.

The strongmen who ruled across a vast crescent of sand rose from the dragon teeth of tribalism, sectarianism, colonialism. They carried the memes of societies still yearning for the glory of the old caliphates and the breath of the sonorous Koran. Oh, we tell ourselves, with an indulgent smile, these men embody a passing moment in history – a feeble resurgence of medievalism – and their power will surely crumble before global capitalism and the Internet. Really? I, for one, doubt that dictators simply betray the deformities of nationalism in a transitional, postcolonial period.

Look deeper, I say. Certainly, all autarchs are not the same; nor do they hide a cloven hoof or carry the mark of a slouching beast. (Gamal Abdel Nasser, for instance, won the admiration of people across the Third World; and in Egypt, only the funeral of an incomparable singer, Um Kulsum, summoned larger crowds to the streets.) Moreover, the domains of the strongmen stretch from the Maghreb to Mindanao and count two billion Muslim heads. These people have no common language, race, or history; and in their time zones flourish the mountain cedar and desert cactus, the scorpion and the snow owl. Can the despots share particular traits beyond their rage for power?

For the sake of simplicity, consider the Arabs, ignoring for the moment Muslim nations such as Indonesia and Iran. In *The Seven Pillars of Wisdom*, T. E. Lawrence spoke of 'desert Semites' who lacked "half-tones in their register of vision," people of "primary colours, or rather of black and white."[12] I expect that truth and falsity mingle in that perception. In any case, though I have known few desert Semites, I propose to focus on the *rhetoric* of Arab leaders, which I do find "primary," a smashmouth, delusionary language that recasts reality in odd, sometimes comical ways. (Remember Saddam's press secretary?)

What sustains this kind of bombast? We know that the rhetoric cohabits with low literacy. We also know that it thrives where misogyny thrives. In its masculine bravado – its tumescence, so to speak – the rhetoric reverts to an earlier time, when words possessed preternatural powers and women embodied deviltry. (But please also note that the denigration of women thrives as well in non-Islamic cultures, in India and China, in Africa and Latin America, a pathogen of violence in quite diverse societies.)

But history moves less like an arrow than a boomerang: the denigration of Arab women has become *more* (not less) acute in modern times – witness the rising crimes against women in Egypt. Current practices of women in Islamic societies would have scandalized female members of my family in Egypt. To them, the un-liberated household was not only *passé* but also *déclassé*. The attitude

---

12 T. E. Lawrence, *The Seven Pillars of Wisdom* [1926] (London: Penguin, 2012): 36.

was rife among the secular, urban, and pseudo-Westernized elements of Egypt, in whom snobbery often posed as an enlightened stance. Today, the headscarf tells another tale. Many Muslim women assume the *yashmak* and *hijab* quite voluntarily, as an act of modesty as much as of cultural assertion, and even of sartorial chic.

No veil, however, can hide racism. In the Egypt of my childhood, as elsewhere in the world, status shaded into color, if not exactly into 'race': the paler the skin, the higher the status. In this bleached logic, the 'white man' could claim to be king of the mountain though, like Humpty Dumpty, he only sat high on a colonial wall. Willy-nilly we're back to colonialism, which, like slavery, compounds class, race, and gender in its scourges. These practices, however, were hardly unique to Europeans. Nearly everyone colonized, nearly everyone enslaved, and most people indulged in racism. The light-skinned Mamelukes, for instance, ruled Egypt more barbarously than the ruddy British, expropriating the land and skewering the fellah on iron spikes.

I review this coalition of miseries because it helps explain the rise of dictators. With one ruthless blow, these men – men, of course – appear to abolish class, race, and colonial influence while retaining absolute power. Smiling or glaring down from their outsize marble pedestals, they pretend to champion the oppressed while cramming their torture chambers and their Swiss bank accounts. Nationalism, populism, Arab socialism, even Islamism, all accrued to the advantage of the satraps, advantages that included palaces, harems, and infinity pools. Till a policewoman – please note, it *was* a woman – slapped a vendor in Sidi Bouzid; till Tahrir Square.

So, who made the despots necessary? They appear like jetsam on the strands of receding empires; they emerge from failed states or warring tribes; above all, they arise in societies lacking a civic tradition, lacking empathy and obligation beyond a particular family or clan. (The contrast between the dreck of public places and the sparkle of affluent, private spaces seems to escape the attention of most tourists.) Yet, for all their oppressions, the satraps pacified their people. As Stephen Pinker remarks in *The Better Angels of Our Nature:* "People were less likely to become victims of homicide or casualties of war, but they were now under the thumb of tyrants, clerics, and kleptocrats. This gives us the more sinister sense of the word *pacification*."[13] Around these squalid, latter-day Ozymandiases, the "lone and level sands stretch far away" – above vast deposits of crude oil. To escape their misrule, the wretched and the gifted fled their homelands.

---

13 Steven Pinker, *The Better Angels of Our Natures: The Decline of Violence in History and Its Causes* (London: Allen Lane, 2011): 58.

Can we consider these despots an engine of diaspora, then, one of several engines, like poverty, corruption, and, yes, the World Wide Web?

Sometimes, to lighten my frustration with my native culture, I imagine an interlocutor more firmly embedded in the Arab world than I am. The sly dialogue, suitably offensive, goes like this:

Q: You complain and complain about colonialism. But why did the British occupy Egypt rather than the other way around?

A: Navies and cool heads. Anyway, the colonies have struck back: headscarves in Glasgow, curry in Birmingham, reggae in the London Tube, not to mention bombs.

Q: So where is the Arab Enlightenment and why did it fail to emerge?

A: The Janissaries of the Grand Turk took care of that, the Great Powers afterwards. We had our Enlightenment in the fourteenth century. Pity it didn't last.

Q: But why is authoritarianism ingrained in all those countries? Even after Mubarak, the zealots and generals continue to rule Egypt by other means.

A: You want me to say we suffer from a Pharaonic Complex? You want me to denounce Patriarchy and Islam? Why did America condone authoritarianism for the sake of stability? Why did it back up Mubarak till Tahrir Square?

Q: Alright, then, tell me why have so many countries, like Saudi Arabia, contributed nothing to the world in five hundred years, nothing beyond oil, terrorism, and domestic abuse?

A: It's the best way to preserve the status quo when you have nothing else to offer.

Q: What about the intellectuals? Where's their self-critical spirit? Not in Sayyid Qutb, the implacable voice of Muslim theocracy. Why do Arabs always point the finger at someone else?

A: Intellectuals were in self-exile, like you, effendi, in America's Dairyland, eating cheese. Otherwise, they languished in prisons or hung by the neck like Qutb. Besides, only recently has the West lent them an ear. What's this sudden concern with our writers and intellectuals? Tell me that. Did the Western conscience finally wake up from its interminable colonial sleep?

Q: OK, forget the intellectuals. When will you stop beating your wives?

A: Not right away. But Islamic societies will be feminized in due course, never fear.

Q: Meantime, what? Nepotism, corruption, litter in the street, not to mention government by torture and assassination – are these all you can manage in the Middle East?

A: You say nepotism and corruption, but they're our way of honoring our tribal past and spreading meager resources? We are warm people; we care about our families, our friends.

Q: Honestly, now, will you and I live to see any real change?

A: Who knows? A struggling democracy here, a failed democracy there, a few police states rising and falling, till literacy and civic pride catch up with the people. Meanwhile, please note that a new sense of self-worth has taken hold of Arabs, a new way of speaking to the world has emerged.

Q: Oh, you mean terrorism?

A: That was a cheap shot!

Q: Sorry! The last question now, a humdinger. What about Israel?

A: What about Israel? It's both inevitable and unspeakable. But what would we do without our bugaboo? We need it to explain our selves and our history. Anyway, don't take everything I say so seriously. A word in Egyptian Arabic can mean itself, its opposite, or a camel.

I don't offer this interchange as an exercise in provocation or levity. (Satire always contains some grain of truth, anyway.) I offer it, rather, to convey the mood of many Arabs now. More, I wanted to puzzle some questions that political correctness ignores, and to ask why the Middle East remains a serpents' nest of irredentist passions.

Before I end my remarks, however, I want to review some traits that still hinder a people – the Arab people – who once contributed mightily to the world, and have now spread out after centuries of isolation. The traits I mention are also motives of diaspora everywhere. To the matrix of Arab culture, I attributed misogyny, poverty, illiteracy, irresponsible elites, a taste for inflated rhetoric, the absence of a liberal, democratic consensus, the lack of a robust critical spirit, a tendency to see the world without nuances, and a postcolonial mood, both vengeful and liberating – aspects, all, of acute nationalism in the so-called 'developing world'. Some of those traits also disfigure nations in the fully developed world: for instance, the varieties of jingoism and bigotry in America. But it's the coincidence of these traits, like a bad conjunction of stars, which thwarts Arab aspirations now.

Explanations of the historical process, however, even when tentative, are notoriously partial. We can never reckon all the variables of the case; and we interpret always according to our needs, as Nietzsche knew. Nor is the principle of causality, implicit in all explanations, itself secure. Thus the larger question behind diaspora continues to haunt and taunt us: why are certain societies friendlier to human lives than others, and why do they promise, if not always deliver, their version of the 'pursuit of happiness'?

People answer the question about happiness with their feet: they just up and leave, often at great peril to themselves, putting their bodies and minds in harm's way. (Remember Toni Morrison's point about the body?) The tyrants themselves have no interest in resolving the issue, only in maintaining their power. They erect walls, dig trenches, and emplace machine guns, trying to perfect that monstrosity of our time, the prison or police state.

But the key issue remains. Though we may not know precisely why some societies favor human dignity more than others, we know that poverty and violence fuel diaspora and exile. Can we take comfort in Pinker's argument that violence has declined dramatically since an arrowhead pierced the skull of Ötzi the Iceman in the Tyrolean Alps five thousand years ago? I'm not sure.

Granting Pinker's erudition and goodwill, we may still fret about his conclusion. Couldn't the decline of violence reverse itself with one apocalyptic blast, given the bellicosity of would-be nuclear states like North Korea and Iran? And how much can we really extrapolate from the past? Short of genetic engineering in a brave new world, we still lack the means to eliminate suffering and evil. Can education perfect the flawed nature of our species?

But it's time to conclude before giving pessimism the last word. In this paper, I've been harsh sometimes, critiquing people whose "blood" – so to speak – runs in my veins. (Remember the fury Hannah Arendt unleashed when she criticized her fellow Jews in *The Banality of Evil?*) That may be the price of self-exile, my distrust of so-called "roots." In any case, I never promised to extirpate, only to sublimate, my prejudices – promised to lay them bare before your eyes. And so, in closing, I want to strike a higher note, not only on behalf of Arabs everywhere, and not only for the disfavored of history, but for the body of humanity at large, which will either founder like the crew of the Medusa or together make port.

Despots will come and go, and Arab women will someday attain their majority. Meanwhile, in the Middle East, something *was* born in Sidi Bouzid as in Tahrir Square, and it was no beast slouching toward Bethlehem. Call it, despite General El Sisi, a new sense of possibility. As one Egyptian woman put it, "We know now the way to Tahrir Square" – know it, perhaps, only too well.

As for myself, by tearing myself away from a certain culture, as countless immigrants have done before me, I joined inadvertently a horde, traveling a distance longer than any Ötzi the Iceman imagined his offspring would travel – a journey across millennia, and across alps and seas, driven by a vision of breaking through into a different landscape. In this visionary landscape, which John

Keats called the "vale of Soul-making," the issues of both Arab nationalism and the biases of an individual speaker like wholly superfluous. In this vale of soul-making, even diaspora becomes irrelevant, since humanity labors ever closer to a unanimous fate.

Meantime, I prefer to place my emphasis not on the sorrows of departure but on the challenges of arrival. And so I remind myself continually of Ovid – Ovid in David Malouf's marvelous novel, *An Imaginary Life* – as the Roman poet contemplates his exile in the wastes of Dacia: *"Here is the life you have tried to throw away. Here is your second chance* [...]. *Now you will become at last the one you intended to be.*"[14] What a wonderful end to diaspora and exile?

---

14 David Malouf, *An Imaginary Life* [1978] (London: Vintage, 1999): 90, emphasis in original.

Pnina Werbner

The Boundaries of Diaspora: A Critical Response to Brubaker

Abstract: Unlike the classic diasporas of old — the Jews, the Armenians, the Greeks — the territorial origins and boundaries of late modern diasporas may be vast and diverse regions, sometimes even stretching globally. Late modern diasporas are distinctive, the chapter suggests, in being fractal and perspectival rather than multi-layered and 'deep.' Home, homeland and belonging may not coincide in such diasporas. The paper thus concurs with Rogers Brubaker's critique of a tendency to essentialise diaspora while contending that, like many other diaspora scholars, Brubaker too fails to theorize the dynamic social principles underlying the shifting boundaries of diaspora formation in the late modern world; the fact that late modern diasporas, and perhaps all diasporas, are not only social fields made up of clusters, networks and activities, but that they have multiple boundaries that are stressed situationally. Like Brubaker, I argue that in the face of the fuzzy boundaries of modern-day ethnic groups, attempts to institute any corporate form of multiculturalism simply cannot work. Nor are Pakistanis in Britain part of one single 'community.' Rather, they belong to a host of moral, aesthetic and interpretive communities, uniting them with other Muslims, women, black people, South Asians, cricket lovers, Labour activists, businessmen and anti-racists, as well as with their fellow-Pakistanis. Nevertheless, in some situations, the boundary of the diaspora periodically surfaces as a momentary reality. Finally, the question the chapter raises is: May we say that the Muslim *ummah* is in some sense a late modern diaspora?

What are the boundaries of late modern diasporas? Where is home for members of such diasporas, what is their imagined homeland and where do they find a sense of belonging? The answers to these questions are by no means as straightforward as it may seem. Unlike the classic diasporas of old — the Jews, the Armenians, the Greeks — the territorial origins of late modern diasporas may be vast and diverse regions, sometimes even stretching globally. Late modern diasporas are distinctive, I want to suggest here, in being fractal and perspectival rather than multi-layered and 'deep.' Home, homeland and belonging may not coincide in such diasporas.

Understanding these features of late modern diasporas is crucial if we are to engage with Rogers Brubaker's critique of a tendency to essentialize diasporas as though they were definite, clearly bounded groups. In a highly influential paper, Brubaker argues trenchantly against the scholarly penchant to take as reality the rhetoric of so-called diaspora or ethnic 'entrepreneurs'; self-appointed spokesmen and women who make claims on behalf of a whole diaspora, often numbering millions, as if that diaspora was unified in its singularity.[1] In invoking the diasporic 'community', diaspora entrepreneurs, Brubaker contends, disguise

---

1 Rogers Brubaker, "The 'Diaspora' Diaspora," *Ethnic and Racial Studies* 28.1 (2005): 1–19.

the reality that members of diaspora often not only disagree with these self-appointed leaders who claim to speak in their name, but do not even identify or recognize them as spokespersons or leaders. He calls this tendency toward reification of social categories such as diaspora or ethnicity "groupism."[2]

There are, I want to suggest, two problems with Brubaker's critique. The first is that few would disagree with him. Virtually all diaspora theorists these days recognize that diasporas in the democratic West are heterogeneous social formations, marked by internal divisions and fuzzy boundaries. Brubaker is, in other words, preaching to the converted. But my second critique is more fundamental. I believe that like many other diaspora scholars, Brubaker too fails to theorize the *dynamic social principles* underlying the shifting boundaries of diaspora formation in the late modern world; the fact that late modern diasporas, and perhaps all diasporas, are not only social fields made up of clusters, networks and activities, but that they have multiple boundaries that are stressed situationally. In order to explain this claim further, I intend to draw on a set of foundational social principles as they were originally theorized by the Manchester School of Social Anthropology. I myself was a student at Manchester at a time when the founders of the Manchester school were still alive and my work as a social anthropologist is deeply indebted to the ideas animating the school as it then was. My aim in this chapter is thus to spell out, explicate and clarify my own foundational assumptions in studying diaspora.

Before going on to outline these principles in detail, let me begin with a literary example of the situationalism of diaspora boundaries and the multiple identities that diasporans bear. It is taken from *The Satanic Verses* by Salman Rushdie, a novel which raised a global controversy and led to a death *fatwa* against the author, issued by the Ayatollah Khomeini of Iran.[3] As many have argued, including Rushdie himself, *The Satanic Verses* is a book about migration. It builds on an allegory of the foundational myth of Islam, the migration of the Prophet Muhammad in the face of persecution from Mecca, the city of his birth, to Medina. According to the Koran the Prophet was welcomed by the citizens of Medina and ultimately made governor of that city, before finally returning to Mecca as conqueror. This myth is also the central allegorical narrative in *The Satanic Verses*. In the book, 'Mahound,' the medieval name for the Prophet meaning false demon or devil, emerges as a true believer who founds a great religion yet is unable to tolerate Baal, the sacrilegious poet. Paralleling Mahound's migration in the novel are two other migrations: one of Chamcha Saladin, who

---

2 Brubaker, "The 'Diaspora' Diaspora," 11–12.
3 Salman Rushdie, *The Satanic Verses* (London et al.: Viking, 1988).

falls from an aeroplane over London. Chamcha is the Anglicized Muslim Indian migrant who leaves home, rejects his father, marries a tweedy Englishwoman, and adopts a pukka English accent, lifestyle, and mode of dress. In the end, Chamcha returns home, to India, rediscovers his love for his father and his love for his Indian childhood sweetheart who has in the meanwhile become a crusading secular Muslim fighting in India against religious communalism and sectarianism. The third migrant figure, also in London, is Gibreel, a famous Indian film star who acts in Indian movies, especially in the roles of various gods, both Hindu and Muslim − hence a tolerant man. Ultimately, however, he betrays his friends and ends by committing suicide.

There are various other migrations and figures in the book but to simplify matters, let us focus on these three figures, each of whom appears to typify a quite different and even opposed character: Mahound, the devout Muslim believer; Chamcha, the anglicized secular modern sceptic; and Gibreel, the passionate lover of Indian film and culture. The question that may be asked is: are they really different? In fact it can be argued that *they may well be one and the same person*. There are many such South Asian migrants or diasporans living in Britain − Muslim believers who love Indian film and music and are highly anglicized in their everyday work lives. Vast numbers of such people exist in India as well, of course, and even in Pakistan. So what are we to make of this apparently paradoxical fact? And how does it reflect on the boundaries of diaspora?

To answer this question I want to make another detour, this time to outline some of the basic principles of social analysis articulated by the Manchester School of Social Anthropology as these were formulated in and through a wide range of rural and urban ethnographies. The principles may be summarized as: (1) situational analysis; (2) conflict theory; (3) the social field; (4) the extended case study or social drama; and finally, (5) social networks.

Let me begin with situational analysis. Situational analysis theorizes the fact that people bear multiple identities and that determining which identity is performed, stressed or highlighted depends on, indeed is often determined by, the social situation. The definition of the situation frames social interactions in terms of one identity rather than another. For example, you may be a South Asian, a Pakistani and British, but as a factory worker, you share interests with fellow workers, irrespective of your ethnic identity. In a famous aphorism Max Gluckman, who founded the Manchester School, argues that an African townsman is a townsman, an African miner is a miner; he is only secondarily a tribesman.[4] Once "he crosses the tribal boundary," Gluckman argues, he is "detribalised."[5] The urban or work situation that a man or woman finds him- or herself in defines who he or she is.

The reverse of this principle is that identities only exist situationally, in opposition, as Stuart Hall too recognizes when he argues that identities are constructed through *différance*.[6] For example, you might define yourself as black vis-à-vis your white neighbors, or a Pakistani vis-à-vis your Indian neighbor, or you and all your neighbors may define yourselves in terms of a shared middle class identity vis-à-vis members of other classes. Of course, there are times when people deliberately set themselves apart, refusing to accept the definition of the situation. They can also construct and create contexts in which their valued identities can flourish, a point I return to below. This is one way that conflict may be caused. But quite often, conflicts at one level are resolved at another level. Another famous aphorism by Max Gluckman is that custom first divides and then unites.[7] By this he means that although there are many divisions in a society, for example, on the basis of class, gender and ethnicity, these divisions do not coincide or reinforce each other; in other words, conflicts hardly ever create a grand divide, total polarisation. Rather than reinscribing the same division, conflicts cut across each other and this creates pressure to make peace. A classic example of this was taken from Africa: the Nuer, an East African nomadic group, marry exogamously, i.e., they take wives from beyond their named tribal segment. When tribal segments feud and blood is spilt, this means that husbands and wives who come from feuding segments are prohibited from eating together. Such cross-cutting ties, as Gluckman called them, create pressure to settle feuds quickly.[8]

Another aspect of conflict theory, one I have argued in relation to the Pakistani diaspora, is that because internal competition and conflict focus around shared central cultural symbols and values – for example, Islam, or honor, such internal conflict or competition paradoxically strengthens and renews the

---

4 Max Gluckmann, "Tribalism in Modern British Central Africa," *Cahier d'études africaines* 1.1 (1960): 55–70, 57–58.

5 Gluckmann, "Tribalism," 57–58.

6 Stuart Hall, "Introduction: Who Needs Identity?" in *Questions of Cultural Identity*, ed. Stuart Hall and Paul du Gay (London: SAGE, 1996): 1–17, 5 and *passim*.

7 Max Gluckman, *Custom and Conflict in Africa* (Oxford: Blackwell, 1955): 1.

8 Max Gluckman, "Analysis of a Social Situation in Modern Zululand," *Bantu Studies* 14.1 (1940): 1–30.

validity of these symbols and values dialectically.[9] This implies that the fact that there are disagreements and divisions within diaspora or ethnic groups does not lead to fragmentation, as one might expect, but to a higher unity, precisely because these conflicts focus around the same symbols and values. As a simple example, during the Rushdie affair, despite deep internal divisions among Pakistanis in the UK, the vast majority united to demonstrate against the publication of the *Satanic Verses* and its author since they all shared the idea that the Prophet as a symbol of Muslim moral perfection had been vilified and blasphemed.[10] Another example might be drawn upon from the Jewish diaspora: Jews who support, and indeed lead, the boycott movement against Israeli goods from the occupied territories, are condemned by the pro-Israel American lobby AIPAC.[11] The irony is that both sides are united by their love of Israel and a desire for its continued existence; they simply interpret the political realities and the Zionist dream differently. Neither is indifferent to the fate of Israel or desires its destruction.

Such an argument presumes a shared space of dialogue, or many spaces where diasporics can debate with one another. I have called such spaces of dialogue the "diasporic public sphere."[12] Whether this diasporic pubic sphere is visible to a wider audience or hidden from view, it has to be created through voluntary efforts and investments by members of the diaspora. It requires labor and funding. Within the diasporic public sphere communication may be conflictual and confrontational, the mutual accusations and recriminations bitter and condemnatory, the political and religious disagreements sharp and unbridgeable. In it many different groups each may claim to speak on behalf of the whole diaspora. But in being focused around shared celebrations, predicaments and places, or arguments of identity, the diasporic public sphere creates bounded arenas or spaces of focused communal value. The multiple conflicts themselves crosscut one another, leading to overarching unities at a higher level. In this sense the divergent perspectives of members of a diaspora about their society, politics,

---

9 Pnina Werbner, *The Migration Process: Capital, Gifts and Offerings among Manchester Pakistanis* [1990] (Oxford: Berg, 2002): 341.

10 Cf. Tariq Modood, "British Asian Muslims and the Rushdie Affair," *Political Quarterly* 61 (1989): 143–160.

11 Cf. "The Unjust Efforts to Delegitimize Israel," <http://www.aipac.org/~/media/Publications-old/Policy%20and%20Politics/AIPAC%20Analyses/Issue%20Memos/2011/The%20Unjust%20Efforts%20to%20Delegitimize%20Israel.pdf> (acc. January 27, 2015).

12 Cf. Pnina Werbner, *Imagined Diasporas among Manchester Muslims: The Public Performance of Pakistani Transnational Identity Politics* (Oxford: James Currey, 2002) and Pnina Werbner, "Theorising Complex Diasporas: Purity and Hybridity in the Diasporic Public Sphere," *Journal of Ethnic and Migration Studies* 30.5 (2004): 895–911.

the world and their place in it, first divide and then unite diasporas, to echo Gluckman's aphorism. The plurality of radical disagreements within diasporic groups does not necessarily lead to the erasing of diaspora boundaries but on the contrary, they unite protagonists within a single interpretive community. Arguments of identity, of who we are, may divide diasporas over key ontological issues, as Clifford and Yuval-Davis have shown for the Jewish diaspora, or Gilroy for the Black diaspora.[13] But the one thing they do share is the arguments. Similarly, the unity and in some instance boundedness of the Pakistani diaspora is, I have proposed, dialectical rather than homeostatic: conflicts and contradictions highlight the shared values competed over, framed in shared spaces of dialogue or social situations.[14]

An important theoretical point is at stake here, related to Frederik Barth's famous insight that ethnic groups are defined by their 'boundaries,' not the cultural 'stuff' these boundaries enclose.[15] The key insight which this classic anthropological view afforded stemmed from Evans-Pritchard's segmentary analysis of the Nuer: identities are essentially social rather than cultural, and they shift situationally; collective identities emerge in contestation, oppositionally. It is the boundary of contestation that marks identity, signalled by diacritical emblems, border posts that 'stand for' a group's distinctiveness.[16] These differences may at times appear objectively insignificant to outsiders. In Bosnia groups sharing the same language in one case, and the same religion in another, were nevertheless willing to murder and rape neighbors marked by minor cultural differences.

Coming back to Brubaker, in modern nation-states, there is no doubt that apparently 'bounded' collective identities and interests – and hence also conflictual relations – are often the product and construction of the 'center' or, indeed, of multiple centers: of a buried intelligentsia locked in arguments of identity among themselves. This center consists as much of artists and writers as of political entrepreneurs. It is the debate among them that determines both the imagined

---

13 James Clifford, "Diasporas," *Cultural Anthropology* 9 (1994): 302–338; Nira Yuval-Davis, "Ethnicity, Gender Relations and Multiculturalism," in *Debating Cultural Hybridity: Multi-Cultural Identities and the Politics of Anti-Racism*, ed. Pnina Werbner and Tariq Modood (London: Zed Books, 1997): 193–208; Paul Gilroy, *The Black Atlantic: Modernity and Double Consciousness* (London: Verso, 1993).
14 Werbner, *Imagined Diasporas among Manchester Muslims*.
15 Frederik Barth, "Introduction," in *Ethnic Groups and Boundaries: The Social Organisation of Cultural Difference*, ed. Frederik Barth (London: George Allen and Unwin, 1969): 9–38.
16 Cf. Edward Evan Evans-Pritchard, *The Nuer: A Description of the Modes of Livelihood and Political Institutions of a Nilotic People* (New York: OUP, 1940).

boundaries of ethnic contestation and the imagination of the community as a bounded whole. Such definitions from the center obscure, however, the everyday, mundane reality that ethnic communal boundaries are shaped by quotidian networks of exchange and sociality, often with outsiders, and are thus variable, changing, fuzzy and indeterminate. Rather than any sharp boundary defining the ethnic or diasporic group, it is the center that imagines the boundary. Sheffer points out that there is no single command structure that determines the diaspora. Following that, I have argued that diasporas are chaordic formations, changing and developing in often predictable ways in different parts of world, without a unified leadership or strategy.[17]

The political imaginaries marking out ethnic communities as 'bounded' are nurtured and publicized by organic intellectuals at the center, including writers, singers and other popular cultural producers. In this specific sense it is the cultural 'stuff' of ethnicity, an unceasing argument of identities produced at the center, which defines ethnic groups as distinct and separate, not the fuzzy boundaries these arguments mask. As early as 1982, well before Brubaker's critique, Michael Walzer recognised that America's immigrant communities were characterized by, as he puts it, a

> centre of active participants [...] and a much larger periphery of individuals and families who are little more than recipients of services generated at the centre. They are communities without boundaries, shading off into a residual mass of people who think of themselves simply as Americans. Borders and border guards are among the first products of a successful national liberation movement, but ethnic assertiveness has no similar outcome. There is no way for the various groups to prevent or regulate individual crossings. Nor can the state do this without the most radical coercion of individuals.[18]

This points to another key term of the Manchester School, that of the *social field*. In their studies of labor migration in Northern Rhodesia, today's Zambia, members of the school recognized that tribes under British colonialism did not simply constitute discrete social and cultural groups since their members were constantly on the move between urban centers and rural peripheries and were, indeed, the product of earlier migrations. So too, for Manchester Pakistanis, as I argued in my book *Imagined Diasporas*, the world is multi-centered and shaped by flows

---

17 Pnina Werbner, "The Place which Is Diaspora: Citizenship, Religion and Gender in the Making of Chaordic Transnationalism," *Journal of Ethnic and Migration Studies* 28.1 (2002): 119 −133; Gabriel Sheffer, "The Emergence of New Ethno-National Diasporas," *Migration* 28 (1995): 5−28.
18 Michael Walzer, "Pluralism in Political Perspective," in *The Politics of Ethnicity*, ed. Michael Walzer et al. (Cambridge, Mass.: Belknap P of Harvard UP, 1982): 1−28, 21.

of ideologies as well as of consumer goods, pilgrims, visiting kinsmen, ambassadors, pop stars, cricketers, religious experts, politicians and media images, the latter originating from Bombay, Mecca, Islamabad, London, New York or Hollywood.[19] The diasporic world which is locally created appropriates and combines these traveling ideas and images into meaningful moral allegories.

In the face of the fuzzy boundaries of modern-day ethnic groups, attempts to institute any corporate form of multiculturalism simply cannot work. Nor are Pakistanis in Britain part of one single 'community.' Rather, they belong to a host of moral, aesthetic and interpretive communities, uniting them with other Muslims, women, black people, South Asians, cricket lovers, Labour activists, businessmen and anti-racists, as well as with their fellow-Pakistanis. Nevertheless, in moments of crisis and celebration, on occasions of fund-raising to alleviate natural disasters or wars in the homeland, or when celebrity film stars or cricketers tour the diaspora, otherwise passive members of the diaspora are mobilized for action, and in these situations the boundary of the diaspora periodically surfaces as a momentary reality.

Thinking about social situations and social fields together, the Manchester School developed what came to be known as the extended case study method. Its members considered what happens when different ethnic or tribal groups come together or encounter each other in particular social situations. The methodological and theoretical importance of studying social situations of this type was first highlighted in Gluckman's "Social Situation in Modern Zululand."[20] The event described was the opening of a bridge in Zululand, built through collaboration between whites and blacks and desired by both communities. The opening was a convivial and harmonious affair which deployed a mixture of Zulu and English colonial ceremonialism. Gluckman uses his intimate knowledge of many of the protagonists, White and Zulu, to highlight his basic paradoxical thesis or conflict theory, of cooperation in the context of division, the peace in the feud. Here the wider conflict is the racial division in Southern Africa between blacks and whites, the 'color bar' as it was known at the time, later institutionalized in apartheid laws. He shows the cross-cutting ties of conflict and cooperation between Africans and Whites which make possible the peaceful opening of the bridge.

Michael Burawoy has argued that if grounded theory, as outlined by Glazer and Strauss, was based on multiple interviews or cases, which gave a bird's-eye vision of society at a particular moment, sacrificing particularity and specificity,

19 Werbner, *Imagined Diasporas*; Werbner, "The Place which Is Diaspora," 119–133.
20 Gluckman, "Modern Zululand," 1–30.

the extended case study method as developed by the Manchester School allows us to see a society in all its complexity as it is becoming and changing.[21] Situational analysis highlights points of resistance to change, cultural encounters, conflicts between rules, instability, anomie, and how these are played out in public and even in the intimate relations of everyday life. It also allows us to study the effects of external forces, even global change, on a micro-society. Hence the relation between micro and macro is played out differently in each methodological approach.[22] The key point stressed by all commentators is that the extended case study is not simply an 'apt illustration' or an interesting 'ethnographic vignette' — writing strategies favored by many anthropologists. The extended case study is an analytic construct that, by abstracting directly from an ethnography of practice, generates a theory of social process, change and conflict, often by following a series of encounters or social situations involving the same or related actors. Each social situation is an indexical event that indexes relations among social categories, ideologies and modes of practice. Seen in its totality, the extended case study method allows us, in other words, to think outside the box, to recognize the rules and values constituting a complex, changing social field, one characterized by shifting borders and political alliances, and hence also by a kaleidoscopic play of identities and competing normative and ethical assumptions. Practice in this method incorporates both discourse and symbolic action, including performance, ritual and ceremony, as well political actions such as elections, mass protests or violent clashes.

In my book *Imagined Diasporas*, my use of the extended case study method led me to a realization that the people I was studying could not simply be labeled a 'Pakistani' diaspora or a 'Muslim' diaspora or a 'South Asian' diaspora. If I wanted to label them, I would have to say that my study was of Punjabi-Pakistani-South Asian-Muslim-British-Mancunians, but this of course only created another reified illusion. There was no single, bounded diaspora that was easily

---

21 Michael Burawoy, "The Extended Case Method," *Sociological Theory* 16.1 (1998): 4–33; Barney G. Glaser and Anselm L. Strauss, *The Discovery of Grounded Theory* (Chicago: Aldine, 1967).

22 For a full discussion, cf. Richard Werbner, "The Manchester School in South-Central Africa," *Annual Review of Anthropology* 13 (1984): 157–185; Kingsley G. Garbett, "The Analysis of Social Situations," *Man* (New Series) 5.2 (1970): 214–227; Jaap Van Velsen, "The Extended-Case Method and Situational Analysis," in *The Craft of Social Anthropology*, ed. A. L. Epstein (Oxford: Pergamon P, 1979): 129–149; and contributions to Terry M. S. Evens, Don Handelman (eds.), *The Manchester School: Practice and Ethnographic Praxis in Anthropology* (Oxford: Berghahn, 2006), particularly Bruce Kapferer, "Situations, Crisis, and the Anthropology of the Concrete: The Contribution of Max Gluckman," 118–156, and Don Handelman, "The Extended Case: Interactional Foundations and Prospective Dimensions," 94–117.

identifiable but instead, there were multiple, cross-cutting diasporas that emerged situationally.

I began my research quite modestly, following a series of Pakistani factional confrontations over control of the Central Jamia mosque in Manchester. I studied cultural performances, commemorative ceremonials, local level debates and meetings, elections that broke up in violence, factional celebrations of victory. The picture that emerged was a complex one – of factional alliances between secularist and Islamic groups, democrats and conservatives, in which the personal and the political were so intermeshed as to create strange allies, following the principle that my enemy's enemy is my friend. Although the actors involved were quite small groups, many were also enmeshed in factional politics in their home villages in Pakistan or Muslim sectarian groups there. Despite their plurality and small size, they managed to create alliances in two solid, opposed factions. The social field at this point looked like the situation depicted in fig. 1.

It was a picture that seemed to confirm the blurred boundaries hypothesized by Walzer or Brubaker, with a core of fragmented and divided activists, politically, culturally, ideologically involved, and a periphery of passive onlookers. But then came, in quick succession, the Rushdie affair, the first Gulf War and the Pakistani cricket team's world cup victory, captained by Imran Khan and followed by his fund-raising visit to Manchester. In all these major international events I was astonished to observe that what seemed to have been small tonga associations, unknown leaders with small groups of followers, came together and coalesced in dramatic, massive nationwide mobilizations for protest. They also came together in celebration after the cricket team's victory. Suddenly it seemed that the Muslim diaspora of Britain, led by Pakistanis or South Asians, was indeed a bounded community. So too was the Pakistani diaspora. Virtually at the same time, however, an explosion of Asian delicatessens and restaurants, British South Asian films, Indian and Pakistani TV soaps, imported and local music, extra-terristrial satellite stations beamed from South Asia, giant weddings, bhangra clubbing and the like, signaled the emergence of a self-conscious *South Asian* diaspora cutting across the Muslim and Pakistani diasporas.

These developments proved that beyond situational analysis – even if building on it – major crises and national events required a theory of social movements. In *Imagined Diasporas* I draw on Alberto Melucci to argue that the invisible local-level diaspora with its internal arguments of identity about who we are, which I had studied through situational analysis, came to be *visibilized* as Pakistanis mobilized in their hundreds and thousands on the wider national and international stage. Later, the wars in Bosnia, Iraq and Afghanistan became further points of mobilization as Pakistanis joined the Stop the War Alliance with other British citizens following the 9/11 bombings. Seditious plots by small

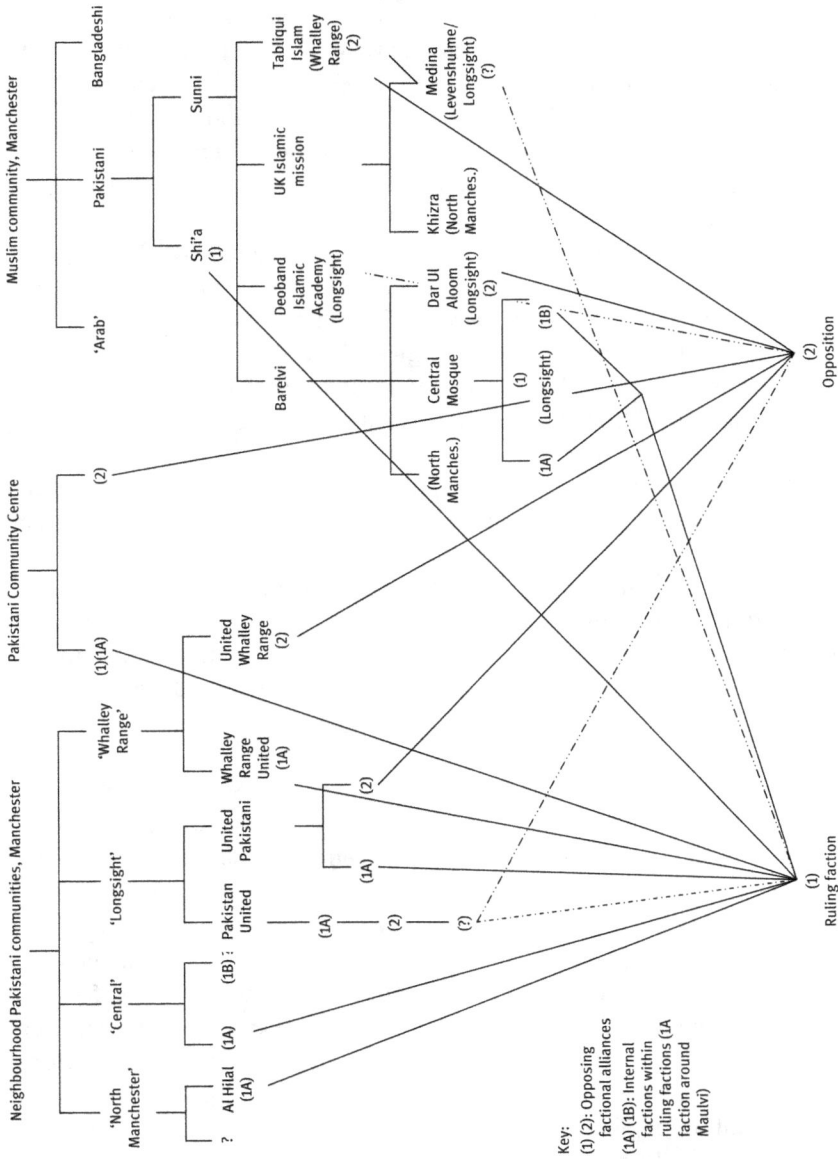

Fig. 1 Factional alliances among Manchester Muslims, 1987–88. Reproduced from Pnina Werbner, *Imagined Diasporas among Manchester Muslims*, 297.

groups of young Pakistanis and other Muslims kept the diaspora community in the public eye. The earthquake in Kashmir, in which 80,000 people were estimated to have died, was another point of mobilization, this time of Pakistanis as patriots and citizens from afar. In the meanwhile, also, well-to-do Pakistanis were initiating good works in Pakistan – building mainly small hospitals and schools. And on top of that, tens of thousands of young, second-generation Pakistanis were marrying spouses from Pakistan.

All these mobilizing events drew boundaries, but the boundaries they drew were around different diasporas despite the fact, although this may seem paradoxical, that they were often composed of the same people. Home, homeland and belonging were articulated differently in each diasporic mobilization. Moreover, it was evident that the diasporas were not stable social formations but constantly changing formations *in process*. This led me to theorize late modern diasporas as complex or segmented diasporas.

Complex diasporas defy any neat typological theorisations of diaspora that look to *national* historical origins exclusively as determining the groups that may be defined as diasporas. In this type of typologizing the Jewish diaspora assumes paradigmatic status and its central features are taken as the starting point in formulating the fundamental parameters of diaspora.[23] This is partly, of course, because the colloquial use of the term diaspora has historically been with reference to the Jewish dispersion. The question thus becomes: how far can a diaspora community deviate from the original prototype and still be called a diaspora?

Complex or segmented diasporas reflect the fact that similar cultural preoccupations, tastes, cuisines, music, sport, poetry, fashion and popular cinema are widely enjoyed across vast geographical regions encompassing several postcolonial nation-states in a globalizing world. This points to a key feature of late modern diasporas (and indeed of some earlier ones) which has remained so far untheorized in the scholarly literature and which cannot easily be assimilated into the archetypical Jewish model of diaspora. That model starts from the fact that Jewish religion, culture and national political orientation to Zion coincide, despite geographical dispersion and despite internal religious or political disagreements. This coincidence is true also of the Armenian and Greek diasporas. But where vast cultural regions of *consumption* do not simply coincide with either religion or national homelands, as is true for South Asians, Middle Easterners, Latin Americans, Africans, Afro-Caribbeans and Chinese, we may talk of complex or segmented diasporas. In such complex diasporas the fact that people

---

23 Cf. William Safran, "Comparing Diasporas: A Review Essay," *Diaspora* 8.3 (1999): 255–291.

from a particular region share a rich material culture of consumption, both high-cultural and popular, and often a dominant religion (e.g., Islam, Catholicism) creates public arenas and economic channels for cooperation and communal en-joyment which cut across the national origins or religious beliefs of performers and participants.

An example of such a complex diaspora is the South Asian one, which in-cludes five nation-states (India, Pakistan, Bangladesh, Sri Lanka and Nepal) and at least five world religions (Islam, Hinduism, Buddhism, Sikhism and Chris-tianity). The South Asian diaspora, seen as a regional diaspora of cultural con-sumption (Ghosh calls it a "diaspora of the imagination"[24]), in no way deter-mines either political loyalties and commitments or more focused exilic yearnings for a lost homeland. It is quite possible for people from a single cul-tural region to be locked in bitter national or religious conflicts as they are in South Asia. In the diaspora, however, the sharing of a regional culture can create cross-cutting ties and the potential for transcendent coalitions and alliances which mitigate such conflicts.

Some contemporary new diasporas still appear to remain confined to a sin-gle nationality – the Japanese spring to mind. But the vast new diasporas of the late modern postcolonial world – such as the South Asian diaspora – are com-plex in new ways: culturally, linguistically, religiously, politically. Their borders are porous, their identities multiple, intersecting and in constant flux, shifting situationally. Nevertheless, they do not simply assimilate. Instead, they retain passionate attachments to aesthetic, religious and national modes of living in the world. At the same time, however, the 'worlds' they inhabit are not defined or limited to the same groups of people, all the time. This is reflected in the com-plexity and plurality of the diasporic public sphere. This final statement may re-quire some explanation.

I argued earlier that diasporas create their own public spheres and more broadly, as Khachig Tölölyan has pointed out, they create a diasporic civil soci-ety composed of a plurality of associations, media, cultural societies and so forth.[25] The notion of a diasporic public sphere rests on theorizations by femi-nists, who have argued for the need to conceptualize the pluralization and com-plexity of the public sphere. Reconsidering Habermas's original notion, which implied a national, unified public sphere, Nancy Fraser argues in an important article that women and other marginalized groups historically created a counter-

---

24 Amitav Gosh, "The Diaspora in Indian Culture," *Public Culture* 2.1 (1993), 73–78.
25 Khachig Tölölyan, "Elites and Institutions in the Armenian Transnation," *Diaspora* 9.1 (2000): 255–291.

civil society to the official, hegemonic public sphere. A truly functioning democracy, she proposes, requires such "subaltern counterpublics" in which oppositional interpretations of "identities, interests, and needs" are formulated.[26] Seyla Benhabib too has argued that the increasing porousness and complexity of the public sphere allows women and other marginalized groups to set new agendas not attended to in the national public sphere.[27] Rather than a single public arena, the point made by these feminist theorists is that such separate and diverse spaces are essential for subalterns and marginal groups to thrash out their own perspectives on public policies and the public good.

If the public good, according to Habermas, was defined through public debate between rational citizens, such later conceptualizations take account of its aesthetic and affective dimensions as well.[28] Paul Gilroy, for example, speaks of a black "alternative" public sphere of "story-telling and music-making."[29] Fraser stresses that "public spheres are not only arenas for the formation of discursive opinion. In addition, as arenas for the formation and enactment of identities," they are in some sense a 'theatre.'[30] In Alberto Melucci's terms, the work of identity is one of first discovering and then negotiating shared identities.[31] Such views reflect the fact that "meaning is always in excess of what can be understood discursively, spilling out beyond the symbolic."[32] Public assemblies, Bruno Latour proposes in an interview with Sánchez-Criado, are as much about 'things' as people or the politics of representation.[33] In her theorization of public arenas in India, Sandria Freitag, it will be recalled, argues that processions and public rituals encompass both the 'political' and 'religious,' the formal

---

26 Nancy Fraser, "Rethinking the Public Sphere: A Contribution to the Critique of Actually Existing Democracy," in *Habermas and the Public Sphere*, ed. Craig Calhoun (Cambridge, Mass.: MIT P, 1992): 109–142, 123.

27 Seyla Benhabib, *Situating the Self: Gender, Community and Postmodernism in Contemporary Ethics* (Cambridge: Polity P, 1992): 94.

28 For an overview, cf. Lincoln Dahlberg, "The Habermasian Public Sphere: Taking Difference Seriously?" *Theory and Society* 34.2 (2005): 111–136.

29 Gilroy, *Black Atlantic*, 200.

30 Fraser, "Rethinking the Public Sphere," 125, 110.

31 Alberto Melucci, *Nomads of the Present: Social Movements and Individual Needs in Contemporary Societies*, ed. John Keane, Paul Mier (London: Hutchinson Radius, 1989).

32 Dahlberg, "The Habermasian Public Sphere," 115; cf. Iris Marion Young, "Impartiality and the Civic Public: Some Implications of Feminist Critiques of Moral and Political Theory," in *Feminism as Critique: Essays on the Politics of Gender in Late-Capitalist Societies*, ed. Seyla Benhabib, Drucilla Cornell (Cambridge: Polity P, 1987): 56–76, 72.

33 Bruno Latour, Tomás Sánchez-Criado, "Making the 'Res Public'," *Ephemera* 7.2 (2007): 364–371.

and informal, elite and popular concerns.[34] My study of the local Pakistani diasporic public sphere similarly highlighted its poetics – the way that political passion and rhetoric allow speakers to reach out persuasively to their audiences.[35] A recognition of the pluralized nature of the diasporic public sphere allows for a theorization of diaspora, community and culture not as a homogeneous, unified, monolithic, harmonious whole but as heterogeneous and conflictual.

By way of conclusion, I want to raise a further issue to consider. Could we say the Muslim *ummah* is in some sense a late modern diaspora of the kind I have been describing so far? After all, Islam is a universal religion and unlike Judaism, Hinduism or Sikhism, for example, it has no home or homeland. While Mecca may be the sacred center of Islam as a world religion, it does not constitute a place of belonging for Muslims wherever they are. Indeed, Muslims are scattered throughout the world, some living outside their national homelands, some in countries where they are long-standing minorities, while others live in majority Islamic countries. It seems far-fetched to describe them all as a diaspora. But even if we narrow the ambit, could we speak of a British Muslim diaspora, for example? They may all feel they belong to a single global *ummah*, but beyond that there is much that divides them – they belong to many different national and ethnic groups and to different Islamic sectarian groups. They speak different languages, have different popular cultural traditions, their cultural practices of Islamic ritual differ, even if they share the same aesthetic sensibilities and some of the same texts and key festivals and customs.

The issue is partly a definitional one. If we expand the term diaspora beyond geographical rootedness, national origin or ethnic belonging, the very term may become so diffuse as to lose any analytic value. But conversely, if we define diaspora as a moral community of co-responsibility, a group whose members recognize an affective bond of fictive brotherhood and sisterhood (*ukhwah* in Arabic) with each other beyond family and kinship, one in which they identify with the sufferings of fellow members of the diaspora elsewhere – Marranci speaks of an emotional Islam[36] – and mobilize to support fellow diasporans politically – then it might be that, indeed, the global Muslim dispersion can be described as a diaspora after all:

---

34 Sandria B. Freitag, *Collective Action and Community: Public Arenas and the Emergence of Communalism in North India* (Berkeley: California UP, 1989): 14.
35 Werbner, *Imagined Diasporas*.
36 Gabriele Marranci, *Understanding Muslim Identity: Rethinking Fundamentalism* (London: Palgrave Macmillan, 2009).

Muslims are a diaspora in...
- being an internationally dispersed *moral community* of co-responsibility
- being an 'imagined' transnational 'community' or *ummah*
- being an *affective and aesthetic community* across borders
- *identifying with the sufferings* of fellow diasporans across borders
- being willing to *mobilise politically and economically* to support fellow diasporans across borders

But they do not...
- constitute a community that yearns for a single homeland
- cultivate a sojourner mentality
- share the same popular culture, music, food, literature.

There has, in fact, been quite a long-standing debate on the intersection of religion and diaspora which recognizes the incorporative role of religion for new immigrants as they establish themselves and claim citizenship in a new country. The issue I am raising, however, is more specifically whether we may talk about a *Muslim* diaspora? Seán McLoughlin speaks of the centrality for Muslims of "translocal and supralocal imaginings."[37] In some ways, in my observation, being a Muslim is *counter-diasporic*. Overseas Pakistanis suffer from what Ghassan Hage has called "migration guilt,"[38] they feel guilty for leaving Pakistan and cultivate a myth of return and a sojourner mentality. In this context embracing Islam fully absolves them from this sense of guilt and temporary abode. They can practise Islam fully in Britain or anywhere else because it is a universal religion. Thus I was told by first-generation Pakistanis that they could not expect their children to feel the nostalgia and loyalty to Pakistan that they did, but it was important that they remain good Muslims.

Nevertheless, I argued in *Imagined Diasporas* that there are situations that arise in which Pakistanis act like a Muslim diaspora, mobilizing for Palestine, Bosnia, Chechniya, Iraq, in terms of their Islamic identity. In those situations

---

37 Seán McLoughlin, "Muslim Travellers: Homing Desire, The *Umma* and British-Pakistanis," in *Diasporas: Concepts, Intersections, Identities*, ed. Kim Knott, Seán McLoughlin (London: Zed Books, 2010): 223–229, 223; for overviews, cf. also Steven Vertovec, "Religion and Diaspora," in *New Approaches to the Study of Religion: Textual, Comparative, Sociological and Cognitive Approaches*, ed. Peter Antes, Armin W. Geertz, Randi R. Warne (Berlin: de Gruyter, 2004) 2:275 –303.
38 Ghassan Hage, "The Differential Intensities of Social Reality: Migration, Participation and Guilt," in *Arab-Australians Today. Citizenship and Belonging*, ed. Ghassan Hage (Carlton South: Melbourne UP, 2002): 192–205.

the boundaries of the Muslim diaspora are defined situationally, both in their discourse and in acts of mobilization and protest. I describe such mobilisations in detail in *Imagined Diasporas*. So we return to the Manchester School and situational analysis. In conclusion, I hope I have demonstrated vis-à-vis Brubaker that diasporas do have boundaries, but that the boundaries of diaspora are defined and highlighted situationally, dialectically and over time, in action, through performance and periodic mobilizations.

Rasha Chatta

Mutations of the *Trans-Migrare:* Reflections on the Aesthetics of Individuation and Un-Homing on the Other Side of Belonging

Abstract: This chapter seeks to approach critically the ready sociological constructs of notions of home and belonging through the literary works of migrant writers. Recent approaches to the field of Migrant literature have tended to force identity constructs on authors' writings, thereby placing them in opposition to a national canon which equates to a nation-state. At the core of this impulse is the assertion that Migrant literature not merely refers to the author's movement away from a (national) home and to a new (national) home, but also does imply a mutation, as the Latin migrare suggests. How then to re-consider notions of home and (un)belonging within this literary phenomenon which tends to work against entrenched frontiers within and between languages, nations, geographic provenances? Examining questions of home and (un)belonging through the imaginative necessities and challenges of individual experience, beyond the social analytical categories of the collective, and from within the texts, offers the possibility of an existential topos, which could lead to a new perspective, beyond the predominantly sociological approaches. The emergent forms of subjectivity possibly constitute the fundamental grounds of the experience of home/(un)belonging and hence the unique nature of the literary output of so-called Migrant literatures. The chapter offers analytic examples drawing on Arab migrant writing in Quebec.

In a lecture entitled "Claiming diasporas, reclaiming diaspora studies" presented at the University of Stockholm on October 23, 2012, Khachig Tölölyan outlined the specificity of diaspora studies as being part of the wider phenomenon of dispersion whose core relies on migration beyond the national configuration,[1] and is as such deemed transnational. Further, one of the main features at the heart of what characterizes the diasporic, he argued, is the predominant focus granted to the binary home/homeland, and we can add, its corollary notion of belonging. In fact, his proposed working definition of what constitutes a diaspora, in opposition to any other community marked by dispersion, such as for example transnational or migrant communities, is the shift operated by distinguishing the homeland from the home.[2] In second, or most generally third generation mi-

---

1 Khachig Tölölyan, "Claiming Diasporas, Reclaiming Diaspora Studies" (May 22, 2013), *Department of Social Anthropology* <http://www.socant.su.se/english/research/research-seminars/transnational-migration-autumn-2012/filmed-lectures/filmed-lecture-by-khachig-tololyan-1. 108780> (acc. September 1, 2013).
2 Khachig Tölölyan distinguishes his object of research and approach from that of scholars of migration and establishes a crucial distinction in the usages of the often-conflated terms 'migration' and 'diaspora'. If, he argues, it is correct to point out that both diaspora and transnationalism derive from migrant mobility, his focus of research remains nonetheless on "the tension

grants, the process of diasporization occurs when the transnational communities of migrants are no longer bound to the homeland primarily by a first-hand account experience of displacement, but rather by a generational distance to it: "[They] develop some familial, cultural, and social distance from their [homeland] yet continue to care deeply about it, not just on grounds of kinship and filiation but by commitment to certain chosen affiliations."[3] That is, Tölölyan elaborates, collectively 'the homeland' survives through some collectivised disposition or a set of shared values and memories that may have a cohesive function. But with the second and third generation, these cohesive nodes begin necessarily to enter a seemingly ever-changing process of negotiating a differentiated identity, an identity that emerges through observable and experiential differences from the social majority of the 'host' country. Transnational and self-fashioning, this emergent identity begins to cement the condition of diasporicity.[4] To put it succinctly, durable diasporas correspond to that moment when "home [becomes] the country of residence while the land of origin is only recognized as the land of ancestors."[5]

This shift from homeland to home is precisely what operates when transnationalism becomes qualified as diasporic. Tölölyan's argument pinpoints an aspect that is at the heart of the debate, not only in diaspora studies, but also in wider multidisciplinary studies involving migration and mobility beyond national borders. This aspect is the conception of home and belonging outside of their traditional usages associated with the national. Tölölyan's insight is particularly significant to migration studies and more specifically migrant literature. What could be seen as initial hermeneutical negotiation of a fundamental relation to a perceived collectivity begins to settle into a dominant signification of meaning, a factuality of history. The conceptual shift in the approach to home as a construct, as I argue here, allows us to reconceive the dynamics of belonging in literary works, and the languages of imaginative necessities they offer, beyond the strictures of disciplinary approaches within migrant studies. The various forms of social analysis have so far tended to conceive of such works sociologi-

---

between the sedentary nodes of diasporic networks and migratory mobility [...] the circuit between [these two]," see Tölölyan, "Claiming Diasporas, Reclaiming Diaspora Studies," 00:02:27.

3 Tölölyan, "Claiming Diasporas, Reclaiming Diaspora Studies," 00:17:36.

4 For more extensive study, see also Khachig Tölölyan's seminal works: "Diaspora Studies: Past, Present and Promise," *IMI Working Papers Series* 55.4 (2012): 1–14; "Rethinking Diaspora(s): Stateless Power in the Transnational Moment," *Diaspora, a Journal of Transnational Studies* 5.1 (1996): 3–36; and "The Contemporary Discourse of Diaspora Studies," *Comparative Studies of South Asia, Africa and the Middle East* 27.3 (2007): 647–655.

5 Tölölyan, "Claiming Diasporas, Reclaiming Diaspora Studies," 00:33:55.

cally as a form of literary production that is locked into a crisis mode, admitting no possibilities for aesthetic or individual, non-normativizing imaginative agency. That is, we must learn from within the field how to read the work of a "migrant" writer first as a work of *literature* and therein recognize in the imaginative languages of urgency the possibility of an alternative imaginary that may lead us to reconceive the limits of categorical disciplinary formations. What we might consider, building on Tölölyan's argument, is the possibility that the original and originating hermeneutical negotiations also survive as the very condition of a cementing collective imaginary. This mode of survival is equivalent to the functions of cultural memory through which a single community negotiates its durable identity (national or otherwise). The fundamental difference here, however is that the diasporic imaginary is by definition necessarily, transnational, trans-historical, trans-locational; it is a creative imaginary of the meaning-giving acts of trans-ing, so to speak. The imaginative mutations of these trans-ing imaginaries, as I argue here, are what potentially offer us aesthetic modalities of individuation, and they are what deliver the literary imagination of the migrare.[6]

In order to be able to pursue home and belonging outside of their traditional usages, which also inform the knowledge-constructs of the disciplines and their categorical impulses, one need only consider the increasing body of literary production by individuals labeled migrant or diasporic. The prominence of such works and authors in the past few decades points to the possibility of a type of world experience that resonates across borders and beyond the questions of national belonging. The way they negotiate this world experience can be said to constitute an activity of un-homing as such, for what they seek to achieve and indeed often succeed in articulating is a way of owning self and space (linguistic, social, national, etc.) against or in the face of the claiming forces of belonging. They forge their own ties so to speak. They imaginatively claim as home the *trans* in the *migrare* and thereby shift the terms of the debate from those of home and homeland or country of origin and host country to home and world, as a space of negotiation beyond the physicality and materiality of borders whether linguistic or spatial.

---

6 It is interesting to note that the Latin term 'migrare' (to migrate) shares the same Indo-European root *MEI- as the Latin term 'mutare' (to mutate; and in biology too, a migrating cell is a mutating cell). The *Online Etymology Dictionary* indicates that the Latin origin of "mutable" could either be 'mutare', ('change') or 'migrare' ('to move from one place to the another'), with the implication that to change oneself is to change places or is akin to changing places (see www.etymonline.com).

In an article entitled "The World and the Home," Homi K. Bhabha resorts to the term 'unhomely' in articulating the aesthetic and cultural complexities of such an experience:

> You must permit me this awkward term – the unhomely – because it captures something of the estranging sense of the relocation of the home and the world in an unhallowed place. [...] In that displacement, the border between home and world becomes confused; and, uncannily, the private and the public become part of each other forcing upon us a vision that is as divided as it is disorienting. In the stirrings of the unhomely, another world becomes visible. It has less to do with forcible eviction and more to do with the uncanny literary and social effects of enforced social accommodation, or historical migrations and cultural relations. The home does not remain the domain of domestic life, nor does the world simply become its social or historical counterpart. The unhomely is the shock of recognition of the world-in-the-home, the home-in-the-world.[7]

While Bhabha ultimately puts forth this concept of the unhomely in the context of negotiations in the House of Fiction, the concept still suggests a kind of incommunicability in the public moment, "a psychic obscurity that is formative for public memory."[8] But it is also what is aesthetically treated in works of literature. "Literature," he says, "asks questions at the border of its historical and disciplinary being."[9] The aesthetic impulse therefore does not seek to document what is seemingly factually saturating the work, its themes, languages and character types; rather it constitutes a foundational act through the investigation of such nodes of incommunicability. The migrant writer carries the task further, what I'm suggesting here as un-homing is a willful negotiation of such borders of literature as well as of linguistic, social and national spaces, in order to bring out the agency of experience as one of presentness.

As Mads Rosendhal Thomsen notes in a chapter entitled "Migrant Writers and Cosmopolitan Literature":

> The writing of migrants is an understudied but increasingly interesting topic in the history of literature, particularly with regard to the effects it has had on modernist and contemporary literature, and in making transnational literature visible as field to be taken seriously in its own right.[10]

---

7 Homi K. Bhabha, "The World and the Home," *Social Text* 31/32 (1992): 141–153, 141.
8 Bhabha, "The World and the Home," 143.
9 Bhabha, "The World and the Home," 143.
10 Mads Rosendhal Thomsen, *Mapping World Literature: International Canonization and Transnational Literatures* (London, New York: Bloomsbury Academic, 2008): 61.

Works classified as migrant literature are difficult to theorize mainly because of the criterion retained by literary critics and academic institutions in labeling a work as migrant writing. Before proceeding further with how the literary aesthetically alienates all such public categories and constructs of identity in order to highlight what is at stake in the human condition of dislocation, it is perhaps important to pause and to consider how the field of migrant literature was constructed. That is, to explore briefly the problematic at stake when considering such notions as home and belonging in multidisciplinary studies that comprise migration.

Disciplinary Formations and the Aesthetics of Estrangement

Since roughly the 1950s and until today, the successive paths towards globalization – "facilitated by new means of transportation, telecommunications, and internationalization of the labor force" alongside the decolonization processes – have practically translated into an increase in the flow of human movement and mobility.[11] This has consequently allowed for the circulation of ideas and varying forms of cultural production across geo-political boundaries.[12] These formative contexts for the field of migrant literature prove important when sketching its disciplinary evolution; it is crucial to inscribe the moment of its emergence in these wider economical and geopolitical contexts, which can be understood to have modeled and shaped its critical reach and method.

The inevitable result was a refashioning of the worldview based partly on the necessity to account for the changes produced by the recent historical developments. This has had a particular implication for literary practices and has urged academic institutions and literary critics to reconsider the traditional classifications of literary history in order to take into account the emergence of new liter-

---

11 Sandra Ponzanesi, Daniela Merolla (ed.), *Migrant Cartographies: New Cultural and Literary Spaces in Post-Colonial Europe* (Oxford: Lexington Books, 2005): 3.

12 See for example the following works, which provide a general overview of the circulation of humans, ideas and cultural products since the 1950s: Gisela Brinker-Gabler, Sidonie Smith (ed.), *Writing New Identities: Gender, Nation, and Immigration in Contemporary Europe* (Minneapolis, London: Minnesota UP, 1997); Homi K. Bhabha (ed.), *Nation and Narration* (London: Routledge, 1991); Homi K. Bhabha, *The Location of Culture* (London: Routledge, 1994); Bill Ashcroft, *Post-Colonial Transformation* (London: Routledge, 2001); Russell King, John Connell, Paul White (ed.), *Writing Across Worlds* (London: Routledge, 1995).

atures,[13] as demonstrated in the earlier debates over the classification and the labeling of "emergent literatures" following the decolonization period. Labels such as "Third World Literature" or "-phone literature" (e. g. "Francophone Literature") designating works often composed in the language of the colonizing power reveal the limitations and complications of literary history in its classical conception and the need to resort to a new language to name a new body of literature which does no longer merely correspond to the national canon, in its narrower sense. Issues of canonical inclusion and exclusion and complex power relations appear to be at the heart of these debates. For what most of these emergent literatures have in common is their defiance to traditional approaches modeled on national literatures. In fact, globalization renders national boundaries highly porous thereby rendering obsolete, to a certain extent, or incomplete, inadequate, the idea equating the national canon with fixed and clearly delineated national borders. Earlier models of European literary histories do generally conflate the national canon with the borders of the nation-state, holding at its core a clearly delineated language sphere. Literary history as conceived in France, for example, constitutes an illuminating model. In the late nineteenth century, Gustave Lanson proposed the first approach to literary history as a modern discipline in his *Histoire de la littérature française* (1895), in which language, literature, and the nation are melded together in an unproblematic union, and France's geographical and political borders correspond to its linguistic borders. Despite the emergence since then of "extra-national" literatures written in French, produced in countries such as the Maghreb or Vietnam to name but a few, the trinity of language, literature and the nation in French literary history still informs much of the resistance and difficulty to envisage literatures in French outside the nation in much of the twentieth century, but especially after the Second World War.[14]

The broad term 'new literatures' which has served as an umbrella embracing such diverse literary categories as Commonwealth Literature, Third World Literature and more recently Migrant Literature, to name some of the major trends, is

---

13 See, amongst others, Gayatri Chakravorty Spivak, *Death of a Discipline* (New York: Columbia UP, 2003); Fredric Jameson, "Third-World Literature in the Era of Multinational Capitalism," *Social Text* 15 (1986): 65–88.
14 See Christie McDonald, Susan Rubin Suleiman (eds.), *French Global: A New Approach to Literary History* (New York: Columbia UP, 2010). The editors' introduction to this volume, entitled "The National and the Global" (ix–xxi) provides an excellent overview of the issues at stake in conceiving of French literary history linearly, and in a framework of analysis that is centred on the trinity of language, literature and the nation. The editors then put forth a new vision and approach calling for the inclusion of French's global dimensions.

deemed 'new' as a possible shortcut attempt to mark the emergence of such differential literary practices that do not fall within a particular national canon. Therefore, at first glance, it represents a corpus of literary works whose main thrust lies in the fact that it is a corpus *other* than the national canon. The implications for authors of these 'new literatures' prove to be problematic in many respects. Labels and categories imposed on these authors clearly state that they do not belong in the national canon, as traditionally conceived, and further poses issues of authenticity and allegiance towards a strictly defined body of literature. Salman Rushdie's dismissal of the label Commonwealth Literature and the arguments he puts forth to justify his refusal to be designated as a Commonwealth author are reminiscent of the impulse behind the labeling of authors as pertaining to migrant literature:

> 'Commonwealth literature' is no more than an ungainly name for the world's younger English literatures. If that were true, or rather, if that were all, it would be a relatively unimportant misnomer. But it isn't all. Because the term is not used simply to describe, or even misdescribe, but also to *divide*. It permits academic institutions, publishers, critics and even readers to dump a large segment of English literature into a box and then more or less ignore it. At best, what is called 'Commonwealth literature' is positioned *below* English literature 'proper' – or [...] it places Eng. lit. at the centre and the rest of the world at the periphery. [...] What is life like inside the ghetto of 'Commonwealth literature'? [...] One of the rules, one of the ideas on which the edifice rests, is that literature is an expression of nationality.[15]

These are rather pointed but still largely relevant insights. Rushdie maps out the literary field as a system which would contain a center – the national canon or, Eng. Lit. – while the rest is distributed hierarchically over a clear divide. One way of highlighting the irony of such a divide is Rushdie's shrewd play with the conception and labeling of authenticity:

> 'Authenticity' is the respectable child of old-fashioned exoticism. It demands that sources, forms, style, language and symbol all derive from a supposedly homogenous and unbroken tradition. Or else. What is revealing is that the term, so much in use inside the little world of 'Commonwealth literature', and always as a term of praise, would seem ridiculous outside this world. Imagine a novel being eulogized for being 'authentically English', or 'authentically German'. It would seem absurd. Yet such absurdities persist in the ghetto.[16]

---

15 Salman Rushdie, "Commonwealth Literature Does Not Exist," in *Imaginary Homelands: Essays and Criticism 1981–1991* (London: Granta, 1991): 61–70, 65–67.
16 Rushdie, "Commonwealth Literature Does Not Exist," 65–67.

The same irony clearly applies to the classification of migratory as against a work recognised by the dominant cultural actors as one belonging to the canon or representative space of the host culture. On the European scene, the examples are numerous, ranging from *Gastarbeiterliteratur* from the 1970s in Germany[17] to the more recent *Letteratura della migrazione* in Italy.[18] The case of migrant literature in Italy provides an illustrative example for my point. It is only since the 1990s that "the publishing industry in Italy has paid attention to 'other' narratives previously ignored" and in a similar process to other European settings,[19] "migrant literature started acquiring visibility thanks to a gradual acquisition of space – in the literal sense, on the shelves of bookstores and in catalogues of publishers."[20]

A close examination of how migrant texts have been tackled thus far reveals the emphasis placed on approaching them merely as sociological or ethnological accounts of the migration experience itself: "So far migrant literature as a category has been relegated to the realm of social studies: therefore it is time to search for new paradigms of interpretation that can assess the value of a literature of migration in its own terms."[21] In her book *Migration Italy*, a volume on migrant literature in Italy, Graziella Parati articulates the point more sharply: "Literary critics in Italy have only marginally studied migration [...] literature because it often is considered a phenomenon that belongs to social studies and is outside the aesthetic concerns of practitioners of literary criticism."[22] Consequently, "defining migrants' writings [...] is complicated by the fact that outside forces tend to define them in categories or genres that are not determined by form, but by [thematic] content, or even more problematically by the author's

---

17 See amongst others Leslie Anderson, *The Turkish Turn in Contemporary German Literature: Toward a New Critical Grammar of Migration* (New York: Palgrave MacMillan, 2005); Kristin Surak, "Guestworkers: A Taxonomy," *New Left Review* 84.11–12 (2013): 84–102; Alfred Cobbs, *Migrants' Literature in Postwar Germany: Trying to Find a Place to Fit In* (Lewiston, New York: Edwin Mellen P, 2007).

18 See amongst others Graziella Parati (eds.), *Mediterranean Crossroads: Migration Literature in Italy* (Madison, NJ: Fairleigh Dickinson UP, 1999); Graziella Parati, *Migration Italy: The Art of Talking Back in a Destination Culture* (Toronto: Toronto UP, 2005); Armando Gnisci, Nora Moll (eds.), *Diaspore europee & lettere migranti* (Rome: Interculturali, 2002); Armando Gnisci, *La letteratura italiana della migrazione* (Rome: Lilith, 1998).

19 Parati, *Migration Italy*, 28.

20 Parati, *Migration Italy*, 63.

21 See Sandra Ponzanesi, Daniela Merolla (eds.), *Migrant Cartographies: New Cultural and Literary Spaces in Post-Colonial Europe* and Russell King, John Connell, Paul White (eds.), *Writing Across Worlds* (London: Routledge, 1995) for a more extensive study of the relation between the social sciences and the humanities in their respective approaches to migrant literature.

22 Parati, *Migration Italy*, 103.

identity."[23] While themes of migration are often, though not always, central in the works of migrant writers, they tend to be overemphasized by the external conditions of market and by critics; the first critical impulse is to prioritize such works underlining a strong autobiographical undertone. I shall analyze the effects of such external conditioning of experience in more detail when discussing the case of Lebanese Quebecois writer Abla Farhoud in the following section.

In Italy, Roberta Sangiorgi, one of the promoters of migrant writing and the founder of the association Eks&Tra in 1995, has been organizing the first literary award for migrant writers since then and has consistently placed the emphasis on the autobiographical element.[24] In some notable cases, editors went as far as co-authoring works written by migrant authors, in order to render them more 'authentic' and to alert the readership's attention to issues closely linked to the migratory experience: for example, editor Mario Fortunato has co-authored Salah Methnani's autobiography in order to render it more 'authentic' to the eyes of the Italian readership. Fortunato justifies his initiative by qualifying Methnani's and other migrant authors' writings as "pre-literary experiences":

> [these writings are] pre-literary experiences that contain a sociological value. These are messages in a bottle that originate from an underground reality that is taking shape. There will be the need of other generations, of a deeper assimilation of the language, of its narrative stylistic features. And surprises will probably originate from this because we cannot exclude that, opening itself to new interpretations, the Italian language could become richer, more eccentric. Or poorer. [25]

The envisioning of migrant authors' writings as mere sociological accounts with no literary value as well as the quest for 'authenticity' and the importance attached to it are clear reminders of Salman Rushdie's own experience of being labeled a 'Commonwealth' writer – a different set of criteria in the evaluation of literary works than those applied to works classified within the national canon as traditionally conceived.

The dichotomy that emerges from opposing a national canon, the public moment in Homi K. Bhabha's terms, that defines what is to be included and what is

---

23 Parati, *Migration Italy*, 16.

24 Graziella Parati notes that this award runs the danger of establishing a creative ghetto that can only marginally contribute to the literature written in one language (Parati, *Migration Italy*, 54–103).

25 Statement contained in Adriana Polveroni, "L'immigrato racconta in italiano," *L'Unità* (April 26, 1995). Translated by Graziella Parati and cited in Parati (ed.), *Mediterranean Crossroads*, 17.

an "other" or in this case "migrant" canon relies mainly on holding the author's background as at once a principle of selection and a principle of explanation. Additionally recurrent themes related to exile, deterritorialization, difficulties in adapting to the "host" country, a here, a there and an in-between are often shared themes. These statements make us question the authorial influence (in terms of identity and its corollaries, such as language) on the text itself and ask to what extent an author with a certain background is expected to write in a certain manner.

What is really problematic is perhaps not so much the will to acknowledge the existence of an important and increasingly visible body of texts written by migrant authors, but the way it has been approached: as the examples within the Italian scene have illustrated, because of the themes put forth and their authors' backgrounds, such works have been seen as testimonial accounts of the experience of migration itself, as if the writing were yet unreflective native expressions of the phenomenon, without agency, much less any form of individuation, and in the manner of cultural practices of a primitive society: the approach here shares with older ethnographic methods how, under the disciplinary gaze, the phenomenon at once *expresses* and *produces* itself.

One early and notable contribution, the first to call for the literariness of the texts to be taken into account, is the volume entitled *Writing Across Worlds* edited by Russell King, John Connell and Paul White, in which the authors claim that the humanities and literature have not concerned themselves directly with research questions dealing with migration:

> Every act of migration reflects wider social, political and economic developments, such as modernisation processes. Thus, one may wish to draw on migrant literature as social evidence. On the other hand, literature is individual, subjective and diverse. It may reflect, but also exaggerate, challenge or invert the social experience that informs it. In finding a voice outside the established social discourse, and exploring the possible beyond the given, it may also resist functionalization as social evidence. Interpretative practice needs to take account of both the individual and the social-historical significance of a text.[26]

Following from these arguments, the question still remains: how do we find this voice "outside the established social discourse"? Where would a critical theoretical reading of texts belonging to migrant literature begin, in the face of an overwhelming sociological approach to the field, which bypasses aesthetic mediation altogether and sees value only in the biographical and historical factuality satu-

---

26 Sabine Fischer and Moray McGowan, "From 'Pappkoffer' to Pluralism. Migrant Writing in the German Federal Republic," in King, Connell, White (eds.), *Writing Across Worlds*: 39–56, 41.

rating the work? This question is precisely what constitutes the point of departure for a critical investigation into that which "resists functionalization as social evidence" in literary practice. More specifically, how does a critical theoretical reading of texts belonging to migrant literature negotiate the constructions of home and belonging?

Farhoud: Traces of the Home Trans-Imaginary

The imaginative mutations of diasporicity, as I have explained briefly, offer us the possibility of reconceiving the collective hermeneutical negotiations of a differentiated identity in aesthetic terms, and as that which the aesthetic impulse explores or grapples with before significations of identity settle into sociological factuality. This aesthetic impulse should therefore be pursued in the terms of a trans-imaginal, rather than those of the transnational. When one begins to consider possible contexts that may aid the analytic investigation of conceptions of the literary, beyond simply positing the questions of a trans-nationalist impulse at work, the case of Quebec emerges as a significant sphere. Indeed, the Quebecois literary scene offers some of the first serious attempts at theorizing migrant literature, at the limits of its own literary systems of circulation. Migrant literature, locally termed *écriture(s) migrante(s)*,[27] has emerged since the sixties and became visible in the eighties, with important nexuses around Quebec City and especially Montreal. The province of Quebec with its diversified cultural and language spaces offers one of the most interesting laboratories in terms of theorization of migrant literature. This is of course closely tied with the important Italian, Irish and more recently Chinese and Arab migrant waves.[28]

The historical and national self-imagining of Quebec as the largest French-speaking community outside France has been strongly influenced by the experience of domination by the rest of Anglo-Saxon Canada, as well as by strong crit-

---

27 The term was coined by Pierre Nepveu, who borrowed it from Robert Berrouet-Oriol, "L'Effet d'exil," *Vice versa* 17 (1986/1987): 20–21. See Pierre Nepveu, *L'Ecologie du réel: Mort et naissance de la littérature québécoise contemporaine* (Montréal: Boréal, 1988): 197–210.
28 See amongst others: Daniel Chartier, "Les origines de l'écriture migrante: L'immigration littéraire au Québéc au cours des deux derniers siècles," *Voix et Image* 27.2 (2002): 303–316; Danielle Dumontet, Frank Zipfel (eds.), *Ecriture Migrante/Migrant Writing* (Hildesheim: Olms, 2008); Marie Carrière, Catherine Khordoc (eds.), *Migrance comparée, Comparing Migration: Les Littératures du Canada et du Québec, The Literatures of Canada and Québec* (Berne: Peter Lang, 2008); Simon Harel, *Les Passages obligés de l'écriture migrante* (Montreal: XYZ, 2005); Pierre Nepveu, *L'Ecologie du réel: Mort et naissance de la littérature québécoise contemporaine* (Montréal: Boréal, 1988).

ical and historical discourses offering an analogy between Quebecois and North African terms of resistance. As such, for example, in a special issue of the journal *Parti Pris* (1963–1968), edited by Pierre Maheu, the author compiled the "portrait of the colonized Quebecois" in reference to Albert Memmi's analyses of the culturally,[29] politically and economically colonized Maghrebians.[30] It is interesting here to note the shift from Maghrebians colonized by France to the French Quebecois "colonized" (although dominated would probably constitute a better-suited term) by the Anglo-Saxon presence. Similarly, in 1968, Pierre Vallières wrote an autobiographical work entitled *Nègres blancs d'Amérique*[31] [translated into English as *White Negroes of Domination*] referring to the suffering of the Quebecois people at the hands of the Anglo-Saxons and with a clear allusion to Frantz Fanon's *Peau Noire, Masques Blancs*[32] [*Black Skin, White Masks*]. As Pierre Nepveu, the Quebecois critic who coined the term *écriture(s) migrante(s)*,[33] writes: "the Quebecois *imaginaire* was largely defined, since the sixties, under the banner of exile [...], of a lack, of an absent or incomplete country; from the heart of this very negative, it has re-emerged as a migrant, plural, and often cosmopolitan awareness."[34] It is therefore not surprising that Quebec presented a most favorable laboratory for approaching and theorizing migrant literature.[35]

Within this complex tapestry, Arab Quebecois writings offer fruitful grounds for the approaches to the literary experience. The literature written by Arab migrants in Quebec was born in the early 1970s, at the hands of First Generation Canadians of Arab descent, which have authored over 150 books, all genres included.[36] About ten to fifteen percent of Arabic-Quebecois literature is produced in Arabic, while over sixty-five percent is written in French, the remainder being written in English.[37]

---

29 *Parti Pris* 11.5 (1965), cited by Lise Gauvin, "Traversal of Languages. The Quebecois Laboratory," in *French Global*, ed. Christie McDonald, Susan Rubin Suleiman: 419–436, 421.
30 Pierre Maheu refers in particular to Albert Memmi, *Portrait du colonisé, précédé de Portrait du colonisateur* [1957] (Paris: Gallimard, 2002).
31 Pierre Vallières, *Nègres blancs d'Amérique* [1968] (Montreal: Typo, 1994).
32 Frantz Fanon, *Peau Noire, Masques Blancs* (Paris: Éditions du Seuil, 1952).
33 See footnote 27.
34 Nepveu, *L'Ecologie du réel: Mort et naissance de la littérature québécoise contemporaine*, 200–201. Cited in and translated by F. Elizabeth Dahab, *Voices of Exile in Contemporary Canadian Francophone Literature* (Lanham, Plymouth: Lexington, 2009): 5.
35 Simon Harel, *Les Passages obligés de l'écriture migrante* (Montreal: XYZ, 2005).
36 Dahab, *Voices of Exile*, viii.
37 Dahab, *Voices of Exile*, 21.

E. Dahab provides a detailed overview of the background of the Arabic-Canadian authors writing in French and their body of literature; she estimates that there are about forty writers: "of whom about twenty-five have produced a major work (one or more books); the rest have a minor production (principally publications in reviews and magazines)."[38] A significant portion of these authors has immigrated to Quebec or Ontario between 1963 and 1974, "while several did so in the fifties, late seventies, or eighties."[39] Farhoud belongs to the first wave of Arab migrants, alongside Naim Kattan, and can be said to have experimented with languages, and different registers in Arabic, French and English, especially in her novels while approaching migrant thematics in an innovative fashion.

Inscribed in this context, Lebanese-Quebecois Abla Farhoud's oeuvre, particularly her novel entitled *Le Bonheur a la queue glissante* (Happiness has a slippery tail),[40] constitutes an interesting case study. Abla Farhoud was born in 1945 in a small village in South East Lebanon. At six years old, she immigrated with her parents to Montreal and settled in a Francophone neighborhood. After four years spent back in Lebanon, Farhoud moved to Paris to study theatre and eventually returned to Montreal where she became a professional actress performing on stage and television. She left the stage in 1990 to devote herself completely to her writing. *Le Bonheur a la queue glissante* is her first novel, published in 1998 for which she received the France-Quebec Prize the following year. Since then three novels have followed: *Splendide Solitude* [Splendid Solitude], *Le Fou d'Omar* [Omar's Madman], and more recently *Le Sourire de la fille juive* [The Smile of the Little Jewess].[41]

In this section, I wish to offer a few reflections on the trans-imagining of home and belonging operated in *Le Bonheur a la queue glissante* through and beyond the negotiation of world experiences across national borders and linguistic enclaves. This novel is indeed significant for the way it illustrates how the author aesthetically alienates the question of home and belonging as public moments in the life of her main character, Dounia. The spaces of migration, while geographically delineated, are woven into the mnemonic refractions of a direct voice that, over the movement of the narrative and memories, slowly begins to emerge. While such spaces are claimed in the urgencies of an individu-

---

38 Dahab, *Voices of Exile*, 11.
39 Dahab, *Voices of Exile*, 17.
40 Abla Farhoud, *Le Bonheur a la queue glissante* [1998] (Montreal: Typo, 2010). Further references in the text, abbreviated as "*BQG.*" Unless otherwise stated, all translations are mine.
41 Abla Farhoud, *Splendide solitude* (Montreal: L'Hexagone, 2001); Abla Farhoud, *Le Fou d'Omar* (Montreal: VLB, 2005); Abla Farhoud, *Le Sourire de la petite juive* (Montreal: VLB, 2011). For more biographical information, see Dahab, *Voices of Exile*, 97–133.

alized sensibility, the voice itself begins to willfully take shape against an externally forced muteness. The main character cannot speak French, but in struggling with this highly symbolic condition, it redeploys the very the possibilities of expressivity in language through the aesthetically alienating native registers. Claiming language and the ability to express, beyond simple communication, in such manner, however, is not the same as claiming Lebanese identity; it is not the sociological act of claiming home in the nostalgia of belonging. The latent expressive force in the idiomatic Lebanese expressions interspersed in the French text, retrieved in the urgency of the present, emerges as mode of relation to the collective beyond the claiming of origins. It turns on the very expressivity of language, beyond the ability to communicate, functionally in French or directly in Arabic as an act of asserting identity, and in so doing turns language itself into a process of individuation. The collective force of language is unhomed in both directions, just as the spaces of belonging are temporized in the acts of retrieval. The centralizing aesthetic in the narrative's projections of language and space emerges as that of an individual sensibility that is the cumulative effect of a sustained 'elsewhereness.'

The novel is centered on the character of Dounia, a Lebanese grandmother in her seventies who has been living in Montreal for the past forty years. The narrative is constructed as an interior monologue, written in the first person, which allows the reader an intimate entry into her psyche. We learn through her monologue that she has started her peripatetic journey first moving from village to village in Lebanon, when she married her husband, and later on in Quebec:

> The other day, I told Abdallah [her son] that I had first emigrated when I got married and went to live in Bir-Barra [her husband's village]. He had a good laugh. For him, to emigrate is to change countries, to cross oceans, to go to the end of the world. [...] Immigrant [...] for me is the right word, because it is while living in my husband's village that I started to make comparisons, to see the differences, to experience lack and nostalgia, to feel like being elsewhere without being able to, to feel a stranger. (BQG, 43)[42]

In the village of her husband, for twelve years, she is perceived and feels an alienated stranger: "For me it (her husband's village) was a different country. For them, I was the foreigner who had stolen Salim (her husband)" (BQG,

---

42 "L'autre jour je disais à Abdallah que j'avais émigré la première fois en me mariant, quand je suis allée vivre à Bir-Barra. Il a bien ri. Pour lui, émigrer, c'est changer de pays, traverser les océans, aller au bout du monde. [...] immigrant [...] pour moi c'est le mot qui convient, parce que c'est en vivant dans le village de mon mari que j'ai commencé à faire des comparaisons, à voir les différences, à vivre le manque et la nostalgie, à avoir envie d'être ailleurs sans pouvoir y aller, à me sentir étrangère."

43).[43] It is significant to note that with each different peregrination – first from village to village within Lebanon, then from Lebanon to Quebec, then within Quebec, then back to Lebanon, and finally within Quebec – the perception the "natives" have of them evolves, offering a complex imaginary of interconnected and yet geographically delineated spaces. The labels attributed to them begin to cumulate: "In Lebanon we were called 'the Americans'; in Canada, during the first years, we were called 'the Syrians'; in my husband's village, I was called by the name of my village. When I think of it, I [realize] I have been called Dounia only in my village" (*BQG*, 105).[44] In fact, particularly significant is the centrality of space and its intimate association with the delineation of a multiplicity of homes – and to some extent, the failure to do so repeatedly. This specific trait participates in reinforcing the feeling of un-belonging throughout the plot. Throughout the narrative thread, effects of zooming in and out constitute recurrent strategies to convey the emotions caused by the change from a place to another: Dounia describes herself as a girl of the mountains. Her village was perched on a mountain and she could see far away into the horizon. When she moved to her husband's village, adjoining mountains were blocking the view, and the air consequently was less fresh. She qualifies this first migration as "suffocating" (*BQG*, 42–44). Later, in Canada, she describes her world as being confined to "these four walls" and in her last moments, her vital space is reduced to a crib in the nursing home (*BQG*, 147–150).

This movement is paradoxical to her migration trajectory, which for her is an opening up to the world:

> Up until my thirties, I thought the world ended at Gharouda, three villages away from mine. After arriving to Beirut and taking the boat, I understood that the world still continued. We crossed the sea. I learned later on that this sea was called the Mediterranean. In Italy, we changed boats and the world kept getting bigger and bigger and I kept getting smaller and smaller [...] does the world end anywhere? [...] The world is too big. (*BQG*, 55–56)[45]

---

43 "Pour moi c'était un autre pays. [...] Pour eux, j'étais l'étrangère [qui] avait volé Salim."
44 "Au Liban, on nous appelait 'les Américains'; au Canada, les premières années, on nous appelait 'les Syriens'; au village de mon mari, on m'appelait par le nom de mon village. Quand j'y pense, je n'ai été appelée Dounia que dans mon village."
45 "Jusqu'à l'âge de trente ans, je croyais que le monde finissait à Gharouda, à trois villages de chez nous. En arrivant à Beyrouth pour prendre le bateau, j'ai bien vu que le monde continuait. Nous avons traversé la mer. J'ai su plus tard que cette mer-là s'appelle Méditerranée, j'avais souvent entendu son nom dans les histoires. En Italie, nous avons changé de bateau et le monde devenait de plus en plus grand et moi, de plus en plus petite [...] le monde est trop grand."

This is as if the crossing of space and time was inevitably leading to death and disintegration. Dounia states:

> To emigrate, to go away, to leave behind that which we will start calling *my* sun, *my* water, *my* fruit, *my* plants, *my* trees, *my* village. When one is in one's native village, one does not say *my* sun, one says *the* sun, and barely mentions it since it is there, it has always been there, one does not say *my* village because one's been inhabiting it... (*BQG*, 43)[46]

In the final pages, she concludes that:

> Emigration has perhaps come to change the normal pace of things. The first emigration, and then the return to Lebanon, which has been very difficult. People say that a tree that has been transplanted too often hardly gives any fruit to be replanted. (*BQG*, 129)[47]

Dounia seems to embody Farhoud's assertion of a constant search for an elsewhere, which complicates the relation between home and belonging. Her emigration is not so much about being in a foreign country as such, as she states: "Some immigrants say: 'I would like to die in the country in which I was born.' Not me. My country is not the country of my ancestors and not even the village of my childhood; my country is where my children are happy" (*BQG*, 23).[48] The discontinuity of space as well as the complex and intricate interplay between the blurring of a clearly delineated home is closely linked to the muteness of the main protagonist. The rupture provoked by her emigration translates into her inability to express herself: Sometimes I would like to be able to speak, with words. I have forgotten, with time (*BQG*, 16).[49]

Because the central thematics in *Le Bonheur a la queue glissante* can easily be read sociologically, critics and interviewers have particularly insisted on questioning Farhoud on the issues confronted by migrant writers. In one particular roundtable in 1994, Farhoud asserted repeatedly that for her, being a migrant writer was peripheral to her work, and somehow accidental. She contended

---

46 "Emigrer, s'en aller, laisser derrière soi ce que l'on va se mettre à appeler mon soleil, mon eau, mes fruits, mes plantes, mes arbres, mon village. Quand on est dans son village natal, on ne dit pas mon soleil, on dit le soleil, et c'est à peine si on en parle puisqu' il est là, il a toujours été là, on ne dit pas mon village puisqu'on l'habite..."
47 "L'émigration est peut-être venue changer le cours normal des choses. La première, et le retour au Liban qui a été très dur. On dit qu'un arbre trop souvent transplanté donne rarement des fruits à planter."
48 "Certains immigrants disent: 'Je voudrais mourir là où je suis né.' Moi, non. Mon pays, ce n'est pas le pays des mes ancêtres ni même le village de mon enfance, mon pays, c'est là où mes enfants sont heureux."
49 "Quelquefois j'aimerais pouvoir parler, avec des mots. J'ai oublié, avec le temps."

that immigration for her is not a major theme, but merely a background land-scape and that her own experience of immigration can stand as a metaphor for human life: "My writing is migrant to the extent that I am always in search of the elsewhere. As a child, I have experienced loss and displacement, as every human being who has had to leave one day his mother's womb. It is in that sense that my immigrant experience is a metaphor for the human trajectory."[50] Moving from village to village becomes a universalizing experience, beyond specific na-tional boundaries. Farhoud can be said to have transcended the specific attrib-utes associated with emigration by portraying characters whose plights have uni-versal resonance. The narrative deploys and consciously embodies the contours of such human experiences of the constant search for an elsewhere.

The sociological approaches to migrant literature seem to have equated home with nationalness, by conceiving it through the prism of either the home country or the host country. As such, they have applied a monolithic dis-course of home, taken in singular terms, on the migrant writers, viewed collec-tively. However, the texts of creative writers of migrant literature offer us the pos-sibility of negotiating home and belonging in multiple terms. If we look closely at the works of migrant writers, we can perceive how people, as individuals, ne-gotiate home outside the collective. In other words, the literary as that which al-lows for the possibility of posing questions at the limit of historical and discipli-nary being can be used as a tool to go beyond the disciplinary boundaries and to conceive of home as that which is claimed on the other side of belonging, the agency of owning experience by claiming not only social space but also the spaces of memory and by claiming language not only as the functionality of so-cial positioning and mobility but as a force of expressivity in the process of ne-gotiating oneself in the world.

---

50 Dahab, *Voices of Exile*, 97–133.

Diasporic Selves: Memory, Identity, Agency

Sonja Fielitz
Hyphenated Homes: Elizabeth Jane Weston and the Diaspora of Early Modern English Catholics

Abstract: This chapter addresses a hitherto neglected aspect of early modern culture, namely, the concept of 'home' for the exiled Catholics under Elizabeth I and James I. 'Home' for them was first of all marked by travel and distance from England, as well as religious opposition to Anglicanism. Their native homeland was by no means a place associated with security and comfort but with severe persecution, torture and execution. Was it exactly their enforced distance that enabled the exiled Catholics to imagine England as their (idealized) home, or did their enforced displacement rather produce a hybridized identity and/or enable them to take action? In how far did their aim to re-catholicize England shape their feeling of home and give a group identity to them? To what extent was their notion of home bound to a unifying language, that is, English, – or rather Latin as the language of the learned but also of the Catholic Church? And, with specific reference to an individual, that is, Elizabeth Jane Weston as one of the most learned women of her time, what role did women, traditionally associated with home in the sense of family and household, play in these dynamics?

Cultural Framework: Early Modern Religious Discourses

Catholics were severely suppressed under Elizabeth I and even more so under her successor James I. During the earlier years of her reign, Elizabeth I still pragmatically acknowledged that Catholics keeping to their faith could yet be her loyal subjects. The Act of Uniformity of 1559 had made a failure to attend church illegal, but Elizabeth I still continued her effort of inter-confessional politics through the 1570s. After the promulgation of Pope Pius V's bull excommunicating Elizabeth in 1570 and her having defeated numerous conspiracies and major threats to her reign, the parliamentary Recusancy Act of 1580 imposed increasingly heavy fines and other penalties on practicing Catholics. The belief prevailed that an allegiance to the Old Faith could ultimately result in a traitorous commitment to foreign powers, such as Spain, which would be ready to invade the country. Religious exiles awaiting or working for the restoration of Catholicism in England were a political menace.

Despite the government's efforts to suppress the Catholic community, early modern England nevertheless remained a religiously divided land, in which a Catholic subculture survived:

[...] husbands submissively attended Anglican services and otherwise upheld public Protestant appearances to try to avoid recusancy fines, while wives at home sheltered priests, took part in conspiracies, held private masses, maintained secret travel networks, and sometimes gained a degree of initiative in religious affairs well beyond what most of their Protestant counterparts could exercise.[1]

The Old Faith had initially been sustained mostly by non-conforming priests from Queen Mary's reign, and later also from missionary priests who had been trained in the foreign seminaries on the Continent as the centers of a vibrant exile community. Exiled Catholic women had the opportunity of entering a convent on the Continent, particularly in France, Spain, and the Spanish Netherlands (today: Belgium). Perhaps the most well-known of them still today is Mary Ward (1585–1645), who founded the Institute of the Blessed Virgin Mary, an order dedicated to the education of women.[2] All in all, neither Elizabeth I nor her successor James I succeeded in quenching Catholicism in early modern England.

The most active agents in the field of Catholic sub-culture were the Jesuits. With specific reference to their activities and the early mission, the publications by Eamon Duffy,[3] the late Ernest Honigmann,[4] Gerard Kilroy,[5] Arthur Marotti,[6] Thomas McCoog S.J.,[7] Alison Shell,[8] Paul Whitfield White,[9] and Richard Wil-

---

1 Louise Schleiner, *Tudor and Stuart Women Writers* (Bloomington: Indiana UP, 1994): 84. After the Act of 1580, married women could not be fined because they were legal nonentities who could own no property. Thus, a surprising inverted gender pattern could develop among the Catholic gentry.

2 On Ward, see, for instance, Kari Boyd McBride, "Recusant Sisters: English Catholic Women and the Bonds of Learning," in *Sibling Relations and Gender in the Early Modern World*, ed. Naomi J. Miller and Naomi Yavneh (London: Ashgate, 2006): 28–39.

3 Eamon Duffy, *The Stripping of the Altars: Traditional Religion in England: c. 1400 – c. 1580*, second ed. (New Haven: Yale UP, 2005); see also his *Fires of Faith: Catholic England under Mary Tudor* (New Haven: Yale UP, 2009).

4 E. A. J. Honigmann, *Shakespeare. The Lost Years*, second ed. (Manchester: Manchester UP, 1998).

5 Gerard Kilroy, *Edmund Campion. Memory and Transcription* (London: Ashgate, 2006).

6 Arthur Marotti (ed.), *Catholicism and Anti-Catholicism in Early Modern English Texts* (Basingstoke: Palgrave, 1999).

7 Thomas McCoog (ed.), *Monumenta Anglia: English and Welsh Jesuits: Catalogues (1555–1629)*, 2 vols. (Rome: Institutum Historicum Societas Iesu, 1992).

8 Alison Shell, *Catholicism, Controversy and the English Library Imagination, 1558–1660* (Cambridge: Cambridge UP, 1999).

9 Paul Whitfield White, *Drama and Religion in English Provincial Society, 1485–1660* (Cambridge: Cambridge UP, 2008).

son,[10] to name but a few, have shown since the 1990s that especially the religious order of the Jesuits was severely suppressed in Elizabethan and Jacobean England, because it actively sent out missionaries. The first Jesuit mission took place in 1580,[11] when Father Edmund Campion and Father Robert Persons were sent to England from Rome.[12] Campion, who had sent his *Ten Reasons* to Parsons in March 1581, was arrested about a year after his landing, and was executed by hanging, drawing and quartering on December 1, 1581:

> Edmund Campion's execution in 1582 [...] was an elaborately contrived piece of political pageantry: paraded through the streets of London to the Tower, he was tied to a horse with a sign in large letters reading 'Campion the seditious Jesuit' pinned to his hat. [...] John Gerard also suffered the excruciating pain induced by the device of the strappado on two occasions in 1597, and the Yorkshire missionary Thomas Bell was hung upside down for three days.[13]

Sovereign power and spectacle sent out clear messages about the duties of religious conformity and obedience.

Persons escaped his pursuers and retired to the Continent in August of the same year where he passed away in Rome in 1610. He saw his vocation in establishing institutions abroad which energetically and effectively helped to support the English Jesuit mission. As a consequence in England, the statute of 1585 Against Jesuits and Seminary Priests made their very presence an act of high treason and ordered them to depart the realm within forty days of the end of the current parliamentary session.[14] Any harboring of Jesuit priests was severely punished, in most cases by death. The subsequent Acts against Seditious Sectaries and Popish Recusants (1593) sent offenders into exile, and in 1606 Jacobean

---

10 Wilson appropriates the topic for a distinctly dissident Shakespeare. See, for instance, his *Secret Shakespeare: Studies in Theatre, Religion and Resistance* (Manchester: Manchester UP, 2004) and "'Blood Will Have Blood': Regime Changes in *Macbeth*," *Shakespeare Jahrbuch* 143 (2007): 11–35.

11 For more details, see John L. La Rocca, "Popery and Pounds: The Effect of the Jesuit Mission on Penal Legislation," in *The Reckoned Expense: Edmund Campion and the Early English Jesuits*, ed. Thomas McCoog (Woodbridge: Boydell & Brewer, 1996): 249–263.

12 For the first missionary tour by Robert Parsons and Edmond Campion lasting from July 18 to October 1580, see Francis Edwards, *The Jesuits in England. From 1580 to the Present Day* (Tunbridge Wells: Burns and Oates, 1985).

13 Alexandra Walsham, *Charitable Hatred. Tolerance and Intolerance in England, 1500–1700* (Manchester: Manchester UP, 2006): 79–80.

14 See G. R. Elton (ed.), *The Tudor Constitution: Documents and Commentary* (Cambridge: Cambridge UP, 1992).

authorities even inserted a clause in the Oath of Allegiance explicitly prohibiting the use of equivocation.[15]

Early Modern Subject-Positions

Recent critical debates have made us aware that 'identity' as well as 'diaspora' are complex and contested terms which cannot be limited to any single type of community or historical situation.[16] They all, however, carry the common feature that communities have settled outside their natal territory and acknowledged that their homeland has some claim on their loyalty and emotions. Thus, "a deep symbolical [...] relation to the 'homeland' – be it an independent nation-state or set in a quasi-mythological distant past – is maintained by reference to constructs of common language, history, culture and – central to many cases – to religion."[17]

In our context of early modern religious discourses, exiles could indeed (as Campion and Parsons had done) return as missionaries to their home country in the hope of strengthening the community of recusant Catholics. Their mission would, however, imply the risk of being captured, tortured, and executed. The Catholics who remained in their exile on the Continent, on the other hand, may have become alienated of their homeland, and may have expressed home-sickness and nostalgic longing for an idealized England.

Exile and diaspora need not only be a cause for lamentation and grief (analogized to the diaspora of the Old Testament Jews), but can also be seen as a culturally *productive* condition. As James Clifford and others have argued, diasporas can also host a constructive potential as 'mediating cultures' instead of implications of exile and loss. In our context, it appears to have been their very status of exiles which did indeed enable Catholics to (subversively) 'mediate' in the sense of organizing activities of resistance, as well as write and publish treatises and pamphlets, since they had access to Catholic presses across Europe at St. Omer in northern France, at Louvain, Antwerp, Douai, and elsewhere. The English colleges on the Continent, for instance, were one means of providing a surrogate public sphere within the context of diaspora enabling them to act from a

---

15 See, for instance, Michael L. Carafiello, "Robert Parsons and Equivocation 1606–1610," *Catholic Historical Review* 79 (1993): 671–680.

16 See, for instance, the list of criteria in Robin Cohen, *Global Diasporas. An Introduction* (Seattle: U of Washington P, 1997), 180.

17 Waltraud Kokot, Khachig Tölölyan and Carolin Alfonso (eds.), *Diaspora, Identity and Religion. New Directions in Theory and Research* (London and New York: Routledge, 2004): 3.

distance. The governmental authorities, however, would interpret their activities as a threat to the nation's cultural boundaries as well as to the state's sovereignty.

Whatever subject-position early modern English Catholics may have taken: in all cases, the experience of persecution and exile would have shaped their idea of home and diaspora. As mentioned above, the exiles' experience was inextricably linked with travel and displacement. To be a Catholic in early modern England implied to have a particular relationship to space, that is, to England, and its borders. Even though English Catholics were dispersed in areas ranging from England to Spain to Brazil to India, this diaspora was bound together by their specific group identity. Almost paradoxically, it was this very experience that enabled – rather than precluded – Catholic participation in constructions of nationhood, home, and belonging.

Elizabeth Jane Weston and (Neo-Latin) Women

As briefly mentioned above with reference to Mary Ward, English women played a major role in Catholic activities on the Continent. They have remained, however, a highly understudied component of the Catholic diaspora.

> Indeed, most feminist scholarship has focused on the lives and works Protestant women and on the limits imposed on women's education by conservative Protestant moralists and educators. This focus, and the concomitant failure to attend to Catholic women's experience, leave our history of women's education in England distorted and incomplete.[18]

Another and equally widely neglected aspect in scholarship has been that Latin was not only (as is commonly known) the language of the educated world (male as well as female) of the time but also of the *Catholic* religious community who did not conform to the linguistic and Anglican nationalism propagating the vernacular. "Catholic translations of the New and Old Testaments came out in 1582 and 1602 respectively, and [...] English and bilingual editions were used in Catholic centers such as Antwerp, and St. Omer."[19] Latin and English thus co-existed, and English was not the sole, or even dominant, vernacular language in the exiles' publications.

---

18 Kari Boyd McBride, "Recusant Sisters," 28.
19 Jane Stevenson, "Women Catholics and Latin Culture," in *Catholic Culture in Early Modern England*, ed. Ronald Corthell, Frances E. Dolan, Christopher Highley, and Arthur F. Marotti (Notre Dame: Notre Dame P, 2007): 52–72, 53.

As sketched above, exiled early modern Neo-Latin female authors did play an important role in the religious discourses of the early modern period. For this purpose, I will in the following mostly focus on the life and writings of Elizabeth Jane Weston (1581–1612), a Catholic exile and famous Neo-Latin woman poet of her time, who has largely been ignored by academic discourse today. In her day, however, she enjoyed greatest international fame and was widely celebrated and acknowledged as one of the most learned women and gifted poets. If critics have dealt with her at all, they have been interested in the construction of her identity as an "English maiden,"[20] as a women poet and as an exile as such, frequently decrying her state by referring to Ovid's *Tristia* (especially in her poem I.39).[21] Highly surprising in the light of early modern studies since the late 1980s, Weston's identity as a *Catholic* refugee appears to have been completely neglected by scholars to date.[22] As I wish to develop in the following, the exciting combination of her identities as a Neo-Latin female poet *and* as a Catholic are apt to throw new light on the discourse of *home and diaspora* in early modern England.

Elizabeth Jane Weston,[23] also known as "Westonia," was born in Chipping Norton in Oxfordshire in 1582, but the precise details of her English biography have been left unspecified to date.[24] What we know is that her father died when she was still an infant, that her mother re-married within a year, that her family left England when she was about one year old and that she spent the rest of her life as a Catholic exile in Prague at the Court of Rudolf II, King

---

20 See Brenda M. Hosington, "Elizabeth Jane Weston and Men's Discourse of Praise," in *La femme lettrée à la Renaissance: Acts du Colloque International*, ed. Michael Bastiaensen (Brussels: Peeters, 1997): 107–118; Donald Cheney, "Virgo Angla: The Self-Fashioning of Westonia," in *La femme lettrée à la Renaissance: Acts du Colloque International*, ed. Michael Bastiaensen (Brussels: Peeters, 1997): 119–128; and Elizabeth Jane Weston, *Collected Writings*, ed. Donald Cheney and Brenda M. Hosington (Toronto: U of Toronto P, 2000): xxi–xxii.

21 See Sylvia Brown, "In Praise of Filia Docta: Elizabeth Weston and the Female Line," in *Acta Conventus Neo-Latini Cantabrigiensis. Proceedings of the Eleventh International Congress of Neo-Latin Studies, Cambridge 30 July – 5 August 2000*, ed. Rhoda Schnur (Tempe, AZ: Arizona Center for Medieval and Renaissance Studies, 2003): 105–113.

22 See, for instance, Carole Levin et al., *Extraordinary Women of the Medieval and Renaissance World. A Biographical Dictionary* (Westport, London: Greenwood P, 2000).

23 This passage on Weston's life is based on Pieta van Beerk, "'Golden Songs of Latin Thread': The Collected Songs of Elizabeth Jane Weston," *Moreana* 41.159 (2004): 87–94, and Schleiner, *Tudor and Stuart Women Writers*, 96–98.

24 For the early life of Elizabeth Jane Weston, see Susan Bassnett, "Revising a Biography: A New Interpretation of the Life of Elizabeth Jane Weston (Westonia) Based on her Autobiographical Poem on the Occasion of the Death of her Mother," *Cahiers Elisabéthains* 37 (1990): 1–8. Bassnett here calls attention to an autobiographical poem hitherto unknown in Western Europe.

of Bohemia and Holy Roman Emperor, where her stepfather, that is, Edward Kelley, had found a permanent position as court alchemist. Edward Kelley was an associate of the magician Dr. John Dee (1527–1608), a celebrity in England, "who had cast the horoscope of Elizabeth I. Elizabeth respected Dee enough to have her coronation on the day he suggested."[25] The Kelley family left England in 1583 on travels to Poland and Bohemia, and Kelley "put down roots in Bohemia (his brother Thomas was married to Ludmilla von Pisnitz, niece of Heinrich, Rudolf's vice-chancellor and mayor of Most, that is in German, Brüx) and stayed on as the Emperor's alchemist."[26] Kelley received a knighthood from Emperor Rudolph II in Prague in 1591. From 1591 onward, however, his fortunes declined, likely as a result of a duel in which he killed a member of the court. He was arrested in May 1591, and died in prison in 1597. After his imprisonment, all his property was confiscated or heavily encumbered by creditors, leaving his wife and his two children, that is Elizabeth Jane (born in 1582) and her brother John Francis (born two years earlier, that is, in 1580), in a destitute situation. John Francis, who had entered the Jesuit College in Ingolstadt (see below), in 1598, passed away there in 1600, and Elizabeth was devastated by his death. In 1603, she married Johann Leo, or Loewe, a lawyer and agent of Christian of Anhalt at the imperial court. In nine years of marriage, she gave birth to seven children (four sons who predeceased her and three daughters who survived). She died on November 23, 1612 and was buried in St. Thomas's church in Prague.[27]

Despite her obscurity today Elizabeth Jane Weston provides fascinating evidence of one of the most learned and talented female authors within the international republic of letters of her time.[28] She "arguably enjoyed the greatest international fame of any English writer who was not – like Sidney or More – of predominantly extra-literary interest to Europeans."[29] "Between 1606 and 1861, there appeared twelve catalogues of famous women in which she featured."[30] Thomas Farnaby's *Index Poeticus* (1663) includes her as only one of seven Eng-

---

25 Levin et al., *Extraordinary Women of the Medieval and Renaissance World*, 281.
26 Weston, *Collected Writings*, xii.
27 See Brenda M. Hosington, "Elizabeth Jane Weston (1581–1620)," in *Women Writing Latin. From Roman Antiquity to Early Modern Europe*, ed. Laurie Churchill, Phyllis R. Brown, and Jane E. Jeffrey, 3 vols (New York, London: Routledge, 2002) 3:217–218, and Levin et al., *Extraordinary Women of the Medieval and Renaissance World*, 281–284.
28 For example, Patricia Demers lists her among "lesser known figures" (Patricia Demers, *Women's Writing in English: Early Modern England* [Toronto: U of Toronto P, 2005]: 63).
29 Cheney, "Virgo Angla: The Self-Fashioning of Westonia," 119.
30 Hosington, "Elizabeth Jane Weston and Men's Discourse of Praise," 117.

lish writers – alongside Thomas More and the first Jesuit missionary Edmund Campion – as the only English woman of any time and place to appear in this list of eminent ancient and modern writers.[31] Furthermore, she was the only female to publish an authored volume of Neo-Latin verse known to exist, that is, *Poemata* and *Parthenicon*. It is safe to say that she definitely belonged to the prominent and distinguished members of the Neo-Latin *Res Publica Litteraria* of her time.

No doubt, in sixteenth- and seventeenth-century Europe, Latin was the *lingua franca* of the learned world, and the world of Neo-Latin literature embraced poets and scholars from across Europe. It thus brought together writers and audiences of different nationalities whose tastes, concerns, and backgrounds were similar. The vast amount of Latin texts produced in the period proves that its appeal was not only limited to a small intellectual and wealthy elite.

Elizabeth Jane Weston had been educated in the town of Most by an immigrant and Oxford man, John Hammond, and was fluent in Latin. Highly interestingly in our context, she chose to write *only* in Latin, although she is said to have spoken four or even five vernacular languages, that is, English, German, Czech and Italian.[32] Latin, however, could pass over national and linguistic boundaries without the slightest difficulty and would have enabled her to reach an international audience, to correspond with and dedicate poems to many of Europe's most well-known men of letters in England, France, Holland, Germany, and Silesia. We know that Elisabeth Jane Weston corresponded, among others, with the Dutch humanist Joseph Scaliger (one of the most outstanding poets of Neo-Latin verse), Jan Dousa (the famous Dutch poet and scholar), the German poet laureate Paul Melissus, Daniel Heinsius, Justus Lipsius, Jiri Carolides (the leading Neo-Latin poet at Rudolph's court),[33] and Georg Martin von Baldhoven, all of whom – independently of their own different religious backgrounds – testify to her extraordinary talent and erudition.

Baldhoven was responsible for the publication of two volumes of Weston's poems including her imitations of Classical poets,[34] and religious verse.[35] The

---

31 Thomas Farnaby, *Index Poeticus* (London, 1663): 271, qtd. in Hosington, "Elizabeth Jane Weston and Men's Men's Discourse of Praise," 107.

32 See Hosington, "Elizabeth Jane Weston (1581–1620)," 219.

33 See J. W. Binns, *Intellectual Culture in Elizabethan and Jacobean England. The Latin Writings of the Age* (Leeds: Francis Cairns, 1990): 113.

34 E.g., "On Ovid's Tristia II" echoes the Roman poet's grief in exile and compares her state as an Englishwoman forced to live in Bohemia with Ovid's banishment to Tomis, recounted in his *Tristia*. For the Latin text and English translation of Weston's poem, see Schleiner, *Tudor and Stuart Women Writers*, 101–104.

first one, entitled *Poemata*, was printed at Frankfurt-on-Oder in 1602, the follow-ing (undated) one, entitled *Parthenicon libri iii*, was printed in Prague,[36] probably in 1605 or 1606. It includes a reprint of the poems of the former volume and also a collection of letters. Copies of both volumes survive in the British Library.

> The *Parthenicon* contains several poems by her well-known contemporary writers who refer to her in most laudatory terms. Paul Melissius praises her beauty, her learning and her abil-ity to speak a wide range of languages ... Baldhofen sees her as '*Venus angla*' and as '*teu-tobritanna.*' Most generous of all scholars, perhaps, is Mattheus Zuber's question: '*Quid na-tura tibi, Westonia docta, negavit? Excepto, quod sis femina nata, nihil.*' ['What did nature deny you, learned Westonia? Nothing, except you are born as a woman'; my translation][37]

Last but not least, Jan Dousa praises her as "writing which it seems no mortal hand could have portrayed, but Charm itself / O Nectar, O words flowing with honey!" ["*Litera, mortalis quam non manus ulla videri / Pinxe, sed ipse Lepos, ipsa Sais poterat. / O suada, O Nectar, O Melle fluentia dicta!*"] (III.37)."[38]

Elizabeth Jane Weston did not only communicate with the most well-known male scholars of her time but was also – hardly seen by scholars yet – part of an impressive female *Res publica Litteraria* in which northern European learned women did eloquently and actively take part by not only contributing to the Neo-Latin revival but also having a significant network of their own.[39] The schol-arly assumption of earlier days, i.e., that Latin literacy was only fundamental to institutions of *male* power and authority, can thus not be upheld any more. As the achievements of Elisabeth Jane Weston and others prove, female authors did play a major role in the erudite Latin discourse of the early modern period. Due to recent scholarly work in this field we know by now that far more women read and wrote Latin than has hitherto been believed.[40] "Latin culture was rea-sonably widespread among Catholic gentlewomen and not simply a peculiarity

---

35 "Weston's verse, like other Neo-Latin poetry, circulated in manuscript and in several copies before it was finally printed" (Weston, *Collected Writings*, xvii).

36 "Poems of praise were one of the most highly regarded forms of Neo-Latin verse, ranging from hymn and encomium to occasional poetry in the forms of epigram, epithalamion, epitaph and elegy. Letters of praise were also a favourite form of epistolary expression amongst Neo-Latin writers. In *Parthenicon* we find both" (Hosington, "Elizabeth Jane Weston and Men's Dis-course of Praise," 109).

37 Susan Bassnett, "Elizabeth Jane Weston – The Hidden Roots of Poetry," in *Prag um 1600, Kunst und Kultur am Hofe Kaiser Rudolfs II*, ed. Hermann Fillitz, 2 vols. (Freren: Luca-Verlag: 1987, 1988) 1:9.

38 Qtd. in Hosington, "Elizabeth Jane Weston and Men's Discourse of Praise," 110.

39 See, for instance, Stevenson, "Women Catholics and Latin Culture," 52–62.

40 See especially Churchill, Brown, and Jeffrey (eds.), *Women Writing Latin*, 1.

of court circles."[41] Latin was the language of educated women as well as of men, and this in terms of various social and political systems, the language of humanists, and also, as mentioned above, of the Christian Church in the West.[42] Elizabeth Jane Weston did belong to a female network, as also, for instance, Maria Jars de Gournay (1565–1645), Montaigne's "fille d'alliance" and editor of his essays, or Anna Maria von Schurman.[43]

> Schurman exchanged letters with the Irish-British Dorothea Moore (in Latin and Hebrew), the British Batsuha Makhin (in Greek), the French Marie Jars du Gurnay, and Marie du Moulin (in French, Latin and Hebrew), the German Elizabeth of Bohemia (in Latin and French), and the Swedish queen Christina and Danish Brigitte Thott (in Latin).[44]

Jane Stevenson has shown that Weston knew Camille de Morelle in Paris,[45] and Joseph Scaliger reports that he "was in correspondence with Elizabeth Weston, the recipient of a Latin poem by Margarethe Bock van Gutmansdorf,[46] and a close friend of the learned 'Dames de Roches' in France.[47]

With reference to the significance of Latin not only as the language of the humanists but also of the Catholic Church, it is worth noting that in 1603, Elizabeth Jane Weston sent some poems to the newly crowned King, James I.[48] This is so remarkable because she must have assumed that James knew who she was,[49] although she had left England as an infant and had been an exile since then. In the light of James' marriage to the Catholic Anne of Denmark, she

---

41 Stevenson, "Women Catholics and Latin Culture," 62.

42 "[T]here existed a female European network [...]: the women's Republic of Letters, if you will. In this network learned women like Anna Maria van Schurman from Holland participated and corresponded with learned women from Ireland, England, Sweden, Denmark, Germany and France (ca. 1636–1660)" (Beerk, "'Golden Songs of Latin Thread'," 90).

43 For a comparison of Schurman and de Gournay, see A.R. De Smet, "'In the Name of the Father': Feminist Voices in the Republic of Letters," in *La femme lettrée à la Renaissance: Actes du Colloque International*, ed. Michael Bastiaensen (Brussels: Peeters, 1997): 177–198; 191–195.

44 "Introduction," in Churchill, Brown, and Jeffrey (eds.), *Women Writing Latin*, 6.

45 Stevenson, *Women Latin Poets*, 191.

46 She appears to have exchanged letters with Martin von Opitz and also wrote Latin verses to Joseph Scaliger; see Stevenson, *Women Latin Poets*, 244.

47 That is, Madeleine Neveu and Catherine Fradonnet (mother and daughter); see Schleiner, *Tudor and Stuart Women Writers*, 421.

48 Later, in 1612, she also addressed poems to Rudolph II's successor, Matthew II of Hungary and Bohemia.

49 "[A]t no point does Westonia suggest that James might not be fully cognizant of their identities (that is, Elizabeth and her mother [my addition]) and their case history in trying to reclaim her father's property confiscated in Bohemia" (Bassnett, "Elizabeth Jane Weston," 11).

may have hoped for reconciliation with Catholic Europe – which leads me to a discussion of her identity as an exiled Catholic.

Exiled Catholic

The fact that Elizabeth Jane Weston decided to publish exclusively in Latin does not only testify to the international intellectual networks to which she belonged (see above) but also to her dedication to the language of the Catholic Church (Protestants much more kept to their vernacular languages). We need only recall that the most famous Jesuit dramatists of the time, i.e. Jakob Gretser, Paul Biedermann and Jakob Balde, all composed their dramas in Latin, and it is commonly known that linguistic choices are likely to carry political and social implications as well. Thus, I will now trace – to my knowledge for the first time in this field – the significance of Weston's Neo-Latin writing for the religious controversies of the time, and here in particular for the early English Jesuit mission under Edmund Campion and Robert Persons. An approach like this appears all the more rewarding because "cultural minorities respond to political and social hegemonies in a variety of ways, including assimilation through mimicry, creative transcendence that simultaneously affirms the mainstream culture and the minority culture, and writings that are subversive in some way."[50]

Being an English Catholic refugee on the Continent first of all implied the experience of geographic dislocation and a position marked by opposition to the nation's dominant Anglican culture. Being exiled need not only cause passivity and depression, however, but, as the example of the Jesuits has proved, can also generate highly productive energies. Thus, in an almost paradoxical sense, Elizabeth Jane Weston as an exile was much more privileged than the oppressed subculture of Catholics in England, because the court of Rudolph II in Prague allowed her to have her ideas circulated. Here, her voice could emerge from her classical learning, her social rank, and her Catholic religious identity which she would not have been able to publicly preserve in England. Rudolph II's court in Prague was a place of rich cultural cross-fertilization hosting a plethora of different languages. What is more, his court appears to have been particularly hospitable to women. As Jane Stevenson has argued, there "seem to be no other Renaissance women Latinists, either poets or prose writers, anywhere else in Bohemia, Hungary, or any other part of Central Europe."[51]

---

50 Churchill, Brown, and Jeffrey (eds.), *Women Writing Latin*, 6.
51 Stevenson, *Women Latin Poets*, 251.

The Significance of Prague for the Early English Jesuit Mission

It is without question that early English Jesuits had numerous and most diverse contacts to the seminaries on the Continent where they were educated, and their books and pamphlets could be printed (see above). In the reigns of Henry VIII and Edward, English Catholics had travelled to the Continent and swiftly established bases in Louvain and Reims, others founded schools, seminaries and colleges in the Low Countries. Hundreds of young men were trained as missionaries in Douai, Rome and in Spain, and innumerable lay people, among them numerous English printers and publishers, sought asylum in France and the Low Countries. Particularly interestingly for our context, Rudolph II's court at Prague did indeed play a major role in the early English Jesuit mission. As I have shown elsewhere,[52] Edmund Campion worked in Prague from 1574 to 1580, and his drama *Ambrosia* was staged there in 1578. And it seems that also Elizabeth Jane Weston engaged in the subversive Catholic activities from her exile on the Continent. Thomas Fuller's *History of the Worthies of England* (London 1622) states[53] that Weston (and her family) was forced to flee England because of Catholic persecution,[54] and indeed she finds comfort in her faith. Although Weston confesses in her poetry and correspondence that she is deeply affected by sorrows, beset by financial problems and having been exiled from her native country, her religious poems include mostly epigrams and Ignatian mediations on biblical topics or liturgical feast days.[55] In the epitaph to her mother, she finds resolution in the final lines: God will bring her consolation and finally reunite her with her loved ones. Last but not least, the motto of her *symbolum album* was 'Spes Mea Christus.'[56]

As we have seen above, Elizabeth Jane Weston was educated in a richly stimulating and international Neo-Latin cultural environment in Prague in which a

52 Sonja Fielitz, "Shakespeare and Catholicism: The Jesuits as Cultural Mediators in Early Modern Europe," *Critical Survey* 21. 3 (2009): 54–68.
53 Brenda M. Hosington, "Elizabeth Jane Weston (1581–1620)," 223.
54 "The nature of this Catholic identity [...] becomes understandable when we recall the extensive record in John Dee's diaries of his and Kelley's taking Catholic sacraments and having theological discussions with Catholics, as well as Dee's utopian scheme, important in his and Kelley's angelic séances, for an ecumenical movement to heal the rift of Christendom. [...] They had various dealings with the ecumenical equivocator and sometime priest Francesco Pucci, eventually executed" (Schleiner, *Tudor and Stuart Women Writers*, 106).
55 See Schleiner, *Tudor and Stuart Women Writers*, 105.
56 Stevenson, *Women Latin Poets*, 247.

number of contacts with the leading intellectuals of her time (male as well as female) existed. In addition, on the political level, the court of Rudolph II, attracted

> a number of interesting Englishmen [...], and Elizabeth Weston mentions her acquaintance with some of them, such as Edward Dyer (1543–1607), the English poet and Chancellor of the Order of the Garter, who paid several visits to Prague, and Sir Stephen Lesieur, James I's Ambassador to the Court of Rudolph II. [...] she writes verses to Oswald Croll, alchemist, physician and Paracelsian, and to Petr Vok, Count of Rosemberg.[57]

What appears to have escaped critics' attention in this context so far, however, is a passage in a letter from Elizabeth's brother which shows that the Weston family itself remained in regular contact with England. On October 12, 1598 John Francis Weston writes to his sister in Prague:

> I have learned for the first time, dearest sister, from information given me by reverend Thomas that our kinswoman by marriage, Ludomilla Kelley, has set off for England, in the company of two of her sons [*Intellexi non ita pridem, charissima soror, ex R. Dn. Thomae ad me datis Dnm. Affnem nostrum Ludomillam Kelleam in Anglicam, assumptis duobus filiis suis*].[58]

Another major detail in the context of Elisabeth Jane Weston and her possible subversive engagement in the early English Jesuit mission is the significance of the town of Ingolstadt. As briefly mentioned at the beginning of this essay, her brother John Francis studied in Ingolstadt in Southern Germany (about 70 kilometres north of Munich) – which was a major Jesuit residence of the time. Even one of the most distinguished scholars and editor of Weston's life and work, Donald Cheney, simply mentions Ingolstadt without apparently being aware that it was a famous Jesuit college.[59] "Weston's brother had been sent to the local Jesuit Clementine school in Prague in 1585 before he was enrolled in Ingolstadt in the summer term of 1598 as 'Ioannis Westonius Oxoniensis Anglus Nobilis'."[60] His kinsman Heinrich von Pisnitz had attended Ingolstadt College as well.[61]

---

57 Binns, *Intellectual Culture in Elizabethan and Jacobean England*, 113.

58 Letter III, 20, in Weston, *Collected Writings*, 210–211. Ludomilla is Ludomilla Pisnitz, that is, the wife of Edward Kelley's brother Thomas.

59 Cheney, "Virgo Angla: The Self-Fashioning of Westonia," 120.

60 Donald Cheney, "Elizabeth Weston as Cultural Icon," in *Acta Conventus Neo-Latini Cantabrigiensis. Proceedings of the Eleventh International Congress of Neo-Latin Studies, Cambridge 30 July – 5 August 2000*, ed. Rhoda Schnur (Tempe, AZ: Arizona Center for Medieval and Renaissance Studies, 2003): 139–144, 140. Cheney refers to *Annales Ingolstadiensis Academiae*, part 2

Elizabeth Weston exchanged numerous letters with her brother in Ingolstadt in which she expresses her concern for his poor health and comments that he says nothing of his studies "you have too coldly satisfied my enquiries about your studies" ["*Mihi porro de studiis tuis quaeritanti nimis fridige satisfecisti*"],[62] while he praises her letters ("in them I see your distinctive style and your elegance" ["*In illis enim video characterem tuum ornatum & elegantiam tuam*"]),[63] and complains of her silence: "I remain in doubt as to when I shall finally hear from you" ["*Temporis dubius persisto, donec tuas litteras accepero*"]).[64] She wrote his epitaph and laments his passing in 1602 in a letter to Baldhofen.

It would appear intriguing to further trace the thesis that Elizabeth Jane Weston was possibly (there is no evidence yet) related to the Jesuit William Weston (1550–1615) who was executed in the wake of the early Jesuit mission (see above). William Weston entered the Society of Jesus in November 1575, made his novitiate in Spain, and reached England on 20 September 1584. He was imprisoned in August 1586 and confined in Wisbech Castle until early in 1599 he was committed to the Tower. In 1603 he was sent to exile and spent the rest of his days in the English seminaries at Seville and Valladolid in Spain. As Susan Bassnett has argued, "the name [Weston] has [...] associations in the Elizabethan context that invite further speculation still, if we recall Father Weston, the catholic priest imprisoned by Elizabeth in 1586."[65] If, in addition, we take into account that Jesuits in many cases adopted aliases, we may recall that the above-mentioned courtier and poet Edward Dyer was the son of a Thomas Dyer of Weston, Somerset.

Conclusion

Early modern England did indeed host multiple and competing cultural constructs of 'home' and 'diaspora'. Under Elizabeth I and James I, English Catholics were forced to leave their home country and thus adopt a hybridized identity. As exiles, they were positioned outside the demand for political and religious homogeneity propagated by the English government. Against this socio-political

---

(Ingolstadt, 1782): 152, qtd. in Götz Freiherr von Pölnitz, *Die Matrikel der Ludwig-Maximilians-Universität* (Munich: J. Lindauer'sche Universitätsbuchhandlung, 1937) 1:1374.

61 Weston, *Collected Writings*, xii.

62 III, 16, in Weston, *Collected Writings*, 202–203.

63 III, 18, in Weston, *Collected Writings*, 206–207.

64 III, 20, in Weston, *Collected Writings*, 210–211.

65 Bassnett, "Elizabeth Jane Weston," 14.

background, the members of early modern diaspora communities found themselves confronted with a multitude of 'others' towards whom different designs of identity were advisable. Thus, 'home' for early modern Catholics was by no means a stable or monolithic entity in a Golden Age, as earlier critics would have it, but a field that was open to contestation and (critical) re-imagining.

Elizabeth Jane Weston has served as our concrete example to throw new light on early modern Catholics' notion of 'home,' and their limits, but also their opportunities of (subversive) activities. Due to her identities as a Neo-Latin female poet and as a Catholic, as well as her hyphenated home of England *and* Bohemia she did not only have the opportunity to act as a cultural mediator for the Catholics' cause, but also kept her own ideal of Englishness. In her letters and (Ovidian) poems, Weston frequently decries the hostile fates that have robbed her of happiness and stability in her life. Torn from her native land as an infant and never able to return, she contstructs a nostalgic image of her homeland and even reminds James I of her loyalty to her native land. In England, however, she would certainly not have benefitted from the same learned network of powerful and learned friends nor, as a Catholic, enjoyed the same freedoms that she in fact had at the court of Rudolf II in Prague.

All in all, Weston provides fascinating evidence of an early modern Neo-Latin poetess who – due to her exile at the Catholic court of Rudolph II in Prague – had the privilege to communicate and act in a public cultural space where she could have a voice of her own. "It was a perhaps unique humanist female voice, emerging from modicum of learning, social positioning, and international Catholic religious identity that she managed to claim"[66] and preserve in Prague. By perseverance, talent and the networks of the early modern Latin world, Weston managed to circulate her manuscripts and also have them printed. She thus impressively created a place for herself in the international network of neo-Latin (male and female) poets and scholars. What is more, as an exiled Catholic authoress who had decided to write exclusively in Latin, that is, not only the language of the learned, but also of the Catholic Church, she may also have played a role in the subversive early English Jesuit mission. Which one this may possibly have been, requires further scholarly investigation. In short, in the words of Donald Cheney and Brenda M. Hosington, "it is obvious that there is still much to be learned about the details of Weston's life and times."[67]

---

66 Schleiner, *Tudor and Stuart Women Writers*, 106.
67 Weston, *Collected Writings*, xi.

Jaqueline Flack

East German Constructions of Home in the Context of Intra-German Migration Movements Since 1989

Abstract: In the wake of German reunification, East Germany has undergone dramatic changes in all aspects of political, social, economic, cultural and private life. Hence, many East Germans have felt uprooted and alienated from where they grew up or lived for many years. These fundamental feelings of foreignness, of subalternity and the desire to belong on the one hand, and enduring distinctive socio-cultural practices, values and norms on the other hand can be described as diaspora-like experiences and practices in East Germany. Furthermore, those who left East Germany did so for various reasons. They migrated to the West in search of better jobs, to escape unemployment, and to study. To put it simply: They moved to live in better and more secure social circumstances. East Germans describe how their migration to the West intensified their perceptions and feelings of being different. Migration is often seen by East Germans as an essential component by which to reflect on a specific East German identity. Thus, the East German diaspora has to be seen as an important supposition to construct an East German homeland and to reflect on socio-cultural belonging. I will reflect on the construction of a homeland in the East German diaspora by analyzing biographical narratives of homeland, identity and a sense of belonging of young East Germans since 1989. Furthermore, I will analyze collectivization practices in the West by reference to the example of the *"Ossi-Stammtisch."*

Since 1989, East Germany has had to deal with far-reaching transformations in all aspects of the political, social, economic, cultural and private life. Almost every aspect of daily life was affected by these tremendous changes. The changes did not take effect gradually but literally 'overnight,' and hence, many East Germans felt that they were uprooted and alienated from where they had grown up or lived for many years. On the one hand, the experience of being uprooted, of foreignness, of subalternity[1] and the desire to belong and, on the other, enduring to a certain extent distinctive socio-cultural practices, values and norms[2] can be described as diaspora-like experiences and practices in East Germany.

---

1 Raj Kollmorgen, "Subalternisierung. Formen und Mechanismen der Missachtung Ostdeutscher nach der Vereinigung," in *Diskurse der deutschen Einheit. Kritik und Alternativen*, eds. Raj Kollmorgen, Thomas Frank, Hans-Liudger Dienel (Wiesbaden: VS Verlag, 2011): 301–359, 325.
2 See, for example, Rudolph Woderich, "Ostdeutsche Identitäten zwischen symbolischer Konstruktion und lebensweltlichem Eigensinn. Schriftfassung des Referates auf der Konferenz 'The German Road from Socialism to Capitalism' " [1999], *Brandenburg-Berliner Institut für Sozialwissenschaftliche Studien e.V.* <http://www.biss-online.de/download/ostdeutsche_identitaeten.pdf> (acc. March 1, 2014); Heiner Meulemann, "Werte und Wertewandel im vereinten

People left East Germany for various reasons: e. g., they migrated to the West to get better jobs, to escape unemployment, to study, or, to put it simply, they moved to live in better and more secure social circumstances. East Germans describe how their migration to the West in particular intensified their perceptions and feelings of continuing to be different. Such migration is often seen by East Germans as an essential element for reflections on a specific East German identity. This is conceptualized as a form of collective identity which is based on shared experiences of living and being socialized in the GDR, experiencing the fall of the Berlin Wall as an existential change and living or growing up in the East German transformation society. What emerges above all from this period and the events that took place "is the *experience* of a profound *discontinuity,*"[3] and the three factors provide reference points in the process of constructing an East German collective identity. However, the individual relevance of those biographical reference points might differ widely. In addition, the construction of a collective East German identity has to be seen as the result of public discourse dominated by hegemonic West German media. In public discourse since 1990 East Germans are described as different, subaltern,[4] or as "symbolic strangers."[5] In this way, East Germans are constructed as a *collective subject* in which diversity and heterogeneity of their social group is eliminated. Those predominantly media-constructed stereotypes still affect both East Germans' perception of themselves as well as their external perception to this day.

Many East Germans tell of social disembedding and disorientation as fundamental and cross-generational aspects of the process of societal transformation since 1989. Beside the confrontation with media constructed stereotypes, experiences of cultural distinctiveness became particularly widespread in the context of inner German migration. Therefore, the extensive migratory movements from East to West Germany since 1989, which represent an important aspect of the East German transformation society, cannot be seen as similar to those, for example, from northern to southern Germany. Although the two nations

---

Deutschland" (September 20, 2004), *Bundeszentrale für politische Bildung* <http://www.bpb.de/apuz/26719/werte-und-wertwandel-im-vereinten-deutschland?p=all> (acc. March 1, 2014).

3 Cf. Stuart Hall, "Cultural Identity and Diaspora," in *Identity: Community, Culture, Difference,* ed. Jonathan Rutherford (London: Lawrence and Wishart, 1990): 222–237, 227.

4 Cf. Raj Kollmorgen, Thomas Frank, Hans-Liudger Dienel (eds.), *Diskurse der deutschen Einheit. Kritik und Alternativen,* eds. (Wiesbaden: VS Verlag, 2011). See also *Die Ostdeutschen in den Medien. Das Bild von den Anderen nach 1990,* eds. Thomas Ahbe, Rainer Gries, Wolfgang Schmale (Bonn: Bundeszentrale für politische Bildung, 2010).

5 Cf. *Der "Ossi." Mikropolitische Studien über einen symbolischen Ausländer,* eds. Rebecca Pates, Maximilian Schochow (Wiesbaden: Springer VS, 2013).

were politically reunified, migrating to the West and vice versa was still crossing a cultural border for many.[6] While West Germans think of themselves as German,[7] the conception of an East German identity becomes particularly relevant in the context of inner German and even transnational migration.

While many East German migrants live in the East and commute to the West to work, others settle where they work or study. Some of those who stay in the West articulate a strong desire to return and a longing for "a place like home." Therefore, many East German migrants foster close relationships with family and friends at home, consider returning, or connect with other East Germans through various networks and associations in the West. Physical or virtual spaces such as online forums (*"Ossi-Forum"*),[8] East German *"Ossi-Stammtische"* (regular group meetings in a bar)[9] or even *"Ossi-Läden"* (shops for purchasing 'typically' East German groceries and goods)[10] allow the homing desire to be satisfied. In the meantime a transregional and transnational network called *3te Generation Ostdeutschland* (3rd East German Generation)[11] has gained publicity as a network focusing on discussing and elaborating specifically East German topics from an inner perspective by aiming to change public discourse about East Germany. Furthermore, recent literary texts, especially those written by younger East Germans, discuss details of East German history, which is seen

---

6 Cf. Jaqueline Flack, "Cultural Distinction and the Example of the 'Third East German Generation'," in *Borders and Border Regions in Europe. Changes, Challenges and Chances*, eds. Arnaud Lechevalier, Jan Wielgohs (Bielefeld: transcript, 2013): 145–156, 147. See also Klaus Roth, Juliana Roth, "One Country – Two Cultures? Germany after Unification," in *Europeans. Essays on Culture and Identity*, eds. Åke Daun, Sören Jansson (Lund: Nordic Academic Press, 1999): 159–180.

7 Cf. Thomas Hanf, Reinhard Liebscher, Heidrun Schmidtke, "Die Wahrnehmung und Bewertung der deutschen Einheit im Spiegel von Bevölkerungsumfragen," in *Diskurse der deutschen Einheit. Kritik und Alternativen*, eds. Raj Kollmorgen, Thomas Frank, Hans-Liudger Dienel (Wiesbaden: VS Verlag, 2011): 249–300, 278, 284.

8 E.g., *Ossi-Forum. Bundesweites Kontakt- und Unterhaltungsforum* < http://www.ossiforum.de/> (acc. March 9, 2015).

9 E.g., *Ossi-Stammtisch Frankfurt a. M.* <http://www.frankfurt-treff.de/>; *Ossi-Stammtisch Fellbach* <http://ossi-stammtisch.beepworld.de/>; *Ossi-Club in Franken* <http://ossi-club-franken.de/ocfweb/ostalgie/ossilclubs.htm>; *Ossi-Stammtisch Augsburg* <http://www.ossiclub.de/> (all acc. March 11, 2015).

10 E. g. *Ossiladen* <http://www.ossiladen.de>; *Ostprodukte Versand* <http://www.ostprodukte-versand.de/>; *Ilando (Im Land Ost)* <http://www.ilando.de/>; *Kaufhalle des Ostens* <http://www.kaufhalle-des-ostens.de/> (all acc. March 9, 2015).

11 The network at present maintains locations in Germany, Switzerland, and the US: <http://netzwerk.dritte-generation-ost.de/>; <https://thirdgenerationost.wordpress.com/2013/10/25/third-generation-east-germany/> (all acc. March 12, 2015).

as essential in the construction of a distinct East German identity.[12] It is experiences of migration from East to West Germany in particular which lead to experiences of distinctiveness and in-depth reflections on the existence of a collective East German cultural identity. Diverse supraregional and transnational practices of collectivization and networking also contribute to (re-)constructing and (re-)producing a collective identity. I will treat the East German migratory experience as a diaspora-like experience in the light of recent debates about the concept of diaspora.[13] These emphasize the state of dislocation and marginalization, the meaning of homeland, the wish to return, cultural hybridity, the construction of "imagined communities"[14] and collective identities in the context of (global) migratory movements. By reference to the example of the Ossi-Stammtisch, I shall analyze East Germans' practices of building a (imagined) community, a home and a cultural identity in the context of inner German migration.

Intra-German Migration since 1989

According to several research papers,[15] approximately 2.7 million East Germans migrated to the West between 1989 and 2002, and with due consideration of the amount of migrations from West to East in this period, this is equivalent to 7.5 percent of the former East German population.[16] This group of migrants features a disproportionally high number of under-thirty-year-olds and young women. According to a 2006 study by Sascha Wolff, East Germany shows "the second highest netto migration of the post-socialist nations in Central and Eastern Eu-

---

12 E.g., Jana Hensel, *Zonenkinder* (Hamburg: Rowohlt, 2002); Jana Hensel, *Warum wir Ostdeutschen anders bleiben sollten* (Munich: Piper, 2009); Anna Schädlich, Susanne Schädlich (eds.), *Ein Spaziergang war es nicht. Kindheiten zwischen Ost und West* (Munich: Heyne, 2012); Andrea Hanna Hünniger, *Das Paradies. Meine Jugend nach der Mauer* (Stuttgart: Cotta, 2011); Robert Ide, *Geteilte Träume. Meine Eltern, die Wende und ich* (Munich: btb, 2009); Sabine Rennefanz, *Eisenkinder. Die stille Wut der Wendegeneration* (Munich: Luchterhand, 2013).
13 E.g., Hall, "Cultural Identity and Diaspora," *passim*; Robin Cohen, *Global Diasporas: An Introduction* (Seattle: U of Washington P, 1997); James Clifford, "Diasporas," *Current Anthropology* 9.3 (1994): 302–338.
14 See also Benedict Anderson, *Imagined Communities. Reflections on the Origin and Spread of Nationalism* (London: Verso, 1983).
15 Cf. Sascha Wolff, "Migration und ihre Determinanten im ost-westdeutschen Kontext nach der Wiedervereinigung. Ein Literaturüberblick" (2006), *Econstor* <http://www.econstor.eu/bitstream/10419/31959/1/515893765.pdf> (acc. March 1, 2014): 2.
16 Wolff, "Migration und ihre Determinanten," 2.

rope [...] after Albania."[17] These data illustrate the great relevance of inner German migration for the East German transformation society since 1989. They also reflect the imbalance of migratory movements between East and West Germany, which represents the pattern of migration between the economically and structurally more peripheral East German regions and the more central West German regions.[18] To understand East-West German migration since 1989, it is important not only to reflect on the number of migrants who moved from East to West and vice versa, but also to consider the different reasons for their migrations and their economic and social determinants. Thus, we can distinguish between highly structurally motivated East-West German migrations [e. g., to avoid unemployment][19] and more individually motivated West-East German migrations [e. g., to improve one's career] in these years.[20] For instance, Nancy, born in 1981, says:

> Just as for many others, the decision to leave my [home region] was job-orientated. Only a few leave their home simply for adventure. It's not a good feeling that you have to leave your home, the place where you grew up, just to achieve something in your job. But as for my career opportunities, West Germany still offers better conditions than East Germany.[21]

---

17 Wolff, "Migration und ihre Determinanten," 2: "Unter den ehemals planwirtschaftlich organisierten Regimen Mittel- und Osteuropas, weist Ostdeutschland damit nach Albanien die zweithöchsten Nettomigrationsraten auf."

18 According to Wallerstein, central regions are economic and political power regions while peripheral regions involve economically and structurally weak(er) regions which economically depend on central regions (Immanuel Wallerstein, *Der historische Kapitalismus* [Hamburg: Argument, 1984]: 48). Jach indicates that this perspective implies a rather mechanistic, divisive model that only focuses on economic and political aspects while it disregards the complexity of cultural processes (Regina Jach, *Migration, Religion und Raum. Ghanaische Kirchen in Accra, Kumasi und Hamburg in Prozessen von Kontinuität und Kulturwandel* [Münster: LIT, 2005]: 17; see also Nikos Papastergiadis, *The Turbulence of Migration. Globalization, Deterritorialization and Hybridity* [Cambridge: Polity P, 2000]).

19 Cf. IfL Leipzig, "Die Studie: Re-Turn – Regionalentwicklung durch Rückwanderung" (2012), *Leibniz-Institut für Länderkunde* <http://www.ifl-leipzig.de/fileadmin/user_upload/Forschung/Raumproduktionen/Re-Turn_ZA_Online-Erhebung.pdf> (acc. March 1, 2014): 3.

20 Cf. Grit Beck, "Wandern gegen den Strom. West-Ost-Migration in Deutschland seit 1990" (Diss. Freie Universität Berlin, 2011) <http://www.diss.fu-berlin.de/diss/servlets/MCRFileNodeServlet/FUDISS_derivate_000000009368/West-Ost-Migration_in_Deutschland_seit_1990.pdf> (acc. March 9, 2015): 79.

21 "Bei der Entscheidung, [meine Heimat] zu verlassen, spielten wie bei so vielen anderen die beruflichen Aussichten eine entscheidende Rolle. Nur wenige verlassen ihre Heimat aus purer Abenteuerlust. [...] Es ist kein schönes Gefühl, dass man die Heimat, in der man aufgewachsen ist, hinter sich lassen muss, um an einem anderen Ort beruflich etwas erreichen zu können. [...] Was aber meine Berufsmöglichkeiten angeht, bietet mir Westdeutschland immer noch bessere Bedingungen als Ostdeutschland" (qtd. in Michael Hacker et al. (eds.), *Dritte Generation Ost.*

At the same time, Nancy claims that she would like to return one day (*DG*, 109–110), and this desire to return is characteristic of many members of diaspora-communities. According to a 2012 study of the Leibniz Institute for Regional Geography, almost seventy-five percent of interviewed East German migrants considered returning to their home regions despite their generally positive experiences in the West.[22] Meanwhile, for individuals who left home chiefly for professional and economic reasons returning would be due to social reasons, e. g., to be closer to family and friends.[23] At the same time, migration from West to East Germany occurred in the 1990s especially when the objective was a unidirectional transfer of expert knowledge in various fields.

The main focus of my research is on young East Germans who experienced the fall of the Berlin Wall during childhood or adolescence. In what follows, I discuss their sense of a loss of *Heimat* [home] and being uprooted after 1989 in the context of East German migration to the West as an important aspect of the process of identity construction for this young generation from East Germany. One relevant publication in this discussion is from the network *3te Generation Ostdeutschland* ["3rd East German Generation"]. The network was founded in Berlin in 2011 by East Germans born between 1975 and 1985 in the GDR, and it intends to connect with young East Germans to reflect on their specific biographies and to present them to a wider public. Furthermore, they intend to initiate a dialogue with the generation of their parents who seem to have had different experiences. The biographical narratives analyzed here illustrate the practices of constructions of home in the context of societal transformation or individual migratory experiences. Many of these young East Germans feel under-represented in public discourse, in particular with reference to their specific and sometimes heterogeneous experiences of growing up in East Germany.

The name of the network, *3te Generation Ostdeutschland*, was inspired by the discourse of the third generation of migrants in Germany with whom they share the experience of being brought up and socialized between two different social systems, respectively distinct cultures. However, sociological academic literature uses different terms to describe this generation of East Germans who experienced the societal transformation during their childhood or adolescence. Researchers refer to them as "the fourth generation," the "*Generation der Unbera-*

Wer wir sind und was wir wollen [Berlin: Ch. Links, 2012]:109–110; further references in the text, abbreviated as "*DG*." All translations are mine; the German original is provided in the footnotes).

22 IfL Leipzig, "Die Studie," 2.

23 Beck, "Wandern gegen den Strom," 5.

tenen" ["unadvised generation"],[24] the *"Mauerfall-Kinder*" ["children of the fall of the Wall"],[25] or the *"Wendegeneration*" ["generation of change"].[26] Sometimes the focus is on different cohorts. Applying a Mannheimian concept of generations,[27] I view the East Germans who experienced the fall of the Berlin Wall during their childhood or adolescence as a single generation. This generation of East Germans grew up in a societal space defined by its "in-betweenness," a space of transition in which a large part of the cultural and social knowledge of their parents' generation seemed to have become obsolete, and in which new cultural rules had to be learned collectively and across all generations of East Germans from scratch. The experience of a radical new beginning in society and of having to fend for themselves at a very important stage of socialization makes those young East Germans as one distinct generation, and it also serves to offer a sense of mutual connection for many of them. Reflections on their own roots and identity seem to be very important to this generation. Hence, the experience of the loss of their home, of being uprooted or alienated, and the construction of a new identity are not only articulated in the context of inner-German migration. The broad transformations of their living environments, thus of the places of home themselves, were described retrospectively as experiences of losing their home. The concrete loss of familiar social and cultural structures – but not of the GDR itself – is widely considered a painful experience. The profundity, the amount, and the speed of the transformations in society, as well as their impact on everyday life, are still felt to have been far-reaching for many of those young East Germans today. Anja Görnitz, born in 1982 in East-Berlin, remarks: "I grew up in a kind of strange and split world which is divided into a past and present

---

24 Bernd Linder, "Die Generation der Unberatenen. Zum Profil der letzten DDR-Jugendgeneration," *Berliner Debatte Initial* 14.2 (2003): 28–34.

25 Tanja Bürgel, "Mauerfall-Kinder. Wie orientieren sich junge Ostdeutsche 15 Jahre nach der Wende?" *Berliner Debatte Initial* 15.4 (2004): 16–25; Tanja Bürgel, "Gibt es eine vom ostdeutschen Umbruch geformte Generation? Zu Prägungen und Perspektiven ostdeutscher Mauerfall-Kinder," in *Die DDR aus generationengeschichtlicher Perspektive. Eine Inventur*, eds. Annegret Schüle, Thomas Ahbe, Rainer Gries (Leipzig: Leipzig UP, 2006): 455–471.

26 See Karl Ulrich, Eva Schulze, *Die Wendegeneration. Lebensläufe des Jahrgangs 1971* (Frankfurt am Main: Campus, 2009). See also Schüle, Ahbe, Gries (eds.), *Die DDR aus generationengeschichtlicher Perspektive, passim.*

27 Mannheim defines a generation as the result of the shared experience of historical events by individuals of a similar age, who develop a collective and distinctive consciousness. Particularly for those who were adolescents at the time of the fall of the Berlin Wall in 1989 and during the following period of profound social change in East Germany, these constitute the main generation building events. See Karl Mannheim, "Das Problem der Generationen," *Kölner Vierteljahreshefte für Soziologie* 7.2 (1928): 158–185.

time, with the present beginning in 1989" (*DG*, 23).[28] Another East German, born in 1976, felt at that time like "being thrown into another world" (*DG*, 83).[29] Therefore, besides other important topics, those transformational experiences should be understood as identity-forming for many young East Germans.

While the broad transformations of social structures in East Germany offer the main point of reference in these biographical narratives to the loss of a homeland, the question of one's own origin mostly arises first in the context of one's own migration to the West. Responding to the question "what *Heimat* means" to her today, K., born in 1976, says:

> I think, since I have been here [in the West] or probably in general, I feel rather homeless because if I went back to my hometown it would no longer be the same place in which I grew up and [...] everything has changed, and not for the better. [...] It makes me kind of sad [...] and I think [...] in this sense there is no home for me any longer. And in comparison to my West German friends, I feel a bit disadvantaged because they can go to the places where they grew up [...] and they are mostly the same, I guess, as they were twenty-five years ago (though they may deny it). At least the names of the streets didn't change, that is one thing. When I am back home now and make an arrangement, I never know the names of the streets and then I think I even don't know the names of the places in my own town.[30]

Spatial and temporal distance intensifies the need of young East Germans to articulate their personal transformational experiences and to redefine their own identity. The concept of diaspora allows us to also gather the positive as well as the more challenging and painful aspects of the process of social transformation in East Germany for this generation. It enables us to capture the inherent

---

28 "Ich bin in einer eigenartigen zweigeteilten Welt groß geworden, sie ist getrennt in früher und heute, wobei heute 1989 beginnt."

29 "[...] wie in eine andere Welt hineingeworfen."

30 Transcript from a biographical interview (May 11, 2013, the translation is mine): "Denn, ich glaube, dass ich mich, seit ich dann hier bin oder generell wahrscheinlich als eher heimatlos [...] empfinde, weil, wenn ich jetzt zurückgehe in meine Heimatstadt, dann ist das ja nicht mehr die-Stadt, in der ich aufgewachsen bin und es hat sich alles verändert, und nicht zu seinem Vorteil. [... D]as macht mich irgendwie traurig und ich denke, so die Heimat in dem Sinne gibt es nicht mehr. Und ich empfinde das immer als eine Benachteiligung gegenüber meinen Freundinnen von hier [i.e., West German friends], die am Wochenende dann [nach Hause] fahren, wo sie aufgewachsen sind und da ist ja vieles noch, bilde ich mir ein – die sagen, es ist auch nicht ganz so – wie vor 25 Jahren. [... A]lso da haben sich keinerlei Straßennamen geändert, das ist auch so eine Sache. Wenn ich jetzt zuhause bin und ich verabrede mich, ich weiß nie wie die Straßen heißen [...] und dann denke ich, ich weiß in meiner eigenen Stadt nicht mehr wie die Plätze heißen."

synchrony in radical social change of the dissolution of boundaries (in a positive sense) and deracination (in a negative sense).

"Our identity is at once plural and partial. Sometimes we feel that we straddle two cultures; at other times, that we fall between two stools":[31] This is how Salman Rushdie describes the diasporic feelings of a migrant, a hybrid kind of belonging and the experience of dual alienation from both one's home and one's place of residence. Although the contexts are widely different, the quotation also reflects the reality of the lives of many young people who grew up during the transformation of East German society. Growing up between two different social systems still produces feelings of inner fragmentation. Anne Wessendorf, born in 1979, says:

> It is as if I have an East-self and a West-self, which have developed successively and are not automatically connected with each other. [...] They are two inner worlds which have to be reconciled and integrated. Even more than twenty years after the official reunification I have to work hard for the unification of these two inner worlds. (*DG*, 84–85)[32]

She goes on to add: "I started to think about this many years later. I became aware only recently of the uncertainty and inner split as a result of social changes" (*DG*, 84–85).[33] At the same time, it is this generation that won previously unimaginable opportunities for personal development and a higher degree of freedom. The East German psychoanalyst Hans Joachim Maaz certifies this generation a distinctly strong resilience in social changes he ascribes to their specific conditions of socialization.[34] Many authors indicate that diaspora groups develop needs for an identity, a home and sense of belonging, as well as a capacity for flexibility, mobility and cultural adaptability.[35] Many young East Germans today experience this kind of tense relationship.

---

31 Salman Rushdie, *Imaginary Homelands. Essays and Criticism 1981–1991* (London: Penguin, 1992): 15.

32 "Es ist, als ob es ein Ost-Ich und ein West-Ich in mir gibt, die sich zeitlich nacheinander gebildet und auch nicht automatisch miteinander verzahnt haben. [...] Es sind zwei innere Welten, die es miteinander zu versöhnen und zu integrieren gilt. Auch mehr als 20 Jahre nach der offiziellen Wiedervereinigung muss ich mir die Vereinigung dieser beiden Welten mühsam weiter erarbeiten."

33 "Das Nachdenken hat erst viele Jahre danach begonnen. Die Verunsicherung und Spaltung, die der Umbruch in meinem Inneren ausgelöst hat, wird mir erst jetzt richtig bewusst."

34 Hans Joachim Maaz, "Intragenerationales Erbe," speech at the annual network meeting of *3te Generation Ostdeutschland* (Berlin: Collegium Hungaricum, November 24, 2013).

35 See, for example, Alois Moosmüller, "Diaspora – zwischen Reproduktion von 'Heimat,' Assimilation und transnationaler Identität," in *Interkulturelle Kommunikation in der Diaspora. Kul-*

Heimat and its Dimensions of Meaning

Contemporary academic literature focusing on the complexity of the German term *Heimat* identifies four main dimensions which characterize the meaning of the term in general: a spatial, a temporal, a social and a cultural dimension of *Heimat*.[36] The widespread changes in East Germany after 1989 concern the spatial, social, cultural and temporal dimensions of *Heimat* as a whole. However, the discourse of *Heimat* in the GDR was highly ideological and functionalized and it shaped the concept of *Heimat* which was institutionally imparted. *Heimatkundeunterricht*, for example, taught from the first to the fourth grade in school, was strongly related to the idea of a socialist nation.[37] Furthermore, the idea of *Heimat* in the GDR, as Frank Hoffmann argues, was not related to a concrete topographic place, but rather to the utopian concept of a socialist nation.[38] But personal concepts of home cannot be reduced to this institutionally, culturally or media constructed idea of *Heimat* which was equivalent to the former ideology. The authors of the anthology *Heimat als Erfahrung und Entwurf* observe that the concept of *Heimat* is more than a mere result of personal constructions, as recent researchers suggest.[39] Accordingly, *Heimat* is characterized as at once a space of personal experiences and a result of social construction.

The process of reflection on one's home is often effected by its loss. A generation that does not discuss questions of home and belonging has its home and knows where it belongs.[40] However, the great political changes in Europe since 1989 have opened "entirely new horizons of experience" for home-making, as

turelle Gestaltung von Lebens- und Arbeitswelten in der Fremde, ed. Alois Moosmüller (Münster, Munich, New York: Waxmann, 2002): 11–28.

36 Cf. Gerhard Handschuh, "Brauchtum. Zwischen Tradition und Veränderung," in *Heimat. Analysen, Themen, Perspektiven*, eds. Will Cremer, Ansgar Klein (Bonn: Bundeszentrale für politische Bildung, 1990) 1:633–874, 653.

37 Cf. Frank Hoffmann, "Region oder Heimat? Räumliche Identitäten der DDR – das Beispiel der Museen," in *Heimat als Erfahrung und Entwurf*, eds. Natalia Donig, Silke Flegel, Sarah Scholl-Schneider (Münster: LIT, 2009): 87–109, 99.

38 Cf. Hoffmann, "Region oder Heimat," 101. See also Jan Palmowski, *Inventing a Socialist Nation. Heimat and the Politics of Everyday Life in the GDR, 1945–1990* (Cambridge: Cambridge UP, 2009).

39 Cf. Natalia Donig, Silke Flegel, Sarah Scholl-Schneider, "Zum Geleit," in *Heimat als Erfahrung und Entwurf*, eds. Natalia Donig, Silke Flegel, Sarah Scholl-Schneider (Münster: LIT, 2009): 9–12, 9.

40 Donig, Flegel, Scholl-Schneider, "Zum Geleit," 9.

well.[41] Many young East Germans still consider East Germany their home. However, in the context of the social transformational process and its social, temporal and cultural dimensions, it appears to be a new, different or sometimes lost kind of home. It has to be reinterpreted, reconstructed and re-familiarized. An East German woman, born in 1981, remarks:

> My home is located neither exclusively in East German Thuringia [where she grew up], nor in West German Hesse [where she now lives]. It is here, where I live and work, where I have built something for myself. And it's also where my roots and childhood memories are. Both places constitute my home, but on the question of where I belong, I still feel torn. At once, I am becoming ever more alienated from my home in Thuringia yet I do not completely belong in the home in Hesse. With mixed feelings and curiosity, I will see how my complicated feelings of where I belong develop over the next few years. (*DG*, 113)[42]

The quotation addresses the hybrid or even 'split' sense of belonging that now constitutes the interviewee's social-cultural identity. The idea of living 'in-between' their former home in the East and their current place of residence in the West is often articulated by East German migrants grappling with their social-cultural belonging. Moreover, the interviewee expresses her experience of discontinuity and uprootedness when she states that she feels still in internal conflict on the question of where she belongs.

Diaspora as the Desire for Home and Identity

Peter Dürrmann observes that *Heimat* is the place on which you look from outside.[43] The relevance of *Heimat* therefore increases in proportion to the distance in time and space from it. In a territorial and temporal conception of home of

---

41 Donig, Flegel, Scholl-Schneider, "Zum Geleit," 9: "Indes haben die politischen Verwerfungen und Entgrenzungen in Europa seit 1989 auch in dieser Hinsicht ganz neue Erfahrungsräume eröffnet."
42 "Meine Heimat befindet sich weder allein im ostdeutschen Thüringen noch allein im westdeutschen Hessen. Sie ist hier, wo ich jetzt lebe und arbeite, mir etwas aufgebaut habe. Und doch ist sie auch dort, wo meine Wurzeln und Kindheitserinnerungen liegen. [...] Beide Gegenden fügen sich zu meiner Heimat, aber mein Heimatgefühl ist doch auch immer zerrissen. Denn einerseits entfremde ich mich meiner thüringischen Heimat zusehends, und gleichzeitig gehöre ich noch nicht vollständig zur hessischen dazu. Mit gemischten Gefühlen betrachte ich also gespannt, wie sich meine zerrissene Heimatverbundenheit in den nächsten Jahren entwickeln wird."
43 Peter Dürrmann, *Heimat und Identität. Der moderne Mensch auf der Suche nach Geborgenheit* (Tübingen, Zurich, Paris: Hohenrain, 1994): 88.

this kind, it represents a place which evokes intimate feelings that are activated by being distanced from it. Avtar Brah overcomes the concept of *Heimat* as a connection to a concrete geographical place.[44] The 'homing desire' she speaks of is not realized through being at a certain place, nor is it necessarily connected to the desire or realization of return. Ultimately, the diasporic feeling does not consist of the desire for a homeland but a homing desire. The diaspora community enables the satisfaction of those homing desires in foreign places as well. But even if a person who has left home returns after a longer time, he or she will inevitably be confronted with historical changes that occurred during his or her absence. The imagined homeland will differ greatly from the reality, and, in this sense, it no longer exists.

However, experiences of exile even whilst still 'at home' are also described, e. g., in post-socialist East German society after reunification.[45] In this case, the home itself changed fundamentally, thus rendering a return to the former homeland impossible. Paula Hannaske, born in 1979 in East Berlin, states: "My original home is different and no longer exists" (*DG*, 49).[46] As a result, practices of remembrance often lead to the creation of an idealized, idyllic home in the memory in which "the childhood in the GDR becomes an imaginary, fairy-tale, a fiction" (*DG*, 17–18).[47] East German journalist Robert Ide (born in 1975) remarks critically:

> Many young East Germans [are proud] to come from this side [of Germany] which appears the more magical the longer ago it disappeared. Especially in foreign places, you are overwhelmed by a homely sensation when you meet people with whom you can share a deep feeling without having to verbalise it: the [shared] experience of the break-up of a country in which you once lived.[48]

The homing desire in diaspora communities appears to be satisfied not only through searching for familiar things, situations, feelings or smells, but it is

---

44 See Avtar Brah, *Cartographies of Diaspora. Contesting Identities* (London: Routledge, 1996).
45 E.g., Bernhard Schlink, *Heimat als Utopie* (Frankfurt am Main: Suhrkamp, 2000):7.
46 "Meine unsprüngliche Heimat ist eine andere, und es gibt sie nicht mehr."
47 Katja Warchhold, "'So etwas ist in meiner DDR nicht vorgekommen.' Erinnerungen an ein Aufwachsen in der DDR und im vereinten Deutschland" (*DG*, 58–72, 67): "Die DDR-Kindheit konnte darüber zu einer imaginären, märchenhaften Heimat, zu einer Fiktion werden."
48 "[V]iele junge Ostdeutsche [sind stolz darauf] von jener Seite zu kommen, die ihnen desto verwunschener erscheint, je länger sie verschwunden ist. Besonders in der Fremde befällt einen ein wohliger Schauer, wenn man Menschen trifft, mit denen man mit Hilfe weniger Worte ein tiefes Gefühl teilen kann – die Erfahrung vom Untergang eines Landes, in dem man selbst gelebt hat" (Ide, *Geteilte Träume*, 67).

also characterized by a strong interpersonal component.[49] This is important in enabling people to identify similarities in cooperating, encountering, making friendships etc., and in realizing the desire for interpersonal understanding and belonging.[50] However, searching for similarities is not the same as eliminating diversity. The similarities claimed to facilitate the creation of a community are the result of a shared way of thinking, perceiving, interpreting and experiencing the world.[51] Nancy, born in 1981, says: "What makes me feel comfortable in Hesse [her West German place of residence] are the many people of different ages who come from East Germany and live and work here, too. Thus, I can share memories with them and preserve a piece of home" (*DG*, 109).[52] Coming together with other East Germans and sharing memories of home serves as a way to create a feeling of home in a foreign place. The interviewee considers this a precondition to "feeling comfortable" in West Germany where she lives now. As mentioned before, a common history represents one of the main aspects for the construction of the collective identity of social groups. The interviewee speaks explicitly of "people (...) who come from East Germany" who make her feel at home, not of people from Thuringia, the federal state from where she originates. It is East Germany in general that she considers as home, not simply the region where she grew up. One may therefore draw the conclusion that the interviewee assumes that there is a distinct East German identity which distinguishes East Germans from West Germans and constitutes an imagined East German community.

Coming Home to the Ossi-Stammtisch

In this section, I discuss the East German Ossi-Stammtisch as an example of the practices of collectivization and construction of identity in the context of East German migration. Dominic Boyer defines the term 'Stammtisch' as follows:

> The *Stammtisch* [...] is a venerable political and social institution in Central Europe where a group of individuals, usually exclusively men, gather together at the same table at the same

---

49 Cf. Moosmüller, "Diaspora," 17–18.
50 Cf. Moosmüller, "Diaspora," 17–18.
51 Not every migrant develops a homing desire in a foreign place or wants to connect with others in a diasporic community. Therefore, not every migrant becomes a member of a diaspora community.
52 "Was mir in Hessen gut tut, sind die vielen Menschen gleichen und unterschiedlichen Alters, die ebenfalls aus Ostdeutschland kommen und hier leben, wohnen und arbeiten. So kann ich mit anderen gemeinsame Erinnerungen teilen und mir so ein Stück Heimat bewahren."

local pub on the same night of every week to discuss the relevant issues of the day and to drink a great deal of beer. [...] *Stammkneipen* (regulars' pubs) were particularly important sites for *gemütliches Beisammensein* (convivial togetherness) among the working class. [...] Now by no means limited to lower-class strata, *Stammtische* continue to serve as local forums for the exchange of news and opinion and avid political debates and as informal loci in intellectual culture for the hermeneutics of everyday life. In this capacity, the open dialogical character of the *Stammtisch* inverts certain formal conventions of the public sphere (*Öffentlichkeit*).[53]

Manfred Prisching characterizes Stammtische as an example of semi-public places of institutional transition from traditional communities to a type of postmodern temporary collectivization. He contrasts these contemporary types of collectivization with the more durable kinds of communities of traditional societies.[54] Collectivizations emerge from being socially disembedded in an insecure, ambivalent, inconsistent, ambiguous "liquid modernity."[55] The experiences described above as characteristic of contemporary life in Western societies are also mentioned as specific to the East German transformational society since 1989.

In contrast to Western societies where modernization, acceleration and social embedding increased gradually, the radical social transformation in East Germany came literally overnight. For this reason, many East Germans experienced it as an existential upheaval. Sociologists point to the uniqueness of a "double modernization"[56] as a "double social upheaval"[57] in East Germany after the Wende. According to Kollmorgen, East German society has to deal with the challenge of the post-socialist transformation and political unification process at the same time as dealing "with specific postmodern formations."[58]

---

53 Dominic Boyer, *Spirit and System: Media, Intellectuals, and the Dialectic in Modern German Culture* (Chicago: U of Chicago P, 2005): 249–250 (emphases in the original).
54 Manfred Prisching, "Paradoxien der Vergemeinschaftung," in *Posttraditionelle Gemeinschaften. Theoretische und ethnographische Erkundungen*, eds. Ronald Hitzfeld, Anne Honer, Michaela Pfadenhauer (Wiesbaden: VS Verlag, 2008): 35–54.
55 Cf. Prisching, "Paradoxien der Vergemeinschaftung," 35; also see Zygmunt Bauman, *Liquid Modernity* (Cambridge: Polity P, 2001).
56 Dieter Klein, "Doppelte Modernisierung im Osten. Illusion oder Option der Geschichte?", in *Umbruch zur Moderne*, eds. Michael Brie, Dieter Klein (Hamburg: VSA, 1991): 9–34, 18.
57 Rainer Land, "Paradigmenwechsel in der Ostdeutschlandforschung," *Berliner Debatte Initial* 16.2 (2005): 69–75, 73; Raj Kollmorgen, *Ostdeutschland. Beobachtungen einer Übergangs- und Teilgesellschaft* (Wiesbaden: VS Verlag, 2005): chapter V.
58 "Die Problematisierung eines *doppelten* Umbruchs stellt klar, dass wir es in Ostdeutschland einerseits mit postsozialistischer Transformation und Vereinigung zu tun haben, andererseits [...] mit spezifischen Formierungen der 'Postmoderne' " (Raj Kollmorgen, "Zwischen 'nachholender Modernisierung' und 'doppeltem Umbruch': Ostdeutschland und deutsche Einheit im Diskurs der Sozialwissenschaften," in *Diskurse der deutschen Einheit. Kritik und Alternativen,*

The statement of a young East German woman about feeling as though she was "thrown into another world" (*DG*, 83)[59] at that time exemplifies the impact of the social transformational process on the individual lives of East Germans since then. Stammtische as forms of temporary collectivization in general satisfy the desire for social embedding and community but lack the strong traditional implications of interpersonal commitment, emotional bonding, continuity and permanence.[60] However, Prisching observes that collectivization supports postmodern individuals in the processes of self-reassurance and searching for identity.[61] The Ossi-Stammtisch specifically satisfies homing desire of those East Germans whose migration to the West is accompanied by feelings of uprootedness, the longing for home and questions of cultural identity. Morover, the practices themselves of building communities at the Ossi-Stammtisch mark a process of identity construction that manifests and reproduces the construct of East Germans as a collective subject with a distinct collective identity.

The kind of East German Ossi-Stammtisch encountered in several larger West German cities can be characterized as a low-threshold, informal institution where East Germans regularly meet to share their transformational and migratory experiences with people who have a similar biographical background and cultural roots. The similarities and specifics of these East German biographical experiences are a strong dimension in shaping the identity of the participants of the Ossi-Stammtisch. East German Stammtische are exclusively to be found outside East Germany, especially in economically stronger regions in the West which became important destinations for East-West German migratory movements after 1989, e. g., Baden-Württemberg, Bavaria, the Rhine-Main area or Hamburg. Therefore, they can be considered the result of the inner German migratory process after 1989.

East Germans of all ages and social backgrounds come to the Ossi-Stammtisch. Hence, a very heterogeneous group of academics and a diverse range of other professionals meet regularly at East German Stammtische in several West German cities. Comparable institutions of West Germans in the East exist, but they are rare.[62] They seem to be more exclusive, but they are not osten-

---

eds. Raj Kollmorgen, Thomas Frank, Hans-Liudger Dienel (Wiesbaden: VS Verlag, 2011): 27–65, 57.

59 "[...] wie in eine andere Welt hineingeworfen [...]."
60 Cf. Prisching, "Paradoxien der Vergemeinschaftung," 38.
61 Cf. Prisching, "Paradoxien der Vergemeinschaftung," 38.
62 Ralf Schuler, "Wessis in Dresden. Die Wendehelfer bleiben Fremde an der Elbe" (August 22, 1998), *Die Welt* <http://www.welt.de/print-welt/article625312/Wessis-in-Dresden.html> (acc. March 1, 2014).

tatiously labelled as "West German" or as "for Wessis" (i. e., West Germans), and they are more difficult to identify for outsiders.

While West Germans tend to identify as "German" or have a more regional identity, many East Germans feel a much stronger identification with "East Germany" in general.[63] The individual motivations for participation at an Ossi-Stammtisch are primarily based on shared experiences marking the biographical interface of East German migrants. Sharing childhood memories, socializing, joining in pastimes, and mutual support in coping with the challenges of daily life constitute the main topics of East German meetings at Stammtische in the West. The participants emphasize that the Stammtisch is neither a circle of frustrated *Nostalgiker* (i. e., people nursing nostalgic feelings for the supposed delights of the former GDR) nor a place where East Germans meet to complain, as a widespread stereotype suggests.[64] Contrary to this, they do not talk of the political dimensions of the GDR very often at all.[65] The common origin of the participants itself rarely constitutes an explicit topic at the Stammtisch. Instead, it is the referential frame of interpersonal exchange about everyday experiences in the past and the present which shapes talk at the Stammtisch. Hence, both the past and present experiences in a new place in the West create an implicit

---

63 Cf. Kollmorgen, Koch, Dienel, *Diskurse der deutschen Einheit*, 278; 284.

64 Cf. the cover of *Spiegel* 39/2004: "Jammertal Ost" ["East German vale of tears"] (September 20, 2014), *Der Spiegel* <http://www.spiegel.de/spiegel/print/d-32205142.html> (acc. March 1, 2014); Kollmorgen, Koch and Dienel, *Diskurse der deutschen Einheit*, 206; Holger Drechsel, "Einmal im Monat trifft sich der Ossi-Stammtisch" (October 1, 2010), *Wa.de – Nachrichten aus Hamm* <http://www.wa.de/nachrichten/nrw/einmal-monat-trifft-sich-ossi-stammtisch-942831.html> (acc. March 1, 2014); Sebastian Röhl, "Ostdeutsche haben es schwer in Hessen: Stammtisch auf Ossi-Art" (October 3, 2010), *Rhein-Main Extra Tipp* <http://www.extratipp.com/news/rhein-main/ostdeutsche-haben-schwer-hessen-stammtisch-ossi-art-940834.html> (acc. March 1, 2014); Christina Hucklenbroich, "Frankfurter 'Ossi-Stammtisch'. Wir waren jung, wir hatten Glück" (August 9, 2009), *Frankfurter Allgemeine Rhein-Main* <http://www.faz.net/aktuell/rhein-main/frankfurter-ossi-stammtisch-wir-waren-jung-wir-hatten-glueck-1838326.html> (acc. March 1, 2014); Julia Gaschik, "Ein Hauch von Heimat im Westen. Ossi-Stammtische beliebt" (November 9, 2009), *ntv* <http://www.n-tv.de/panorama/Ossi-Stammtische-beliebt-article580069.html> (acc. March 1, 2014).

65 E.g., "Die DDR-Vergangenheit spielt bei unseren Treffen keine Rolle." In Röhl, "Ostdeutsche haben es schwer in Hessen, Stammtisch auf Ossi-Art, 1. E.g., "Über die DDR, sagen sie, reden sie gar nicht so oft – nicht einmal im 20. Jahr nach dem Mauerfall. Die Zeit vor der Wende war zuletzt vor einem halben Jahr Gegenstand der Stammtischgespräche." In Hucklenbroich, "Frankfurter Ossi-Stammtisch," 1.

symbolic meaning that seems to be an important dimension connecting those who meet at the Stammtisch.[66]

Collective remembrance at the Ossi-Stammtisch appears dissociated from the political dimensions of the GDR. Instead, participants seek to establish a predominantly apolitical, interpersonal dialogue based on their current everyday experiences. Many of them describe the sensation of foreignness, difficulties in bonding or socializing in the West, and some report open confrontations with prejudices against and stereotypes of East Germans in general. In their strongest and most offensive versions, these ended in blatant and outright rejections. Andreas (who goes by "Mercy"), an East German technician, born in 1971, describes his personal experiences at work after migrating to southern Germany to a journalist:

> He was called 'UDO' by the Wessis, which is short for 'Unser Dummer Ossi' [our stupid Ossi/East German]. He has been called a 'lazy pig,' as well. His Swabian colleagues declared that he and all the other 'UDOs' did not have the slightest idea what it really means to work. [...] He felt like a second-class citizen, at the very least.[67]

Gabi, an East German woman born in 1968, likewise relates that

> in 1989 she came to southern Germany looking for a better life. She soon found work as a hairdresser. She had finished her training [at home] with highest grades. [...] However, in the West her qualifications were worthless. Nobody wanted to let her cut their hair. 'She is from the East,' she frequently heard the clients saying. After fourteen days, she quit her job.[68]

---

66 See Rill's analysis of the symbolic dimension of cultural identities in Ingo Rill, *Symbolische Identität. Dynamik und Stabilität bei Ernst Cassirer und Niklas Luhmann* (Würzburg: Königshausen und Neumann, 1995): 169–170; see also Pates, Schochow (ed.), *Der "Ossi"*.

67 "Mercy hieß bei den Wessis Udo – für 'unser dummer Ossi.' Manchmal wurde er auch 'faules Schwein' genannt. Seine schwäbischen Kollegen erklärten ihm, er und all die anderen Udos hätten nicht den blassesten Schimmer davon, was echte Arbeit sei. [...] Er fühlte sich wie ein Deutscher zweiter Klasse. Mindestens" (Verena Mayer, "Stammtisch in Stuttgart. Heimatabend unter Ossis" [October 3, 2013], *Stuttgarter Zeitung* <http://stuttgarter-zeitung.de/inhalt.stamm tisch-in-stuttgart-heimatabend-unter-ossis.6845faa0-5784-45e1-84f9-890dedd99f05.html> [acc. March 1, 2014]: 1).

68 "Gabi kam 1989 [...] auf der Suche nach einem besseren Leben in den Süden. Rasch fand sie eine Stelle als Friseurin. Gabi hatte ihre Ausbildung mit Bestnote abgeschlossen. [...] Im Westen jedoch war ihr Können nichts wert. Niemand wollte sich von Gabi die Haare schneiden lassen. 'Die ist doch aus dem Osten,' hörte die Friseurin häufig die Kunden raunen. Nach 14 Tagen gab Gabi ihre Stelle auf" (Mayer, "Stammtisch in Stuttgart," 2).

Other participants report that they had very positive experiences and, although they already feel at home in the West, they use the Stammtisch as a platform to connect with people who have a similar mentality or share the same cultural roots. Andrea, another East German woman, born in 1961, reports that she had only positive experiences in a smaller city in North Rhine Westphalia and that she was made to feel very welcome there.[69] The members of the Stammtisch describe it as a place where "they feel like coming home"[70] and observe that attending it satisfies their desire for their homeland. Furthermore, since they share a longing for "closer social interactions,"[71] the Stammtisch gives them the opportunity to connect and make new friends far from home faster. For Andrea, for example, the Stammtisch became "almost a family meeting place. A place for chatting, laughing and feeling at home."[72] Torsten, born in 1975, states that "at the beginning he went home almost every weekend. But in the meanwhile he made friends in the West as well, especially at the Stammtisch."[73] Similarly, Gabi, another East German woman, born in 1966, relates that while she had been living in the West for about nineteen years, it took her ten years to feel at home there.[74]

---

69 "Andrea [...] hat 'nur gute Erfahrungen in Hamm gemacht. Ich wurde hier mit offenen Armen empfangen' " (Drechsel, "Einmal im Monat trifft sich der Ossi-Stammtisch," 1).

70 "Für die Älteren ist es ein Stück Nach-Hause-Kommen," and: "Dass er in Frankfurt am Main schnell heimisch geworden sei, habe er auch dem 'Ossi-Stammtisch' zu verdanken, erzählt der 32-Jährige. Zwar findet er nicht, dass ein Neuanfang im Westen grundsätzlich schwieriger ist als im Osten – aber an die Mentalität der Frankfurter musste er sich gewöhnen. 'Die Ostdeutschen sind etwas offener, lassen einen eher an sich heran' " (Gaschik, "Ein Hauch von Heimat im Westen," 1).

71 "Der DDR traure sie nicht hinterher, betont die Wahl-Nürnbergerin, die sehr gern reist und das Eingesperrtsein immer 'schrecklich' fand. Allenfalls vermisse sie das engere Miteinander von früher. [...] Doch da sorgt der Stammtisch, um den ein regelrechtes Netzwerk entstanden ist, für Ausgleich" (Silke Roennefahrt, "Der Ossi-Stammtisch hilft auch gegen Heimweh" [November 21, 2009], *Nürnberger Nachrichten* <http://www.nordbayern.de/nuernberger-nachrichten/nuern berg/der-ossi-stammtisch-hilft-auch-gegen-heimweh-1.603839> (acc. March 1, 2014): 2; Gaschik, "Ein Hauch von Heimat im Westen," 1).

72 "Für sie ist der Stammtisch schon fast so etwas wie Familientreffen. Ein Ort zum Klönen, zum Lachen, zum sich heimisch fühlen" (Drechsel, "Einmal im Monat trifft sich der Ossi-Stammtisch," 1).

73 "Am Anfang sei er noch jedes Wochenende nach Hause gefahren; mittlerweile habe er sich aber auch hier einen Freundeskreis aufgebaut. 'Vor allem über den Stammtisch,' sagt er" (Hucklenbroich, "Frankfurter Ossi-Stammtisch," 2).

74 "Ich lebe jetzt 19 Jahre hier und brauchte zehn Jahre, um mich hier zu Hause zu fühlen" (Drechsel, "Einmal im Monat trifft sich der Ossi-Stammtisch," 1).

A place like home at the Ossi-Stammtisch is constructed through telling stories, sharing experiences of the past and the present, remembering things and, above all, using the same language, such as a particular vocabulary or dialect, a shared knowledge of implicit contexts of meanings and of communication rules. The members of the Stammtisch consider it a "question of mentality" that brings people from the East together at an East German Stammtisch, similar to Bavarians or Germans from northern parts of the country.[75] Katja, born in 1980, emphasizes that it is this shared mentality that makes it much easier to get in contact. She states that: "Here one can interact immediately about issues. [...] Initially, there is that feeling that Wessis are more superficial. It takes longer to discover what kind of person they really are and to become [closer] friends."[76] Cynthia (born in 1971) for example, an East German woman married to a West German, accepts the differences between East and West Germans and remarks: "We should not act like there are no longer any differences between East and West. [...] This will not change even in a hundred years. And why should it change? Why do we not just accept the differences?"[77] Married to a 'Wessi', she is living proof that differences need not constitute an insurmountable obstacle.[78] Rather, she enjoins more Wessis to participate in the Stammtisch to overcome cultural prejudices against East Germans and to understand "what we are really like."[79]

Using the modifier "Ossi," i.e., East German, in the name of the Stammtisch marks a practice of the construction of a collective identity. It postulates the existence of a social group which understands and identifies with the implicit ascriptions of the word. The linguistically marked exclusiveness of the Stammtisch presupposes a shared social knowledge of the categories of 'Ossi' and 'Wessi' which is reinforced, reproduced and passed on through social communication

---

75 Hucklenbroich, "Frankfurter Ossi-Stammtisch," 3.
76 "Hier kann man sich sofort über Dinge austauschen. [...] Im ersten Moment hat man bei 'Wessis' manchmal das Gefühl, dass sie oberflächlicher sind. Es dauert länger, bis man den Menschen dahinter erkennt und Freundschaften schließt" (Hucklenbroich, "Frankfurter Ossi-Stammtisch," 2).
77 "Man sollte nicht so tun, als gebe es keine Unterschiede zwischen Ost und West. [...] Und bei uns wird sich in 100 Jahren auch nichts ändern [...]. Warum auch? Warum akzeptiert man die Unterschiede nicht einfach?" (Drechsel, "Einmal im Monat trifft sich der Ossi-Stammtisch," 1).
78 "Und dass Unterschiede keine unüberwindbare Mauer begründen, beweist sie selber. Cynthias Mann Jörg, auch mit am Tisch, ist schließlich Westfale. Lupenreiner Wessi" (Drechsel, "Einmal im Monat trifft sich der Ossi-Stammtisch," 2).
79 "Wäre schön, wenn auch mehr Wessis zu unserem Stammtisch kämen. Damit sie sehen, wie wir wirklich sind" (Drechsel, "Einmal im Monat trifft sich der Ossi-Stammtisch," 1).

to subsequent generations.[80] The act of verbalization firstly constructs 'Ossi' and 'Wessi' as social entities. The subordination of individuals under a collective subject like 'Ossi,' for example, emphasizes the community building character of shared social experiences. Furthermore, it constructs an imagined community, relating an individual "I" to a collective (imagined) "Us." Gabi, the East German woman quoted earlier, founded an Ossi-Stammtisch herself after she had undergone several difficult social rejections and painful disrespect for her professional qualifications. She describes this as "bringing together my own crowd," and defines her social identity through belonging to a specific social group, the 'Ossis.'[81] At the same time, she marks a distinction, excluding those who made her feel different and subaltern. Participants feel that the Stammtisch is a place where the social structure of the everyday world can be suspended (as well as associated experiences of subalternity and foreignness).[82] Thus, it constitutes a refuge from public discourse which enables the East German participants to emancipate themselves from the negative descriptions and hegemonic constructions in the media.

An important mechanism for coping with the stereotypes in public discourse is self-deprecation and humor. Mary Douglas describes the joke as an "anti-rite" which helps to deconstruct hierarchies and to destroy social orders.[83] Freud similarly emphasizes the liberating potential of humor. He states that

> humour has in it a liberating element. But it has also something fine and elevating [...]. It refuses to be hurt by the arrows of reality or to be compelled to suffer. It insists that it is impervious to wounds dealt by the outside world, in fact, that these are merely occasions for affording it pleasure. [...] Humour is not resigned; it is rebellious. It signifies the triumph not only of the ego, but also of the pleasure-principle, which is strong enough to assert itself here in the face of the adverse real circumstances.[84]

Joking at the Stammtisch helps to create a mental distance to the ascriptions made by others, taking the force out of disrespectful utterances. Asking the interviewer if they were expected to have a flag of the former GDR on the table or joking they would use a specific kind of East German script are examples

---

80 Also see Peter L. Berger, Thomas Luckmann, *The Social Construction of Reality: A Treatise in the Sociology of Knowledge* (New York: Anchor Books, 1967): 173–179, 173.
81 "'Ich pfeife meine eigenen Leute zusammen,' dachte sie sich. Die Geburt des Ossi-Stammtisches. Ein bisschen Nähe in der Ferne" (Mayer, "Stammtisch in Stuttgart," 1).
82 See Kollmorgen, "Subalternisierung," 301–302.
83 Mary Douglas, "The Social Control of Cognition," in *Man, New Series* 3.3 (1968): 361–376, 369.
84 Sigmund Freud, "Humour," *The International Journal of Psycho-Analysis* 9 (1928): 1–6, 2.

of this kind of self-deprecatory practice of identity *de*construction.[85] Further-more, humor has an important social function in constructing group identities, because laughing together connects people.[86]

Conclusion

In summary, the Ossi-Stammtisch can be said to serve as a place that gives con-crete support to East Germans for coping with the challenges of everyday life in a new place in the West. It enables the participants to develop individual strategies for coping, and to share these in interpersonal exchanges and networking with similar others. In this sense, the Ossi-Stammtisch has a highly practical everyday dimension with a focus on managing the challenges of the present rather than remembering the past. The interpersonal exchanges provide individuals with op-portunities to experience the non-singularity of their perceived foreignness, while mutual understanding and social acceptance can finally evoke the desired feelings of coming home. Ossi-Stammtische can at once construct and stabilize the participants' collective cultural identity of being East German. Furthermore, participants assume that there is a clearly recognizable cultural identity of East-German*ness*. The community of Stammtisch participants shares an implicit knowledge of who can be categorized as an 'Ossi' and who cannot. Based on these indicators, the Stammtisch participants differentiate between the in-group ("us," i.e., 'Ossis') and outsiders ("others," i.e., 'Wessis'). This differentia-tion contributes to the distinctive character of the Stammtisch.

---

85 "Am Stammtisch schreiben Walter und Fred ihre Adressen auf einen Zettel. Damit sie in den Ossi-Verteiler kommen. 'Kannst du das lesen?', fragt Walter Gabi. – 'Geht so.' – 'Das ist Ost-Schrift.' – Lachen" (Mayer, "Stammtisch in Stuttgart," 3); "Der Ankündigung, beim nächsten Mal komme ein Fotograf mit, begegnen sie grinsend mit der Frage, ob sie dann eine DDR-Fahne auf den Tisch stellen sollen" (Hucklenbroich, "Frankfurter Ossi-Stammtisch," 2).
86 Boyer also characterizes *Stammtische* as places where joking plays an important role for in-teracting (Boyer, *Spirit and System*, 250–251).

Frank Jacob
Reflections on the Korean Diaspora in Manchuria

Abstract: Like many other aspects of the Modern History of Korea, the Korean Diaspora in Manchuria was created by Japanese imperial ambitions in East Asia. However, the nature of the diaspora itself was largely determined by the region the Koreans found themselves in. Manchuria, which had been regarded as a kind of 'No Man's Land' for centuries, became a new home for Korean ambitions, leading to local conflicts with other minorities in this multi-ethnic region. Chinese, Japanese, Korean, Manchurian, and Russian ambitions met in this specific region of the world, and personal rather than political ambitions created a sphere where new forms of transnational diasporas came into existence. The following chapter will try to explain the establishment of visionary diasporas by using Korea between 1905 and 1945 as a specific historical example. The establishment and development of this diaspora and its consequences will be discussed in detail and brought into a broader context of diaspora studies.

Introduction

A diaspora can be created by different factors, e.g., war, political or economic crises, etc. We are seeing a growing number of global diasporas connected to the use of modern technology, which provides those who no longer live in their ancestors' country with a tremendously important tool to keep their cultural heritage.[1] As a consequence, we witness the establishment of a growing number of "ethnonational communities,"[2] which are increasingly the focus of scholarly work. Because of these trends, it is important to establish precisely what I mean by the Korean diaspora in Manchuria. It was the movement of people, forced to leave their home country because of political developments caused by the Japanese annexation. They moved north to Manchuria, where a 'No Man's Land' awaited them. There they could continue their life as Koreans, undominated by Japanese rule. However, they also used their ethnic identity to segregate themselves from the other settlers in the region. Consequently, an ethnonational form of diaspora was created by external pressure, leading to a resettlement of settler colonials in Manchuria with the aim of creating a new sphere of "real free Koreanness."

---

1 Cf. Kim D. Butler, "Defining Diaspora, Refining a Discourse," *Diaspora. A Journal of Transnational Studies* 10.2 (2001): 189–219, 190.
2 Butler, "Defining Diaspora," 190.

This development was strongly impacted by Japanese ambitions; the modern history of Korea was determined by Japanese expansionist ambitions, from the forced opening of the Korean peninsula in 1876 until the end of the Second World War in 1945. We can clearly trace the line of these Japanese ambitions: from the discourse surrounding an invasion of Korea (Seikanron) in 1873, bypassing the opening of Korea, the war with China in 1894–1895, and the Russo-Japanese War, which was fought to gain a hegemonic position in Korea, the Katsura-Taft agreement, through which the United States and Japan drew the borders of their imperialist aims in Asia, to the step-by-step annexation of the Korean state, which became part of the Japanese empire in 1910. The main aim of the Meiji policy was total control of Korea.[3] Between 1905 and 1910, the Japanese government enforced Japanese rights in Korea by decreasing the independent status of the Korean government.[4] The Koreans were unable to stop this development, and the international community was not willing to interfere in favor of the Korean state, even when a delegation attended the peace conference in The Hague in 1907.

This was the reason for an increasing diasporic emigration of Korean people, especially to Manchuria, where they found a new home. But this new environment would not remain safe for long. The Koreans who had been forced to leave faced several problems in their new home. This chapter outlines the situation in their new home in the Manchurian borderlands.[5] It will begin with an analysis of why the Koreans emigrated to Manchuria, followed by an overview of the new Korean settlers' problems. It will then be shown that their situation became paradoxical, because they were simultaneously seen as stateless rebels by the Japanese and agents of Japan's imperialism by the Chinese and Russian Manchurians.

---

3 Cf. Deuk-sang Kang, *Chôsen dokuritsu undô no gunzô. Keimô undô kara San-ichi undô he* (Tokyo: Aoki Shoten, 1984): 5.
4 Cf. Kang, *Chôsen dokuritsu undô no gunzô*, 8.
5 Since the second half of the nineteenth century, Manchuria provided a borderland where people could settle quite easily, as it resembled the Chinese periphery and there was no active border control. Thus it provided a large space for anyone in search for a new home. On the borderland discourse in general, and for a survey of some important borderland regions, see the following major works: Leo K. Shin, *The Making of the Chinese State: Ethnicity and Expansion on the Ming Borderlands* (Cambridge: Cambridge UP, 2006); *Peopling the Russian Periphery: Borderland Colonization in Eurasian History*, eds. Nicholas Brezfolge, Abby Schrader, Willard Sunderland (London: Routledge, 2007); *Shatterzone of Empires: Coexistence and Violence in the German, Habsburg, Russian, and Ottoman Borderlands*, eds. Omer Bartov, Eric D. Weitz (Bloomington: Indiana UP, 2013).

Thus their new home was not destined to be safe for long. The Wanpaoshan Incident in 1931 changed everything. The different ethnic groups in Manchuria could not live in harmony. This provided Japan with an opportunity to interfere in Manchuria because the Japanese saw the Koreans as Japanese citizens and the Manchurian incident was a direct consequence of the tendency to anti-Korean violence in Manchuria. The new home of the Korean emigrants became a new sphere of Japanese influence. Finally, the Koreans lost their new home due to the ambitions of the Japanese: In 1945, when the Japanese had to leave again, most Koreans were forced to leave Manchuria as well. The period of Korean settler movement in southern Manchuria came to an end, and after fifty years their new home outside the Japanese sphere of influence became dangerous again. But why did the Koreans choose Manchuria in the first place?

The Geographical and Historical Settings

Korea had been of essential importance to Japanese foreign policy since 1868. Toyotomi Hideyoshi (1537–1598)[6] laid the ground for expansionist ambitions by trying to invade in the late sixteenth century, and after the forced opening of Japan in 1853 the expansionist forces of Japan demanded a second invasion. As early as 1873, just two decades after Japan's own opening from foreign imperialism, the Japanese government discussed a plan to invade Korea (*seikanron*).[7] It was decided that the time was not yet suitable, but just three years later Japan became the driving force behind the opening of Korea.

Since the late 1870s, Japan had been trying to increase its influence on the Korean peninsula. They felt it was near to Japan's southern island, Kyûshû, where nationalist forces feared an invasion.[8] Thus the Japanese need for security was the reason for the increased expansionist engagement in Korea. Japan waged war against China in 1894/95[9] and against Russia in 1904/05[10] to protect

---

6 For a biographical study of Toyotomi, Mary Elizabeth Berry, *Hideyoshi* (Cambridge, Mass.: Harvard UP, 1982) is still valuable reading.

7 The party voting for an invasion was assembled by Saigô Takamori. Cf. Charles L. Yates, *Saigo Takamori: The Man Behind the Myth* (New York: Kegan Paul International, 1995): 136.

8 Due to this fear nationalist tendencies remained tremendously strong in Southern Japan, where secret societies like the *Gen'yôsha* (Black Ocean Society) demanded a more aggressive Japanese foreign policy. Cf. Frank Jacob, *Die Thule-Gesellschaft und die Kokuryûkai: Geheimgesellschaften im global-historischen Vergleich* (Würzburg: Königshausen & Neumann, 2013), 185–190.

9 S. C. M. Paine, *The Sino-Japanese War of 1894–1895: Perception, Power, and Primacy* (Cambridge: Cambridge UP, 2003).

its influence. Their victory against the tsarist empire in 1905 secured unchallenged Japanese control and, as a consequence, several treaties were made in the following years, until the final annexation of Korea in 1910 tightened the control over the Korean Hermit Kingdom.[11]

The Korean population was Japanized step by step, even as the Korean community was eager to keep its personal cultural heritage alive.[12] Many Koreans left their homes to seek a new fortune in Manchuria. This bordering territory was the homeland of the Manchu, a branch of the Tungusic people, who took over rule of China and founded the Qing dynasty,[13] which ruled the Chinese empire from 1644 until 1912. In 1668 the new rulers prohibited the settlement of common Han Chinese in their homeland in order to secure their power base, but in the late nineteenth century this prohibition was lifted and Chinese settlers moved to the northern territory. There they met with fleeing Koreans and Russians, who settled there as a consequence of Russia's expansionist ambitions in the Far East. What developed was a multi-ethnic state. Koreans made up the majority in some of the provinces of the Manchurian no-man's-land, and were seen as Japanese subordinates after 1910. As a result, the Japanese government and especially the military were eager to enforce their influence in this territory, because they had received the Russian rights to the South Manchurian Railway after the end of the Russo-Japanese War. The railway became a tool for Japanese imperialism, and the Koreans were used as a scapegoat. The Kwangtung Army[14] also wanted to create a Japanese sphere of influence in Manchuria and provoked the Mukden Incident in 1931,[15] after which Manchuria was occupied. Finally, the puppet state of Manchukuo[16] was created in 1932 to control the area and the Koreans became part of the Japanese empire again. Pan-Asianism, "an ideology that served not only as a basis for early efforts at regional integration in East-

---

10 For a short introduction, see Geoffrey Jukes, *The Russo-Japanese War 1904–1905* (Oxford: Osprey, 2002).

11 For a survey of this process, see Peter Duus, *The Abacus and the Sword: The Japanese Penetration of Korea* (Berkeley: U of California P, 1998).

12 Jun Uchida, "A Sentimental Journey: Mapping the Interior Frontier of Japanese Settlers in Colonial Korea," *The Journal of Asian Studies* 70.3 (2011): 706–729, 710.

13 For a valuable survey of the history of the Qing dynasty, see Richard Joseph Smith, *China's Cultural Heritage: The Qing Dynasty, 1644–1912* (Boulder: Westview P, 1994).

14 Cf. Yamakawa Akira, *Nihon no senreki. Manshû teikoku no tanjô – Kôtei Fu Gi to Kantôgun* (Tokyo: Gakushû Kenkyûsha, 2001): 46.

15 Long-hsuen Hsu, Chang Ming-kai, *History of the Sino-Japanese War (1937–1945)* (Taipei: Chung Wu, 1971) gives a detailed introduction on the reasons of the Second Sino-Japanese War.

16 Cf. Louise Young, *Japan's Total Empire. Manchuria and the Culture of Wartime Imperialism* (Berkeley: U of California P, 1999): 3–20.

Asia, but also as a cloak for expansionism and as a tool for legitimizing Japanese hegemony and colonial rule"[17] was used to justify Japanese rule, because Japan was described as a helping guide that was merely interested in Asian freedom. But there were more aggressive readings of Japanese Pan-Asianism, because in truth, Japan was mainly interested in securing its own hegemonic position in Asia. These Japanese expansionist tendencies and ambitions were responsible for the start of the Korean diaspora in Manchuria, as well as the subsequent re-integration of the emigrants into the Japanese colonial empire. Japanese rule would last until 1945 when the empire met its end, and the Koreans had to face a second diaspora.

Emigration to Manchuria

Manchuria was traditionally a "largely borderless terrain"[18] to the north of Korea to which people could travel free and without restrictions. This free transition was responsible for the creation of "deep historical links between the two regions,"[19] which became more attractive with the expansion of imperialist Japanese ambitions in Korea. Most of the Koreans who decided to leave their home country were peasants looking for a better life on their own soil, but critics and opponents also left Korea to find a new home in the urban centers of Manchuria.[20] The northern border remained uncontrolled and was the easiest route to a non-Japanese future. It was the ideal place for a new home in the north.

Since the latter half of the nineteenth century, when the Qing dynasty abolished the prohibition of 1668 to settle in their traditional homeland, more and more people from China, Korea and Russia had been moving to a region which was open for reinterpretation and reinvention.[21] Through Japanese economic expansion, the Korean market became commercialized and a gap emerged between the rich, powerful landowners and the poor peasants, who were not

---

17 Sven Saaler, "Pan-Asianism in Modern Japanese History: Overcoming the Nation, Creating a Region, Forging an Empire," in *Pan-Asianism in Modern Japanese History. Colonialism, Regionalism and Borders*, eds. Victor J. Koschmann, Sven Saaler (London, New York: Routledge, 2007): 1–18, 1.

18 Michael Kim, "The Lost Memories of Empire and Korean Return from Manchuria, 1945–1950: Conceptualizing Manchuria in Modern Korean History," *Seoul Journal of Korean Studies* 23.2 (2010): 195–223, 197.

19 Kim, "Lost Memories," 197.

20 Cf. Hyun Ok Park, *Two Dreams in One Bed: Empire, Social Life, and the Origins of the North Korean Revolution in Manchuria* (Durham: Duke UP, 2005): 24–63.

21 Cf. Kim, "Lost Memories," 205–206.

able to succeed in the transformation process.[22] Due to the Japanese railway construction in Manchuria, many Koreans moved there, where they were able to settle as farmers. They were followed by their families and others who thought they could start a new life following their agrarian tradition.[23]

By 1910, 171,543 Koreans had emigrated to Manchuria, but this number increased to 219,217 by 1919. The annexation of Korea and the subsequent Japanization forced many Koreans into exile. As a result, more and more people left Korea. But they were not all forced; some were encouraged, to provide an excuse for more aggressive Japanese foreign policy in Manchuria, because they would not be just settlers, but Japanese citizens, for whose sake Japan could intervene in China. Thus between 1932 and 1940, around 732,000 Koreans left for the northern state of Manchukuo, where their number reached 1,400,000 in 1940. By 1945, over 2,160,000 Koreans were living in Manchuria.[24]

But the Koreans in exile were not just a favorable factor in the Japanese plans for foreign intervention. Since 1907, when the Korean delegation to The Hague was unsuccessful in convincing the world of Korea's status as a sovereign country, several guerilla forces had taken military action supported by their political leaders, who had previously emigrated to Manchuria. In 1908, 1,451 incidents were registered.[25] The annexation of Korea created another wave of emigration in 1910, as well as the March 1st Movement in 1919. The oppression of the revolutionary movement in Korea after the First World War led to another emigration wave, this time politically motivated.[26]

In contrast to this forced emigration, in the aftermath of the Second World War the Japanese started to encourage the Koreans to leave their home country. They were seen as a tool to broaden Japanese influence in Manchuria, because the Korean people had been Japanese citizens since 1910. So Japan constructed a Japanese minority in the region. In addition to this, those leaving made room for

22 Cf. Gi-Wook Shin, *Peasant Protest & Social Change in Colonial Korea* (Washington: U of Washington P, 1996): 27–30.
23 Cf. Jae Eun Kang, *Manshû no Chôsenjin paruchizan. 1930 nendai no Tôman – Nanman wo chûshin toshite* (Tokyo: Aoki Shoten, 1993): 17.
24 Cf. Ku Dae-yeol, *Korea under Colonialism: The March First Movement and Anglo-Japanese Relations* (Seoul: Seoul Computer P, 1985): 17; Kim, "Lost Memories," 203, 215.
25 Cf. Dae-yeol, *Korea under Colonialism*, 3.
26 For the Movement of March 1, see Deuk-sang Kang, *Chôsen dokuritsu undô no gunzô*, 19; Kawase Takaya, *Shokuminchi Chôsen no shûkyô to gakuchi. Teikoku Nihon no manazashi no kôchiku* (Tokyo: Seikyûsha, 2009): 122–123; Richard S. Kim, "Diasporic Politics and the Globalizing of America: Korean Immigrant Nationalism and the 1919 Philadelphia Korean Congress," in *Asian Diasporas. New Formations, New Conceptions*, ed. Rhacel S. Parreñas, Lok C. D. Siu (Stanford: Stanford UP, 2007): 201–224.

Japanese settlers in Korea. In 1919, alongside the political emigrants, many people were supported in their wish for emigration. Consequently, 45,000 Koreans left for the north.[27] Japanese contemporary historians went even further when they spread a singular history of both regions, the so-called *Mansenshi*, after the Russo-Japanese War.[28] This propaganda made it clear that both regions needed to be unified under Japanese rule. Once again, historiography was instrumentalized by Japanese expansionist ambitions. But despite these constructions of a united ethnic heritage, the situation of the Koreans in their new home in Manchuria was very paradoxical.

A Paradoxical Situation

The Koreans who sought a new home far away from Japanese rule were successful. They introduced paddy farming and monopolized the rice trade in a very short time. Having previously belonged to a traditional agricultural society, the settlers were able to use their broad knowledge of farming to produce a larger amount of rice, making them prosperous. But they were not only farmers; industrialists were also interested in this new economic sphere. They invested in new factories and were eager to sell their products to the new market of old customers. In particular, Korean products were successfully exported to the Korean settlers in Manchuria.[29]

The Manchurian Koreans were good customers, but they were no longer seen as Koreans in an official sense. By 1945, there were up to 600,000 Koreans in Manchuria who were stateless. They had found a new home far away from the political control of their Japanese enemy, but when the Japanese founded the new multi-ethnic state of Manchukuo after the Manchurian Incident in 1931, these people were not able to be a part of the new state. To become a citizen, they needed to be registered in colonial Korea. Because most Koreans had left their homes as a consequence of the annexation, they were not registered there, and now were unable to become citizens of Manchukuo. They were stateless again, and their home became Japanized once more.[30]

This was not the only paradoxical factor of Korean life in the new homeland. Although they had left as suppressed people searching for a free home, they were seen by their Chinese and Russian neighbors as agents of Japanese impe-

---

27 Cf. Dae-yeol, *Korea under Colonialism*, 7.
28 Cf. Kim, "Lost Memories," 201.
29 Cf. Kim, "Lost Memories," 220.
30 Kim, "Lost Memories," 220.

rialism in Manchuria. The pre-existing settler community in the Manchurian borderland thus saw the Korean newcomers as a threat, one which might lead to
Japanese domination in the region. From a historical retrospective this seems
to be the case, even if the Korean community was not willingly acting in that
sense. However, their presence to the north of the Japanese border was naturally
used Japanese with imperialist ambitions as an excuse for subsequent military
intervention in this region. Consequently, the increasing immigration of Korean
farmers was considered a negative trend for the future of Manchuria itself. In the
long run the diasporic situation for the Korean people was double-edged. The
Koreans lost their home in the south to settle in the north, where they were greeted with stereotypes about the Japanese Empire, which made aggressors out of
victims. However, the Koreans themselves established an ethnonational self-
image based on anti-Japanese feelings and the wish to create a new sphere of
national strength and wealth. The antagonism of the pre-existing Chinese and
Russian settler communities provided another danger. This awkward situation
was ultimately responsible for the worsening of the Manchurian position in general, as the different claims for regional supremacy between the different interest
groups made it easier for Japan to take over the region and proclaim "unification" under Japanese leadership. Violence between the settler communities
could not be prevented for long.

This trend was increased by cultural differences between the new settlers
and the Chinese communities. Even though there had been long-term relations
between China and Korea, the common population feared the new and strange
element. The Koreans pretending to be national Koreans themselves were settler
colonialists, who by definition wanted to settle and not integrate. They wanted to
achieve something new: a de-Japanized version of Korea in Manchuria. Therefore
integration was of no interest and the tensions over influence, possession of
land, and economic domination worsened the situation in this region. The settlers spoke another language, dressed like Koreans, had their own cultural habits, and were not willing to integrate into a new state system, instead wanting to
maintain their own way of living in the new setting. These settlers did not leave
Korea to start a promising life in another culture or another country; they left because they were no longer allowed to be typically Korean in their own country,
which had become a victim of Japanese imperialism and Japanization. They ultimately created an ethnonational diaspora, where they intended to keep their
Koreanness, something that was already starting to be suppressed by the Japanese in the south, where Koreans were forced to subsequently abandon their cultural heritage to become Japanese citizens of the Greater Asian Empire of Japan.

The Wanpaoshan Incident

The Wanpaoshan Incident (*Manpôzan jiken*)[31] provided an excuse for further Japanese northward expansion: the Manchurian Incident of 1931. But in this case, what happened and what was reported were completely different. On July 1, 1931, near to the Manchurian city of Changchun, Koreans started to dig a ditch around the land they had leased from a Chinese broker. The Chinese farmers were angry about this and protested, because they thought the ditch would pass through their own land. They met in protest at the ditch, causing the Japanese consular police to fire some shots, but no one was injured.[32] The problem was ultimately not the event itself, but the way the press reported it. Korean and Japanese newspapers embellished the story, and people in Korea were informed that many people had died during the incident. This led to anti-Chinese riots throughout Korea, and what followed was described by the Chinese Journal P. T. Times on August 28, 1931 as "the most shocking exhibition of mob barbarity in recent history."[33]

Chinese traders in Korea – there were 24,000 in 1920 – were particular victims of this excessive press campaign. They were attacked, 142 people died across Korea, 546 were wounded and the economic damage cost 4.1 million Yen. The traders finally decided to leave the hostile environment.[34] The vacuum created by their leaving was filled by Japanese and Korean traders. In Japan, ultranationalist groups like the Black Ocean Society (*Gen'yôsha*) and the Amur Society (*Kokuryûkai*) organized the Mediation Union (*Kaiketsu dômeikai*) to provide an antidote to the societies' Pan-Asianist agenda. The groups longed for a harmonious Manchuria, in which Japan would take the lead over the other ethnic groups. In July the union met around ten times and propagated the idea of a

---

31 21 Shôwa 6 nen, 8 gatsu, 28 nichi kara Shôwa 6 nen 8 gatsu 31 nichi, Gaimushô gaikô shiryôkan B-A-1-1-113; Mansen mondai ni kansuru, 1931, National Institute for Defensive Studies of the Ministry of Defence of Japan, Kaigunshô-kôbun-bikô S6–140–4242; Shimada Toshihiko, *Kantôgun. Zai-Man rikugun no dokusô* (Tokyo: Chûô Kôronsha, 1965): 99–100; Yamakawa Akira, *Nihon no senreki. Manshû teikoku no tanjô – Kôtei fugi to Kantôgun* (Tokyo: Gakushû Kenkyûsha, 2001): 49–51.
32 Cf. Michael Kim, "The Hidden Impact of the 1931 Post-Wanpaoshan Riots: Credit Risk and the Chinese Commercial Network in Colonial Korea," *Sungkyun Journal of East Asian Studies* 10.2 (2010): 209–227, 210.
33 21 Shôwa 6 nen, 8 gatsu, 28 nichi kara Shôwa 6 nen 8 gatsu 31 nichi, Diplomatic Archive of the Foreign Ministry of Japan B-A-1-1-113.
34 Cf. Kim, "Hidden Impact," 209–215.

multi-ethnic state in Manchuria.[35] Under this argument, the Koreans were used as an excuse for Japanese intervention, which would bring peace to Manchuria in general and the Wanpaoshan region in particular.

Japan's Instrumentalization of the Manchurian Koreans

The Japanese nationalists and military circles saw expansion as the only solution to the problem of growing population. They adopted a more aggressive foreign policy, and their ideas became more radical. Hashimoto Kingorô, a founding member of the Cherry Blossom Society (*Sakurakai*), a radical secret society whose members belonged to the Japanese military, explained the problem at the end of the 1930s as follows:

> We are like a great crowd of people packed into a small and narrow room, and there are only three doors through which we might escape, namely emigration, advance into world markets, and expansion of territory. The first door, emigration, has been barred to us by the anti-Japanese immigration policies of other countries. The second door, advance into world markets, is being pushed shut by tariff barriers and the abrogation of commercial treaties. What should Japan do when two of the three doors have been closed against her?[36]

As well as employing direct force, the members of the Black Ocean society, the Amur Society, and many other nationalist organizations achieved indirect expansion by using the ideology of Pan-Asianism as a camouflage for their real aims. In this context, Pan-Asianism was a "tool for legitimizing Japanese hegemony and colonial rule"[37] mainly "based on the Japanese belief that the Japanese share common physical traits with their continental neighbors, Koreans and Chinese, or that they belong to an East Asian world system with historical roots."[38]

The Japanese believed that Manchuria was a special sphere of Japanese influence, where raw materials could be collected for the economy in Japan, and

---

35 Mansen mondai ni kansuru, 1931, National Institute for Defensive Studies of the Ministry of Defence of Japan, Kaigunshô-kôbun-bikô S6–140–4242.

36 Hashimoto Kingorô, "The Need for Emigration and Expansion," in *Japan 1931–1945. Militarism, Fascism, Japanism? Problems in Asian Civilizations*, ed. Ivan Morris (Boston: D. C. Heath, 1963): 64–65, 64.

37 Saaler, "Pan-Asianism," 1.

38 Miwa Kimitada, "Pan-Asianism in Modern Japan: Nationalism, Regionalism and Universalism," in *Pan-Asianism in Modern Japanese History. Colonialism, Regionalism and Borders*, eds. Victor J. Koschmann, Sven Saaler (London, New York: Routledge, 2007): 21–33, 21.

the South Manchurian Railway of Gotô Shimpei was used as a tool of indirect expansion in this area.[39] To secure this area for Japanese interests, the Korean emigrants were used as justification to solve the problem of the Korean peninsula (*kanshima mondai*), because the emigrated Koreans, who made up almost 60–95 percent of the Manchurian population in some of the four provinces (especially the southern provinces), were seen as a dangerous political factor to the north of Japan's borders.[40] Uchida Ryôhei, the chair of the Amur Society, published a memorandum in 1920 in which he asked for Japanese intervention against the Koreans in Siberia and Manchuria. In the nationalist argument of the memorandum, the Korean population was the reason for the unrest in Korea itself.[41] Later, in June 1931 the Amur Society and the Greater Japanese Production Party (*Dai-Nihon seisantô*) organized meetings with the Manchurian Youth League in Japan, where the Pan-Asianists of both regions met to discuss the foundation of the Pan-Asianist future of Manchuria.[42] During this time, Uchida received 50,000 Yen through military channels to make the Manchurian case public and to promote Japanese interest in this region. By doing this, Uchida maintained a close relationship with the military which can be traced back to 1901, when his society was founded.

Ultimately, the military decided the fate of Manchuria, which was occupied during the Manchurian Incident[43] in September 1931, and the creation of Manchukuo put an end to the borderless and informal zone in the north of Korea. The Korean emigrants were once again caught by Japanese imperialism, which brought them back under colonial control.

Conclusion

Ultimately, the Koreans were forced to leave their homes on the Korean peninsula due to the changes enforced by the Japanese rule. They found a new home in Manchuria, a 'No Man's Land' in the north of Korea. There, the Koreans were able

---

39 Cf. Ramon H. Myers, "Japanese Imperialism in Manchuria: The South Manchuria Railway Company, 1906–1933," in *The Japanese Informal Empire in China, 1895–1937*, eds. Peter Duus et al. (Princeton: Princeton UP, 1989): 101–132, 125; Akira, *Nihon no senreki*, 46.
40 Cf. Kang, *Manshû no Chôsenjin paruchizan*, 18.
41 Cf. Dae-yeol, *Korea under Colonialism*, 269.
42 Cf. Hiroharu Seki, "The Manchurian Incident 1931," in *Japan Erupts. The London Naval Conference and the Manchurian Incident, 1928–1932, Japan's Road to the Pacific War*, ed. James William Morley (New York: Columbia UP, 1984): 139–230, 181–182.
43 For the Manchurian Incident see Kang, *Manshû no Chôsenjin paruchizan*, 28–29.

to build new homes, where the more experienced farmers were successful and conquered the economically important rice trade. They had created an ethnonational diaspora, antagonistic to other settler communities in the region, one which yearned to establish a non-Japanese Korea north of the Yalu River.[44] But the Japanese knew that a sizeable independent Korean population might be a danger to their colonial rule. Furthermore, the Koreans could be used as a scapegoat for Japanese expansion in this area.

Nationalist societies enforced action against these dangerous factors, and the multi-ethnic region of Manchuria would be united under Japanese hegemony; a thought spread using Pan-Asian slogans of unity and prosperity. The antagonism of the Korean and Chinese settlers in Manchuria finally laid the ground for another annexation. The Wanpaoshan Incident provided a reason for intervention, and the military started the Manchurian Incident just two months later to put an end to the independent state in this area. Manchukuo was founded, and the Koreans were ruled by the Japanese once again.

It seems ironic that the Koreans, who suffered so much under Japanese rule, were forced to leave the region again after 1945 because the Chinese and Manchurian people thought they had been advocates of the harsh Japanese regime. The collapse of the Japanese empire was responsible for one of the largest migration movements in the aftermath of the Second World War.[45] These experiences were not just Korean, because the Japanese settlers were forced to leave their new homes as well and were now able, possibly for the first time, to better understand the Koreans' fate.[46] The Korean diaspora was Japanese-made, and the new home in the north was not far away from the Japanese expansionist aims. The Koreans were suppressed again, and later experienced a second forced emigration.

---

44 The Yalu River marked the border between Korea and Manchuria.
45 Cf. Kim, "Lost Memories," 203.
46 Fujiwara Tei, *Nagareru hoshi wa ikite iru* (Tokyo: Hibiya Shuppansha, 1949) describes the return of Japanese settlers to Japan after 1945. It seems paradoxical, but due to the harsh memories, the diasporic experiences of the Japanese and Koreans became the same in the aftermath of the collapse of the Japanese empire. Due to this, Fujiwara's book became a bestseller in Korea as well, even it was written by a Japanese.

Andreas Niehaus and Tine Walravens

Home Work: Post-Fukushima Constructions of *Furusato* by Japanese Nationals Living in Belgium

Abstract: Rogers Brubaker remarks that "as a category of practice, 'diaspora' is used to make claims, to articulate projects, to formulate expectations, to mobilize energies, to appeal to loyalties."[1] It is in times of crisis and trauma, we will argue in this paper, that these practices construct and intensify an awareness of community, generated by emotion, feelings, and affect. When the 3/11 Triple Disaster struck Japan in 2011, Japanese nationals living abroad took a diasporic stance and immediately showed their commitment and loyalty to the homeland by organizing fundraising and charity events as well as moral support activities. Interpreting these events from the perspective of gift-giving (Marcel Mauss), it can be argued that remittances and material gifts served to show solidarity of an individual as well as a group to the homeland (furusato) and thus strengthening the feeling of belonging to it. Yet, what is the "homeland" that they support? The idea of homeland is a concept that is culturally and thus historically negotiated, and diasporic communities tend to develop a romantic idea of it. In Japanese, the English term "homeland" would be captured by the term *furusato*, which already embraces a strong element of nostalgia and memory (similar to the German "Heimat"). It originally refers to one's place of birth and is recently used to point to the "idea of originary, emotive space."[2] Based on fifteen in-depth interviews with both short-term and long-term Japanese residents in Belgium, this paper sets out to analyze the effect the triple disaster of 2011 had on the Japanese diasporic communities in Belgium.

On March 11, 2011, the northern Tôhoku region of Japan was struck by a massive magnitude-9 earthquake. In the wake of this earthquake, a tsunami destroyed vast areas along the north-east coast, which also resulted in the meltdown of three reactors in the Fukushima nuclear power plant, due to which an area of approximately twenty kilometers around the stricken areas has been evacuated and designated as no-go zone. As of today, the number of casualties is officially estimated to be about 16,000, and by September 2013 there were still around 290,000 people who had to stay in emergency shelters.[3] However, the long-term psychological implications as well as the environmental consequences cannot be estimated yet, and radioactive polluted water is still leaking into the Pacific Ocean.

---

1 Rogers Brubaker, "The 'Diaspora' Diaspora," *Ethnic and Racial Studies* 28.1 (2005): 1–19, 12.
2 Christine Yano, *Tears of Longing. Nostalgia and the Nation in Japanese Popular Songs* (Cambridge, London: Harvard UP, 2002): 19.
3 Japan Today, "Nearly 290,000 people still living in shelters 2 1/2 years after Tohoku disaster" (September 18, 2013) <http://www.japantoday.com/category/national/view/nearly-290000-people-still-living-in-shelters-2-12-years-after-tohoku-disaster> (acc. January 20, 2015).

It has been argued in anthropological disaster studies that disasters "mobilize forces of cultural change,"[4] and potential fields of research vary because disasters affect every aspect of human life, be it social, economic, environmental, political, or even biological.[5] However, existing theoretical approaches on the cultural effects of disaster have a blind spot because the object of their studies are members of societies and cultures that were directly struck by disaster, which thereby spatially limits the research to the affected areas. Excluded from the existing research are analyses of diasporic communities, whose members have – by definition – been absent from their homeland during a disaster but still retain a strong emotive connection to the homeland and for whom the homeland is still part of their own identity. Emotions, feelings, and affect increase an awareness of one's identity and intensify loyalty towards the home country during times of crisis. Disasters also increase a sense of what Ghassan Hage in his work on Lebanese migrants termed the "guilt of migration."[6] As Amanda Wise explains: "Such guilt derives from the disruption of a moral economy of social belonging, whereby members of a community are indebted to that community in a reciprocal gift-exchange relationship."[7] Hage argues that this relationship is guilt-inducing and that the feeling of guilt is increased in times of crisis: "when you do not share the fate of the collective which gave you social life, you are guilty of letting others pay alone for a debt you are collectively responsible for."[8] Starting from these considerations, this paper sets out to analyze the effect the triple disaster of 2011 had on the Japanese diasporic communities in Belgium. Based on fifteen in-depth interviews with Japanese short-term and long-term residents, our research will show that notions of *furusato* were negotiated and temporary diasporic *communitas* of disaster[9], based on practice, came into being.[10] Further-

---

4 Susannah M. Hoffman, Anthony Oliver-Smith, "Why Anthropologists Should Study Disaster," in *Catastrophe & Culture. The Anthropology of Disaster*, eds. Susannah M. Hoffman, Anthony Oliver-Smith (Santa Fe: School of American Research P, 2002): 3–22 9.
5 See Oliver-Smith, "Theorizing Disasters: Nature, Power, and Culture," in *Catastrophe & Culture. The Anthropology of Disaster*, eds. Susannah M. Hoffman, Anthony Oliver-Smith (Santa Fe: School of American Research P, 2002): 23–48, 23–24.
6 Ghassan Hage, "The Differential Intensities of Social Reality: Migration, Participation and Guilt," in *Arab Australians Today: Citizenship and Belonging*, ed. Ghassan Hage (Melbourne: Melbourne UP, 2002): 192–205, 203.
7 Amanda Wise, *Exile and Return Among the East Timorese* (Philadelphia: U of Pennsylvania P, 2006): 94.
8 Hage, "The Differential Intensities," 203.
9 For *communitas* of disaster see Edith Turner, *Communitas: The Anthropology of Collective Joy* (New York: Palgrave Macmillan, 2012).
10 The interviews will be marked Source: I 1–15.

more, by applying Marcel Mauss's approach on gift-giving, we will argue that remittances serve to be recognized and accepted by the homeland and that the
"need of return" played a crucial role in the apolitical position the Japanese diasporic communities took in Belgium.

Japanese Nationals in Belgium

The Kingdom of Belgium, with a population of 9,832,010 (2011), is divided into
three parts. The division is based on language, which, amongst other issues,
fuels political and social conflict. Belgium has three official languages: Dutch,
French, and German. The Dutch speaking community is situated in the economically strong northern region of Flanders and the French speaking population in
the Southern region of Wallonia. A minority of German speaking Belgians lives
in the Eastern part of Wallonia. According to the most recent statistical data provided by the EUROSTAT population census, a total of 4,458 Japanese nationals
were living in Belgium on January 1, 2011, of which 2,020 were male and 2,438
female.[11] There are 901 long-term residents with Japanese nationality.[12] However,
the majority of Japanese nationals who come to Belgium do so for remunerative
reasons or family reunification with a Japanese national and will only stay short
term.[13] In 2010, the permits issued for remunerated activities numbered 293,

---

11 ADSEI (Algemene Directie Statistiek en Economische Informatie) gave 4,457 as the total for
the Japanese population (<http://statbel.fgov.be/nl/modules/publications/statistiques/bevolk-
ing/downloads/bevolking_per_nationaliteit_per_gemeente_01–01–2011.jsp> [acc. October 10,
2014]; however, this link is currently inactive. For the latest statistics available, we refer to
the statistics of 2010 as mentioned below.) As of January 1, 2010, a total of 4,543 Japanese
were registered in Belgium. For 2010, see also the data of ADSEI Algmene Directie Statistiek
en Economische Informatie (<http://statbel.fgov.be/nl/modules/publications/statistiques/bev-
olking/population_natio_sexe_groupe_classe_d_ges_au_1er_janvier_2010.jsp> [acc. October
10, 2014]). According to the Japanese Embassy, 5,335 Japanese nationals were registered in Belgium in October 2011. Source: I 1, interview with representatives of the Japanese Embassy in
Brussels (Tuesday, May 22, 2012).
12 Of those 901 Japanese citizens registered as long-term residents in Belgium, 72.6 percent
(655) were female (*Eurostat* <http://epp.eurostat.ec.europa.eu/portal/page/portal/population/
data/database> [acc. October 10, 2014]).
13 The first permits issued for family reasons and remunerative reasons are interrelated; from a
total of 512 first permits for family reasons, 373 were issued on the basis of "person joining a
non-EU citizen." In these cases, Japanese employees are joined by spouses, partners, and children. However, it is interesting to note that the number of first permits for persons joining an EU
citizen more than doubled between 2010 (58) and 2011 (139), whereas the persons joining non-
EU citizens decreased in absolute numbers from 412 in 2010 (see *Eurostat* <http://epp.eurostat.

which is actually a significant decrease of 40 percent since 2008. This trend reflects the growing economic crisis in Japan, which resulted in the reduction of overseas staff members, closure of overseas offices or the decision not to open new offices.[14] The statistical data show the Japanese expat community in Belgium as being comparable to other communities in Europe, for example, in Germany or the Netherlands, where a transient community of Japanese, primarily male, employees and their families, working for transnational companies or for governmental institutions, is concentrated in urban centers like Düsseldorf or Amsterdam. Because Brussels is the capital of Belgium, home to NATO headquarters and primary seat of the EU, it attracts a great number of Japanese companies and lobbies and also houses Japanese governmental and semi-governmental organizations.[15] In 2011, there were approximately 260 Japanese companies registered in Belgium, 60 percent of them in the county of Brussels, eight percent in Antwerp.[16] Additionally, governmental organizations including the Japanese Embassy to the Kingdom of Belgium, The Mission of Japan to the EU, The EU-Japan Centre for Industrial Cooperation, Japan External Trade Organization office (JETRO), and The Belgium-Japan Association & Chamber of Commerce operate from Brussels.

Brussels houses a large international corporate and political expatriate community, whose members are well paid. They live in the more exclusive parts of the city, and their social contacts often stay within the limits of this international expatriate community. Also, the rotating, short-term Japanese residents living in Brussels are not well integrated into the host city but constitute a parallel society. However, the Japanese residents receive little to no attention from the host

---

ec.europa.eu/portal/page/portal/population/data/database> [acc. October 10, 2014] and compare also Centrum voor gelijkheid van kansen en voor racismebestrijding [ed.], *Jaarverslag Migratie 2011* [Brussels, 2012] and Centrum voor gelijkheid van kansen en voor racismebestrijding [ed.], *Jaarverslag Migratie 2010* [Brussels, 2011]). First permits issued for remunerative activities accounted for 334 permits in 2011, with the majority issued for a period less than a year (303). Only 62 permits were issued for educational purposes, of which 58 were for studies, and 54 received a permit for less than a year (see *Eurostat* <http://epp.eurostat.ec.europa.eu/portal/page/portal/population/data/database> [acc. October 10, 2014]). The number of Japanese students coming to Belgium has dropped from 91 in 2008 to 58 in 2011. See also Centrum voor gelijkheid van kansen en voor racismebestrijding (ed.), *Jaarverslag Migratie 2010* (Brussels, 2011).
14 International migration flows and residence permits, *Eurostat* <http://epp.eurostat.ec.europa.eu/portal/page/portal/population/data/database> (acc. July 20, 2013).
15 According to the BJA, there are about 220 Japanese companies registered in Belgium. See Belgium-Japan Association, Chamber of Commerce (ed.), *Editorial* 92 (2011). Of these companies, 60 percent are situated in the county of Brussels (Source: I 9).
16 Source: I 1.

country. It seems that there is no direct need for the Japanese to integrate into the society of Brussels.[17] Brussels is actually situated in the Flemish part of the country but is mainly French speaking. Within the circles of the international corporate and diplomatic community of Brussels, English and French are the languages most commonly spoken, whereas Dutch plays no significant role. Accordingly, there is no practical reason for short-term Japanese residents to learn Dutch.[18]

Members of transient communities tend to reside in close proximity to each other, thus creating a sense of home, what the Japanese post-structuralist philosopher Nishitani Osamu in another context terms: "to recreate the union with one's origin."[19] This is also true for the community in the county of Brussels, where the majority of Japanese nationals in Belgium resides. Of the Japanese residing in Brussels, 68.7 percent are living concentrated in only three municipalities from a total of 23 municipalities, which are St. Lambrechts Woluwe, St. Pieters Woluwe, and Oudergem. When these data are cross-referenced with the prices on the real estate market in Brussels, it shows that St. Lambrechts Woluwe and St. Pieters Woluwe have the highest rent for apartments in Brussels and that the prices in Oudergem are also generally above average. Members of transient communities are also generally aware of the fact that they will only stay for a short while in the host country. Thus, they are less inclined to socialize with members of the host country or to adjust their lifestyle. These communities, therefore, create a sort of cultural island that can be seen as a replica of the homeland in which members of the community can live a life according to their standards, needs, and interests.[20] Katarzyna Cwiertka argues concerning short-term employees in the Netherlands:

> [T]he 'employees' follow the logistic decisions of their employers with little influence on their destinations. This, along with the temporary character of their residence, is the

---

17 This has also been argued by Christian Tagsold concerning the Japanese diasporic community in Düsseldorf (Christian Tagsold, "Das Schriftzeichen des Jahres 2011 als Antwort auf das gefühlte Auseinanderbrechen der Gesellschaft?", in *Japan: Politik, Wirtschaft und Gesellschaft*, eds. David Chiavacci, Iris Wieczorek [Berlin: VSJF, 2012]: 143–168, 160).
18 However, even within the circles of highly-integrated, long-term Japanese residents living in the Flemish province, English is generally the lingua franca because the partners often do not speak Japanese (Source: I 12).
19 Osamu Nishitani, *Fushi no wandarandô* (Tokyo: Kodansha, 1996): 230.
20 André Leroi-Gourhan describes this process as the "symbolic domestication of space" with the purpose of constructing social order. See André Leroi-Gourhan, "Die symbolische Domestikation des Raums," in *Raumtheorie*, eds. Jörg Dünne, Stephan Günzel (Frankfurt am Main: Suhrkamp, 2006): 228–243.

most important factor responsible for the formation of suspicious feelings towards foreign culture and a tendency to recreate a Japanese lifestyle outside Japan in order to leave their identity as untouched as possible.[21]

However, Merry White also convincingly linked the creation and maintenance of a "Japanese" environment to the question of return, "ascertaining that a Japanese lifestyle will make the reentry into the Japanese culture easier."[22]

In Brussels, the Japanese infrastructure includes supermarkets, restaurants, recreational clubs, and the Nihonjinkai (Association of Japanese), which is closely involved with the Japanese school. This Japanese school provides an education conforming to the Japanese educational system on weekdays with additional Japanese language education on Saturday mornings. Children from the transient community generally attend the Japanese curriculum on weekdays, whereas the members of the permanent community tend to enroll their children in the Belgian educational system and additionally send them to the Japanese school on Saturday mornings if they live in Brussels or the vicinity. The infrastructure in Brussels is concentrated around the previously mentioned three communes and the Flagey neighborhood close to the European Union institutions. It is noteworthy that despite the infrastructure near the city center of Brussels, the majority of Japanese living in the county of Brussels tend to live in the richer outskirts of the city. Japanese restaurants situated on the outskirts of Brussels target Japanese customers and are owned by Japanese nationals.

Belgium is a rather small country, approximately 30,500 square kilometers, but the Japanese nationals living outside the direct vicinity of Brussels, such as the Japanese in Ghent, have hardly any contact with the Japanese nationals living in Brussels, Japanese organizations, or even cultural activities that can be found in the capital. This is also true for the Japanese living in the city of Ghent. Ghent has a population of approximately 250,000; the city is situated in the Flemish region about 50 kilometers northwest of Brussels. The number of Japanese nationals registered in Ghent on December 31, 2011 was 62.[23] Against the general overall trend seen in Belgium, the number of Japanese residing in Ghent is actually increasing. The group of Japanese expatriates in Ghent consists primarily of female Japanese who are married to Belgian nationals. Most of those

---

21 Katarzyna J. Cwiertka, "Eating the Homeland. Japanese Expatriates in the Netherlands," in *Asian Food. The Global and the Local*, eds. Katarzyna J. Cwiertka, Boudewijn Walraven (London, New York: Routledge, 2002): 133–152, 148.

22 Merry White, *The Japanese Overseas: Can They Go Home Again?* (Princeton, NJ: Princeton UP, 1992): 106.

23 See data provided by the city of Ghent: <http://www.gent.be/docs/Departement%20bevolk ing%20en%20Welzijn/Dienst%20bevolking/demo2011_6.pdf> (acc. January 13, 2013).

women are, in contrast to the professional housewife of the short-term Japanese community, working outside of the household. Through their partners as well as their work environment, they are generally well integrated into the Flemish community, although the interviews suggest that social contacts are mainly with other Japanese or expatriates from other nations. Ghent also lacks the infrastructure for maintaining a Japanese lifestyle, such as supermarkets to obtain ingredients for Japanese meals. There are a number of Japanese restaurants located in Ghent, but they depend on non-Japanese customers and are owned by non-Japanese who are taking advantage of the recent sushi hype. The children from the Japanese long-term residents living in Ghent are enrolled in the Belgian school system and on Saturdays additionally attend the Japanese school in Lille or, to a lesser extent, the Japanese school of Brussels. The choice of Lille, which is located just across the border with France, is firstly economically motivated because the fees there are considerably lower. Secondly, Lille's popularity arose from to the "Japaneseness" of the school in Brussels, as explained by one of the interviewees:

> their [school in Lille] primary targets are half-blood children. But, that is my opinion, the quality of education in Brussels is also very good, but they try to do everything as it is done in Japan. The school in Lille is more for children who have another language [other than Japanese] as mother tongue.[24]

Whereas the short-term residents choose an education based on the Japanese system in order to make the reintegration of their children into the Japanese school system easier, "doing it the Japanese way" is considered to be a disadvantage for the children of long-term residents because they are used to the Belgian system and will not need to adapt to the Japanese school system in the future.

Home Work: Constructing *furusato*[25]

The complex and changing relationship between diasporic communities and *furusato* has recently been discussed in different studies.[26] These studies show that

---

24 Source: I 12.
25 The phrase 'home work' is adapted from the concept of 'nation work'; Timothy Brook and Andre Schmid, *Nation Work: Asian Elites and National Identities* (Ann Arbor: U of Michigan P, 2003): esp. 6.

the definition of "homeland" and "home" is culturally negotiated, determined by and highly dependent on historical context. In the interviews as well as on websites maintained by different groups of the diasporic community in Belgium, "Japan" as homeland is referred to as *furusato* (故郷, literally "old village").[27] Marilyn Ivy has argued that the notion of *furusato* as a modern concept is a reaction to the challenges of modernity and especially to the exodus of people in search of work in the cities at the beginning of the twentieth century.[28] By linking the concept of *furusato* to Freud's definition of the "uncanny,"[29] Ivy shows that:

> The countryside literally became regressive, opposed to the "progressive" powers of urban-based capitalism. Yet urban domination could not be sustained as such, but in time became open to the uncanny returns that such repression inevitably ensures. The rural homeland became a sign of infantile yearnings and was simultaneously valorized as the source of true Japanese virtue.[30]

She further states that "[t]he *furusato* is, then, properly uncanny, because it indicates a return of something estranged under the guise of the familiar."[31] At this point, it can be argued that there is no antecedent *furusato:* continuously and discursively constructing, that is, to narrate *furusato* is a performative act that confirms and reasserts the idea that there actually is a *furusato*.[32]. With

---

26 See, for example, André Levy and Alex Weingrod (eds.), *Homeland and Diasporas. Holy Lands and Other Places* (Redwood City: Stanford UP, 2005).
27 The term '*furusato*,' which Yano describes as "the focal point of nostalgia and memory," on the one hand refers to one's (rural) place of birth, but on the other hand is also used to point to the "idea of originary, emotive space" (Yano, *Tears of Longing*, 17). See also Jennifer Robertson, *Native and Newcomer: Making and Remaking a Japanese City* (Berkeley: U of California P, 1991): 5, 14, 25–37. Although dictionaries mention up to 22 synonyms for the terms 'home' and 'homeland' (e.g. 故郷 *kokyô*, 故国 *kokoku* 田舎 *inaka*, etc.), the term '*furusato*' is used almost exclusively in the conducted interviews.
28 Marilyn Ivy, *Discourses of the Vanishing. Modernity Phantasm Japan* (Chicago, London: U of Chicago P, 1995): 21, 100–108.
29 Sigmund Freud, "Das Unheimliche," *Imago. Zeitschrift für Anwendung der Psychoanalyse auf die Geisteswissenschaften* 5/6 (1919): 297–324.
30 Ivy, *Discourses of the Vanishing*, 107.
31 Ivy, *Discourses of the Vanishing*, 107.
32 In Japanese, this process of constructing "home" has been captured by the term *furusato-zukuri* (see, for example, Robertson, *Native and Newcomer*, 14). The German philosopher Peter Sloterdijk has argued in his *Sphären* trilogy that the construction of home also answers to the basic human need to create a protective and secure environment as a social being (Peter Sloterdijk, *Sphären II* [Frankfurt am Main: Suhrkamp, 1999]: 633; see also Leroi-Gourhan, "Die symbolische Domestikation," 228–243). This approach has also been pursued by Yi-Fu Tuan, *Space and Place: The Perspective of Experience* (Minneapolis: U of Minnesota P, 1977), where he de-

the increased globalization of the Japanese economy and more Japanese leaving Japan for remunerative reasons, the *furusato* as an emotive space of nostalgic sentiments was taken out of its local context and elevated to the level of the nation: turning the local onto the national and the national onto the local. *Furusato* continued to carry nostalgic and emotive notions of one's origin, linking the question of space with questions of identity and of Japaneseness. But what exactly is the relationship between one's place of birth, one's *furusato* and oneself? Nishitani argues that the human being is not born in Heimat – here understood as place of origin – but "born by forming his place of birth as himself," thus creating a kind of organic entity of self and space.[33] From this perspective, the spatial and emotional alienation from one's *furusato* in modernity consequently results in an alienation from the self. This line of thought also engulfs a nostalgic tendency because *furusato* must be regained, not in the sense of returning to the origin but

> to let the origin return within the present, to make the present a repetition of the past and by that recreate the union with one's origin. The present has to get its depth through one's origin, one's Heimat. "Loss" means "destruction," and "oblivion" is "blindness." "Loss" as well as "oblivion" guide the human towards the uncanny.[34]

In this sense the uprooting of modernity and the concept of one's origin are linked to the uncanny. What does this actually mean for the reaction of diasporic communities after the triple disaster?

Websites and flyers for support events organized by Japanese nationals in Belgium tended to display elements of a stereotypical and romantic – even nostalgic – construction of Japan and Japaneseness as well.[35] The triple disaster, as the interviews also suggested, increased both a sense of being Japanese and the awareness of a Japanese cultural identity.[36] A good example can be seen in a

---

fines the need for protection and security as one of the reasons for the emotional bond with one's home and homeland.

33 Nishitani, *Fushi no wandârando*, 230.
34 Nishitani, *Fushi no wandârando*, 230.
35 For diaspora and Japaneseness, see Eyal Ben-Ari, "The Japanese in Singapore. The Dynamics of an Expatriate Community," in *Global Japan: The Experience of Japan's New Immigrant and Overseas Communities*, eds. Roger Goodman, Ceri Peach, Ayumi Takenaka, Paul White (London, New York: Routledge, 2003): 116–130.
36 This practice of preserving and even exhibiting a distinctive identity vis-à-vis the host society can be linked to one of the core elements of a diaspora, which according to Brubaker is boundary maintenance (see Brubaker, "The 'Diaspora' Diaspora," 1–19).

message by Japanese artists written in Japanese to the victims of the 3/11 disaster, posted on the ACT FOR JAPAN website:

> We are trying to unite our efforts and act to support our home country (*furusato*). From Belgium, where we are blessed with a rich cultural environment and opportunity to share our art, we pray for Japan's rebirth and declare the message that no matter how hard it may be, Japan will rise up and shine again, just like the sun always rises in the morning. In this time of darkness, Japan needs your support. Until the day we overcome the difficulties and smile again, we will join our hands and act for Japan.[37]

"Japan will shine and rise again, just like the sun rises in the morning" is a metaphorical and even religious allusion that features prominently in conservative and right wing texts, referring to a historically unspecified time of glory, which is then defined as the pure expression of the Japanese character. Fredric Jameson has described metaphorical allusions as a characteristic of nostalgia, a blurring of "official contemporaneity" that makes the illusion of some eternal decade beyond historical time possible.[38] By defining what must be regained, the "Act for Japan" website creates an idea of a "happy-before-the-catastrophe-*furusato*," ignoring or placing the ongoing economic, social, and political crisis that has been characteristic of the last ten years into oblivion. And it comes as no surprise that some see the catastrophe as a catalyst for cultural change, to bring back what were considered to be real Japanese virtues that had been lost before. *Furusato*, therefore, becomes the emotive space where that which has been lost – whether it be real or imaginary – can be found. But the question of what is actually coming back in the wake of and only because of the catastrophe remains unanswered.[39]

---

[37] *ACT FOR JAPAN* <http://www.actforjapan.be/?page_id=20> (acc. December 30, 2012). The website also displayed a message to the victims of the triple disaster in the Tôhoku region. It is striking that the term '*furusato*' was used when referring to Japan: "What had happened in our home(land)." The metaphorical use of "shining" and "sun" in context of the nation can semantically also be linked to the Shinto sun goddess Amaterasu.

[38] Fredric Jameson, *Postmodernism, or, The Cultural Logic of Late Capitalism* (Durham, NC: Duke UP, 1991): 19–21.

[39] One short-term resident from Brussels, who also creates a semantic field of darkness and light, remarked: "We became aware again about the bad and good sides of being Japanese. There are good things like immediate organization of reconstruction, but the chaos also let the dark sides of the people come to light, like profiting from the confusion, taking away or stealing things from others, not take into consideration the situation at hand. We are used to thinking that these things do not exist in our society, but they do. The will to survive, to protect oneself, and to rescue was overwhelming" (Source I 8).

Nevertheless, the interviews suggest that one of the main frames that is now "colonizing" the space of *furusato* is a feeling of solidarity among fellow Japanese nationals:

> Even before [the triple disaster] I had met these people [who were organizing the flea market], but I also met other Japanese people through them, and by organizing this flea market together, it felt as though the power of solidarity (*danketsuryoku ga umareta*) as Japanese emerged.[40]

This quote is especially striking, as is the phrase *danketsuryoku ga umareta* ("power of solidarity emerged"), which can also mean the "ability to join activities emerged." The quote primarily refers to something that was felt to be absent so far, namely a feeling of solidarity as being Japanese, a feeling that Japan lacked a civil society,[41] or as another female respondent put it: "Before I used to think that Japanese are egoistic, but this is changing now. They now know that we have to help each other. [...] They are more concerned. Their heart's eye has opened."[42]

The interviewee mentions the sense of helping each other, but it is striking that she is creating a complex field of inclusion and exclusion. Although defining herself as Japanese, she is creating an emotional distance with the Japanese back home by using the grammatical markers of "I," "we," and "they." The feeling of exclusion, which is found here as part of a self-perspective, is also created externally by a discursive exclusion from the others who are still inhabiting the homeland, a homeland where members of diasporas are often seen "as not Japanese enough."[43]

---

40 This statement was made by a short-term resident in Brussels and is taken from an online questionnaire conducted by the BA3 and MA students of Ghent University in 2011.

41 For the definition of the term 'civil society' in Japan, see Isa Ducke, *Civil Society and the Internet in Japan* (London, New York: Routledge, 2007). In Japan the redefinition of the cultural and social system and the rediscovery of the civil society is coined in the term *kizuna* (bonds; connection), which was chosen as the word of the year 2011. For the controversial discussion of the term *kizuna* in Japan see Tagsold, "Das Schriftzeichen des Jahres 2011," 309–328. Already in December 2011 a new political party named *New Kizuna* (*Shintô Kizuna*) was founded, which exploited the term *kizuna* for political ends. The party was dissolved already before the general election in December 2012. The main political aims were economically oriented and directed against the proposal to raise the consumption tax as well as against the Trans-Pacific Partnership Agreement.

42 Source: I 3.

43 See Merry White, *The Japanese Overseas: Can They Go Home Again?* (Princeton, NJ: Princeton UP, 1992). However, it can also be argued that from the perspective of the diasporic community the disaster at the same time created a sense of solidarity because the Japanese in the homeland

After having elaborated on the concept of *furusato* in Japan, we would now like to ask whether members of a diaspora will belong to what Edith Turner has coined "communitas of disaster" in order to describe the feeling of togetherness that will result from a shared experience of a trauma.[44] Turner seems to suggest that "sharedness" is a given: either one has experienced a disaster or not. However, the parameter "shared experience" is one of perspective as well as degrees of sharedness. Therefore, sharedness as a category creates different communitas as well as exclusion.

Turning towards the Tôhoku Triple Disaster, "shared experience" can refer to the victims in Tôhoku who may have lost family members, friends, or their homes due to the disaster. It can, however, also refer to relatives and friends of victims not living in the areas struck. The experience is discursively also extended to the Japanese nation, in contrast to other nations that were spared from the catastrophe. But what is the experience of the Japanese diaspora? They certainly consider themselves to be Japanese as well members of the Japanese nation that was hit by the triple disaster. Yet, they lack the direct, unfiltered experience of the catastrophe. Additionally, it has been shown by several studies on Japanese nationals living abroad that although they are Japanese by nationality and feel Japanese, they will often be considered as no longer Japanese "enough" by the Japanese living in Japan. From that perspective, Japanese nationals living abroad are excluded from the shared experience of disaster by mainland Japanese. The breach with the homeland can also be seen on the abovementioned website formed by the group of Japanese artists after the triple disaster to support the homeland. On the website, we read: "We were only able to make the direct experience as eye witnesses through media and Internet." Thus, the perceived lack of shared experience becomes an additional barrier for Japanese nationals to be accepted members of the Japanese homeland, and this rejection also complicates the construction of the homeland.

---

had also lost their *furusato* either precisely in the sense of one's hometown or in the broader sense of homeland since parts of the stricken area literally have become an empty non-*furusato* that cannot be entered.

44 Turner, *Communitas*, 76.

Gifting Communitas: Japanese Nationals in Belgium Supporting Home

The catastrophe certainly endangered the re-creation of the union with one's origin as well as threatened the "replica" homeland in Brussels not only because of the economic implications of the catastrophe but also because of the food import restrictions placed by the EU following the nuclear incident. Because food is a major factor in creating a sense of home, shortage of certain ingredients for Japanese meals jeopardized this mirror homeland. The problem of the Japanese-brand food supply was mentioned in several interviews. The emotional binding to the *furusato*, the need to demonstrate solidarity and reintegration for the transient members of the community, created a wave of donations and support activities as well as fundraising activities organized by Japanese individuals as well as Japanese companies in Belgium. Niko Besnier argues that

> intrinsic to giving and accepting is the mutual recognition of the other party, and thus the basis of self-conscious selfhood, which places the gift right at the center of a moral order. Remittances, then, bind the participants in a common moral order of mutual recognition. And so does that particular kind of remittances, gifts provided to help relief efforts in the wake of disaster.[45]

By linking remittances with the "crisis of return," it can be argued that gift-giving will serve to show solidarity of an individual as well as a group to the *furusato* and thus strengthening the feeling of belonging from both sides.[46] In this sense, gift-giving secures a smooth return to the homeland for the short-term residents.

It is not possible to speak of "the" Japanese diaspora in Belgium as a whole. Rather, we have to speak of different communities bound together by different frames, such as space, period of stay, age of children, company affiliation, and social background. The support activities organized in Belgium show a striking difference between long-term and short-term residents. Whereas long-term residents organized charity events within their informal networks, also reaching out to the host community, the events organized by the short-term diasporic com-

---

45 Niko Besnier, "Diasporas: Communities of Practice, Communities of Affect," unpublished conference paper given in Ghent at the international conference *Transnational Responses to Catastrophe: Japanese Diaspora Communities and the March 2011 Triple Disaster* (June 22–23, 2012).

46 With regard to gift-giving, we refer to Marcel Mauss, "Essai sur le don. Forme et raison de l'échange dans les sociétés archaïques," *L'Année Sociologique, seconde série* (1923–1924): 30–186.

munity of Japanese nationals stayed within the community and were highly institutionalized and able to embed the individual into the community of Japanese living abroad.

Japanese Nationals in Brussels

Institutions such as the Embassy of Japan and the Nihonjinkai, an association for and by Japanese living in Belgium, did not organize any support actions. This tendency could be explained by the fact that the Nihonjinkai considers itself as a receiving partner.[47] The same is true for the embassy. The embassy did not contact Japanese citizens actively, and none of the respondents from the interviews had contacted the embassy. A representative in Brussels explained that the embassy's limited role towards charity actions is due to the Japanese legal framework.[48] Constrained by this framework, the embassy can neither take up a responsible role nor organize charity events by themselves; they are limited to supporting fundraising activities indirectly, for example, through patronage. As such, the embassy was a patron of six support events. The embassy acted as an intermediary for the donations and tried to assist by disseminating information on several levels, such as on their website and during cultural activities. The embassy also functioned as the official representative of the government and seemed to concentrate on restoring people's trust in the government and economy, thus limiting the economic damage. At an event attended by more than 800 invited guests and held in the Hilton Hotel in Brussels one year after the Triple Disaster, Ambassador Yokota Jun, speaking on behalf of the Nihonjinkai and the Ambassador of Japan to the European Union, Shiojiri Kojiro, openly addressed politicians and policy makers, asking them to lift the import restrictions and to support the Japanese economy.[49] The event also included a minute of silence and promotional wine tasting. Also, JETRO focused worldwide on building

---

47 Source: I 9.

48 Source: I 1.

49 Ambassador Yokota Jun also expressed his regret about EU import restrictions on Japanese products during a memorial service at the Japanese Garden in the city of Hasselt on November 3, 2012, which was attended by about 100 Japanese and Belgians. As part of the ceremony, Yokota Jun together with the president of the Belgium-Japan Association planted a cherry tree; a plaque donated by the Belgium-Japan Association was placed. The event was framed by the female Japanese chorus of Brussels and a group playing Japanese drums. The photograph that was placed above the internet article in the Belgian newspaper *De Morgen* actually showed Asian faces with white face masks and candles. The photograph was not of the ceremony in Hasselt but of a 'memorial demonstration' in Brussels mainly attended by anti-nuclear energy supporters.

up foreign investors' trust in the Japanese economy in general and in the stricken areas by organizing conferences and briefings for companies and business organizations. JETRO Brussels, for example, jointly with the Mission of Japan to the European Union, held a briefing for European companies and business organizations to explain countermeasures taken in response to the Great East Japan Earthquake.[50]

One example of institutionalized support activities that ought to be mentioned is the HOPE project of Japanese car manufacturers in Belgium (Isuzu, Mazda, Nissan, Subaru, Suzuki and Toyota), through which these companies transferred €20 per sold car between March 11 and April 15, 2011 to the Japanese Red Cross Society. One of the key organizations in Belgium-Japan business and cultural relations is certainly the Belgium-Japan Association, Chamber of Commerce (BJA). The BJA, with a primarily corporate-oriented membership, supported activities (for example, charity concert by Seikyo Kim, May 13, 2011) and published a call for donations already on March 14–15, 2011.[51] By March 30, thus within only fifteen days, the BJA collected €263,138, a sum that they then transferred to the Red Cross.[52] These events displayed a male-gendered official face, which stands in contrast to the female face of the grassroots activities organized within long-term Japanese networks, for example, in Ghent, where one interviewed long-term female resident remarked: "Japanese men organizing? Zero."[53] In the case of the short-term resident community in Brussels, it can be argued that organizations and companies, rather than individuals, functioned as hubs. Japanese organizations and companies located in Brussels engaged in calls for financial support, donated money, and logistically supported or participated in events. When events were organized, they stayed within the community as far as participation is concerned. The Japanese School of Brussels can serve as an example in this case: the school was contacted to participate in and promote different activities.[54] It decided to focus on events that were somehow connected to children and education, for example, with the European School of Brussels and Dyslexia International. They forwarded messages of sup-

---

50 *The Mission of Japan to the European Union* <http://www.eu.emb-japan.go.jp/Counter measures%20for%20the%20Great%20East%20Japan%20Earthquake.html> (acc. October 10, 2014).
51 See Belgium-Japan Association, Chamber of Commerce (ed.), *Trade Flows & Cultural News* 92 (2011): 2.
52 See Belgium-Japan Association, Chamber of Commerce (ed.), *Trade Flows & Cultural News* 91 (2011): 3.
53 Source: I 11.
54 However, requests to use the school grounds for fundraising activities were denied.

port from different international schools in Brussels to Japan. The school itself organized a "writing characters of support" event and collected money as well,[55] but these activities stayed within the boundaries of the school.[56]

One of the main charity events organized in Brussels was certainly the Japanese charity flea market on April 3, 2011 at the Notre Dame Church in Stockel, Sint-Pieters-Woluwe, a neighborhood with a high density of Japanese expatriates. The initiative of the flea market came from a female Japanese long-term resident in Brussels who also had experienced the Great Hanshin earthquake in 1995.[57] The flea market was officially coordinated on a volunteer basis by Misc Netto, a website organized by Japanese female volunteers living in Brussels, and the web company Beru tsû.[58] Both supported the Japanese short-term community in Belgium by organizing "sayonara sales" and providing useful information on life and living in Belgium.[59] Beru tsû, with 35,000 visitors per month on their website, is also well connected with social media, hosts a staff blog for members, distributes a "mail magazine," and created a webpage devoted to the triple disaster.[60] The service offered by these websites is crucial for the Japanese expatriate community in Belgium, and the organizers were able to activate a broad network, which attracted, according to the organizers, more than 3,000 participants and resulted in €25,614 from sales as well as donations. The funds were transferred to the embassy, which then donated the money to the Japanese Red Cross. The organizers also reached out to the Japanese School in Brussels,[61] and information about the fundraising events was spread through the short-term community's information bulletin (minikomi) Petits-Pois (Puchi Powa). Thus, the organizers could rely on a well-established, institutionalized, and structured network. The volunteering participants were generally short-term Japanese residents in Brussels. The flea market also included a Japanese café, chocolate and cake shop, a shiatsu and origami workshop, a Japanese drum demonstration, and a concert by Japanese musicians, thus creating a "Japanese" atmosphere. Taking into account the special situation of Brussels, flyers were printed in four lan-

---

55 The money collected by the Japanese School was partially donated to a Primary School in Miyagi, through contacts of the former school director.
56 Source: I 14, 15.
57 Source: I 15.
58 *Misc Netto* <www.misc-net.com> (acc. January 13, 2013); *Beru tsû* <www.bel2.jp> (acc. January 13, 2013).
59 The company name Beru tsû can be translated as "Belgium Connoisseur." *Beru* can also mean "bells," which are represented in the logo.
60 *Beru tsû* <http://www.bel2.jp/home/earthquake.html> (acc. January 13, 2013).
61 Source: I 15.

guages (Japanese, French, Dutch, and English) and distributed mainly in the Japanese community as well as in cultural and corporate circles with a strong connection to Japan. The Japanese flyer, in contrast to the French, Dutch, and English versions, explicitly made clear that the goods sold were donated following a call for donations and that all participants in the event, including the staff members of the organizing companies, were volunteers and that accordingly 100 percent of the earned and donated money would go to the victims. On the Japanese language website of *Beru tsû*, it becomes clear that the charity bazaar was seen as an activity by a group of Japanese nationals who came together because they shared the same experience and wanted to do more than "just" individually donate money: "Even if it is just a little help for the victims from the distant Belgium [...]."[62] The impression of a "Japanese-helping-Japanese" event is also supported by the "Thank You Letter" (*Orei to hôkoku*) placed on the website.

Japanese Nationals in Ghent

When talking to long-term residents in the city of Ghent, we realized that the four participants in our interviews did not consider themselves as part of a Japanese diaspora although they certainly considered themselves to be Japanese. They belonged to different informal "Japanese" subgroups, formed by the parameters of children (age and school), work place, and social activities. These subgroups form loose networks that are held together by the identity marker "homeland" and by practice, such as New Year's dinner each year, occasional "ladies nights," and activities with children. All long-term interviewees in Ghent participated in several fundraising and support activities, generally organized by Japanese friends or acquaintances. The members of the overlapping networks informed other members to spread the information about fundraising activities to an extent that one interviewee from Ghent remarked: "It was impossible to go to all support events. There were just too many."[63] The activities organized were directed towards an "outside" non-Japanese audience, mainly Belgians who were also in one way or another connected to Japan economically or culturally, such as students of Japanese studies, martial arts clubs, people who went to a Japanese concert or movie. The activities of these groups show a high degree of cultural knowledge about the host country because they are using the events and net-

---

62 See *Beru tsû* <http://www.bel2.jp/PNG/home/bazaar/bazaar%20flyer%20JP.pdf> (acc. January 13, 2013).
63 Source: I 11.

works of daily Belgian social life. The support and fundraising events were not initiated by an established and well-defined group but by individuals who functioned as hubs. On the one hand, the support events as a reaction towards the shared experience of shock also strengthened the networking system of the Japanese citizens and brought the participants closer together (albeit just for a short period of time), but on the other hand, preexisting trenches were reaffirmed: "The support activities did not really change the community of Japanese in Ghent, but people who did not want to do anything gave a weird feeling and the friendship has cooled down. We didn't want to press. We are disappointed."[64] Examples of activities include a flea market charity sale by a Japanese businesswoman and the folding and selling of *origami* cranes by the "*tsuru* ladies" ("origami-crane ladies") in companies and schools, during a film festival and in a judo club.

The flea market sales at the church of St. Jacob in Ghent is a traditional, semi-professional flea market with regular stands and is held every week from Friday to Sunday; it is an excellent example of how the support actions of the permanent community were embedded into Belgian community life. An unmarried, Japanese businesswoman and long-term resident in Ghent organized the charity sales action at this flea market, which was supported by other long-term female residents and their Belgian husbands. Selling on long-established, local markets requires a permit, which cannot be obtained easily. In the case of the support action, however, the organizer was able to use the reserved space of a friend and just needed a permit for this particular event. Friends and acquaintances, contacted via e-mail, telephone, Twitter, and Facebook, donated the products to be sold. These were typical products that could be expected to be on sale at flea markets as well as products of Japanese origin. It was clearly marked that the products were sold for charity reasons and a charity box with a short explanatory text in Dutch and a *hinomaru* (flag of Japan) was placed on the sales stand as well. Because regulations prohibit placing charity boxes on sales stands, a special permit was also obtained from the city hall. Using a traditional Belgian flea market for a support action requires cultural, structural, and administrative understanding as well as an engagement with the city and its people. Short-term residents cannot obtain this kind of specific cultural knowledge, which also shows a certain degree of embeddedness into the host community and its social network. When arguing from the point of network analysis, we can state that the organizer(s) were able to find a common code of cultural communication, a code that could be understood by the mem-

---

64 Source: I 12.

bers of the home community.[65] The flea market itself was broadcast live on a video on the Ricobel blog, which is linked to the company of the organizer and targets Japanese with an interest in Belgian culture.

In the case of the flea market in Ghent, the way the money was donated also shows a high degree of social network within the host community. Most charity actions donated the money directly to the Red Cross in Japan or Belgium. In the case of the flea market sale in Ghent, the organizers bought toys and sweets for children and sent these to the city of Kanazawa, from where they were finally forwarded to the areas hit by the triple disaster. Choosing Kanazawa seems odd at first because Kanazawa is about 420 kilometers away from Fukushima prefecture. However, the organizer was aware of the fact that Ghent and Kanazawa are sister cities, and through personal contacts in Ghent's city hall, she was able to use her social network for this action. In this sense, the action also strengthened the Ghent–Kanazawa connection.

In the second example, another individual female employee in Ghent utilized her work environment for organizing support activities. She functioned as hub in at least two fundraising events. Inspired by the example of the sister of a Japanese colleague who folded and sold origami cranes (*tsuru*) in Japan, she, together with the colleague, participated in the Orizuru_PrayforJapan support activity and folded origami cranes together with volunteering colleagues. On the Orizuru_PrayforJapan website, the company received special thanks from the organizers.[66] The organizers visited other offices in their building and sold the cranes for the victims of the disaster for the price of €1. This activity was extended to the private context by organizing crane origami activities at the schools of the interviewees' children and also at the judo club of one of the children. The paper crane is a basic origami figure that can easily be folded and is thus very well suited for a group activity involving children. In one case, after obtaining the permission of the school director, the two Japanese women – dressed in kimono – visited all classes in this school over a period of two days and folded cranes together with the attending schoolchildren. The children then went home to sell the cranes to their parents, friends, and neighbors. In a second activity, the annual Japanese film festival "Japan Square," of which one inter-

---

65 On network analysis, see especially Herbert Blumer, "Der methodologische Standort des symbolischen Interaktionismus," in *Kommunikationstheorien: Ein Textbuch zur Einführung*, eds. Roland Burkart, Walter Hömberg (Vienna: Wilhelm Braumüller, 1992): 23–39.
66 *Orizuru_PrayforJapan* <http://orizuruprayforjapan.blogspot.be/> (acc. December 27, 2012).

viewee is board member, served as platform for a *tsuru* sale action.[67] In both cases, the organizers donated the money to the Red Cross Flanders and also received the permission to use the Red Cross logo.[68]

In contrast to the above mentioned flea market activity, the *tsuru* activity was based on and made use of stereotypical and easily recognizable elements of Japanese culture for their fundraising activity, thereby making the activity readily identifiable as an activity related to Japan.[69] The crane is a bird of cultural significance in Japan, expressing hope, long life, recovery from illness and injury, peace, and now increasingly stands for solidarity. Through the tragic story of the Hiroshima atom bomb victim Sasaki Sadako, the crane is well known also in Belgium as a symbol of nuclear disarmament. The link with the nuclear catastrophe of Fukushima made the crane a symbol that could also be interpreted as protest against nuclear energy. The Japanese embassy also received a number of origami cranes (single or in a string of 1000 *senbazuru*), which were displayed in a special exhibition at the Cultural and Information Centre of the embassy as token of gratitude following the triple disaster.[70]

When analyzing support activities from the perspective of gift-giving and the motivations connected to gift-giving, we need to understand that the practice of giving must necessarily be communicated in order to secure mutual recognition. It was, therefore, no surprise to find that the support activities of diasporic communities were "advertised" in Japan. However, the degree to which this happened was surprising because not only Twitter and Facebook but also local newspapers and even the national TV NHK reported on the donations by Japanese living abroad. One example is the dissemination of the activities organized

---

67 Source: I 12, 13. On March 11, 2012 the film festival also showed the film *Sketch of Mujo*, a documentary on the Tohoku disaster. For more information on the filmfestival, see <http://www.japan-square.be/filmfestival/> (acc. January 18, 2014).

68 See *Orizuru_PrayforJapan* <http://orizuruprayforjapan.blogspot.be/> and *Cinematoday* <http://www.cinematoday.jp/page/N0031568> (acc. December 27, 2012).

69 In the official magazine, *Trade Flows & Cultural News*, of the Belgium-Japan Association, Chamber of Commerce, which has a circulation of 2,500 print copies, this activity was referred to as "Japan Square – Tsuru Ladies." See Belgium-Japan Association, Chamber of Commerce (ed.), *Trade Flows & Cultural News* 92 (2011): 5.

70 Also other Japanese or Belgians who organized fundraising events or moral support activities also used the crane as trademark that could easily be recognized, for example, the *Dinner of the Rising Sun* in the Palace of the Colonies (Tervuren/Brussels) on May 26, 2011. For the price of €200, which was donated to the Red Cross, guests were served a four-course dinner by Japanese and Belgian top chefs. The event was organized by a non-profit organization, whose representative is the sushi-chef of the Antwerp-based restaurant Ko'uzi, Kawada Junko, a long-term resident. The names of the chefs as well as the names of their restaurants were mentioned on the advertisement.

by an unmarried businesswoman living in Ghent, who had organized the afore-mentioned charity flea market sale, which in itself is quite interesting to analyze. With the money earned, she bought toys and sweets for children in the affected areas. Her activities were noted in two newspaper articles of the *Hokkoku Shimbun*, a regional tabloid from Kanazawa. The toys and sweets were clearly marked as gifts from an individual Japanese female living in Ghent, Belgium. The first headline read: "From Belgium to the children of the stricken area. Mrs. XXX from Ghent entrusts the city with toys and sweets,"[71] and the second headline refers to the gifts as "Belgian toys to the stricken areas. Mrs. XXX from Ghent city. Entrusting sister city Kanazawa."[72] The latter article also shows two photos of the gifts being placed on a conference table and arranged by a Caucasian woman (in one photo also watched by a Japanese woman), who can be identified, although not mentioned in the article, as the (Belgian) Coordinator of International Affairs at Kanazawa City Hall.

An excellent example for the importance of communication is also the production of three videos by the abovementioned businesswoman with messages of support and sympathy for the victims in Japan. Thus, support activities were not limited to providing financial and material support but expanded to activities such as messages of solidarity that were meant to give moral support. The moral support aspect was considered to be equally as important as financial or material support. The people who appeared in the two videos, "A support message from Belgium (1) / (2): Be strong, Japan! (*Berugî kara ôen messêji (1) / (2) Ganbare Nippon!*)," were Ghent citizens, one city official, local traders or teachers, and students from Ghent University, all somehow related to Japan, the Japanese living in Ghent or visiting the city. Among them was the chocolatier on the Korenlei (a famous tourist spot) who can count many Japanese tourists among his clientele. The third video was a personal message from the mayor of Ghent, Daniël Termont. The oral English or Japanese messages were subtitled in Japanese and placed on YouTube as well as on the Ricobel blog.[73] The com-

---

71 *Hokkoku Shimbun* (April 21, 2011).

72 *Hokkoku Shimbun* (April 23, 2011).

73 Daniël Termont, "Message from the Mayor of Gent" (March 16, 2011), *Youtube* <http://www.youtube.com/watch?v=-l1xP65o12Q>; ricobel, "A support message from Belgium (1): Be strong, Japan! (Berugî kara ôen messêji (1): Ganbare Nippon!)" (March 15, 2011), *Youtube* <http://www.youtube.com/watch?feature=endscreen&v=cTLr8HV3nYM&NR=1> (more than 17,000 hits on December 31, 2012); and ricobel, "A support message from Belgium (2): Be strong, Japan! (Berugî kara ôen messêji (2) Ganbare Nippon!)" (March 24, 2011), *Youtube* <http://www.youtube.com/watch?v=H45 L7MkWDxc> (all acc. January 13, 2013). For the website and the blog of the company, see: <http://www.ricobel.com/> (acc. January 13, 2013).

ments posted on both sites as well as the numerous letters sent to Ghent University show that Japanese in the homeland indeed seemed to notice and appreciate the messages sent. The Japanese national TV station NHK chose certain scenes for a sequence of support messages from all over the world that were shown regularly in commercial breaks during the months following the Triple Disaster. The messages from Ghent were clearly marked with a "Thank you" note to Ricobel Company.

The Blind Eye of Solidarity: Voices of Protest?

In Japan the Triple Disaster, and especially the nuclear catastrophe, resulted in large-scale protests and a comeback of what might be termed a political civil society. Despite our respondent's critical remarks concerning Japanese politics in general and also against nuclear energy and TEPCO (Tokyo Electric Power Company) in particular, it can be stated that the diasporic community in Belgium limited itself to support activities without participating or organizing social and political protests. Even in the case of the *tsuru* ladies and the use of the crane as cultural symbol and potential symbol of anti-nuclear protest, no effort was made to engage in nuclear protests.

Several reasons might have contributed to the lack of politicization. The first reason is demographic. Students under the age of 30 and *furiitaa* (freelance or unemployed) over the age of 50 who carried out and sustained the protests in Japan following the Fukushima catastrophe.[74] However, most Japanese nationals in Belgium are between 30 and 50 years old and are career oriented. The Japanese nationals in Belgium are also well integrated into a social network based on corporate affiliation (Nihonjinkai) with close ties to governmental institutions. The second reason is that media coverage might have played a role. Although Japan witnessed the largest grassroots protests since the 1960s with sometimes over 100,000 participants, media either hardly covered or outright ignored the citizens' demonstrations of discontent. More importantly, politicians also succeeded in linking the protest to sentiments of anti-patriotism by claiming that in times of crisis it was a patriotic duty to support the official disaster management and attempts to restore normality. The aforementioned "crisis of return," the need to reintegrate after returning to Japan, then implied that mem-

---

74 For the protests in Japan following the nuclear catastrophe, see Katrin Gengenbach, Maria Trunk, "Vor und nach 'Fukushima': Dynamiken sozialer Protestbewegungen in Japan seit der Jahrtausendwende," in *Japan: Politik, Wirtschaft und Gesellschaft*, eds. David Chiavacci, Iris Wieczorek (Berlin: VSJF, 2012): 261–282.

bers of the community in Brussels took a supportive stance and didn't take an openly critical position towards the political establishment because "reentry [into Japanese society] raises questions of identity that can be silenced only by strict conformity and virtual denial of the foreign experience."[75]

Conclusion

We have argued that a group creates or reconfirms itself (from within) through practice. Despite the differences between both long-term and short-term diasporic communities, the triple disaster and its aftermath served as a catalyst for increased communication on a personal level within the community. As such, the (closed) community of short-term Japanese nationals strengthened and reinforced their ties within the Japanese community, while the permanent Japanese nationals in Belgium strengthened their contacts with other Japanese, and also reached out to Belgian nationals for participation in charity events. However, the strengthening of togetherness was – because the practice of support was limited in time – only a temporary manifestation and limited to the months immediately following the triple disaster. The support events also served as a means to define network boundaries further because not all Japanese nationals were equally willing to participate in volunteer activities. The organization of support actions thus strengthened preexisting divisions and provided an acceptable reason for further alienation. Whereas support activities served to create temporary communitas of disaster in Belgium, they also served as a token of solidarity towards the homeland (*furusato*). The catastrophe strengthened not only the discursive construction of *furusato* but also the awareness of "Japaneseness" and of being Japanese. By interpreting the support activities from the perspective of gift-giving rather than aid or charity, we could show that moral as well as financial and goods support served to show solidarity and strengthen the bond with the homeland. Because the gift-giving was communicated extensively in the homeland, it verified the Japaneseness of short-term and long-term diaspora members. Moreover, the activities at least temporarily added the notion of a "civil society" as a new element of Japaneseness: the ability to stand together and support each other in times of catastrophe not only individually or locally but also (trans)nationally. In Japan, this feeling of solidarity also meant a politicization of civil society, whereas the support activities of the Japanese diaspora in Belgium, in essence, remained apolitical and supportive of the existing political system.

---

75 White, *The Japanese Overseas*, 106.

Anita Janassary
Diasporic Individuals – A Hidden Peace Building Capacity?

Abstract: There are currently no research publications which systematically evaluate the involvement of diasporic individuals in peace building efforts in their places of origin, because they are seen as part of the local staff force rather than a unique peace building staff type. This assumption is based on the still commonly held territorial definition of diaspora within contemporary peace building practice, which describes diaspora as a temporal phenomenon. However, a spatial understanding of the term 'diaspora' posits diasporic individuals as autonomous actors who may even – when included in the design of peace building measures – function as bridge builders between 'the local' and 'the international.' Additionally, since the concept of the 'local turn' in peace building studies claims that the integration of 'the local' is crucial for contemporary peace building efforts, diasporic individuals may be capable of fulfilling a prominent role in peace building. In the future, empirical research has to clarify whether diaspora individuals can act as bridge builders and are thus able to bring 'the local' into contemporary peace building. This chapter concludes that these hypotheses, which derive from both recent peace building studies and ongoing discussions amongst practitioners, should be probed through empirical qualitative case studies.

The United Nations' *Independent Report of the Senior Advisory Group* on *Civilian Capacity in the Aftermath of Conflicts*[1] discusses the concept of local ownership[2] as a key factor in successful (post-conflict) peace building.[3] Consequently, it argues that the staffing of recent peace building efforts should be reconsidered:

---

[1] UN, *Civilian Capacity in the Aftermath of Conflict: Independent Report of the Senior Advisory Group* (UN, 2011).

[2] According to Mary Martin et al. the local ownership approach is a principle which describes and aims for a process of transferring full responsibility from international organizations to local authorities. The concept further implies that all measures undertaken within peace operations should be adapted to local contexts. For further readings see: Mary Martin et al., "Exiting Conflict, Owning the Peace: Local Ownership in International Peace Operation," *Friedrich Ebert Stiftung – Policy Paper* (Berlin: Friedrich Ebert Stiftung, 2012).

[3] Depending on the definition of peace as a process or a status-quo, the term peace building is sometimes used with the attribute 'post-conflict' to emphasize a violent situation which has to be managed by building peace (status-quo term). If the term is instead defined as process-related, efforts to build peace would be a permanent task since conflicts also exist in peace time, although they may not be dealt with violently. Thus, the attribute post-conflict would be obsolete. Furthermore, success of peace building is often defined differently according to the applied definitions of 'peace'. This chapter does not dispute the question of success in peace building and applies a quite narrow definition in this regard: Peace building is successful if organized major violence is absent and a majority of the local population perceives the implementation of peace building measures as successful.

In some cases, the needed capacities are just not available. It is difficult, for example, to find people who can rebuild a judicial system. Conflict may have weakened capacities at home and the international market has not been able to provide enough talented people with the right skills, language and cultural fluency who can deploy at short notice and will stay long enough to be effective.

Often, however, there is more national capacity than is at first apparent. Even countries ravaged by conflict have latent capacities that must be protected and nurtured. And despite some persistent gaps, there is more deployable capacity in the international system than has been fully used. Diasporas offer one potential reservoir.[4]

In this short passage the UN Senior Advisory Group touches on an as yet neglected topic that deserves serious examination: diasporic individuals as peace building capacity. The role of diasporas in conflict is frequently analyzed in the field of peace and conflict studies. However, such studies tend to problematize diasporas and focus on diasporas as groups settled somewhere other than their places of origin.[5] Thus, research efforts often focus on the long-distance activities of diasporas with regard to violent conflicts or regime transformation processes in their places of origin.[6] On the other hand, practitioners in particular point out the peace building capacity of diasporic individuals when they are engaged as staff members in conflict and crisis management projects implemented in their places of origin.[7] Additionally, the recent shift within studies of peace building

---

4 UN, *Civilian Capacity*, 3.

5 On the tendency of the problematization of the diaspora phenomenon – meaning focusing on research questions which deal with the challenges connected to diasporas rather than on questions which ask whether opportunities also arise with the phenomenon of diasporas – see for example: Jana Braziel, Anita Mannur, "Nation, Migration, Globalization: Points of Contention in Diaspora Studies," in *Theorizing Diaspora: A Reader*, ed. Jana Braziel, Anita Mannur (Malden: Blackwell, 2009): 1–22; Yossi Shain, "The Role of Diasporas in Conflict Perpetuation or Resolution," *SAIS Review* 22.2 (2002): 115–144; and Judith Vorrath, "Engaging African Diasporas for Peace: Cornerstones for an Emerging EU Agenda," *EU ISS Occasional Paper* 98 (2012): 2–43.

6 For example: Terrence Lyons, Peter Mandaville (ed.), *Politics from Afar: Transnational Diasporas and Networks* (New York: Columbia UP, 2012); Gabriel Sheffer, *Diaspora Politics: At Home Abroad* (Cambridge: Cambridge UP, 2003).

7 For practitioner publications on the peace building capacity of diaspora, see for example: Cindy Horst et al., "Participation of Diasporas in Peacebuilding and Development: A Handbook for Practitioners and Policymakers," *PRIO Report* 2 (2010); Stabilization & Peacebuilding Community of Practice (SPCoP), "E-Discussion Report on Participation of Diaspora in Peacebuilding and Development" (International Stabilization and Peacebuilding Initiative, Bonn International Center for Conversion, March 19, 2011), *civcap.info* <https://www.civcap.info/fileadmin/user_upload/e-discussions/report_3_e_discussion_daispora.pdf> (acc. February 14, 2012); The Advocates for Human Rights, *A House with Two Rooms: Final Report of the Truth and Reconciliation Commission of Liberia Diaspora Project* (Saint Paul, MN: DRI P, 2009).

from a rather structure- or system-centered (macro-level) perspective[8] to an actor-centered approach (micro-level perspective)[9] when analyzing the success and failure of peace building, opens the floor for discussions of diasporic individuals as peace building capacity. Taking these considerations into account, this chapter seeks to answer the question of whether it is worthwhile to study the peace building capacity of diasporic individuals. Before explaining why diasporic individuals are rarely considered deployable as staff members in peace building activities, I define and contextualize peace building within the frame of civilian crisis and conflict management. Subsequently, I argue that the peace building capacity of diasporic individuals is obscured due to the still common territorial definition of diaspora – even though diaspora theories have turned to a more complex understanding of the term.[10] I then go on to compare diasporic individuals to the two main peace building staff types: international and local/national staff. I assume that diasporic individuals offer a hybrid profile, combining the average profile of international and local staff.[11] Finally, I discuss concerns of partiality which are often explicitly or implicitly attributed to diasporic individuals when arguing against their involvement as staff members in peace building before concluding with a plea for an empirical-qualitative

---

8 Studies with a macro-level perspective include Paul Collier et al., *Breaking the Conflict Trap: Civil War and Development Policy* (Oxford: Oxford P, World Bank, 2003) and Francis Fukuyama, "The Imperative of State-Building," *Journal of Democracy* 15.2 (2004): 17–31.

9 This shift is especially reflected in publications dealing with the concept of 'the everyday' or the 'local turn' within peace building, such as: Audra Mitchell, "Quality/Control: International Peace Interventions and 'the Everyday'," *Review of International Studies* 37.4 (2011): 1623–1645; Michael Pugh, "Local Agency and Political Economies of Peacebuilding," *Studies in Ethnicity and Nationalism* 11.2 (2011): 308–320; Roger Mac Ginty, Oliver P. Richmond, "The Local Turn in Peace Building: A Critical Agenda for Peace," *Third World Quarterly* 34.5 (2013): 763–783.

10 See for example: Rakesh M. Bhatt, "In Other Words: Language Mixing, Identity Representations, and Third Space," *Journal of Sociolinguistics* 12.2 (2008): 177–200; Michel Bruneau, "Diasporas, Transnational Spaces and Communities," in *Diaspora and Transnationalism Concepts, Theories and Methods*, ed. Rainer Bauböck, Thomas Faist (Amsterdam: Amsterdam UP, 2010): 35–49; Isti Siti Saleha Gandana, "Exploring Third Spaces: Negotiating Identities and Cultural Differences," *The International Journal of Diversity in Organisations, Communities and Nations* 7.6 (2008): 143–150; Khachig Tölölyan, "The Contemporary Discourse of Diaspora Studies," *Comparative Studies of South Asia, Africa and the Middle East* 27.3 (2007), 647–655; Steven Vertovec, "Cosmopolitanism," in *Diasporas: Concepts, Identities, Intersections*, ed. Kim Knott, Seán MacLoughlin (London: Zed Books, 2010), 63–68.

11 For the argument that diasporic individuals may have a unique profile especially compared to international staff in peace building, cf. Séverine Autesserre, *Peaceland: Conflict Resolution and the Everyday Politics of International Intervention* (New York: Cambridge UP, 2014), 14.

study to analyze the impact of diaspora involvement as staff members in peace building efforts.

Peace Building

The term 'peace building' describes an instrument of crisis and conflict management which was introduced to the wider public in 1992 with the publication of *Agenda for Peace: Preventive Diplomacy, Peacemaking and Peace-keeping*[12] by former UN Secretary-General Boutros Boutros-Ghali. He subscribed to Johan Galtung's differentiation of peacekeeping, peacemaking and peace building[13] while he clearly favored (post-conflict) peace building as a conflict management and resolution tool[14] and argued "towards the re-shaping of societies."[15] Only five years later, John Paul Lederach published his book *Building Peace: Sustainable Reconciliation in Divided Societies* and systematically set out the concept of peace building.[16] He defined it less as an activity undertaken to maintain peace, but more as a concept which aims to maintain the social structure of societies which have the capacity to adapt to social change and are therefore able to deal with social conflict:

> [...] I suggest that 'peacebuilding' is more than postaccord [also often referred to as post-conflict] reconstruction. Here, peacebuilding is understood as a comprehensive concept that encompasses, generates, and sustains the full array of processes, approaches, and stages needed to transform conflict toward more sustainable, peaceful relationships. The term thus involves a wide range of activities and functions that both precede and follow formal peace accords. Metaphorically, peace is seen not merely as a state in time or a condition. It is a dynamic social construct.[17]

In contrast to peacekeeping and peacemaking, peace building does not involve military assistance per se, but is rather a civilian tool of crisis and conflict man-

---

12 Boutros Boutros-Ghali, "An Agenda for Peace: Preventive Diplomacy, Peacemaking and Peace-Keeping" (United Nations Security Council, June 17, 1992), *United Nations Rule of Law* <http://www.unrol.org/files/A_47_277.pdf> (acc. June 25, 2013).
13 Johan Galtung, "Three Realistic Approaches to Peace: Peacekeeping, Peacemaking, Peacebuilding," *Impact of Science on Society* 1.2 (1976): 103–115.
14 Boutros-Ghali, "An Agenda for Peace," 5.
15 Vivienne Jabri, "Peacebuilding, the Local and the International: A Colonial or Postcolonial Rationality?," *Peacebuilding* 1.1 (2013): 3–16, 9.
16 John Paul Lederach, *Building Peace: Sustainable Reconciliation in Divided Societies* (Washington, DC: USIP P, 1997): 20–21, 73–85.
17 Lederach, *Building Peace*, 20.

agement.[18] The underlying normative assumption of peace building as a concept is that any society's main goal is peace. In this context the understanding of conflict is non-pathological, meaning conflict is an inherent phenomenon within any society that contributes to its development.[19]

Mainly, in light of the implementation of state building measures according to international liberal and democratic standards, peace building in practice is often called 'liberal peace building' by those who study the causes of success and failure in contemporary peace building efforts.[20] Often these studies conclude that 'the local' is marginalized in contemporary peace building, even though the implemented measures are supposed to be designed to benefit local populations in (post-)conflict regions or those regions undergoing transformation processes.[21] At the same time, 'the local' is identified as a key factor in successful peace building and more research into the everyday dimension[22] and the involvement of the local is called for.[23] Such studies demand the adaptation of international standards and particular peace building project templates to the ground-based context where peace building measures are implemented. These studies emphasize the recognition of the local context as crucial peace building factor while degrading international standards from the status of best practices to starting point. Hence, the central perspective of peace building is

---

18 Cf. Boutros-Ghali, "An Agenda for Peace," 15–16. Cf. Lederach, *Building Peace*, 20.
19 Cf. Charles Tilly, "War Making and State Making as Organized Crime," in *Bringing the State Back in*, eds. Peter Evans, Dietrich Rueschemeyer, Theda Skocpol (New York: Cambridge UP, 1985): 161–191.
20 See for example: Jabri, "Peacebuilding, the Local and the International," 7–8; Daniel Philpott, "Introduction: Searching for Strategy in an Age of Peacebuilding," in *Strategies for Peace*, ed. Daniel Philpott, Gerard Powers (Oxford: Oxford UP, 2010): 3–15; Oliver P. Richmond, Audra Mitchell, "Peacebuilding and Critical Forms of Agency: From Resistance to Subsistence," *Alternatives: Global, Local, Political* 36.4 (2011): 326–344.
21 See for example: Autesserre, *Peaceland*, 8–9; Mac Ginty, Richmond, "The Local Turn," 763–764.
22 Audra Mitchell gives a brief definition of the concept of 'the everyday' and says: "The 'everyday,' I shall argue, is the set of experiences, practices and interpretations through which people engage with the daily challenges of occupying, preserving, altering and sustaining the plural worlds that they occupy" (Mitchell, "Quality/Control," 1624). Referring to Oliver P. Richmond's concept of 'the local' she argues: "'the local' refers to a universal set of practices, rather than a reference to parochial, spatially, culturally or politically bounded places" (Mitchell, "Quality/Control," 1628).
23 Autesserre, *Peaceland*, 8–9; Michael Lund, "A Toolbox for Responding to Conflicts and Building Peace," in *Peacebuilding: A Field Guide*, eds. Luc Reychler, Thania Paffenholz (Boulder: Lynne Rienner Publishers, 2001): 16–20, 16.

shifted from a macro- to a micro-level, from the global to the local scale – this is what is called the 'local turn' in peace building studies.

When it comes to the staffing of peace building efforts, the complaint is often made that peace building staff lack local expertise[24] which does not change over the duration of their assignments because their interactions with the local population are limited.[25] Since the Brahimi Report[26] was published in 2000 and pointed out, among other things, the unpreparedness[27] of staff in UN peace operations,[28] there have been ongoing discussions regarding changes to recruitment methods and the human resource requirements of peace building organizations.[29] In these discussions, it is assumed that the integration of diasporic individuals could increase the involvement of 'the local' due to the characterization of diasporic individuals as carriers of local expertise, and that this local expertise might result in their functioning as bridge-builders between international standards and local contexts.[30] As I have illustrated, the direction in which contemporary peace building is developing makes the engagement of diasporic in-

---

24 Following the definition of Autessere, local expertise includes "an intimate understanding of the place's history, key actors, and political, social, cultural, and economic dynamics" (Autessere, *Peaceland*, 69).
25 Cf. Autesserre, *Peaceland*, 25; Mojca Vah Jevšnik, *Building Peace for a Living: Expatriate Development Workers in Kosovo* (Ljubljana: ZRC Publishing, Zalozba ZRC, 2009): 90; UN, *Civilian Capacity*, 3.
26 United Nations Security Council, "Report of the Panel on United Nations Peace Operations" ['Brahimi-Report'] (United Nations Security Council, August 21, 2000), *United Nations* <http://www.un.org/en/ga/search/view_doc.asp?symbol=A/55/305> (acc. June 23, 2013).
27 Cf. Luc Reychler, Thania Paffenholz, "Preface," in *Peacebuilding: A Field Guide*, eds. Luc Reychler, Thania Paffenholz (Boulder: Lynne Rienner Publishers, 2001): xiii–xiv, xiii.
28 UN peace operations are a tool of the international community to maintain or re-build peace. They may include peacekeeping, peacemaking and peace building measures and, therefore are not limited to military or civilian activities. Next to the UN also other regional organizations conduct peace operations as for example the African Union or the European Union. For further insights see for instance: Michael W. Doyle, Nicholas Sambanis, *Making War and Building Peace: The United Nations Since the 1990's* (Princeton: Princeton UP, 2006).
29 These discussions are reflected, for example, in the UN human resources reform process (General Assembly of the United Nations, "Human Resource Management Reform at the United Nations" [General Assembly of the United Nations, December 2012], *France at the United Nations: Permanent Mission of France to the United Nations in New York* <http://www.franceonu.org/france-at-the-united-nations/thematic-files/un-reform/human-resources-management-reform/france-at-the-united-nations/thematic-files/un-reform/human-resources-management-reform/article/human-resource-management-reform> [acc. February 12, 2013]) or in SPCoP, "E-Discussion report"; UN, *Civilian Capacity*; Vorrath, "Engaging African Diasporas."
30 SPCoP, "E-Discussion report," 4.

dividuals as staff members a legitimate and logical field for research. Moreover, the topic links peace building studies with the study of diaspora and migration.

Diasporas as Temporary Phenomenon

I argue that diasporic individuals are (still) a hidden peace building capacity, firstly due to the commonly applied definition of diaspora in a territorial sense,[31] and secondly because recruitment methods in many cases do not allow for the hiring of diasporic individuals.[32] In diaspora studies the understanding of the term 'diaspora' underwent several conceptual shifts. The classical understanding of the term refers to the "Jewish experience."[33] In the attempt to make generalizations, social scientists began to use the term for other "categories of people"[34] who left their places of origin and settled elsewhere.[35] William Safran saw that such a comprehensive definition of the term would result in a loss of all conceptual functionality and suggested applying the concept of diaspora to "expatriate minority communities" which share certain features.[36] These features describe the relationship of diasporas to their places of origin and settlement and thus build on territorial references. This territorial understanding of diasporas is criticized by constructionist scholars who, inter alia, argue that the concept of diaspora should rather emphasize diasporic identities

---

31 Cf. Tölölyan, "The Contemporary Discourse," 648.

32 For example, due to application requirements diasporic individuals are excluded from applying for international job positions within EU peace missions, unless they are in the possession of a EU passport or gained the nationality of a third contributing country (see: European Rule of Law Mission Kosovo (EULEX), "Job Opportunities: Frequently Asked Questions" [EULEX], *European Union: External Action* <http://www.eulex-kosovo.eu/en/jobs/> [acc. March 3, 2011]. Similar human resources requirements are conducted for political missions of the OSCE (see: Organization for Security and Co-operation in Europe [OSCE], "Employment: FAQ" [OSCE], *Organization for Security and Co-operation in Europe* <http://www.osce.org/employment/23> [acc. April 23, 2014]). The distinction of national/local and international posts is not limited to the EU or OSCE and can be found in international organizations as well as in non-governmental organizations (cf. Autesserre, *Peaceland*, 84–87).

33 Robin Cohen, *Global Diasporas: An Introduction* (London: Routledge, 2008), 1.

34 William Safran, "Diasporas in Modern Societies" [1991] in *Migration, Diasporas, and Transnationalism* eds. Steven Vertovec, Robin Cohen (Cheltenham, Northhampton: Edward Elgar, 1999): 83–99, 83.

35 Safran, "Diasporas in Modern Societies," 83.

36 Safran, "Diasporas in Modern Societies," 83.

which are "at once local and global"[37] and thus deterritorialized.[38] Territorial references are not sufficient in describing the diaspora phenomenon. However, according to Robin Cohen, diaspora studies are now in a consolidating phase, because

> [t]he social constructionist critiques were partially accommodated, but were seen as in danger of emptying the notion of diaspora of much of its analytical and descriptive power. While the increased complexity and deterritorialization of identities are valid phenomena and constitutive of a small minority of diasporas (generally those that had been doubly or multiply displaced over time), ideas of home and often the stronger inflection of homeland remain powerful discourses [...].[39]

This brief overview of the development of the term diaspora over the last four to five decades is not exhaustive. It exemplifies the shifts from a specific, to a territorial, to a deterritorialized, to a consolidated understanding of the term diaspora within diaspora studies. Nonetheless, when the term is used in peace building practice, it still widely applies the territorial meaning. For example, *The Africa Briefing Report – Diaspora Groups in Peace Processes: Lessons Learned and Potential for Engagement by the EU* summarizes the discussion of experts, policymakers, researchers and civil society representatives on the engagement of diaspora groups in peace building.[40] While it states that diasporas may obtain "transnational sets of norms and values", it stresses the potential problem of difficult "homeland" or "hostland" relations, e. g., due to "hidden agendas" shaped by the national affiliation of diasporas.[41] Another example is *The Final Report of the Expert Forum – Capacity Building for Peace and Development: Roles of Diaspora*, which conceptualizes diaspora as territorial, defining it only in terms of diasporic individuals' relationship to their places of origin and settlement.[42]

The territorial definition of diaspora focuses on territorial references and emphasizes that collective diaspora identities are produced based on a direct and

---

37 Avtar Brah, *Cartographies of Diaspora: Contesting Identities* (London, New York: Routledge, 1996): 196.
38 Cohen, *Global Diasporas*, 1.
39 Cohen, *Global Diasporas*, 2.
40 Any Freitas, *Diaspora Groups in Peace Processes: Lessons Learned and Potential for Engagement by the EU* (Brussels: European Union Institute for Security Studies, 2012).
41 Freitas, *Diaspora Groups in Peace Processes*, 4.
42 University for Peace, "Capacity Building for Peace and Development: Roles of Diaspora" (Final Report of the Expert Forum held in Toronto: University of Peace, October, 19–20 2006), *United Nations Institute for Training and Research* <http://www.unitar.org/ny/sites/uni tar.org.ny/files/UPEACE%20Report.pdf> (acc. April 8, 2014).

permanent differentiation regarding their places of origin and settlement.[43] Even definitions which stress the autonomy of diasporas with regard to their places of origin and settlement may still refer to territorial categories because while diasporic activities may take place within a deterritorialized social space, they are nevertheless often addressed to territorialized political or economic matters within certain (often national or sub-national) territories.[44] Consequently, diaspora concepts which put emphasis on territorialities do not identify diasporas nor diasporic individuals as independent actors. Such definitions rather stress the interim-status of diaspora and diasporic individuals as phenomena which eventually disappear, either by a return to a place of origin or by integration into the communities of places of settlement. Hence, the term diaspora in a territorial sense cannot be applied to research on diasporic individuals as staff members in peace building activities in their places of origin, since individuals who have returned to their place of origin would no longer be considered diasporic.

In order to carry out such research, I therefore argue for a definition of diaspora which stresses deterritorialized features of diasporas and diasporic individuals as it allows them to be identified as autonomous actors. This understanding, which is supported by spatial definitions of diaspora, argues that diasporas and diasporic individuals produce transnational social spaces[45] which are sometimes called 'diaspora space',[46] 'diasporic space'[47] or 'third spaces'.[48] In these spaces, members of transnational communities negotiate and translate values, ideas and practices which bear meanings inherited from their communities of origin and settlement.[49] By reorganizing these aspects within transnational so-

---

43 See for instance: Arjun Appadurai, *Modernity at Large: Cultural Dimensions of Globalization* (Minneapolis: U of Minnesota P, 1996); Peggy Levitt, *The Transnational Villagers* (Berkeley: U of California P, 2001); Karen F. Olwig, "Defining the National in Transnational: Cultural Identity in Afro-Caribbean Diaspora," *Ethnos* 88 (1993): 361–376.

44 Cf. Bruneau, "Diasporas," 36–37; Terrence Lyons, "Diasporas and Homeland Conflict," in *Globalization, Territoriality and Conflict in an Era of Globalization*, ed. Miles Kahler, Barbara Walter (Cambridge: Cambridge UP, 2006): 111–132.

45 I am following Henri Lefebvre's definition of social space: "[Social space] subsumes things produced, and encompasses their interrelationships in their coexistence and simultaneity – their (relative) order and/or (relative) disorder. It is the outcome of a sequence and set of operations, and thus cannot be reduced to the rank of a simple object" (Henri Lefebvre, *The Production of Space* [1974] [Oxford: Blackwell, 2005]: 73).

46 Brah, *Cartographies of Diaspora*, 181.

47 Bruneau, "Diasporas," 37.

48 Cf. Homi K. Bhabha, *The Location of Culture* [1994] (London: Routledge, 2009): 55–56; Bhatt, "In Other Words," 182.

49 Cf. Bhabha, *Location of Culture*, 55–56.

cial spaces, communities of hybrid identity are produced.[50] The results are new, or rather transformed and synthesized values, ideas and practices[51] which may not be found as such within the diasporas' or diasporic individuals' communities of origin or settlement.[52] This means that even when external inputs from the communities of origin and/or settlement are blocked, the hybrid identity persists. Hence, diasporic individuals who are bearers of ideas, values and practices within these spaces can be identified independently from their actual locality. Possible evidence for the diasporic space is provided by the case studies of Basch et al.[53] In these case studies, the diasporic individuals interviewed possessed an identity that was different from the collective identities of both their communities of origin and settlement. Moreover, they shared specific "social experiences" which were not part of the social experiences of the other two communities.[54]

Types of Peace Building Staff

Distinct from a territorial diaspora definition, a spatial understanding of diaspora allows for the identification of diasporic individuals as research subjects independent from their locality. Moreover, the local turn in peace building studies makes the topic of the involvement of diasporic individuals in peace building especially relevant. As I have also mentioned, recent studies regarding the success and failure of peace building have shown that the local in contemporary peace building is underestimated. This underestimation is reflected in the emphasis on the professional background[55] of peace building staff while local ex-

---

50 Cf. Bhabha, *Location of Culture*, 55; Gandana, "Exploring Third Spaces," 148; Stuart Hall, "Cultural Identity and Diaspora" [1990], in *Migration, Diasporas, and Transnationalism*, eds. Steven Vertovec, Robin Cohen (Cheltenham, Northampton: Edward Elgar, 1999): 222–237, 235.
51 Bhabha, *Location of Culture*, 37.
52 Cf. Linda Basch et al., *Nations Unbound: Transnational Projects, Postcolonial Predicaments, and Deterritorialized Nation-States* (New York, London: Gordon and Breach, 1994): 8; Bhatt, "In Other Words," 182.
53 Basch et al., *Nations Unbound*, 7.
54 Basch et al., *Nations Unbound*, 7.
55 The term 'professional background' refers, among other things, to thematic or technical expertise gained through formal education: "'thematic knowledge' or 'technical expertise' [...] relies on an in-depth understanding of particular aspects of intervention work [respectively, peace building]. These may be general aspects, as in conflict-resolution, development, or humanitarian aid, or they may be specialized ones, as in project management, public finance, or agricultural engineering" (Autesserre, *Peaceland*, 69).

pertise is not viewed as a requirement for peace building personnel.[56] This presumption is transmitted into the human resources structures of peace building organizations, be they inter-governmental or non-governmental.[57] This means "subordinate" posts are usually filled by local staff and management posts are assigned to international staff.[58]

International personnel can be described as "high-skilled, high-wage professionals who regularly cross borders as part of their employment obligations, usually migrating from first world countries to less developed countries to take part in various development [and peace-building] activities."[59] As Mojca Vah Jevšnik explains in *Building Peace for a Living: Expatriate Development Workers in Kosovo*, international personnel rarely integrate into local population and she describes a system of parallel social spaces which hardly intersect.[60] This causes a lack of communication between international staff – who are supposed to support the establishment of a safe and secure ground needed for peace building activities[61] – and the local population, which should benefit from these efforts.[62] Hence, peace building activities are often not tailored to the needs of the local population. Nevertheless, it is the local population which has to live with the results of the implemented activities, while those who planned them may be long gone.[63]

Séverine Autesserre comes to a similar conclusion in her recent *Peaceland: Conflict Resolution and the Everyday Politics of International Intervention*, where she states that even though local people are involved in the implementation of peace building measures (as national staff members, for example), they are, with few exceptions, not usually involved in the design of such measures or peace building strategies.[64] In her view, the reason for this is the lack of international experience and professional background among local staff, both highly

56 Cf. Autesserre, *Peaceland*, 72.
57 Cf. Autesserre, *Peaceland*, 72–73.
58 Autesserre, *Peaceland*, 95.
59 Vah Jevšnik, *Building Peace for a Living*, 85.
60 Vah Jevšnik, *Building Peace for a Living*, 90.
61 United Nations Peacebuilding Support Office, "UN Peacebuilding: an Orientation" (United Nations, 2010), *United Nations* <http://www.un.org/en/peacebuilding/pbso/pdf/peace building_orientation.pdf#page=1&zoom=auto,–223,510> (acc. March 8, 2014), 9.
62 See also: Leopold von Carlowitz, "Migranten als Garanten? Über die Schwierigkeiten beim Rechtsstaatsexport in Nachkriegsgesellschaften," *HSFK Standpunkte: Beiträge zum demokratischen Frieden* 6 (2004): 1–12.
63 Vah Jevšnik, *Building Peace for a Living*, 90.
64 Cf. Autesserre, *Peaceland*, 85–86.

prized in peace building organizations.[65] While she stresses the importance of fresh and innovative inputs often provided by international staff who therefore should not be excluded from peace building projects, she also cites a number of examples she came across during her studies and her work as a peace building staff member that showcase the benefits of individuals who combine a professional background with local expertise (because they have integrated into the society which is on the receiving end of the conducted peace building measures, have stayed for a longer period of time, or have personal ties to the region and society, for instance through marriage or family).[66] Diasporic individuals usually fit such a hybrid profile, and this is what differentiates them from most international peace building staff members. Additionally, they may contribute technical skills (professional background) and international experiences of peace building which most local staff members cannot offer since the chances of going abroad for education or professional reasons are significantly decreased in (post-)conflict regions.[67] However, diasporic individuals are often excluded from application processes for international posts.[68]

In addition to practitioners' recommendations to look more closely at the peace building capacity of diasporic individuals, the empirical studies of Autesserre and Vah Jevšnik both point in this direction. In order to close the "knowledge" gap between international staff and local population, it is worthwhile to look into alternative staffing concepts in the field of peace building and, since human resources directives of international and regional organizations are relatively restrictive regarding the adoption of alternative concepts, it might also be of benefit to include alternative concepts in the field of NGO development work or that of governmental organizations into a comprehensive analysis. Programs which address this challenge can be divided into two kinds: those which point to the huge capacity of returnees and therefore offer recommendations relating to how diasporic individuals may be attracted to return permanently and work in the field of peace building and development,[69] and those which highlight the potential of diasporic individuals who are permanently settled abroad but who may

---

65 Cf. Autesserre, *Peaceland*, 84–87.
66 Autesserre, *Peaceland*, 14.
67 Cf. von Carlowitz, "Migranten als Garanten?," 8–9.
68 See footnote 32, above.
69 E.g., International Organization for Migration (IOM) – Afghanistan, "Return of Qualified Afghans Project" (IOM Afghanistan, 2012), *Diaspora and Development* <http://diaspora.iom.int/return-qualified-afghans-rqa-programme> (acc. April 12, 2013).

be willing to work in the field of peace building and development temporarily.[70] Both sources appear relevant to the analysis of diasporic individuals as peace building capacity.

A Question of Impartiality

I have argued that diasporic individuals are a hidden peace building capacity. But before a study on diasporic individuals as peace building capacity can be undertaken, a frequently mentioned concern must be addressed: the belief that diasporic individuals are partial agents.[71] If this is true, further research in this area is pointless as peace building organizations require their staff to remain impartial.[72] However, it is my contention that, on the contrary, there is no evidence that international staff members might be less partial than diasporic individuals.[73] Moreover, recent developments show that the assumption of impartiality as crucial peace building principle is contested and may not even be a key factor in successful peace building.[74]

While diasporas and therefore diasporic individuals often are perceived as partial by the communities of their places of settlement,[75] the perception of (im-)partiality varies within their communities of their places of origin.[76] Also, Anderson et al. showed that if peace building staff members have a local background, the implemented efforts gain credit with the local population, and therefore the outcome of the measures may be more sustained than they would be if implemented by international staff lacking such background.[77] Thus, the involve-

70 E.g., Horst et al., "Participation of Diasporas"; IOM Afghan Expatriate Services Program, "Afghan Expatriate Program (AEP)" (IOM Afghanistan, 2012), *Islamic Republic of Afghanistan: Independent Administrative Reform and Civil Service Comission: General Directorate, Program Design & Management* <http://www.afghanexperts.gov.af/?page=Page-AEP-Menu&lang=dr> (acc. June 20, 2013).

71 Cf. Freitas, *Diaspora Groups in Peace Processes*, 4.

72 See for example: United Nations, *United Nations Peacekeeping Operations Principles and Guidelines* (New York: UN Peacekeeping Best Practices Section, 2008): 33; OSCE, "OSCE Code of Conduct," 1.

73 Autesserre, *Peaceland*, 235.

74 Autesserre, *Peaceland*, 236.

75 Sheffer, *Diaspora Politics*, 194; Cohen, *Global Diasporas*, 193–194.

76 Von Carlowitz, "Migranten als Garanten?," 10.

77 Mary B. Anderson et al., *Time to Listen: Hearing People on the Receiving End of International Aid* (Cambridge: CDA Collaborative Learning Projects, 2012), 49–50.

ment of local expertise increases the legitimacy of peace building measures in the eyes of the population who is supposed to benefit from them.[78]

Autesserre even questions whether impartiality is a crucial success factor in peace building, since her studies demonstrated that being and staying impartial is difficult for anyone working in the field: "Many interveners are so shocked by the horrors they witness that they form strong opinions in favor of or against certain belligerents."[79] She further states: "Target populations prefer organizations that side with them to nonpartisan actors."[80] Such conclusions have prompted several peace building agencies to change their principles and no longer include the principle of impartiality.[81] This shows that the question of impartiality can be targeted from two different perspectives. Firstly, assuming that impartiality is crucial for the success of peace building efforts, it is not reasonable to claim that diasporas and diasporic individuals are per se perceived as partial within the communities of their places of origin. Secondly, a key factor to successful peace building may even lie in partiality or rather solidarity as Autesserre indicates. So, whether impartiality is discussed as a matter of perception or as a matter of fact, it seems that impartiality is neither a crucial factor in peace building nor an attribute which can be used to describe international staff. Therefore, when it comes to peace building, partiality should not be the reason for excluding diasporic individuals as peace building capacity.

Diasporic Individuals as Peace Building Staff

There are many examples of diasporic individuals working in peace building in their places of origin. I encountered this first hand during my assignment at the 'German Centre for International Peace Operations,' a government-funded non-profit recruitment, training and deployment agency of German civilians for multilateral peace building efforts.[82] My observations were confirmed during my research field work in the Western Balkans where I had the chance to interview at least forty diasporic individuals who are working as peace building personnel in their places of origin.[83] Such persons can be divided into three groups: one group

---

78 Anderson et al., *Time to Listen*, 49–50.
79 Autesserre, *Peaceland*, 235.
80 Autesserre, *Peaceland*, 236.
81 Autesserre, *Peaceland*, 236.
82 For further information see *Zentrum für Internationale Friedenseinsätze* <http://www.zif-berlin.org> (acc. June 23, 2014).
83 The field work referred to here is part of my PhD project and will be published in 2016.

working for development organizations which seem to be more open towards diasporic individuals as staff members, another group of diasporic individuals who possess the nationality of the countries of their places of settlement and are therefore assigned to international posts, and a third group working as local staff in peace building, although not in managerial positions.

The identification of diasporic individuals in peace building organizations can be difficult since human resources departments do not usually keep relevant data because diasporic individuals are not considered as potential staff members for managerial positions, as previously mentioned. It follows that individuals who are assigned to an international post may not inform human resources that they are also passport holders of a local nationality in order to avoid being rostered as local staff. While human resources departments usually keep track of language skills, the ability to speak a local language fluently is not synonymous with being a diasporic individual.[84] Ultimately, identifying those who fit the hybrid diasporic profile and work in peace building organizations in their country of origin is often done on a word-of-mouth basis.

Conclusion

I have argued that diasporic individuals should be considered as autonomous actors within peace consolidation processes and, despite the fact that they may be perceived as partial, their bridge building capacity to bring 'the local' into contemporary peace building efforts is reason enough to consider diasporic individuals a relevant research subject in peace building studies. More importantly, the results of such research efforts would support personnel management of peace building organizations by offering insight into the still rather hidden capacity of diasporic individuals. However, because human resource data are sensitive and often do not evaluate ratios regarding diaspora features, it is difficult to identify diasporic individuals for research efforts. Therefore, I suggest that research on diasporic individuals' peace building capacity has to be conducted in the manner of an empirical qualitative case study. Such an approach would take recent theoretical developments into account and also offers the opportunity of accessing a not yet systematically investigated field of research.

---

84 Cf. Sheffer, *Diaspora Politics*, 95.

Gesa Bierwerth

The Process of Integration among German Expellees in the GDR

Abstract: This chapter explores the process of integration amongst German expellees who settled in the Soviet occupation zone and later German Democratic Republic in the aftermath of
the Second World War. More specifically, it examines how these expellees balanced their longing
for their old home and their need to belong to their new place of settlement. Based on ethnographic fieldwork with expellees from East Prussia, this reflection sheds light on the stages towards a new sense of home in spite of their continuing existence in diaspora amongst German
compatriots. The narratives of the interviewed expellees reveal that they sometimes undertook
integration efforts compelled by the circumstances and due to their desire for acceptance by society. Despite the oppressive politics aiming to enforce integration, the expellees usually found
niches to keep memories alive and even to pass them on. Since the fall of the Iron Curtain, they
have had new possibilities to reconnect with the former homeland and with its old and new inhabitants, and have thus been able partly to overcome their nostalgic feelings. A new sense of
home and belonging emerges.

The Second World War, the German defeat, and the Potsdam Agreement of 1945
led to the loss of more than a quarter of the German territories, mostly the Eastern territories. Their population fled from the Red Army during the invasion or
was expelled. Fourteen million Germans were displaced; about two million people died during flight and expulsion.[1] Most survivors settled in the new, divided
Germany and could generally not return to their former places of living for decades because of the Cold War. The Federal Republic of Germany received almost
8 million expellees, which represented sixteen percent of its population, while
the German Democratic Republic (GDR) received about 3.6 million people,
which meant nineteen percent of its population at the beginning of the 1950s.[2]
The management of these migration flows and the incorporation of a significant
number of refugees into the new German societies demanded particular strategies from the authorities. One of the first measures was the dispersal of the
new arrivals. The Occupation forces wanted the total and quick fusion of the
new inhabitants. They imposed a general interdiction for gathering and aimed

---

1 Hans-Ulrich Wehler, "Einleitung", in *Die Flucht: Über die Vertreibung der Deutschen aus dem
Osten*, eds. Stefan Aust, Stephan Burgdorff (Bonn: Bundeszentrale für politische Bildung, 2005):
9–14, 10.
2 Rainer Münz, "International Migration of Ethnic Germans," in *International Encyclopedia of
the Social & Behavioral Sciences*, eds. Niel J. Smelser, Paul B. Baltes (Oxford: Elsevier, 2001):
7799–7804, 7801.

to mix people of different origins and religious beliefs.[3] The question of the refugees constituted the "problem number one" of postwar Germany.[4] For a long time, national German historiography presented the integration of the homeless from the East as a success or even as a postwar miracle. However, recent research calls into question the myth of the smoothly running assimilation in the 1940s and 1950s. Insight is gained into the difficulties that the expellees faced after displacement, especially from studies with emphasis on the hostility on the part of the local society, like the work of Kossert. Yet not enough attention has been paid to the very personal struggles in the integration process of the expellees. Especially research about the former GDR focuses on official politics and is not primarily attuned to the people who had to cope with its consequences.[5] In fact, research on the expellee problem and especially on their integration in the GDR host society had been impossible for decades, at least up until the end of the 1970s.[6] Schwartz deplores the fact that the state of source material on expellees in the GDR is poor, especially for what goes beyond the first decade after 1945 because the statistics did not chart the refugees and expellees anymore and because no other significant information on them was recorded. Thus, Schwartz concludes that long-run analyses on the integration of expellees in the GDR could only rely on personal accounts and would be limited to individual retrospection.[7] Nevertheless, this kind of study on individual integration should be undertaken. As a matter of fact, it is high time to ask the last survivors about their experiences in the German postwar society. Empirical research on flight and expulsion as well as autobiographical accounts usually put emphasis on the very proceeding of flight and expulsion and neglect to shed light on the fur-

---

3 Hermann Bausinger, Volkskunde *ou l'ethnologie allemande: De la recherche sur l'antiquité à l'analyse culturelle*, trans. Dominique Lassaigne, Pascale Godenir (Paris: Éditions de la Maison des sciences de l'homme, 1993): 163.

4 Andreas Kossert, *Kalte Heimat: Die Geschichte der deutschen Vertriebenen nach 1945* (Munich: Siedler, 2008): 87.

5 Cf. Michael Schwartz, *Vertriebene und "Umsiedlerpolitik": Integrationskonflikte in den deutschen Nachkriegsgesellschaften und die Assimilationsstrategien in der SBZ/DDR 1945–1961* (Munich: Oldenbourg, 2004); Heike Amos, *Die Vertriebenenpolitik der SED 1949 bis 1990* (Munich: Oldenbourg, 2009); Manfred Wille, "Die 'Umsiedler'-Problematik in der DDR-Geschichtsschreibung," in *Sie hatten alles verloren. Flüchtlinge und Vertriebene in der sowjetischen Besatzungszone Deutschlands*, eds. Manfred Wille, Johannes Hoffmann, Wolfgang Meinecke (Wiesbaden: Harrassowitz, 1993): 3–11.

6 Wille, "Die 'Umsiedler'-Problematik in der DDR-Geschichtsschreibung," 3. According to Wille, the GDR conception of history was the main reason for the absence of such work: Talking about the refugees and expellees would have required to study flight and expulsion and to talk about the expellers as well. But the system did not permit such an approach.

7 Schwartz, *Vertriebene und "Umsiedlerpolitik,"* 43.

ther developments towards merging into the host society. It is relevant to ask how the expellees coped with their traumatic past, their feelings of longing and belonging and the oppressive GDR politics and how all this translated into daily life. The ethnological methods of semi-structured interviews and life story telling provide insights into the personal apprehension of the past and up to the present. This reflection is about German expellees from East Prussia, an ancient German province that ceased to exist in 1945. Parts of the territory were from now on under Polish, Lithuanian and Russian administration. The argumentation is based on interviews with former East Prussian inhabitants who settled in the Soviet occupation zone and later GDR, which means that they passed from one dictatorship to another. The first generation witnesses interviewed between 2008 and 2013 were children when they went through war, flight and expulsion.[8] They currently live in the German federal state Mecklenburg-Vorpommern.

The objective of this chapter is to shed light on the process of integration amongst German expellees from an emic perspective. It points out different stages and dimensions which have an impact on the individual's nostalgic feelings, for example the traumatic experiences of flight and expulsion, the arrival in a hostile environment and the new beginnings. It shows how these displaced people balanced their longing for their old home and their desire to belong in their new place of settlement in the GDR. Concerning the memories and the attachment to the former homeland, the research participants reveal various ways in which they responded and bypassed the State's coercive politics on their behalf. The analysis also shows the importance of family ties, of factors like the age of an individual and the role of souvenir objects for remembrance. Finally, the chapter discusses how these expellees have perpetuated, expressed and even renewed their attachment to the former home since the end of the Cold War and the opening of the European East for international tourism.

Each of the German states relied on different strategies in order to assimilate the new arrivals quickly. The Federal Republic of Germany proceeded in keeping with the politics imposed by the Western Allies. The objective was to enforce economic, social and political assimilation. For the Soviet occupation zone and later GDR, it seemed to be admitted that the dictatorship got the refugee problem out of the way by applying its ideology and by introducing a taboo around the phenomenon.[9] The state systematically denied the existence of the expellees al-

---

8 All interviews were conducted in German. Translations are mine.
9 Michael Schwartz, "Der historische Osten in der Erinnerungskultur der DDR," in *Die Vertreibung der Deutschen aus dem Osten in der Erinnerungskultur*, colloquium of the Konrad-Adenauer-

though they represented a fifth of its population. In some districts, the rate of expellees could exceed fifty percent. Multiple "politics of memory,"[10] or rather of forgetting, were put in place. The mere existence of the measures implemented in this context is evidence enough to show that the regime deemed it necessary to assimilate the new arrivals and to avoid any references to their actual fate by the use of euphemisms. For example, a vocabulary suppressing all references to flight and expulsion was imposed: The refugees and expellees became "resettlers" (*Umsiedler*) from 1945 and "former resettlers" (*ehemalige Umsiedler*) from 1950.[11] This terminology expressed the communist regime's acceptance of the frontiers traced by the Potsdam Conference and acknowledged that the Germans from the Eastern provinces would not return to their homelands. The recognition of the frontiers was also part of the strategies aiming to achieve more stability. In this way, the State tried to establish a good relationship (principally of economic nature) with the Eastern Bloc.[12] The communist regime feared expellee gatherings and fought their tendency of self-organization. An unofficial *Heimat* day[13] was organized in Leipzig in 1950 and other meetings followed in Halle. Several hundred people came together until massive arrests put an end to these large gatherings in 1953.[14] The regime utilized repression against individ-

---

Stiftung and the Institut für Zeitgeschichte (Berlin: Konrad-Adenauer-Stiftung, 2004): 69–84, 69.

10 Cf. Rainer Schulze, "The Politics of Memory: Flight and Expulsion of German Populations after the Second World War and German Collective Memory," in *National Identities* 8.4 (2006): 367–382.

11 Schwartz, "Der historische Osten in der Erinnerungskultur der DDR," 71.

12 Schwartz, "Der historische Osten in der Erinnerungskultur der DDR," 73.

13 Heimat means home and homeland in German. It implies a highly emotional bonding towards the places of origin. Rather than referring to a specific place, it invokes identity through place. Blickle conceptualizes it as "both a spiritualized province (a mental state turned inside out) and a provincial spirituality (a spatially perceived small world turned outside in)" (Peter Blickle, *Heimat: A Critical Theory of the German Idea of Homeland* [Rochester: Boydell & Brewer, 2006]: 7). The complex concept of Heimat has multiple social, cultural, political, individual as well as collective dimensions. Heimat days sought to bring together the otherwise dispersed fellows from the former Eastern territories. They were occasions for commemoration and political demonstration. These events were aborted in the German Democratic Republic, but the expellees joined their fellows immediately after the fall of the Iron Curtain in 1989. Heimat days as well as other regional and national expellee gatherings are still performed seventy years after flight and expulsion in the unified Federal Republic of Germany.

14 Cf. Schwartz, "Der historische Osten in der Erinnerungskultur der DDR," 75. Beyond Schwartz's general observation, Amos offers a more nuanced analysis of ongoing efforts to meet as well as of the GDR government's efforts to inhibit such gatherings (Amos, *Die Vertriebenenpolitik der SED*).

uals who talked about their origins, who participated in expellee gatherings in West Germany, who obtained and distributed journals intended for expellees, and so on. The fact that expellees had a proper culture and a distinct identity was rejected. There was no place for their memories and experiences, nor for any expression of them in the public sphere. The repressive and assimilating politics were maintained until the collapse of the system in 1989. The research participants mention these political aspects. They talk about the pressure they were subjected to and how they dealt with it.

Forced Departure and Hope of Immediate Return

Flight and expulsion were often traumatic, and longing for the former homeland influenced by the forced and sudden departure. It needs to be underlined that the nostalgic feelings are not just a kind of emotional longing but that the expellees lost their possessions, often several family members, their accustomed environment, their status within society, and so on. It is a real, violent loss beyond repair. In addition to this loss of all their points of reference came an uncertain future, at least during the first years after the war. The sense of loss is central to the expellees' nostalgic feelings. This is confirmed by Hans-Jürgen, who is head of a refugee group in his region of residence. In his group he regularly discusses the feeling of longing and belonging. He summarizes the accounts of the group members:

> In conversations, expellees often reveal that the sudden and unprepared departure – everything had been left behind, only some things taken in a hurry – as well as the belief that it would only be for a limited duration, imprinted that nostalgia profoundly in the consciousness of many expellees.

For most East Prussians, the displacement started during the cold winter of 1945. Flight and expulsion were real odysseys: weeks or months of wandering and a difficult journey. Entire villages joined the exodus. Elderly people, women and children had to walk for long distances, some had carts. The long treks moved slowly. Some parts of the journey were eventually made by train, freight cars, or ship. Millions of people fled without knowing where to go. The interviewee Gerda recalls the incertitude: "It was not decided where to go. Westwards, they always said. No, we did not even know for how long we would be on the road." The whole way, the refugees came face to face with death: People around them did not have the strength to continue and were given up in the ditch; others died due to hunger and severe cold. The enemy armies conducted air raids on the treks; soldiers threatened the refugees, raped women and carried out executions as it pleased them. All of the interviewees recount such events. The odyssey of the flight is generally told in chronological order. Especially striking experiences are integrated in the narrative. For example, Alfred recalls a stretch on the train. The wagon's insides were covered in ice, brought about by the condensation of the breath of the refugees enclosed in the carriage. He points out: "The worst thing was relieving oneself. Everybody shouted: It's too cold, don't open the door! There was one chamber pot for the whole train. It went round…" Alfred recalls that the elderly could not wait for relief. The smell was terrible. People lost their minds. As the train arrived at the final station, several people were no longer able to walk. Their legs were black due to the icy temperature and the lack of blood circulation. Everybody lacked food, as Gerda remembers:

> We snatched sorrel from the ditch and ate it. […] Mum covered us with wooden boards; we slept in the open air. Once we found an old barn and we said to one another: We're lucky. We'll have a roof over our heads tonight. Yes, and then… the roof was completely destroyed, we hadn't noticed it before … and there was intense rain… I don't know… How we could stand all this!

Some expellees establish a relationship between their longing for the old home and the way in which the exodus took place. Thus, a particularly violent loss of the home, extreme experiences during flight and expulsion as well as intense suffering due to hostility in the host society justify the continuous interest in the old homeland as well as the need for retrospection, sharing recollections and even return journeys. For example, Eva relates that her current neighbor does not understand why she goes back to visit her old home and accuses Eva of being a revanchist looking to regain her lost possessions. But Eva shakes her head and explains that her neighbor's displacement cannot be compared to her own experience of flight and expulsion: The neighbor took a train to reach her family, where she slept in a bed and ate her fill; the new place of settlement was her former holiday destination. According to Eva, that woman's experience differs greatly from the weeks of stray, fear and hunger that so many other expellees experienced. "We walked over corpses," Eva insists. In some way, the research participants are astonished about their own survival.

Starting off a New Life Elsewhere

The end of the odyssey generally led to camps. Then, the refugees were sent to live with local residents: "They were all distributed somewhere" (Dietmar). Homeowners were obliged to accommodate expellees. Every family had to cede a room or two, ordinarily small spaces under the roof. Bruno, his two sisters and their mother arrived in Thuringia after expulsion and they did not have any sign of life from their father. American officers suggested going on to Bavaria, as Benno explains: "But my mother stayed. She knew that father was in the East [soldier on the east front] and that he would be released to the East [Soviet occupation zone] [...]. We all lived with only 75 Ostmarks a month. The years 1945–1949 were years of hunger and privation." Gerda's family fled by train. When the first refugees were allowed to get off the train, the mother took her four little girls. As she did not know where to go, she did not want to go any further. She was sent to a village where the family obtained a small room: "And that's where we lived for years. I don't know... the five of us slept in two beds. We didn't have sheets, but we got old coats." Alfred and his family were allocated to a farmer who already housed another family in the same room. The latter was furnished with two beds: the first occupied by Alfred's mother and his two brothers and sisters, the second by two women and a girl. Alfred slept on the floor. Dietmar recalls that even "each barn corner was occupied by the refugees." Being a little boy, he looked through the windows of a big hall where refugees laid down in the hay, using blankets to improvise compartments in order to separate the families.

Many families had anticipated meeting points in the case of dispersal, generally at some relative's place in other parts of Germany. However, measures in order to prevent further migration flows obliged every person who wanted to move to get a proof of housing in the new place. Actually, the lack of housing often restrained quick family reunion. The expellees were rarely kindly welcomed in the new places of settlement. Due to the precarious postwar situation, compatriots were seen as competitors for resources. In addition, some Germans regarded the Eastern provinces as foreign countries because of their distance from the more urban and economically more flourishing parts of Germany. Thus, East Prussians were sometimes considered intruders. Kossert even speaks in terms of "German racism" to refer to the attitude of Germans towards their eastern fellow citizens.[15] The research participants recall that they were called Poles or gypsies. Moreover, some expellees seem to have internalized this discourse to a point that they describe themselves in similar terms: "We came to the villages like gypsies!" (Eva). They came poor and hungry. Alfred remembers that the farmer who housed his family did not give any sheets to them. They were hungry. But they did not get more to eat than the food rationing although the farmer had a lot of food in stock. "And the farmer's wife grumbled: 'If you are

---

15 Kossert, *Kalte Heimat*, 71.

refugees, why didn't you take your cooking pots with you?'" Sixty-five years later, Alfred still concludes bitterly that he did not make many good experiences with the people from Pomerania. This includes experiences with his relatives, namely his grandmother who lived in Stralsund, Western Pomerania, and who did not want to house the family. Astonishingly, the grandmother had herself experienced deterritorialization after the First World War, when her hometown Memel became part of Lithuania and she left because she would otherwise have been obliged to adopt Lithuanian citizenship. Nevertheless, she did not have pity with Alfred's family. The interviewee recounts that his grandmother continuously complained about their presence, although his mother and the children searched for food and even provided it for other family members. He recalls that in June 1945, the Russian Commander of Stralsund called for refugees to go back to their homelands.[16] In order to stimulate their return, they did not receive food rationing any longer. The grandmother then pushed Alfred's mother to go back to East Prussia in order to save her husband's goods. But the way back home turned out to lead directly into Russian captivity. His mother, his brother and his sister could leave Russia in 1948. "But they kept me until 1949 as cheap labor, only for some food and drink and wretched clothes. Or you had to find it all on your own" (Alfred).

The hostility and mistrust of the local population towards the expellees perpetuated for several years until a certain normality set in: "We really felt like... we were called the riffraff of refugees... in the village, at school, everywhere" (Gerda). At school, Gerda spent the breaks with her sister. Contact to other children was very limited. She recalls that she did not have beautiful clothes like the other kids, that she could not have a meal with them and that they made fun of her. Renate, whose family was expelled from West Prussia, recalls that new children continuously arrived in the classes and that these refugees came from different regions. According to her observations, these children were intimidated and fearful, but as time went by, and especially if they succeeded well at school, they regained assurance.

---

16 The Russian position towards the refugees was inconsistent. For example, some Russian Commanders encouraged the return to their places of origin in June 1945, while they were not allowed to cross over the Oder and Neiße rivers, and even while the Poles had begun to expel the Germans at the end of the same month. This inconsistency is reported in the early 1950s in the first volume of the documentary of the expulsion of the Germans from East-Central Europe (*Die Vertreibung der deutschen Bevölkerung aus den Gebieten östlich der Oder-Neiße*, in collaboration with Werner Conze, Adolf Diestelkamp, Rudolf Laun, Peter Rassow and Hans Rothfels, ed. Theodor Schieder [Bonn: Bundesministerium für Vertriebene, Flüchtlinge und Kriegsgeschädigte, 1954]: 72–73).

For some expellees, the struggle to be accepted carried on for decades. Alfred tried hard to acquire the local dialect, but he did not manage to pass unnoticed. He quotes the people who commented on his accent: "You can speak *Platt* [a low-German dialect] but you will never be a real Mecklenburger [a native of Mecklenburg, Alfred's new region of residence]." Generally, the younger children got used to the new environment more quickly. Their parents did not keep them from assimilating because they wanted them to grow up without suffering.

In addition to flight and expulsion, the postwar experiences, particularly the lack of material resources and food, as well as the lack of warm human relationships, can also be considered as traumatic. Hardship determined the priorities of the early years after the war. Adolescents became responsible adults almost overnight and started to work immediately after resettlement. The expellees did usually work very hard in order to regain safety and to acquire material belongings. They struggled to improve their personal situation, to gain a place in society and to be recognized as individuals. Despite the difficulties, the Germans from the Eastern territories often managed to reach a social status that they themselves found satisfactory. They went their own ways and found their place within the host society. Nevertheless, it was due to the worry for survival that people conformed and integrated to the new places of living. In this sense, the integration of the refugees was formally a success.

Longing for the Places of Origin and Remembrance of the Old Home

Given the combination of postwar hardship, individual priorities and oppressive politics, no profound work of memory was undertaken by the new arrivals. Actually, they had been steadily undergoing difficulties since the enforced departure. Under these circumstances, the affected could not face the loss of the home and the homeland, but there was no complete suppression of *Heimweh* either (that is, the longing for the place one feels one belongs to). The East Prussians kept longing for their region of origin for years. In fact, some of them still feel homesick today and continue to feel that they belong to East Prussia. "My home is there [in East Prussia], I only live here," declares Edith. Obviously, the formal integration did not go together with full acceptation of the new places of residence as home.

For the first years after the war, postal addresses for official use continued to refer to the old home; the current address was followed by the old one. As Dietmar recalls, they would follow their own names with that of the person they were currently living with, "like it used to be during holidays." He does not remember when they stopped writing their address in this way. More generally, it is not easy to identify when the idea of the definite return was given up. The participants' accounts reveal the hope for a final return that persisted in their mind although they objectively knew that there would be no return. Kurt explains: "The wish to go back had always been there, but it wasn't realistic." The longing, which is highly emotional, resists facts and reason. A survey of the GDR's single party shows that an important minority of the population (22 percent) had not yet recognized the regime's decision to surrender the German Eastern territories in 1965 although it had been made official in 1950.[17] Nevertheless, the thesis is encountered in academic studies as well as in some expellees' accounts that the quick recognition of the new frontiers by the officials had supported the integration of the expellees in the GDR because it took away all "illusions of return."

Among adults, those who were conscious of the danger of expressing their attachment to the old home adjusted to the official GDR demand and pretended to conform. But they were afraid of their children's behavior. Children could easily say something that went against the grain of the official position, and this might have consequences for the whole family. So it happened frequently that adults chose to lower their voice or that they completely avoided talking about the old home in the presence of their children. This had been seen as a necessary evil in order to protect the younger ones as well as the family from external repressions on the one hand, and on the other hand as a way of guarding the children from the adult's suffering. Alfred and Hedwig, a couple of East Prussians who were fifteen and thirteen years old when they fled, decided not to talk about their origins with their children. Hedwig says: "We did not want to burden them." Alfred adds: "It had always been difficult. Our whole family lived in the West [i.e., West Germany]." Those who tried to maintain close contact across the border between the two German states were observed and questioned on their political convictions. Thus, the people from the Eastern territories did not only have to cope with their altered circumstances as expellees, but also with the threats and pressures that weighed on the whole population under the dictatorship. Dietmar describes the consequences: "People retreated into their private lives. It was typical for people in the GDR to retreat to the family, to the garden, to shut themselves off from the world around them, to isolate themselves from all public things." In the family circle, one was able to talk more frankly. Thus, their former home still existed and was remembered, but only behind closed doors.

---

17 Cf. Schwartz, "Der historische Osten in der Erinnerungskultur der DDR," 73.

The expellees searched for and created occasions in order to maintain a relationship towards the places of origin, as Benno explains: "In the GDR, according to the official version, we were emigrants. Nevertheless, there were niches to commemorate the Heimat." Benno availed himself of a "work and holiday camp"[18] and two trips with music groups "to find out more about the situation of the Eastern territories." He knows that some retired people participated in gatherings in West Germany. As they had finished their active working lives, the risk of repression by the State was smaller. It is also reported that expellees met in churches and that the former homeland was a topic on the church's threshold after service. One of the interviewees describes the church as a meeting point: "The church was open to everybody. Families met. Afterwards, the men played cards together" (Editha). Bendel argues that church could even become a new kind of Heimat.[19] But the GDR regime mistrusted religious activities, so church might present a niche, but affiliation to religious groups could lead to pressure from the system. An individuals' risk for exclusion could double if they were a religious expellee.

Some expellees state that solidarity and a deep bond, which did not really need to be made explicit, characterized the relationship between East Prussian expellees: "At school, we gathered, without saying a word and we ate our East Prussian cake" (Benno). People identified each other by their accent. Favors could be exchanged amongst expellees with the same origins. Alfred obtained a job thanks to an East Prussian nurse who facilitated his examination. Siegfried recalls that refugees from East and West Prussia as well as Bessarabia came together in the village. As the village children knew each other and used to play together, the refugees also banded together. The two groups of children played games against each other. According to Siegfried, origins were also significant when it came to dating, as the refugees did not have a good standing amongst the native people. He personally married an East Prussian girl. Siegfried recalls that differentiation began to vanish at the beginning of the 1960s. In contrast, Helga, who did not leave East Prussia until 1948, did not experience any solidarity, not even with fellow expellees. "We were not integrated. Nobody supported us," is how she sums up her experience after resettlement. Instead, mutual support within the family was essential for survival. Helga reports that after the fall

---

18 *Lager für Arbeit und Erholung*, an optional program for pupils during summer vacation with daily working hours as well as cultural activities.
19 Cf. Rainer Bendel, "Einführung," in *Vertriebene finden Heimat in der Kirche: Integrationsprozesse im geteilten Deutschland nach 1945*, ed. Rainer Bendel (Cologne, Weimar, Vienna: Böhlau, 2008): 1–12.

of the Berlin Wall she was surprised to learn that there were so many East Prussians around her.

The expellees' conception of their Heimat is directly related to personal memories and accounts from close relatives. Thus, their idea of Heimat covers the childhood home: the parental house and the immediate environment. Considering that the interviewees were still young when they left East Prussia, the places they used to frequent are very limited. Research participants aged ten and older when they had to leave their home argue that memories of one's own of the places of origin are needed to be able to feel real homesickness. As positive memories from the former home are mixed up with negative memories from war, flight and expulsion, their comprehension of homesickness is bittersweet. According to these older expellees, their younger brothers or sisters who do not have direct memories are somehow privileged because they do not carry the burden of bad memories. Nevertheless, interviews with expellees who were younger than ten when they left East Prussia reveal ways of developing a 'Heimat consciousness' anyway. Dietmar explains that he grew up with two old aunts who were like grandmothers to him. He constantly heard them talking about Königsberg and East Prussia. Given the fact that Dietmar, his brothers and sisters, his parents and the two aunts all originated from the same city, and given that they all still lived close together after the war, they could easily share memories and recall different aspects of the former home. Thus, it is mostly from family accounts that Dietmar learned about his place of birth. "And I continued to live in this family, and home was always East Prussia." Dietmar cannot say for how long this idea of the home persisted. Curiously, he explains that this was the case much longer for himself than for his older brothers or sisters. The latter quickly left the house in order to work while young Dietmar stayed at home and soaked up the accounts he listened to. He concludes that he is "emotionally" linked to the former home while his older brother, who was already a teenager when he left Königsberg, is "internally" linked to it, meaning that he internalized the feeling over there. More precisely, Dietmar states that his brother's emotional attachment has a real basis, an experienced space. When Gerda is asked in which situations the former home was mentioned within her family, she answers without hesitation that this occurred at Christmas. She can give an account of anecdotes that her mother told frequently. But she also explains that she does not personally recall that these episodes took place in East Prussia. For sure, Christmas is generally a festive moment shared with the family. But Gerda's family struggled hard to survive and lost their father and their accustomed environment because of the war. According to Gerda, it was difficult for her mother to talk about her old home. The Heimweh in this case is composed of a few good memories passed on to the children. Gerda's account reveals that her mother did not try to transmit a special image of the Heimat or to perpetuate the Heimweh. Asked what kind of thing was mentioned, Gerda reconstructs the domestic interior of the old house in East Prussia thanks to her mother's descriptions. She repeats that she was six when she left:

> I can... I know... I cannot... what... where there was the bedroom, I know that. In the sitting room, I remember – not the wallpaper; there was wall paint done by Uncle Emil. And then, I don't know... mum always said that we had a vertiko [piece of storage furniture with two doors and a drawer] in there. And... no, not a sofa, but a *chaise longue*. And in the front, there was a table with chairs. Yes, when I tried to remember... yes... but not really. But what I recall very clearly is that in the kitchen we always sat around a big table and we ate together and so on. And where there was the kitchen cupboard. And she [the mother] had an older wardrobe with two doors; she put our winter clothes in it, during the summer. But I do not know anything else... you know, we were not really interested in it.

In this quote, Gerda mixes up descriptive elements about the disposition of furniture with memories about her family as well as her own memories and those of her mother. Her final sentence ("we were not really interested in it") is an excuse that she is not able to reconstruct better, but it is also an admission: interest was limited. Nevertheless, the quote shows that the former home and particularly the former house were a topic within her family. Dietmar's family reminisced over the homeland in folksongs sung everywhere and all the time. Up until now, Hans-Jürgen has chosen this kind of intangible heritage in order to express his attachment to the former homeland. Dietmar's parents tracked down several friends from a Königsberg sports club who were then living in West Germany. According to Dietmar, these contacts contributed to remembering the old homeland.

Souvenir objects can play an important role for memory and remembering amongst migrants. As Lowenthal underlines, "[t]o own a piece of the past can promote a fruitful connection with it."[20] Fourcade studied the place that items reminding diasporics of their origins hold in the domestic sphere, as well as their function in identity construction.[21] Her research reveals that such objects gain heritage value whether they are for decorative purpose or for daily use, and that they enable the diaspora to grow roots again.[22] The German expellees in the GDR could not reach a state of re-rooting with the very few objects they might have owned. Usually, flight and expulsion did not allow taking along

---

20 David Lowenthal, *The Past is a Foreign Country* (Cambridge: Cambridge UP, 1985): 44.
21 Marie-Blanche Fourcade, *Habiter l'Arménie au Québec: Ethnographie d'un patrimoine domestique en diaspora* (doctoral thesis, Université Laval, 2007).
22 Fourcade, *Habiter l'Armémie au Québec*, 410.

many objects. Gerda remembers her luggage: "Three of us, Erika, Ulla and me, already went to school. Mum put things into our school bags: a shirt for each of us, a pair of briefs for each of us, and I think a towel, too. That was all." Russian soldiers often confiscated the few objects of more value that the expellees had with them, such as watches or wedding rings. Pillaging occurred along the escape route. Gerda retains two photographs of the pre-flight period: the first shows the mother and three of her daughters, the other is a wedding photo of her parents. Gerda does not have any memory of her father, a soldier. An aunt gave her the pictures, which are framed and placed on the table close to Gerda's bed. She gets up and fetches the picture to the interview table: "That's the only picture we have. Everything stayed behind." Renate explains: "That was something for the refugees, too... that they did not have anything from their past for their proper identity. Nothing, nothing." Alfred keeps an object from his father, a sculpted moose that survived the war. The moose is an emblematic animal of East Prussia and Alfred explains, not without pride, that his particular region of origin was known for its game. Charlotte also keeps a handcrafted moose in her small room in a residential home for the elderly. The artifact does not only stand for the East Prussian homeland, it also reminds her of her husband who carved it in Russian captivity. This moose is nowadays her most important personal item. It is well visible from her bed where she has to spend the whole day. Finally, the aforementioned objects are as much related to the family memory as they evoke the places of origin. Altogether, the souvenir items are kept in special spots in the expellees' living space or are even worn on their body. In the days of the Berlin Wall, Charlotte wore a neck chain with an East Prussian pendant. The need to keep a material souvenir with her constantly was so important that – although she was an openly devoted communist – she ignored the fact that such avowals for the former homeland were not tolerated by the system. The pendant hidden under her jersey from the controlling gaze of committed communist spies represents a silent and private way to express the love for the Heimat.

Return Tourism

As the years went by, the impossibility of final return was increasingly recognized. A temporary return became the new objective. The longing then meant that the expellees' only wish was to see the old places again. With the fall of the Iron Curtain in 1989, this kind of return became possible. People did not have exaggerated expectations towards the former home. They did not expect to find the lost paradise because they knew that the war had brought large-scale destruction to the Eastern territories. They further knew from their own experience in a communist state that the neighboring countries of the Eastern Bloc would not have engaged much in reconstruction or conservation of historic structures. However, a realistic attitude does not prevent the expellees from pain once they undertake the journey back to their native villages and towns. The visits caused intense emotional and physical responses. The immediate contact with the places of origin enabled the returnees to enter into a dialogue with their own past. They situate themselves in the encountered space and in relation to eventually found objects. The physical presence in the authentic sites sets off a narrative about the places, and it also promotes auto-narration. Although uprooted, the tourists still somehow feel they belong to the territory, and their belonging is revealed and justified by their memories of the place.

Psychotherapy recognizes narration for its healing functions. Pennebaker et al. show that the therapeutic effect does not take place if an individual simply goes through experiences and emotions again and again, but only when they are cognitively structured, as is the case with narratives: "This structure promotes the assimilation and understanding of the event and reduces the associated emotional arousal. In other words, translating traumas and their accompanying images and emotions into language demands that all features of the experience be encoded and stored in a more organized, coherent, and simplified manner."[23] Thus, the expellees put their experiences into words, and moreover, they explicitly engage in a reflection in order to comprehend their own past, to understand their emotions and their place attachment. These reflections translate into a certain awareness and interpretation of the return experience. Hans-Jürgen describes the phenomenon as follows: "Throughout the return, it's like entering into the inner self." It constitutes an act of introspection, an effort to analyze one's own state of mind. The tourists question themselves about their nostalgia, whether aiming to justify it or to comprehend it, in order to come to terms with it. Each individual looks for their own way to make sense of what they perceive as a senseless past. Introspection is part of a process of distancing from past experience. It initiates a more general reflection about one's biography. Despite various difficulties like traumatic experiences of war and displacement, loss of the homeland and family members, postwar misery and poverty, limited possibilities as regards to education and formation, political constraints, and so on, the unanimous current discourse of the expellees is one of success. The individuals assert that their success is the fruit of their courage, their tenac-

---

23 James W. Pennebaker, Tracy J. Mayne and Martha E. Francis, "Linguistic Predictors of Adaptive Bereavement," in *Journal of Personality and Social Psychology* 97.4 (1997): 863–871, 864.

ity, their strength and sometimes their ingenuity. Today, these elderly tourists draw a positive balance of their life. The return visits enable them to engage in a process of critical remembrance, to obtain a certain distance to their past and to gain quietude in the last stage in their life. For many expellees, this "therapeutic" effect unfolds thanks to repeated journeys. And physical strength permitting, the most assiduous are ready to leave again on route to their roots: "Every year, I say to myself that it might be the last trip. In spring, I decide whether I can leave again, if my health allows it" (Eva). Surprised by the will and the strength of the elderly tourists a tour guide shouts: "The Heimat heals!" (Friedhelm). Even if the urge to go back again and again might seem "pathological," as Edith declares with a wink, actually, the return visits initiate reflections and narrations which go far beyond the travel period.

During the return visits, not only old images and imagination are compared to the present reality but new images are perceived and memorized. New impressions add to remembrance, perhaps overwriting it: Memory is updated. Kurt reveals that images well-kept for decades suddenly disappear: "What happened to me is that I had memorized everything, even the smallest detail. And when I came back for the first time [to the old home], memory dissolved." Memory constitutes an "invisible luggage" that the expellees have carried around since their forced departure in the 1940s. This luggage may sometimes be a heavy burden when the painful or even traumatic memories are stressed. During the return visits, the expellees can take this weight off their shoulders. Actually, several expellees explain that recurrent dreams and nightmares disappeared once they had gone back to the old home. Thus, the return can have a liberating effect of "forgetting." Faced up to their difficult past, the expellees manage to leave bad memories behind at least partially. However, they actively try to keep good memories. The latter are usually linked to positive emotions. Thus, it is not important whether memories are real or constructed. More essential is the work of memory and the mourning[24] that this kind of return tourism allows them to fulfil. Nevertheless, the older generation, expellees born before 1935, continue to feel particularly attached to their native villages and towns. The tour guide Friedhelm observes that those who grew up in the old Heimat feel the need to savor their return intensively. According to him, the older tourists want to spend several hours or a whole day around the former home in order to walk again on the old paths. They undertake the journeys to refresh their

---

24 Cf. Jean-Didier Urbain, "Tourisme de mémoire: Un travail de deuil positif," in *Cahier Espaces. Tourisme de mémoire 80*, ed. Mylène Leenhardt-Salvan (Paris: Éditions touristiques européennes, 2003): 5–7, 7.

memories. The guide Manfred adds that for these elderly people, the circle of life doubles back to the starting point. As a matter of fact, the rediscovery of the childhood home leads to the completion of a lifelong quest. The visits allow them to get close to the old house, to touch it, to re-dwell symbolically, to unite with the place. They eliminate the long-lasting physical distance. Subsequently, they can distance themselves from their nostalgia as well as from traumatic memories. The return as a form of accomplishment provides emotional stability. The expellees achieve inner peace. Furthermore, they realize the new reality of the places of origin. To think profoundly about their own experiences allows them to objectivize their relation towards the places of origin. Often, the individual return becomes less important throughout time and with recurrent return experiences. In parallel, the collective dimension of organized return tourism activities gains importance. This is of particular interest considering the fact that the expellees who lived in the GDR did not have many opportunities to meet fellow expellees and to exchange past experiences with them. The group tours put emphasis on the discovery of a larger East Prussian region and on a collective German heritage stretching back to the Middle Ages. In that way, return tourism allows the expellees to identify otherwise with their former homeland and to renew their relationship towards it beyond their very personal experiences.

As for the younger tourists, a guide explains that their quest during the return visits is different from what the elderly look for:

> The younger ones, those who know their places of origin mostly from their parents' reports, they say: Well, I want to be in the authentic sites again, where I once lived, where I was born, where my parents were... Only to see all this again, go and see what the sky looks like over there, or pick a flower, and so on. It's more like a gesture. (Friedhelm)

Actually, some tourists believe that it is possible to leave nostalgia and the old home behind:

> Considering that the Heimat no longer exists and that the old life cannot be re-established, the wheel has come full circle [...], a sense of irreversibility and finiteness emerges. That's how an inner distance towards the past can be achieved, a definitive goodbye, like a case of bereavement [which is closed] after mourning. (Dietmar)

The accomplishments of the return journeys as well as individual reflections lead to such conclusions. Souvenirs can be brought from the return visits. Some expellees display objects brought back from recent journeys to East Prussia. Pictures showing landscapes and buildings that are typical for the region are encountered in several expellee houses. Amber is also very common amongst expellees. It evokes the East Prussian coast of the Baltic Sea, a region that boasts the biggest open air amber mines in the world. The amber brought back can be jewelry, a keychain, a gift for family and friends, and so on. In addition to these souvenirs, some other things now available can be charged with sense and emotions. For example, Alfred welcomes me sitting at a big table cleaned up for the interview. He has a great number of maps in front of him. When he starts his account unfolding a map very carefully, he declares: "What the bible means to a Christian, is what my maps of East Prussia mean to me."

By Way of Synthesis: Emergence and Decrease of a Diaspora-like Community

It is not the purpose of this reflection to show that the Germans from the former Eastern territories actually fit in any definition or model of diaspora. Following Tölölyan, "[i]t may be best to think of diaspora not as the name of a fixed concept and social formation but as a process of collective identification and form of identity."[25] The German expellees have been going through this process for seven decades now. Considering the period since the war allows, on the one hand, to offer a more differentiated picture of the integration processes the expellees have undergone, and, on the other hand, to examine tendencies of community building. The results show that feelings of longing and belonging amongst East Prussian expellees change throughout this period. Tölölyan underlines that collective displacement due to catastrophe forges diasporas to which the work of memory, commemoration and mourning are central, and who have, amongst others, the salient characteristic of a rhetoric of return.[26] The GDR prohibited an open expression of all those. Nevertheless, the need for recognition and commemoration as well as the wish to see the East Prussian home again were latently present during the oppressive GDR era. The ethnological approach offers insights into the way in which the loss of the East Prussian home, longing and belonging were experienced and expressed and how integration ultimately took place. Thus, acclimatization to the new places of settlement is fashioned by the personal experiences of flight and expulsion, the postwar period, the attitude towards the GDR dictatorship, the niches found, and so on. The narratives of the interviewed expellees reveal that they sometimes made integration efforts compelled by the circumstances and due to their desire to be accepted by society. The ex-

25 Khachig Tölölyan, "The Contemporary Discourse of Diaspora Studies," *Comparative Studies of South Asia, Africa and the Middle East* 27.3 (2007): 647–655, 649–650.
26 Tölölyan, "The Contemporary Discourse of Diaspora Studies", 649.

pellees in the GDR factually recognized the non-return to their home, but they experienced continuous emotional longing. Those who had experienced flight and expulsion as adults felt a strong urge to speak of their places of origin. Although their degree of commitment varied, they conveyed some knowledge and emotions linked to the former homeland to their children. The latter, in turn, chose whether or not to pass the memory on to their descendants. Their decision was guided by the will to protect their children from both, the oppressive regime and the potentially burdening family history. Also, responding to external circumstances and the politics which aimed to prevent the creation of communities, the expellees individually retained their memories, but they did not experience a sense of collectivity. The fall of the Iron Curtain represents the turning point that was needed for the expellees in the GDR to engage with their collective past. For two and a half decades now, the expellees have been able to exchange ideas more openly about their past, they can experience community with fellows and make up for decades spent in comparative isolation. Thus, gatherings, monuments, commemoration ceremonies and return tourism as collective practices only became possible after 1989. These diasporic activities allow them to renew their relationship to the former home and help to overcome the strong feelings of homesickness. The expellees' conception of home is widened: from the childhood home and parental house to which they are linked by personal memories towards a larger collective and historical homeland, that is, East Prussia as a whole. They actively engage in reflections about their Heimat consciousness.

The situation of the GDR expellees quickly adjusted to the one of their fellow expellees in West Germany. The latter largely supported this development. Moreover, the political changes not only allow visits to the former homeland, but they also enable the establishment of close contacts between former and current inhabitants of the former German Eastern territories. The Germans provide humanitarian help and they engage in the safeguarding of cultural heritage. Reconciliation takes places from below. Tölölyan highlights that a "sustained and organized commitment to maintaining relations with kin communities elsewhere, and with the homeland" are a fundamental characteristic of diasporas.[27] But just as quickly as an expellee community (including those living in the former GDR) developed after 1989, it is current declining. Most of the survivors have become so old that they can no longer attend expellee activities. Moreover, what the elderly are allowed to express today is rarely passed on to their descendants. Especially in the former GDR, there is so much to clear up about the past and

---

27 Tölölyan, "The Contemporary Discourse of Diaspora Studies", 649.

history after the breakdown of the communist regime. People who grew up within the system and additionally with the taboo surrounding flight and expulsion and the Eastern territories rarely develop a sustained interest in East Prussia. After the fall of the Berlin Wall, they had to adjust to a new system and maybe to address their own experiences under the GDR dictatorship. Indeed, their FRG counterparts seem to be more engaged in personal quests about their being grandchildren of the war. For example, they focus on the effects of the war on their parents' attitude, their upbringing and internalized behaviors. But this kind of personal quest is not specific to descendants of expellees. However, it can take the latter to travel to the family's places of origin. Yet, the collective aspect important to those who consciously experienced flight and expulsion appears to be removed. The former Eastern territories no longer evoke a sense of longing and belonging in these later-born generations. Finally, the integration politics from above as well as the integration efforts from below led to the completion of the integration process several decades after the war.

Anke Patzelt
Notions of Home and Belonging for *Alteinwanderer* and *Neueinwanderer* in the German-Speaking Community in Ottawa

Abstract: By drawing on in-depth interviews and participant observations, this chapter examines the extent to which members of the German-speaking community in the city of Ottawa, Canada, construct notions of home and belonging. A special focus is placed on the differences in the understanding of these terms between the so-called *Alteinwanderer* – German speakers who migrated to Canada in the era immediately after the Second World War, and the *Neueinwanderer* – German speakers who migrated more recently, i.e., in the last twenty-five years. Factors such as the different social circumstances framing migration processes, age, time of residency in Canada, as well as communication and transportation possibilities are taken into consideration when analyzing the categories of home and belonging. The results show that the Alteinwanderer, after having lived in Canada for most of their lives, have developed strong ties to the country and perceive it as their permanent home, although they maintain their "Germanness." The Neueinwanderer, on the contrary, perceive Canada as a new temporary home, whereas Germany is seen as their true homeland.[1]

In recent years, international migration has increased significantly. More and more people are moving across national borders and settling in regions outside their country of origin, both temporarily and permanently. It is argued that nowadays, as a result of this development, identities are multiple in character.[2] Formerly stable categories, such as nation-states, which used to determine collective identities, have been undermined by increased international mobility, e.g., in past decades, the notion of national identity has been challenged by global as

---

1 This chapter partly draws on material I collected as part of a field study for a master thesis project within the German speaking community of Ottawa in the spring of 2013. Parts of this chapter, such as the theoretical perspectives, the historical background, the description of the research environment and parts of the analysis, therefore heavily draw on the final version of my master thesis with the title: *Of 'Modern Immigrants' and 'German Bread': A Case Study of Ethnic Identity Construction Amongst Contemporary German Immigrants in the City of Ottawa, Canada* which was defended upon completion of the two-years master's program of International Migration and Ethnic Relations at Malmö University in August 2013.
2 Stuart Hall, "Introduction: Who Needs 'Identity'?", in *Questions of Cultural Identity*, eds. Stuart Hall, Paul du Gay (London, Thousand Oaks, New Delhi: SAGE, 1996): 1–17, 4; Wsevolod W. Isajiw, "Definition and Dimensions of Ethnicity: A Theoretical Framework," in *Challenges of Measuring an Ethnic World: Science, Politics and Realities: Proceedings of the Joint Canada-United States Conference on the Measurement of Ethnicity April 1–3, 1992*, ed. Statistics Canada, US Bureau of the Census (Washington, DC: US Government Printing Office, 1993): 407–427.

well as local identities.[3] Migrants moving across borders – physical, social, and cultural ones – construct identities which go beyond those borders. One's participation – economically, socially, politically, and culturally – in a new host society, whilst maintaining ties with one's original home country, further promotes a multidimensional construction of identities. Accordingly, migrants shape new understandings and images of themselves.[4] In these processes, the connection to and the identification with their home country, as felt by the people residing in immigrant situations, play an important role. This chapter explores the notions of home and belonging amongst Germans residing in immigrant situations. By drawing on in-depth interviews and participant observations conducted amongst first-generation German immigrants, it examines the ways in which members of the German-speaking community in Canada's capital, Ottawa, construct these notions. The chapter particularly focuses on the differences in the understanding of these terms between the so-called *Alteinwanderer* – German speakers who immigrated to Canada immediately after the Second World War, and the *Neueinwanderer* – German speakers who migrated more recently, i.e., in the past twenty-five years. It argues that the changing social and political circumstances in Germany since the end of the Second World War, e.g., from a war-torn country to a politically, socially, and economically stable democracy; but also those circumstances existing on a global level, e.g., new possibilities within communication and transportation, have caused these differences. Moreover, this chapter shows that other factors, such as one's age and time of residency in Canada, need to be taken into consideration when analyzing the distinctive understandings and perceptions of home and belonging amongst the two groups.

Theorizing Home, Homeland and Belonging

The concepts of home, homeland and belonging have been widely discussed in the fields of diaspora and transnational studies. The ways in which these concepts are constructed and seen in diasporic societies can yield important information about the immigrants' relationship with their old and new homeland and, thus, about the extent to which they identify with it. Even though, originally, the term diaspora was used for describing "the exile of the Jews from their historic homeland and their dispersion throughout many lands, signifying as

---

3 Stuart Hall, "Ethnicity: Identity and Difference," *Radical America* 23.4 (1989): 9–20, 12–13; Stuart Hall, "Culture, Community, Nation," *Cultural Studies* 7.3 (1993): 349–363, 354.
4 Vijay Agnew, "Introduction," in *Diaspora, Memory, and Identity. A Search for Home*, ed. Vijay Agnew (Toronto, Buffalo, London: U of Toronto P, 2004): 3–17, 5.

well the oppression and moral degradation implied by that dispersion,"[5] the traditional definition of diaspora has undergone significant changes in recent years. Nowadays it is used in a number of different contexts and, according to some scholars, it is used to describe what might otherwise be called immigrant societies or minorities.[6] James Clifford, for example, states that "diasporic forms of longing, memory, and (dis)identification are shared by a broad spectrum of minority and migrant populations,"[7] and Canadian sociologist Anne-Marie Fortier argues that "immigrant populations experience 'diasporic moments'."[8] In a similar way, Sheffer puts forward the following definition of what he calls "ethno-national-diasporas":

> [T]hey were created as a result of either forced or voluntary migration (most of the more recent incipient and established diasporas have been created as a result of voluntary rather than imposed migration); they consciously maintain their ethno-national identity; they create communal organizations, or are on the way to creating them; equally consciously, they maintain explicit and implicit ties with their homelands; even if only in a rudimentary form, they develop trans-state networks connecting them with their respective homelands and their brethren in other host countries and they face grave dilemmas concerning dual and divided loyalties to their homelands and host countries.[9]

A detailed examination of the term diaspora would go beyond the scope of this chapter; however, what needs to be highlighted here is its almost interchangeable use with terms such as 'immigrant societies,' its transnational character and, finally, its close connection to ideas of home and homeland. Thus, the connection to, and the identification with, the old homeland play an important role in the formation and life of both diasporic and immigrant societies. Diasporas and immigrant communities often have a transnational function and thus create a sense of belonging and ethnicity that is not limited to the territory of a nation-

---

5 William Safran, "Diasporas in Modern Societies: Myths of Homeland and Return," *Diaspora* 1.1 (1991): 83–99, 83.
6 Agnew, "Introduction"; James Clifford, "Diasporas," *Cultural Anthropology* 9.3 (1994): 302–338; Safran, "Diasporas in Modern Societies: Myths of Homeland and Return"; Gabriel Sheffer, "A New Field of Study: Modern Diasporas in International Politics," in *Modern Diasporas in International Politics*, ed. Gabriel Sheffer (London: Croom Helm, 1986): 5–28; Khachig Tölölyan, "The Nation State and its Others: In Lieu of a Preface," *Diaspora* 1.1 (1991): 3–7.
7 Clifford, "Diasporas," 304.
8 Anne-Marie Frontier, "Bringing It All (back) Home. Italian-Canadians' Remaking of Canadian History," in *Communities across Borders. New Immigrants and Transnational Cultures*, eds. Paul Kennedy, Victor Roudometof (London, New York: Routledge, 2002): 103–115, 104.
9 Gabriel Sheffer, "The Emergence of New Ethno-National Diasporas," *Migration* 28 (1995): 5–28, 9.

state. However, the dichotomy between here and there, between the old and the new home(land), is always present.[10] This dichotomy is not merely a result of the movement of migrants, but also of the process of globalization. The time-space compression which has resulted from the process of globalization allows today's immigrants to maintain close ties with their home country, both in terms of family and social, as well as political, economic and cultural, relations.[11] These circumstances are assumed to have an influence on the consciousness and, thus, also on the identity construction of people residing in diasporic or transnational situations. It is claimed that diasporics often have "a double consciousness," which "is caught between 'here' and 'there'."[12] People feel that they belong to their old home country but simultaneously feel attached to their new host society. Thus, notions of home and belonging are created in "dynamic processes, involving the acts of imagining, creating, unmaking, changing, losing and moving 'homes'."[13]

From a traditional and more static viewpoint, home is often seen as the physical place where one is living and finds shelter.[14] Beyond this, the term is frequently related to ideas such as "'family', 'community' or 'homeland/nation'," or, quite simply, the place to which one feels one belongs.[15] In more recent years, however, this relatively stable conceptualization of home has been undermined by processes of globalization and increased international movement.[16] Home could be the place of birth, or the place of current residence.[17] Moreover, it is no longer seen solely as a physical place, but also as a symbolic space in which meaning is created.[18] As such, home becomes a signifier for cultural and social values and moreover can be found in routines and practices, as

---

10 Agnew, "Introduction," 4.

11 Michael Kearney, "The Local and the Global: The Anthropology of Globalization and Transnationalism," *Annual Review of Anthropology* 24 (1995): 547–565, 551; Agnew, "Introduction," 11; Paul Kennedy, Victor Roudometof, "Transnationalism in a Global Age," in *Communities across Borders. New Immigrants and Transnational Cultures*, eds. Paul Kennedy, Victor Roudometof (London, New York: Routledge, 2002): 1–26, 13.

12 Agnew, "Introduction," 14; Paul Gilroy, "It Ain't Where You're From, It's Where You're At...: The Dialectics of Diasporic Identification," *Third Text* 5.13 (1991): 3–16, 4.

13 Nadje Al-Ali, Khalid Koser, "Transnationalism, International Migration and Home," in *New Approaches to Migration? Transnational Communities and the Transformation of Home*, eds. Nadje Al-Ali, Khalid Koser (London, New York: Routledge, 2002): 1–14, 6.

14 Mary Douglas, "The Idea of Home: A Kind of Space," *Social Research* 58.1 (1991): 287–307.

15 Al-Ali, Koser, "Transnationalism, International Migration and Home," 6.

16 Al-Ali, Koser, "Transnationalism, International Migration and Home," 7.

17 Avtar Brah, *Cartographies of Diaspora. Contesting Identities* (London: Routledge, 1996): 3.

18 Al-Ali, Koser, "Transnationalism, International Migration and Home," 7.

well as "in styles of dress and address, in memories and myths, in stories carried around in one's head."[19] Thus, it "brings together memory and longing, the ideational, the affective and the physical, the spatial and the temporal, the local and the global, the positively evaluated and the negatively."[20] Therefore, home is an important vessel for one's sense of belonging. It describes not only the place, but also other more abstract categories of where one belongs.

Similarly, the notion of homeland is relatively fluid. It is commonly claimed that migration reinforces and strengthens identification with one's homeland.[21] The literature offers numerous definitions and understandings of the term.[22] The homeland can be anything from a fixed geographical location, a politically defined state, or a more abstract understanding.[23] It is often associated with such aspects as "language, nation, home, family, community, tradition, landscape, region, or place."[24] In today's common understanding and discourse, homeland is often understood as the country where one was born, or from where one's ancestors originate. However, even though the homeland might be perceived in spatial terms, it is mainly a "mental image" which is captured in the passage of time: "The true homeland exists in the mind of the migrant," and furthermore, "[w]hat is peculiar about the homeland is that it emerges as a mental image in a recollection once one is no longer there. [...] It represents a lack of something, a missing piece. It is nostalgia."[25] In this regard, the notion of memory becomes important. As Vijay Agnew stresses: "Memories establish a connection between our individual past and our collective past (our origins, heritage, and history). The past is always with us, and it defines our present; it resonates in our voices, hovers over our silence, and explains how we came

---

19 Nigel Rapport, Andrew Dawson, "The Topic of the Book," in *Migrants of Identity. Perceptions of Home in a World of Movement*, eds. Nigel Rapport, Andrew Dawson (Oxford: Berg, 1998): 3–18, 7.
20 Rapport, Dawson, "The Topic of the Book," 8.
21 Orm Øverland, "Old and New Homelands, Old and New Mythologies. The Creation of Ethnic Memory in the United States," in *Migrants and the Homeland. Images, Symbols, and Realities*, ed. Harald Runblom (Smedjebacken: Fälth & Hässler, 2000): 43–73, 43.
22 Felicita Medved, "The Concept of Homeland," in *Migrants and the Homeland. Images, Symbols, and Realities*, ed. Harald Runblom (Smedjebacken: Fälth & Hässler, 2000): 74–96, 76.
23 Harald Runblom, "Introduction: Homeland as Imagination and Reality," in *Migrants and the Homeland. Images, Symbols, and Realities*, ed. Harald Runblom (Smedjebacken: Fälth & Hässler, 2000): 9–30, 10.
24 Medved, "The Concept of Homeland," 76.
25 Charles Westin, "Migration, Time, and Space," in *Migrants and the Homeland. Images, Symbols, and Realities*, ed. Harald Runblom (Smedjebacken: Fälth & Hässler, 2000): 33–42, 41–42.

to be ourselves and to inhabit what we call 'our homes'."[26] Agnew accentuates that our past, and thus our memories, influence and even construct the way in which we perceive our present.[27] Through remembering and communicating our memories we present our past (and present) and thus construct an important part of our identity. This is, however, not a fixed construction, but one which changes over time, as the way in which we remember constantly evolves, depending on the context and situation.[28] Thus, the image of the homeland is dynamic, influenced by circumstances including, for example: age, social and family status, time of residency, as well as level of education, in both the receiving and the sending society.[29] This is true nowadays more than ever due to the international media, communication and transportation networks, which allow an up-to-date contact with the homeland.[30]

German Migration to Canada from the 1950s until Today

According to statistics, German-Canadians form the third largest ethnic group of European origin in Canada. Today, around 400,000 people live in Canada whose mother tongue is German[31] and around 3.2 million claim to be of German ethnic origin.[32] With migration from German-speaking areas starting in the sixteenth century, 'Germans' can look back on a long and enduring migration history to Canada.[33] One of the most significant immigration periods from Germany to Canada were the years between 1951 and 1957.[34]

---

26 Agnew, "Introduction," 3.
27 Agnew, "Introduction," 3.
28 Agnew, "Introduction," 9–10.
29 Runblom, "Introduction: Homeland as Imagination and Reality," 9–10.
30 Westin, "Migration, Time, and Space," 35–36.
31 "Census Profile. 2011 Census" (24 October 2012), *Statistics Canada*, Catalogue no. 98–316-XWE, Ottawa <http://www12.statcan.gc.ca/census-recensement/2011/dp-pd/prof/index.cfm?Lang=E> (acc. October 15, 2014).
32 "2006 Census of Population," *Statistics Canada*, Catalogue no. 97–562-XCB2006006 <http://www12.statcan.gc.ca/census-recensement/2006/dp-pd/tbt/Rp-eng.cfm?LANG=E&APATH=3&DETAIL=0&DIM=0&FL=A&FREE=0&GC=0&GID=0&GK=0&GRP=1&PID=92333&PRID=0&PTYPE=88971,97154&S=0&SHOWALL=0&SUB=0&Temporal=2006&THEME=80&VID=0&VNAMEE=&VNAMEF> (acc. December 8, 2012).
33 Hartmut Froeschle, *The German-Canadians. A Concise History / Die Deutschkanadier. Geschichtlicher Überblick* (Toronto: Historical Society of Mecklenburg Upper Canada, 1992).

During the Second World War, Canada had halted immigration for all German citizens, lifting the ban only in 1950.[35] With the withdrawal of this restriction, a migration boom of German immigrants to Canada began. Having lost the war, Germany was facing severe social and economic crises. Thousands of ethnic Germans from the eastern territories of Europe had been displaced from their homes, now seeking refuge in the western parts of Germany, which led to overpopulation. The country was in ruins, there was a lack of food, of housing and employment. As a result, many people did not see a future in their home country.[36] Canada, on the other hand, had survived without any major economic losses, its territory untouched by the war. Thus, the country was intact and its economy was flourishing.[37] Indeed, Canada was in need of an increased labor force during that time and, thus, for the millions of Germans who were without a job, it was a desirable destination.[38] In the postwar influx, between 1951 and 1957, approximately 200,000 national and ethnic Germans arrived in Canada, representing 17.6 percent of all immigrants coming to the country during this period.[39]

It was only at the end of the 1950s, when conditions in Germany improved, that this influx of German immigrants to Canada started to decline.[40] During the 1970s, the number of German newcomers decreased to around 5,000 per year. In the following decades this decline continued, although immigration never entirely stopped.[41] Today, Canada is still amongst the top eleven destination countries attracting German immigrants[42] with about 3,000 Germans moving there

---

34 Roland E. Schmalz, "Former Enemies Come to Canada: Ottawa and the Postwar German Immigration Boom, 1951–57," Diss. U of Ottawa, 2000: 1–2.

35 Gerhard Bassler, "Deutsche Einwanderung und Siedlung in Kanada" [1983] in *Adler auf dem Ahornbaum. Studien zur Einwanderung, Siedlung, Kultur- und Literaturgeschichte der Deutschen in Kanada*, ed. Hartmut Froeschle (Toronto: German-Canadian Historical Association, 1997): 1–12, 11.

36 Schmalz, *Former Enemies Come to Canada*, 5, 65; Manuel Meune, *Les Allemands du Québec. Parcours et discours d'une communauté méconnue* (Montreal: Méridien, 2003): 26; John C. Walsh, "Re-thinking Ethnic Boundaries: The Negotiation of German-Canadian Ethnic Identities in Ottawa, 1945-1975," MA thesis U of Ottawa, 1996: 9.

37 Schmalz, *Former Enemies Come to Canada*, 31–33.

38 Schmalz, *Former Enemies Come to Canada*, 6–9, 33–34; Meune, *Les Allemands du Québec*, 53.

39 Schmalz, *Former Enemies Come to Canada*, 1–2.

40 Schmalz, *Former Enemies Come to Canada*, 5, 67.

41 Meune, *Les Allemands du Québec*, 53.

42 Lenore Sauer, Andreas Ette, *Auswanderung aus Deutschland. Stand der Forschung und Erste Ergebnisse zur Internationalen Migration Deutscher Staatsbürger*, Materialien zur Bevölkerungswissenschaft 123 (Wiesbaden: Bundesinstitut für Bevölkerungsforschung, 2007): 32–34.

each year.[43] Compared to those Germans who migrated during the postwar period, the profile of subsequent generations of Germans coming to Canada was substantially different. With changing conditions in Germany at the end of the 1950s and at the beginnings of the 1960s, the motivations of people wanting to migrate to Canada also changed. The most dominant reason for migrating to Canada, originally the seeking of economic security and trying to escape from Germany's past, was replaced by a lust for adventure. During this time, people were often better informed about their new country of residence, had better knowledge of the English language, and sometimes even received a work contract before arrival in their new country of residence.[44] This is also true for Germans migrating to Canada in recent years. Most of them are highly qualified, and their reasons for migrating are not primarily caused by the social or political situation in Germany, as was the case in the post-war period.[45]

In the meantime, Germany had developed from being run by a totalitarian dictatorship, in the 1930s and 1940s, to becoming a democracy. By virtue of this development, processes of democratization and liberalization took place in Germany after the Second World War. These changes profoundly altered the country's social environment.[46] Moreover, Germany, just like other Western countries, has been influenced by the process of globalization. New communication and transportation technologies have created an increasingly mobile and flexible population. Thus, the circumstances in which German immigrants from the 1950s lived and under which they decided to migrate are significantly different from those of more recent migrants, especially in terms of their political, cultural and social situations.

---

43 Statistisches Bundesamt, *"Bevölkerung und Erwerbstätigkeit. Wanderungen 2011"* (February 20, 2013), *Destatis Statistisches Bundesamt* <https://www.destatis.de/DE/Publikationen/Thematisch/Bevoelkerung/Wanderungen/Wanderungen2010120117004.pdf?__blob=publicationFile> (acc. October 24, 2013): 78.

44 Matthias Zimmer, "Deconstructing German-Canadian Identity," in *A Chorus of Different Voices. German-Canadian Identities*, eds. Angelika Sauer, Matthias Zimmer (New York: Peter Lang, 1998): 21–39, 26; Meune, *Les Allemands du Québec*, 29; Daniel Geyer, "Die alte Welt verlassen -- in der neuen Welt angekommen? Wanderungsbiographien deutschsprachiger Migranten in Montreal/Kanada," PhD diss. U of Bonn, 2012: 3, 46.

45 Zimmer, "Deconstructing," 26.

46 Zimmer, "Deconstructing," 27.

Research Environment: The German-Speaking Community in Ottawa and Its Community Life

The following analysis builds upon field research conducted within the German-speaking community in Ottawa. Like the rest of Canada, Ottawa experienced an enormous influx of German-speaking immigrants in the period between 1951 and 1957. During this time, the German population in Canada's capital more than tripled, reaching nearly 9,500. After the German immigration boom during the 1950s, only a relatively small number of new German immigrants settled in Ottawa. Today, there are around 10,000 (single answers)[47] people claiming German ethnic origin that live in Canada's capital and its surrounding areas.[48] With the high influx of German-speaking immigrants in the post-WWII period, a vivid and flourishing network of German clubs, organizations, associations, shops, services and activities for a German-speaking public was soon established in Ottawa. Today, two German churches – Martin-Luther Gemeinde and St. Albertus Pfarrgemeinde – remain, offering services and other religious activities. In addition, the facilities of the German Lutheran church are also used for and by a seniors club, a children's playgroup, a German book club, meetings, concerts and other events.[49] Moreover, other clubs and associations, such as the German Benevolent Society, the Maple-Leaf Almrausch Club, a German Language School and a German Kindergarten can be found in Ottawa. These amenities are complemented, amongst others, by the German Embassy and the Goethe Institut. Interest in these facilities differs significantly between the older and more recent waves of German immigrants residing in Ottawa. While these facilities are regularly visited by the older German immigrants, Germans who have immigrated more recently show little interest in joining such organizations.

---

47 When asked about their ethnic origin in the Canadian census, people can name more than one ethnicity. "Single answers" thus means that people claimed only to be of German ethnic origin (cf. "Ethnic Origin Reference Guide, 2006 Census" [April 5, 2011], *Statistics Canada* <http://www12.statcan.gc.ca/census-recensement/2006/ref/rp-guides/ethnic-ethnique-eng.cfm> [acc. February 19, 2013]).

48 "Population by Selected Ethnic Origins, by Census Metropolitan Areas (2006 Census) (Montréal, Ottawa-Gatineau)" (August 14, 2009), *Statistics Canada* <http://www.statcan.gc.ca/tables-tableaux/sum-som/l01/cst01/demo27e-eng.htm> (acc. October 10, 2012).

49 Dieter Kiesewalter, *Kanada – Gelobtes Land? Aus dem Leben einer deutschen Auslandsgemeinde* (Ottawa: MCC, 1994): 216; Martin-Luther-Gemeinde Ottawa <http://www.glco.org/GLCO/Home.html> (acc. February 18, 2013); Service Handouts Martin-Luther Church (March 10, 2013; March 17, 2013; April 14, 2013; April 21, 2013).

In total, thirty-five interviews with first-generation German immigrants to Canada were conducted in March and April 2013. These interviews included Germans who had emigrated to Canada between 1951 and 2007. As this chapter focuses on a comparison between the so-called Alteinwanderer and Neueinwanderer, only interviews conducted with Germans who entered the country in the immediate post-war period (Alteinwanderer), or after the German reunification in 1990 (Neueinwanderer) were selected for discussion. Hence, eight interviews for each of these groups form the basis of this chapter. As a result of the methods used for sourcing the interview partners, most of the persons that were contacted had some connections with the different organizations and associations of the German-speaking community. However, when looking at the number of people residing in the Ottawa region who claim German ethnic origin, the proportion of the German-speaking population that has an active role within the community is relatively small. This may have placed a certain bias with regard to the analysis and should be kept in mind when reading this chapter. The interview material is complemented by participant observations, which were conducted by, e.g., attending different events of German organizations and associations. The first part of the analysis investigates the experiences of the Alteinwanderer, whereas the second part examines the situation of the Neueinwanderer. Both parts are structured in the same way, by: (1) giving an overview of the reasons for migration and the social circumstances during the respective time periods of migration; (2) describing the ways in which the immigrants maintained ties to Germany, and how this changed over time; (3) examining the reasons for participating in German organizations, associations and clubs; and (4) discussing the feelings the interviewees have towards both Germany and Canada, and the ways in which home and belonging are defined amongst the two groups. The findings are compared and discussed in the concluding section.

The Experiences of the Alteinwanderer

The interviewees belonging to the Alteinwanderer have very diverse backgrounds. Two of them come from the former eastern territories of Germany which today are part of Poland, respectively the Czech Republic. Both had to leave their home towns and flee to the western parts of Germany during the Second World War. The other six interviewees are from other regions in Germany, e.g. Bavaria or Schleswig, which both during the Second World War and today form part of the national territory of Germany. Most of them had experienced some form of displacement during or after the Second World War (e.g., as a result of the evacuation of children in Germany during the Second World War), and their lives had been influenced in one way or the other by the consequences of this war (e. g., due to bombings or the loss of family members). All of the interviewees immigrated to Canada between 1951 and 1965, and their age structure at the point of the interviews varied from 75 to 91 years. Three of the interviewees brought their families to Canada, whereas the rest came on their own. Their educational backgrounds upon arrival in Canada differed significantly. Some interviewees had completed a school education in Germany but had not obtained any professional education. Others had completed an apprenticeship or university degree before migrating to Canada. Likewise, their English language skills upon arrival in Canada varied from some being almost fluent, to some merely knowing school English, to some having no knowledge at all of the English language, depending on their respective social situation and their age at the time of migration.

The reasons cited for migrating were diverse, but were often in some way connected to the events of the Second World War and its consequences. Hedwig M.[50] (91) relates that her husband and brother were the ones who had made plans for migrating to Canada, since she "would have never done it alone."[51] However, since her hometown had been bombed and destroyed due to the Second World War, she and her family did not see any opportunities there. Canada, on the other hand, promised a better future for the small family. Hans O. (79), who arrived in Ottawa together with his wife Gertrude O. (75) in 1957, had slightly different reasons. He says that he himself was seen as a refugee in Germany, belonging to the thousands of displaced persons from the former eastern territories of Germany, in his case Silesia,[52] who were seeking shelter in the country. For him, even though he grew up with the German language and culture, the region he was forced to move to in Germany was foreign to him and he neither felt that he belonged there nor did he establish a feeling of home there. Therefore, he decided to leave Germany and start a new life elsewhere. Originally, he had planned to migrate to Australia; however, since he had fallen in love with a "German girl," his present wife, the money he had saved was not enough to cover the travel costs for both of them. Since the journey to Canada was cheaper, they finally decided to move there. Otto H.'s (84) decision to move to Canada in 1957 was mainly motivated by the fact that he did not want to be drafted to the military, which had been reintroduced in Germany during that time. With the rising tensions between the US and the Soviet Union, which had become particularly vir-

---

50 The names of all interviewees have been changed in order to secure confidentiality.
51 Translations of all interviews from German into English are mine.
52 Silesia mainly belongs to Poland today.

ulent in the divided country, he furthermore wanted to get away from the conflict zone, fearing the outbreak of another war. The main reasons for leaving Germany and moving to Canada cited by all the interviewees were the fact that they were seeking a better life and wanted to escape Germany's past, as well as the miserable situation in Germany after the war.

For the Germans who arrived in Ottawa during the 1950s and 1960s, it was difficult to maintain close ties with family and friends who had stayed behind. The transportation system was still poor. Most of the people arriving in Canada during this period had to cross the Atlantic by ship on a journey that could take up to ten days or more. Airfares did not become widely affordable until the late 1960s, when prices began to fall and more and more airlines began to operate. Moreover, (tele)communication possibilities were limited. Without computers and the internet, the only way to stay in touch with family and friends back home was via telephone or by writing letters. Since phone calls were expensive and the quality of transatlantic calls low, most of the interviewees had to rely on letter writing. When talking about how she maintained contact with her family and friends at the beginning of her stay, Sarah L. (79) says: "We did not have any means of contact, the only thing we could use were letters. No other contact. [...] People wrote to each other." Likewise, when asked about how she maintained contact with her family in Germany, Hedwig M. (91) remembers: "Only by writing, only by mail." Furthermore, she says that the only people with whom she maintained contact were her siblings. She did not maintain any contacts with friends or other relatives. She also remembers that she first returned to Germany during the 1970s, roughly twenty years after her migration to Canada. By that time, many things had changed in Germany, and Hedwig M. (91) had difficulties coming to terms with these changes to her home country. Similarly, Karl-Heinz R. (80) reports that he first returned to Germany after having lived in Canada for fifteen years: "In the beginning you neither had the time nor the money. I couldn't leave my family here, without any money, and spend some thousand dollars [to visit Germany]. I first returned to Germany after fifteen years and, after that, I maybe went every fifth year." With a few exceptions, most of the interviewees were unable to return to Germany for a long time after they entered Canada. These circumstances, together with the poor communication facilities available during this time, resulted in a disconnection between the Germans in Ottawa and the developments going on in their home country. This has changed in recent years due to new inventions, especially within the sector of communication technology, that have made it possible to take part in the life of another country and to get up-to-date information at any time.

As outlined, most of the interviewees could not return to Germany or maintain close ties with the country due to a lack of communication and transportation options. Two different patterns for approaching this situation could be observed amongst the Alteinwanderer: (1) people either reacted by trying to maintain the "German way of life" in Canada, e. g., by founding German organizations and associations and, thus, in a way recreating their homeland and preserving the German culture and language; or (2) they tried to quickly assimilate to the Canadian society and to adjust to the new living situation. Participation in German organizations, clubs and associations, varied amongst the interviewees of the Alteinwanderer, depending on their social situations, and their ability to learn the new language and to adjust to the living situation in Canada. Some of the interviewees who came on their own and married a Canadian spouse were not at all active within the German community. Sarah L. (79) says: "Due to the fact that I got to know my husband and married into his family, I was completely disconnected from the German world, completely." Others, such as Martin A. (79), did not face any difficulties when integrating into the Canadian society. Martin A. already knew the English language perfectly and, thus, was quickly able to build a social network. Several other interviewees, however, took an active part in German organizations from the very beginning of their stay in Ottawa. Language difficulties as well as the fact that they were finding it hard to adjust to the new living situation in Canada, were reasons why some were seeking the comfort of German organizations and clubs. Trying to find companionship and support due to the lack of family and friendship networks were others. Otto H. (84) recounts that especially in the beginning of his time in Canada, he was seeking contact with other German immigrants. As reasons for this, he mentions: "Well, it was because you were feeling helpless. In the beginning you would be trying to seek support from your compatriots." Gertrude O. (75) mentions: "But it was also for our children. We didn't have a grandma to support us; we didn't have grandparents, no uncles. [...] But our choristers [from the German choir], those are the people who today still play the role of uncles for our children."

Thus, depending on their situation upon arrival in Canada, levels of participation and engagement in German organizations varied significantly amongst the interviewees belonging to the group of the Alteinwanderer. However, what unified this heterogeneous group once they reached the age of senior citizens was that all of them took part in different events and organizations which were specifically addressed towards German-speakers in Ottawa. Most of the time, this was explained by a common nostalgic longing towards Germany as their homeland, which became stronger in old age. This nostalgic longing was partly explained by the fact that before retirement, people were fully involved in their work and family duties and thus concentrated on their lives in Canada. At retirement, they had more time to think, both about their past and present life and to reactivate contacts with family and friends in Germany, and with the country as a whole. Interviewees report that childhood memories became more present again, as did memories of their life in Germany before their emigration. Talking and reflecting about these memories with non-Germans, however, proves difficult, as the latter cannot relate to them due to their different socialization experiences. Therefore, especially for the Alteinwanderer, German institutions, organizations and clubs have gained importance, as they seem to function as a remedy for them missing their homeland. In these environments, they have the possibility of exchanging experiences and memories, to talk about "old times," to use their mother tongue, and to maintain certain German traditions and holidays in the way they used to know them. Observations made while visiting a meeting of the *Frohe Runde*, a German seniors club, underline the crucial role that these entities play in determining the wellbeing of older German immigrants in Ottawa:

> Upon arrival at the Martin-Luther Church, where the Frohe Runde meets, there was already a lively atmosphere, with some of the participants in the kitchen preparing coffee and food. I could hear cheerful chatter from the room next door, where others had gathered around a table with a set of *Rummikub* [a parlor game for two to four persons] in front of them, which appeared to be very popular amongst the people in the room. I learned from a few people there that this meeting was actually the "highlight of their week," and that they were constantly looking forward to it. A few of the people who came to the Frohe Runde were happy to just meet people like them, to play Rummikub, and to be able to speak German for the five hours during which the group meets every Thursday. Others also take advantage of different activities that are offered during the meetings, e.g. today, a *Heimatfilm* [a movie about the homeland] was shown. Later, at around noon, everyone gathered in the main room to eat lunch together: "a good traditional German soup," which I was informed was a common choice during their gatherings. They invited me to eat with them, and one woman smiled and gave me a sandwich, saying that I needed to taste it, since it was "just like the good bread back in Germany, not like the sticky white bread that you can find here".[53]

Most interviewees have strong emotional ties to both Germany and Canada. They still perceive Germany as their homeland; however, Canada has likewise become their home and is perceived as their new homeland. In fact, all interviewees feel more at home in Canada due to the long time – up to sixty years – they have been living there, compared to the relatively short period of their lifetime that was spent in Germany. Gertrude O. (75) says that she was always happy when returning to Canada after having visited Germany, and explained it as follows:

---

53 Field Notes, *Frohe Runde*, April 4, 2013.

> Germany is the country where I was born and where I spent the first twenty years of my life, only twenty years! In the meantime, I have been living in Canada for 55 years, and that disconnects you. When going back to Germany, you remember places where you have been, but it is more nostalgia. [...] Well, I am still proud to be German. But once you have children here [= Canada], that makes you feel much more connected to Canada. And then there are the grandchildren, and I have one son who is buried here. So I don't want to leave again. These things connect you to this country.

Otto H. (84) describes how he still sees Germany as his homeland. However, he stresses that he does not have a highly sentimental connection to the country as such, but rather feels a strong emotional attachment to his "Germanness."[54] Canada has become his home, where he feels very comfortable. It is the place where he has spent most of his life, where he has established his own business, and where he has his family. He describes this perception metaphorically: "You use the German aspect, the *Heimat*, and it is a bit like a foundation upon which the rest of your life is built. Well, in my case, the rest of the life is Canada. I mean, I have been living here [in Canada] for 60 years already. And, in practical terms, the house is Canadian, but the foundation is German." That is also true for Hedwig M. (91) who states that Canada became her home and the place where she feels she belongs. She longs for Canada, when traveling, but she still feels a strong connection to her "Germanness": "Well, the Germanness is there. I am German, but I have to be very thankful to this country [= Canada], because it allowed us to enter and build a new life." The fact that Canada became their new home(land) over time is also reflected by Klara V. (77). She says that life is a lot better in Canada compared to Germany, especially when arriving there directly after the Second World War. She did not have any possibility of returning to Germany and, thus, it was important for her to settle down and immerse herself into Canadian society, which she perceived as her new home. Although she kept a sense of home, a *Heimatgefühl* towards Germany, over time, she became more and more Canadian. After having lived in Canada for sixty years, she has strong feelings of being at home in and belonging to Canada.

The Experiences of the Neueinwanderer

All interviewees belonging to the group of the Neueinwanderer came to Canada in the last twenty-five years, the earliest arriving in 1990 and the most recent in

---

54 The interviewees defined "Germanness" in the sense of maintaining the German language, culture and traditions and strongly identifying with the same.

2007. Hence, all of them had been living in Canada for at least six years at the point of the interviews. They came from a variety of different regions in Germany and their age varies between 40 and 54 years. All but one participant, who had completed an apprenticeship, had obtained a university degree, and, thus, all of them were highly qualified upon arrival in Canada. Most of the interviewees also had previous experiences of living abroad for some time, in connection with e. g., university exchanges or other working experiences. Moreover, all interviewees had previous language knowledge in either English or French, or both languages before immigrating to Canada. Although some of them had to improve or deepen their language skills, generally, the level of English and/or French was high. The interviewing sample of the Neueinwanderer contains Germans who are married to either Canadian-born partners (both Anglophone and Francophone) or partners who hold Canadian citizenship and have themselves immigrated to the country, as well as Germans who came to Canada with their families.

In contrast to the older German immigrants who immigrated to Canada with hopes and expectations for a better life, who were escaping hunger, homelessness and unemployment after the Second World War, more recent German immigrants came to Canada because of a job offer or because of the fact that they were in a relationship with a Canadian citizen. A number of the more recent immigrants in Ottawa say that they had not necessarily planned to live in Canada. Initially, rather, they had a desire to go out and discover the world, and "by accident, got stuck" there, but felt that they could have just as well ended up somewhere else. This feeling is effectively described by Klaus A. (41):

> I have always felt that I got stuck here somehow; I mean, I could just as well be somewhere else. Some people might have a 'dream': I want to come to Canada at some point, like this is my 'dream.' For me it wasn't like that. I had always wanted to get out, but theoretically it could have been somewhere else as well. But, I mean, Anne [his wife] is Canadian. [...] I have talked to people and they have told me: Ah well, you immigrated here. And then I always thought: Yes, well, I did that, but it was more [pause] well, let's say it was more unconsciously. I mean, I actually feel that I am a German and that I am more on a transit or something. That's how I feel. So I could be somewhere else as well.

When trying to describe her situation in Canada, Frida B. (46) uses the term "modern immigrant," which she thinks characterizes her best as a person. For her, moving to Canada had nothing to do with wanting to leave Germany, but was a decision made on a family level, as her Canadian husband wanted to return to Canada after having lived in Germany for some years. She does not feel that she had immigrated to Canada but rather feels that she had moved there, just as if she had moved elsewhere in Germany or in Europe. She lives in Canada now, but may return to Germany some day in the future. Imke M. (40) describes her life in Canada in a similar way: "I don't know, it's more like I have the feeling of being somewhere on a long holiday. You don't want to go back home, but it is neither as if you [pause] Well, actually, I don't know whether I will spend my whole life here or not." She continues to recount that in the beginning of her stay in Ottawa, she was convinced that she and her family would move back to Germany sometime in the near future. However, as time passed, she did not feel as strongly about returning to Germany any longer.

Those interviewees who migrated to Canada at the beginning of the 1990s especially report that communicating with Germany has become much easier during recent years. Whereas most of them used the telephone and letters to communicate with family and friends in Germany at the beginning of their time in Canada, nowadays modern means of communication such as email, Facebook and Skype facilitate communication and have become dominant. Klaus A. (41) recounts:

> Yes, it has become much, much, much easier. Well, take a look at telephone rates, for example. Fifteen years ago, the prices for phoning back home were incredible high and now it no longer costs anything. [...] [T]oday, I call the normal way, half an hour, an hour, it doesn't cost anything. But this has changed dramatically. Certainly, email and Skype and all the other things have facilitated things a lot.

The new possibilities of maintaining contact, which have been caused by improvements in technology, are also described by Beate K. (48): "[M]y kids have an iPad, my parents have an iPad, and so they can walk through the house and talk to each other and, yes, well, I think it is a bit different today." Relationships with family and friends are also maintained with regular visits to Germany. Although all interviewees report that they go home to Germany on a regular basis, this often varies amongst individuals, depending on their social and financial situation. Most interviewees state that they visit Germany at least once a year. Imke M. (40) says: "Well, during the first two years, we went back twice a year, during summer and for Christmas. [...] But now it has become common to go there [i.e., to Germany] once a year, for six weeks in summer." Heinz W. (45) also visits Germany at least once a year. He says that during these visits, he usually stays with his family for a while, and also meets with a group of six to seven good friends with whom he maintains close and regular contact. Besides personal relations, the interviewees also maintain other types of contact with Germany. The majority of interviewees keep themselves informed about both the social and political situation in Germany to some extent. In this regard, most of them say that they were using the internet in order to watch the news or to read German newspapers online. Some of them do so on a daily basis, whereas others do it more occasionally. In addition to using these online resources, a few of the interviewees also mention that they watch the German foreign broadcasting service *Deutsche Welle* or access German newspapers available in Canada. Apart from staying informed about current events in Germany, some also use social media to access other German TV shows, movies or magazines. Frida B. (46) says: "And I read the *Brigitte* [a German women's magazine] on my iPad, that makes me really happy," and Heinz W. (45) mentions: "I watch *Lindenstraße* [a German soap opera] regularly every week, every episode." Thus, in today's multimedia world, the number of ways to maintain ties to one's country of origin has increased, and, hence, this has improved dramatically compared to the situation about twenty years ago.

Although most of the interviewees have some connection to German organizations in Ottawa, the extent to which they participate in ethnic institutional organizations differs significantly depending on their social and family situation as well as their personal interests. In general, interest in the two German churches in Ottawa is quite low. Only Eva P. (43) regularly attends the Lutheran Martin-Luther Church where she, for example, organizes the children's services. Other interviewees who were unwilling to be involved with religious facilities cited as reasons for this the fact that they were not able to identify with the older members of the two German churches, as well as simply not being religious. Imke M. (40) remembers that she had participated in the German playgroup when her children were younger, and had sent them to the German Saturday school for some years:

> We went there [i.e., German Language School] [...] for three years, I think. But then it felt as if my children's German had become too good and they weren't really learning anything new there. And also, it was on Saturday mornings, and my son decided that he would rather do sports on Saturday mornings at some point. Well, and then it didn't really fit with our schedule any longer.

Most interviewees sent their children to the German Language School for some time, and one of them, Beate K. (48), began working in the school as a teacher this way. Others, such as Heinz W. (45) and Sara L. (54), were occasionally involved in the work of German organizations as part of their job teaching German language and culture. One of the main factors that contributed to interviewees not joining other voluntary organizations, such as the Mapleleaf-Almrausch Club and the German Benevolent Society, was that they could not identify with the ideas of current members. The variety of different cultures and traditions within Germany, depending on the region people were coming from, was seen as a further reason. Imke M. (40), for example, thinks that there is no consensus amongst the German immigrants, because "[w]hat is perceived as being typically German by some, is not at all typically German for others." Furthermore, she points out that according to her experiences it seems as if most people of her generation have a high interest in informal gatherings, such as parties or BBQs, rather than in formal clubs and associations. Other reasons for not joining German organizations are emphasized, for example, by Klaus A. (41), who assumes that the more recent German immigrants might not have such a high interest in German community life because they are too busy with their work and family life to regularly attend club meetings. Furthermore, he refers to the fact that there is no longer any need to specifically join German clubs or associations, as "[t]oday, you can be in Canada, but you can watch German TV, you can Skype, you can fly home once a year or more often. Yeah, today, you can be anywhere, so you do not need to rebuild your home."

The feelings of the interviewees towards Germany and Canada are very diverse, and so are the emotions and memories connected to the two countries. Most of them continue to feel a close attachment to Germany and view it as their homeland. Reasons which are given for this are that it was the country in which they grew up in and, to a large extent, formed their personalities. Canada, on the other hand, is seen as a new home by most, in a sense of being the place where they live and take care of their families, and where they feel comfortable. Frida B. (46) says that she had developed a feeling of home when she first moved away from her hometown, Freiburg. She describes this feeling as follows: "Well, I had already developed such a feeling back then: Yes, that's where I come from, from the Black Forest. And the landscape and everything, that feels like – when you stand somewhere in that area, and the panorama and the base slope, well, yes, that's where I like to be and that's where I belong." Whereas when talking about Canada, she stresses: "[T]hat's where I live, that's where I earn my money and where I raise my family, raise my kids [...] I am living here, I think it is a nice place to be, but I don't think that I have a highly emotional attachment to the country." Eva P. (43) feels the same and describes Germany as her homeland, whereas Canada represents her present home, where she can find the comfort of a home, and has her social environment and, of course, her family. When trying to explain the terms "homeland" and "home", she points out:

> Well, *Heimat* refers to the land on which you have walked, the paths, streets, surroundings, flora, fauna, air, noises, neighborhood, maybe events, memories from school, certain places where you can eat and drink certain things, [pause] places which you visited and especially liked, such as a special museum, which cannot be found here [i.e., in Canada] or a castle or a particularly beautiful château which is part of the *Heimat*. And home is [pause] what is learned and what you are used to. It's where you feel comfortable, where you can relax, where you are around people that you can trust and who support, love and help each other, where you can reach out or look for the things you would like to do. It is the place

where you know that the people you are responsible for are taken care of and are provided with everything they need. I do not to any extent connect these things with Germany right now. Germany, rather, is an emotional homeland, in practical terms, so to speak. Well, I think, this is the difference.

In the same respect, other interviewees view Germany as their homeland that had shaped them, but feel that Canada is offering them a better life and suited their personalities better or simply makes them feel better. Peter J. (47) sees Germany as his homeland, whereas Canada symbolizes adventure and is seen as his "adopted home." He is happy when going back to Germany and values his German heritage. However, he feels that Canada suits him better at present and that it is the place he belongs at the moment. He describes a certain vibe which Canada and the Canadian mentality generates, which causes this feeling of belonging. Sara L. (54) has found that the longer she lives in Canada, the more she feels at home there. When describing how she feels when going back to Germany, she emphasizes that she enjoys the atmosphere there, but somehow feels trapped, whereas she feels free in Canada. She summarizes her feelings in metaphorical terms as follows: "Well, let's say – Canada, my feeling towards Canada is breathing freely. Germany: asthma, I have to gasp for breath. I am getting respiratory problems." Although her feelings towards Germany are rather negative, she acknowledges Germany as her country of origin that shaped her identity. Canada, on the other hand, is her home now, a place where she has changed a lot and found a new identity.

Summary and Discussion of Results

Although German immigrants in Canada cannot be seen as a traditional diaspora group, they qualify as an "ethno-national diaspora" as defined by Sheffer.[55] As such, they maintain, e. g., their national identity, have created some communal organizations, and to a certain extent keep up ties to their homeland. While exploring the ways in which German immigrants in Ottawa identify with Germany and Canada and construct notions of home and belonging, it became obvious that significant differences exist between participants belonging to the Alteinwanderer and the Neueinwanderer. I showed that these differences are caused by various factors such as the social situation, the possibilities of maintaining ties with the country of origin, and the time spent in the receiving country.

---

55 Sheffer, "The Emergence of New Ethno-National Diasporas," *passim.*

After the end of the Second World War, when Germany was in ruins, most of the Alteinwanderer left the country in search of a better life. Canada offered them the possibility to start over and to build a new life in a socially, economically and politically secure environment. These circumstances, paired with the fact that these people often did not have a choice about returning to Germany, led to their acceptance of Canada as their new permanent home. In contrast, the Neueinwanderer did not have to leave Germany because of their social situation but moved there mostly because they fell in love with a Canadian. The majority of these interviewees perceived themselves as "modern immigrants," currently living in Canada, but who could easily be living in Germany or elsewhere. Thus, Canada was seen as a new temporary home, whereas Germany remained their true homeland.

When the Alteinwanderer came to Canada during the 1950s, they hardly had any possibilities of maintaining close ties with relatives and friends in Germany as the communication and transportation system was poor. Visiting Germany was too expensive and letters were often the only way to communicate. Moreover, several of the German immigrants during that period did not have any previous language knowledge, which made it difficult for them to settle in and adjust to their new living situation. This resulted in the foundation of a variety of different German organizations and associations where people were seeking support and companionship and tried to maintain their "German way of life." For the Neueinwanderer, the situation is completely different. With modern forms of communication and transportation, they can maintain close ties with Germany in virtually all spheres and at any possible time. They can move back and forth between the two countries, having the possibility to visit Germany on a regular basis. Thus, they are able to maintain closer ties with Germany and their German heritage, without feeling the urge to rebuild their German life in Canada, leading amongst others to a lower interest in participating in German organizations. These findings confirm what has been stated by various authors, e.g. Kearney, Agnew, and Kennedy and Roudometof, which is namely that the time-space compression which has resulted from processes of globalization allows immigrants, in this case contemporary waves of German immigrants in Ottawa, to maintain close ties to their country of origin in all dimensions of life.[56]

Finally, when looking at the influence of age and the time spent in Canada, significant differences can also be observed. The Alteinwanderer feel more at home in Canada, having spent most of their lives there. Factors such as family,

---

[56] Kearney, "The Local and the Global"; Agnew, "Introduction"; Kennedy, Roudometof, "Transnationalism in a Global Age."

friends and property, which are all in Canada, tie them to the country and create the feeling of belonging there. This goes with a more traditional definition of home, as is for example highlighted by Douglas as well as by Al-Ali and Koser.[57] However, they have also developed a strong emotional connection to Canada as their home, which is emphasized, e. g., by Rapport and Dawson.[58] Germany – or more accurately, German language and culture – is still perceived as their emotional homeland, which represents an important component of their lives in Canada. This is what Medved refers to when highlighting that one's homeland is associated with such aspects as, e. g., language, community and traditions.[59] Especially when reaching the age of senior citizens, it was reported that they developed a nostalgic longing for their homeland, which expressed itself in a stronger identification with their "Germanness." This can be connected with Westin's understanding of the homeland, which he defines partly as a "mental image" and partly as "nostalgia."[60]

The situation is different amongst the Neueinwanderer. Most of the interviewees still feel a strong attachment to Germany, feeling that it is their homeland and has shaped their personalities, and that it still exerts an influence on their daily lives. Thus, the past or memories of the past, i. e., the time spent in Germany up until the point of emigration, has shaped the interviewees' perception of themselves and who they are today. This is what Agnew refers to when he says that the past defines our present and, thus, is an important part of our identity.[61] Moreover, the findings show that the homeland (Germany) is not only associated with a geographical location, but also with more abstract aspects, such as family and friends, the diversity of the German culture, or certain memories. This indicates the variety of definitions existing with regard to the homeland, as outlined by Runblom and Medved.[62] Canada is seen as a new temporary home by most. The notion of home in relation to Canada has other connotations than in relation to Germany, and is rather perceived as the place where they are currently living and which has provided comfort and security to their families. Hence, different understandings of the concept of home seem to apply for the interviewees. For them, home does not only represent the region or country where they were

---

57 Douglas, "The Idea of Home"; Al-Ali, Koser, "Transnationalism, International Migration and Home."
58 Rapport, Dawson, "The Topic of the Book," *passim.*
59 Medved, "The Concept of Homeland," *passim.*
60 Westin, "Migration, Time, and Space," 41–42.
61 Agnew, "Introduction", *passim.*
62 Runblom, "Introduction: Homeland as Imagination and Reality"; Medved, "The Concept of Homeland."

born, but it also represents the physical place where they are currently living and where their families reside.[63] Moreover, Canada is perceived as home in a more symbolic or affective sense[64] by some interviewees, as it provokes a feeling of being free, or the country's mentality is perceived as being a better fit to one's own lifestyle. Both the social circumstances of migration as well as the age and time spent in Canada exert an influence on the way in which German immigrants identify with Germany as their country of origin, and with Canada, the country in which they currently reside, as well as the ways in which they construct notions of home and belonging. Identities and the construction of home and belonging are fluid concepts that constantly evolve. Therefore, it remains to be seen whether, and in which ways, these feelings may change for the Neueinwanderer as their time spent in Canada increases.

---

63 Cp. Douglas, "The Idea of Home"; Al-Ali, Koser, "Transnationalism, International Migration and Home."
64 Rapport, Dawson, "The Topic of the Book," *passim.*

Milena Uhlmann
Home and Belonging in a Semi-Diasporic Setting: Converts to 'Reflexive Islam' in West European Societies

Abstract: Muslims and Muslim communities in Western Europe were and are conceived as alien elements by European majority societies with their Christian-secular background. In public and media discourse, Islam is often deemed to be a threat to 'Western' culture and norms as well as national security, notwithstanding the fact that Muslims make up only a small proportion of Europe's population. Based on findings from 27 narrative interviews with converts to 'reflexive Islam' in Berlin, London and Paris, this chapter discusses their motifs for conversion as well as what their conversions entails for the way they relate to their society of origin.

In recent history, migration movements emerging in the second half of the twentieth century resulted in the rising presence of Muslims in Western European countries, making encounters between Muslims and non-Muslims and thus conversions to Islam more likely. After the Second World War, a high demand for blue-collar workers arose in Western Europe which could not be met by domestic manpower. To counterbalance this shortage, foreign 'guest workers' (*Gastarbeiter*) from different countries – in the case of France and the United Kingdom also immigrants from their colonies – were contracted in large numbers. Usually they were employed in fields with poor working conditions and low wages without a perspective for professional advancement or social mobility.[1] Furthermore, the Gastarbeiter were allocated to housing areas of low social status, resulting in their relative separation from majority society.

Orienting themselves along ethnic lines, immigrant groups often reproduced the traditions and network structures of their regions of origin.[2] Following hefty

---

1 Germany concluded agreements with Italy in 1955, Greece and Spain in 1960, Turkey in 1961, Morocco in 1963, Portugal in 1964, Tunisia in 1965 and Yugoslavia in 1968. Until impeded by the Iron Curtain, Britain contracted workers from Eastern Europe for a brief period shortly after the Second World War. While workers from Southern Europe were more inclined to head for France, Germany, Switzerland and Austria, the UK's 1948 citizenship regime legislation had granted citizenship together with the according social, political and economic rights to all of its 600 million colonial subjects. As a consequence, West Indians, Indians and Pakistanis migrated to the UK in large numbers (cf. Randall Hansen, "Migration to Europe since 1945: Its History and its Lessons," *Political Quarterly* 75.1 [2003]: 25–38, 25–27).
2 Alain Boyer, "La diversité et la place de l'Islam en France après 1945," in *Histoire de l'Islam et des musulmans en France, du Moyen Âge à nos jours*, ed. Mohammed Arkoun (Paris: Albin Michel, 2006): 762–783, 771; Charles Husband, "The Political Context of Muslim Communities' Participation in British Society," in *Muslims in Europe*, eds. Bernard Lewis, Dominique Schnap-

national debates resulting from controversies about societal conflicts induced by decolonization and immigration, more restrictive immigration laws were implemented in Britain between 1962 and 1971.[3] In France and Germany, official recruitment was stopped due to the economic recession in the context of the oil crisis in 1972 (France) respectively 1973 (Germany).

Despite these restrictive measures, immigration – neither intended nor fancied, neither by government institutions nor the public – did not cease in reality, but continued by mechanisms of chain migration. The former 'guests' had built lives in the respective countries, often joined by family members from their countries of origin.[4] This practice of family reunions gradually led the general public to realize that the presence of foreign-rooted persons was not temporary and that their countries thus had evolved into countries of substantial immigration. This did not result in a pragmatic assessment and acceptance of the factual situation, but rather an attitude of hostility towards the immigrants. While facing individual, institutional and structural discrimination, they were usually either marginalized and ignored or stigmatized and pressured to assimilate into majority society.[5]

per (London: Pinter, 1994): 79–97, 80; Rémy Leveau, "Der Islam in Frankreich: Wandel und Kontinuität," in *Der Islam in Europa: der Umgang mit dem Islam in Frankreich und Deutschland*, ed. Alexandre Escudier (Göttingen: Wallstein, 2003), 12–25, 15; Quintain Wiktorowicz, "Anatomy of the Salafi Movement," *Studies in Conflict & Terrorism* 29.3 (2006): 207–239, 55.

3 Randall Hansen, "Citizenship and Immigration in Postwar Britain: The Institutional Foundations of a Multicultural Nation" *Paper for the Political Studies Association – UK 50th Annual Conference* (London, April 10–13, 2000) <http://www.ibrarian.net/navon/paper/Citizenship_and_Immigration_in_Postwar_Britain__T.pdf?paperid=11229> (acc. March 30, 2015): 2, 14, 22–23; Hansen, "Migration to Europe," 28; Rosemary Sales, "Britain and Britishness: Place, Belonging and Exclusion," in *Muslims in Britain: Making Social and Political Space*, eds. Waqar Ahmad, Ziauddin Sardar (New York: Routledge, 2012): 33–52, 46.

4 Boyer, "La diversité," 764, 769; Hansen, "Migration to Europe," 25–27; Husband, *Political Context*, 79; Edouard Mills-Affif, "Sur le petit écran: de l'immigré au musulman," in *Histoire de l'Islam et des musulmans en France, du Moyen Âge à nos jours*, ed. Mohammed Arkoun (Paris: Albin Michel, 2006): 976–986, 976, 978; Catherine Wihtol de Wenden, "L'intégration des populations musulmanes en France, trente ans d'évolution," in *Histoire de l'Islam et des musulmans en France, du Moyen Âge à nos jours*, ed. Mohammed Arkoun (Paris: Albin Michel, 2006): 800–821, 800.

5 Cf. Franck Frégosi, "La représentation institutionnelle de l'islam en France," in *Histoire de l'Islam et des musulmans en France, du Moyen Âge à nos jours*, ed. Mohammed Arkoun (Paris: Albin Michel, 2006): 837–855, 839; Yehudit Ronen, "Der Nexus zwischen Terrorismus und islamischer Immigration: Europas radikale Importe," in *Globaler Terrorismus und Europa: Stellungnahmen zur Internationalisierung des Terrors*, ed. Peter Nitschke (Wiesbaden: VS Verlag, 2008): 79–97, 90.

Following changing perspectives in public debate, the categorization of persons with a migration background shifted from "foreigners" to "Turks" (in the German case) respectively "Arabs" (in the French case) or "Pakistanis" (in the British case) during the 1990s to "Muslims" in the 2000s. Previously ignored, the religious affiliation of immigrants has in the meantime become a topic of special interest,[6] usually in the context of what is framed as a 'clash of civilizations' between essentialized concepts of Muslim and non-Muslim culture.[7] Political scientists Hendrik Meyer and Klaus Schubert note for the German context that this shift was induced by the realization that the so-called Gastarbeiter where in the country to stay.[8] This hints at the prevalence of a mindset which – instead of accepting the diversification of the population as a consequence of globalization processes – persistently focusses on what makes those who are regarded as 'others' different from 'us'; and thus entails never-ceasing, ever-continuing othering.

The inability to constructively deal with the de-facto diversification of the local population induced by the immigration of people with differing cultural, ethnic and religious origins led to social tensions and – often aggressive – debates about the definition and essence of cultural respectively national identity in England, France and Germany. One of the symptoms reflecting the difficulties these societies were and still are experiencing in the context of coming to terms with a diverse and often ambiguous social reality is the reaction to the presence of Muslims in these countries in general and to the phenomenon of conversion to Islam in particular.

---

6 Cf. Hendrik Meyer, Klaus Schubert, "Politik und Islam in Deutschland: Aktuelle Fragen und Stand der Forschung," in *Politik und Islam*, ed. Hendrik Meyer, Klaus Schubert (Wiesbaden: VS Verlag, 2011): 11–26, 12; Riem Spielhaus, *Muslime in der Statistik: Wer ist Muslim und wenn ja wie viele? Ein Gutachten im Auftrag des Mediendienst Integration* (Berlin: Mediendienst Integration, 2013) <https://mediendienst-integration.de/fileadmin/Dateien/Muslime_Spielhaus_MDI.pdf> (acc. March 30, 2015): 4–5.
7 The catchphrase of the "clash of civilizations" was coined by political scientist Samuel P. Huntington. He conceptualized cultures as fundamental determinants of human action and inherent characteristics of civilizations. Cultures shape the identities of the individuals belonging to the respective culture and are transnational by concept. In Huntington's model, the main features of the "fault lines" between civilizations are of cultural and religious nature and "particularly prevalent between Muslims and non-Muslims" (Samuel P. Huntington, *The Clash of Civilizations and the Remaking of World Order* [New York: Simon & Schuster, 1996]: 207–210).
8 Meyer, Schubert, "Politik und Islam," 12.

General Perceptions of Muslims and Converts to Islam

Comparing Europe with other regions in the world, the Religion Monitor states that "Europe in particular exhibits a certain fundamental fear of Islam."[9] Islam is generally conceived as a monolithic religious bloc by the general public. Contrary to this perception, the nature of Islam in Western Europe is as diverse as the background of the Muslims residing there. They differ with respect to national and ethnic background, age, how long ago (if at all) their ancestors immigrated, religiosity and orthopraxy as well as which current of Islam they ascribe themselves to. Intertwined with this perception is the nature of public dialogue on Islam and Muslims which is characterized by friction and distrust since the events of 9/11 as well as a focus on security and integration issues.[10] Islam is perceived as a foreign (and often violent) menace,[11] upholding a conception propagated in Europe since the Middle Ages.[12]

The Religion Monitor links this perception to "specific contexts and events as well as the link between Islam and terrorism in the minds of the population."[13] For France, violent conflicts in the context of the French colonies' struggle for independence had politicized the public's perception regarding the presence of foreign workers from the colonies. This was the case especially for Algerians, who in the light of violent conflicts within metropolitan France in the context of the Algerian War (1954–1962) as well as terrorist acts in the 1990s were in-

---

9 Gert Pickel, *Religion Monitor: Understanding Common Ground. An International Comparison of Religious Belief* (Gütersloh: Bertelsmann Stiftung, 2013): 12. The Religion Monitor was developed by the German Bertelsmann Foundation as "an instrument for helping to shed light on the interactions between religion and society" (Liz Mohn, "Preface," in Gert Pickel, *Religion Monitor: Understanding Common Ground. An International Comparison of Religious Belief* [Gütersloh: Bertelsmann Stiftung, 2013]: 6–7, 7). Its analysis is based on the responses of 14,000 people from thirteen countries to a questionnaire of about 100 questions (Mohn, "Preface," 7).
10 Cf. Franck Frégosi, "La perception de l'islam en France: vieille rhétorique et habits neufs," in *Histoire de l'Islam et des musulmans en France, du Moyen Âge à nos jours*, ed. Mohammed Arkoun (Paris: Albin Michel, 2006): 961–971, 961–963; Werner Schiffauer, *Parallelgesellschaften: Wie viel Wertekonsens braucht unsere Gesellschaft? Für eine kluge Politik der Differenz* (Bielefeld: Transcript, 2008): 11; cf. Katrin Rosenow, Matthias Kortmann, "Die muslimischen Dachverbände und der politische Islamdiskurs in Deutschland im 21. Jahrhundert: Selbstverständnis und Strategien," in *Politik und Islam*, eds. Hendrik Meyer, Klaus Schubert (Wiesbaden: VS Verlag, 2011): 47–86, 47; Wihtol de Wenden, "L'intégration," 800–802.
11 Boyer, "La diversité," 772; Pickel, *Religion Monitor*, 28.
12 Cf. Frégosi, "La perception," 966–967.
13 Pickel, *Religion Monitor*, 12.

creasingly perceived as posing a security threat.[14] This topos strongly influenced national discourse about immigrants and has become part of France's collective memory. Events such as what is often referred to as the "affaire du foulard" (headscarf debate) which originated in 1989 in the Paris suburb of Creil,[15] the 9/11 terrorist attacks in the United States and the riots in several French *banlieues* (suburbs) in November and December 2005 furthered the opinion prevalent in the French majority society that Muslims are not capable of integrating and the view of Islam as a form of communitarism importing not only foreign habits alien to French culture, but also external conflicts.[16] This perception was aggravated by the French republican ethos which demands absolute assimilation to the cultural and social norms prevalent in French society.[17]

---

14 Cf. Boyer, "La diversité," 764; Wihtol de Wenden, "L'intégration," 815.

15 Robert Leiken points out that the French headscarf affair coincided with the Rushdie affair, the triumph of jihad in Afghanistan and the birth of the Algerian Front islamique du Salut (FIS, Islamic Salvation Front), further stirring up the debate (cf. Robert S. Leiken, *Europe's Angry Muslims: The Revolt of the Second Generation* [New York: Oxford UP, 2012]: 22). In October 1989, the principal of a secondary school in the Paris suburb of Creil expelled three girls from his school because they refused to take off their headscarves. This was the beginning of a protracted dispute that would last for several years (cf. Leiken, *Europe's Angry Muslims*, 23). In the opinion of those opposing the headscarf, it was an instrument of the suppression of Muslim women which must be contained by a law. At the same time, they saw the headscarf as a threat to the 'French way of life,' symbolizing an alleged rejection to commit to 'French values' (cf. Jytte Klausen, *The Islamic Challenge: Politics and Religion in Western Europe* [New York: Oxford UP, 2007]: 175–176). This debate went far beyond the issue of headscarves in schools and initiated further disputes over the presence of a growing Muslim minority in France and its relationship to the non-Muslim majority society (cf. Leiken, *Europe's Angry Muslims*, 23). Although the Conseil d'État, France's highest administrative court, disclosed that wearing the headscarf does not violate the principle of secularism and despite that the government of Socialist Prime Minister Lionel Jospin decreed that the decision about the admission of headscarves should be left to the the the rectors of the respective schools, teachers of various schools went on strike in order to express their disagreement with the veil. The controversy again gained momentum when the two teenage daughters of a Jewish attorney and a Catholic schoolteacher converted to Islam during the summer vacation in 2003. Coming back to school after the vacation, they wanted to attend classes wearing the headscarf and as a result were expelled from school. President Jacques Chirac of the center-right Union for a Popular Movement declared the headscarf incompatible with the principle of secularism and as a disturbance of public order. A commission charged with updating the 1905 Law on the Separation of Church and State which codified their separation of by establishing the principle of laïcité recommended the prohibition of wearing of conspicuous religious symbols. The French National Assembly followed this recommendation with a large majority. Subsequently, a law was passed banning religious and political garments in public schools (cf. Klausen, *The Islamic Challenge*, 174–176).

16 Cf. Wihtol de Wenden, "L'intégration," 810; cf. Leveau, "Der Islam in Frankreich," 13.

17 Cf. Frégosi, "La représentation," 839; Ronen, "Der Nexus," 90.

In Britain, the growth of Muslims communities had largely been ignored until the 1980s. Increasingly emerging demands for *halal* school lunches led to widespread media coverage and large-scale discussions. The debates following the Rushdie affair of 1989 set a turning point. The public burning of a copy of Salman Rushdie's *The Satanic Verses* during a demonstration against his book in January 1989 in Bradford as well as Ruhollah Khomeini's fatwa calling for Rushdie's death led to fierce disputes.[18] Next to politicizing British Muslim communities, these events also resulted in increased public awareness regarding Muslim presence in Britain.[19] As Islamic scholar Kate Zebiri noted for the British context, there seems to be "a reluctance among some sections of the media to disrupt the familiar image of Muslims as foreign immigrants."[20]

In Germany, where "being Muslim is the current cipher for the foreign and threatening,"[21] intensive debates about so-called 'honor killings,' 'import brides' and the alleged emergence of parallel societies contributed to negative associations regarding Islam.[22] An analysis of German media reporting dating from 2013 highlights the media's role in this context, concluding that the German media predominantly portrays Muslims as "objects of failed integration." Furthermore,

---

18 Religious scholar Gereon Vogel provides an analysis of the controversial nature of Rushdie's book (Gereon Vogel, *Blasphemie: Die Affäre Rushdie in religionswissenschaftlicher Sicht: Zugleich ein Beitrag zum Begriff der Religion* [Frankfurt a. M.: Peter Lang, 1998]).

19 Cf. Kees Groenendijk, Astrid Meyer, Rinus Penninx, Jan Rath, *Western Europe and its Islam* (Leiden, Boston: Brill, 2001): 227–228, 230–232.

20 Kate Zebiri, *British Muslim Converts: Choosing Alternative Lives* (Oxford: Oneworld, 2008): 82.

21 Deniz Baspinar, "Wie man zum Moslem gemacht wird" (November 3, 2013), *Zeit Online* <http://www.zeit.de/gesellschaft/generationen/2009-11/migranten-islam-auslaender> (acc. June 28, 2014).

22 Schiffauer, *Parallelgesellschaften, passim*. The best-known honor killing case was that of Hatun Sürücü, a 23-year-old second-generation immigrant of Kurdish origin. At the age of fifteen, she was taken out of high school in Germany and forced to marry a cousin in Turkey. Following the birth of her child in Berlin, she refused to return to Turkey. Shortly after, she left her parents' home and began an apprenticeship as an electrician. She was murdered by her 18-year-old brother in order to restore 'family honor' in light of the 'immoral life' she was living. The term 'import bride' refers to a woman who is brought from her country of origin to a foreign country to be married to a countryman who lives there. Such arranged marriages are widely contested in European societies, especially since the bride often is forced to marry. Furthermore, the bride usually does not speak the language of her host country and is not familiar with its culture. Thus she will be deprived of her chances to integrate and ascertain her rights.

the study criticized media reporting relating to Islam since the 9/11 events as "crisis-oriented."[23]

A 2009 study focusing specifically on German journalists' coverage of the phenomenon of conversion to Islam came to similar conclusions. Converts to Islam were usually portrayed either as what the authors dubbed the "wild thorns frame," highlighting the convert's emotional hardships before or during their conversion, often referring to socio-economic problems, a broken family situation, low educational achievement, pre-conversion drug and alcohol abuse. Alternatively, journalists might use the "fifth column frame," focusing on a presumed national security risk posed by "fanaticized individuals who from their physiognomy look like 'us,' but think totally different and decided to fight against their native society." Finally, they might use the "Islamophobia frame" which implicitly triggers fears of an 'Islamization' of European societies.[24] A subsequent study dating from 2011 noted a dramatic increase of news items around the excavation of the so-called Sauerland group in 2007 and the beginning of the trail against the group's members in 2009, equally providing evidence for the above-mentioned crisis-oriented, negative reporting.[25] Yet, the Religion Monitor notes that the "diffuse fears" of Islam prevalent in Europe

> do not necessarily result in a wholesale rejection of other religions, still less of their adherents. The feelings of threat associated with ideas about a given religion decrease sharply when people rather than names of religions are mentioned: 'Muslims' provide less cause for concern than 'Islam,' and trust in the adherents of another faith is not significantly lower than trust in members of the *respondents' own religion*. [...] Overall, a wait-and-see, pragmatic attitude to religious pluralism was observed, though it must be said that people are easily influenced by public discourse and political decisions since their attitudes are often based on emotions rather than on knowledge.[26]

---

23 Cf. Gunilla Finke, Jan Schneider, Anne-Kathrin Will, "Muslime in der Mehrheitsgesellschaft: Medienbild und Alltagserfahrungen in Deutschland" (2013), *Sachverständigenrat deutscher Stiftungen für Integration und Migration* <http://www.svr-migration.de/wp-content/uploads/2013/03/Medienbild-Muslime_SVR-FB_final.pfd> (acc. February 8, 2015), 10.

24 Keren-Miriam Tamam, Milena Uhlmann, "How German Journalists Cover Converts to Islam: Who Are You – One of 'Us' or One of 'Them'?" (2009), *The Hebrew University of Jerusalem: European Forum at the Hebrew University* <http://www.ef.huji.ac.il/publications/Tamam%20&%20Uhlmann.pdf> (acc. October 31, 2014).

25 Keren-Miriam Tamam, Milena Uhlmann, "The Media Visibility of Converts to Islam in Germany: From the Phenomenon of a Colorful Peacock to a Worrisome Lion's Roar" (2011), *The Hebrew University of Jerusalem: European Forum at the Hebrew University* <http://www.ef.huji.ac.il/publications/Tamam-Uhlmann2011.pdf> (acc. October 31, 2014).

26 Pickel, *Religion Monitor*, 12.

Figures on Muslims and Conversions to Islam in England, France and Germany

For all three countries, generating reliable figures regarding the number of conversions is impossible, which contributes to the above-mentioned lack of knowledge. Since the Muslim community has no formal clergy, there is no central institution that could take up the task of registering Islam's adherents or keep track of the number of conversions to Islam. Furthermore, the process of converting to Islam consists of a simple ritual which requires no formal registration. In order to become Muslim, the person wanting to convert simply speaks out the *šhahāda* (declaration of belief in the oneness of God and acceptance of Muhammad as his prophet) in front of two Muslim witnesses.[27] Therefore, estimates referring to the number of converts must be regarded as dubious.

In general, registration offices in the three countries do not keep record of religious affiliations, as religion is considered a private issue. Germany constitutes an exemption, as the government collects church tax on behalf of the two biggest Christian denominations which are governed by public law (the so-called *öffentlich-rechtliche Religionsgesellschaften*).[28] However, the numbers issued relate only to the Roman-Catholic and Protestant denominations. The latest census mentions 49.1 million (61.2 percent of the total population which amounts to 80.2 million) Roman-Catholics respectively Protestants residing in Germany as of May 9, 2011, the reference date of the census.[29] As for the Muslim population, it indicates the number at about 1.5 million (1.9 percent).

This figure stands in stark contrast to the number issued by the *Bundesamt für Migration und Flüchtlinge* (Federal Office for Migration and Refugees; BAMF) in 2009 when the BAMF estimated a total of 3.8 to 4.3 million Muslims (about 5

---

27 The corresponding phrase is *ašhadu 'al-lā ilāha illā-llāhu* ("I testify that there is no god except God") *wa 'ašhadu 'anna muhammadan rasūlu-llāh* ("and I testify that Muhammad is the messenger of God"). The first part confirms the uniqueness and oneness of God (*tauand*), the second part acknowledges the finality of God's revelation as proclaimed by his prophet. Muslim scholars disagree on the necessity of a declaration of intent (*niya*) prior to the recitation of the *šhahāda* (cf. Clarke, "Conversion," 160).

28 Cf. Spielhaus, *Muslime in der Statistik*, 3.

29 Cf. Statistische Ämter des Bundes und der Länder, *Zensus Kompakt: Ergebnisse des Zensus 2011* (Stuttgart: Statistisches Landesamt Baden-Württemberg, 2013): 8, 16. Germany uses a combination of a register-based census with a household survey of circa 10 percent of the country's population on the basis of a random sampling to obtain information on issues which is not held in registers (cf. Statistisches Bundesamt, *Zensus 2011: Bevölkerung Bundesrepublik Deutschland am 9. Mai 2011* [Wiesbaden: Statistisches Bundesamt, 2013]: 4–5).

percent of the total population) to reside in Germany.[30] Since the census and the BAMF study used different data bases acquired by differing methodological designs of data collection,[31] the divergences of the result do not necessarily represent a change in numbers or a trend.[32] It must also be taken into consideration that 17.4 percent of those interviewed for the census declined to provide information regarding their religious affiliation.[33]

The BAMF study yielded an interesting result which spurs further analysis in the context of this paper: 10 percent of those who categorized themselves as Muslim stated to be "rather not believing" and 4 percent "not believing."[34] This hints at another dimension of what self-identifying as a Muslim may signify: In the context of West European societies in which Islam constitutes a stigmatized minority religion, identifying as a Muslim can serve as a means to stabilize one's identity in the light of discrimination. In consequence, it does not necessarily have to constitute a religious indicator, but can (also) refer to an identity marker

---

30 Cf. Sonja Haug, Stephanie Müssig, Anja Stichs, *Muslimisches Leben in Deutschland* (Nuremberg: Bundesamt für Migration und Flüchtlinge, 2009): 84–85.

31 This kind of fallacy is a typical pitfall when it comes to the comparability and usage of opinion polls. Also, differing research designs (and research questions) lead to differing findings. The difficulty in acquiring reliable statistics about religious affiliation becomes obvious when looking at the question of which characteristics a person must meet in order to qualify as an adherent of a specific faith as defined by the survey-designers and the researchers analyzing the collected data. Moreover, categorization as attributed by survey-designers, poll-takers, or analyzing researchers may differ from the intended self-ascription of the researched subjects (cf. Spielhaus, *Muslime in der Statistik*, 6–10). In addition, the wording and question types (e.g. open vs. closed, asked in a one- or two-stage process) of the particular questionnaires will yield different outcomes (cf. Antonius Liedhegener, Anastas Odermatt, "Religious Affiliation in Europe: An Empirical Approach" (2013), *Swiss Metadatabase of Religious Affiliation in Europe (SMRE)* <http://www.smre-data.ch/results/workingpapers/> (acc. October 28, 2014).

32 Cf. Spielhaus, *Muslime in der Statistik*, 8. The Pew Research Center's Religion and Public Life Project estimated the percentage of Christians for 2010 at 68.7 percent (56.5 million) and the percentage of Muslims at 5.8 percent (4.76 million) in its 2012 benchmark survey (cf. Pew Research Religion and Public Life Project, "Table: Religious Composition by Country, in Percentages" [December 18, 2012] <http://features.pewforum.org/grl/population-percentage.php> (acc. June 29, 2014). The Center's estimates are based on the 2005 Generations and Gender Survey and the 2008 International Social Survey Programme (cf. Pew Forum on Religion and Public Life, "Appendix B: Data Sources by Country," (n.d.) <http://www.pewforum.org/files/2012/12/globalReligion-appB.pdf> (acc. June 29, 2014): 73.

33 Cf. Spielhaus, *Muslime in der Statistik*, 7.

34 Cf. Haug, Müssig, Stichs, *Muslimisches Leben*, 139. 36 percent stated to be "very believing," while 50 percent characterized themselves as "rather believing" (cf. Haug, Müssig, Stichs, *Muslimisches Leben*, 139).

beyond religious affiliation.[35] The point of reference in this context is thus not necessarily constituted by one's religious identity, but may be strongly influenced by the polarized and politicized debate about Islam, thus serving as an indicator for a sense of belonging to society as a whole.

In 2006, a report compiled by the *Zentralinstitut Islam-Archiv Deutschland* (ZIIAD) at the request of the German Federal Ministry of the Interior suggested a rise of conversions to Islam in Germany amounting to approximately 20 percent compared to the time before the attacks of September 11, 2001, with about 5,000 people converting between July 2005 and June 2006.[36] However, as the head of the institute admitted himself, many Islamic institutions which had been asked to provide figures about conversions that took place in their communities included numbers from a time span well before July 2005,[37] thereby distorting the information on the conversion rate. Moreover, the institute has been criticized for intransparent proceedings.[38] The BAMF study mentioned above estimates referring to between 13,000 to 100,000 converts in Germany, but deems them not valid.[39]

In England and Wales, the population amounted to 56 million on March 27, 2011, the reference date of the most recent census.[40] Among them, 33.2 million categorized themselves as Christian and 2.7 million as Muslim. A comparison of the new data to the findings of the 2001 census shows that while the number of Christians dropped substantially from 72 percent (37.2 million) to 59 percent, the number of Muslims rose from 3 percent (1.5 million) to 5 percent of the population. At the same time, the percentage of the population categorizing them-

---

35 Cf. Boyer, "La diversité," 771–777; Gilles Kepel, *Die neuen Kreuzzüge: Die arabische Welt und die Zukunft des Westens* (Munich, Zurich: Piper, 2004): 329–330, 348–350; Leveau, "Der Islam in Frankreich," 15; Saphirnews, "Mosquées: à 2,1 ou 5 millions, les musulmans manquent toujours de places" (March 21, 2011), *Saphirnews* <http://www.saphirnews.com/Mos quees-a-21-ou-5-millions-les-musulmans-manquent-toujours-de-places_a12337.html> (acc. June 28, 2014); Ronen, "Der Nexus," 89–90; Spielhaus, *Muslime in der Statistik*, 9–11.
36 Information provided by the head of the Institute, Muhammad Salim Abdullah, in a telephone interview with the author on November 2, 2006.
37 Muhammad Salim Abdullah, in a telephone interview with the author on January 27, 2007.
38 Thomas Lemmen, *Muslime in Deutschland: Eine Herausforderung für Kirche und Gesellschaft* (Baden-Baden: Nomos, 2001): 112–113.
39 Cf. Haug, Müssig, Stichs, *Muslimisches Leben*, 58.
40 Office for National Statistics, "Census 2011, table ID QS210EW: Religion (detailed)" (January 30, 2013), *Office for National Statistics* <http://www.nomisweb.co.uk/census/2011/ QS210EW/view/ 2092957703?cols=measures> (acc. June 28, 2014). In the United Kingdom, the census is conducted via a complete survey of the whole population (cf. Statistische Ämter des Bundes und der Länder, "Wie zählen andere Staaten ihre Bevölkerung?" (n.d.) <https://www. zensus2011.de/DE/Zensus2011/Ausland/Ausland_node.html> (acc. June 29, 2014).

selves as having no religion rose from 15 percent (7.7 million) to 25 percent (14.1 million). 89 percent of the Christians were born inside the UK, compared to 47 percent of the Muslims residing in the country. 86 percent of them have an Asian background.[41] 7 percent (4 million) did not state their religious affiliation.[42] Drawing on data from the 2001 census as well as a survey of British mosques, a 2010 study focusing on conversions to Islam in the United Kingdom estimated the number of converts in England and Wales at 59,445. However, the report advises caution regarding the reliability of this estimate, especially concerning the accuracy of the information given by the mosques.[43] Indeed, the study seeks to validate its estimates as effectively as possible; yet, many 'ifs' subsist.

The French census counts a total average population of 65.7 million for 2013,[44] but does not offer information on religious affiliation. The last census providing information on this matter was conducted in 1968.[45] In 1978, a law was passed which forbade the collection and processing of certain personal data including information on "racial or ethnic origins, political, philosophical or religious opinions."[46] Hence, the figures referring to the number of Muslims

---

41 Office for National Statistics, "What Does the Census Tell Us about Religion in 2011?" (May 16, 2013) <http://www.ons.gov.uk/ons/rel/census/2011-census/detailed-characteristics-for-local-authorities-in-england-and-wales/sty-religion.html> (acc. June 28, 2014).

42 Office for National Statistics, "Census 2011, table ID QS210EW." The Pew Research Center's Religion and Public Life Project estimated the percentage of Christians for 2010 at 71.1 percent (44.1 million) and the percentage of Muslims at 4.4 percent (2.74 million) (cf. Pew Research Religion and Public Life Project, "Table: Religious Composition"). The Center's estimates are based on the 2010 Office for National Statistics Annual Population Survey and 2001 Census for Northern Ireland (cf. Pew Forum on Religion and Public Life, "Appendix B," 73).

43 Cf. Kevin M. Brice, *A Minority Within a Minority: A Report on Converts to Islam in the United Kingdom* (December 28, 2010): 3, 11.

44 Institut national de la statistique et des études économiques, "Démographie: Population moyenne de l'année: France hors Mayotte" (January 28, 2014) <http://www.bdm.insee.fr/bdm2/affichageSeries.action?idbank=001641584&codeGroupe=62> (acc. June 28, 2014). France uses a "rolling census," not surveying all of the country's inhabitants on one single reference date, but continuously polling smaller segments of the population (cf. Statistische Ämter des Bundes und der Länder, "Wie zählen andere Staaten ihre Bevölkerung?").

45 Cf. Wihtol de Wenden, "L'intégration," 801.

46 Légifrance, "Loi no 78–17 du 6 janvier 1978 relative à l'informatique, aux fichiers et aux libertés, article 8, paragraphe I" (March 19, 2014) <http://www.legifrance.gouv.fr/affichTexte.do?cidTexte=LEGITEXT000006068624&dateTexte=2011045> (acc. June 28, 2014). Original text in French: "Il est interdit de collecter ou de traiter des données à caractère personnel qui font apparaître, directement ou indirectement, les origines raciales ou ethniques, les opinions politiques, philosophiques ou religieuses ou l'appartenance syndicale des personnes, ou qui sont relatives à la santé ou à la vie sexuelle de celles-ci." Collecting data on French citizens' religious

in the country are often projections extrapolating derivations based on the 1968 poll as well as the countries of origin of France's inhabitants. In consequence, these figures construct a religious community based on ascribing religious characteristics merely because of a person's origin in a country with a Muslim majority and are not based on actual religious affiliation and practice.[47] A study issued by the French Ministry of the Interior in 2010 sought to account for this problem. It counted between 5 and 6 million Muslims 'by culture' of which 33 percent (about 1.8 million) had declared themselves as believing and practicing.[48]

Two other state institutions which are exempt from the interdiction to collect data on religion are the *Institut national de la statistique et des études économiques* (National Institute for Statistics and Economic Studies, INSEE) and the *Institut National d'Études Démographiques* (National Institute for Demographic Studies, INED).[49] In 2013, the INED published a study numbering France's Muslims in the age group of 18 to 50 years at 4.1 million (1 percent) as compared to 12 million Christians (48.5 percent).[50] Out of the 4.1 million Muslims, 2.1 million declared themselves as religious.[51] One of the authors estimated the number of Muslim converts in the age group of 18 to 50 years between 70,000 and 110,000.[52] The study was based on data from a survey with 21,000 people residing in France conducted by INSEE and INED between September 2008 and February 2009.[53]

---

beliefs would run counter to the country's constitutional principle of laicism (cf. Maurice Barbier, *La laïcité* [Paris: L'Harmattan, 1995]: 23–24).

47 Cf. Boyer, "La diversité," 773; Saphirnews, "Mosquées." This is a common practice in all three countries, resulting in problems when it comes to assessing the number of believing and practicing Muslims as well as further difficulties regarding the comparability of the existing surveys.

48 Thomas Vampouille, "France: comment est évalué le nombre de musulmans" (April 5, 2011), *Lefigaro.fr* <http://www.lefigaro.fr./actualite-france/2011/04/05/01016-20110405ART FIG00599-france-comment-est-evalue-le-nombre-de-musulmans.php> (acc. June 28, 2014).

49 Cf. Légifrance, "Loi n° 78–17 du 6 janvier 1978 relative à l'informatique, aux fichiers et aux libertés, article 8, paragraphe II, 7," (19 March 2014) <http://www.legifrance.gouv.fr/affich Texte.do?cidTexte=LEGITEXT000006068624&dateTexte=20110405> (accessed June 28, 2014). Opinion polls are permitted, but they lack the precision of a census (cf. Vampouille, "France").

50 Cf. Patrick Simon, Vincent Tiberj, *Sécularisation ou regain religieux: la religiosité des immigrés et de leurs descendants* (Paris: Institut National d' Études Démographiques working paper 196, 2013): 6.

51 Cf. Vampouille, "France."

52 Saphirnews.com, "Mosquées."

53 The Pew Research Center's Religion and Public Life Project estimated the percentage of Christians for 2010 at 63 percent (40 million) and the percentage of Muslims at 7.5 percent (4.7 million) (cf. Pew Research Religion and Public Life Project, "Table: Religious Composi-

To sum up, definite, clearly-defined, reliable and comparable statistics regarding how many Muslims – be they converts or not – live in the three countries are not existent.[54] At the same time, it is clear that converts constitute only a very small portion of Europe's total Muslim population. Although it is impossible to generate concrete numbers, certain trends are palpable which seem to reflect the influence of certain factors for the choice to convert to Islam. Theologian and expert on conversions to Islam Ali Köse suggested an increase of British converts especially to Sufism in his empirical study dating from 1996,[55] emphasizing Islam's spiritual appeal.[56] As Köse states himself, this assumption cannot be backed with hard data.[57] Yet the statement seems legitimate as it fits within the rising interest in and conversion to New Religious Movements (NRM) in the 1960s and 1970s, some of which possessed similar features to Sufism, such as Baghwan Movement, Hare Krishna and other NRM focusing on spiritual awakening. Pargeter holds Sufism to be attractive first and foremost to the intelligentsia. She considers the development of political Islam in the Middle East in the 1980s a root of what she calls "a new breed of converts" who are reflecting the trend in the Middle East by taking on more politicized interpretations of Islam.[58]

Conversion Narratives

Empirical investigations of conversions usually rest upon interview data acquired ex post a conversion. The inevitable retrospectivity not only of a conversion, but of any bygone event, provokes the question to what extent this event can be given account of 'objectively,'[59] as the researcher has access only to the

---

tion"). These assessments are based on analyses of different surveys: the 2005 Generations and Gender Survey of the International Institute for Applied Systems Analysis (IIASA), the above-mentioned 2008/2009 study by INSEE/INED and multiple surveys between 2007 and 2008 by the French Institute of Public Opinion (cf. Pew Forum on Religion and Public Life, "Appendix B," 73).

54 Liedhegener, Odermatt, "Religious Affiliation in Europe," A 2.

55 Cf. Ali Köse, *Conversion to Islam: A Study of Native British Converts* (London, New York: Kegan Paul International, 1996): 20.

56 Cf. Ali Köse, "The Journey from the Secular to the Sacred: Experiences of Native British Converts to Islam," *Social Compass* 46.3 (1999): 301–312.

57 Köse, *Conversion to Islam*, 7.

58 Pargeter, *The New Frontiers*, 168.

59 Cf. Ivonne Küsters, *Narrative Interviews: Grundlagen und Anwendungen* (Wiesbaden: VS Verlag, 2006): 34.

life story as it is *told*, not as it has been actually *lived*.[60] Moreover, since for different reasons certain information will be blanked out when narrating a bygone event, the narration is inherently selective.[61] When telling about their conversion, the convert sums up their biography in the light of the conversion – it is the ledger of the logic, structure, and meaning of their narration. Sociologists of religion Roger Finke and Rodney Stark note that converts tend to emphasize theological aspects when talking about the motifs for their conversion.[62] Conversion narratives do not only serve to explain one's conversion, but are also a means to legitimize and validate it retrospectively not only towards the interviewer, but also towards oneself as well as one's pre- and post-conversional peer group. Given that religion is by definition of transcendent, extramundane, metaphysical nature, the mentioning of reasons for conversion other than theological ones may pose a threat to the validity and authenticity of the individual's religious conversion motif. Hence, the reply might be subjected to response bias. This should be taken into account when analyzing conversion narratives.[63] It is for this reason that sociologist of religion Bryan Taylor pleads for using conver-

---

60 Cf. Gabriele Rosenthal, *Erlebte und erzählte Lebensgeschichte. Gestalt und Struktur biographischer Selbstbeschreibungen* (Frankfurt a. M., New York: Campus, 1995), *passim*.

61 Cf. Monika Wohlrab-Sahr, *Konversion zum Islam in Deutschland und den USA* (Frankfurt a. M., New York: Campus, 1999): 486.

62 Cf. Roger Finke, Rodney Stark, *Acts of Faith: Explaining the Human Side of Religion* (Berkeley: U of California P, 2000): 122.

63 The narrative interview technique (which I also used for generating my data) as conceptualized by Fritz Schütze (cf. Fritz Schütze, "Biographieforschung und narratives Interview," *Neue Praxis* 13.3 [1983]: 283–293) is a useful tool aimed at avoiding biased replies. When using this technique, narratives are structured by 'inherent demands of narration' (Gerhard Riemann, "Zugzwänge des Erzählens," in *Hauptbegriffe qualitativer Sozialforschung*, eds. Ralf Bohnsack, Winfried Marotzki, Michael Meuser [Opladen: Leske und Budrich, 2003]: 157–167, 167; cf. Wohlrab-Sahr, *Konversion zum Islam*, 490–491) initiated by improvised narration (*Stegreiferzählung*). The inherent demands of narration produce a narrative flow which reduces the 'risk' of the interviewee structuring and predetermining their narration prior to the interview. Instead, replies will be intuitive and spontaneous (cf. Ralf Bohnsack, *Rekonstruktive Sozialforschung: Einführung in qualitative Methoden* [Opladen, Farmington Hills: Budrich, 2007]: 93). The dynamic and associative nature of the narration makes it more likely for the interviewee to bring up topics which he/she might have blanked out or suppressed (cf. Schütze, "Biographieforschung und narratives Interview," 286). As a consequence, the interviewee is stimulated to present his or her subjective reality as authentically as possible. The interview data yielded by this technique thus allows the researcher to take on the task of reconstructing the respondent's attitudes and relevances (cf. Bohnsack, *Rekonstruktive Sozialforschung*, 93–94; Michael Häder, *Empirische Sozialforschung: Eine Einführung* [Wiesbaden: VS Verlag, 2006]: 262; Jan Kruse, *Einführung in die Qualitative Interviewforschung* [Freiburg: October, 2011]: 129; Riemann, "Zugzwänge des Erzählens," 167).

sion narratives to make statements only about the individual's *post*-conversional identity, not to analyze the research subject's pre-conversional mindset and relevances.[64]

Since the acquisition of 'neutral' data regarding an individual's conversion (and his/her conversion motifs) is not possible, biography analysis will not yield a one-to-one reconstruction of the personal history of the person in question.[65] As a consequence, none of the existing tools can claim to 'uncover' the 'true' conversion motifs and the actual course of the conversion. Despite these limitations regarding the analysis of conversion narratives, they are nonetheless useful to assess the mindset and relevances in place at the time of the interview. The emphasis an individual puts on certain life events respectively topics provides a useful indicator in that context.[66] Even if specific topics had not intrinsically been important to them, but were 'introduced' by a third party – be it persons from their original social context or from the Muslim community they relate to – those issues were important enough to the respondent in order to be taken up and addressed and thus have become of relevance in their post-conversion context.

Converting to Islam

With the foregoing cautioning remarks regarding conversion narratives as well as conversion motifs in mind, I am discussing the way to Islam as well as the reasons for converting as presented by my respondents in the following. Conversions to Islam constitute a multi-faceted and very complex phenomenon. There are as many ways to Islam as there are converts; thus, a unique mix of influencing factors initiates each conversion to Islam. As conversions to any religion whatsoever do not take place in a vacuum, but constitute a product of the society the would-be convert lives in, his or her immediate social environment, and the individual's personal characteristics, the context within which the respective person converted has to be taken into consideration when analyzing their conversion. I will hence firstly cast a glance at the factors that influ-

---

64 Cf. Bryan Taylor, "Conversion and Cognition: An Area for Empirical Study in the Microsociology of Religious Knowledge," *Social Compass* 23.1 (1976): 5–20, 18.

65 Cf. Gabriele Hofmann, *Muslimin werden: Frauen in Deutschland konvertieren zum Islam* (Frankfurt a. M.: Institut für Kulturanthropologie und Europäische Ethnologie, 1997): 17; Wohlrab-Sahr, *Konversion zum Islam*, 67–68.

66 Cf. Monika Wohlrab-Sahr, "Biographieforschung jenseits des Konstruktivismus?", *Soziale Welt* 50.4 (1999): 483–494, 487–488.

enced the respondents' path to conversion. Although given the described negative perception of Islam among the non-Muslim majority societies in the three countries this may seem somewhat startling, at the same time genuine interest in Islam has emerged. In a number of conversion narratives, the interest initiated by the (often critical) examination of Islam constitutes a first step on the way towards conversion.[67]

The sample I examined consisted of twenty-seven individuals. Fifteen were females, twelve males. Their ages ranged from a seventeen-year-old high school student to a mother-of-five in her early sixties. Fifteen interviewees had obtained an A-level degree, eleven had completed an apprenticeship, four were undergoing educational training. All either had a job, were still in school or apprenticeship, or taking care of their families. Eight had a migration background, and three had been born into a nominally Muslim family – i.e., one or both of their parents were Muslims, but not practicing the religion. Six of my respondents had experienced heavy conflicts in their families. In three cases, my interviewee's parents were divorced. Five had been raised by a single parent. Seven had converted aged 16 to 19, eleven between 20 and 29, four between 30 and 37 and two in their early fifties.

Among them, a considerable proportion of respondents expressed that the inducement for them to learn more about Islam derived from wanting to find out more regarding issues such as the alleged link between Islam and violence in general and terrorism in particular as well as women's rights within Islamic religious parameters. Correspondingly, a large share of those whom I interviewed converted after 9/11: three respondents converted towards the end of the 1970s, two at the end of the 1980s, one at the end of the 1990s, and seventeen between 2001 and 2011 – thirteen of the last-mentioned group in the second half of the 2000s. In the case of those of my interviewees who were intrigued to learn about Islam by this negative stimulus, initial critical skepticism changed to fascination about the religion through the process of acquiring knowledge about Islamic values, ultimately resulting in their conversion.

Seventeen respondents specifically mentioned that personal contacts to practicing Muslims had played a crucial role for initiating their interest in Islam. Six interview partners referred to friends, four to their spouses and seven to other social contacts, e.g. schoolmates. These persons had introduced them to religious contents and norms as well as an Islamic way of life which

---

67 Milena Uhlmann, *Konversionen zum Islam und ihr gesellschaftlicher Kontext: Biographische Interviews deutscher Muslime* (unpublished diploma thesis, U of Potsdam, 2006); Milena Uhlmann, *Konversionen zum Islam in westeuropäischen Gesellschaften: Eine explorative Studie*, forthcoming.

– except in two cases – had impressed the future converts in a positive way.[68] In consequence, they developed interest in the religion. Five of the interviewees stated to have been religious seekers, while two converted in an ad-hoc decision under peer-pressure. 21 respondents decided to convert after a long process of critical examination of the religion as well as the pros and cons of joining it, which usually went on over months or even years.

Usually, there wasn't one sole reason for converting which was referred to, but a mix of the following was mentioned: Islam was conceptualized by the converts as being not only a religion, but a way of life which provided a wholesome meaning, goal and direction and thus integrated those aspects of the individual's life which had been compartmentalized by the mechanisms of differentiation of West European (post-)modern societies. Furthermore, the compelling logic and coherence of Islamic dogmas was emphasized, often by juxtaposing them to those of Christianity (such as the trinity, the divine sonship of Jesus and original sin). Additionally, an emotional attraction towards Islam as well as social aspects such as the benevolence, solidarity and sense of community among Muslims was emphasized and contrasted to the egoism prevalent in society. Transforming their socio-critical analysis to the individual level and themselves, the converts applied Islam as a tool to work on reducing their individual egoism and reform their own character.

The converts' access and relation to Islam most of the time was highly cognitive, reflexive, individualized and active: cognitive, because they assessed Islam intellectually; reflexive, because they scrutinized their own biography as well as Islam, developing a critical distance to both; individualized, because they worked out their very own understanding and conceptualization of Islam quite independently at a speed corresponding to their needs (i.e., not pushing themselves too much when a norm of conduct risked overexerting them[69]) and progress of understanding the meaning behind Islamic norms; and active, because most of the time, they retained agency. As a result of their reflective and individualized approach to the religion, they developed a high degree of ambiguity tolerance towards other interpretations of Islamic principles and norms. Because of these reasons, I named them converts to 'reflexive Islam.'

---

68 In one case, the respective future convert's interest to learn about Islam initially stemmed from wanting to find weaknesses in the religion in order to prove to her husband that the Christian belief was superior to Islam. In the other case, the would-be convert who at that time was an esoteric at the initiative of a schoolmate went to a talk about esotericism in a mosque with the goal to involve the speaker into a dispute.

69 For example as it was the case for most of the female converts regarding the use of the headscarf.

While discussing the impact of their conversion on their lives, it became very clear that one of the most important aspects of this process was to learn how they can contextualize their 'exotic' faith within their Western context. One recurrent topic connected to this endeavor was the question of how to reorder their social bonds and how they should relate to the context of belonging they originated from. In her analysis based on interviews with converts to Islam in Germany and the United States which she conducted in the end of the 1990s, sociologist of religion Monika Wohlrab-Sahr identified a strong tendency to functionalize Islam as a means to demarcate oneself from mainstream society.[70] Quite in opposition to the observations Wohlrab-Sahr made for her sample, my respondents put a lot of effort in contextualizing their new faith within their British, French or German social and societal environment. While scrutinizing and assessing their (soon to be) new religion, the (potential) converts tried to 'de-culturize' Islam from an 'oriental' context. Their aim was to put themselves in a position where they could differentiate between Islam as a religion and Muslim culture, so as to be able to identify 'true' Islamic norms and values instead of adopting cultural customs. As a result, the converts empowered themselves in their self-identity as new Muslims vis-à-vis born Muslims. Simultaneously, this process of reflection reordered their references of belonging. Having spent considerable time on studying Islam and developing their own individualized understanding of the religion, my respondents more often than not came to the conclusion that is it perfectly possible to live an Islamic life within a West European context. In fact, they believed that the semi-diasporic setting – belonging to majority society and a minority religion at the same time – was much more favorable in this respect than the setting in countries with a Muslim majority, as in their view Muslims living there often do not differentiate between culture and religion. The authoritarian nature of those countries' regimes, limiting civil liberties such as freedom of religion, was seen as further contributing to a 'culturalization' of Islam, disconnecting the orthopractic elements of the religion from its spiritual and moral essence. Liberal democracy and pluralist societies however, despite all of their flaws and shortcomings the converts identified, were appreciated for providing the possibility for choosing a self-determined way of life as a British, French or German Muslim convert.

On the social level, my interviewees emphasized an exigency to 'heal' their more often than not strained post-conversion relationship to their parents as well as a pronounced wish to counter negative attitudes prevalent in their social environment by means of demonstrating their 'benevolence' in their daily interac-

---

70 Wohlrab-Sahr, *Konversion zum Islam*, 388.

tions with non-Muslim majority society. By putting special attention to behaving in a non-aggressive, empathic way and with the goal of reconciliation, they aimed at abolishing or at least ameliorating what is perceived as a deplorable state of distance between Muslims and non-Muslims stemming from ignorance resulting in fear. This effort was as complex as are the mechanisms and societal relations structuring it. With it came a fair amount of frustration with the stereotyping, stigmatization and ignorance the converts were facing with respect to the more abstract public discourse as well as their immediate social environment.

Strategies for coping with these frustrations were either (more often than not only intermittently) to abstain from these efforts, or – and this is the more common case – to develop an even deeper introspection and reflection of one's own behavior, as well as a more intense preoccupation with Islamic principles and norms so as to better be able to elaborate and explain them while at the same time demonstrating the steadfast dedication to values perceived as having a positive effect on society as a whole, be its members Muslim or not. A side effect of this – as could be seen from the statements made by my respondents – is the stabilization of the convert's self-understanding and self-perception as a Muslim as well as the growth of his or her self-confidence, also stemming from the expansion of the respective individual's expertise in Islamic matters. Hence, the self-identity of the convert is reinforced and stabilized, which likewise strengthens his or her position with respect to fellow Muslims. This is not implemented at the expense of a non-Muslim interaction partner, but in the empathetic reaction to his or her perceptions and anxieties. The result is a broadening of the convert's perspective, not a retraction, and usually a very fine understanding of the subtleties of issues connected to home and belonging.

Conclusions

Looking at the way my sample recomposed their pre-and post-conversional identity and how they try to deal constructively with their social and societal environments, the fear and mistrust towards converts surfacing in public discourse seems exorbitant and out of place. The deficit-oriented media coverage contributes to the negative attitude towards converts to Islam. At the same time, West European societies are struggling with the fact that the diversification of their population demands adaptive performance not only for those who deliberately change their way of life (be it by migration or conversion), but also from those who are affected by these phenomena. The abstract fear of this impact in the case of converts to Islam often results in their denunciation as traitors and/or a menace.

Although not representative in a statistical sense, the cross-country comparative design of my study, drawing its respondents from different Muslim communities as well as interviewing persons not connected to one, points to a rather widespread diffusion of the mindsets and relevances I described. As a multi-faceted, complex phenomenon, conversion to Islam must be approached with an open mind. We need to take a close look in order to come to a reality-based assessment. The exploration of what conversion to Islam means and entails for the actual converting or converted individual is the key.

─────

Home-Making: Space, Virtuality, Ideology

Nina Gren

Being Home through Learning Palestinian Sociality: Swedish-Palestinian Houses in the West Bank

Abstract: This chapter discusses diasporic constructions of home and belonging through a case study of houses in the West Bank, owned by Swedish-Palestinians (i.e., existing or planned houses). The chapter builds on ethnographic fieldwork among Swedes with Palestinian backgrounds and family in the West Bank. My informants all travel regularly to the West Bank and many have or plan to construct a house or an apartment there. There are several social, emotional and political reasons behind why these houses are built. I will focus on one particular reason, namely my informants' desires to teach their children about Palestinian customs and norms while growing up in exile. I discuss my material with inspiration from scholarly literature on migrants' houses, diasporic practices and material culture. I argue, firstly, that these houses are part of a diasporic project and, secondly, that children and youth growing up in Sweden learn Palestinian cultural values by staying in their houses and interacting with them. The designs of the houses, and the ways in which they are used, mediate Palestinian sociality of how to relate to others, focusing on notions of hospitality and a rich social life. I claim that this sociality is a building block in creating a sense of diasporic belonging to Palestine and opens up for several cultural competences.

Background and Fieldwork

Palestinians have a long history of migration, often in search of better educational opportunities and improved quality of life. However, Palestinian diasporic life truly began in 1948, with the first Israeli-Arab war and the following flight of about 750,000 Palestinians from their homes inside today's Israel.[1] These events are referred to as *al-nakba* in Arabic, meaning the disaster, and point to the severe impact it had on Palestinian lives. Most 1948 refugees ended up in the Middle East. The Palestinian dispersal has however been ongoing since *al-nakba*, due to statelessness (in Iraq post- Saddam Hussein for instance), civil wars (in Lebanon in the 1980s and in Syria today), along with political persecution and economic stagnation in the occupied territories and elsewhere. It has

---

1 Ilan Pappe, *A History of Modern Palestine: One Land, Two People* (Cambridge: Cambridge UP, 2004): 139.

been estimated that 191,000 people of Palestinian descent currently live in Europe.[2]

There has been little research carried out on Palestinians in Sweden.[3] However, Palestinians are not usually registered as Palestinian when settling in Sweden. They are usually categorized as "stateless" (which also includes other groups) or of "unknown citizenship." Lindholm estimated that about 13,000 Palestinians resided in Sweden in the late 1990s, while *Le Monde Diplomatique* mentioned a figure of 15–18,000 and Abdul Ghani 10,000.[4] In my view, those figures are far too low and/or do not take descendants of Palestinian migrants into account. A prominent activist in Swedish-Palestinian diaspora circles hypothesized that there are approximately 40,000 people residing in Sweden who came from Palestinian refugee camps in Lebanon alone, while 10,000 have arrived from the West Bank and 5,000 from Gaza.[5] That would total about 55,000 individuals. In addition, Palestinians have arrived to Sweden from Syria, Iraq and other Middle Eastern countries. In this research, I focus on people who self-identify as Palestinian or of Palestinian origin despite how Sweden identifies them. Since the majority of my interlocutors hold Swedish citizenship or permanent residency and since the boundaries of the "group" are difficult to distinguish, the term "Swedes

2 Abbas Shiblak, "Reflections on the Palestinian Diaspora in Europe," in *The Palestinian Diaspora in Europe: Challenges of Dual Identity and Adaptation*, ed. Abbas Shiblak (Jerusalem and Ramallah: Institute of Jerusalem Studies, Shaml Palestinian Refugee & Diaspora Center, 2005): 7–18, 12.
3 The exceptions are Helena Lindholm Schulz, Juliane Hammer, *The Palestinian Diaspora: Formation of Identities and Politics of Homeland* (London: Routledge, 2003); Dalal AbdulGhani, "Caught Between Two Worlds: The Case of the Palestinian Community in Sweden," in *The Palestinian Diaspora in Europe: Challenges of Dual Identity and Adaptation*, ed. Abbas Shiblak (Jerusalem and Ramallah: Institute of Jerusalem Studies, Shaml Palestinian Refugee & Diaspora Center, 2005): 44–51, who have written briefly on Palestinians in Sweden. In neighboring Denmark, two PhD theses in social anthropology about Palestinians in impoverished urban areas have been completed: Anja Kublitz, *The Mutable Conflict: A Study of How the Palestinian-Israeli Conflict is Actualized among Palestinians in Denmark* (unpublished dissertation, Copenhagen: U of Copenhagen, 2011); Mette-Louise E. Johansen, *In the Borderland: Palestinian Parents Navigating Danish Welfare State Interventions* (Copenhagen: DIGNITY Danish Institute Against Torture Publication, 2013). These more extensive works have been inspirational for me although they both deal more with issues of integration in Denmark than with transnational relations and diaspora issues.
4 Lindholm, *The Palestinian Diaspora*, 84; Philippe Rekacewicz, "La diaspora palestinienne dans le monde" (February 1, 2001) *Le Monde Diplomatique*, <http://www.monde-diplomatique.fr/cartes/refugiesdiasporapaldpl2000> (acc. February 14, 2014); AbdulGhani, "Caught Between Two Worlds," 45.
5 Personal communication, February 2014.

with a Palestinian background" or "Swedish-Palestinians" are, in my view, more accurate and relevant labels than "Palestinians in Sweden."

This chapter builds on my fieldwork in southern Sweden on people who have Palestinian background and who maintain regular contacts with relatives in the West Bank through visits. The fieldwork contains twenty-five qualitative interviews. I also conducted participant observations of political events in Sweden (demonstrations and lectures) and people's daily lives in Sweden and in the West Bank.[6] I made a month long visit to the West Bank to meet and interview some of my informants during their family visits as well as some of their West Bank relatives. My main focus has been on three families of which at least one parent had arrived to Sweden in the 1960s or 1970s. I have used snowball sampling using contacts from my earlier research in the West Bank as well as my personal networks in Sweden.[7] Though all have a Palestinian background, they constitute a heterogeneous group regarding socio-geographical backgrounds in the Palestinian territories. Some come from a remote village, others from urban Jerusalem, others from small towns and yet others from refugee camps. Such geographical differences lead to differences in access to buildable land. Camp refugees, for instance, come from families who lost their land in 1948, though some have managed to buy other plots. My interlocutors also live in diverse social settings in Sweden; ranging from fancy parts of inner cities to marginalized and impoverished city outskirts or small towns and suburban villa quarters. Some of my informants were born in the Palestinian territories, while others were born in Sweden. Among my group of interlocutors, there are both Muslims and Christians. Since Palestinian Christian exile has been comparatively larger than its Muslim counterpart, the percentage of Christians in this study is larger than that of the West Bank population.

The Swedish authorities' reasons for giving residency to my informants do not always display how migrations are related to politics and Israeli dominance. Although some of my interlocutors were accepted as refugees due to political persecution in the 1970s, other elderly informants came as work migrants as early as the 1960s. Such work migration was however related to the economic

---

6 All names mentioned in this text are pseudonyms and some biographical details have been changed as to ensure the anonymity of my informants. Interviews were mostly carried out in Swedish, but a couple of them in Arabic or in English. Thanks to my earlier research in the West Bank, I encounter few obstacles when attempting to establish trust and informed consent among my interlocutors.

7 Nina Gren, *Each Day Another Disaster: Politics and Everyday Life in a Palestinian Refugee Camp in the West Bank* (Gothenburg: U of Gothenburg, 2009).

constraints following *al-nakba* and dire conditions under Jordanian rule.[8] Some informants are former students who were denied return to or were deported from the occupied territories or who decided to stay outside the homeland for various reasons.[9] Amongst my informants, single men would migrate to Sweden in the 1960s or the 1970s and were later married to women from the West Bank. These women would arrive through family reunification. These couples' children were then born in Sweden and became Swedish citizens, as did their parents. As this second generation of Swedish Palestinians has grown up, many of them have married Palestinians from the West Bank. Another wave of family reunification in Sweden thus started. A couple of younger women, born in Sweden, also moved to Palestine for their spouses. One of my informants arrived as an asylum-seeker rather recently. Sweden was in this case chosen as a country of refuge, because this person had relatives already residing in the country.

While in the West Bank, my interlocutors either stay with close family or in their own house or apartment (if they have one). They might also stay in a family house that they will inherit or have inherited part of. Most use a couple of weeks of their summer vacations for these visits, while some retired informants spend half the year in Palestine,[10] in a kind of "seasonal retirement migration." Though emotionally and politically charged, Palestine in a sense becomes a sort of holiday destination, a getaway from mundane routines.

Swedish-Palestinian Migrant Houses as Diasporic Project

Swedish-Palestinian houses in the West Bank have many similarities with other migrants' houses in different parts of the world. This has been described in previous migration research (see below). There are however things that distinguish the houses I deal with here from the bulk of migrants' houses and this is related to the fact that Swedish-Palestinian houses are built in a very politicized context.

---

8 Maya Rosenfeld, *Confronting the Occupation: Work, Education and Political Activism of Palestinian Families in a Refugee Camp* (Stanford, California: Stanford UP, 2004): 33–34; Benny Morris, *Righteous Victims: A History of the Zionist-Arab Conflict 1881–1999* (New York: Alfred A. Knopf, 1999): 260.

9 Cf. Lindholm, *The Palestinian Diaspora*, 84.

10 I am well aware that strictly speaking there is no state called "Palestine." In this text, I sometimes use this word since this was the most frequently used term by my interlocutors when referring to one of their homelands.

Although I find it problematic to speak of diasporas as groups,[11] it is important to underline that Palestinian exiles can and should be understood as a type of "victim diaspora."[12] Their dispersal is accompanied by the collective memory of a single traumatic event (*al-nakba*) along with repeated persecution and political violence.[13] As noted about Palestinians in Sydney and in Athens, there are close connections between political and cultural identities.[14] In my view, the wider use of the word diaspora for any group of migrants (who are spread out in several countries and keep engaged in the country of origin) carries with it problematic aspects, since it undermines our ability to understand more unsettling experiences of flight such as Palestinian, Tamil, and Kurdish, amongst others.

Brubakers's claim that the over-application of the term 'diaspora', which threatens to render it useless, has caused the concept to lose its discriminating power.[15] Diasporas vary greatly in type and location. The term is assigned to a variety of different experiences as Armenian expulsion, a global gay community and Hindu exile. In addition, Brubaker and I see the risks of essentializing diasporas as bounded, homogeneous units, which avoid the complexities of identity politics and of people's diverse relations to place. Belonging to a diaspora should not merely be about counting ancestry. Brubaker's suggestion is that research instead should focus on diaspora as a category of practice that is used to make claims, to start projects and mobilize energies. "It is often a category with a strong normative change. It does not so much *describe* the world as seek to *remake* it," writes Brubaker.[16] Diaspora formation is a way of formulating the identities and loyalties of people. Diasporas, understood in this way, help us think about political communities through their actions; how they mobilize, strategize and effect change locally, nationally and transnationally.[17] In sum, rather than to

---

11 Rogers Brubaker, "The 'Diaspora' Diaspora," *Ethnic and Racial Studies* 28.1 (2005): 1–19, 10.

12 Robin Cohen, *Global Diasporas: An Introduction* (London: UCL P, 1997): 39–40.

13 This does not exclude that forced dispersals may bring some positive change for individuals and groups, neither does it exclude the possibility that identity formation may be a direct outcome of such tragedies.

14 Jeremy Cox, John Connell, "Place, Exile and Identity: The Contemporary Experience of Palestinians in Sydney," *Australian Geographer* 34.3 (2003): 329–343; Elizabeth Mavroudi, "Palestinians in Diaspora, Empowerment and Informal Political Space," *Political Geography* 27 (2008): 57–73.

15 Brubaker "The 'Diaspora' Diaspora," 3.

16 Brubaker "The 'Diaspora' Diaspora," 12.

17 Daphne Winland, "Why We Come Back to Diasporas: Heterogeneous Groups and the Persistent Dream of Political Action," *Diaspora: A Journal of Transnational Studies* 16.1/2 (2007): 254–264, 262.

speak of "the diaspora" as an ethno-cultural unit, it is more fruitful and precise, to speak of diasporic stances, projects, claims, idioms, practices, and so on. I return to the diasporic part of my informants' house-projects below.

As shown in case studies worldwide, many migrants have an interest in investing in houses in their country of origins,[18] as do Swedes with Palestinian origins. Within migration research, house-building has frequently been discussed in relation to remittances and investments.[19] To my knowledge, the only scholarly attention paid to Palestinian migrants' houses is an article by Escribano and El-Joubeh and a discussion about remittances in a book by Moors.[20] Remittances to the Palestinian territories have largely been spent on housing in addition to university fees and wedding expenses.[21] Building houses in the Palestinian territories often requires buying land, which is another form of investment. House construction also offers employment opportunities and helps local salesmen when building material is bought locally. On the other hand, houses and land are hotly contested issues in the Israeli-Palestinian context. The Israeli state continues to demolish Palestinian houses[22] and to confiscate Palestinian-owned land.[23] To some extent this renders housing a precarious investment for

---

18 See for instance Marta Bivand Erdal, "'A Place to Stay in Pakistan': Why Migrants Build Houses in their Country of Origin," *Population, Space and Place* 18 (2012): 629–641; Dimitris Dalakoglou, "Migrating–Remitting–'Building'–Dwelling: House-making as 'Proxy' Presence in Postsocialist Albania," *Journal of the Royal Anthropological Institute* 16 (2010): 761–777; Lothar Smith, Valentina Mazzaucato, "Constructing Homes, Building Relationships: Migrant Investments in Houses," *Tijdschrift voor Economische en Sociale Geografie* 100.5 (2009): 662–673.
19 Filomeno Aguilar, "Labour Migration and Ties of Relatedness: Diasporic Houses and Investments in Memory in a Rural Philippine Village," *Thesis Eleven* 98 (2009): 88–114.
20 Marisa Escribano, Nazmi El-Joubeh, "Migration and Change in a West Bank Village: The Case of Deir Dibwan," *Journal of Palestine Studies* 11.1 (1981): 150–160; Annelies Moors, *Women, Property and Islam: Palestinian Experiences, 1920–1990* (Cambridge: Cambridge UP, 1995).
21 Nobody seems to know the amount of remittances that reach the West Bank and Gaza Strip. My impression is that the remittances are mostly sent from people in exile to their parents and siblings rather than to other family members.
22 The Israeli army claims to have two main reasons for destroying Palestinian houses; the first is if the house has been built without permission (which is the usual reason for demolishing houses built inside Israel) and the second is the wide category 'military/security needs,' including destroying the homes of Palestinians who are suspected of carrying out attacks against Israelis. See Amnesty International, *Under the Rubble: House Demolition and Destruction of Land and Property* <http://www.amnesty.org/en/library/info/MDE15/033/2004> (acc. February 6, 2015) (Amnesty International, 2004); UN OCHA, *East Jerusalem: Key Humanitarian Concerns* (East Jerusalem: UN OCHA, 2011).
23 Yehezkel Lein, Eyal Weizman, *Land Grab: Israel's Settlement Policy in the West Bank* <http://www.btselem.org/download/200205_land_grab_eng.pdf> (acc. February 6, 2015) (B'Tselem – The Israeli Information Center for Human Rights in the Occupied Territories, 2002); UN

Palestinian migrants and locals.[24] However, as have been noted by several anthropologists and other social scientists, remittances are more than financial transactions and rational investments; they are moral obligations that may inform us about processes to create and maintain social relations, in particular kinship.[25]

Migrants, in general, seem to build houses for both practical and symbolic reasons. The other major scholarly approach is to view migrant houses as relational places in transnational social spaces, upholding bonds in dispersed families despite geographical distances. Or phrased differently, "making [...] houses is synonymous with the (re-)making of relationships."[26] In the Palestinian case, kinship has proven to be a crucial component in counteracting social disintegration and economic deprivation in exile. It has been given special prominence since relatives are usually relied upon for various types of support.[27] Housebuilding, both practically and symbolically, often strengthens the cooperation between family living abroad and family in Palestine (although it may also jeopardize a relationship if serious conflict emerges under construction). When a Swedish-Palestinian family builds a house in the West Bank, a close male relative is usually the one responsible for watching over its construction. The house also becomes a physical manifestation of the migrant's connection to the home-

---

OCHA, *The Humanitarian Impact on Palestinians of Israeli Settlements and Other Infrastructure in the West Bank*, (East Jerusalem: UN OCHA, 2007).

24 It is not new that houses are contested in the Israeli-Palestinian context; the British authorities blew up houses as a form of reprimand during the peasant revolt in the 1930s. See Ted Swedenburg, *Memories of Revolt: The 1936–1939 Rebellion and the Palestinian National Past* (Fayetteville: U of Arkansas P, 1999): 173. Village houses were also razed by Israel after the Palestinians fled in 1948. Not only do Israeli policies today politicize Palestinian houses, but so too does Palestinian resistance. For instance, the lost village houses are often evoked in Palestinian nationalistic poetry. See Susan Slyomovics, *The Object of Memory: Arab and Jew Narrate the Palestinian Village* (Philadelphia: U of Pennsylvania P, 1998): 176.

25 Lisa Åkesson, "Remittances and Inequality in Cape Verde: The Impact of Changing Family Organization," *Global Networks* 9.3 (2009): 381–398; Silvia Grigolini, "When Houses Provide More Than Shelter: Analyzing the Uses of Remittances within Their Sociocultural Context," in *Migration and Economy: Global and Local Dynamics*, ed. Lilian Trager (Walnut Creek, Lanham, New York, Oxford: Rowman & Littlefield, 2005): 193–224.

26 Dalakoglou, "Migrating–Remitting–'Building'–Dwelling," 772.

27 Shafeeq N. Ghabra, *Palestinians in Kuwait –The Family and the Politics of Survival* (Boulder, London: Westview P, 1987), *passim*; Diane Baxter, "Honor Thy Sister: Selfhood, Gender, and Agency in Palestinian Culture," *Anthropological Quarterly* 80.3 (2007): 737–775, 762; Julie M. Peteet, "Transforming Trust: Dispossession and Empowerment among Palestinian Refugees," in *Mistrusting Refugees*, eds. Valentine E. Daniel, John C. Knutson (Berkeley: U of California P, 1995): 169.

land and to the family. As I will explain further on, in the Palestinian territories, people most often live close to their families, on top of or next to parents' and other relatives' flats and houses. The migrants thus literally build a space for themselves in the family and establish a presence by proxy in their place of origin even if living far away.[28]

Again I return to diasporic practices and wonder: Can the planning and building of houses in the West Bank be categorized as such? At first glance, these practices may seem transnational rather than diasporic, but in an extremely politicized context such as in Israel and Palestine, it is difficult to consider them apolitical. Even if many of my informants may prefer *not* to think about their family trips and house building in the West Bank as political, their actions are forced into a political frame by the Israeli authorities and the wider context of the Israeli-Palestinian relationship. The Swedish-Palestinians are not mere tourists or expats coming home for the summer but Israel considers, suspects, and deals with them as "security threats." Swedish citizens of Palestinian descent, who have at some point been registered in the occupied territories by the Israeli state, are also denied travel privileges from Ben Gurion Airport (near Tel Aviv).[29] They are instead required to travel through Jordan via the Allenby Bridge. This was a major concern for them as well as the harassment my informants experienced due to their Palestinian origins by Israeli border guards (whether they have been registered in the occupied territories or not), and was often brought up in interviews. The harassment ranged from being endlessly questioned at the airport or the Jordanian border and verbal threats of violence to less frequent arrests and deportations. Crossing the border was thus an unpleasant experience and created much uncertainty, but it also politicized the visits to Palestine. I am tempted to say that my informants became "more Palestinian" by such annoyances, since these Israeli practices underlined and confirmed their "Palestinian-ness."[30]

For my interlocutors who reside in Sweden, houses "back home" came to represent a commitment to the West Bank family and to the country in general; the houses represent social, emotional *and* political statements. Israeli settlements in the occupied territories are often referred to as "facts on the ground"

---

28 Dalakoglou, "Migrating–Remitting–'Building'–Dwelling," *passim*.

29 The Swedish General Consulate in Jerusalem are well aware of these problems and write about it (in Swedish) at the following home page: Swedish General Consulate, "Reseinformation Jerusalem och Palestina" <http://www.swedenabroad.com/sv-SE/Ambassader/Jerusalem/Reseinformation/Reseinformation-Jerusalem/> (acc. February 26, 2014).

30 Cf. Rashid Khalidi, *Palestinian Identity: The Making of a Modern National Consciousness* (New York: Columbia UP, 1997).

that may influence future peace agreements and an establishment of permanent borders between Israel and a future Palestinian state.[31] From a political and pa-triotic viewpoint, one reason to build in the West Bank is to establish Palestinian "facts on the ground," opposing Israeli settlement policies. House-building is in this context a sort of defiance strategy. This was more or less confirmed by my informants. For example, Fuad, sixty years old, had lived in Sweden for about thirty-five years when I interviewed him in his house in a suburb of a major Swedish city. He had not built a house in Palestine but he owned some land that for him clearly represented an act of resistance:

> I have 5,000 square-meters. It is agricultural land planted with olive trees. I've bought it myself. As, I told you earlier, I gave my blind brother the piece of land I inherited. I bought the land with money I had earned in Sweden. [...] Nina: Why is it important with land [in Palestine]? –It is important! It's my roots. I don't want to be pulled away from there. And it is in defiance of the paper I had to sign [when I was deported by Israel]. You can't act like that. Israelis do as they like. They have committed all crimes but they are always forgiven.

The dream of returning to places of origin is not only part of individual migrants' lives, but often constitutes an element in diasporic identity formation, although it seldom leads to actual repatriation.[32] Although many migrants acknowledge that it is not likely they will actually return, building houses seem to be "the pos-sibility of sustaining the myth [which] enables them to keep at a distance the painful consciousness that they will never go back 'home'."[33] In the Palestinian case, strong nostalgia, which is commonly expressed by exiled communities, is reinforced by a deep sense of injustice from being robbed of a homeland. UN Resolutions also states that the refugees from the Israeli-Arab war in 1948 should have the right to return to their homes and to be compensated for their losses.[34] For many Palestinians, "return to Palestine" is imperative and includes complex political, material, moral and existential dimensions, although individuals may

---

31 According to the Israeli human rights organization Btselem there were 125 government-sanctioned Israeli settlements in the West Bank in 2012 (excluding East Jerusalem and Hebron) along with about 100 unauthorized 'outposts.' It is estimated that half a million settlers live in the West Bank B'Tselem, "Statistics on Settlements and Settlement Population" (January 1, 2011), *B'Tselem – The Israeli Information Center for Human Rights in the Occupies Territories* <http://www.btselem.org/settlements/statistics> (acc. February 26, 2014).
32 See, for instance, Julianne Hammer, *Palestinians Born in Exile: Diaspora and the Search for a Homeland* (Austin: U of Texas P, 2005); William Safran, "Diasporas in Modern Societies: Myths of Homeland and Return," *Diaspora* 1.1 (1991): 83–99.
33 Erdal, "A Place to Stay in Pakistan," 635.
34 It is the UN General Assembly Resolution 194 (III), December 11, 1948, which is most fre-quently referred to when discussing the Palestinian refugees' right of return.

have different opinions about the likeliness and pragmatics of return.[35] The quest for return has become a significant part of Palestinian national identity, reaching much further than those Palestinians fleeing during *al-nakba*. It symbolizes Palestinian history. The strong implications to return were also notable in some of my informants' narratives. For others, it seemed to remain a context that was impossible to forget.

In addition to the discourse on return, Palestinian political leadership has also highlighted the importance of remaining inside the historical homeland by showing *ṣumud* (steadfastness).[36] *ṣumud* is a complex emic concept that carries several intertwined meanings, both in nationalist rhetoric and in daily life. For instance, the word *ṣumud* is used in relation to refusing to surrender one's land, by remaining in refugee camps and inside the Palestinian homeland. Israeli right wing politicians also continue to talk about "transfer," which refers to the forced deportation of Palestinians from the occupied territories. Steadfastness is thus a resistance to these threats. Palestinians living in Sweden have of course failed to remain steadfast in Palestine. They have either left voluntarily or by force. Maintaining contact with their homeland and building houses is therefore an attempt to, despite patriotic failures, remain committed and at least open to the possibility of return. Those practices also establish a sense of diasporic belonging to the Palestinian homeland.

A House in the West Bank

Vivianne lives in a city in Southern Sweden. She and her family also own a house in the town where she grew up. She left almost forty years ago when she moved to Sweden for marriage. During my visit to her West Bank house, Vivianne points out the buildings outside her family's kitchen window. She and her husband are related to practically everyone in this neighborhood. One of their daughters married a man from this town and also lives nearby. To Vivianne, one of the most important things about her time spent in Palestine is being close to her daughter and her grandchildren.

Like most Palestinian houses, in Vivianne and her husband's, you step directly into a large reception room when entering. There is no hallway and the kitchen and bedrooms are normally hidden in the interior of the house. To a first time guest,

---

35 Gren, *Each Day Another Disaster*, 158–162.
36 Raja Shehadeh, *The Third Way: A Journal of Life in the West Bank* (London, Melbourne, New York: Quartet Books, 1982).

these rooms often remain out of sight. Except for the rather large reception room with three different groups of sofas, they have two bedrooms: one occupied by Vivianne and her husband and one currently occupied by their youngest daughter and her husband and baby. The daughter and her family are here on vacation from a Gulf country where they live. In the house there is also a bathroom, a fully-equipped kitchen and a spare room used for storage and ironing. The house is surrounded by a huge veranda with a splendid view of the valley below. There is no sign of luxury or excessive spending, but the apartment design seems ordinarily middle class Palestinian. The lower floor of the house is rented out to a family who lives there year round.

I ask Vivianne how they have been able to build this house and she explains that they have been working hard in Sweden and have spent all their money on building the house. They started the construction in the mid-1980s and have been constructing it step-by-step over time. Her husband inherited the land they built on from his father so it did not cost them anything. In Sweden, on the other hand, Vivianne and her husband live in a rented apartment.

In the West Bank, it is "normal" to build a house; essentially "everybody" attempts to build a house. This is especially true for young men. Bachelors should ideally prepare a house or apartment for potential brides. House-building is thus linked to establishing a family.[37] It is also common that people who have been renting for years save up to build a house before retirement. Most prefer to own their houses rather than to pay rent. House ownership is culturally significant, since autonomy, in the sense of a household being independent of others, is greatly valued.[38] In urban areas and among prominent families, houses signify social status and "deep-rootedness;" the material evidence of a family that dates back hundreds of years. In villages, a large part of one's income is spent on building a house. Camp refugees who lost their houses in 1948, also spend money on improving their housing in the camps, even if they do not own the land on which these houses are built.[39] Refugees with financial means have also bought land and built houses outside of the camps.[40] By building a house in Palestine, the Swedes with Palestinian backgrounds thus become "like everybody else" among West Bankers. Some migrants also experience pressure from their West Bank relatives to build houses. It is possible that some build

---

37 Gren, *Each Day Another Disaster*, 122.
38 Moors, *Women, Property and Islam*, 46.
39 Moors, *Women, Property and Islam*, 46.
40 Gren, *Each Day Another Disaster*, 172.

out of guilt from leaving their families behind. For others, houses "back home" prove that they have succeeded abroad as migrants.[41]

A large portion of one's house is not intended for those who live there, but instead for its visitors. In Vivianne's reception room, she could easily find seats for fifteen guests without bringing in extra-chairs or rearranging. In the West Bank, an ideal Palestinian is said to be generous, hospitable and caring about others,[42] although such concepts are interpreted differently depending on family traditions, class and local area. Also for migrants, who decide to build a house, it seems expected and self-evident that houses are designed for receiving many visitors. An adult Palestinian needs a home for receiving guests, to show hospitality and to perform generosity. In Palestinian villages there used to be public spaces or houses where village men received guests. Those guesthouses had different names depending on local areas and were for instance called *diwan, madafah, diwaniyye* or *saahah*.[43] It is said that the coffee always needed to be kept warm in the guesthouses in case a stranger came by. Guesthouses were also meeting places for related kin groups, common in many Arab societies.[44] Today, no such communal guesthouse exists in the West Bank, so people find other ways to receive guests. Depending on one's economic situation, each household or extended family has a reception room, or *saloon* in colloquial Arabic, with sofas, armchairs and coffee tables where guests are entertained. In the poorer strata of society, families that cannot afford furniture put mattresses or plastic chairs in this room. The *saloon*, according to local standards is a room kept tidy by the women of the family in case someone unexpectedly would drop by. Although the communal guesthouses of the past were part of a male sphere, in the present day both men and women use the *saloon* to accommodate guests.

In Sweden, on the other hand, houses and apartments are often designed differently. An ordinary rented apartment in Sweden, similar to the one Vivianne lives in, is strikingly different from a Palestinian house because it has been built primarily for the people who live there, not for accommodating many guests. The space for accommodating guests is normally a minor part of a Swedish living room today; it is mostly for the people who live in the house, for watching TV

---

41 Cf. Escribano, El-Joubeh "Migration and Change in a West Bank Village," 154.
42 Julie M. Peteet, "Male Gender and Rituals of Resistance in the Palestinian *intifada:* A Cultural Politics of Violence," *American Ethnologist* 21.1 (1994): 31–49.
43 Slyomovics, *The Object of Memory*, 137.
44 Slyomovics, *The Object of Memory*, 137.

or spending time together.[45] If Vivianne would have fifteen guests in her Swedish apartment she would need to move the furniture and bring in extra-chairs. If she were to expect many guests she might even rent a hall. When looking at the design of Swedish apartments and houses, it is also striking that the hallway or the entrance is an important room. The hallway has a practical function: in the harsh Swedish climate, this is where people leave their jackets, umbrellas, hats, gloves and boots. Year around, most Swedes leave their shoes in the hallway, either while they are visiting someone or in their own homes. This room clearly marks inside from outside and symbolically establishes boundaries between private and public spheres. In contrast, and as Sayigh noted about houses in Palestinian refugee camps in Lebanon, Palestinian houses often have rather flexible boundaries.[46] Depending on your age, gender, and relationship to a family, you are or are not allowed entrance to different parts of a house. Palestinian homes are not characterized, in Sayigh's words, by the "unbreachable boundaries of individual privacy and exclusion" from the members of a household as are houses in Northern Europe but, on the contrary, are open to members of the extended family and to close friends and neighbors. However, there are limits to this openness. Not just anyone can walk into someone else's bedroom; it is a question of kinship, gender and the nature of the relationship. As mentioned above, first time guests usually only get to see the *saloon.*

So who visits migrants' houses in the West Bank? Most often visitors consist of relatives and in-laws. Some neighbors and old friends also come by frequently. Neighbors may in fact also be relatives, since in the West Bank people tend to live in "kin-based living arrangements, despite the prevalence of nuclear households."[47] An individual's parents and siblings or in-laws may live in the same building and uncles or other close family members may live across the street. Kinship ties have a socially constructed nature even in Palestinian society, where blood relations are often discursively underlined. As Rothenberg writes, proximity is central to the practices of affirming kinship and for enforcing fam-

---

45 Before functionalism arrived in Sweden in the 1920s and 30s, there was a Swedish tradition of having a kind of reception room or a room only used for special occasions. It was referred to as *finrum* or *salong.*
46 Rosemary Sayigh, "A House is Not a Home: Permanent Impermanence of Habitat for Palestinian Expellees in Lebanon," *Holy Land Studies Journal* 4.1 (2005): 17–39.
47 Peggy Johnson, "Living Together in a Nation of Fragments: Dynamics of Kin, Place, and Nation," in *Living Palestine: Family Survival, Resistance, and Mobility under Occupation*, ed. Lisa Taraki (Syracuse, New York: Syracuse UP, 2006): 92.

ilial ties and obligations.[48] With continuous dispersal of Palestinian families, due to migration and restricted mobility in the occupied territories, ties and obligations are weakened and must be re-affirmed by different practices, such as courtesy visits.

West Bank hospitality *(karamat iddayaafe)* includes offering tea, coffee, soft drinks, sweets, fruits, nuts, cookies and sometimes a full meal if guests linger. Being able to attend to many people is a virtue.[49] Guests are not supposed to move around in the house or to serve themselves. Even if you are busy, you are expected to give your guests time – anything else would be rude. Even though people more and more tend to call before they attempt to visit someone's home, it is often acceptable to drop by unannounced. In my experience, hosts do not always feel they need to "do something" with their guests, but in most cases emphasis is put on pampering guests and "sitting together" as it is often expressed locally. It can be about the simple pleasure of drinking tea or smoking together. Swedish-Palestinians are also invited to numerous dinners hosted by kin and friends; these invitations are generally impossible to turn down out of courtesy. In a house in the West Bank, one often invites people back to establish a temporal reciprocal equilibrium.

A practical reason for building houses in one's country of origin is to have somewhere to stay while visiting during the holidays.[50] Among my Swedish-Palestinian informants, this reason was prominent. Although Swedish-Palestinians may stay with different relatives during visits to Palestine, many prefer to have a place of one's own. Socializing in the West Bank can be intense. By having one's own house, the visiting family can have privacy and act more independently from one's relatives, my informants explained. It is considered more appropriate to have one's own place and to not burden one's relatives if visiting the West Bank yearly. Social life in the West Bank differs from most of my informants' social lives in Sweden. Especially for those who have grown up in Sweden, gossiping and interference in other people's lives can be experienced as overwhelming. Some also noted that many Palestinian families fight a lot, which was considered tiring and difficult to deal with, especially while sharing a house. One can thus note some ambivalence about West Bank sociality among Swedish-Palestinians. It seems that the houses help to manage these ambivalent emotions.

---

48 Celia E. Rothenberg, *Spirits of Palestine: Gender, Society, and Stories of the Jinn* (Lanham, Oxford: Lexington Books, 2004): 86.
49 Cf. Andrew Shryock, "The New Jordanian Hospitality: House, Host, and Guest in the Culture of Public Display," *Society for Comparative Study of Society and History* (2004): 35–62.
50 Erdal, "A Place to Stay in Pakistan," 629.

Feeding Our Children's Roots

For many adults, spending holidays in Palestine offers an important way to teach children, who grow up in exile, about Palestinian culture. I met up with a married couple in their forties, Jamil and Nada, in his native village. They had decided to build an apartment on top of Jamil's parents' house and had already ordered the house plans. While we were having coffee, Jamil said that he really enjoyed spending time in the village where he grew up. To him, there was something special about this particular village: Here, he felt at home even after two decades in Sweden. "I enjoy sitting on the veranda in the evenings, drinking tea with my parents. There is something special here to me that has little to do with the country as a whole. It is also about guiding our children towards knowing where they come from." According to Jamil, parents need to help their children know their roots so they can find a balance between "the Swedish" and "the Palestinian" way. Although Nada was hesitant about the building project, since she was afraid they could not afford it, she also agreed that the trips and the house were vital for their children. Commenting on the large amount of money the family spent on their West Bank vacation, Nada said: "But we do this for our children, for their roots. Palestinians always need to fertilize their roots." Such statements were common among my interlocutors and hint at a political context where Palestinian presence is threatened.

Behind parents' wishes to teach their children about their cultural heritage, is the fear of losing one's children to Swedish norms and life styles.[51] An interesting parallel to those concerns can be found in Escribato's and El-Joubeh's article about a Palestinian village marked by emigration: Wives and children were often left behind, while men migrated, because people wanted their children to be raised in the village.[52] Several of my interlocutors worried that their children would get married to a Swede and then end up divorced since divorce rates in Sweden are high.

For most of my informants children should learn the vague "Palestinian ways" (*det palestinska* in Swedish). These concentrated on practicing Arabic, getting to know the family in the West Bank, and learning about religion and ways of socializing. Also, bringing one's grown up or young adult children to the West Bank, makes it possible to introduce them to potential future spouses in hopes that the children will fall in love with a local Palestinian without matchmaking from their relatives. Owning a house or apartment facilitates bringing up chil-

---

51 Cf. Erdal, "A Place to Stay in Pakistan," 635.
52 Escribano, El-Joubeh, "Migration and Change in a West Bank Village," 153.

dren in "the Palestinian way." Rami provides a good example of this "successful socialization process." He was born in a middle-sized Swedish town in the early 1970s. He speaks Arabic well although he doesn't know how to write and read. Since early childhood he spent most summers in the small town from which his parents originate. Some of his best friends live in this town. After marriage to a Swedish woman that ended in separation, he also met and fell in love with his present Palestinian wife from the West Bank, who now lives with him in Sweden. In an interview in Sweden, he commented on his parents' decision to build a house in the West Bank:

> I'm so happy my dad built [the house] because I have cousins who live [in Sweden] and who don't speak a word of Arabic. Their parents came at the same time as mine, but they took another path somehow. They didn't travel [to Palestine] that often, they never built a house down there. Maybe they didn't have the same strong contacts as my parents kept with Palestine and they [my cousins] hardly understand any Arabic. And they don't like to travel there, they think it's boring and that there is nothing to do. While I can travel there and there might be a curfew and I sit and just talk with two friends and I still think that it's the best summer of my life. They don't understand what I mean, but somehow I still have this inside me. I don't need to do much when I'm in Palestine, but I'm with my friends and I rest and take it easy.

"Sitting and just talking with a friend" even during curfew is an example of the kind of sociality, which is, at least ideally, promoted in Palestine. While Rami was positive about the West Bank and the family house there, others were more ambivalent. Nada's and Jamil's teenage son, Salim, enjoyed being in his father's village, but did not really care about the planned apartment since he felt the political situation was too uncertain and that the village and its land was threatened by neighboring settlements. "It is over here. [...] I will die in Sweden. It would have been different if it had been more unsafe there, in Sweden."

The Power of Diasporic Houses

Bourdieu wrote that the inhabited space, especially the house, is "the principal locus for the objectification of the generative schemes."[53] In his view, the house is central to *habitus* and thus to how a child learns the logics of his or her culture. Houses are the locus of social and cultural reproduction as well as creativ-

---

53 Pierre Bourdieu, *Outline of a Theory of Practice* (Cambridge, New York, Melbourne: Cambridge UP, 1979): 89.

ity. Miller remarks that houses, what he calls "the elephants of stuff," silently carry messages like other material things:[54]

> There is a natural humility to things, in that they work best as the frame that guides our sense of what is appropriate, rather than as things we pay regard to in their own right. [...] When [a] message is carried, not by a hectoring voice, but well hidden within the mere substance of apparently silent stuff, we are less likely to sense our disempowerment.

In this chapter, I argue that by interacting with the houses in the West Bank children of Palestinian descent born and raised in Sweden are disempowered by a Palestinian sociality that is built into the houses. Houses are tools to construct Palestinian subjects. There are power discrepancies built into the houses as children's opinions about construction and design might not be of concern to their parents. It is also likely that power affects individual adults' possibilities to decide how houses will look. For instance, a husband may make more decisions than his wife or the opinions of a migrant who spends the majority of his or her time in Sweden might be overruled by a relative in charge of construction. Often, people are not the sole agents behind the material world through which they live.[55]

According to Miller's "accommodating theory", people can relate to their houses in three distinct ways.[56] Firstly, as mentioned, the Palestinian-Swedes have a need for accommodation while spending time in Palestine. By providing accommodation for themselves in their own house, they are free from obligations with their extended family and can establish a kind of normalcy "as if not living abroad or even if living abroad." They are also able to invite, receive and entertain guests on their own accord.

Secondly, accommodating is an appropriation of the home by its inhabitants. It may imply the altering of a home to suit one's needs, but it can also imply the need to change oneself to suit his or her accommodation. Miller takes the example of his own house in the UK, which was built in 1906. Theoretically, he can alter the house as he pleases since he owns it, yet he cannot. The house is, according to Miller, "too good-looking." Every time he brings a new item home he feels ashamed of not being able to fully live up to the aesthetics of the house. In relation to the houses discussed in this chapter, we might wonder whether the physical layout of the house affects the social activities that take place within the house. Is it appropriate not being a good host in a house built

---

54 Daniel Miller, *Stuff* (Cambridge, Malden: Polity P, 2010): 82.
55 Miller, *Stuff*, 84.
56 Miller, *Stuff*, 96.

for welcoming guests? I would say: not really. It might be possible of course, but not likely. For instance, Rami or Jamil's children become "more Palestinian" in that they focus more on hospitality and social relations, while staying in a Palestinian house. Failing to have many visitors in the Palestinian house is also likely to cause loneliness. Do children learn these values merely by visiting? Or must they actively participate in having a house in the West Bank? I would say they learn to be guests by visiting others. They may observe how their grandparents and other relatives accommodate guests or how they act as hosts themselves in others' houses. However, if the Swedish-Palestinian family has their own house, the process seems to be accentuated.

Thirdly, according to Miller, we can think about accommodation as a willingness to compromise on behalf of the other, a convenient arrangement to settle a dispute. In the case of Swedes with a Palestinian background, the West Bank houses seem to achieve balance between the Swedish-ness of their everyday lives and their Palestinian origins. Accommodation, in this sense, reflects what Homi K. Bhabha referred to as cultural *side-by-side-ness*.[57] My interlocutors were not cultural "hybrids," but they were most often able to move rather freely between the Palestinian and Swedish parts of their lives. However, according to Vivianne, "when I'm here I long for my life in Sweden and when I'm there I long for Palestine." Apart from being a cultural compromise, it is also a political one. Through the house, the family residing in exile maintains presence in the West Bank while being absent, steadfast despite having left.

Turning houses into homes is indeed a dynamic process. Home may refer to a place of living for mundane practices, be bound up with national imaginaries and constitute a mobile concept within a transnational world.[58] The homeliness of domestic spaces cannot be taken for granted, but interacts with individuals' different experiences of home, depending on, for instance, family dynamics, gender, age, race, sexuality and personality. I hesitate to call the houses discussed in this chapter "homes," because the ones I have visited were at least in my view not very "homely," but strikingly empty, almost ghost-like. Others were not yet built. What differentiates the appearance of Vivianne's house for instance from many other Palestinian homes in the area is that it looked new and unused. There were very few knickknacks and decorative items, except from curtains and cushions. The walls were more or less empty of paintings and family photos and "empty" in comparison to their homes in Sweden. In Swedish exile, people,

---

57 Homi K. Bhabha, "Living Side By Side: On Culture and Security," keynote address, *Diasporic Constructions of Home and Belonging* conference, University of Münster, September 22–24, 2013.
58 Alison Blunt, Robyn Dowling, *Home* (London: Routledge, 2006): 29.

especially those who have migrated, tended to build "a little Palestine" or "Palestine shrines" in their homes by decorating with Palestinian flags, Palestinian embroideries and pictures of *Al Aqsa* mosque in Jerusalem.[59] They also display photos of family. It is possible that the uncanny house is a precondition for accommodation in its third sense, for balancing between different cultural and political contexts and remaining both Swedish and Palestinian, but this needs to be further investigated.

Conclusion

In sum, due to their politicized context, Swedish-Palestinian migrants' houses in the West Bank are part of a diasporic project and the houses mediate Palestinian cultural values about hospitality and a rich social life to children and youth who grow up in Sweden. By interacting with the houses, children and youth become "more Palestinian" and the houses establish a balance between life in Sweden and life in Palestine. The mastering of Palestinian sociality is both an important ingredient in a political sense of diasporic belonging to Palestine and for cultural side-by-side-ness.

Beyond the empirical uniqueness of this case study, a focus on house-building as a diasporic practice is part of a material approach to issues of home and belonging. As a researcher interested in diaspora, it is easy to discuss intangible feelings of identity with one's informants. A focus on material expressions of belonging such as houses, home decorations or passports and other identity papers open up new possibilities to understand diasporic identities.

---

59 Lindholm, *The Palestinian Diaspora*, 178.

Annette Kern-Stähler

The Sanctification of Home in Late Medieval England

Abstract: This article considers home as a sacred space. For a long time, studies of medieval sacred spaces focused only on consecrated buildings such as churches, chapels and shrines and excluded the home. However, recent scholarship has challenged our understanding of the sacred and the profane as two distinct categories (Eliade, Durkheim) and has emphasized the fluidity between the boundaries of the sacred and the profane. This article explores late medieval practices of transforming the profane space of the home into a sacred space.[1]

In what has been described as one of the "most astonishingly inventive compositions" of the late fifteenth-century,[2] the first full-page miniature in the Book of Hours of Mary of Burgundy (illuminated *c.* 1470–75) shows the owner of the manuscript, probably Mary of Burgundy (1457–82), daughter of Charles the Bold, Duke of Burgundy, and wife of the Holy Roman Emperor Maximilian (fig. 1).[3] She is seated by a window, absorbed in a book of hours, her prayer beads to hand – an intimate scene in a domestic setting which displays all the attributes of Mary's noble station: a small lapdog, jewels, cut irises in a crystal vase, two buds of dianthus, a veil, an embroidered purse, and a valuable book of hours covered with a protective chemise. The window of her chamber overlooks a sacred space: the choir of a gothic church, in which Mary of Burgundy appears once more, this time in veneration of the Virgin and Child. Read from front to back, the image illustrates the process of Mary's religious meditation: in the foreground the act and the tools of devotion (prayer book and beads), in the background the visualization of her contemplation. Such a reading is supported by the large initial "O" on the open page of Mary's book, which is the first letter of the *incipit* of two popular prayers to the Virgin: "Obsecro te" ["I beseech you"]

---

1 I would like to thank the members of the *Berner Mittelalter Zentrum* for their helpful comments on an earlier version of this paper.
2 Alixe Bovey, "Renaissance Bibliomania," in *Viewing Renaissance Art*, eds. Kim Woods, Carol M. Richardson and Angeliki Lymberopoulou (London: Yale UP in association with the Open University, 2007): 3:93–129, 112.
3 The debate about the identity of the young woman in the miniature and the ownership of the manuscript is summed up in Thomas Kren, "Revolution and Transformation: Painting in Devotional Manuscripts, circa 1467–1485," in *Illuminating the Renaissance. The Triumph of Flemish Manuscript Painting in Europe*, eds. Thomas Kren, Scot McKendrick (Los Angeles: Getty Publications, 2003): 121–229, 137–141.

Fig. 1 Mary of Burgundy at prayer. Book of Hours of Mary of Burgundy (illuminated *c.* 1470–75). Cod. Vind. 1857, fol. 14v. By kind permission of the Austrian National Library, Vienna.

and "O intemerata" ["O immaculate virgin"].[4] Indeed, the miniature suggests that, assisted by the prayers in her book of hours, Mary of Burgundy is able, on the strength of her contemplative practice, to transcend the space of her mundane domestic interior and to enter an imaginary sacred space which allows her to approach the object of her devotion.

It is the transformation of a domestic profane space into a sacred space illustrated by this illumination which will be the concern of this article. More specifically, I will explore medieval practices of, and models for, adapting the domestic space to accommodate worship and devotion, of integrating the sacred into the profane space of the home and of investing the home with a sacred meaning.

Drawing on the scholarship of Émile Durkheim and Mircea Eliade, who conceived of the sacred and the profane as two mutually exclusive categories,[5] studies of medieval sacred spaces tended to exclude the domestic sphere and were restricted to those buildings and locations which were consecrated and publicly recognized as holy sites, be they churches, chapels or shrines. The understanding of sacred and profane spaces as specific and distinct locations was suggested by the verbal dichotomy of the Latin terms *sacer* and *profanus*, both of which have primarily a spatial meaning: the *sanctum/sacrum* refers to a place set apart for religious use from the space around it (*sancire*); this, in turn, was *profanus* or, literally, outside the temple. This dichotomous model has more recently been challenged. Indeed, it has been shown that the profane often penetrates the sacred and vice versa. Reviewing recent scholarship on medieval and early modern sacred spaces in their introduction to the volume *Defining the Holy* (2005), Sarah Hamilton and Andrew Spicer consequently note an increased "emphasis on the fluidity between boundaries" of the sacred and the profane.[6]

This new emphasis is, I think, largely due to a growing awareness in the field of archaeology that in order to comprehend how people in the past understood, defined and used space, it is not sufficient to study the archaeological records of

---

4 Bovey, "Renaissance Bibliomania," 112; Christine Havice, "Women and the Production of Art in the Middle Ages," in *Double Vision: Perspectives on Gender and the Visual Arts*, ed. Natalie Harris Bluestone (Cranbury, NJ et al.: Associated UP, 1995): 67–94, 78.

5 Émile Durkheim, *The Elementary Forms of the Religious Life*, trans. J. W. Swain (London: George Allen & Unwin, 1915): 36–42; Mircea Eliade, *The Sacred and the Profane: The Nature of Religion*, trans. Willard R. Trask (New York: Harcourt Brace, 1959).

6 Sarah Hamilton, Andrew Spicer, "Defining the Holy: The Delineation of Sacred Space," in *Defining the Holy: Sacred Space in Medieval and Early Modern Europe*, eds. Sarah Hamilton, Andrew Spicer (Aldershot: Ashgate, 2005): 1–10.

early buildings alone.[7] While earlier, structuralist approaches to the study of material culture read material remains as external projections of social and mental processes, as a body of signs which encode, and make observable, past actions and ideas,[8] more recent poststructuralist archaeological approaches focus on the ways in which people interact with architecture.[9] While they acknowledge that space imposes a certain set of restrictions on its users, they emphasize that space is, at the same time, open to interpretation and transformation by its users.

Significant means of effecting such a transformation are specific objects and the activities associated with these objects. As the cultural anthropologist Amos Rapoport suggests, the function of a room may be transformed entirely through "the changes of the semi-fixed elements and the varied activities of the occupants."[10] With this conception of the agency of the user of space, Rapoport invites us to expand earlier notions of the sacred which were based on the claim of the structuralist anthropologist Claude Lévi-Strauss that "being in their place" is what makes sacred objects sacred.[11] Indeed, it seems that both observations should not be read as mutually exclusive and that in the medieval imagination the sacred, be it a sacred space, a sacred object or a sacred practice, had a "contagious" effect, as Dawn Marie Hayes puts it,[12] and in fact potentially performed the sanctification of whatever it came into contact with. Following Rapoport's reasoning (so neatly illustrated by the illumination of Mary of Burgundy) and drawing on a variety of sources, such as inventories, wills and devotional texts and images, I will therefore consider archaeological records in conjunction with the objects available, and the activities performed in, the late medieval home in order to conceptualize the sanctification of home in this period.

---

7 See further Annette Kern-Stähler, *"A Room of One's Own": Reale und mentale Innenräume weiblicher Selbstbestimmung im spätmittelalterlichen England* (Frankfurt a. M. et al.: Peter Lang, 2002): 6–12.

8 Claude Lévi-Strauss, *Structural Anthropology* (New York: Doubleday, 1967): 285. See further Bill Hillier and Julienne Hanson, *The Social Logic of Space* (Cambridge: Cambridge UP, 1984): 1:3–5; Ian Hodder (ed.), *Symbolic and Structural Archaeology* (Cambridge: Cambridge UP, 1982).

9 Roberta Gilchrist, "Medieval Bodies in the Material World: Gender, Stigma and the Body," in *Framing Medieval Bodies*, eds. Sarah Kay, Miri Rubin (Manchester: Manchester UP, 1994): 43–59, 45.

10 Amos Rapoport, "Systems of Activities and Systems of Settings," in *Domestic Architecture and the Use of Space: An Interdisciplinary Cross-Cultural Study*, ed. Susan Kent (Cambridge: Cambridge UP, 1990): 9–20, 13.

11 Claude Lévi-Strauss, *The Savage Mind* (Chicago: U of Chicago P, 1966): 10.

12 Dawn Marie Hayes, *Body and Sacred Place in Medieval Europe 1100–1389* (New York, London: Routledge, 2003): 5.

Sacred Spaces in the House

The integration of a sacred space into a domestic building is particularly manifest in the domestic chapel. This was initially a feature of noble residences but became increasingly popular in the fourteenth and fifteenth centuries, first in castles and manor houses, but later also in town houses – and not only in noble households. As Kate Mertes puts it, "[o]ne could in a sense bring Christ into the living quarters, within the very heart of one's own life, by the creation of a private chapel."[13] Some domestic chapels were lavishly decorated, including wall and panel paintings and stained glass, and were supplied with vestments and relics. Often the private apartments of the head of the household and his family overlooked the interior of the chapel through windows. Notable examples are Membury Court in Devon (*c.* 1290–1300), Broughton Castle in Oxfordshire (fourteenth century), and Ashby de la Zouch in Leicestershire (*c.* 1470).[14]

The domestic chapel defines one particular area of the house as a sacred domain. It is set apart (*sanctum*) for religious use by the act of consecration and thus separated from the surrounding area, the *profanum*.[15] Devotion, however, was not restricted to custom-built and consecrated chapels but also penetrated to other rooms of a house. An increase in spatial differentiation and a greater emphasis on private accommodation meant that smaller rooms gradually emerged in the medieval house. These provided rooms for prayer and private contemplation. In his monograph, *A Secret History of Domesticity* (2005), Michael McKeon has pointed at the significance of the devotional closet for private devotion in the seventeenth century. The concept of the closet, he explains, is based on a literal understanding of the biblical text of the 1611 version of Matthew 6:6: "But thou, when thou prayest, enter into thy Closet."[16] Significantly, however, the closet had already been in frequent use as a private room in the late medieval period (*OED* 'closet'), not only for reading and writing but also for prayer.[17] Sim-

---

13 Kate Mertes, *The English Noble Household 1250–1600: Good Governance and Politic Rule* (Oxford: Blackwell, 1988): 147.
14 See Mark Girouard, *Life in the English Country House: A Social and Architectural History* (New Haven: Yale UP, 1978): fig. 28; Margaret Wood, *The English Medieval House* (London: Phoenix House, 1965): 232–237. For further examples see Kern-Stähler, *A Room of One's Own*, 55–56.
15 The three phases of the rite of consecration are described in Hayes, *Body and Sacred Place*, 11–13.
16 Michael McKeon, *The Secret History of Domesticity: Public, Private, and the Division of Knowledge* (Baltimore: Johns Hopkins UP, 2005): 40.
17 See, for example, Cicely Neville's and Margaret Beaufort's use of their respective closets, discussed below, and Girouard, *Life in the English Country House*, 56, 156.

ilarly, the oriel, or oriel chamber, a recess with a window often at the upper end of the hall (*OED* 'oriel'), served as a multifunctional retreat for reading, writing and prayer.[18] Some of these multi-purpose rooms were equipped with a portable altar, for which a papal licence was required.[19] The bedchamber, too, was widely used as a place for prayer (oratory). Late medieval courtesy books recommended prayers to be said in the bedchamber on retiring at night and on rising in the morning.[20] The Chevalier de la Tour Landry, for example, admonishes his daughters in his conduct manual composed in the late fourteenth century and translated into English in the late fifteenth century: "whan ye ryse oute of youre bedde, thenne entre in to the seruyse of the hyhe lord and begyn ye your matyns"; and at the end of the day they ought to "pray for hem that ben departed oute of this world."[21] The garden, too, offered a space of seclusion and thus lent itself to private devotion.[22] An instance of this is cited in the Paston Letters. In 1453, Agnes Paston wrote to her son John that shortly before his death, one "Ser Jon Henyngham [...] seyd to hese wyf that he wuld go sey a lytyll devocion in hese gardeyn."[23]

The residences of Margaret Beaufort, Countess of Richmond and Derby and mother of Henry VII, are particularly interesting in relation to the sanctification of home. Margaret was known for integrating her devotional exercises into a very busy public life.[24] Several of her homes, such as her principal residence at Collyweston in Lincolnshire, contained a consecrated and well-supplied chapel, which was accessible from her private chambers.[25] Oddly, as the plan of her house in Sampford Peverell, Devon, indicates, this residence of hers did not include a chapel (fig. 2). Does this house, then, lack a 'sacred space'?

---

18 Wood, *English Medieval House*, 99–100.

19 Girouard, *Life in the English Country House*, 56, 156; Nicholas Orme, "Church and Chapel in Medieval England," *Transactions of the Royal Historical Society* 6 (1996): 75–102, 80; George R. Keiser, "Patronage and Piety in Fifteenth-Century England: Margaret, Duchess of Clarence, Symon Wynter, and Beinecke MS 317," *Yale University Library Gazette* 60 (1985): 32–46, 37.

20 See further John Schofield, *Medieval London Houses* (New Haven, London: Yale UP, 1994): 66; Mertes, *English Noble Household*, 140; Nicholas Orme, *Medieval Children* [2001] (New Haven: Yale UP, 2003): 208.

21 *The Book of the Knight of the Tower*, trans. William Caxton, Early English Text Society (London, New York, Toronto: Oxford UP, 1971): 16.

22 For the garden as a space of seclusion see Teresa McLean, *English Medieval Gardens* (London: Collins, 1981): 103.

23 *The Paston Letters, A.D. 1422–1509*, ed. James Gairdner, 6 vols. (London: Chatto & Windus, 1904) 2:286.

24 Orme, *Medieval Children*, 208.

25 See Richard W. Pfaff, *The Liturgy in Medieval England: A History* (Cambridge: Cambridge UP, 2009): 549.

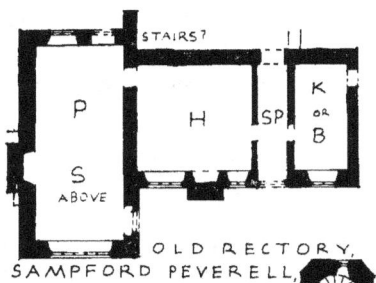

Fig. 2 Old Rectory, Sampford Peverell, Devon. Early 16th century. Floor plan. Reproduced from W. A. Pantin, "Medieval Priests' Houses in South-West England," *Medieval Archaeology* 1 (1957): 118–146, 142 (fig. 26).

I would argue that it does not. Bearing in mind Rapoport's argument that the function of a room can be altered by semi-fixed elements and the activities of the occupants, it proves helpful to consider the objects which were kept in Margaret's rooms as well as the activities associated with these objects. In late medieval England, numerous devotional books and images were in private hands: richly illuminated books of hours, alabaster reliefs and ivory sculptures, portable altarpieces, crucifixes and small shrines bearing relics.[26] Diane Webb has pointed out that when we look at these images today, they "cannot tell us in what physical setting they were originally located or used, or indeed by whom."[27] While this is certainly the case for the objects themselves, I argue that wills, inventories and other textual evidence help us to understand who owned these objects and sometimes also where they were kept. Thus, the inventory of Margaret Beaufort's closet next to her bedchamber, which was drawn up at her death, allows us to trace the objects with which she was surrounded. Apart from various legal documents pertaining to her dependants and herself, the inventory registers prayer and service books and a number of devotional images: "a plate sylver and gylt with the ymage of the salutacion of oure lady," "a smal shryne gilt with reliques and glased," "a littel bag conteyning a hert of reliques."[28] The devotional objects and the devotional exercises performed with the help of these objects charged this room with sanctity and transformed it temporarily into a devotional room. And indeed, from a sermon delivered shortly after her death by her confessor

---

26 See Kern-Stähler, *A Room of One's Own*, 90–91.

27 Diane Webb, "Domestic Space and Devotion in the Middle Ages," in *Defining the Holy: Sacred Space in Medieval and Early Modern Europe*, eds. Sarah Hamilton, Andrew Spicer (Aldershot: Ashgate, 2005): 27–47, 45.

28 Michael K. Jones, Malcolm J. Underwood, *The King's Mother: Lady Margaret Beaufort, Countess of Richmond and Derby* [1992] (Cambridge: Cambridge UP, 1995): 189.

John Fisher (1509), we know that Margaret used to say matins with her confessor in this closet every morning.[29]

Other laypeople, too, used chambers and closets as prayer rooms. Joan, Lady Cobham, for example, was praised by John Sheppey, the Bishop of Rochester, in the sermon he prepared for her funeral, for praying every morning in her chamber:

> as regards prayers, every day was a feast day with her. For unless there was some greater necessity, on no day would she willingly come down from her chamber or speak with any stranger, until she had said matins and the hours of Our Lady, the seven psalms and the litany, almost every day.[30]

From the will of Cicely Neville, Duchess of York (1495), we know that she kept a mass book and a psalter for use in her closet: "a masse-boke that servith for the closet [...] and a sawter that servith for the closett covered with white ledder."[31] In addition, the anonymous "Rules and Orders of the Princess Cecill" (1485–95), which document her daily routine, mention that she offered the last prayer of the day in her "pryvie closette."[32] Cecily's daily custom incorporated both public and private devotion in formal and informal devotional spaces: prayers in her chamber, divine service in the chapel, a *lectio* of "holy matter" at her dining-table, and evening prayers in her bedchamber.[33]

Such efforts to integrate the sacred into the realm of the domestic must be seen in the context of the "mixed life," the *vita mixta*, which was propagated as a way of life for laypeople who sought to lead a religious life not in a monastic institution but in the world.[34] In England, the earliest text to provide a guide for such a way of life was *The Mixed Life* by Walter Hilton, a mystic from Yorkshire (composed around 1380). In this treatise, Hilton advised his readers to alternate

---

29 "The moneth mynde of the noble prynces Margarete countesse of Rychemonde & Darbye," in John E. B. Mayor (ed.), *The English Works of John Fisher, Bishop of Rochester*, Early English Text Society, extra series, 27 (London: Trübner, 1876): 289–310.

30 Cited in William A. Pantin, *The English Church in the Fourteenth Century* (Cambridge: Cambridge UP, 1955): 256.

31 John G. Nichols and John Bruce (eds.), *Wills from Doctors' Commons: A Selection from the Wills of Eminent Persons Proved in the Prerogative Court of Canterbury, 1495–1695*, Camden Society, first series, 83 (London: Camden Society, 1863): 4.

32 "Orders and Rules of the House of the Princess Cecill," in John Nichols (ed.), *A Collection of Ordinances and Regulations for the Government of the Royal Household, made in Divers Reigns, from King Edward III to King William and Queen Mary. Also Receipts in Ancient Cookery* (London: Society of Antiquaries, 1790): 37–39, 37.

33 "Orders and Rules of the House of the Princess Cecill," 37.

34 See further Kern-Stähler, *A Room of One's Own*, 223–240.

between the "werkes of actif liyf" (following the model of Martha) and times for "goostli occupacion" (following the model of Mary Magdalene):

> thou schalt oo tyme with Martha be bisi for to rule and gouerne thi houshoold, thi children, thi seruantis, thi neiʒbours, thi tenauntes [anothir tyme] thou schal with Maria leue bisi-nesse of the world, and sitten doun at the f[ee]t of oure lord bi mekenesse in praiers and in hooli thoughtis and in contemplacioun of him [...]. And so schalt thou goon from the toon to the tothir profitably and fulfille hem bothe.[35]

Sacred Homes: The Homes of Saints

The lives of saints, and especially of the Holy Family, served as a model for pursuing a devout life at home. A large number of late medieval devotional texts and images focus on the home of the Holy Family. Affective piety, which was promoted by the Franciscans from the thirteenth century onwards, encouraged the faithful to meditate on the humanity of Christ, to respond to his love for them with compassion and to engage emotionally with the suffering and joys of Jesus and his mother. To stimulate the much sought-for compassion of late medieval affective piety, devotional art and literature showed scenes which offered what Denise Despres calls a "sentimental gaze on the concrete life of Jesus."[36] In numerous embellishments of the gospel on the early years of Jesus, ample attention was paid to scenes of everyday life and to the Holy Family's domestic arrangements.

The most influential text in the tradition of affective spirituality was the *Meditationes Vitae Christi*, wrongly attributed to Bonaventure but probably composed around 1300 by a Franciscan from Tuscany, John of Caulibus. The *Meditationes* imaginatively recreates the life of Christ, embellishing the gospel events in order to elicit an emotional response in the reader:

> You must not believe that all things said and done by Him on which we may meditate are known to us in writing. For the scale of greater impressiveness I shall tell them to you as

35 S. J. Ogilvie-Thomson (ed.), *Walter Hilton's Mixed Life, edited from Lambeth Palace MS 472* (Salzburg: Institut für Anglistik und Amerikanistik, 1986): 9–10 and 11. I have silently changed the 'thorn' in this edition to 'th'.
36 Denise Despres, *Ghostly Sights. Visual Meditation in Late-Medieval Literature* (Norman, OK: Pilgrim Books, 1989): 25.

they occurred or as they might have occurred according to the devout belief of the imagination and the varying interpretations of the mind.[37]

This text was particularly popular in late medieval England, with a large number of manuscripts held in English libraries and seven Middle English adaptations extant.[38] The only adaptation of the full Latin text, the early fifteenth-century *Mirror of the Blessed Life of Jesus Christ* by Nicholas Love, prior of the Carthusian house of Mount Grace in Yorkshire, survives in 51 manuscripts and has been referred to as the "most popular book of the fifteenth century."[39]

While the *Meditationes* was addressed to a religious woman, the intended audience of Love's adaptation was "lewd men and women."[40] To lay people, the attention this text pays to the humanity of Christ would have been particularly appealing. Among the many human details added to the scriptural account are the domestic arrangements of the members of the Holy Family: "For as we mowe ymagine thei hade no grete house bot a litel, in the whiche thei hade thre seuerynges [partitions, partitioned spaces] as it were thre smale chaumbres, there specialy to pray & to slepe."[41] After 'communal family time,' these rooms offer each member of the family a retreat for their individual prayers:

> aftir mete how thei speken to gedire, & also perantre othirwhile in hir mete, not veyn wordes or dissolute: bot wordes of edificacione ful of wisdome & of the holi goste, & so as thei weren fed in body, thei were miche better fed in soule. And then aftur siche manere recreacione in comune. thei wenten to praiere by hem self in hir closetes.[42]

37 *Meditations on the Life of Christ. An Illuminated Manuscript of the Fourteenth Century*, trans. Isa Ragusa, ed. Isa Ragusa and Rosalie B. Green (Princeton, NJ: Princeton UP, 1961): 5.
38 On the popularity of the *Meditationes* see e. g. Denise N. Baker, "The Privity of the Passion," in *Cultures of Piety: Medieval Devotional Literature in Translation*, ed. Anne Clark Bartlett and Thomas H. Bestul (New York: Cornell UP, 1999): 85–106, 85–86.
39 Denise N. Baker, "Mystical and Devotional Literature," in *A Companion to Medieval English Literature and Culture, c. 1350–c. 1500*, ed. Peter Brown (Oxford: Blackwell, 2007): 423–36, 433. Baker draws on Deanesly's influential study on the vernacular books documented in late medieval wills: Margaret Deanesly, "Vernacular Books in England in the Fourteenth and Fifteenth Centuries," *Modern Language Review* 15 (1920): 349–358.
40 Michael G. Sargent (ed.), *Nicholas Love's Mirror of the Blessed Life of Jesus Christ. A Critical Edition based on Cambridge University Library Additional MSS 6578 and 6686*, Garland Medieval Texts, 18 (New York, London: Garland, 1992), 10.
41 Sargent (ed.), *Mirror*, 64. In my quotations from the *Mirror*, I have silently converted the Middle English 'thorn' in this edition to 'th'.
42 Sargent (ed.), *Mirror*, 64.

In late medieval art, too, the Holy Family was portrayed as an ordinary family, as a family not only absorbed in prayer but also engaged in the household chores and pastimes of everyday life so well known also to the beholder. In an illumination from the fifteenth-century Book of Hours commissioned for Catherine of Cleves, Duchess of Gueldern, and executed around 1435 by an unknown Flemish painter (fig. 3), we see the Holy Family in a domestic interior – Mary weaving, Joseph the carpenter with the tools of his trade, and the little Christ Child strolling around in a contemporary baby-walker, a common device in late medieval Europe. The recognition of the everyday familiar which such representations evoked served by association also to draw the sacred events for which they provided the setting into the reality of the beholder.

Thus, in the late medieval imagination, the home became also the celebrated setting for a crucial moment in the story of salvation: "et angelus ingressus" (Luke 1:28), which formed the basis for all theological discussions and legendary embellishments of the annunciation, suggests an interior space, but the notion of Mary's home in Nazareth was a medieval specification. Bernard of Clairvaux explains that Mary retreated into a "cubiculum" and avoided the company of others, and Albertus Magnus situates the annunciation in Mary's chamber ("conclave").[43] In the *Meditationes Vitae Christi*, Gabriel meets Mary in a bedchamber of her little house ("in thalamo domunculae").[44] In his Middle English adaptation of this text, Nicholas Love puts a further stress on the seclusion of Mary, situating her encounter with Gabriel "in her priue chaumbure that tyme closed."[45] In John Lydgate's poem "Ave Jesse, Virgula," Mary is in the "closet" at the time of the annunciation,[46] and in the fifteenth-century *N-Town Cycle* Gabriel visits Mary

---

43 Bernardus, "Super missus est homilia" and Albertus Magnus, "Enarrationes in primam partem evangelii Lucae," both cited in Klaus Schreiner, "Marienverehrung, Lesekultur, Schriftlichkeit: Bildungs- und frömmigkeitsgeschichtliche Studien zur Auslegung und Darstellung von 'Mariä Verkündigung'," *Frühmittelalterliche Studien* 24 (1990): 314–368, 327–328.

44 Sven Lüken, *Die Verkündigung an Maria im 15. und frühen 16. Jahrhundert: Historische und kunsthistorische Untersuchungen* (Göttingen: Vandenhoeck & Ruprecht, 2000): 36.

45 Sargent (ed.), *Mirror*, 21. I have written elsewhere on the didactic aspect of the emphasis on Mary's enclosure (*A Room of One's Own*, 30–35). The gloss to this text ascribes this addition to Bernard but, as Carol Meale suggests, it goes back to the revelations of St Elisabeth of Hungary: Carol M. Meale, "'Oft siþis with grete deuotion I þought what I miȝt do plesyng to God': The Early Ownership and Readership of Love's Mirror, with Special Reference to its Female Audience," in Shoichi Ogura, Richard Beadle, and Michael G. Sargent (eds.), *Nicholas Love at Waseda: Proceedings of the International Conference 20–22 July 1995* (Cambridge: Brewer, 1991): 19–46, 41.

46 Henry Noble MacCracken (ed.), *The Minor Poems of John Lydgate*, 2 vols., Early English Text Society, extra series, 107 and original series 192 (London: Oxford UP, 1911–1934) 1:299–304, 301, verse 75.

Fig. 3 The Holy Family at work. Hours of Catherine of Cleves. Utrecht, *ca.* 1440. New York, Pierpont Morgan Library MS M.917/945, 149. Purchased on the Bella de Costa Green Fund and with the assistance of the Fellows, 1963. Photographic credit: Pierpont Morgan Library, New York.

in the "lytyl praty hous" in which she is reading her psalter during Joseph's absence.[47] Late medieval art, too, situated the annunciation in Mary's home, depicted as a contemporary home and thus inviting the empathetic response of the beholder: most famously, perhaps, in the center panel of Robert Campin's Mérode Altarpiece,[48] which sets the Annunciation within a carefully detailed domestic interior rather than in a church setting.[49]

In the late medieval imagination, then, the house was an important setting in the story of salvation. Several devotional texts suggest that the sacredness of the events situated in the house is passed on to the location so that the house partakes in the holiness of the occupiers and the sacred story. The meditation on the "Incarnacion of Jesu, and the feste of the Annunciacion" in Nicholas Love's *Mirror of the Blessed Life of Jesus Christ*, for example, marvels at Mary's house in Nazareth on account of the holy events that occurred there: "A lord, what house is that, where such gestes bene & sech thinges ben don!"[50] Similarly, in a meditation on the Visitation of Mary to Elizabeth, the house of Elizabeth is being praised on account of its inhabitants and visitors: "A lord god what house was that, what Chaumber & what bedde in the which delleden to gedire & resteden so worthi Moderes with so noble sones, that is to sey Marie & Elizabeth, Jesus & Jon,"[51] which is taken up in the *N-Town Play:*

A Lord God, what hous was this on
that [held] these childeryn and here moderys to
As Mary and Elizabeth, Jesus and John,
And Joseph and Zakarye also.[52]

In fact, England as a whole came to partake of the sacredness of Mary's house. In the Holy Land, no building existed which could claim to be the 'original' site of the annunciation. According to legend, the house where Mary was born and where she was saluted by Gabriel had been translated by angels to Italy in the

47 Stephen Spector (ed.), *N-Town Play: Cotton Vespasian D.8*, 2 vols., Early English Text Society, supplementary series, 11–12 (Oxford: Oxford UP, 1991) 1:109.
48 The household objects on display are of course highly symbolic of Mary's virginity, like the stalk of white lilies or the highly polished bronze laver and candlestick. At the same time, they serve another function: to situate Mary in a contemporary town house, which the medieval onlooker could identify with.
49 See David M. Robb, "The Iconography of the Annunciation in the Fourteenth and Fifteenth Centuries," *Art Bulletin* 18 (1936): 480–526 and Lüken, *Die Verkündigung*, 32–64.
50 Sargent (ed.), *Mirror*, 22.
51 Sargent (ed.), *Mirror*, 31.
52 Spector (ed.), *N-Town Play*, 1:138. I have silently changed the 'thorn' in this edition to 'th'.

late thirteenth century, where it became an important pilgrimage site: Santa Casa di Loreto. English pilgrims did not have to travel to the Holy Land or to the Santa Casa in Loreto for that matter, for they had miraculously been given a replica of Mary's Nazareth house in Walsingham, a little village in Norfolk, which became one of the most important centers of Marian devotion in late medieval Europe. The origin of the shrine is founded on the belief that the Virgin Mary and her house appeared in the eleventh century in a vision to a widow from Norfolk, Richelde of Faverches. In this vision, Mary told Richelde to note the length, width and height of her house so that she could erect a copy of it. The house was subsequently built with the help of local craftsmen and a host of angels. In the earliest written account of this miraculous event, a ballad written around 1460 and printed by Richard Pynson in 1495, the house became known as the "newe Nazareth."[53] In what Stella Singer has called a "sanctification of English space,"[54] the angelic re-creation of Mary's home in Nazareth in a village in England (the "newe Nazareth") transferred some of the sacredness of the Holy Land to home.[55]

The home of saints feature prominently also in late medieval saints' lives. Catherine of Siena (1347–1380) and Zita of Lucca, two female saints particularly venerated in late medieval England, served as models for those who aspired to lead a contemplative life not in a monastic institution but in their own homes. The life of Saint Catherine, written by her confessor Raymond of Capua between 1385 and 1395 and documented in the *Acta Sanctorum*,[56] describes the painstaking attempt of the young Catherine to lead a life of prayer and devotion amidst difficult circumstances. When her parents urged her to get married, she refused and cut her hair, which led her parents to deprive her of both the location and the time for prayer: "ut et locus et tempus orandi [...] sibi aufferrentur."[57] Her own chamber was taken away from her and Catherine had to do all the household chores previously done by the domestic servant, while being abused by her family. As Raimund writes, Catherine nevertheless managed to keep up her devotional regime by applying two tactics: after the family took away her chamber

---

53 The so-called Pynson ballad is reproduced at <http://www.walsinghamanglicanarchives.org.uk/pynsonballad.htm> (acc. July 1, 2014).
54 Stella A. Singer, "Walsingham's Local Genius: Norfolk's 'Newe Nazareth'," in *Walsingham in the Literature from the Middle Ages to Modernity*, eds. Dominic Janes, Gary Waller (Farnham: Ashgate, 2010): 23–34, 26.
55 See further J. C. Dickinson, *The Shrine of Our Lady of Walsingham* (Cambridge: Cambridge UP, 1956) and Gary Waller, *Walsingham and the English Imagination* (Farnham: Ashgate, 2011): 1–38.
56 Raimundus Capuanus, "Vita S. Catharinae Senensis," in *Acta Sanctorum...editio novissima*, eds. Joanne Carnandet et al. (Paris: V. Plame, 1863–1983), Aprilis III: 862 ff.
57 Raimundus, "Vita S. Catharinae Senensis," 874.

in which she used to pray, she built herself an inner cell (*a cella interior*) which no one, as the text emphasizes, would ever be able to take away from her: "nunc facta cella interior, quae sibi auferri non posset, numquam ipsa egrediebatur."[58] And what is more, in her imagination Catherine replaced her family with the Holy Family. When serving her family, she imagined her father to be Jesus Christ, her mother his mother, and her siblings and other members of the household to be the disciples. When she was in the kitchen, she imagined to be in the *sancta sanctorum*: "sique in coquina existens, simper erat intra Sancta Sanctorum."[59] Thus, Catherine transcended from the real space, her parental home and its domestic chores into a sacred space of her imagination.

Zita of Lucca (*c.* 1218–1272) was sent at the age of twelve as a maidservant to the Fatinelli family in Lucca. According to the *Acta Sanctorum*, her life was marked by tiring and hard work, during which she continued her prayers: she slept on the bare floor or on a wooden table, tired from her labor, and from countless devotional exercises, yet she served God with inner love, during her work and after: "Nam ambulans et sedens, laborans et vacans, intus et foris, adeo erat oration mentis intent, ut Deo videretur non solum quidquid erat cordis et corporis, verum etiam temporis et operis dedicasse."[60]

Both Catherine and Zita were extremely popular in late medieval England. Catherine's principal work, *Il Dialogo*, was translated into Middle English in the early fifteenth century and was printed in 1519,[61] and her vita was printed by Wynkyn de Worde in Middle English translation *c.* 1493 and was upheld as a "fructuous example of virtuous liuinge."[62] Zita's life circulated both in Latin in manuscripts of the fifteenth century and in English translation.[63] Images of

---

58 Raimundus, "Vita S. Catharinae Senensis," 874.

59 Raimundus, "Vita S. Catharinae Senensis," 875.

60 Fatinellus di Fatinelli, "Vita Zitae," *Acta Sanctorum*, Aprilis III, 504–515, 503.

61 The translation of *Il Dialogo*, *The Orcherd of Sion*, was probably produced for a nun at Syon Abbey. After it was printed by Wynkyn der Worde in 1519, it circulated more widely: Michael G. Sargent, "Minor Devotional Writings," in *Middle English Prose: A Critical Guide to Major Authors and Genres*, ed. A. S. G. Edwards (New Brunswick, NJ: Rutgers UP, 1984): 147–76, 151; Norman F. Blake, "Middle English Prose and its Audience," *Anglia* 90 (1972): 437–55, 442.

62 This is taken from the incipit of "The Lyf of Saint Katherin of Senis," an anonymous Middle English translation of Raymond's vita, which was printed by Wynkyn de Worde ca. 1493 together with the Revelations of St Elizabeth of Hungary (STC 24766). See Sarah McNamer's introduction to *The Two Middle English Translations of the Revelations of St Elizabeth of Hungary, ed. from Cambridge University Library MS Hh.1.11 and Wynkyn de Worde's printed text of ?1493*, ed. Sarah McNamer (Heidelberg: Universitätsverlag Winter, 1996): 9–50, 27.

63 See Thorlac Turville-Petre, "A Middle English Life of St Zita," *Nottingham Medieval Studies* 35 (1991): 102–105, 104.

Zita adorned a number of churches in late medieval England, with more than 50 extant examples from the fifteenth century.[64] The iconography of this saint, with the attributes of keys and rosary, already point at a combination of prayer and household work.[65] It has been argued that her cult would have been specifically attractive to young people in late medieval England who went to service in another household as part of their socialization.[66]

Conclusion

In late medieval devotional art and literature, the house is an important setting for the story of salvation and for embellishments of the gospel which catered for a growing interest in the humanity of Christ and in details of the everyday domestic life of the Holy Family. A large number of laypeople in late medieval England followed the example of the Holy Family and adapted their homes to accommodate worship and devotion: consecrated domestic chapels and less formal closet chapels and oratories were increasingly part of the medieval house. Prayer books and devotional images, like alabaster sculptures and portable altarpieces, were kept in medieval homes. These devotional tools and the devotional practices associated with them could turn any room into a devotional space. Moreover, these objects and practices were also a means of transcending the physical space of the home and enter an imaginary sacred space, like St Catherine's *cella in mente* which was filled with figures from the gospel, or the visionary space of the gothic church choir in the Book of Hours of Mary of Burgundy with which I started my article. The constructions of home in the late medieval period as a setting for scenes from the gospel and as a space of devotion challenges the binary opposition between sacred and profane and strongly suggests that the house is one of the " 'secret-sacred' spaces" which demand more attention.[67]

---

64 Sebastian Sutcliffe, "The Cult of St Sitha in England: An Introduction," *Nottingham Medieval Studies* 37 (1993): 83–89, 87; Eamon Duffy, "Holy Maydens, Holy Wyfes: The Cult of Women Saints in Fifteenth- and Sixteenth-Century England," in *Women and the Church*, eds. W. J. Sheils, Diane Wood (Oxford: Blackwell, 1990): 175–96, 178–79.
65 Duffy, "Holy Maydens, Holy Wyfes," 178.
66 Sutcliffe, "The Cult of St Sitha." On life-cycle service in late medieval England see P. J. P. Goldberg, *Women, Work and Life-Cycle in a Medieval Economy: Women in York and Yorkshire c. 1300–1520* (Oxford: Oxford UP, 1992): 1–15.
67 Spicer and Hamilton, "Defining the Holy," 4–5.

Annegret Pelz and Marianne Windsperger

Constituting Transareal Convivence via Portable Collection Books: Home and Belonging in Times of Uprootedness and Increased Mobility

Abstract: Albums and collection books are portable property. As portable objects, they move across spatial and temporal divides and therefore bear the traces of multiple usage and inscriptions of different people. With their ability to draw together and transport images of living spaces and objects, these portable paper media gain importance in connection with the increased mobility of people in global networks. Through the creative processes of collecting, selecting and assembling, the album provides a distinct territorial texture and structure with an important relation to the homelike as a form of belonging. The rules regulating access to the portable archive, meaning decisions about what is and what is not included in the private archive and the question of to whom it is shown, operate to filter out the effects of external dis-order. In this chapter, we provide theoretical considerations and historical context on the topic of portable media in times of increased mobility and we direct our attention to different types of albums and collection books as well as forms of writing connected to albums.

In her novel *The Museum of Unconditional Surrender* (1997), former Yugoslav writer Dubravka Ugrešić tells an anecdote about Ratko Mladić, who had to stand trial at the International Criminal Tribunal for the former Yugoslavia in The Hague for crimes against humanity:

> There is a story told about the war criminal Ratko Mladić, who spent months shelling Sarajevo from the surrounding hills. Once he noticed an acquaintance's house in the next target. The general telephoned his acquaintance and informed him that he was giving him five minutes to collect his 'albums', because he had decided to blow the house up. When he said 'albums', the murderer meant the albums of family photographs. The general who had been destroying the city for months, knew precisely how to annihilate memory. That is why he 'generously' bestowed on his acquaintance life with the right to remembrance. Bare life and a few family photographs.[1]

This anecdote describes the transition from concrete places to a practice of re-territorialization through media: In times of war, humanitarian catastrophes and political upheavals, living spaces and social surroundings are transferred into a portable archive. Uprooted from his dwelling, a refugee can only remember and tell his story when he can draw on a materialized archive. That is why for

---

1 Dubravka Ugrešić, *The Museum of Unconditional Surrender* [1997], trans. Celia Hawkesworth (London: Phoenix House, 1998): 7.

a dislocated life the small paper-sized format of the album with its origins in diasporic contexts gains essential importance as a portable personal archive. The right to remember – as stated in the quotation above – is vital for a stable life and the constitution of transgenerational continuity. On this account, this paper highlights the difference between refugees who possess such transportable and material bearers of memory and those who do not. The aspects of diasporic situations described in the aforementioned novel are the point of departure for the central thesis of our contribution, which states that individuals and groups localize and stabilize convivence and create a sense of home and belonging in times of crisis, migration, diaspora, uprootedness and increased mobility via portable media like albums and collection books.[2]

The portable album or collection book can be seen as a center of stability, a small-dimensioned place of refuge that can be described as the communicative practice of taking up residence[3] – the embedding into a familiar context in order to confront the new and integrate the unusual. In situations of migration, interiors are transferred into the album, spaces of living become transportable and new homes therefore can be reconstructed against the backdrop of images and help to build new centers of stability. The temporary refuge within the protected space of the album or collection book subsequently triggers the opening up of this space and helps to confront the unforeseeable in the world. In this sense, the possession of this kind of personal archive not only serves retrospective processes of commemoration and remembering but also brings about a willingness to embrace the future. Hence, the portable collection book is a medium that opens up the perspective on a transareal space of interaction as well as a framed object that, through the combination of inscriptions and images on the space of the pages, represents complex social fabrics.

We will first provide preliminary theoretical considerations and historical contexts for the topic of portable media and the constitution of convivence in di-

---

2 We present preliminary findings emerging from our research conducted within the scientific platform *Mobile Cultures and Societies. Interdisciplinary Studies on Transnational Formations* at the University of Vienna. The platform comprises researchers from the fields of social, cultural, philological and media studies. The disciplines involved focus on reexamining key concepts that have currently emerged in Mobility Studies. It is in the cross-fertilization of Social Sciences and Cultural Studies that we see an opportunity to critically investigate and bring together case studies of migration, mobility, diaspora and home-making with the reflections emerging by the study of cultural texts and media. The research platform with its seven subprojects was launched at the University of Vienna in April 2014 and can be accessed via <https://mobilecultures.univie.ac.at/>.

3 Vilém Flusser, "Wohnung beziehen in der Heimatlosigkeit," in *Von der Freiheit des Migranten. Einsprüche gegen den Nationalismus* (Bensheim and Düsseldorf: Bollmann, 1994): 15–30.

asporic situations. In the second part, we will look at two examples of albums and their role in shaping forms of belonging. In general, the collection on the pages of albums has the purpose to record living spaces and assemble friends and family members as well as significant events as completely as possible. In our contribution, we want to emphasize the different forms of creating stability by immigrants with such albums and refugees without personal archives. In the third section, we focus on literary forms of "taking up residence" and the experimental adoption of album-like poetics in fragmentary forms and modes of diasporic writing. We direct our attention to new ways of understanding the historical and contemporary role of network-media in the building of transareal convivence.

Writing Transareal Convivence

Our understanding of albums and collection books as diasporic media draws on Ruth Mayer's critical investigation of diasporic concepts, in which she points out that communities that have been uprooted from their original context to at least two other geographical settings need to shape a sense of belonging and a common future in medial forms.[4] Thus, the uprooted and transportable album and collection books can point to a long history of network-organization and convivence of communities that no longer define themselves in a territorial sense.

In our contemporary age of post-traditional and fluid communities that are marked by the disappearing proximity of their members to the social space, new situational forms of associating and new modes of coming together regulate the nomadic community life into which the individual only occasionally immerses himself, but to which he is not permanently bound.[5] As early as the 1970s, Roland Barthes pointed out that for this new mode of life shared language is the genuine place of community building. In his lecture entitled *How to Live Together*, Roland Barthes turns to the literary simulation of spaces that are bound to a specific form of living together. Thus, for example in Thomas Mann's novel *Der Zauberberg (The Magic Mountain)* (1924), the Sanatorium represents the special

---

4 Ruth Mayer defines 'diaspora' as a group of people leaving one place for at least two other geographical settings. In this case, diaspora can be defined locally (one origin), by dispersal worldwide, and a sense of belonging (community) worldwide. Cf. Ruth Mayer, *Diaspora. Eine kritische Begriffsbestimmung* (Bielefeld: transcript, 2005): 13.
5 For further information on fluidity und situativity of post-traditional communities, cf. Hartmut Rosa et al., *Theorien der Gemeinschaft. Zur Einführung* (Hamburg: Junius, 2010).

place in which this peculiar form of conviviality unfolds.[6] Ottmar Ette follows Roland Barthes theoretical considerations and comes up with the concept of "literary convivence" in order to describe multiple relations within transareal networks and diasporic situations that shape our sense of belonging.[7] In a world that is marked by the constant movement of individuals and groups, convivence has to be understood as situational form of living together in peace and amidst cultural difference.[8] In order to contextualize the term convivence, we want to draw attention to the Latin origin of this word: *convivium* describes a table fellowship. The Berlin-born American sociologist and economist Albert O. Hirschman uses the term *commensality* in order to describe a table fellowship located at the boundary between the public and private sphere. In his view the table is essential for constituting consent in community-life.[9] Hannah Arendt – in her book *The Human Condition* (1958) – defines the function of the table in a table fellowship as keeping the intermediate space free so that in this community of equal beings every member can speak from their respective place autonomously and feel integrated.[10] In diasporic communities, the materiality of portable media acts as the table top: The blank pages of an album or collection book grant every member of the community their own place that at the same time can bridge and keep open the gaps between the positions.[11]

Coming back to Roland Barthes and the importance of the shared language for community building, we emphasize that the increased mobility of people creates interconnected cultural spaces and therefore communication as a form of living together is marked by multiple processes of translation. "Literatures without a fixed abode"[12] are distinguished by a specific knowledge on convivence in these interconnected spaces: first, these literatures are on the move and marked by the search for a common language. Second, migration, problems, conflicts and misunderstandings in culturally diverse communities are represented and

---

6 Roland Barthes, *How to Live Together. Novelistic Simulations of Some Everyday Spaces*, trans. Kate Briggs (New York: Columbia UP, 2013).

7 Cf. Ottmar Ette, *ZusammenLebensWissen. List, Last und Lust literarischer Konvivenz im globalen Maßstab* (Berlin: Kadmos, 2010).

8 Cf. Ottmar Ette, *Konvivenz. Literatur und Leben nach dem Paradies* (Berlin: Kadmos, 2012): 58 –102.

9 Albert O. Hirschman, *Tischgemeinschaft. Zwischen öffentlicher und privater Sphäre* (Vienna: Passagen, 1997): 20. Hirschman refers to Georg Simmel, *Das Individuum und die Freiheit* (Berlin: Wagenbach, 1984).

10 Hannah Arendt, *The Human Condition* (Chicago: U of Chicago P, 1998): 58.

11 For a take on "conviviality" in the postcolonial context, cf. Paul Gilroy, *After Empire. Melancholia or Convivial Culture?* (Abingdon: Routledge, 2004): vii–xii , 133–168.

12 Cf. Ottmar Ette, *ZwischenWeltenSchreiben*.

dealt with in the literary works. Thus, literature provides an experimental space for diverse forms of knowledge about convivence. In our project, we are concerned with the constitution of transareal community through the book forms that serve as imaginary points of reference in diasporic communities. Albums and collection books assemble inscriptions, images and paper objects in fragmentary constellations. The activity of collecting in situations of uprootedness serves the function of creating a detailed and complete documentation of what has been left behind.

In recent research, the origin of the album as a diasporic object of network-organization is traced back to the student circle of Luther and Melanchton. Over the course of the sixteenth century, protestant theologists started to write down notes on the blank pages or in the margins of their students' bibles when they were leaving for the European diaspora.[13] This practice gained further importance at the universities and in aristocratic circles during the sixteenth and seventeenth centuries. The portable property[14] of the album in the form of the *Philothek* or friendship book played a significant role in the aristocratic self-fashioning and served as a career-promoting proof of network-building: the *Album Amicorum*, originating from the academic circles surrounding humanistic thinkers, documents the networks of scholars and artists and the communities of professors, doctors, geographers and writers.

In the Jewish diaspora, the appearance of collections and *Memorbooks* as a deterritorialized practice of shaping communities can be traced back to the thirteenth century. These books not only listed the names of the deceased and of outstanding community members, they also included accounts of events that had been of major importance for the community life. After the great waves of migration of Eastern European Jews to the United States, Canada, Palestine, Australia and Latin America at the end of the nineteenth and the beginning of the twentieth century and during and after the Second World War, the Memorbook-tradition found its continuation in the *Yizker bikher:*[15] In the diaspora the so-called

---

13 Werner Wilhelm Schnabel, "Das Album Amicorum. Ein gemischtmediales Sammelmedium und einige seiner Variationsformen," in *Album. Organisationsform narrativer Kohärenz*, eds. Anke Kramer, Annegret Pelz (Göttingen: Wallstein, 2013): 213–239, 219.

14 Cf. John Plotz, *Portable Property. Victorian Culture on the Move* (Princeton: Princeton UP, 2008).

15 *Yizkor* means "remember" in Hebrew and generally refers to the memorial prayer recited for the deceased. The Yiddish term yizker-bikher is used for the large number of memorial books commemorating Jewish communities in Eastern Europe that have been destroyed during the Second World War. Hundreds of these books were produced in the aftermath of the Holocaust, generally they are in Yiddish and Hebrew. Cf. Jonathan Boyarin, "Yizker-bikher" (November 10,

landsmanshaftn became important organizations for immigrants coming from the same villages, towns and cities in Central and Eastern Europe. These landsmanshaftn were built within the framework of existing social, political and religious organizations. They provided newly arrived immigrants with financial assistance, medical care, and help in administrative matters. Within the framework of these homeland associations, so-called yizker bikher were created in large numbers after the Second World War by the collaboration of migrants who had left their homes at the beginning of the twentieth century or in the Interwar period and survivors of the Shoah. These books had the function of commemorating the destroyed communities of Eastern and Central Europe and represented an imaginative attempt of "going home again."[16] Jack Kugelmass and Jonathan Boyarin point to the extraordinary project of the *Kurow yizker bukh*, in which 200 former inhabitants of Kurow came together in order to reconstruct the topographical surrounding of their hometown and to come up with a list of their former neighbors: "[T]hey sat around a table, and began to review the town and its inhabitants, building by building. They then sent the list to surviving landsmen around the world. The final list numbered some 2,800 people."[17] Through the collection of material documents, photographs and memorial accounts as well as hand-drawn maps of the former hometowns and the process of naming the former inhabitants, these network media aimed at creating a web of multiple connections. Organized in book form, fragmentary knowledge and missing records of the town's history were given a context and in turn established stability for the new diaspora community.[18] In Jewish history, attempts to collect and record have a long-standing history and – in the twentieth century – are closely connected to the founding of the YIVO, the *Yidisher Visnshaftlekher Institut* (Yiddish Scientific Institute), in the year 1925.[19] Yizker bikher stabilize memory by

---

2010), in *YIVO Encyclopedia of Jews in Eastern Europe* <http://www.yivoencyclopedia.org/article.aspx/Yizker-bikher> (acc. October 10, 2014).

16 Jack Kugelmass and Jonathan Boyarin, *From a Ruined Garden. The Memorial Books* (Bloomington, IN: Indiana UP): 28.

17 Kugelmass and Boyarin, *Ruined Garden*, 12.

18 Cf. Alfed Bodenheimer, *Ungebrochen gebrochen. Über jüdische Narrative und Traditionsbildung* (Göttingen: Wallstein, 2012).

19 In 1891, the historian Simon Dubnow reacted to the secularization of Jews by calling for the material documentation of the Eastern European past. His approach to history was that documentation was to be achieved by a mass movement of common people, "history from below" as we might call it today. This form of documentation through collecting found its continuation in the *zamler*-movement (collectors' movement) in the 1920s and 1930s which helped to assemble ethnographical, historical and philological material and data for the Yiddish Scientific Institute, the YIVO. The collected material did not only have the purpose to document the past, but

creating a collective voice, they enable community-building in the present and therefore establish generational continuity for the future.[20] Today the yizker bikher have found their way into the internet: through their digital availability global networks of former hometowns expand their outreach to younger generations, the yizker bikher are re-read with a generational delay, information is corrected and the names and dates of missing relatives are added.[21] In the online-representation, the movement of "going back" becomes an important feature that bridges the gap between past and future. The album and the collection book primarily emerge in situations where people have to collect and place their scattered belongings and fragmentary knowledge into a new context in order to stabilize their ruptured lives.

Taking Up Residence in Albums

If the apartment is a place where things remain static, the album is the medium that puts things into movement. With reference to Vilém Flusser's[22] concept of dwelling as a modern, detached, abstract and not spatially but medially and communicatively located form of existence, we want to show how in a situation of migration and exile the function of being at home is transferred to an album. We do this by turning to the genesis of the special album that accompanied Freud into his exile in London on June 4, 1938: *Professor Sigmund Freud's Wohnung im Hause Wien, 9., Berggasse 19. Zur Erinnerung.*[23]

In May 1938, the 82-year-old Sigmund Freud and his family were granted permission – through diplomatic intervention and the payment of the so-called "Reichsfluchtsteuer" – to emigrate and to take with them a few things from his doctor's office and apartment. The young photographer Edmund Engelman was sent to Freud's apartment at Berggasse 19 in order to document as thorough-

---

also to gather evidence of contemporary cultural developments. Cf. Cecile Esther Kuznitz, "YIVO" (November 10, 2010), in *YIVO Encyclopedia of Jews in Eastern Europe*. <http://www.yivoencyclopedia.org/article.aspx/YIVO> (acc. October 10, 2014).

20 Cf. Kugelmass and Boyarin, *Ruined Garden*, 9–45.

21 Cf. *JewishGen* <http://www.jewishgen.org/JewishGen/> (acc. March 13, 2014); "Yizkor Books Online," *New York Public Library* <http://yizkor.nypl.org/> (acc. March 13, 2014).

22 Vilém Flusser, "The Challenge of the Migrant," in *The Freedom of the Migrant: Objections to Nationalism*, ed. Anke Finger, trans. Kenneth Kronenberg (Champaign: U of Illinois P, 2003), 1–15.

23 For a more detailed depiction, cf. Annegret Pelz, "Wohnung beziehen – im Album," in *Dinge des Exils. Exilforschung. Ein internationales Jahrbuch* 31 (2013), eds. Doerte Bischof, Joachim Schloer (Munich: Edition Text und Kritik, 2013): 205–214.

ly as possible the place where Freud had been living and working since 1891. This quite risky move was initiated by the pedagogue and psychoanalyst August Aichhorn, who wanted to capture the "birthplace" of psychoanalysis "in all detail [...] to enable [...] the creation of a museum when the storm of the years is over."[24] The plan was to create the basis for future remembrance through photographic documentation of the unique and soon-to-disappear ensemble of Freud's working and living space.

The photographs that to the present day have shaped the image of Freud's Viennese apartment in Berggasse 19 were taken by the Viennese photographer Edmund Engelman, who emigrated to America in the year 1939. In Engelman's autobiographical retrospective, he describes the dangers and the time constraints under which the approximately 150 famous images came into being. Engelman had to work without flash and lighting in order not to be discovered, since the apartment in the Berggasse was under surveillance by the Gestapo. Fully aware "that one day these photographs could come to be the last available records enabling the reconstruction of Freud's working and living space,"[25] the photographer tried to create a complete inventory by taking the pictures in such a way that they would overlap each other. A byproduct of this systematic "photographic program intended to capture one room after the other in an image"[26] was a series of small prints that Engelman developed in the darkroom and "pasted into an album with the intention of giving them to Freud before his departure."[27] Thus, an album of twenty pages with 28 images was created and dedicated to Sigmund Freud with the inscription "Professor Sigmund Freud's Wohnung im Hause Wien, 9., Berggasse 19. Zur Erinnerung." He handed the album to Freud with the words:

> "As a memory and to take to England with you." He [Freud] looked at it carefully, page after page and image after image. Slowly he started to smile and finally he laughed with ease. His seriousness returned and he said: "I thank you sincerely. This will mean a lot to me."[28]

---

24 Edmund Engelman, *Rückblick*. In: *Sigmund Freud, Wien IX. Berggasse 19. Photographien und Rückblick*, introd. Inge Scholz-Strasser (Vienna: Brandstätter, 2004), 89–105 (here and in the following translated by Marianne Windsperger). Edmund Engelman died at the age of 92 in Manhattan in April 2000, cf. his obituary: Wolfgang Saxon, "Edmund Engelman, 92, Dies; Took Freud Photos" (April 16, 2000), *The New York Times* <http://www.nytimes.com/2000/04/16/nyregion/edmund-engelman-92-dies-took-freud-photos.html> (acc. October 13, 2014).
25 Engelman, *Rückblick*, 99.
26 Engelman, *Rückblick*, 99.
27 Engelman, *Rückblick*, 99.
28 Engelman, *Rückblick*, 100.

Through the intervention of his friend Edmund Engelman, Sigmund Freud became an immigrant with a portable archive. In the aftermath of the Holocaust, however, having a materialized memorial archive was a privileged position. A large number of Eastern European Jews who fled persecution and destruction were not able to take photographs of their homes and relatives with them. Therefore, images of Eastern European Jews, houses, living and working environments taken by the photographer Roman Vishniac and published in book form as early as 1947 replaced missing family albums.[29] Referring to the appropriation of these images of everyday living spaces by a large number of American Jews, the author Dara Horn states that "every suburban Jewish family had one"[30] of Roman Vishniac's books. The pictures that had been integrated into the publication created an image of a timeless and unchanging "authentic society captured in amber."[31] Roman Vishniac's accounts of the dangers involved in the journey to the Eastern European towns in the 1930s, the narrative of taking the pictures with a hidden camera and the subsequent miraculous salvaging of the photos by a friend have added to the pictures the symbolical meaning of being last testimonies of a vanished world:[32] "I am walking – we are walking – behind Roman Vishniac, and we are caught by a thousand glances which enliven the alleys of the little Jewish villages. Our eyes, too, see two things at once: living beings yesterday, a void today."[33] The comments that accompanied the pictures of Vishniac as well as the frame provided by the foreword (1947 by Abraham Joshua Heschel, 1983 by Elie Wiesel) seem to capture an image of a world that could not be revisited again and had shaping and formative character for Jewish Americans right after the events of the Second World War and in the subsequent years of upward mobility: Roman Vishniac's images enabled new immigrants to reunite with lost family members and friends and helped to integrate into the new life in the United States memories of traditions and ways of life left behind. For a Jewish-American society on its way to Americanization, these pictures provided a sense of

---

29 Roman Vishniac, *Polish Jews: A Pictorial Record*, introd. Abraham Joshua Heschel (New York: Schocken Books, 1947).

30 Dara Horn, "The Vanishing Point," *The Jewish Review of Books* 13 (2013): 39–42.

31 Alana Newhouse, "A Closer Reading of Roman Vishniac," *New York Time Magazine* (April 4, 2010): 36–43, 42.

32 Only after Roman Vishniac's death was the real purpose of his travels to Eastern Europe in the 1930s discovered: On commission of the American Joint Distribution Committee, he documented the poor life of Eastern European Jews in the villages and towns in the years 1935 to 1938. The purpose of the collection of images was to raise funds in the United States for Jewish communities in Eastern Europe (cf. Newhouse, "Closer Reading", 36–43).

33 Elie Wiesel, "Foreword," in Roman Vishniac, *A Vanished World* (New York: Farrar, Straus & Giroux, 1983): n. pag.

collective belonging, of continuity and of stability. The pictures were exhibited at different places in New York City[34] and were reproduced in numerous publications,[35] they reached a large public and enabled the adoption of now public photographs for missing private archives. Just like the pictures of Sigmund Freud's living and working space, these photographs came to be seen as a last-moment-documentation of living environments that had been destroyed by the Second World War. Therefore, they were formative for future remembrance and the creation of stability.

In the literary reworking of diasporic constellations, the possibility of the imaginative re-territorialization within a materialized memorial archive is of major importance. In the literary adaption of the album, the primary interest of creating a collection that is as complete as possible shifts to experimenting with album-like writing techniques. Thus the Viennese art historian and author Wolfgang Georg Fischer conceptualized a trilogy of novels: *Wohnungen* [*Apartments*] (1969), *Möblierte Zimmer* [*Lodgings in Exile*] (1972), and a third unpublished one that was to represent a collection of contemporary events entitled *Tausendjährige Dinge* [*Thousand-year-old Things*].

In his search for a narrative stance between New Objectivity and New Realism that only records the visible, his first volume, *Wohnungen,* outlines his characters against the background of two Viennese Fin de Siècle apartments. In doing so, he puts into contrast worlds of objects, forms of living, fitment and furniture and creates a characterization and inventory of Viennese society in the early twentieth century. After the loss of the apartment in the year 1938, the perspective is mobilized in the second volume, *Möblierte Zimmer,* which is dedicated to all those "who said no in April 1938."[36] Here, the setting switches to the train compartment, the "real space of the emigrant."[37] The mobile form of living in the compartment replaces the relational proximity and the lively continuity of the urban living space with the panoramatic view out of the window of the train

---

34 The exhibitions were "Life Everywhere" at the New School for Social Research (1942), "Children of Want and Fear: Europe Before the War" at the Teacher's College der Columbia University (1943), and finally the two exhibitions at the YIVO Institute for Jewish Research in New York, "Pictures of Jewish Life in Prewar Poland" (1944) and "Life in The Carpathians" (1945). Cf. the photographic archive at "Roman Vishniac," *International Center of Photography* <http://vishniac.icp.org/> (acc. March 13, 2014).

35 For example, in Isaac Bashevis Singer, *A Day of Pleasure. Stories of a Boy growing Up in Warsaw* (New York: Farrar, Straus & Giroux, 1969), the entire book is illustrated with images by Vishniac and private pictures of the author.

36 Wolfgang Georg Fischer, *Möblierte Zimmer* (Munich: Hanser, 1972): 5.

37 Fischer, *Möblierte Zimmer,* 7 (here and in the following translated by Marianne Windsperger).

and therefore with the spatial experience of a vanishing reality.[38] In this situation, the text – interspersed with dream sequences and imaginary pictures – is not a coherent whole but narrates in "snapshots," "flashes," "slides" and "image sequences" from an imaginary "photo album that does not really exist"! The entries are numbered and have titles: "From the photo album that does not exist snapshot no. 1 (flash)," "From the photo album that does not exist snapshot no. 2," or simply "From the photo album that does not exist." The literary album consists of a collection of "image sequences," "collages of words" and "scraps of words" that "lie in the air" of national-socialist-dominated everyday life in Vienna since March 1938: "*Words* spinning around on advertising columns, *words* taking the tramway together with advertisements, *words* being thrown from the sky together with fliers, *words* that have not existed yesterday, but today already are words of tomorrow."[39] At the end of the book, we find a dream protocol in which "albums that are cut in half" are brought into secure hiding places.[40] In this dream an album that has been taken into emigration is cut in half. It contains not only private portraits, snapshots, group-photographs and official photos but also so-called "snaps of evidence," images of the protagonist's Jewish father who fled to England. These pictures represent a potential threat to the son when he returns to Vienna in 1940.[41] For this reason, the pages of the family album are cut into parts – reflecting the fact that the family has been divided – and the compromising images are "surgically removed."[42]

The album's ability to integrate, represent and symbolically work through all other medial and cultural forms can also be extended to whole cities: this is shown in Fred Heller's *Familienalbum einer Stadt* (*Family Album of a City*), published in Buenos Aires by the publishing house of the German-speaking population in exile, Editorial Cosmopolita in the year 1948.[43] This "family album" of a Viennese writer, theater producer and journalist assembles the observations and chance finds of a flaneur in the streets, alleys and squares of Montevideo. The corresponding sections are given the following headings: "City with a double-life"; "A Tenant moves out"; "Melody of the Alleys"; "Occurrences of a Week" or "Waves of Football and Opera" and form a collection of short stories, anec-

38 For further information on panoramatic travelling, cf. Wolfgang Schivelbusch, *Geschichte der Eisenbahnreise. Zur Industrialisierung von Raum und Zeit im 19. Jahrhundert* (Frankfurt a. M., Berlin, Vienna: Hanser, 1979): 51–66.
39 Fischer, *Möblierte Zimmer*, 56; italics in the original.
40 Fischer, *Möblierte Zimmer*, 263–266.
41 Fischer, *Möblierte Zimmer*, 264.
42 Fischer, *Möblierte Zimmer*, 265.
43 Fred Heller, *Familienalbum einer Stadt* (Buenos Aires: Editorial Cosmopolita, 1948).

dotes, accounts and reports about a European immigrant's voluntary and involuntary participation in community-life.[44] The design of the book cover clearly draws a comparison with a "real album", but does not explicitly refer to this form of representation. The poetic presence of the "family album," however, becomes clear in the last short story entitled "Meeting point of the Europeans."[45] This story contrasts the lively presence of the city as it is inventoried in the album – packed stores and the abundance of delicious foods in display windows are understood as part of everyday life – with the "unreality" of far-off Europe starving and dying. These two worlds are connected with each other through the mail office where the European immigrants meet.[46] While the letters and packages are addressed to a spatially and temporally distant Europe, the album collects the contemporary evidences of life of immigrants that over the "past years have become attached to the foreign soil," "live their lives under new conditions" and now "think in new lines of thought."[47]

Whereas the examples of Wolfgang Georg Fischer's and Fred Heller's writings show how literary techniques related to the album are used to describe the fragmentary perception of immigrants and exiles, the experience of migration also resonates in the succeeding generations. A trans-generational rereading of different forms of collection books, albums and yizker bikher can be observed in contemporary Jewish-American literature: in their search for cultural belonging, authors such as Jonathan Safran Foer, Nicole Krauss and Dara Horn turn to family histories that connect New York and Jewish Eastern Europe, the past and the present. Drawing on archival material, photographs and objects, these authors place the materiality of books, images and objects in the center of their novels. In search for the family past, they experiment with different forms of writing: letters, lists, diagrams are integrated into their novels, parts of the books are overwritten, pages are left blank or only have one line of inscription. Material archival documents and antiquarian objects play a central role in the way in which these authors engage with the ruptures in the family history that have been caused by migration, war, displacement and annihilation. In her novel *The History of Love*, Nicole Krauss shows how a book is appropriated through processes of reading, writing and translating by different people, demonstrating that every book becomes a collection book bearing traces in forms of inscriptions or translations.[48] In the novel *Everything is Illuminated*, Jonathan

---

44 Heller, *Familienalbum*, 83 (here and in the following translated by Marianne Windsperger).
45 Heller, *Familienalbum*, 192–196.
46 Heller, *Familienalbum*, 196.
47 Heller, *Familienalbum* 193, 196.
48 Nicole Krauss, *The History of Love* (London: Penguin, 2005).

Safran Foer experiments with different forms of collecting: Spaces in Eastern Europe are archival spaces with boxes full of material, the moment of looking at photographs together plays a crucial role in the narrative and shows how the fragmentary parts of the novel – letters of the protagonists to each other – are connected to each other.[49] If we talk about fragmentary forms in the context of migration, mobility and diaspora, we have to direct our attention to another book project by Jonathan Safran Foer that shows that every book becomes fragmentary when it is removed from its context and when traces of its origin have been erased: In his creative engagement with Bruno Schulz' stories *The Street of Crocodiles* (*Sklepy cynamonowe*,1934), he not only re-reads and re-works the literary works, but he makes the creative processes involved in literary reception visible by cutting out parts of Bruno Schulz' writings, placing them in a new context and leaving the holes visible.[50]

Conclusion

If residing or dwelling – in keeping with Walter Benjamin – means to leave traces, the practices of assembling in books and the literary reworkings of these practices show how these forms of collecting traces are of major importance for a new perspective on transcultural phenomena in the field of Cultural and Media Studies. The use of collection books has historically developed in the context of mobile cultures and diasporic constellations and therefore this medium – with its ubiquitous availability and transportability as well as with its openness for entries of archival material, images and writing – is especially suited to assemble the evidence of a life marked by multiple ruptures. The knowledge of the great role that the old book medium plays for the communication and the memory of mobile, deterritorialized cultures and dislocated communities has until now not emerged from research, but from the medial practices in literature and arts. The contemporary artistic ideas of the album draw attention to an increasing interest in archival and material-aesthetic processes that – in keeping with Didi-Huberman – have to be called fragmentary and porous. Collection book-like poetics assemble disordered remains being surrounded by destruction, aggression and arbitrary or unconscious breaks and in its core refer to the gap from which they have been ripped out.

---

49 Jonathan Safran Foer, *Everything is Illuminated* [2002] (New York: Perennial, 2003).
50 Jonathan Safran Foer, *The Tree of Codes* (Keure: Visual Editions, 2010). Bruno Schulz was born in 1892 in Drohobych, Galicia (today's Ukraine). He died at the hands of a German Nazi officer in 1942. Parts of his writings were lost or destroyed during the Holocaust.

Today, *facebook* can be called the most prominent practice of the collection 'book' on a transareal scale.[51] With its users numbering over one billion and it being one of the most visited online sites worldwide, we see *facebook* as a global album constituting transareal convivence that represents a change in the public sphere in general: the movement from large to small fragmentary and transmedial forms. In literature, we can notice a similar development: With Roland Barthes we observe a movement away from the grand novel to the album that is characterized by an organizing structure of recurrence and multiple layering.[52] The here presented transareal texts assemble their entries album-like, alinear with cracked and porous surfaces that show the fragmentary web of small inscriptions. On a textual level, the books represent reworkings of migration and diaspora in a trans-generational perspective and have their origin in experiences of uprootedness, migration and expulsion. These texts refer to the album or the collection book as archive or technique and position themselves in a line with the generally open and transmedial form of these books: They assemble material traces of lives marked by the experience of uprootedness, they draw together fragmentary knowledge and point to the holes in the narrative.

---

51 The name *facebook* points to practices of collecting and assembling in college and highschools yearbooks. Through the invitations to write on the *facebook* wall and the opportunity to regulate public access, practices associated with *facebook* can be linked to old album media.
52 Cf. Anke Kramer, Annegret Pelz, "Einleitung," in *Album. Organisationsform narrativer Kohärenz*, eds. Anke Kramer, Annegret Pelz (Göttingen: Wallstein, 2013): 7–22.

Wim Weymans

At Home Abroad? International House New York and the Cité Universitaire in Paris: Cosmopolitan versus Diasporic Internationalism

Abstract: What would it mean for people living abroad to literally find a new "home away from home," that is to say to share the same house or space with other expats, be it of their own nationality or a different one? To answer that question, this chapter looks at two experiments, International House New York and the Cité Universitaire in Paris in which expats live under the same roof, thus creating a new home abroad. Though inspired by the same internationalist spirit of fostering understanding between nations, they each choose to host foreign students rather differently. In New York, hundreds of students from all over the world live under the same roof, whereas in Paris thousands of students from all nations live in the same park but each in their own national house. This chapter suggests that these experiments reflect different forms of internationalism, *cosmopolitan internationalism* (in New York) and *diasporic internationalism* (in Paris). It focuses on the differences between these two models by using archival documents that reveal how Americans looked at the Parisian experiment and tried to make it more cosmopolitan. It shows that exporting American ideas of how people from different nations should live together proved harder than expected.

If we reflect on how people living abroad create a home in their new host country, we normally think about the ways they create communities, networks or relationships. By a "home," then, we refer to a home in a metaphorical sense. Yet, what would it mean for expats, foreign students, uprooted "cosmopolitans" and other people living abroad to *literally* find a new "home" or "house," that is to say to share the same house or space with other expats, be it of their own nationality or a different one?[1] To answer that question, we can look at concrete experiments in which different expats live under the same roof, thus creating a new home. In this paper I will look at two contemporary experiments, International House New York and the Cité Universitaire in Paris. Though inspired by the same internationalist spirit of fostering understanding between different nations, they each choose to host foreign students rather differently. In New York, hundreds of students from all over the world live under the same roof, whereas in Paris thousands of students from all nations live in the same park but each in their own national house. To simplify the picture rather drastically one could perhaps

---

1 I use "home" in a very specific sense as in the expression "a home away from home," which, according to the *Oxford English Dictionary* means "a place where one is as happy, relaxed, or comfortable as in one's own home."

say that these two experiments reflect two different forms of internationalism, *cosmopolitan internationalism* (in New York) and, for lack of a better word, *diasporic internationalism* (in Paris). I will focus on the differences between these two models by using letters and other archival documents, written between 1925 and 1953, that reveal how Americans looked at the Parisian experiment and tried to make it more cosmopolitan.[2] Yet, as we shall see, exporting American ideas of how people from all nations should live together proved harder than expected.

Two Attempts to Create Peace

The international exchange of academic ideas and practices paradoxically started as a nationalistic project whereby nations exchanged ideas through, for example, scholarly conferences in order to prove that they were the best. While such competitive nationalistic form of internationalism continued after the First World War, the postwar years also saw the start of a new form of internationalism "as a way to increase collaborative efforts and downplay the bellicose patriotism that surfaced during the war."[3] In the same vein, many politicians and philanthropists during the interwar period tried to foster international peace through for example diplomatic initiatives such as the League of Nations.[4] Reis explains the new model of peaceful internationalism through education and exchange as follows: "[...] rather than introduce what each nation had accomplished independently, contributors to the new model hoped for the creation of novel ideas through shared interaction. Therefore, collaboration between educators across national boundaries as a means of effacing national differences in the hopes of forging future wars became the diplomatic definition of the interwar international education mouvement."[5] It is in this context that the original

---

2 This paper is based in part on research done at the Rockefeller Archive Centre, Tarrytown, NY (hereafter "RAC") in September 2012 and April 2013. I would like to thank the archivists Tom Rosenbaum and Nancy Adgent for facilitating my archival research. I also thank Jeffrey Wayno for his helpful comments on a previous draft. I did this research as a Postdoctoral Research Fellow of the Fund for Scientific Research – Flanders (Belgium) attached to the University of Leuven (KU Leuven). This research was also supported in part by a Career Integration Grant (CIG) awarded by the European Commission through the Marie Curie Actions.
3 Jehnie I. Reis, "Cultural Internationalism at the Cité Universitaire: International Education between the First and the Second World Wars," *History of Education* 39.2 (2010): 155–173, 156.
4 For a recent history of such diplomatic initiatives, see Mark Mazower, *Governing the World. The History of an Idea* (London: Penguin, 2013).
5 Reis, "Cultural Internationalism," 156.

idea emerged of creating peace by allowing students from all nations to live together, which would increase understanding between students from different countries. Almost simultaneously two such attempts were made, one in New York and one in Paris. Though similar in their goals, they were very different in set up.

The New York model consisted of one dormitory – appropriately called International House – in which 500 students "from sixty to seventy countries," lived together "beneath one roof."[6] It opened its doors in 1924, a few years after Harry Edmonds (1883–1979), YMCA secretary for metropolitan New York, succeeded in convincing the philanthropist John D. Rockefeller, Jr. (1874–1960)[7] of the necessity to construct such a building.[8] Some ten years before the idea of an "International House" emerged, Edmonds had already become aware of the need to organize activities for foreign students:

One day in 1909 Harry Edmonds [...] said good morning to a passing Chinese student. The student stopped him with this comment: "Do you know, you are the first person who has greeted me in the three weeks I have been in the city." Struck by the young foreigner's loneliness, Edmonds invited him to supper the following Sunday, and out of this incident grew the institution of Sunday suppers for foreign students at the home of Mr. and Mrs. Edmonds, an institution which soon overran its limited quarters and was moved to Earl Hall at Columbia University, where it became the Intercollegiate Cosmopolitan Club. Here was developed an imaginative program for introducing the hundreds of foreign students in the city's colleges and universities not only to each other but to American students and homes.[9]

After meeting Rockefeller, Edmonds could convince him to plan "a building to house this new international program."[10] While Edmonds can be seen as the enthusiastic founding father of International House, Rockefeller soon became an equally passionate supporter of the idea.

Although one-third of the residents were still American, International House New York aimed "to gather a considerable number of nationalities into one com-

6 Harry Edmonds, "International House," *Religious Education: The Official Journal of the Religious Education Association* 26.2 (1931): 149–152, 149.
7 In this chapter, John D. Rockefeller Jr. is referred to as "Rockefeller" and occasionally also as "Junior." On Rockefeller, cf. Raymond B. Fosdick, *John D. Rockefeller, Jr.: A Portrait* (New York: Harper, 1956) and John Ensor Harr, Peter J. Johnson, *The Rockefeller Century. Three Generations of America's Greatest Family* (New York: Charles Scribner's Sons, 1988).
8 On the history of International House New York, see: Lee Hall, *Living in the Future. International House New York. 75 years* (New York: International House New York, 2000).
9 Fosdick, *John D. Rockefeller, Jr.*, 390–391.
10 Fosdick, *John D. Rockefeller, Jr.*, 392.

munity for the purpose of furthering peace through the fellowship of living together."[11] Additionally, on a more practical level, it also served "as a residence and social center for foreign students, most of whom found themselves barred from joining American fraternities and sororities."[12] Edmonds explained how all this worked in practice: "There are, in reality, three separate buildings in one: a distinctly separate dormitory for women, another for men and a portion open to all members. The latter includes social and dining rooms, assembly hall, gymnasium, and so forth."[13] He continued:

> International House is a miniature world which includes all races and creeds [...] The members of this varied group are not brought together for a conference of a week or two; they *live* together for an academic year or longer. In close proximity, in one corridor, using a common room where they bathe and shave, there may be men of a dozen or more nationalities; and on the other side of the House, in a commodious laundry, the women see their common humanity through the medium of a common task in washing their choice bits of clothing.[14]

As their dormitory rooms were small, students were encouraged to use the often huge common or social spaces such as the social and dining rooms, assembly hall or gymnasium where they could interact and meet each other. For Edmonds, "The social rooms, large and small, corresponding to the living rooms of a private house, bring the family together for social and intellectual intercourse, just as informally and naturally as in the case of a small family in a small house."[15]

Rockefeller's ambitions for peace and internationalism went beyond New York. As he explained: "if buildings for foreign students, comparable to International House in New York, were located in half a dozen or more of the leading student centers of the world, they would exert an influence toward international understanding and world peace that might be very far reaching in its results."[16] Soon after New York, Rockefeller built International Houses in Berkeley (opened in 1930) and Chicago (opened in 1932).

But not in Paris, or at least not yet. In Paris, a French politician and senator, André Honnorat (1868–1950), had already been inspired by the same ideals of

---

11 Edmonds, "International House," 149.
12 Harr and Johnson, *The Rockefeller Century*, 166.
13 Edmonds, "International House," 149.
14 Edmonds, "International House," 149–150.
15 Edmonds, "International House," 150.
16 Junior to Gunn, August 29, 1938, folder 1012, box 132, series educational interests, RG III 2 G, RAC.

peace, yet he had a somewhat different idea about how to turn these ideals into reality. Rather than having students from all over the world live under the same roof, his idea was to construct a huge park at the southern edge of Paris in which there would be "national buildings, housing national groups."[17] Unlike Rockefeller, Honnorat was not a rich philanthropist, so he had to convince wealthy donors to construct dormitories where students of a certain nationality could live. The Cité Universitaire (or "halls of residence"), as the huge park was called, opened its first building in 1925 and in just a decade construction had already begun on Canadian, Belgian, American, Danish, Argentinian, Greek, Armenian, Cuban, French and Japanese houses.[18]

Just like in New York, these houses at the Cité were more than merely dormitories, since "each house has its dining room, recreation room and library, and the idea is to foster social life among the students."[19] As one observer described it, "in this special village, the foreign student does not feel like a stranger [*dépaysé*]; he finds himself in an intimate and national environment [*cadre*] and at the same time he is in contact with students from other nationalities with whom he can exchange his language, his culture, his ideas."[20] Still, contact between houses was limited, because "resident students are not expected to visit the other houses at all, unless when invited by someone in them."[21]

So in the Cité Universitaire internationalism seemed to mean that nationalities shared a park with other nations but not a house. Living abroad still meant living abroad with people from one's own nation. Once one felt at home, one

---

17 Rose to Mrs. Rockefeller, March 3, 1926, folder 1010, box 132, series educational interests, RG III 2 G, RAC.

18 For the origins and early history of the Cité Universitaire, see Dzovinar Kévonian and Guillaume Tronchet (eds.), *La Babel étudiante. La Cité internationale universitaire de Paris (1920 −1950)* (Rennes: Presses Universitaires de Rennes, 2013) and Reis, "Cultural Internationalism," 155−173. For an overview of the different buildings and their history, see Pascale Dejean (ed.), *La Cité Universitaire de Paris. Architectures paysagées* (Paris: Editions L'œil d'Or, 2010). See also Brigitte Blanc, *La fondation Émile et Louise Deutsch de la Meurthe* (Paris: Somogy éditions d'art, 2010).

19 From Dr. Paeree's diary, January 26, 1925, folder 1010, box 132, series educational interests, RG III 2 G, RAC.

20 Georges Martin-Charpenel, "La Cité Universitaire de 1920 à 1933," *La Cité Universitaire: Revue internationale des etudiants de la Cité Universitaire de Paris* 1.1 (1933): 3−4, 4. The French original reads: "Dans ce village si spécial, l'étudiant étranger n'est pas dépaysé; il se retrouve dans un cadre intime et national analogue à celui où s'est écoulée son enfance et en même temps il est en contact avec des étudiants d'autres nationalités avec lesquels il lui est possible d'échanger sa langue, sa culture, ses idées."

21 Walter A. Troy to Mr. Keebler, June 29, 1935, folder 1011, box 132, series educational interests, RG III 2 G, RAC.

could perhaps start to reach out to students of other nations. The American version of internationalism, by contrast, meant that different nationalities had to live not in the same park but under the same roof from the very start. These two versions of internationalism perhaps correspond to two ways expats choose to belong to a community. When living abroad, some choose to stay close to other people of their nationality or religion, as is still the case in "China-Town" or "Little Italy" in some cities. This model can be called, for lack of a better word, a diasporic approach to internationalism, and can be found at the Cité Universitaire. Diaspora and diasporic are terms that can mean many different things. Here it refers to "the connections migrants form abroad and the kinds of culture they produce."[22] In speaking of diasporic, I refer to migrants who establish connections abroad with other migrants of the same homeland. Other expats, however, feel closer to fellow-expats than to people from their home country. For them feeling at home abroad means building a community with people who share not the same home-community but rather share the same feeling of being away from home. This second model, one could say, corresponds to a cosmopolitan version of internationalism that inspired International House New York.

Converging Internationalisms?

Now back to our two internationalist experiments. Soon after they started operating, these two internationalist enterprises learned of each other's existence. It comes as no surprise that Rockefeller did not like Honnorat's idea of student dormitories based on nationality. As he wrote, "the principle on which the *Cité* was established was just the opposite from the principle on which International House was founded."[23] Little wonder that Rockefeller even denied a request by the American house at the Cité for financial help, precisely because subsidizing a national house would be "contrary to the principles of international house."[24]

Rockefeller explained why his view of internationalism was superior by comparing the Cité unfavorably to his own International House:

---

22 Kevin Kenny, *Diaspora. A Very Short Introduction* (Oxford: Oxford UP, 2013): 12.

23 Junior to Gunn, August 29, 1938, folder 1012, box 132, series educational interests, RG III 2 G, RAC.

24 Raymond Fosdick to Junior, January 28, 1928, folder 1010, box 132, series educational interests, RG III 2 G, RAC.

The Cite [sic] is composed of a number of separate national buildings each housing the students of its own country, and keeping them separate and apart. International House, on the other hand, brings together under one roof students from fifty or sixty different countries and throws them into constant association in the ordinary routine of daily life as well as in social matters.[25]

In the Cité in those early days exchange between students indeed appears to have been minimal. It is true that in its first decade the Cité planned to encourage student participation and intended to foster student activities and exchanges between the different national houses while avoiding "nationalism." In 1927 Honnorat had already visited Rockefeller's International House in New York, which apparently inspired Honnorat to increase exchanges between students in his own Cité Universitaire.[26] Moreover, since March 1933 the Cité even published a magazine called *La Cité Universitaire* that was scheduled to appear every two weeks. Despite all this, participation still turned out to be quite limited and mostly focused on sports.[27]

Yet for Rockefeller not all hope was lost in Paris, because he believed that it remained possible to turn the Cité in Paris into something that would resemble International House New York. From an American perspective there was still the need and possibility in Paris for "a building providing for a common life and conducted as International House in New York is being conducted. This building need not provide living rooms, but should provide for the common life."[28] Soon Rockefeller offered help to his French counterpart in constructing, amidst the different national houses of the Cité, an international house called the Maison Internationale, where residents of the different national houses could meet. The French accepted the offer and, after some quarrels about the architecture, the huge building – that was modeled after a French *Château* – was built and opened its doors in 1936. Given that the house was not mainly a dormitory, there was even more space for common rooms and meeting places than in New York. In Paris there was not only a restaurant but also a library, several meeting places, a theatre, a concert hall and even a state-of-the-art swimming pool.

25 Junior to Gunn, August 29, 1938, folder 1012, box 132, series educational interests, RG III 2 G, RAC.
26 See Frank Sereni, "Quelques réflexions sur les sociabilités étudiantes à la Cité internationale universitaire de Paris (années 1920–1950)," in Kévonian, Tronchet, *La Babel étudiante*, 117 −126, 117−119.
27 Sereni, "Quelques réflexions," 118−123, and Reis, "Cultural Internationalism," 169−171.
28 Rose to Mrs. Rockefeller, March 3, 1926, folder 1010, box 132, series educational interests, RG III 2 G, RAC.

The French expected a lot from the new Maison Internationale. In one essay the new building was presented to the residents in a newspaper of the Cité. The essay concluded by describing the ambitious aims that the new international house should fulfill:

> The [...] aim [...] consists in making the entire Cité a new intellectual home kept alive by young men and women from five corners of the world, each with their race, language, religion, knowledge and ignorance, prejudice, flaws and qualities. All those who arrive have two things in common: they are twenty years old and have to study. In what the Cité has to become, they will be able to get to know each other, to discuss, mutually enrich each other and learn how friendship and politeness between individuals can prepare friendship and politeness between nations. For many years this cosmopolitan friendship has already been developing under the roofs of the different foundations [the national houses] of the Cité. The international house will constitute the field where it can appear.[29]

Seen from a French perspective the construction of the Maison Internationale was indeed a huge improvement for social life of the students in the Cité, especially for sports and culture.[30] The Americans, in turn, believed that they had succeeded in turning the Cité into one huge International House, whereby, for Edmonds, "[t]he Maison Internationale corresponds to the common space in the New York House."[31] Seen from this perspective the Maison Internationale in the Cité even had the potential of overshadowing its New York counterpart. While in New York only a couple of hundred students from all nations lived under the same roof, in Paris many *thousands* of students of many more different nationalities lived in the same park, scattered over different national houses. So in principle students from different parts of the world could interact on an even larger scale in Paris than in New York.

---

29 Pierre Durieu, "La Maison Internationale," *La cité universitaire. Revue internationale des étudiants de la cité universitaire de Paris* 4.6 (1936): 5–10, 10. My translation; the original reads as follows: "Le [...] objectif [...] consiste à faire de l'ensemble de la Cité un foyer intellectuel nouveau entretenu par des jeunes gens et des jeunes filles venus de cinq parties du monde avec chacun sa race, sa langue, sa religion, son savoir et son ignorance, ses préjugés, ses défauts et ses qualités. Deux points communs entre tous ces arrivants: vingt ans et des études à faire. Dans ce que doit devenir la Cité, ils pourront se connaître, discuter, s'enrichir mutuellement et apprendre comment l'amitié et la politesse entre les individus peuvent préparer l'amitié et la politesse entre les nations. Cette camaraderie cosmopolite est depuis plusieurs années en germe sous les toits des différentes fondations de la Cité. La maison internationale va constituer le champ où elle pourra éclore."
30 Sereni, "Quelques réflexions," 122–123.
31 Harry Edmonds to Senator Honnorat, September 20, 1936, page 2, folder 1012, box 132, series educational interests, RG III 2 G, RAC.

Yet, from an American perspective the Maison Internationale turned out to be much less internationalist than its counterpart in New York. Initially the Americans were hopeful. As Edmonds, who followed the Maison from close by, noted:

> In my opinion, the House has had a favorable beginning. The students are much pleased, and the superior environment has already made an improvement in their conduct. Only the food service is open, but there is every indication that they can be trusted to use the rest of the building with propriety as rapidly as it is opened to them.[32]

But as time went on, the Americans who visited the Maison became increasingly appalled by what they saw. Many years later the same Edmonds would even exclaim dramatically: "one of the greatest opportunities in the world for furthering understanding and peace is being lost."[33] What went wrong? Why were the Americans disappointed? And whom did they blame?

One group they held responsible for the lack of success of the Maison were the directors of the existing national houses surrounding it. As one could expect "most of the directors of the different national houses are indifferent to the central building."[34] Rockefeller explained: "Naturally, each manager is more interested in his own house than he is in the new central building and its possibilities."[35] One American wrote that "the directors of the different buildings [...] do not understand or are incapable of understanding the international aspects of the Maison Internationale."[36] A possible explanation for the directors' lack of interest in the new internationalist Maison was their age. As Edmonds observed after meeting them: "look at them: of 14 directors present last night [...] 8 were bald, [...] all but 2 were grey; 12 appeared to be 60 or over [...] And yet, there they are, leading the 2500 youth of the Cité Universitaire; you see the problem?"[37] When visiting the Cité in 1947, John Mott, the then director of Internation-

---

32 Harry Edmonds to Nelson [Rockefeller], May 1, 1936, folder 1021, box 133, series educational interests, RG III 2 G, RAC.

33 Harry Edmonds to David Rockefeller, July 1, 1953, folder 1015 A, box 132, series educational interests, RG III 2 G, RAC.

34 Selskar Gunn, Notes on interview with Senator Honnorat, March 10, 1939, folder 1012, box 132, series educational interests, RG III 2 G, RAC.

35 Junior to Gunn, page 2, August 29, 1938, folder 1012, box 132, series educational interests, RG III 2 G, RAC.

36 Selskar Gunn, Interview with Horatio Krans, December 21, 1938, folder 1012, box 132, series educational interests, RG III 2 G, RAC.

37 Harry Edmonds to Nelson [Rockefeller], May 26, 1936, page 2, folder 1021, box 133, series educational interests, RG III 2 G, RAC.

al House New York, went further. For him the directors not only lacked interest in the Maison Internationale but even saw their own interests as opposed to those of the Maison. An activity organized by the Maison was, for example, seen by the directors as "taking their students away from their own Houses" and as a result the director of the Maison "had to drop this program which was designed to bring the whole Cite [sic] together."[38] Mott thus realized that the Maison Internationale could only live up to its promise if the surrounding houses also became more international:

> I emphasized that, unless the Directors and students of the Cite [sic] take full advantage of the facilities and opportunities of International House, the Cite [sic] could easily in the years ahead become a place which emphasizes nationalism instead of internationalism. I also suggested that [...] each national House should be made more and more international by accepting students from as many different countries as possible.[39]

Part of Mott's last idea would eventually become a reality. Through a so-called "*brassage*" system of student-exchange, today every national house of the Cité is obliged, at least in in principle, to send out around 30 percent of its own residents to other national houses and to open, in return, 30 percent of its own rooms to residents of different nationalities from other houses.

It was not just the directors of the national houses that were to blame; the Maison Internationale was part of the problem too. According to the Americans this lack of interest on the part of the directors was indeed exacerbated by the fact that the staff of the Maison lacked the necessary "know-how" of organizing appropriate activities. One observer concluded that "the chief difficulty is the lack of a driving person who would have a knowledge of the techniques necessary to develop international activities."[40] This "knowledge of techniques" could be about very simple things. When sending food to the Cité Universitaire in the postwar years, Mott for example made the following suggestion to his French counterpart, Robert Spitzer:

> I realized how much the largely attended programs which we have here in International House may be due to the fact that we are able to give the students in the House refreshments in the form of tea, coffee, cakes, or a Sunday Supper along with a program. I believe that if you were in a position to provide refreshments of the same type, or even of a much

38 John L. Mott, Report on Visit to Maison Internationale, February 21, 1947, page 5, folder 1019, box 133, series educational interests, RG III 2 G, RAC.
39 John L. Mott, Report on Visit to Maison Internationale, February 21, 1947, page 6, folder 1019, box 133, series educational interests, RG III 2 G, RAC.
40 Selskar Gunn, Interview with Mr. Lowrie, December 23, 1938, folder 1012, box 132, series educational interests, RG III 2 G, RAC.

simpler type, at a party on Sunday afternoon or evening or at other times in the week, you may be able to attract from their various Houses a considerable number of students of all nationalities.[41]

So when Mott went on to send food to his counterpart in Paris, this was not just to feed hungry students in postwar Europe but also to help the Cité fulfill its internationalist mission.

Yet for the Americans the directors and staff of the Maison Internationale not only lacked basic "know-how" but also, and more fundamentally, failed to appreciate the importance of international participation. In the eyes of the Americans, Honnorat himself – the founding father of the Cité – and to a lesser extent also Spitzer – the French director of the International House – did not understand what internationalism was all about. As one observer noted: "I doubt if Honnorat quite grasps the basic international idea of international house."[42] One American wrote: "If [...] he could be shown how far short the Paris International House comes to the work done by any of the International Houses in the States, he might be willing to urge some changes in the present administration."[43] And Edmonds deplored: "Hardly anyone knows what it is all about. Or if they do, their concept is different from ours."[44] The French and the Americans indeed seemed to have very different conceptions of internationalism. As one observer summarized it: "The international aspects of the question are not understood by Honnorat or by the directors of the different national buildings. This conception is essentially an American one."[45]

So, what, then, was the main difference between the French and the American interpretation of the role that the central Maison Internationale could play? For the Americans, the French merely focused on the buildings and the landscape, yet failed to see the importance of the actual *use* of the house and its social activities. For Edmonds, the French confuse "for the inner spirit what we

---

41 John Mott to Robert Spitzer, May 29, 1947, folder 1019, box 133, series educational interests, RG III 2 G, RAC.
42 Selskar Gunn to Junior, July 17, page 2, 1939, folder 1012, box 132, series educational interests, RG III 2 G, RAC.
43 Donald Lowrie to John D. Rockefeller 3rd, April 15, 1938, folder 1012, box 132, series educational interests, RG III 2 G, RAC.
44 Harry Edmonds to John D. Rockefeller 3rd, April 7, 1938, page 2, folder 1012, box 132, series educational interests, RG III 2 G, RAC.
45 Selskar Gunn, Interview with Mr. Lowrie, page 2, December 23, 1938, folder 1012, box 132, series educational interests, RG III 2 G, RAC.

think of as merely outward forms."[46] For the French, as long as the building looked nice, everything was fine. Yet for the Americans the building was only the beginning and required student activities and participation to have it fulfill its internationalist mission. Like many others, Mott saw Honnorat as the embodiment of these French ideas. He wrote: "Honnorat [...] tends to think of the House as a museum or a show place rather than a place to be lived in."[47] And he concluded: "Honnorat himself is one of the real problems of the Cite [sic]."[48] All this explained why the Americans were disappointed when they saw that the French administrators of the Cité did not use the building for what it was intended. One American estimated that the House "is being used to not more than about twenty-five per cent of its capacity."[49] For Edmonds "the Paris House is nothing more than a glorified restaurant."[50] And according to Rockefeller's son John "the house [...] is now merely serving as more or less of an hotel."[51] He added: "The great international hall is always locked except when used in connection with some fete which may be once or twice a year. All the smaller rooms, except the writing room, are locked all the time."[52] According to another American, a decade later, the house "appears to be hardly used at all."[53]

The main complaint thus appears to have been the lack of student participation in the Paris house. As Rockefeller's son John stated: "there are no activities organized by the House in which students participate."[54] Moreover, interaction between students of different houses remains limited because "visiting, if not in-

---

46 Harry Edmonds to John D. Rockefeller 3rd, April 7, 1938, page 2, folder 1012, box 132, series educational interests, RG III 2 G, RAC.
47 John L. Mott, Report on Visit to Maison Internationale, February 21, 1947, page 3, folder 1019, box 133, series educational interests, RG III 2 G, RAC.
48 John L. Mott, Report on Visit to Maison Internationale, February 21, 1947, page 6, folder 1019, box 133, series educational interests, RG III 2 G, RAC.
49 John D. Rockefeller 3rd to Junior, March 28, 1938, page 2, folder 1012, box 132, series educational interests, RG III 2 G, RAC.
50 Harry Edmonds to John D. Rockefeller 3rd, April 7, 1938, folder 1012, box 132, series educational interests, RG III 2 G, RAC.
51 John D. Rockefeller 3rd to John Mott, January 17, 1938, folder 1012, box 132, series educational interests, RG III 2 G, RAC.
52 John D. Rockefeller 3rd to Junior, March 28, 1938, page 2, folder 1012, box 132, series educational interests, RG III 2 G, RAC.
53 Harmon Goldstone to Dana Creel, page 6, December 26, 1952, folder 1015 A, box 132, series educational interests, RG III 2 G, RAC. A few years earlier, Mott painted a less gloomy picture, see: John L. Mott, Report on Visit to Maison Internationale, February 21, 1947, page 3, folder 1019, box 133, series educational interests, RG III 2 G, RAC.
54 John D. Rockefeller 3rd to Junior, March 28, 1938, page 2–3, folder 1012, box 132, series educational interests, RG III 2 G, RAC.

vited, is not welcomed between the various houses."[55] One of Rockefeller's collaborators describes the Cité as a "city without souls," lamenting that "the residents look like ghosts."[56]

This lack of student participation could again be explained by different ideas and practices in France and the US. Mott explained how French students are different:

> Another serious difficulty facing the Paris House is that two thousand of the three thousand students in the Cite [sic] are French, and that their background and characteristics are different from an American student group. They do not know or understand the type [of] program of activities which we have in the average American university or International House.[57]

The French explained the lack of student participation by "the fact that students in Paris worked much harder than in American universities and had very much less time for social activities."[58] One American admitted that in France "it is a fact that most of the students have a hard time."[59] Spitzer added that "French students [...] are more than ever wildly individualist. Whatever we do, we shall never have here in France Student Committees composed of the best and the brightest among them with that sense of discipline which you so commonly find in England and America."[60] One American observed that in France "there is nothing like the solidarity of student opinion and action"[61] that one finds in the US. Even when compared to their German counterparts French students "were not creating a community of fellow students with whom they could identify and interact."[62] While this seems to have been a specifically French problem,

55 Walter A. Troy, Maison Internationale, Information on operations [1935], page 17, folder 1011, box 132, series educational interests, RG III 2 G, RAC

56 Leon de Rosen to David [Rockefeller], April 23, 1948, page 2, folder 1015 A, box 132, series educational interests, RG III 2 G, RAC.

57 John L. Mott, Report on Visit to Maison Internationale, February 21, 1947, page 7, folder 1019, box 133, series educational interests, RG III 2 G, RAC.

58 Selskar Gunn, Visit to International House, March 29, 1939, folder 1012, box 132, series educational interests, RG III 2 G, RAC.

59 Leon de Rosen to David [Rockefeller], April 23, 1948, page 3, folder 1015 A, box 132, series educational interests, RG III 2 G, RAC.

60 Robert Spitzer [to John Mott], January 22, 1948, page 2, folder 1015 A, box 132, series educational interests, RG III 2 G, RAC.

61 Selskar Gunn, Interview with Horatio Krans, December 21, 1938, folder 1012, box 132, series educational interests, RG III 2 G, RAC.

62 Reis, "Cultural Internationalism," 159.

one can imagine that this French work-ethos and individualism also affected foreign students studying in France.

All this can be explained by different views on university education. Consider the following interesting distinction that Simon Leys finds in John Henry Newman:

> In his classic *The Idea of a University*, he made an amazingly bold statement: he said that if he had to choose between two types of universities, one in which eminent professors teach students who come to the university only to attend lectures and sit for examinations, and the other where there are no professors, no lectures, no examinations and no degrees, but where the students live together for two or three years, he would choose the second type. He concluded, "How is this to be explained? When a multitude of young men, keen, open-hearted, sympathetic and observant as young men are, come together and freely mix with each other, they are sure to learn from one another, even if there be no one to teach them; the conversation of all is a series of lectures to each, and they gain for themselves new ideas and views, fresh matter of thought and distinct principles for judging and acting day by day."[63]

With this in mind, one could perhaps say that the Anglophone model puts more emphasis on student-activities and extra-curricular activities as an integral part of university education, whereas the French model focuses more on lectures and exams, to the detriment of extra-curricular activities. This cultural difference may in part explain the difference in student-activities at the Cité Universitaire compared to International House New York.

For the Americans, this lack of student participation was not just caused by differences in work-ethos or social behavior of the French students, but also by the way their superiors treated them. The Rockefellers observed that the French administrators "seem to greatly fear the students,"[64] especially "the possibility of the students getting out of hand"[65] and go on strike or damage the furniture of the building. This is why they were not allowed to use many social rooms or become involved in theatre or cinema. No wonder that students protested. Yet their complaints were dealt with in a, from an American perspective, very formal way, thus failing "to win the confidence and interests of the students."[66] Edmonds re-

---

63 Simon Leys, *The Hall of Uselessness. Collected Essays* (New York: New York Review of Books, 2013): 12–13.
64 Junior to Gunn, page 3, August 29, 1938, folder 1012, box 132, series educational interests, RG III 2 G, RAC.
65 John D. Rockefeller 3rd to Junior, March 28, 1938, folder 1012, box 132, series educational interests, RG III 2 G, RAC.
66 Selskar Gunn, Interview with Mr. Lowrie, December 23, 1938, folder 1012, box 132, series educational interests, RG III 2 G, RAC.

gretted that there was thus "no sign of the students being recognized or consulted in an undertaking which will never succeed [...] without their enthusiastic help, not as mere onlookers, but as actual participants."[67] For the Americans, the conclusion was clear: "the central building will never become a vital and effective influence in the life of the students until they have been made to feel that it is their building and have been given responsibility for initiating, organizing and carrying on the student activities in it."[68]

We can now see why Edmonds described the house he helped create as a "splendid ship" which remained "tied to the dock unused."[69] A disappointed Edmonds concluded: "the Paris House is like a marvelous telescope to look at the stars, but the "astronomers" can't even manipulate it above the horizon."[70] The cultural differences also explain why the French almost tragically praise the functioning of the international house with the same passion as the Americans criticize it. Where the Americans saw missed opportunities and failure, the French saw near-perfection. Seemingly unaware of the huge disappointment by the Rockefellers, Spitzer, the French director of the International House could still write: "I firmly believe that the purpose of Mr. Rockefeller in offering the International House to France has been fully carried out."[71]

Some Lessons

What can we learn from this tragic story of internationalism misunderstood? I believe that there are at least three lessons to be learned. First, this paper showed that there are at least two different ways to offer international students a home away from home. They can feel at home by living together with other students from their home country – the philosophy behind the Cité Universitaire – which makes it harder for them to foster contacts with students from other countries. Or they can feel at home abroad by living together with students who do

---

67 Harry Edmonds to Senator Honnorat, September 20, 1936, page 2, folder 1012, box 132, series educational interests, RG III 2 G, RAC.

68 Junior to Gunn, page 3, August 29, 1938, folder 1012, box 132, series educational interests, RG III 2 G, RAC.

69 Harry Edmonds to Senator Honnorat, September 20, 1936, folder 1012, box 132, series educational interests, RG III 2 G, RAC.

70 Harry Edmonds to John D. Rockefeller 3rd, April 7, 1938, page 2, folder 1012, box 132, series educational interests, RG III 2 G, RAC.

71 Robert Spitzer [to John Mott], January 22, 1948, page 2, folder 1015 A, box 132, series educational interests, RG III 2 G, RAC.

not come from the same home country but who do share the experience of being abroad, which also creates a common bond. This perhaps explains why expats often prefer to meet up with other expats rather than with the local population.

This brings us to a second lesson. Both the US and Europe have universities that welcome students from abroad. Yet from the story I have told we can infer that Europe finds it much harder to create truly cosmopolitan spaces for international students. International Houses still exist today but almost only in the Anglophone world. Is this because Europe is less open to international exchange or is it because Europe has a different form of campus life? One conclusion could be that, when it comes to internationalism, the US appears to be ahead of Europe. Contrary to the cliché that Americans are isolationist and not very interested in the world, the story of the two International Houses shows that when it comes to fostering international student interactions Europeans can perhaps still learn something from the Americans. In France's defense, one must admit that the Cité Universitaire has recently announced a new campaign to expand its capacity by 30 percent, adding 1,800 new rooms in ten new houses (including, amongst others, a Korean and probably also a Chinese and a Russian house).[72] It is, of course, a hopeful sign that such special student dormitories can still be built even when the big era of philanthropy, embodied by the Rockefellers, is over. Yet, an American like Rockefeller would probably have complained that these are again mostly national houses rather than truly cosmopolitan places.

A third and final conclusion is that internationalism paradoxically appeared to be a *national* trait and that it thus depends on specific national values. The Cité Universitaire shows that the issue is not so much funding as a mentality and a matter of priorities. Building a sense of community through extra-curricular activities just seems less of a priority for European students compared to their Anglophone counterparts. So to make internationalism work, one needs not only buildings but also a culture, mentality and series of practices that involve, organize, and bring together other students. Conversely, it may require a climate in which students are treated like equals. This lesson is not without relevance at a time when the Cité Universitaire is expanding.

These lessons resonate in contemporary policy-making, where American ideas are imported to Europe. Think of European policy makers who try to copy features of American universities, often without looking at the specific context in which they originally operated. Just as the Maison Internationale required

---

72 Fondation nationale, Cité internationale universitaire de Paris, Rapport annuel 2012 (Paris), 30–31.

not just a building but also certain practices, so European universities that want to compete with their American counterparts likewise require values and practices such as meritocracy at universities and philanthropic practices in society. And just as it is easier to construct a building than to import practices, so it is likewise more difficult to import practices and values than to just raise more money. But that is yet another story.

Maria Jakob

"Unfortunately, there is no plural for 'Heimat' in German": Home and Belonging in German Naturalization Ceremonies

Abstract: How do people reflect on and make sense of belonging and "home" in the context of migration, settlement and naturalization? In this chapter, a sequential and comparative analysis of speeches given at German naturalization ceremonies is used to enquire about the contingent and essentialist character the concepts of home and belonging can assume, focusing on reflections on "home" made by naturalized speakers and politicians as well as on the use of metaphoric speech from the metaphoric fields of "housing" and "plants." While there are indeed some elaborate reflections on the constructivist character of the concept of "home," the essentialist notion that the immigrants' home is their country of origin dominates the speeches, thus inferring the naturalization candidates as "diasporic by ascription."

The transition from immigrant to citizen can be perceived as the epitome of definite settlement in a country. Are naturalized immigrants, then, still members of diaspora communities and do they maintain close ties to their home countries, or do they become ordinary members of the population, with or without migration background? Instead of attempting to answer these questions analytically, I intend to take a close look at how the newly naturalized people themselves perceive their social position, and at how they are in return perceived by the host society. Host society in this case equates to local politicians – the speakers at naturalization ceremonies. The questions are thus: What conceptions of "home" do naturalization candidates have? And what do representatives of host societies think of where the candidates' "home" is located?

Alongside naturalizing and becoming citizens of their country of residence, many migrants reflect on their position in society and their relationship both to their country of origin and the country in which they live and into which they naturalize. This is also mirrored in the public and media discourses. In Germany, until the 1990s migrants were perceived as "guests" (more precisely: "guest workers") who would be welcome to enter the country, but who were not expected to settle or to make themselves at home.[1] After legislative reforms (most no-

---

[1] Between 1955 and 1974, more than a million guest workers had been recruited to West Germany, most of them from Italy, Greece, Spain and Turkey. While a significant part of them did return to their country of origin, some decided to settle. See also Cord Pagenstecher, "Die 'Illusion' der Rückkehr: Zur Mentalitätsgeschichte von 'Gastarbeit' und Einwanderung," *Soziale Welt* 47.2 (1996), 149–179; Rita Chin, *The Guest Worker Question in Postwar Germany* (Cambridge: Cambridge UP, 2007).

tably the reform of 2000 which introduced some *ius soli* elements into German naturalization law, which until then had been based on *ius sanguinis* only, as Thomas Faist and Triadafilos Triadafilopoulos as well as Kay Hailbronner eluci- date),[2] this notion has changed. The fact that many of the immigrants do stay permanently is now a more widely accepted element of the discourse. This, how- ever, does not mean that Germany is now regarded as the home or *"Heimat"* of the immigrants. As Katharina Inhetveen argues,[3] there have been some shifts in the conceptualization of Heimat since the Second World War, arriving at a pres- ent notion of Heimat as an unchangeable affiliation to the place of birth. There is also still widespread discussion in politics and society about whether the Turk- ish minority – which is the largest minority in Germany, consisting of about three million people – and "Islam" in general do belong to Germany or not. Since the 1990s, the notion of a "parallel society" of Turkish Muslims gained political rele- vance, depicting Turkish immigrants as a diasporic group unwilling to integrate into German society.[4]

Different conceptualizations of "home" are explicitly elaborated at natural- ization ceremonies. For many decades such ceremonies have been a standard part of the naturalization process in states such as the US, Canada and Australia. In Germany, however, they are a very recent phenomenon: Naturalization cere- monies were only introduced from 2007 onwards. After the reform of the natural- ization law in 1999/2000 and some succeeding changes – the introduction of a naturalization test and an obligatory pledge of allegiance to the constitution (*"feierliches Bekenntnis"*) – ceremonies were introduced in order to provide a cer- emonial framing for this ceremonial pledge.

Today, most of the naturalization ceremonies in Germany are organized by local governments, but some ceremonies are held at district or federal state level.[5] The ceremonies feature speeches, both by administration officials – most- ly city mayors – and by naturalized women or men. The national anthem is sung,

---

2 Thomas Faist, Triadafilos Triadafilopoulos, "Beyond Nationhood: Citizenship Politics in Ger- many since Unification," *University of Toronto Munk Centre for International Studies Occasional Paper* 1 (2006); Kay Hailbronner, *EUDO Citizenship Observatory Country Report: Germany. Re- vised and updated October 2012* (San Domenico di Fiesole: European University Institute, 2012).
3 Katharina Inhetveen, "Der Flüchtling," in *Diven, Hacker, Spekulanten: Sozialfiguren der Gegen- wart*, eds. Stephan Moebius, Markus Schroer (Berlin: Suhrkamp, 2010): 148–159.
4 Wolf-Dietrich Bukow, "Die Rede von Parallelgesellschaften. Zusammenleben im Zeitalter einer metropolitanen Differenzgesellschaft," in *Was heißt hier Parallelgesellschaft? Zum Umgang mit Differenzen*, eds. Wolf-Dietrich Bukow, Claudia Nikodem, Erika Schulze, Erol Yildiz (Wiesbaden: VS, 2007): 29–51.
5 At federal state level, the Länder of Brandenburg, Saxony, Saxony-Anhalt and North Rhine- Westphalia have their own naturalization ceremonies.

there is music and some drinks are offered. Curiously, the very pledge that was the reason for introducing the ceremonies in the first place is only part of some of the ceremonies. Many administrations prefer to carry out the pledge and the handing over of the naturalization certificate individually and then to hold a common ceremony for all applicants once or twice a year.

In my opinion, the naturalization ceremonies offer the unique opportunity to analyze how both officials and migrants talk about belonging, naturalization and "home." I draw from a sample that consists of about 95 manuscripts of speeches from naturalization ceremonies from all over the country, as well as of participant observation data from fifteen ceremonies held between 2010 and 2013. Some of the manuscripts are interpreted in depth using sequential analysis adapted from Ulrich Oevermann's objective hermeneutics methodology.[6] This will form the basis of a first approach towards the data in this article: I will present some statements made by naturalized people and by local politicians about belonging and "home" and analyze their respective structures of sense-making. The second main analytical approach will consist of a comparison between cases and statements that will take into account the whole data corpus. This approach is derived from the Constant Comparative Analysis Method developed within Grounded Theory by Barney Glaser and Anselm Strauss and is here used to understand the scope of meanings attached to the concepts in the data.[7] My presentations of two main metaphors that are used to depict belonging ("house" and "plant") are based on this approach, as well as the subsequent summary of contingent versus essentialist notions of home and belonging. I will conclude my presentation by explaining my hypothesis that at German naturalization ceremonies the notion of a "diaspora by ascription" is upheld. I will also look at some consequences this may have for the naturalized people and for the very concepts of "home" and "belonging."

---

6 Kai-Olaf Maiwald, "Competence and Praxis: Sequential Analysis in German Sociology," *Forum Qualitative Sozialforschung/Forum: Qualitative Social Research* 6.3 (2005) <http://www.qual itative-research.net/index.php/fqs/article/view/21/45> [acc. March 12, 2015]; Ulrich Oevermann, Tilman Allert, Elisabeth Konau, Jürgen Krambeck, "Structures of Meaning and Objective Hermeneutics," in *Modern German Sociology,* eds. Volker Meja, Dieter Misgeld, Nico Stehr (New York: Columbia UP, 1987): 436–447.
7 Hennie Boeije, "A Purposeful Approach to the Constant Comparative Method in the Analysis of Qualitative Interviews," *Quality & Quantity* 36.4 (2002): 391–409; Barney G. Glaser, "The Constant Comparative Method of Qualitative Analysis," *Social Problems* 12.4 (1965): 436–445.

Reflections on "Heimat" in a Speech by a Naturalized Woman

The first quotes I present are taken from the speech by a woman at a naturalization ceremony I attended in a small town in southern Germany in 2010. In an exemplary way and very explicitly, her speech provides an insight into how the naturalized people themselves try to figure out how to belong and what to call "home". The speaker was born in Zambia and grew up there. After explaining to the audience how she had met her German husband and how she had decided to move to Germany with him, she uses her speech to share some thoughts about the concepts "home" and "Heimat":

> But how does one become a German? In the German language, there is this wonderful term "Heimat." The word Heimat cannot adequately be translated into English or other languages, because through translating it, important parts of its comprehensive meaning are lost. Heimat is more than a place or a country. Heimat also means social relationships and cultural identity. Heimat is also a feeling and it gives us comfort.[8]

The speaker reflects on "Heimat" in the context of "becoming a German." Moving from one country to another and thus exchanging one "Heimat" for another, is a turning point in her life, and encourages her to engage in some fundamental reflections about what it means to belong. Strikingly, in this passage she reflects on the language-dependency of the concept. For the woman, "Heimat" is a "wonderful term" as it allows her to understand home in a way that is new to her. The acquisition of a second language opens up new possibilities to make sense of the world and her life.

According to the speaker, the German term "Heimat" cannot be adequately translated. Therefore she tries to grasp the meaning of the term by describing its vital elements: Compared to the English word "home," which she defines as limited to a spatial dimension, "Heimat" encompasses social relationships, cultural

---

[8] "Aber wie wird man nun zum Deutschen? In der deutschen Sprache gibt es das wunderbare Wort 'Heimat.' Das Wort Heimat kann man nur unzureichend ins Englische und wohl auch in andere Sprachen übersetzen, ohne dass von seiner umfassenden Bedeutung wichtige Teile verloren gehen. Heimat ist mehr als die Bezeichnung für einen Ort oder ein Land. Heimat bedeutet auch soziale Beziehungen und kulturelle Identität. Heimat ist auch ein Gefühl und sie gibt uns Geborgenheit" (naturalized woman at a ceremony in Heilbronn, 2010; manuscript provided by speaker). All quotations from speeches are presented in my own English translation and in the original German in the footnotes. Diagonal slashes within quotations (/ /) indicate insertions or reactions by other people; emphases are italicized.

identity, and "comfort" (for which she actually uses another German word that is hard to translate: "Geborgenheit"), thus social, cultural and emotional dimensions are explicitly added to the spatial conceptualization.

The woman then continues to speak about the implications of exchanging one "Heimat" for another with a more personal tone:

> I left my old Heimat Zambia in 1997 and arrived in my new Heimat, Germany. But how did I make myself at home here? In my case, my husband and most of all my children played a huge part in this. My children have grown up here. They are Germans and they feel like Germans. Their Heimat is this country and there future lies in this country. Through them, this land, its culture and its people have become more and more familiar to me.[9]

The speaker states that she has two homes now: An old one and a new one. She describes "making herself at home" as a task she had to accomplish individually. Thus she is pointing out that the feeling of "being at home" is not something essentially pre-determined, but something that can be achieved for practically every place in the world. For her, "Heimat" and home is where her family is. Identifying one's "home" with one's family may not be so extraordinary, but as we have seen "Heimat" means more than just "home" in German and the speaker's family here functions as an agent of Heimat-making in a sense that encompasses more than just the private realm: "this land, its culture and its people have become more and more familiar."

Concluding this process of "making herself at home," the speaker then describes her way of managing her two affiliations:

> Today, two hearts are beating in my chest. The Zambian one and the German one. In my house, we speak German and English. We eat *Spätzle and Maultaschen*, but also Rice and Beans and *Nshima* – which is an African dish made of corn, similar to polenta. It is with joy that I report about Zambia in Germany and I am proud to speak about Germany in Zambia. I will pass my language, my culture and my story on to my children and in doing so I hope they will grow up as open-minded, tolerant people.[10]

---

9 "Ich hatte 1997 meine alte Heimat Sambia verlassen und war nun in meiner neuen Heimat Deutschland. Aber wie wurde ich "heimisch" hier in Heilbronn? In meinem Fall haben mein Mann und vor allem meine Kinder großen Anteil daran. Meine Kinder sind hier aufgewachsen. Sie sind Deutsche und sie fühlen sich als Deutsche. Ihre Heimat ist dieses Land und ihre Zukunft liegt in diesem Land. Durch sie wurden mir das Land, seine Kultur und seine Menschen immer vertrauter" (naturalized woman, Heilbronn, 2010).
10 "In meiner Brust schlagen heute zwei Herzen. Das sambische und das deutsche. Bei uns zu Hause wird Deutsch und Englisch gesprochen. Wie essen Spätzle und Maultaschen, aber auch *Rice and Beans* und *Nshima*. Mit Freude berichte ich in Deutschland über Sambia und mit Stolz spreche ich in Sambia über Deutschland. Ich werde meine Sprache, meine Kultur und

The reference to the "two hearts" at the beginning of this part of the speech clearly indicates the emotional relevance of the concept of "home," thus the emotional nature of the attachment to a place or an environment. For the speaker, the statement that she now has "two hearts" indicates an additive notion of affiliations. She does not have to make "room" in her heart for another reference area, the affection towards her first "Heimat" does not need to be diminished. Instead, there is enough room in her chest to accommodate double the amount of belonging.

Subsequently, the speaker explains what this double affiliation means for the daily practices in her family, in her "house" where two languages are spoken. Taking into account her earlier statement about the wonderful German term Heimat, it can be stated that a bilingual household allows for a wide range of communicative concepts, enabling the speakers to switch between languages or mix them at convenience. Here, we also find an additive sense of references. The same applies to the second example, which is food. Food is often referred to at the naturalization ceremonies, as it can be seen as very direct bodily exposure to different cultures and as eating habits can be regarded as very tightly connected with cultural and regional affiliations. When it comes to food, the speaker (along with her family) also manages to integrate two different spheres, as they have both the Swabian dishes of "*Spätzle*" (a regional form of homemade pasta) and "*Maultaschen*" (meat dumplings), as well as the supposedly Zambian dishes "rice and beans" and "*Nshima*," which the speaker explains to the audience connecting it to "Africa" and comparing it to the apparently more universally known polenta.

Her two affiliations are a source of communication and stories for this woman, as she explains that she often speaks about Zambia in Germany and the other way round, with "joy" and "pride" respectively. The attribution of "joy" to Zambia and "pride" to Germany may be a hint to a more emotional connection to the country of her childhood, and a rather rationalizing view on the country of her adult residence (understanding "pride" as a feeling that refers to some accomplishment). At the end of this passage, the speaker delivers a kind of mission statement about how she intends to handle her dual belonging concerning her kids. As she has already demonstrated that "her" language, "her" culture and "her" story[11] are additive rather than distinct features that include both belongings, the audience can understand that for her, representing those features

---

meine Geschichte an meine Kinder weitergeben und hoffe, sie dadurch zu weltoffenen und toleranten Menschen zu erziehen" (naturalized woman, Heilbronn, 2010).

11 The German term "*Geschichte*" can refer to both her biographical "story" as well as to a more globally understood "history" of a country or a social group.

is a means of encouraging her children to become "open-minded" and "tolerant."

In conclusion, this speech clearly reveals the contingency of "home" and "Heimat": Instead of being a fixed reality, Heimat is prone to being changed, supplemented, and worked on. By learning German as her second language, the naturalization candidate is led to contemplate the concepts of belonging in a new way. Thus, there are two factors at play here that enable the speaker to reflect on her belonging: The experience of migration and integration into a host society, and the acquisition of another language with new concepts and new possibilities. It is also important to again emphasize the role of the family in this process: For the speaker, feeling at home in a society or a nation depends on starting a family in these new surroundings. Without giving up her own "language, culture and history," the speaker manages to produce a degree of uniformity concerning her belonging and that of her family members.

Ascribed and Reflected Homes: The Mayors' Statements

As I have shown so far, the naturalized speaker's concept of home has become a rather flexible one. However, not at every German naturalization ceremony is a naturalized person invited to speak. Only speeches by politicians – mostly mayors or other highly ranked representatives of administration or local and federal parliaments – are ubiquitous. These speeches feature a broad range of meanings that are attached to "home." At a ceremony held at federal state level in Dresden, one speaker tells the new citizens: "Maybe more people from your home countries will soon come to Saxony. Maybe you will have the chance to assist your fellow countrymen."[12] The "home countries" mentioned here are clearly and exclusively the countries of origin, and the "fellow countrymen" of the already naturalized men and women are not fellow Germans, but still the citizens of the country they have emigrated from. Moreover, the existence of solidarity ties is implied between the naturalized citizens and these "countrymen."

---

12 "Vielleicht kommen bald auch aus Ihren Heimatländern noch mehr Menschen nach Sachsen. Vielleicht werden Sie die Gelegenheit haben, Ihren Landsleuten unter die Arme zu greifen" (Markus Ulbig, Minister of the Interior of the federal state of Saxony, ceremony in Dresden, 2011; <http://www.landtag.sachsen.de/dokumente/sab/110521_Reden-EiFest.pdf> [acc. March 12, 2015]).

A similar notion of "home" informs the statement of the head of a district authority in a rural area in Saxony-Anhalt as he addresses a young boy of Vietnamese descent who was born and raised in Germany. However, according to the speaker, the boys' "home" is not Germany or the region he has been living in his whole life, but the country where his family originates: "So you are one of those people who presumably knows their home, yes who know their home from *visiting*. /Boy: Yes./ yes, who are otherwise born in Germany."[13] "Home" here is not an entity someone creates or chooses, but one that is determined by ancestry. This view underlies the somewhat curious perception that someone has to get to know his "home" by visiting during holidays. The same speaker finally concludes, speaking to the whole group of naturalization candidates present at the ceremony: "The relationships to your ancestral home is [sic] thus very diverse."[14] By describing the homes of the immigrants with the metaphor "angestammt," which lexically derives from "Stamm," the German word for "stem" or "trunk," the speaker is inferring a naturalistic and essentialist view of "home" and belonging. We will return to this point shortly.

On the other hand, there are also statements in the speeches that rely on a contingent and more liberal conceptualization of home and belonging. The mayor of Frankfurt am Main for example concludes her speech by saying: "we, the city of Frankfurt am Main, your home city, cordially welcome you."[15] The mayor here refers to a notion of "home" appearing quite often at the ceremonies, which is that "home" is connected to a narrowly defined place, a city or a region. This view reflects the differences probably many of the immigrants have in determining which of the two (or more) countries, to which they have ties, is their actual "home." When it comes to the city they live in, there is seldom such confusion. They can call the city they have lived in for some time (if not their whole life) their "home city," regardless of whether they otherwise identify themselves as Germans or Turks or whatever else. This notion is clearly indicated in the words of a naturalized speaker of Italian origin who is invited to speak after the mayor. At one point in his speech he professes his identification with his city (also, like the speaker presented earlier, speaking of his "heart") and is greeted with loud and spontaneous applause from the audience: "In my

---

13 "Sie gehören also zu denen, die ihre Heimat wahrscheinlich ja die ihre Heimat von *Besuchen* her kennen /Junge: Ja./ ja, ansonsten in Deutschland geboren worden sind" (district administrator, Halberstadt, 2012; personal recording; emphasis in the recording).

14 "Die Beziehungen zu Ihrer angestammten Heimat ist [sic] also sehr unterschiedlich" (district administrator, Halberstadt, 2012).

15 "[...] heißen wir Sie, die Stadt Frankfurt am Main, Ihre Heimatstadt, ganz ganz herzlich willkommen" (Petra Roth, mayor, Frankfurt am Main, 2010, personal recording).

heart I am – my apologies to those originally from Turkey – a fake ("turked") Italian, / some laughs / or a Germanized foreigner. Or a German with migration background. Or something. But one thing is certain: I am a Frankfurter."[16] On some occasions, the politicians even try to take on the perspective of the immigrants, as in the following statement of the mayor of Berlin's Mitte district at the first naturalization ceremony held by a German Bundespräsident:

> As a local politician and as the mayor of Mitte I also want to draw from my practical experience. Unfortunately, there is no plural for Heimat in German. Heimat only exists in the singular. Actually, this word doesn't describe the attitude towards life of many of our people. Because they generally have, many of those who immigrated, two "Heimate," if I may say so, however grammatically incorrect.[17]

By inventing the plural "Heimate," the mayor tries to adapt German language to the experiences of the immigrants. This reflects a common problem with language(s): It limits our thinking to the concepts that are expressible in the respective language. As long as there is only the singular "Heimat" in German, people who speak and think only (or predominantly) German tend to essentialize the notion of "Heimat" – even if in daily life they witness the potential or capacity of people to have more than one "Heimat." The mayor of Mitte tries to surmount these linguistic limitations. By adjusting the linguistic possibilities to social reality, he goes even one step further than the speaker from Zambia introduced earlier, who reflected linguistic possibilities and used two languages simultaneously, but did not go as far as altering and adapting language itself. To her, "Heimat" is a wonderful term because it widens her scope of conceptual possibilities. For the mayor, however, the same concept bears inherent conceptual limitations that he tries to overcome.

---

16 "[...] im Herzen bin ich also, Pardon für die Vielen, die das mal waren, ein getürkter Italiener / vereinzeltes Lachen / oder ein eingedeutschter Ausländer. Oder ein Deutscher mit Migrationshintergrund. Oder so. Ganz bestimmt bin ich eins: Ein Frankfurter" (naturalized man, Frankfurt am Main, 2010, personal recording).

17 "Ich will als Kommunalpolitiker, als Bürgermeister von Mitte aber natürlich auch berichten von meiner praktischen Erfahrung. Leider hat unsere deutsche Sprache keine Plural für Heimat. Heimat gibt es eigentlich nur im Singular. Und eigentlich können wir damit gar nicht beschreiben, was das Lebensgefühl vieler unserer Menschen ist. Denn sie haben in der Regel, viele die zugewandert sind, eben zwei Heimate, wenn ich das grammatikalisch falsch aber trotzdem so sage" (Christian Hanke, mayor of Berlin Mitte, ceremony at Schloss Bellevue, 2011, personal recording).

"House" and "Plant" as Metaphoric Conceptualizations of Belonging

Besides these explicit reflections presented so far, notions of "home" and "belonging" are also featured as metaphoric speech at naturalization ceremonies. An analysis of the metaphoric imagery applied in the reflections can offer us an insight into the social logic behind the statements, as "norms, values and attitudes are concentrated in metaphoric concepts."[18] An analysis of metaphoric speech is a means to reconstruct social and communicative sense-making, because the use of metaphors indicates the speaker's position and their subconscious general conceptualizations about their concern or topic.[19]

Following Rudolf Schmitt and Jan Kruse et. al., I conducted a systematic analysis consistent of collecting, comparing and interpreting the use of metaphoric speech in naturalization ceremony speeches.[20] Not all of this process can be documented here, instead I limit the presentation to the interpretation of the most prominently and flexibly applied metaphors. Taking into account the material collected at all the naturalization ceremonies, two commonly applied metaphoric concepts come into view when focusing on how belonging and settling are described on a figurative level:[21] The metaphoric concepts of "house" (constructed environment) and "plant" (natural environment). "House" is typically used as a metaphor for the nation, as one speaker quite explicitly states:

> A nation is like a large house, on whose roof one stands. One has not built it on one's own – and ultimately, one could be standing on the roof of another house altogether. But one's parents were born in this house – or moved into it once, like all of you moved to our German house.[22]

---

18 Rudolf Schmitt, "Metaphernanalyse," in *Handbuch qualitative Forschung in der Psychologie*, eds. Günter Mey, Katja Mruck (Wiesbaden: VS, 2010): 676–691, 685.
19 Jan Kruse, Kay Biesel, Christian Schmieder, *Metaphernanalyse: Ein rekonstruktiver Ansatz* (Wiesbaden: VS, 2011): 76.
20 Rudolf Schmitt, "Metaphernanalyse als sozialwissenschaftliche Methode: Mit einigen Bemerkungen zur theoretischen 'Fundierung' psychosozialen Handelns," *Psychologie & Gesellschaftskritik* 21.1 (1997): 57–86; Rudolf Schmitt, "Methode und Subjektivität in der systematischen Metaphernanalyse," *Forum Qualitative Sozialforschung / Forum: Qualitative Social Research* 4.2 (2003); Kruse, Bieder, Schmieder, *Metaphernanalyse, passim.*
21 Metaphoric concepts can be understood as semantic categories of metaphors (Schmitt, "Metaphernanalyse," 678–679).
22 "Eine Nation ist wie ein großes Haus, auf dessen Dach man steht. Man hat es nicht selbst gebaut – und letztlich könnte man auch auf dem Dach eines ganz anderen Hauses stehen.

By depicting society or nation as a "house," a notion of factitiousness is attributed to these concepts. Houses are constructed, reconstructed, torn down. Building a house means settling at a place, but this settlement is not automatically bound to last forever.

A closely connected metaphor is that of a key. Language skills and the German passport are presented as "keys" to German society,[23] one speaker even refers to the knowledge of German culture as a "master key" to integration.[24] With this metaphor, however, the house loses much of its constructed character and becomes a closed entity that can only be entered by certain people. Here, the focus is on the limiting and bordering quality of a house, and not on the possibilities of building, furnishing and inhabiting the house.

Similarly, the metaphor of "rooms" is used to visualize different features of the German political system and German values: There is a "room of justice" and a "room of gender equality."[25] In this picture, the immigrant has to move into a

---

Aber die eigenen Eltern kamen in diesem Haus zur Welt – oder haben es einst bezogen, wie Sie alle unser deutsches Haus" (Werner Patzelt, guest speaker [professor at local university], Dresden, 2008; source: leaflet published by state administration).

23 "So halten Sie beispielsweise mit dem deutschen Personalausweis nun einen der weltweit begehrtesten Schlüssel in Ihren Händen, der Ihnen die Tür in annähernd jedes Land dieser Erde öffnet" [Hence, for instance, the German passport you are holding is one of the most sought-after keys in the world that will open the door to almost every country on earth] (mayor, Krefeld 2012; <http://krefeld.de/C1257478002C7A8D/html/37B8B3375D8B3F2FC 1257AD200564F40/$FILE/einbuergerungsempfang_2012.pdf> [acc. March 12, 2015]). "Der Spracherwerb ist der Schlüssel, um zu verstehen – hier die Deutschen, ihre Denkweise, aber auch um verstanden zu werden und die eigenen Anschauung vermitteln zu können" [Language acquisition is the key to understanding the Germans and their way of thinking, but also to being understood and being able to convey one's own opinions] (Meryem D. Çelikkol, guest speaker, Hamburg 2011; <http://www.youtube.com/watch?v=O_yY0aRdzdI> [acc. March 12, 2015]).

24 "Darüber hinaus gibt es aber einen wertvollen und eigentlich unverzichtbaren Zugang zu diesem Land und seinen Menschen, eine Art Generalschlüssel, und das ist seine Kultur" [Furthermore, there is a precious and virtually indispensable access to this country and its people, a sort of master key, and that is its culture] (Joachim Meyer, guest speaker, Dresden 2009; <http://www.landtag.sachsen.de/dokumente/sab/110521_Reden-EiFest.pdf> [acc. March 12, 2015]).

25 "Da gibt es etwa das 'Zimmer der Justiz.' Denn in unserem 'demokratischen Haus' gibt es eine unabhängige Justiz und eine vorbildliche Gewaltenteilung. Da gibt es das 'Zimmer eines freiheitlichen Landes mit einem funktionierenden demokratischen System.' Da gibt es das Zimmer, wo die 'Gleichheit von Mann und Frau' als Teil unseres Rechts untergebracht ist und heute bereits als ein Teil unserer kulturellen Identität verankert ist" [There is, for instance, the 'room of the judicial system.' Because in our 'democratic house' there is an independent judicial system and an exemplary separation of powers. There is the 'room of a free country with a

furnished apartment, accepting the role of a tenant who cannot change the arrangements the landlord has made in advance. Another metaphor that falls into the scope of the metaphoric depiction of the nation as built environment is that of the nation as a hotel: "A journalist asked me once: How do you feel, here in Germany? My honest answer was: Like in a hotel. Like in a good, well-kept, quiet hotel. But in a hotel – not like at home."[26] This statement points out that it indeed takes time to "make oneself at home"– and that this task cannot be fulfilled by the recipients or the host country. The comparison to a "hotel" clearly indicates that even if the guest is politely and whole-heartedly received, he still is the "guest" of the "hotel" and not the "cohabitant." The speaker therefore criticizes the notion of "new home" that is also often applied in the speeches at the naturalization ceremonies. In his view, belonging is not simply a matter of differentiation, of simply adding a "new" or "second" home to an old or "first" one, but something that takes work, effort and, most importantly, time.

As a second main metaphoric domain in the speeches, references to nature are used to describe and visualize belonging. "Trunk" and "roots" are widely used concepts to speak about the immigrants and their ties. At first sight, these metaphors tend to depict belonging as "natural" in a sense of elemental, unchangeable affiliation. This notion is indeed present at some of the ceremonies that were analyzed. One mayor says: "We all cling to our roots, to our culture and our origins."[27] Another speaker reassures his audience: "We don't expect you to cut your cultural roots, to question your whole life before now. We don't want that."[28] In these statements – as well at the numerous occasions when speakers describe people as "stemming" from some other country – belonging is presented as something that never changes, but that sticks with a person forever. For if we think of people as "plants" or "trees," it is an unnatural

---

functioning democratic system.' There is the room where 'equality of men and women' is accommodated as part of our laws and is today already rooted as a part of our cultural identity] (district administrator, Heidenheim, 2010, published online, not publicly available anymore).

26 "Damals wurde ich von einem Journalisten gefragt: Wie fühlst du dich hier in Deutschland? Ich habe ganz ehrlich geantwortet: Wie in einem Hotel. Wie in einem guten, gepflegten, ruhigen Hotel. Aber in einem Hotel – nicht wie zu Hause" (Juri Rosov, chairman of the Foreigners' Advisory Council, Rostock, 2012; <http://www.das-ist-rostock.de/artikel/47143_2012-01-15_ein gebuergert/?type=98> [acc. March 12, 2015]).

27 "Wir alle hängen an unseren Wurzeln, an unserer Kultur und Herkunft" (mayor, Krefeld, 2012).

28 "[Wir erwarten] nicht von Ihnen [...], dass Sie Ihre kulturellen Wurzeln abschneiden. Dass Sie Ihr ganzes bisheriges Leben in Frage stellen. Das wollen wir nicht" (mayor, Worms, 2006; published online, not publicly available anymore).

process for them to move. Cutting off the roots of a tree, cutting off branches of a stem means killing the plant or its parts in the long run.

There is, however, another use of the "roots" metaphor: The possibility to "establish roots" in another place: "We will present you with a little flower, this flower is a symbol of our hope that you as new Germans will find roots in the FRG or establish roots."[29] Another speaker states: "Some of you have been living and working here for ten, twenty, or thirty years, and you have started families and grown roots."[30] This rather active notion of "growing roots" complements the notion of roots and stems as unalterable features.

At this point we can conclude that there is no simple division between a flexible house metaphor and an image of unchangeable roots. Both metaphoric concepts can be used to express both notions. The metaphoric level thus mirrors the ambiguity of belonging in the situation of naturalization: For some participants of naturalization ceremonies, belonging is something that can be adapted, enhanced, altered. For others, belonging is a rather stable attachment to a certain place (and that place only). By using metaphoric concepts that encompass both of the two notions, the speakers manage to uphold communication in this ambiguous situation. More than with the cognitive reflection over concepts as "home" and "Heimat," which are also featured in the speeches, through the metaphoric conceptualizations the audience can understand and even sense the values and definitions attached to constructed and naturalized notions of belonging. The implicit nature of metaphors allows them to direct action in social interaction, because "they don't verbalize what they say."[31]

Comparing the reflections made by naturalized speakers and the politicians to the assumptions and sense-making incorporated in the metaphoric concepts of "plant" and "house," it can be discovered that when speakers (as the Zambian woman and the mayor of Berlin Mitte) deliberately reflect on the meanings of linguistic concepts and daily practices, they arrive at a rather constructive and individualistic notion of belonging and "home." Other speakers, who do not start to analyze the concepts and terms often stay within the realm of a static, essentialist sense of "home" and social ties. Concerning metaphoric speech, however,

---

29 "Wir werden Ihnen ein kleines Blümchen überreichen, dieses Blümchen ist ein Symbol dafür, dass wir hoffen, dass Sie als neue Deutsche in der BRD Wurzeln finden oder Wurzeln fassen" (mayor, Rüsselsheim, 2012, personal recording).
30 "Zehn, zwanzig und dreißig Jahre leben und arbeiten Sie teilweise schon hier und haben Familien gegründet und Wurzeln geschlagen" (chief officer of the Immigration Authority, Schwäbisch Hall, 2009; published online, not publicly available anymore).
31 Matthias Junge, "Der soziale Gebrauch der Metapher," in *Metaphern in Wissenskulturen*, ed. Matthias Junge (Wiesbaden: VS, 2010): 265–277.

this distinction between reflected versus non-reflected notions cannot be upheld: Metaphors allow for an illustrative rather than reflective communication about concepts of belonging and what it means to be "at home." As the comparison between the concepts of "nature" and "constructed environment" has shown, they can both be employed to transmit both constructivist as well as essentialist notions of belonging.

Constructivist versus Essentialist Notions of Belonging

Having made this quite simplistic statement that the notions depend on their contexts and communicative framings, I will finally look for some answers to the questions that arise from the analysis made so far: Is there a tendency towards one of the two poles after all? Do the statements of the migrants in general differ from the statements of the politicians?

After collecting and coding all statements in the data where "home" is mentioned,[32] I merged them into a scheme of four quadrants as presented in Table 1. The sorting was carried out comparatively, focusing on the features that are assigned to conceptualizations of "home" by asking about what the coded concepts have in common and what main distinctions could be made. In addition to the distinction between contingent (that is, constructivist) notions of belonging – that belonging can be changed – versus essentialist belonging – that belonging is an unalterable feature, a second distinctive dimension was developed: the distinction between belonging as a feature of an individual person versus belonging as a supra-individual feature that all members of a certain group have in common.

I found that four different types of "home" stand out at naturalization ceremonies. First, there are notions that convey a contingent/individual sense of belonging. Here, "home" is presented as a mode of perception, as something to be constructed (as a wish or project), and as something that can also appear in plural (as in the speech of the Zambian woman presented earlier). Second, there are notions that still present home as an individual feature but this time in an essentialist way. Everyone has their own "home," but this home is a static entity that one can long for or arrive at. Some notions here, however, point into the direction of a more contingent view. The acquisition of or the addition of "homes" still

---

32 Juliet Corbin, Anselm L. Strauss, *Basics of Qualitative Research: Grounded Theory Procedures and Techniques*, third ed. (Thousand Oaks: SAGE, 2008): 65–86, 159–194.

sees them as essences outside of individual control, but at the same time they are no longer exclusive. Third, the contingent/collective positions perceive "home" as collectively constructed. Home here is always "our home" and is connected to language or customs. Fourth, home is understood as essentialist and collective feature. Here, "home" is the feature of a nation, a common destiny, and something that ties populations to their countries of birth forever.

1 Contingent/Individual notion	3 Contingent/Collectivizing notion
Home as perception	Old home/new home
Home as experience	Finding a home
Wanting to be at home	Time as main factor
Plural for "Heimat"	"Our home"
"Ubi bene, ibi patria"	Language as home
Building a house	Home as reflected in customs
Searching for a home	Region or town as home

2 Essentialist/Individual notion	4 Essentialist/Collectivizing notion
Feeling at home	Country of origin as "home"
Homesickness	Germany as a house
Home as individual attribute	Home as assignment
Arriving	Home as normative concept
Acquiring a home	"Native"
Addition of "homes"	

Table 1 Classification of codes[33]

While all these notions are represented at naturalization ceremonies, there is, however, a tendency towards more essentialist representations of belonging. This can be determined by looking at the quantitative distribution of the statements to the quadrants,[34] but, more importantly, by taking into account (1) the interpretative authority of the politicians at the naturalization ceremonies, where they function as both host and main commanders of the situation and its meanings, (2) the naturalistic character of the metaphors that operate with essentialist concepts of "plant" and "tree" that make metaphors belonging to

---

33 Some of the codes do not fit in only one category; these are therefore allocated to the category that most of the statements coded respectively would fit into.
34 The quantitative distribution of the statements over the four quadrants indicates both a predominance of collective over individual and of essentialist over contingent notions. This applies to both naturalized speakers and politicians. Because the sample is by no means representative, this can be no more than illustrative evidence.

that concept intuitively reasonable for the audience, as well as (3) the socially defined character of the statements coded as contingent/collectivizing. This places them in a field where "home" is not completely up to individual choice, and therefore adds up to a predominance of statements that indicate if not straightforward essentialist, then at least reified notions of home and belonging.[35]

Interestingly, even the naturalized speakers that purposely and consciously reflect on notions of home and belonging apply reified and essentialist concepts. The overall logic of the statements of all the speakers is thus not so different after all: A majority of the statements convey the image that "home" is an unchangeable fact, that it cannot be modified or complemented. Based on this observation, I would like to characterize the predominant notion of home and belonging at naturalization ceremonies as "diaspora by ascription." Drawing on Rogers Brubaker, who proposes to "treat diaspora not as a bounded entity but as an idiom, stance and claim,"[36] I would like to point out that at German naturalization ceremonies, an ascriptive concept of "diaspora" is implemented: The idea that the newly naturalized citizens withhold primary allegiance to their first countries and that their primary reference point lies in and perseveres with their countries of origin. This is most clearly expressed in the first quote by a representative of the host country I have presented: "Maybe more people from your home countries will soon come to Saxony. Maybe you will have the chance to come to the aid of your fellow countrymen."[37] It also underlies the statement of another mayor who proposes the predominance of primary allegiances to the "*Landsmannschaften*," the fellow countrymen: "you have become bridge-builders to your fellow countrymen. We really have different *Landsmannschaften* hier, and for me it would mean a lot if you reported on this event today to your circle of friends to your *Landsmannschaften*."[38] The notion of solidarity ties between fellow countrymen or "Landsmannschaften" – a term that is generally used to depict groups of ethnic Germans displaced from Eastern Europe after the Second World War that maintain close allegiance within – conveys an image

---

35 Peter Berger, Thomas Luckmann, *The Social Construction of Reality. A Treatise in the Sociology of Knowledge* (Garden City: Doubleday, 1967).
36 Rogers Brubaker, "The 'Diaspora' Diaspora," *Ethnic and Racial Studies* 28.1 (2005): 1–19.
37 "Vielleicht kommen bald auch aus Ihren Heimatländern noch mehr Menschen nach Sachsen. Vielleicht werden Sie die Gelegenheit haben, Ihren Landsleuten unter die Arme zu greifen" (Markus Ulbig, Minister of the Interior, federal state of Saxony, ceremony in Dresden, 2011).
38 "Sie sind zu Brückenbauern zu Ihren Landsleuten geworden. Wir haben ja hier wirklich unterschiedlichste Landsmannschaften, und mir wäre es wichtig, wenn Sie einfach aus der Veranstaltung heute in Ihrem Bekanntenkreis in Ihren Landsmannschaften berichten" (mayor, Halle/Saale, 2013, personal recording).

of many little diasporas in Germany, and that every naturalized person is a member (and continues to be a member) of such a diaspora.

What do these findings imply for a diagnosis of current notions of belonging in Germany and for further research on the issue? Three theses and questions can be concluded from my analysis.

First, the notion of a Turkish diaspora in Germany: There is an obvious contradiction in many of the speeches given at naturalization ceremonies. On the one hand, naturalization candidates are presented as individual cases with individual histories. On the other hand, there is the notion that the immigrants' "homes" are collective-essentialist and that these are still identified with the countries of origin (or the parents' origins). Why is this? I assume that many of the speakers deal with immigration in Germany having immigrants from Turkey in mind. While the Turkish minority is the largest minority in the country and is discursively represented as a Muslim "parallel society," the misapprehension that all naturalization candidates are members of a "diaspora" means to wrongly generalize an assumption made about Turkish immigrants.

Second, a question of loyalty: What does it imply for the question of belonging in Germany that newly naturalized men and women are still perceived as having another "home", that they are perceived as belonging to another place? By ascribing the concept of "diaspora" to the new citizens, their credibility and their loyalty to the German state and society are put in limbo. While the German naturalization process contains written and spoken avowals of loyalty exactly to the purpose of testing and promoting the candidate's loyalty, the speeches at naturalization ceremonies put that in question. A strict differentiation between "natives" and "foreigners" is thus perpetuated even after the "foreigners" are assimilated in status by naturalization: The native Germans "really belong," and every other person "does not really belong."

Third: Is the concept of home contingent? A last and more general question concerns the concept of "belonging to a home." Belonging, as we have seen, is questioned and thought about at naturalization ceremonies. That is because naturalization can stipulate reflections about one's ties to countries, family and social environment. But even in this situation, belonging is often described as an essential and unalterable fact. One may ask, is there a mental need for a definite and primary affiliation? Is there a social requisite to be unambiguous about one's belonging? What is the social or biographical function of definite belongings? Further qualitative enquiries into the social field, the literature and the discourses about diasporic situations and "diaspora by ascription" may be able to provide more refined answers to these questions.

Qianqian Li
Becoming an American: Rethinking the United States Naturalization Policy

Abstract: Not long after Barack Obama's inauguration for his second term of presidency, he gave a speech on immigration reform and repeated the phrase "now is the time" several times to emphasize its urgency. One of the main principles of this reform, Obama proposed, is that there should be a pathway for the eleven million illegal immigrants in the country to earn citizenship. Once again, the topic of naturalization is brought to the spotlight. This article traces the United States naturalization policy back to the Naturalization Act of 1790 and examines the main changes of the policy through time. I argue that although the US immigration policy seems to have achieved a revolutionary reform in the past centuries, its core remains the same, namely, the prerequisite of naturalization has only been changed from being physically white to being innerly white. In other words, contrary to some existing scholarly opinions, assimilation and acculturation are still crucial components in the US naturalization process, and they are the fundamental means for immigrants to become "white."

Introduction

In passing the Naturalization Act of 1790, the First Congress specified that only "a free white person, who shall have resided within the limits and under the jurisdictions of the United States for the term of two years, may be admitted to become a citizen."[1] Furthermore, this person has to make "proof to the satisfaction" of the court that "he is a person of good character," and take "the oath or affirmation prescribed by law."[2] In 1921 and 1924, two Quota Acts were passed, which limited annual admissions of immigrants and even denied "admission to all aliens who were 'ineligible for citizenship'."[3] Today, a person can be naturalized regardless of ethnicity, national origin, or gender. Lyndon B. Johnson emphasized the need for this change in his annual message to Congress on the State

---

1 "Acts of the First Congress of the United States," in *The Public Statutes at Large of the United States of America from the Organization of the Government in 1789, to March 3, 1845*, ed. Richard Peters (Boston: Charles C. Little and James Brown, 1845): 23–225, 103; Library of Congress, "A Century of Lawmaking for a New Nation: U.S. Congressional Documents and Debates, 1774–1875" (May 1, 2003), *Library of Congress* <http://rs6.loc.gov/cgi-bin/ampage?collId=llsl&fileName=001/llsl001.db&recNum=226> (acc. December 11, 2014).
2 "Acts of the First Congress," 103.
3 Erika Lee, "A Nation of Immigrants and a Gatekeeping Nation: American Immigration Law and Policy," in *A Companion to American Immigration*, ed. Reed Ueda (Malden: Wiley-Blackwell, 2011): 5–35, 12.

of the Union in 1964, saying "a nation that was built by the immigrants of all lands can ask those who now seek admission: 'What can you do for our country?' But we should not be asking: 'In what country were you born?'"[4] The Immigration and Nationality Act of 1965 finally symbolizes America's open gate to the world, stating that "[n]o person shall receive any preference or priority or be discriminated against in the issuance of an immigrant visa because of his race, sex, nationality, place of birth, or place of residence."[5] In comparison of the two time periods, the US immigration policy seems to have achieved a revolutionary reform.

Partly because of this immigration reform, and partly because of the fact that the United States now includes a variety of ethnicities and cultures, many scholars began to suggest that assimilation is dead. In David Hollinger's book *Posethnic America: Beyond Multiculturalism*, he states that among "academic and popular political voices, [... t]he figure of the melting pot, encumbered with assimilationist connotations, lost favor to the salad bowl, the mosaic, and the garden of plants each with its own autochthonous roots."[6] He further notes that "[t]he United States came increasingly to be represented as a complex patchwork of distinctive communities."[7] According to Michael Lind, multiculturalists believe that the United States "is a nation of nations, a federation of nationalities and cultures sharing little or nothing but a common government."[8] In his book *The Next American Nation*, he also introduces the term "Multicultural America," which, he believes, is "the de facto orthodoxy of the present American regime" formed in the late 1960s and the early 1970s.[9] Despite these opinions, I argue that assimilation and acculturation are still important elements in the naturalization process, and the idea of the US naturalization policy has not changed much even though the words sound more inclusive.

I will examine both the naturalization policy itself and its consequences for applicants to demonstrate the similarities between the current naturalization policy and the Naturalization Act of 1790. I will elaborate on four important as-

---

4 Lyndon B. Johnson, "State of the Union Address," in *State of the Union Addresses by United States Presidents: State of the Union Addresses by Lyndon B. Johnson*, ed. Jim Manis (Hazleton: Penn State Electronic Classics Series Publication, 2003): 3–11, 9.
5 United States, 89th Cong., *Immigration and Nationality Act of 1965*, Public Law 89–236, 79 Stat. (Washington: Government Printing Office, 1965): 911–922, 911.
6 David Hollinger, *Postethnic America: Beyond Multiculturalism* (New York: Basic Books, 1995): 64–65.
7 Hollinger, *Postethnic America*, 65.
8 Michael Lind, *The Next American Nation: The New Nationalism and the Fourth American Revolution* (New York: The Free Press, 1995): 1.
9 Lind, *The Next American Nation*, 97.

pects in the current naturalization process – the naturalization oath of allegiance, benefits of the United States from naturalized citizens, citizenship education, and morality – which will help shape an ideal model of a naturalized citizen. This new ideal model, when analyzed closely, resembles the one created by the first Naturalization Act more than two centuries ago.

Naturalization Oath of Allegiance to the United States of America

The naturalization oath of allegiance has been an indispensable step for applicants for naturalization to gain citizenship. It requires applicants to renounce all allegiance to any foreign sovereignty and support the Constitution. According to the US Citizenship and Immigration Services (USCIS), before 1906, "there were as many as 5,000 courts with naturalization jurisdiction," and "[e]ach court could develop its own procedures" how applicants take the oath.[10] The Basic Naturalization Act of 1906 unified the procedures. Since then, the oath of allegiance appears on the applicants' "Declaration of Intention"[11] form or their "Petition for Naturalization"[12] form, and applicants have to take the oath of allegiance again in a formal naturalization ceremony before they become citizens. Every word in the oath of allegiance is mandatory in the naturalization ceremony except the last formula "so help me God."

A standardized form of the oath of allegiance appeared in 1929 and was modified in 1950. The current version of the oath of allegiance is as follows:

> I hereby declare, on oath, that I absolutely and entirely renounce and abjure all allegiance and fidelity to any foreign prince, potentate, state or sovereignty, of whom or which I have heretofore been a subject or citizen; that I will support and defend the Constitution and laws of the United States of America against all enemies, foreign and domestic; that I

---

10 United States Citizenship and Immigration Services, "Naturalization Oath of Allegiance to the United States of America" (June 25, 2014), *U.S. Citizenship and Immigration Services* <http://www.uscis.gov/us-citizenship/naturalization-test/naturalization-oath-allegiance-united-states-america> (acc. December 11, 2014).
11 Applicants for naturalization can file their Declaration of Intention after they meet the physical presence requirement (usually 30 months or eighteen months if the applicant is married to a US citizen). The Declaration of Intention is also known as First Papers.
12 After five years of permanent residency or three years if the applicant is married to a US citizen, applicants are allowed to submit their Petition for Naturalization, also known as Second Papers or Final Papers. It usually takes six months for a judge or the USCIS to approve naturalization.

will bear true faith and allegiance to the same; that I will bear arms on behalf of the United States when required by the law; that I will perform noncombatant service in the armed forces of the United States when required by the law; that I will perform work of national importance under civilian direction when required by the law; and that I take this obligation freely without any mental reservation or purpose of evasion; so help me God.[13]

The renunciation symbolizes that the United States requires applicants to cut the bonds to their origins and fully integrate into the American nation. In this sense, applicants have to surrender at least part of their original identity in order to gain American citizenship. Therefore, the process of naturalization functions more like a melting pot, not the salad bowl multiculturalists suggest.

In addition, modifications of the oath of allegiance only *added* mandates to the text. At the very beginning, applicants only had to renounce allegiance to any foreign sovereignty and support the Constitution. After 1906, the modified Naturalization Act implemented a text that requires applicants to defend the Constitution against all enemies. The Immigration Act of 1950 further introduced a requirement that "forced" all applicants to serve in the military.[14] Therefore, the change in the naturalization process is that applicants today have more responsibilities, but they face the same situation as applicants did in the past regarding the loss of original identity. Scholars define this phenomenon as "rational-choice models,"[15] where the "decision [of applicants] to naturalize derives from weighing the benefits vs. the costs of becoming a citizen."[16]

Causes of Change in Naturalization Laws

The main changes in the naturalization laws are usually caused by the US political and economic necessities, not by the belief in multiculturalism. Since being white was a prerequisite according to the Naturalization Act of 1790, the courts had to define and redefine "white" every time race seemed to have crossed the boundaries. For example, as Peter Schrag notes,

[l]awsuits seeking to answer the racial question had begun in 1878 [...] – suits in which the courts ruled repeatedly that the Chinese weren't white, that the Japanese weren't white, that Hawaiians weren't white, that Filipinos weren't white, and that Burmese weren't white.

---

13 USCIS, "Naturalization Oath."
14 USCIS, "Naturalization Oath."
15 Jennifer Van Hook, Susan K. Brown, Frank D. Bean, "For Love or Money? Welfare Reform and Immigrant Naturalization," *Social Forces* 85.2 (2006): 643–666, 646.
16 Van Hook et al., "For Love or Money?", 646.

There were also decisions that Armenians were white. [...]. In 1919 two courts ruled that Asian Indians were white (one other court, in 1919, ruled they probably weren't). After 1923, the courts ruled that Asian Indians, sometimes "Hindoos," weren't white and (in 1925) that Punjabis weren't white. Four pre-1917 decisions had ruled that Syrians were white, and three that they weren't. Then came rulings that Koreans weren't white; that Afghanis weren't white, followed in 1945 by a decision that they were; and that "Arabians" weren't white, again followed by a Board of Immigration Appeals ruling (in 1941) that, because European civilization had originated in the Middle East, that they were white.

By the late 1930s, Mexicans were considered white for most official purposes. Court decisions going back to the turn of the century also held that persons who were half white, one-fourth Chinese, and one-fourth Japanese weren't white. Following what appeared the one-drop-of-blood standard, there were similar decisions for all mixed-race individuals, including one, as late as 1938, that ruled that a person who was three-fourths American Indian and one-fourth African was not African and thus not entitled to naturalization.[17]

These lawsuits indicate that courts have the ability to deny naturalization whenever they consider the applicant not fit for assimilation. It is contradictory, for instance, that Syrians, who are supposed to be of the same race if races are to be categorized by region as they were done in the United States, can be sometimes white and sometimes not; and why, even according to the unreasonable one-drop-of-blood rule, was the person who had one-fourth of African blood not African? Erika Lee states that the prerequisite of being white mirrors "Congress's confidence in the ability of European immigrants to assimilate and become worthy American citizens."[18] Chinese were thought to be too foreign and unassimilable, so the 1882 Chinese Exclusion Act prohibited naturalization of all Chinese immigrants. The Immigration Act of 1917 further "denied entry to aliens living within a newly conceived geographical area called the 'Asiatic Barred Zone' [and] effectively excluded all immigrants from India, Burma, Siam, the Malay States, Arabia, Afghanistan, part of Russia, and most of the Polynesian Islands."[19]

However, there were exceptions in times of war. Irene Bloemraad and Reed Ueda note that "[i]n 1935, President Roosevelt signed the Nye-Lea Act, providing for the naturalization of all Asian veterans by exempting them from the racial bar applied to foreign-born Asians,"[20] because national security topped assimilation

---

17 Peter Schrag, *Not Fit for Our Society: Immigration and Nativism in America* (Berkeley: U of California P, 2010): 111.

18 Lee, "A Nation of Immigrants," 9.

19 Lee, "A Nation of Immigrants," 12.

20 Irene Bloemraad, Reed Ueda, "Naturalization and Nationality," in *A Companion to American Immigration*, ed. Reed Ueda (Malden: Wiley-Blackwell, 2011): 36–57, 41.

to be the first concern of the United States. Today's oath of allegiance also shows America's preparation for recruiting soldiers – a benefit the United States gains from naturalized citizens. Yet, in some respects, this oath eliminates the possibility for an applicant to be pacifist, which contradicts civil liberties enjoyed by US citizens. What actually ended the exclusion of Chinese immigrants in 1943, six decades after the exclusion, was the Second World War, because the United States felt the urge to unite China as a war ally. Similarly, as Lee puts it, "Congress also [...] allowed for the naturalization of immigrants" from India and the Philippines in 1946 "to shore up support from Asian allies."[21] The Japanese, on the other hand, were excluded from naturalization because they were the enemy during the war, and even those who had already become US citizens "were summarily stripped of their rights, freedom, and property and shipped off to [...] 'war relocation camps'."[22] Notwithstanding the discrimination against the Japanese, the Second World War "helped glorify the idea of America as a nation of immigrants, turned Ellis Island into a symbol of historic triumph and belonging, and made the whole idea of immigration less toxic."[23]

The Immigration and Nationality Act of 1965, which abolished "all racial, gender, and nationality barriers to citizenship,"[24] symbolizes America's open gate to the world. However, the act "introduced a system of preference categories"[25] for immigrants with "exceptional ability in the sciences or the arts" and for "skilled laborers,"[26] who, as the act frankly points out, "will substantially benefit prospectively the national economy, cultural interests, or welfare of the United States."[27] Not long after Barack Obama's inauguration for his second term of presidency, he gave a speech on immigration reform on January 29, 2013, and proposed that there should be a pathway for the eleven million illegal immigrants in the country to earn citizenship. One reason for this reform is that it will "encourage them to come out of the shadows so they can pay their taxes and play by the same rules as everyone else."[28] In other words, if illegal immigrants can play by the rules and earn their legal status, the United States will not only benefit from their contribution to the country such as in the fields of agri-

---

21 Lee, "A Nation of Immigrants," 16.
22 Schrag, *Not Fit for Our Society*, 153.
23 Schrag, *Not Fit for Our Society*, 154.
24 Lee, "A Nation of Immigrants," 17.
25 Lee, "A Nation of Immigrants," 17.
26 US, 89th Cong., *Immigration and Nationality Act of 1965*, 913.
27 US, 89th Cong., *Immigration and Nationality Act of 1965*, 913.
28 Barack Obama, "Earned Citizenship" (January 29, 2013), *The White House* <http://www. whitehouse.gov/issues/immigration/earned-citizenship> (acc. December 11, 2013).

culture and construction, but it can also expect an increase in tax revenues. President Obama's immigration reform indicates that changes in immigration policy are usually driven by the expectation of economic growth.

Education in the Naturalization Process

Education in the United States functions as a tool of Americanization. Strong interest in educating immigrants dates back to as early as 1907 when New Jersey passed the first state legislation to support evening classes in English and civics for the foreign-born.[29] Later, the interest escalated to the national level, for "[f]rom 1914 to 1920 the Bureau of Naturalization of the Immigration and Naturalization Services waged an intensive nationwide campaign to interest the public schools in establishing classes for English and the essentials of good citizenship to the foreign-born."[30] In addition, in 1916, the Bureau of Education was founded, which "publicized the approved methods of instructing foreigners, continuing its support of the Americanization movement."[31] According to Bloemraad and Ueda, "[e]ducators throughout the decades of the early twentieth century sought to prepare immigrants for naturalization by imbuing their teaching of English, civics, and history with veneration for the nation-state and its historic traditions."[32] By doing this, "an individual could incorporate him or herself democratically into American nationality through the voluntary internalization of the civic code and patriotic actions, reinforcing the image of civic loyalty."[33] This kind of education is also a necessity for applicants for naturalization, for the Naturalization Act of 1906 "raised the qualifications for naturalization by demanding a rudimentary knowledge of American history and civics, a basic ability to speak and understand English, and proof of moral worth."[34]

Although scholars and thinkers have been questioning Americanization, arguing that immigrants should maintain their cultural pluralism, and that the United States will benefit the most if it preserves "separate cultures side by side within its boundaries,"[35] civics and language requirements remain until

---

29 Ezri Atzmon, "The Educational Programs for Immigrants in the United States," *History of Education Journal* 9.3 (1958): 75–80, 75.
30 Atzmon, "The Educational Programs," 75–76.
31 Atzmon, "The Educational Programs," 77.
32 Bloemraad and Ueda, "Naturalization and Nationality," 41.
33 Bloemraad and Ueda, "Naturalization and Nationality," 41.
34 Bloemraad and Ueda, "Naturalization and Nationality," 40.
35 Atzmon, "The Educational Programs," 80.

today, and applicants for naturalization continue to rely on citizenship education programs. Michael Olneck summarizes David Miller's argument in *On Nationality* and points out that language, myths, symbols and rituals, a common history, and shared vernacular culture are the most significant aspects of national identity.[36] Therefore, naturalization tests on English and American civics are an effective method to accelerate the speed of Americanization.

The USCIS offers study pamphlets to help applicants prepare for civics and English tests. These pamphlets provide not only questions applicants may encounter during their naturalization interview, but also accepted answers and brief commentaries on these questions and answers. The civics test is divided into three parts – American government, American history, and integrated civics. Questions about American government include principles of American democracy, system of government, and rights and responsibilities; questions on American history cover the colonial period and independence, the 1800s, and recent American history and other important historical information; and integrated civics concerns geography, symbols, and holidays. The pamphlet also states the importance of understanding American civics, which embeds the connotation of highlighting American values. For example, under "American government," it states that

> [c]itizens in the United States shape their government and its policies, so they must learn about important public issues and get involved in their communities. Learning about American government helps you understand your rights and responsibilities and allows you to fully participate in the American political process.[37]

This underlines the political rights and responsibilities of American citizens and reminds applicants of their duties once they become American citizens. In the section of American history, the USCIS emphasizes that the United States is a land of freedom, unity, and justice, which can raise feelings of patriotism:

> For more than 200 years, the United States has strived to become a "more perfect union." Its history has been one of expansive citizenship for all Americans. By learning about our shared history, you will be able to understand our nation's traditions, milestones, and common civic values. Our country is independent because of the *strength, unity,* and *determination* of our forefathers. It is important for future Americans to know this story. We are people working toward *great ideals* and principles *guided by equality and fairness.* This is

---

36 Michael R. Olneck, "Assimilation and American National Identity," in *A Companion to American Immigration*, ed. Reed Ueda (Malden: Wiley-Blackwell, 2011): 202–224, 202.
37 USCIS, *Learn About the United States: Quick Civics Lessons for the Naturalization Test*, 1.

important to keep our country free. As Americans, we have been committed to each other and our country throughout our history.[38]

Integrated civics helps immigrants understand the uniqueness of the United States, through which respect for the country emerges. As it states in the section,

> [t]he geography of the United States is unusual because of the size of the country and the fact that it is bordered by two oceans that create natural boundaries to the east and west. Through visual symbols such as our flag and the Statue of Liberty, the values and history of the United States are often expressed. Finally, you will also learn about our national holidays and why we celebrate them. Most of our holidays honor people who have contributed to our history and to the development of our nation. By learning this information, you will develop a deeper understanding of the United States and its geographical boundaries, principles, and freedoms.[39]

To some extent, applicants for naturalization not only learn American civics from reading materials provided by the USCIS, but they also learn American values and the reasons to be patriotic.

As mentioned above, language is a significant aspect of national identity. Therefore, understanding English is fundamental to obtaining American identity. The House of Representatives of the 59th Congress reported in 1905 that

> if [an immigrant] does not know our language he does in effect remain a foreigner, although he may be able to satisfy the naturalization laws sufficiently to secure our citizenship [...]. The Commission is aware that some aliens who can not learn our language make good citizens. They are, however, exceptions, and the proposition is incontrovertible that no man is a desirable citizen of the United States who does not know the English language.[40]

It seems most likely that the education on English has strongly affected second-generation immigrants. According to Michael Olneck, surveys show that "[t]oday's immigrant parents, like those of the past, are encountering the refusal of their children to use their native language, and many report that their children speak primarily English among their friends."[41]

---

38 USCIS, *Learn About the United States*, 15 (emphasis added).
39 USCIS, *Learn About the United States*, 24.
40 United States, 59th Cong., House, *Report to the President of the Commission on Naturalization* (Washington: Government Printing Office, 1905): 11.
41 Olneck, "Assimilation and American National Identity," 212.

Morality and Loyalty in the Naturalization Process

During the naturalization process, applicants have to demonstrate to the USCIS that they have good moral character (GMC). Volume twelve, Part F of the *USCIS Policy Manuel* specifically defines what GMC is. Permanent bars to GMC include murder, aggravated felony, persecution, genocide, torture, and severe violations of religious freedom. More precisely, aggravated felony covers murder, rape, sexual abuse of a minor, illicit trafficking in controlled substance, illicit trafficking in firearms or destructive devices, money laundering offenses (over 10,000 dollars), explosive materials and firearms offenses, crime of violence (imprisonment term of at least one year), theft offense (imprisonment term of at least one year), demand for or receipt of ransom, child pornography offense, racketeering, gambling (imprisonment term of at least one year), prostitution offenses (managing, transporting, trafficking), gathering or transmitting classified information, fraud or deceit offenses or tax evasion (over 10,000 dollars), alien smuggling, illegal entry or reentry by removed aggravated felon, passport or document fraud (imprisonment term of at least one year), failure to appear sentence (offense punishable by at least five years), bribery, counterfeiting, forgery, or trafficking in vehicles, obstruction of justice, perjury, bribery of witness, failure to appear to court (offense punishable by at least two years), and attempt or conspiracy to commit an aggravated felony.[42] There are other conditional bars to GMC including one or more crimes involving moral turpitude, aggregate sentence of five years or more, controlled substance violation, incarceration for 180 days, false testimony under oath, prostitution offenses, smuggling of a person, polygamy, gambling offenses, habitual drunkard, failure to support dependents, adultery, and unlawful acts.[43]

Some of the permanent and conditional bars seem overlapping, and the overlap indicates the undesirableness of such immigrants to the United States. Although felonies such as murder and violence are globally unacceptable, some bars to GMC are legal in some countries. For example, both permanent

---

42 USCIS, "Chapter 4: Permanent Bars to GMC" (October 28, 2014), *U.S. Citizenship and Immigration Services: USCIS Policy Manual: Volume 12, Part F: Good Moral Character*, <http://www.uscis.gov/policymanual/HTML/PolicyManual-Volume12-PartF-Chapter4.html> (acc. December 11, 2014).
43 USCIS, "Chapter 5: Conditional Bars for Acts in Statutory Period" (October 28, 2014), *U.S. Citizenship and Immigration Services: USCIS Policy Manual: Volume 12, Part F: Good Moral Character* <http://www.uscis.gov/policymanual/HTML/PolicyManual-Volume12-PartF-Chapter5.html> (acc. December 11, 2014).

and conditional bars mention prostitution offenses. However, if an immigrant comes from a country where prostitution is not an offense (e. g., Germany or the Netherlands), this immigrant may have been involved in prostitution without breaking the law in his or her original country, but is thus eliminated from GMC in the United States. In a broader sense, GMC is the American ideal, and demonstrating GMC symbolizes immigrants' acceptance of the American ideal and their determination of becoming a good citizen.

Morality and loyalty play an extremely important role in the naturalization process. Susan Gordon notes that

> [w]hen the US government first developed educational materials to help immigrants prepare for that exam in the early twentieth century, the bureaucrats at the Bureau of Naturalization chose, [...], to privilege morality and loyalty (attachment) over the requirement that immigrants demonstrate their knowledge of US history and government. In doing so, they designed an educational program that focused more on inculcating standards of proper American behavior than on civics and history.[44]

She further gives an example of the court's decision on the naturalization of Ricardo Rodriguez, a Mexican national. The court "dismissed [his] inability to explain the principles of the constitution," but "[i]nstead, [...] relied on testimony by a white acquaintance of Rodriguez, who explained that [he] was hard working, honest, law-abiding, [and] peaceable."[45] The emphasis on morality and loyalty, together with the "citizenship education,"[46] as Gordon points out, "has contributed to the social practice of becoming a citizen and, as such, to the manufacturing of ideas of 'the good citizen'."[47] In the aftermath of the 9/11 attacks, the US government finds it more necessary than ever before to "encourage immigrant attachment to the United States and immigrant adoption of 'American values'" through citizenship education.[48] In this sense, the US naturalization process functions as a filter for the fittest citizens, who accept American values and morality, and who will integrate fully into American society.

American values were introduced by White Anglo-Saxon Protestants, who then called themselves "native Americans" even though they were not.[49] Neither actual Native Americans, nor people of other ethnicities had any voice in estab-

---

44 Susan M. Gordon, "Integrating Immigrants: Morality and Loyalty in US Naturalization Practice," *Citizenship Studies* 11.4 (2007): 367–382, 368.
45 Gordon, "Integrating Immigrants," 372.
46 Gordon, "Integrating Immigrants," 372.
47 Gordon, "Integrating Immigrants," 373.
48 Gordon, "Integrating Immigrants," 379.
49 Schrag, *Not Fit for Our Society*, 25.

lishing these values. As a result, accepting American values more or less equals assimilating into the white society. John Tehranian points out in his article that

> [s]uccessful litigants demonstrated evidence of whiteness in their character, religious practices and beliefs, class orientation, language, ability to intermarry, and a host of other traits that had nothing to do with intrinsic racial grouping. Thus, a dramaturgy of whiteness emerged, responsive to the interests of society as defined by the class in power – an "evolutionary functionalism" whereby courts played an instrumental role in limiting naturalization to those new immigrant groups whom judges saw as most fit to carry on the tradition of the "White Republic." The courts thereby sent a clear message to immigrants: The rights enjoyed by white males could only be obtained through assimilatory behavior.[50]

Therefore, the American sense of "white" is not one race, but it is more related to Americanism, and immigrants, regardless of ethnicity or race, can become "white" through assimilation. Schrag notes that "[t]o be that special creature, the American, there always had to be the Other."[51] In current American society, this "Other" is most likely to be those who are un-American. In this sense, assimilation and acculturation are decisive in the process of naturalization, and even though today's naturalization policy has no racial, gender, or nationality barriers, it still creates an ideal model of naturalized citizen which does not differ much from the model in 1790.

Expectation of Assimilation and Contradiction

"Assimilation" is not a popular term in the United States in the twenty-first century, but the naturalization process still quite fits in the definition of social assimilation, which "was 'the name given to the process or processes by which peoples of diverse racial origins and different cultural heritages, occupying a common territory, achieve a cultural solidarity sufficient at least to sustain a national existence'."[52] There are four factors to measure immigrant assimilation, namely, socioeconomic status, spatial concentration, language assimilation, and intermarriage.[53] The US naturalization process can more or less steer the degree of immigrant assimilation. For example, socioeconomic status is largely

---

50 John Tehranian, "Performing Whiteness: Naturalization Litigation and the Construction of Racial Identity in America," *Yale Law Journal* 109.4 (2000): 817–848, 819.
51 Schrag, *Not Fit for Our Society*, 26.
52 Qtd. in Richard Alba and Victor Nee, "Rethinking Assimilation Theory for a New Era of Immigration," *International Migration Review* 31.4 (1997): 826–874, 828.
53 Mary C. Waters and Tomás R. Jiménez, "Assessing Immigrant Assimilation: New Empirical and Theoretical Challenges," *Annual Review of Sociology* 31 (2005): 105–125, 107–108.

shaped by "educational attainment,"[54] which the USCIS tries to reinforce through citizenship education. Studies show that many "1.5-generation (those who arrive before age 13) and second-generation children" even have better performance at school than their "native-born schoolmates."[55] Furthermore, Richard Alba and Victor Nee point out that socioeconomic assimilation can be achieved by immigrant minority's "participation in institutions such as the labor market [...] on the basis of parity with native groups of similar backgrounds,"[56] and immigrant minority does not necessarily show disadvantage among such native groups. The naturalization policy also encourages language assimilation by requiring an English test in the naturalization process. Studies suggest that there is "a strong association between a foreign-born person's time in the United States and his or her ability to speak English well,"[57] and while second-generation immigrants are usually bilingual, "the third generation speaks English only."[58]

Despite the efforts the US government spends on immigrant assimilation, the immigrant generation cannot fully assimilate. For example, some still show signs of low education and poverty,[59] and many, though having made some progress, continue to use their native language primarily.[60] In addition, spatial concentration (e.g., China Town and Little Italy) remains essential in the settlement of the immigrant generation. Therefore, there is a contradiction between the written policy which shows the expectation of the US government that naturalized citizens should assimilate and the reality that naturalized citizens, being the immigrant generation, cannot fully abandon their original identity. Even those who score the highest in their naturalization tests preserve their original identity to some extent, because the cultural and social impacts of their home country are embedded in their thinking.

Because assimilation in the immigrant generation is not complete, scholars define the change in the cultural behaviors of these immigrants as acculturation. Acculturation is an "individual or group process,"[61] where "the ability to function in another culture is added to [the immigrant's] repertoire of skills without

---

54 Waters and Jiménez, "Assessing Immigrant Assimilation," 107.
55 Waters and Jiménez, "Assessing Immigrant Assimilation," 108–109.
56 Alba and Nee, "Rethinking Assimilation Theory," 836.
57 Waters and Jiménez, "Assessing Immigrant Assimilation," 110.
58 Waters and Jiménez, "Assessing Immigrant Assimilation," 110.
59 Waters and Jiménez, "Assessing Immigrant Assimilation," 108.
60 Waters and Jiménez, "Assessing Immigrant Assimilation," 110.
61 Raymond H. C. Teske and Bardin H. Nelson, "Acculturation and Assimilation: A Clarification," *American Ethnologist* 1.2 (1974): 351–367, 351.

displacing [his or her] prior cultural identity."[62] Moreover, acculturation is not a one-way, but a two-way process. Alba and Nee note that

> [t]he influence of minority ethnic cultures can occur also by an expansion of the range of what is considered normative behavior within the mainstream; thus elements of minority cultures are absorbed alongside their Anglo-American equivalents or are fused with mainstream elements to create a hybrid cultural mix.[63]

The two-way process is probably the reason why many scholars suggest that assimilation is dead in the United States. However, the foreign elements in the United States are not necessarily derived from abroad. For example, the well-known Chinese specialty "Chop-suey (based on the Cantonese word for miscellany) first saw light not in China but in San Francisco in the late 1800s," and the famous "fortune cookie was invented in Los Angeles" in the 1920s.[64] Therefore, America's multiculturalism might be a result of acculturation of immigrants, and the seemingly foreign elements in the American culture can be different from the "real" culture in those foreign countries. Randolph S. Bourne pointed out this phenomenon in 1916 in his article "Trans-national America," stating that in the United States there are "masses of people who are cultural half-breeds, neither assimilated Anglo-Saxons nor nationals of another culture."[65] He sees America not as "a nationality but a trans-nationality," and thus "it is spiritually impossible for [America] to pass into the orbit of any [nation]."[66] Although Bourne's article mainly demonstrates that it is impossible for Anglo-Saxon culture to fully assimilate other cultures in the United States, his view also indicates that non-Anglo-Saxon cultures have changed in the United States as immigrants have become "cultural half-breeds."

Conclusion

The current US naturalization policy eliminates all racial, gender, and nationality barriers to citizenship, and it seems to have achieved a revolutionary reform compared to the Naturalization Act of 1790. However, after analyzing the policy,

---

62 Eamonn Callan, "The Ethics of Assimilation," *Ethics* 115.3 (2005): 471–500, 471.
63 Alba and Nee, "Rethinking Assimilation Theory," 834.
64 Bill Bryson, *Made in America* [1994] (London: Black Swan, 1998): 269–270.
65 Randolph S. Bourne, "Trans-national America" (July 1, 1916), *The Atlantic* <http://www.theatlantic.com/magazine/archive/1916/07/trans-national-america/304838/?single_page=true> (acc. December 11, 2014).
66 Bourne, "Trans-national America."

it is evident that applicants for naturalization have to accept American values and surrender at least part of their original identity, and naturalization laws were usually modified to meet the country's political and economic needs. Therefore, the main difference between the Naturalization Act of 1790 and today's naturalization policy is that the basic requirement was at some point altered from being physically white to being innerly white. Peter Schrag calls the Second World War the "biggest whitener"[67] and describes the modification of naturalization policy as "the Great Awhitening."[68] Naturalized citizens may be of different ethnicities, but their behaviors should highly assimilate into the Anglo-American norm. In other words, assimilation can be nonwhite immigrants' pathway to become "white."

The US naturalization policy still intends to assimilate naturalized citizens, and the United States is trying to achieve this goal by providing citizenship education. Nevertheless, there is a tension between the government's expectation of assimilation and the reality of the assimilation progress. The immigrant generation has difficulty to Americanize fully. As a result, acculturation occurs where naturalized citizens absorb Anglo-American culture and add it to their original culture. Thus, assimilation and acculturation are significant components in the US naturalization process, and the term "melting pot" seems to continue to be the preciser description of immigration in the United States than "the salad bowl."

Assimilation does not necessarily have a negative connotation in regard to naturalization, because it is likely that naturalized citizens will face fewer difficulties or conflicts in their new society if assimilated, and it is not realistic that different ethnic groups under one nation have nothing in common but the government. When Barack Obama was running for president, many Americans with immigrant background were inspired by his speech at the Democratic National Convention in Boston where he said that "[t]here's not a black America and white America and Latino America and Asian America; there's the United States of America."[69] Although he was not suggesting assimilation per se, one essential way to achieve this cohesion is that Americans share the same political values, and it is impossible to reach this state if every culture remains unblended. In this sense, the term *e pluribus unum* (out of many, one) – the words used on the seal

---

67 Schrag, *Not Fit for Our Society*, 152.
68 Schrag, *Not Fit for Our Society*, 139.
69 FDCH E-Media, "Transcript: Illinois Senate Candidate Barack Obama" (July 27, 2004), *The Washington Post* <http://www.washingtonpost.com/wp-dyn/articles/A19751–2004Jul27.html> (acc. December 20, 2013).

of the United States which symbolize unity and strength – is strongly implied in Obama's speech with the "melting pot" connotation.

Annika Bauer

Chris Abani's *GraceLand:* Constructing a Diasporic Space in a Postcolonial Metropolis

Abstract: In this chapter, I argue that the relationships of unrelated characters in Chris Abani's *GraceLand* (2004) are enforced by the metropolis; thus, the issue of constructing a home away from home is raised. I examine the notion of the protagonist Elvis, as well as other characters in the novel, living in an intra-national diaspora in Lagos. The analysis constitutes a discussion of 'diaspora' as defined by William Safran and contextualized by Rogers Brubaker, Robin Cohen and Khachig Tölölyan. I also provide further arguments in favor of a metropolitan diasporic space within Lagos by touching on Benedict Anderson's theory of imagined communities offering an explanation for constructing an urban society based on the concepts of comradeship and forms of being imagined as well as on Paul Gilroy's notion of conviviality, a concept indicating that a metropolis is required to harbor and converge the residents' diverse feelings and ideas of belonging.

This chapter examines the novel *GraceLand*[1] by Nigerian author Chris Abani, who resides and works in the US. Abani belongs to the so-called Third Generation of Nigerian writers who often treat postcolonial themes using the English language. However, these Nigerian writers are not so much concerned with colonialism and its aftermaths explicitly. Rather, their major subjects have become "the meeting and mixing of cultures and subjectivities"[2] in the literary environment of Lagos after independence[3] as well as in the context of their Nigerian history and heritage. *GraceLand*, thematically, is an example for this development since the novel contains not only a representation of the metropolis of Lagos; it also features elements of a cityscape and a coming of age novel as seen in the story of the protagonist Elvis Oke. Both genres can be recognized by the division of the plot into two parts. One story line is set in the village of Afikpo. There, Elvis' early childhood is shaped by Igbo heritage and traditions as well as loss and violence within the family. The second plot commences with fourteen-year-old Elvis living in the city of Lagos after having been forced to leave his home village. In the metropolis' slum Maroko in 1983, the familial community

---

1 Chris Abani, *GraceLand* (New York: Picador, 2004). References in the text, abbreviated as "*GL*".
2 Chielozona Eze, "Cosmopolitan Solidarity: Negotiating Transculturality in Contemporary Nigerian Novels," *English in Africa* 32.1 (2002): 99–112, 100.
3 See Chris Dunton, "Entropy and Energy: Lagos as City of Words," *Research in African Literatures* 39.2 (2006): 68–78, 68; Rita Nnodim, "City, Identity and Dystopia: Writing Lagos in Contemporary Nigerian Novels," *Journal of Postcolonial Writing* 44.4 (2008): 321–332, 323.

is no longer available to Elvis; instead, he is supported by people to whom he is not related, and, yet, they become indispensable to the boy's upbringing and survival in Lagos. The spatial and temporal division of the story, however, does not indicate that both parts are independent of each other: frequent switching between the urban and rural plots indicates their interwoven nature. Thus, readers follow Elvis' life and actions in Lagos, and, simultaneously, learn about the influences from his childhood in the village, which have shaped his character and world view as a youngster in the metropolis.

Although *GraceLand* is not an autobiography, the life of the character Elvis bears strong resemblance to the experiences of the author Abani.[4] These experiences forced the latter to leave Nigeria and are now partly the basis for my analysis of the Nigerian metropolis of Lagos as literary space hosting an intra-national diaspora as well as enforcing international diasporic movement in the novel. I discuss the appearance of diaspora in Abani's fictional Lagos with reference to the features of diaspora as stipulated by William Safran and further reviewed by Rogers Brubaker, Robin Cohen, and Khachig Tölölyan. Oliver Bakewell's essay on the subject of diasporas within Africa[5] is discussed when analyzing the development of an intra-national African diaspora in Nigeria, which is strongly indicated by the rural and urban setting of the novel. Thus, it will be shown that the multi-faceted and conflicting metropolitan setting of Lagos as well as the characters' negotiation of it promote the formation of an intra-national Nigerian diaspora. As Cohen has outlined, "[t]he most important nodes in this spatial lattice [of the world economy] are what have come to be called 'world cities' or 'global cities',"[6] and he concludes:

> [T]he location of global economic, political and communication power is now debouching to particular cities, diasporas are often concentrated in such cities and profit from their cosmopolitan character. Deterritorialized, multilingual and capable of bridging the gap between global and local tendencies, diasporas are able to take advantage of the economic and cultural opportunities on offer.[7]

What will become obvious in analyzing Abani's literary representation of Lagos is that the construction of community within the city's slum Maroko crosses the

4 This opinion is based on a forum contribution by Abani – see Chris Abani, "UCF: On The Issues – Human Rights in Politics and Art" (January 27, 2009), *UCF On the Issues Archive* (U of Central Florida) <https://www.youtube.com/watch?v=9Eg4XmK4k6 A> (acc. August 8, 2013).
5 Oliver Bakewell, "In Search of the Diasporas within Africa," *African Diaspora* 1 (2008): 5–27.
6 Robin Cohen, *Global Diasporas. An Introduction*, second ed. (London, New York: Routledge, 2008): 146.
7 Cohen, *Global Diasporas*, 155.

border of communities built on kinship or common origin. Rather, the diasporic experience of characters from all over Nigeria arriving in Lagos and living together under the pressure of a limited urban space and the wish to make a better life than before create a diasporic community characterized by versatility and cooperation. This almost hopeful view is not supposed to hide the fact that the main urban setting of the novel, a slum, is an extremely precarious space and that most of the slum dwellers are destitute, unemployed and/or homeless. Nevertheless, the sense of community deriving from these harsh circumstances shared by Maroko's inhabitants is meant to highlight the quality of living in such a restricted urban space. My argument that a functioning diasporic community can be based on diverse origins is supported by Benedict Anderson's argument that 'imagined communities' are not merely based on blood relations but on mutual agreement and lifestyle.[8] Moreover, Paul Gilroy's comments on conviviality stress that multiculturalism is a feature of postcolonial metropolises,[9] and his concept thus offers a point of view strengthening the analysis of a diverse intra-national diasporic community not constituted by common heritage, religion or political world view, but instead by cohabitation and interaction of individuals.

The Metropolis as a Space of Diasporic Communities

GraceLand contests the notion of the city as the better living place as compared to the village in the countryside and vice versa. On the one hand, the mega-city is characterized by an excess of human capital and indifference towards the metropolitan community as a whole. On the other hand, the village is neither utterly romanticized nor is the reader spared from encountering extreme cruelty among the villagers, specifically among members of Elvis' family. Nevertheless, to the child Elvis, the imminent displacement from the countryside to the metropolis comes as something of a shock:

> "So what now?" Elvis asked [...].
> "Well, your father thinks he can get anoder job in Lagos and I heard him telling a friend dat if he lost de election he would take it," Aunt Felicia said.
> "*Lagos? But that is over eight hundred miles away!* What about you? Are you coming?" Elvis asked, voice shrill. (*GL*, 217, emphasis added)

---

8 Benedict Anderson, *Imagined Communities: Reflections on the Origin and Spread of Nationalism* (London: Verso, 1994).
9 Paul Gilroy, *Postcolonial Melancholia* (New York: Columbia UP, 2004): xv.

The protagonist sees himself confronted with being forced away from his home village and into Lagos. From a child's point of view overhearing adults talk, the reader learns that this is the aftermath of Elvis' father, Sunday, losing in the elections after Nigeria's first military junta in 1980 and being bankrupt as a result of it as well. Sunday is offered a job in Lagos and, therefore, takes his son to the metropolis in hope of a fresh start and return to a financially comfortable and socially respected lifestyle. However, this dream does not come true: Father and son live in one of Lagos' slums, Maroko. Lured into the metropolis and being disappointed by it, Sunday becomes a heavy drinker and a man haunted by the ghost of his late wife. For these reasons, Elvis has to endeavor to grow into an early adulthood imposed upon him by the metropolis. This forcefulness evokes Heinz Reif's description of a metropolis as a "machine[] of integration,"[10] in which human diversity "resulting from immigration defines the everyday life of the city as a space of encounter, hybridity, and mixture."[11] Farías and Stemmler offer an explanation for why this "machine of integration" presents an eventually insurmountable obstacle to defining a new home for Elvis in Maroko. They describe the historical and economic development of a mega-city as a binarism of center and periphery, such as in Latin America where a metropolis is a central entity controlling peripheral satellite cities. Yet, an identification with the metropolitan area as a whole does not take place among the inhabitants of the satellites.[12] In the 1970s and 1980s – the era in which the novel is set – the geography of Lagos already reflected this development. The metropolitan area comprised Lagos Island as well as neighboring cities and more and more rural areas on the mainland.[13] The urban population tripled from about 1.5 million in 1970 to over 4.5 million in 1990.[14] In this developing urban macrocosm, the city's single districts, regardless of whether they are official ones or not, represent seemingly

---

10 Heinz Reif qtd. in Ignacio Farías, Susanne Stemmler, "Deconstructing 'Metropolis': Critical Reflections on a European Concept," *CMS Working Papers Series* 004 (2006): 1–16, 3.
11 Farías, Stemmler, "Deconstructing 'Metropolis'," 3.
12 Cf. Farías, Stemmler, "Deconstructing 'Metropolis'," 7.
13 Cf. Ludger Schadomsky, "Zwischen Nobelvorten und Slums: Afrikas Städte – am Beispiel Lagos," in *Afrika – Mythos und Zukunft*, eds. Katja Böhler, Jürgen Hoeren (Bonn: Herder, 2003): 86–95, 90–94.
14 Sonja Ernst, "Lagos: Hyperwachstum – ungebremst und informell," (October 19, 2006), *bpb: Bundeszentrale für politische Bildung* <http://www.bpb.de/gesellschaft/staedte/mega staedte/64606/lagos?p=all> (acc. January 23, 2015). This high growth rate continued and made Lagos a mega-city with over 15 million inhabitants already by 2003 (Schadomsky, "Zwischen Nobelvorten und Slums," 94.

independent habitats, or satellites. Maroko is, or rather was,[15] such a peripheral area in terms of economic and political influence since it is an informal dwelling location, and it involuntarily becomes Elvis' place of residence in the novel. This involuntariness complemented by the boy's age and limited experience are strong causes for his difficulties in identifying with the city and creating a new home for himself. In what follows, Elvis' enforced dispersal from the village and his problematic attempts to fit into an urban community and to establish a feeling of home will be analyzed in order to argue that Elvis, indeed, can be seen to be living in an urban diaspora.

Discussing intra-national diasporas in Africa, Oliver Bakewell sheds light on the relationship between the African continent and diaspora. His argument is based on the observation that "in [...] literature on African diasporas, very little attention has been paid to African diasporas within the continent."[16] For Bakewell, a main point of criticism of current works on African diasporas is the all-encompassing terminology itself, "African diaspora," and that its various diaspora groups are not being differentiated from each other.[17] In his analysis of several theories of diasporic developments in Africa, Bakewell also cites P. T. Zeleza who refers to events which led to an era of structural adjustment after the change from a military dictatorship to a democratic government in Nigeria in the early 1980s. Diasporic movements due to the successes and failures of the Nigerian democracy at that time are reflected in the novel *GraceLand*. Bakewell nevertheless criticizes Zeleza for merely describing examples of inter-national diasporas, despite the latter's reference to the possibility of an intra-national diaspora in Nigeria. Wary of the risk of creating diasporas where there actually are none, Bakewell thus calls for more research that would investigate the "common blind spot" of African diaspora-research – the continent itself.[18]

GraceLand represents an intra-national diaspora. To a large extent, this is indicated when resemblances between the author's personal experiences and the characterization of the protagonist are highlighted. In a forum contribution at

---

15 A major event in Abani's novel is the demolition of Maroko. The actual slum residents were evicted and their homes bulldozed by the Nigerian government in 1990. Such methods were highly questionable attempts of the government to solve the problem of inadequate living conditions and to develop valuable real estate (cf. Tunde Agbola, A.M. Jinadu, "Forced Eviction and Forced Relocation in Nigeria: The Experience of Those Evicted from Maroko in 1990," *Environment and Urbanization*, 9.2 [1997]: 271–288, 271–272). This is still an on-going practice in Lagos.
16 Bakewell, "In Search of the Diasporas within Africa," 7.
17 Cf. Bakewell, "In Search of the Diasporas within Africa," 12.
18 Cf. Bakewell, "In Search of the Diasporas within Africa," 12–14.

the University of Central Florida in 2008, Abani reflected on his life and how he became a writer, thereby drawing strong parallels to his fictional character Elvis: Abani's mother is a white English woman, and his father a black Nigerian man. He originates from the Igbo village Afikpo – obviously the inspiration for the name of the fictional village. In an account of the development of his appreciation for literature, Abani says that due to his father's work in a prestigious political office – Elvis' father is a politician as well –, Abani had access to many libraries in small towns; therefore, he feels that his introduction to literature was a "sort of middle class privilege and intellectual privilege" for a "kid from the suburbs."[19] By comparison, Elvis' strong interest in literature is initiated and fueled by his mother's journal writing and her urge to make him read (which he follows quite willingly, particularly later as a teenager). Furthermore, besides the international roots inherited from his parents, the author says that he was also strongly influenced by his Indian primary school teacher. These recollections lead Abani to the description of having grown up in a "mish-mash" of cultures. This feature is transferred to the fictional character through his interest in Western movies, rock 'n' roll music and a wide range of literature from Rilke to the Koran (*GL*, 46). The writer, and the protagonist too as is strongly suggested in the novel (*GL*, 318–321), now lives in the US after being forced to flee from Nigeria as well as from London because of political persecution and the threat thereof.[20]

Abani's love for literature led him to start writing at a very young age and to realize the importance and power of this art form. He won his first literary award at sixteen. After having been confronted with brutality in his home country, becoming a refugee and coming into contact with diverse cultures, Abani says:

> I realized that literature, that art, is one of the most powerful things in the world. That it can intervene in things, in ways you don't think are possible. And that has essentially become my life's work – [that] is to catalogue, to organize and to present, to put into difficult situations of conflict, human beings who are often like us, and sometimes not like us. And I push them into these difficult positions to see if it is actually possible to have any kind of transformation, if it is even possible that we can find out what it truly means to be human. And so over the course of my writing career, I've come to believe one thing very true: that we are never more beautiful than when we are most ugly, because that's the only time we can really understand what we are capable of, and that's the only time we really begin to understand what goodness can really mean.[21]

---

19 Abani, "UCF – Human Rights in Politics and Art," 00:02:01–00:03:48; 00:08:27–00:08:35.
20 Cf. Abani, "UCF – Human Rights in Politics and Art," 00:14:58–00:15:32.
21 Abani, "UCF – Human Rights in Politics and Art," 00:05:03–00:06:04.

Abani sums up his opinion by explaining that, for him, literature is a place in which human beings can talk about life, about happiness and atrocities on equal ground[22] – a point of view which is epitomized by Elvis who uses literature to process the positive and negative he has experienced in his home village and in the metropolis. Alongside the brief insight into his life story, this shows how Abani uses his personal experiences of the diaspora as inspiration for the protagonist's story.

The following analysis of features of the diaspora and of the feasibility of applying them to the characters of *GraceLand* is conducted in light of Bakewell's warning on overstraining definitions of diaspora, or, as Brubaker writes:

> As the term has proliferated, its meaning has been stretched to accommodate the various intellectual, cultural and political agendas in the service of which it has been enlisted. This has resulted in what one might call a " 'diaspora' diaspora" – a dispersion of the meanings of the term in semantic, conceptual and disciplinary space.[23]

Nevertheless, Khachig Tölölyan sees in this proliferation of the term across the border of diaspora studies into German, classical or queer studies, to name just a few of his examples, a chance for advancing diaspora research:

> Each of these [studies] [...] has its own specific approach to diaspora studies, shaped by both local exigencies and the ideas and methods it draws from and contributed to the shared supradisciplinary procedures of diaspora studies, which thrives because of that exchange.[24]

The ways in which this exchange might influence diaspora studies cannot be predetermined, not even in the near future, for it "will depend on a configuration of factors too complex to catalog, because they will include elements ranging from the unpredictable elements of post 9/11 [...] to simplifications that the [...] media will deploy to explain diasporas to their audience."[25] Still, Tölölyan is convinced that, in academia, a certain set of defining elements of diaspora will be adhered to, even if each field of research will probably construct and value these diaspora elements "discipline-specific," and that they will contribute to the

---

22 Abani, "UCF – Human Rights in Politics and Art," 00:16:03–00:16:25.
23 Rogers Brubaker, "The 'Diaspora' Diaspora," *Ethnic and Racial Studies* 28.1 (2005): 1–19, 1.
24 Khachig Tölölyan, "The Contemporary Discourse of Diaspora Studies," *Comparative Studies of South Asia, Africa and the Middle East* 27.3 (2007): 647–655, 655.
25 Tölölyan, "The Contemporary Discourse of Diaspora Studies," 655.

"rapidly evolving conceptual vocabulary" of diaspora which derives from the su-pradisciplinary exchange.[26]

The discussion of a high potential for diaspora formation in metropolises as well as of a literary representation of diaspora by utilizing personal experience and of the dangers and opportunities of cross-disciplinary diaspora definitions forms the backdrop for the analysis of a metropolitan diasporic community in Abani's *GraceLand*. William Safran's explanation of diaspora from the early 1990s seems to be a suitable starting point insofar as it has been described as being "certainly the best way to specify a complex discursive and historical field."[27] Yet, it is also a rigid definition which is being criticized as posing the danger of enforcing an "ideal type" of diaspora effectively excluding ambivalent histories or futures.[28]

Regarding the first diasporic feature, Safran states that people must have been dispersed from their homeland, one's personal "center," to at least two "pe-ripheral" places.[29] Reading Abani's novel as a representation of diaspora, we have seen that Elvis is forced to move to a city 800 miles away from his home village. This instance partly reflects the feature of dispersal and simultaneously demonstrates some limitations. Although it is an involuntary dispersion in Elvis' case, it should still be noted that Brubaker writes that "[Safran's] passive formu-lation does not allow for voluntary dispersion. Cohen and others see this as too limiting."[30] Moreover, Elvis' experience of dispersal does not only suggest a sec-ond place of his family diaspora in the US, but also consecutive dispersals. In the end of the novel, it is indicated that Elvis is going to leave Lagos for the US to unite with his aunt who is one of his main caregivers during his childhood in Afikpo after his mother's death. This second instance of applying dispersion into diaspora, though still pending by the end of the novel, is a means of resolv-ing the character's conflicting relationship to the metropolis, in which he fails to make a living legally or illegally, loses his father and is imprisoned and tortured. There is also a more explicit example for another consecutive event of dispersal

---

26 Tölölyan, "The Contemporary Discourse of Diaspora Studies," 655.

27 James Clifford, "Diasporas," *Cultural Anthropology* 9.3 (1994): 302–338, 306.

28 Clifford points out that the Jewish diaspora, which is generally regarded as a prime case of diaspora, would be excluded from Safran's definition since it did not exist before the proclama-tion of Israel as the Jewish homeland. By referring to even earlier definitions of diaspora, Kha-chig Tölölyan also criticizes the constraining and exclusive nature of the concept which domi-nated its definition until revisions in the current period of globalization. See Tölölyan, "The Contemporary Discourse of Diaspora Studies," 648.

29 William Safran, "Diasporas in Modern Societies: Myths of Homeland and Return," *Diaspora* 1.1 (1991): 83–99, 83.

30 Brubaker, "The 'Diaspora' Diaspora," 15.

within the metropolis representing an intra-national diaspora: In the latter half of the novel, when Maroko is destroyed by the Lagosian government, Elvis and the other slum inhabitants are subsequently forced to move to other parts of the metropolis. Thus, the limited yet versatile setting of urban space is transformed to accommodate the sociopolitical shift. However, the instability of the communal space resulting from this shift is one of the causes of Elvis' incompatibility with the metropolis and, subsequently, of his departure. The feature of dispersion, as represented in these instances from the novel, also indicates a victim diaspora.[31] On the African continent, the development of this form of diaspora is grounded in "the experience of slave trade and forced migration."[32] In *Grace-Land*, the destruction of Maroko represents victimization due to forced migration. Moreover, the issue of being victimized also relates clearly to the third diasporic feature stating that the expatriates believe that "they are not [...] fully accepted by their host country."[33] The destruction of Maroko with the intention of dispersing the slum dwellers from valuable real estate is probably the most prominent instance of this aspect. That Elvis is troubled by the host community is further described aptly by his best friend, Redemption: "Your type no fit survive here long" (*GL*, 318). Elvis comes to realize this early in the novel, too: "It seemed like every mendicant in Lagos was able to help him" (*GL*, 48). Brubaker argues that the notion of (partial) acceptance by a host society should be expanded to include "boundary maintenance." In his explanation of this term, he highlights "the preservation of a distinctive identity vis-à-vis a host society" and says that it can function bilaterally: "Boundaries can be maintained by deliberate resistance to assimilation [...] or as an unintended consequence of social exclusion."[34] The latter is represented by the very existence of Maroko and other slums. Their inhabitants are excluded from the metropolis, especially with regard to living conditions and infrastructure, which are both (per definition of 'slum') the opposite of modern, a term usually attributed to the entity 'metropolis'. This also emphasizes Lagos' structure consisting of peripheral satellites which do not, or even cannot, identify with the metropolis as a whole. The former aspect of

---

31 For more information about victim diasporas, especially in the African context, see Cohen, *Global Diasporas*, 39–59.

32 Cohen, *Global Diasporas*, 42.

33 Safran, "Diasporas in Modern Societies," 83. Furthermore, another limitation of Safran's definition becomes evident: By using the term "country," he does not include the existence of intra-national diasporas. I use this diaspora feature in the sense of host community or "host society (or societies)" (see Brubaker, "The 'Diaspora' Diaspora," 6) in order to describe diaspora formation within the same nation and the same metropolis in the novel.

34 Brubaker, "The 'Diaspora' Diaspora," 6.

boundary maintenance, i.e., deliberate resistance to assimilation, is also visible in *GraceLand:* The slum dwellers as a group (naturally) protest against the destruction of their homes. One can also conclude from the bulldozing of Maroko that the host community is blocking assimilation. This concept of boundary maintenance, aside from containing the notion of not being fully accepted, is indispensable for diasporas since it allows for the identification of distinctive diasporic groups in the first place.[35]

Further features of diaspora as stipulated by Safran are closely connected. Cohen notes "four of the six features mentioned were concerned with the relationship of the diasporic group to its homeland." Assessing the list and deeming it somewhat repetitive, Cohen still acknowledges the "crucial importance" of the homeland and suggests adding to and "tweak[ing]" the list of features defining diaspora.[36] Brubaker, by comparison, appears more rigorous, for he consolidates the four features under the heading "Homeland Orientation," thereby assigning this "orientation to a real or imagined 'homeland' as an authoritative source of value, identity and loyalty."[37] Thus, he follows the trend of de-emphasizing the discussion of the homeland by describing it as one out of three distinct features of diaspora.[38] Nonetheless, it remains a defining aspect and, therefore, needs to be discussed in relation to the novel's construction of diasporic identity. Safran's four criteria offer a guideline to the issue of the homeland – again, neither Brubaker nor Cohen exclude these features from explaining diaspora; rather, both stress the importance of the homeland and reinterpret its relation to the diaspora.

One feature of homeland orientation is to maintain a "memory, vision, or myth about their original homeland."[39] In *GraceLand*, this feature is addressed explicitly: For the reader, the alternating story line between the village and the city clearly connects Elvis' childhood memory to his diasporic experience in Lagos. For instance, in the village he is dancing with the women (*GL*, 42); in Lagos, Elvis tries to make a living from singing and dancing as his namesake's impersonator (*GL*, 12). Moreover, each chapter is preceded by part of a description of the kola-nut ritual, reminding the reader of a tradition which expresses respect and hospitality, as well as a recipe from Elvis' mother's journal. The latter, a collection of letters, notes and recipes, is all that the youngster has left of his mother as his only means to conjure up memories of her life since she died of

---

35 Cf. Brubaker, "The 'Diaspora' Diaspora," 6.

36 Cohen, *Global Diasporas*, 6.

37 Brubaker, "The 'Diaspora' Diaspora," 5.

38 Brubaker, "The 'Diaspora' Diaspora," 5–6.

39 Safran, "Diasporas in Modern Societies," 83.

cancer when Elvis was nine years old (*GL*, 11). The other three features concentrating on the role of the homeland, as stipulated by Safran, focus on the wish to eventually return to the homeland, the commitment to maintain or restore it and a continuing identity-defining relationship with it.[40] With regard to these three aspects, it becomes even clearer that Elvis' connection to the homeland, the village Afikpo, is ambivalent. Throughout the novel, it does not seem to be his wish to literally return to the soil of Afikpo; neither does he seem prone to actually maintain it nor to be defined by the land itself. His diverse experiences in Afikpo appear quite clearly to be one reason for this ambivalence: The village is characterized by a patriarchal system, but Elvis feels no affinity to traditions such as marking the coming of age as a man of his tribe by killing an animal (*GL*, 17–22). Even as a young boy, he is more comfortable with being surrounded by women, dancing with them and trying on make-up. The movies of John Wayne and Elvis Presley's music also have a strong impact on his identity. Thus, instead of desiring an actual family life in the village, Elvis' relationship to his homeland is represented in a figurative manner: He could reunite with his aunt as a representative of the female side of his family with whom he has been connected closely from the beginning of the novel (*GL*, 317). Through his mother's journal and his love of reading instilled by her, he maintains the memories and impressions which are important to him for defining his homeland.[41] It is also the loss of his mother that brings Elvis closer to his father since they share that tragic experience. Through this, they also have a continuing relationship to the homeland in common which influences both their identities. That the feature of identity formation is being approached figuratively in *GraceLand* emerges even more strongly when seen in the context of Bakewell's analysis of intra-national diasporas in Africa. Bakewell explains that such diasporas seem to have retained rather a metaphorical attachment to their homeland than an actual one due to a high frequency of mobility within the continent.[42] One example for this mobility is the tribe to which the character Elvis, as well as the author Abani, belongs to: the Igbo. Since the Biafran war in the late 1960s, they moved rather often through Nigeria following economic fluctuations, as represented by the story of Elvis' father (*GL*, 19). Bakewell further notes that there appears to be a rising expectation that young Igbos leave their African homeland to permanently live

---

40 Safran, "Diasporas in Modern Societies," 83–84.
41 These biographical details of the fictional character are most certainly a reflection of the author's own experiences of growing up with international art and popular culture as well as feeling privileged for having access to these sources in the first place.
42 Cf. Bakewell, "In Search of the Diasporas within Africa," 7.

abroad.[43] This statement further suggests a development towards a mainly figurative connection to the homeland especially for diasporic Igbos[44] as is exemplified by Elvis' intention to leave Nigeria at the end of the story.

The representation of the protagonist's development from living in a rural environment to his experiences in an urban one suggests the formation of an intra-national metropolitan diaspora. This is not an "ideal type" of diaspora as defined by Safran, which, according to Clifford (as well as Cohen, Brubaker and Tölölyan), is unlikely to occur.[45] However, since such a type represents a prototypical case, scholars examine diaspora "by acknowledging and evaluating the extent of real life deviation from the ideal type"[46] – in the case of *GraceLand*, the deviation from the ideal type is caused by the literary representation of the diaspora in question. In this context, Elvis and his father's experience can be described as living in an "imperfect" form of urban diaspora which, in their case, does not indicate that a return to the homeland would be an option. Yet in their diasporic consciousness, the memory of the homeland has a strong presence mostly maintained by the ghost of the wife and mother, which is often conjured up in Sunday's frequent drunk spells. He appears to be haunted by his wife, whose voice eventually leads him to a renewed sense of self-esteem shortly before his death in the slum by imploring him: "This is the hour of your death. Go out and fight for your honor" (*GL*, 287). In following her bidding, he becomes a leading figure in the fight against the destruction of the urban diasporic community in Maroko. Elvis is also burdened by the ghost of the past since he misses the benefit of a supportive village community. His experiences consist of violence among family members and traditions which are forced upon him. In his diasporic life in Lagos, he is guided through the unknown sphere of adolescence as well as the still unfamiliar, even inaccessible, metropolis by his mother's journal. For the reader, her presence symbolizes the homeland, albeit in a phantasmagorical light, represented through the alternating urban and rural settings in the novel and through the formulaic chapter introductions.

---

43 Cf. Bakewell, "In Search of the Diasporas within Africa," 20.
44 Bakewell, however, also highlights the temporary identification of Igbo people with their host communities and a strong sense of belonging to Igboland by quoting O. Uduku: "For Igbos in the diaspora within Nigeria their new situation and identification with their host community was seen as clearly temporary or transient. Clearly with Nigeria's shifting geopolitics, one's relationship with one's home town and with other Igbo kin was all that could be assured" (Bakewell, "In Search of the Diasporas within Africa," 19).
45 Cf. Clifford, "Diasporas," 59.
46 Cohen, *Global Diasporas*, 17.

Constituting a Diasporic Community in Lagos

How does a diaspora made up of so seemingly few members – Elvis and his father – function in the novel? In the fictional Lagos, Elvis and Sunday are not living as recluses or in a community solely comprised of diasporic Igbos. Myriads of people of different origins, traditions and beliefs inhabit the metropolitan area. In the novel, the slum dwellers of Maroko seem to form a community based on these differences and seem to feel the need to create a home away from home. In order to function as a community, these individuals with their diverse ways of living have to be connected. How does the author create a common and inhabitable environment out of such a large number of characters? And how does he shape their different backgrounds into a recognizable diaspora?

Benedict Anderson's concept of imagined communities and his observation that "all communities larger than primordial villages of face-to-face contact (and perhaps even these) are imagined"[47] offers the basis needed to concentrate on a particular piece of urban space without disregarding the importance of the city as a whole. In a metropolis, the characteristic of the size of an imagined community becomes obvious, since, especially there, no one can know everyone personally. Yet, the actual number of human beings belonging to a community is not relevant: Whether it is a nation of millions or a town of thousands, the size of a population will always be limited. Rather, community, according to Anderson, can be identified by "a deep, horizontal comradeship [...] regardless of the actual inequality and exploitation."[48] Such comradery is one factor which influences the formation of community in *GraceLand*. Moreover, Anderson states that community is recognized "by the style in which [it is] imagined."[49] This style refers to the specific historical circumstances in which communities are artificially constructed. For instance, as Wendy Griswold explains, it was thought that a national community would develop naturally due to blood relation and emotional connection to a particular area.[50] Yet with regard to places such as a metropolis with millions of inhabitants and slums with their unofficial numbers of residents, it becomes evident that kinship and a relationship to a common homeland among the community members are less likely. Rather, as suggested by Anderson, many of them feel connected to the community through comradeship and

---

47 Anderson, *Imagined Communities*, 6.
48 Anderson, *Imagined Communities*, 7.
49 Anderson, *Imagined Communities*, 6.
50 Wendy Griswold, "The Writing on the Mud Wall: Nigerian Novels and the Imaginary Village," *American Sociological Review* 57.12 (1992): 709–724, 709.

historical circumstances. For instance, as represented in the fictional Maroko, they share the experience of being forced from their respective homelands, of trying to maintain their memories and of lacking acceptance within the larger metropolitan host community; the latter is most evident in the destruction of the actual as well as fictional slum.

Moreover, within the restricted space of the metropolis, the high number of inhabitants means a high concentration of different lifestyles, which can be described as niches within the fabric of the city for creating one's personal space, and which, in turn, characterize the urban space. Hilary Dannenberg describes this development as follows:

> [T]he urban identity maps of *GraceLand* [...] are constructed out of an interplay with spaces beyond inner-urban spaces, in order to produce detailed maps of both life trajectories and a vision of the wider national and global contexts to which that character belongs. [...] Each city is therefore characterized in contrast to, also in correspondence with, different spaces.[51]

Dannenberg's reading of identity formation in the literary metropolis as consisting of different yet interconnected spaces is in line with my argument that an intra-national diasporic community in Lagos is constructed out of many diverse, overlapping personal spaces being negotiated among the slum dwellers in *GraceLand*. Rita Nnodim concurs that there is a correlation between the impact of urban spaces on their residents and the activities and movements of the residents on urban spaces, thus constructing "habitats of meaning," intersecting individual or collective lifestyles, in *GraceLand*.[52] One can argue that the huge number of single habitats is made accessible to the reader by the protagonist Elvis as a medium linking the spaces of Maroko's residents. As the novel puts it: "Elvis read the city, seeing signs not normally visible. [... He] traced patterns in the cracked and parched earth beneath his feet. There is a message in it all somewhere, he mused, a point to the chaos" (*GL*, 306–307). In this instance, Elvis demonstrates a degree of awareness of the construction of the slum community by factors other than kinship – i.e., comradeship and the style of invoking relationships create communal familiarity. An actual example of how Elvis

---

51 Hilary Dannenberg, "Narrating the Postcolonial Metropolis in Anglophone African Fiction: Chris Abani's *GraceLand* and Phaswane Mpe's *Welcome to Our Hillbrow*," *Journal of Postcolonial Writing* 48.1 (2012): 39–50, 40.
52 Nnodim, "City, Identity and Dystopia," 322, 331. Ulf Hannerz also uses the term "habitats" to refer to (transnational) categories of people inhabiting urban spaces ("The Cultural Role of World Cities," *Transnational Connections: Culture, People, Places* [London/New York: Routledge: 1996]: 127–139, 131).

himself forms a relationship in the slum by these means can be found in his relationship to Okon, a poor man he gives food. When they meet again later, their imagined communal connection becomes visible, albeit slowly:

> "Elvis!"
> He spun around. A man stood in the open door of the buka dressed like Superfly. Elvis did not recognize him, and the man, noticing his confusion, explained.
> "It's me Okon."
> It hit him. It was the man he had fed barely a week ago, at this same buka. [...] Elvis smiled at Okon, straining to mask his thoughts. He really wasn't in the mood for company, but his hunger got the better of him, so he went back. They sat facing each other [...]. "Yes. It's me. Okon. Okon" – as if this mantra would bond them. (*GL*, 74–75)

The two have a meal together and Okon tells Elvis how relatively well life has treated him since the last time both met and Elvis was the one helping out the other slum dweller. In the chaos of the urban slum with its seemingly infinite lifestyles, their rather randomly emerging relationship, which develops into a comradeship without regard to inequality and exploitation in the second half of the novel, demonstrates that diasporas are "adaptive forms of social organization."[53] As such, the intra-national diaspora in Abani's novel represents a literary construction of community brought about by interconnecting a diverse group of characters in a limited metropolitan area.

A Lagosian Imagined Community with a Diasporic Consciousness

A closer look at habitats of meaning, or converging lifestyles, in the fictional Maroko highlights the fact that a diverse intra-national diasporic community is not made manifest in the novel by assigning common origin, religion or political world view to its characters, but instead by detailing the cohabitation and interaction of the individuals. One such habitat is occupied by Elvis' closest friend Redemption. He is a character who uses the corruptive society instead of allowing himself to be used by it (*GL*, 25). Redemption continuously raises the stakes: He starts out playing checkers, later becomes a gigolo, peddles drugs and, finally, gets involved in human trafficking. Despite his risky lifestyle, Redemption always has a safety net: a fake American passport which would allow him to leave

---

53 Cohen qtd. in Diana Brydon, "Postcolonialism Now: Autonomy, Cosmopolitanism, and Diaspora," *University of Toronto Quarterly* 73.2 (2004): 691–706, 701.

Nigeria. Throughout the novel, the passport evokes a certain degree of anticipation that a resident of Maroko is going to live in a diaspora in the US. This anticipation is also part of the relationship between Redemption and Elvis, for Elvis' diasporic experiences, which render him able to connect to his friend's habitat of meaning, also show that it is extremely difficult for him to live in Lagos. Sunday, Elvis' father, follows another lifestyle which is open to intersecting with others. In Lagos, he lives an almost traditional village life with a woman and her three children. Furthermore, he appears to become an established member of the slum community leading the people of Maroko during the riot in which their homes are destroyed. Yet, he is also a drunk and disrespected by his own son (*GL*, 5). Another example for a habitat of meaning is that of Okon, Elvis' former-beggar friend. As exemplified in the quotation above, he is a grateful and generous character: When he receives help from Elvis in a time of need, the poor man promises to return the favor, and he stands true to his word several times in the course of the novel. Elvis has long been unsure of Okon's motives, and it is only towards the end of the story that he finally becomes convinced of the former beggar's sincerity – now that Okon has become a respectable businessman. Furthermore, Okon is described as a sensitive and wise friend who does not force himself on Elvis after a traumatic event (*GL*, 308).

None of the three habitats show that their inhabitants strive towards a common achievement or are directly connected to each other. It is their individual relationships to Elvis that joins Redemption, Sunday and Okon. And again, it is Elvis' diasporic experience which renders him able to connect to these different characters in their particular habitats of meaning. To corroborate this point, I refer briefly to Paul Gilroy's notion of conviviality. This humanistic form of social order is based on "processes of cohabitation and interaction that have made multiculture an ordinary feature of social life [...] in postcolonial cities,"[54] or in other words, it is based on the "everydayness of living."[55] In this everydayness, Gilroy states, human differences are acknowledged and embraced. "Supposedly impermeable boundaries of race, culture, identity and ethnicity"[56] are subverted in favor of this all-encompassing multicultural point of view. A metropolitan community with limited space, a high number of inhabitants and diasporic features is a likely entity for observing conviviality. The three habitats described demonstrate Gilroy's notions: Looking again at the youth becoming a

---

54 Gilroy, *Postcolonial Melancholia*, xv.
55 Theresa Enright, "Postcolonial Melancholia" (October 2, 2009) *Politics and Culture* <http://www.politicsandculture.org/2009/10/02/theresa-enright-postcolonial-melancholia/> (acc. July 23, 2013).
56 Gilroy, *Postcolonial Melancholia*, xii.

gangster, the provincial politician becoming a slum leader, and the beggar becoming a prolific community member, it can be observed that features creating hierarchies such as race, age, social class or place of origin do not separate these three characters socially from each other. Each is well-integrated in Maroko and able to adapt to changes in the community in his own way. Rather, it is the versatile urban environment and its plethora of opportunities to make a living which hardly lets their paths cross. In the dynamic of the Lagos metropolis and within the smaller unit of the slum, Elvis becomes a tool through which the reader can make sense of how characters create new ways of living and merge into in a coherent community. Elvis' ability to relate to the other characters in the novel is derived from his experiences providing him with a diasporic consciousness. His lifestyle in the metropolis is characterized by his rural experiences of female and male coming of age rituals, of violence among family members, of loss, of the instilled interest in international literature, films and music, contrasted with the experience of social decline and the attempt to survive on his own, of the vastness and the velocity of life in the urban environment. His diasporic consciousness is further enhanced by his comradeship with the other slum dwellers, especially Redemption, and the offer to go abroad with the help of his friend's fake passport which holds the promise of yet another imaginary diasporic community outside the urban community of the constantly fluctuating metropolis of Lagos which renders it impossible for Elvis to create a home away from his homeland.

Stella Butter

No Place like Home? Conceptualizations of 'Home' in Salman Rushdie's "At the Auction of the Ruby Slippers" and Roshi Fernando's *Homesick*

Abstract: This chapter analyzes different conceptualizations of home in the diasporic imaginary by concentrating on four dimensions of home: home as (1) a place of origin, (2) a social unit, (3) the materiality of home and (4) scales of home. The cultural ideal of home is associated with a sense of coherence, safety and community in both Salman Rushdie's short story "At the Auction of the Ruby Slippers" and Roshi Fernando's *Homesick*. In Rushdie's story, the bidders at the auction identify home as a place of origin they long to return to. Rushdie rejects this ideal of home as a dangerous fetish that destroys all possibilities of 'doing home' in the here and now. This fetish is shown to be steeped in nostalgia and commodity culture. *Homesick* offers a reconceptualization of home in terms of 'from hereness' and practices of intimacy. The structure of Fernando's literary text is endowed with added significance because the book presents itself as a house and a specific type of home or community. This literary model of community is not coded as a metonymic model for the nation because *Homesick* critically questions seemingly smooth transitions between different scales of home.

The emotional appeal of home and its ideological fabric go a long way in explaining why it is often the focus of diasporic desire. Home as an "embryonic community" is featured as a site of belonging, security and comfort in popular images of home.[1] These cultural ideals of home intersect with notions of national belonging as the easy slippage between the scales home and homeland indicates.[2] It is precisely this issue of belonging or the vexed question of 'who is at home in the nation?' that is of crucial importance for the diasporic subject. The dislocation resulting from the migratory experience gives rise to a "homing desire," i.e., a wish for social inclusion and the experience of feeling at home.[3] Such a homing desire of the diasporic subject "[need not] sustain an ideology of 'return'," as Avtar Brah emphasizes in her discussion of *Cartographies of Dia-*

---

1 Mary Douglas, "The Idea of a Home: A Kind of Space," in *The Domestic Space Reader*, eds. Chiara Briganti, Kathy Mezei (Toronto, Buffalo, London: U of Toronto P, 2012): 50–54, 51.
2 On the interplay between home and homeland, see Alison Blunt and Robyn Dowling, *Home* (London, New York: Routledge, 2006): 70–75, 140–188; David Morley, *Home Territories: Media, Mobility and Identity* (London, New York: Routledge, 2000): 31–55.
3 Avtar Brah, *Cartographies of Diaspora. Contesting Identities* [1996] (London, New York: Routledge, 1998): 180.

spora.[4] The conceptual category 'home' is hence inscribed by different components: it can mean the place of origins (homeland) or the "lived experience of
a locality,"[5] a social unit, a set of feelings, and it can also refer to a material dimension, e.g., the physical structure of one's dwelling place.[6] Moreover, home
may be situated on various scales, ranging from one's body and the private
home to the local neighborhood or the nation or even the world.[7]

When comparing visions of home in the diasporic imaginary, it is useful to
examine which specific dimensions of home are activated (e.g., home as social
unit or physical structure) and how these intersecting elements of home operate
in a 'diasporic space' inscribed by power relations.[8] Such an approach refrains
from working with a pre-given definition of home, but is instead attuned to different configurations of home in literary texts. This approach underpins my
analysis of Salman Rushdie's short story "At the Auction of the Ruby Slippers"
(1992) and Roshi Fernando's award-winning book *Homesick* (2012). These two
texts make for an interesting comparison due to their explicit play with the multiple meanings of the term 'homesick' in the context of diasporic geographies.
While literary stories dealing with the experience of diaspora inevitably address
issues of dispersal and settlement, not all of them use the ambivalences of the
term 'homesick' as a focal point for complicating and enriching the discussion
of diasporic longing and belonging. Taken together, Rushdie's and Fernando's
texts provide a nuanced exploration of what homesickness might mean for carving out spaces of belonging in the diasporic here and now. Their stories render
the idea of homesickness ambiguous by suggesting that the diasporic subject
may not only be sick *for* home, but may also become sick *through* home. This
is the case when the diasporic yearning for home becomes implicated in dangerous processes of fetishization so that desiring home appears as a pathology in
need of rejection. Another variant is introduced by foregrounding how individu-

---

4 Brah, *Cartographies of Diaspora*, 180. See also Ruth Mayer, *Diaspora: Eine kritische Begriffsbestimmung* (Bielefeld: Transcript, 2005): 13.
5 Brah, *Cartographies of Diaspora*, 193.
6 On the multiple meanings of 'home' discussed in scholarly literature, see Shelley Mallett,
"Understanding Home: A Critical Review of the Literature," *Sociological Review* 52.1 (2004):
62–89.
7 Blunt and Dowling, *Home*, 27.
8 The expression 'diaspora space' refers to "the intersectionality of diaspora, border, and dis/
location as a point of confluence of economic, political, cultural and psychic processes. It addresses the global condition of culture, economics and politics as a site of 'migrancy' and 'travel'
which seriously problematises the subject position of the 'native'. [...] The concept of *diaspora
space* (as opposed to that of diaspora) includes the entanglement of genealogies of dispersion
with those of 'staying put' " (Brah, *Cartographies of Diaspora*, 181).

als are sick *of* home because the so-called home space features as the site of violence and oppression. As will be shown in the following, Rushdie's text concentrates on diagnosing the 'sickness' of the diasporic imaginary of home, while Fernando's moves beyond this diagnosis by exploring ways of curing the homesickness of the diasporic subject without recourse to regressive fantasies.

Salman Rushdie's "At the Auction of the Ruby Slippers" (1992): Home as a Fetish

"At the Auction of the Ruby Slippers" draws on the American fairytale *The Wizard of Oz* as a key intertext: the ruby slippers mentioned in the story title refer to the shoes that bring Dorothy home.[9] In the world of magical realism opened up in Rushdie's story, 'displaced persons of all sorts' come to an auction to bid for precisely this material promise of home. Set in a dystopian world ridden by violence and peopled by exiles who dwell in underground bunkers, the home these exiles long for is one which renders them "invulnerable to witches [and sorcerers],"[10] where "a lost state of normalcy" (*AARS*, 92) is restored and a reunion with "deceased parents" (*AARS*, 93) is possible. According to this list, the home that answers to the "numberless needs" (*AARS*, 93) of the bidders is defined by a sense of coherence (you are part of normality), a sense of control or safety ('invulnerability') and a sense of community ('reunion with family members').[11]

9 On *The Wizard of Oz* as an American fairytale or myth see Alissa Burger, *The Wizard of Oz as American Myth: A Critical Study of Six Versions of the Story, 1900–2007* (Jefferson, NC, London: McFarland, 2012).
10 Salman Rushdie, 'At the Auction of the Ruby Slippers,' in *East, West* (London: Jonathan Cape, 1994): 85–103, 92. Further references in the text, abbreviated as "*AARS*". For a contrastive analysis of Rushdie's short story with Frank Baum's *The Wonderful Wizard of Oz* (1900), see Justyna Deszcz-Tryhubczak, "The Global Bidding for Dorothy Gale's Magical Shoes: Salman Rushdie's 'At the Auction of the Ruby Slippers' as a (Self-) Reflection on the Post-Frontier Predicament," in *Global Fragments: (Dis)Orientation in the New World Order*, eds. Anke Bartels, Dirk Wiemann (Amsterdam, New York: Rodopi, 2007): 105–113. For a discussion of Rushdie's interpretation of the MGM movie *The Wizard of Oz* and his rewriting of the Oz myth in *Haroun and the Sea of Stories*, see Barbara Schmidt-Haberkamp, "Salman Rushdie und *The Wizard of Oz*," in *Inklings: Jahrbuch für Literatur und Ästhetik* 19 (2001): 88–108.
11 These attributes of home correspond with the meanings of *Heimat* ('homeland') analyzed by Beate Mitzscherlich in her psychological study on this German concept (Beate Mitzscherlich, *"Heimat ist etwas, was ich mache"*. *Eine psychologische Untersuchung zum individuellen Prozeß von Beheimatung* [Herbholzheim: Centaurus, 2000]: 56). In her study, Mitzscherlich emphasizes

Home is a specific experience of the individual and a social situation. More than that, being or feeling at home is shown as crucial for a stable sense of self or identity. The first person narrator emphasizes that when bidding for the ruby slippers he is bidding "perhaps literally – for [...] [him]self" (*AARS*, 101). Home is, however, perceived as unattainable by ordinary means because it is firmly located in a nostalgic past that one longs to return to. Due to this identification of home as a place of origin, most of the displaced persons "are [home]sick" (*AARS*, 87) in the 'here and now.'

The issue of homesickness takes on an added urgency in Rushdie's short story because the text drastically foregrounds sedentarism as a cultural norm in the Western world. The reader is told that the "homeless tramps" (*AARS*, 90) who have turned up at the auction will be

> removed, clubbed into unconsciousness and driven away. They will be deposited some distance beyond the city limits, out there in that smoking no-man's-land surrounded by giant advertising hoardings into which we venture no more. Wild dogs will gather around them, eager for luncheon. (*AARS*, 91)

People without a fixed abode or dwelling place to call their own are literally stripped of their subjectivity and reduced to meat. The treatment of the tramps drastically foregrounds that the loss of home means losing one's place in the cultural order. The result is 'wasted life,' i.e., human life that is "excluded and assigned to waste [the waste-yard, the rubbish heap]."[12] The transformation of the tramps into disposable waste is predicated on a sedentarist perspective that equates

---

that 'Heimat' as a psychological concept combines a "sense of community, sense of control and sense of coherence" (138; my translation).

12 Zygmunt Bauman, *Wasted Lives: Modernity and Its Outcasts* (Cambridge: Polity P, 2004): 16. In his book, Bauman highlights how the "production of 'human waste', or more correctly wasted humans (the 'excessive' and 'redundant', that is the population of those who either could not or were not wished to be recognized or allowed to stay), is an inevitable outcome of modernization [...]. It is an inescapable side-effect of *order-building* (each order casts some parts of the extant population as 'out of place' [...]) and of *economic progress* [...]" (5). The bidders at the auction in Rushdie's story fit Bauman's following description of 'wasted lives': "When it comes to designing the forms of human togetherness, the waste is human beings. Some human beings who do not fit into the designed form nor can be fitted into it. Or such as adulterate its purity and so becloud its transparency: [...] hybrids who call the bluff of ostensibly inclusive/exclusive categories" (30).

a culture [...] with a people and that people with a particular geographical place or territory. [...] From this metaphysics then flows a further set of binary oppositions – between 'us and them', 'here and there' and 'our own and other' cultures or societies.[13]

One may add to this list the binary opposite between 'home' (as a fixed place of origin) and 'exile or displacement.' The bidders at the auction of the ruby slippers seem to have internalized the "metaphysics of sedentarism" because they seek to find a way of returning to the only form of home they allow for: the place of their origins.[14] This homeland is shown to take on mythic qualities in the diasporic imagination.[15] The imaginary quality of what is perceived as home is emphasized by the "permeation of the real world by the fictional" (*AARS*, 94). This implosion of the boundaries between reality and fiction, the saturation of the lifeworld by media images, can be read as an effect of commodity fetishism and its aesthetization of everyday life.[16] The non-material component of the ruby slippers, their promise of a specific experience of home, is the result of medial representations. *The Wizard of Oz* is an "immediately recognizable popular culture icon" and as such an integral part of America's cultural memory and arguably also global memory if one takes the submission of Victor Fleming's *The Wizard of Oz* (1939) to the UNESCO Memory of the World Register into account.[17] One of the central themes of *The Wizard of Oz* is home, and it is precisely

---

13 Morley, *Home Territories*, 39.

14 Lisa Malkki qtd. in Morley, *Home Territories*, 39.

15 Michael Meyer, "Nachwort," in Salman Rushdie, *East, West*, ed. Michael Meyer (Stuttgart: Philipp Reclam, 2002): 245–275, 264.

16 Don Slater, *Consumer Culture and Modernity* (Cambridge: Polity P, 1997): 195.

17 For a discussion of *The Wizard of Oz* as part of America's cultural memory, see Burger, *The Wizard of Oz as American Myth*, 5. To view the inscription of Fleming's *The Wizard of Oz* in the Unesco Memory of the World Register, see <http://www.unesco.org/new/en/communication-and-information/flagship-project-activities/memory-of-the-world/register/full-list-of-registered-heritage/registered-heritage-page-8/the-wizard-of-oz-victor-fleming-1939-produced-by-metro-goldwyn-mayer/> (acc. March 27, 2015). I draw on the term 'global memory' to refer to "new forms of collective memory [...] and *cultural memory*, which [emerge] [...] in an increasingly *globalized* world. Whilst much scholarly discourse in the past has discussed memory within national frameworks [...], an increasing recognition of and focus on the impact of globalization has caused Andreas Huyssen to remark that, by the beginning of the twenty-first century, 'The form in which we think of the past is increasingly memory without borders rather than national history within borders. Modernity has [...] expanded our horizons of time and space beyond the local, the national and even the international' " (Jessica Rapson, "Global Memory," in *The Routledge Companion to Critical and Cultural Theory*, eds. Simon Malpas, Paul Wake, second ed. [London, New York: Routledge, 2013]: 233–234, 233).

this theme that continues to be negotiated in the manifold adaptations and re-visions of *The Wizard of Oz* as Rushdie's own story illustrates.[18]

In the dystopian world of Rushdie's story, commodity culture is not under-stood as offering materials or resources for the creative construction of self, but is instead only perceived in its alienating effects: everything is subsumed under the logic of the market. As a result, home is rendered a marketable com-modity and a fetish in itself. This fetishization of home has disastrous implica-tions for the interaction with other subjects. They are not perceived as individu-als, but instead are reduced to functioning as an empty canvas for nostalgic projections of home. A case in point is the narrator's relationship with his cousin Dorothy Gale. By buying the ruby slippers for her, the narrator hopes to revive their love relationship. He emphasizes that

> there was nothing abnormal about our love-making, nothing, if I may put it thus, *fictional*. Yet it satisfied me deeply [...], especially when she chose to cry out at the moment of pen-etration: '[...] Home, baby, yes – you've come home!' One day, [...] I came home to find her in the arms of a hairy escapee from a caveman movie. (*AARS*, 95)

This is an obvious satirical gloss on the well-worn psychoanalytical claim that the desire for what is termed 'home' is nothing more than a regressive 'caveman' fantasy: home is the maternal, for which all women stand in. The price the women pay for embodying the male birthplace, the place of safety and plenti-tude, is the annihilation of self.[19]

Rushdie's story connects the portrayal of home as a regressive or narcissistic fantasy with the triumph of the 'hyperreal' (Baudrillard).[20] After their split-up, the narrator happens to see his cousin Gale again in a bar. She is watching the news coverage on a sad astronaut stranded on Mars singing songs of home with no hope of being rescued. She is crying while watching this. Instead of "go[ing] across to comfort her" (*AARS*, 97), the narrator adopts the position of a voyeur with the comment that Gale "had become my chosen programme" (*AARS*, 97). The narrator eschews closeness or intimacy with Gale at this moment precisely because she is not important to him as a unique embodied individual, but as a signifier for home. If Gale is his chosen TV program, then she appears as

---

18 Burger, *The Wizard of Oz as American Myth*, 11.
19 On home as the site of the maternal, see Christoph Türcke, *Heimat: Eine Rehabilitierung* (Springe: Zu Klampen, 2006). For a feminist critique of this idea of home, see Iris Marion Young, "House and Home: Feminist Variations on a Theme," in *Intersecting Voices: Dilemmas of Gender, Political Philosophy, and Policy* (Princeton, NJ: Princeton UP, 1997): 134–164, 135.
20 For a Baudrillardian reading of Rushdie's story, see Michael Meyer, "Nachwort," 245–275.

hyperreal and hence as the product of media images without any depth or anchoring in concrete social relations that have developed over time.[21] In his stance towards the auction and to Gale, the narrator displays what Don Slater terms the 'hyperawareness' of the postmodern consumer, meaning he is well aware of the capitalist game that is being played with all its cynicism.[22] The narrator oscillates between a critique of a commodity fetishism catering to the diasporic yearning for home and his own desire to return home by means of the magic slippers.

In the light of the fetishization of home and the concomitant reduction of the Other to a consumable sign, homesickness does indeed appear as a sickness in the most negative sense possible. Worshipping home is seen as a pathology that destroys all possibility of intimate social relations because it is implicated in narcissistic fantasies and processes of commodification. The motto of *The Wizard of Oz*, 'there is no place like home,' which is quoted in the story, thus takes on an ambivalent hue, as critics and also Rushdie himself have emphasized: it refers to the longing for home, while implying that this longing can never be fulfilled because home is a fetish that contributes to alienation and hence works against the making of home in the here and now.[23]

While Rushdie's story does not offer a cure for the diagnosed homesickness, there are indications regarding the form such a therapy might take. Here are the narrator's thoughts on the magic slippers:

> They promised to take us *home*, but are metaphors of homeliness comprehensible to them, are abstractions permissible? Are they literalists, or will they permit us to redefine the blessed word? (*AARS*, 93)

The redefinition of home may offer a means for disrupting home's complicity with a specific form of nostalgia. The word 'nostalgia', which combines the Greek word *nostos* ('return home') with *algos*, the word for pain, refers to "a longing for a home that no longer exists or has never existed."[24] Feelings of loss and yearning are hence bound up with suffering from the irreversibility of time as

---

21 Don Slater, *Consumer Culture and Modernity*, 200.

22 On the hyperawareness of the postmodern consumer, cf. Slater, *Consumer Culture and Modernity*, 197. On commodity culture and globalization in Rushdie's short story, see also Deszcz-Tryhubczak, "The Global Bidding for Dorothy Gale's Magical Shoes."

23 Michael Meyer, "Nachwort," 264. For an analysis of *AARS* based on Bhabha's concept of 'third space,' see Thomas Wägenbaur, "'East, West, Home's Best': Homi K. Bhabha's and Salman Rushdie's Passage to 'Third Space'," in *Colonizer and Colonized*, eds. Theo D'Haen, Patricia Krüs (Amsterdam: Rodopi, 2000): 109–122.

24 Svetlana Boym, *The Future of Nostalgia* (New York: Basic Books, 2001): xiii.

one desires "something in the past [that] is no longer accessible."[25] This tempo-ral dimension of nostalgia is foregrounded by the narrator in Rushdie's short story when he claims that the ruby slippers are both "space machines" and "time machines" (*AARS*, 93). The home that the ruby slippers promise to trans-port their owners to is always already situated in the past. The bidders' fixation on a return to a prelapsarian past corresponds with what Svetlana Boym calls "[r]estorative nostalgia."[26] This type of nostalgia views the past as a golden age and and is bent on "the reestablishment of stasis" by resurrecting the myth-ical lost home.[27] While restorative nostalgia does not, Boym explains, under-stand itself as nostalgia but as "truth and tradition," the form of nostalgia she calls "reflective" eschews a restorative conservatism because it conjoins affective memories of home with a critical stance that is attuned to the contradictions and tensions in historical development and collective memories.[28] Rushdie's short story concentrates exclusively on restorative nostalgia, which explains why home appears as nothing else but a fetish in the diasporic imagination. While such a fetishization of home is emphatically rejected, the story leaves the ques-tion unanswered how home could or should be redefined. Such a redefinition of home is offered, however, in Roshi Fernando's book *Homesick*.

Roshi Fernando's *Homesick* (2012): The Multi-Dimensionality of Home

Homesick traces the lives of a closely knit Sri Lankan community in southeast London from the 1970s to post-7/7 Britain. Their lives are told in seventeen inter-connected stories, each of which has a separate title and which weave back and forth in time. In the following, I will first concentrate on the notion of home as a place of origin before discussing home as a social unit and the material dimen-sion of home.

The first story with the programmatic title 'Homesick' introduces the main characters of Fernando's book and its key theme of home. The story is set in the eve of the year 1982 and Victor and his family are preparing for a New Year's party. At first glance, the story seems to introduce the nostalgic ideal of home that Rushdie satirically attacked in his short story. The opening lines fea-

---

25 Andreas Huyssen, "Nostalgia for Ruins," *Grey Room* 23.1 (2006): 6–21, 7.
26 Boym, *The Future of Nostalgia*, 41.
27 Boym, *The Future of Nostalgia*, 49.
28 Boym, *The Future of Nostalgia*, xviii, 49.

ture Victor reminiscing about his childhood in Sri Lanka – home appears as a sugar-coated and feminized place of origin filled with "voices of people long left behind" or deceased so that there is no going back.[29] While this notion of home as the place of one's 'roots' surfaces also in other stories, the book is quick to undermine such a nostalgic view of the family home and Sri Lanka as homeland by emphasizing the presence of violence in home spaces.

The return of what is repressed in idealized images of home gains center stage in the story "The Fluorescent Jacket." The story is about Kumar, who belongs to Victor's extended family and who came to Britain to find employment. His favorite past-time in England is digging up earth because he feels this gives him a connection to the land:

> When he is at the park, digging earth, he feels happy. Earth is earth, whatever its colour. In Sri Lanka, the earth is red and dusty, [...] but here the earth feels heavy and is black [...]. It feels good in his hands, it feels like he holds people in his hands, people from pasts he has no knowledge of. When he dies, he does not want to be swallowed up by this country, to become part of the heavy blackness. He will go back to Sri Lanka, he thinks, to die. To disappear into dust there, that is his ambition. (*H*, 45)

This love of earth, with its associations of 'roots,' is a heavy-handed metaphor for home as a feminized place of origin. The gendered coding of native soil is drastically foregrounded when the earth yields the dead bodies of black and white girls at exactly the moment when Kumar is vividly imagining himself back "home, in the hills" (*H*, 49) of Sri Lanka while he is digging or clearing the ground in an English park for the city council. The surfacing of the corpses links the feminized earth as a signifier of home to violence against female selves. This linkage stages a critique of patriarchal politics of home that is similar to the one articulated in Rushdie's story: it targets the annihilation of the female self entailed in transforming women into embodiments of home/land. Rushdie's narrator admits that he is unable to perceive the 'real' Gail, or rather Gail as an individual, because he has reduced her to a signifier for home. In "The Fluorescent Jacket", the erasure of the female self in the gendering of home/land is not explicitly addressed but suggested through the *motif* of the unearthed female dead bodies. *Homesick* strengthens its feminist critique of patriarchal notions of home/land by foregrounding how home spaces function as sites of oppression for females. Forms of abuse against women and girls in the family home are repeatedly shown throughout Fernando's book. One of the girls, for example, re-

---

29 Roshi Fernando, *Homesick* (London et al.: Bloomsbury, 2012): 2. Further references in the text, abbreviated as "*H*".

mind Kumar of his young cousin Lolly, whom he is sexually abusing while living at her mother's home.

The dismantling of home as a nurturing space is not restricted to the female experience of home in *Homesick*. In abusing Lolly, Kumar is replicating the sexual abuse he himself experienced as a young boy in Sri Lanka when he was sold to a German tourist. The bodies the earth yields while Kumar is nostalgically thinking of his homeland can also be linked to the war crimes against civilians during the Sri Lankan civil war, which is featured in a later story. Against this backdrop, the title of the book *Homesick* does not only refer to the longing to belong ('I am homesick'), but also to the fact that one's alleged 'home' or homeland can literally make you sick: it can leave you scarred, wounded and even dead.

The book as a whole distances itself from defining home as a (feminized) place of origin. Instead, home means 'from-hereness' as Victor insists in the following programmatic statement: " 'We belong *nowhere*,' he says. 'But if we belong anywhere, it is *here*. I have chosen *here*.' He stands. '*We* have chosen *here*' " (*H*, 18). This 'from hereness' is created through family networks and memories. In the last story, the meanwhile aged family members gather together at a funeral and end up singing the popular Sri Lankan song "Ma bale kale," which Victor had played at the beginning when he was fondly remembering his boyhood days in Sri Lanka. The book thus has a circular structure: it stages the cycle of life and returns to Victor's boyhood days. This circular movement can be interpreted as a 'coming home.' Only in this case, the homecoming does not refer to a going back to a previous place, but to the experientiality of 'from hereness,' at least if one focuses on his wife Nandini: "Nandini has no memories of her life with Victor before this room, this house. Here they had all grown up. Here, their life had happened" (*H*, 292). This quality of 'from-hereness' amounts to what Avtar Brah describes as

an image of 'home' as the site of everyday lived experience. [...] It is a discourse of locality, the place where feelings of rootedness ensue from the mundane and the unexpected of daily practice. Home here connotes our networks of family, kin, friends, colleagues and various other 'significant others'. It signifies [...] a community 'imagined' in most part through daily encounter.[30]

While not all portrayed diasporic characters experience such a feeling of 'from hereness' or 'feeling at home,' this specific conceptualization of homeland forms an important intervention in the political discourses on belonging to the

---

30 Brah, *Cartographies of Diaspora*, 4.

nation.[31] In this context it is striking to note the strong correspondences between Fernando's fiction of home and current attempts to redefine *Heimat* as 'from hereness' in ethnology.[32]

Homesick ties the feeling of 'from hereness' or belonging to everyday patterns of family life. In this way, the meaning of home as a social unit is emphasized. Again, the first story of *Homesick* is programmatic for the whole book. What one finds in this opening story is the conceptualization of home as 'being-with-the-Other.'[33] As the New Year's party progresses, Victor becomes befuddled from drink, gets confused, scared and even angry. In this emotional state he starts looking for Nandini: "Nowhere he can find [sic!] home, but if he found Nandini, it would be there, in her, and he would be safe again" (*H*, 16). When he does finally find her, he says "I was homesick for you" (*H*, 18). It is significant to note that Victor says this to Nandini after having insisted on defining home as from-hereness. This foregrounds that Nandini does not allegorically embody Sri Lanka (i. e., a place of origins) for Victor.[34] Instead, 'doing intimacy' is depicted as a form of 'doing home' and hence as a practice that contributes to feelings of belonging in the here and now.

This form of home-as-being-with-the-Other encompasses the same experientiality that was also associated with home in Rushdie's story: a sense of safety, coherence and community. The crucial difference is, however, that 'homesickness' may be cured in Fernando's book because 'home' is created through intimacy with a significant Other. It is the strong focus on intimacy that gives the 'embryonic community' of home its special hue in the novel. Many of the characters are homesick in terms of longing for physical, emotional and/or cognitive intimacy. In this context, *Homesick* is also very much about queering home by portraying gay and lesbian relationships.

---

31 The book intervenes also in other ways by, for example, countering the stereotype of the terrorist as a radical Muslim fundamentalist (see the stories "Mumtaz Chaplin" and "The Terrorist's Foster Grandmother").

32 See, for example, Ullrich Kockel, "Being From and Coming To: Outline of an Ethno-Ecological Framework," in *Radical Human Ecology: Intercultural and Indigenous Approaches*, eds. Lewis Williams, Rose Roberts and Alastair McIntosh (Farnham: Ashgate, 2012): 57–71, 66: "being *from here* is not so much about nationality, ethnicity or religion, but rather about being defined in active relation to a particular place of dwelling, which may even include movement."

33 For a discussion of this notion of home, see Kuang-Ming Wu, "The Other is My Hell; The Other is My Home," *Human Studies* 16.1–2 (1993): 193–202.

34 I will shelve the discussion of Victor's problematic gendered visions for another time. All in all, *Homesick* veers between a deconstruction of patriarchal gender stereotypes and an affirmation of these.

There are many instances in Fernando's book that clearly identify practices of intimacy as a form of 'doing home.' In the story "Honey Skin," for example, an old widow named Dorothy, who is plagued by her lust for young women, reflects on the intimacy she had experienced in her long marriage to Hugo:

> For Hugo, the sex was centred about *her* and her alone. Her body's changes had only increased his desire, as if each pocket of fat or crease or stretch mark were decorative proofs of his infinite love, as if she were a house, which in its subsidence became safer. [...] For Dorothy, sex was an insular game. [...] When he made love to her, he knew she fantasised. Here she lied to him; here, she never told what she really thought of [= making love to a woman; SB]. [...] It was not satisfactory to think – oh, I was a lesbian all along – because she had not been. She had loved Hugo with an intensity and fire that raged and burnt [...]. (*H*, 253–254)

What is striking about this passage is not only that Dorothy's body is a house and arguably a home for Hugo, but that intimacy does not take the form of what Lynn Jamieson terms "disclosing intimacy," meaning that one discloses one's innermost thoughts and feelings to the other. Instead, Fernando's book highlights an array of other practices that create intimacy, for example caring for the other in sickness.[35] There is a lingering sense of the closeness Dorothy experienced with Hugo throughout the story, especially at the end when Dorothy wakes up from a lesbian sex dream with the sound of her own and Hugo's bemused laughter in her ears. This joint laughter points to reciprocal acceptance as a crucial element of the portrayed intimacy. To quote the philosopher Kuang-Ming Wu: "Being at home means that you accept me (as I am), I accept your acceptance of me, and I am born in this reciprocal acceptance."[36]

The conceptualization of 'home' as a relation of intimacy – as something that one does and not just 'has' – follows traditional associations of home with categories that tend to overlap with intimacy, namely the family and privacy. However, this focus on intimacy as a way for the diasporic subject to 'do home' gains added significance in the context of the pronounced racism portrayed in Fernando's book. Such an intimacy entails what Gabriele Griffin de-

---

35 Lynn Jamieson, "Intimacy as a Concept: Explaining Social Change in the Context of Globalisation or Another Form of Ethnocentricism?" *Sociological Research Online* 16.4 (2011): <http://www.socresonline.org.uk/16/4/15.html> (acc. November 28, 2013). In her article, Jamieson emphasizes that "disclosing intimacy is [...] only [one] item in the repertoire of practices of intimacy."
36 Wu, "The Other is My Hell," 194.

scribes as "efforts to inhabit that inalienable but simultaneously culturally alienated space": the non-white body.[37]

As one can see from the description of Dorothy and Hugo's relation, intimacy is linked to the motif of houses in the book. This motif points to the third dimension of home: the materiality of home. What makes *Homesick* such a fascinating read is that this text as a whole presents itself as a house and arguably also as a specific type of home because it features moments of feeling at home on the level of content. The reading of this book as a house is triggered by a metafictional passage in the opening story. Here we are told that "Victor takes another journey around the theatre of his house, imagining the characters who will be there shortly" (*H*, 4). This metafictional analogy invites perceiving *Homesick* itself as a house where the lives of these characters are played out. The motif of the house is emphasized through the frame structure of the book, which can be read metaphorically as the enclosed space a house offers. With this analogical model, *Homesick* inscribes itself in a long tradition of thinking about literary texts in terms of architecture.[38]

The specific form that *Homesick* takes as a house can be seen to express the diasporic subjectivity of its inhabitants. Preethi, Victor's daughter, angrily gives voice to the diasporic dilemma: "here we are, in England, and we're different, and there we are in Sri Lanka, and we're different. Nowhere is home, nowhere! And it makes me *so angry!* I want to feel I *belong*" (*H*, 290). The diasporic subjects portrayed in Fernando's text are both of Sri Lanka and of Britain. This multi-locationality translates on the level of form into the difficulty of categorizing *Homesick* in terms of genre: is it a cycle of short stories or a novel? In keeping with this multi-locationality is the fact that the chronotopos of this house is not restricted to Britain, but includes Sri Lanka. Not only are some of the stories set in Sri Lanka, but a double coding of the temporal frame is introduced right at the beginning of the book. The references to political tensions in Sri Lanka in the opening story "Homesick" endows the new year about to begin with added significance: 1983 is the year in which Sri Lankan civil war broke out. While the action of this first story may be set 'here' in England, the events over 'there' in Sri Lanka are equally present.

In terms of the analogical model, the individual stories of *Homesick* can be seen as the rooms of the house. These rooms are not shut-off rooms, but instead

---

37 Gabriele Griffin, *Contemporary Black and Asian Women Playwrights in Britain* (Cambridge: Cambridge UP, 2011): 81.
38 On the tradition of thinking about literature as a house, see Chiara Briganti and Kathy Mezei, "Literary Spaces," in *The Domestic Space Reader*, eds. Chiara Briganti, Kathy Mezei (Toronto, Buffalo, London: U of Toronto P, 2012): 321–323.

interlinked through leitmotifs and connections between the different protagonists, especially relations of kinship (and this includes foster care). The characters are also connected through friendship or mutual acquaintances. In this way,
communal relations are highlighted. Fernando's staging of a literary house or
home with many rooms inhabited by different, but interconnected people may
be termed a 'communal narrative.' At the same time, the book presents an ambivalent view of community. The Sri Lankan community and the family offer support, but they also exert pressure on the individual to conform to social expectations.

Against this backdrop, the fact that the building blocks of this book appear
as short stories gains added significance. The multiperspectival structure is a
comment on the model of community *Homesick* privileges: it rejects totalizing
notions of community by emphasizing the incommensurability of the individual.[39] The experiential life worlds depicted in each of the stories with their different protagonists often stand in tension to each other. This means that the individual cannot be simply subsumed under a larger collective. Instead, we find the
individual in conflict with a larger collective in many of the stories. A case in
point is, for example, Preethi's brother Rohan, who rigidly suppresses his homosexual leanings because these are not tolerated by his family. In contrast to this
emphasis on social conformity, *Homesick* champions a model of community that
allows for difference, contradictions and tensions.

What is important to note is that the model of community *Homesick* stages
with its self-presentation as a house is *not* coded as a metonymic model for the
nation. The easy slippage between home and homeland rests on a suppression of
incommensurability because each unit is completely subsumed under the next
higher level. The family home is seen as part of the local community as home,
which is in turn subsumed under the nation as home. While home may be situated on different social scales, the movement up the hierarchy of terms does not
correspond to a simple logic of inclusion. Instead, the move from one level to the
next is shaped by intersecting identity categories such as ethnicity, gender, religion and class. In his discussion of the cultural functions of conceptual hierarchies, Albrecht Koschorke describes the complex translation between scales of
inclusion as follows:

---

39 For a full discussion of how the short story cycle may be used to explore tensions between
'commonality and difference' as well as 'separateness and connection,' see Elke D'hoker, "The
Challenges of Community in Rachel Cusk's *Arlington Park*," *Anglistik: International Journal of
English Studies* 26.1 (2015): 13–23.

Not all qualities of the individual are included in the conceptual category local community; there is a rest that resists being subsumed. Conversely, specific characteristics of the individual are produced through his or her identification with a local community. Hence, the subsumption is not only incomplete, but also strongly affects the repertoire of elements that are to be subsumed. And this repeats itself from one level of the hierarchy to the next. [...] Inclusion is a question of power, and the movement from one sphere of inclusion into another takes place within gravitational fields of power.[40]

Homesick offers numerous examples of disruptions between the different scales of home and how these are tied to issues of power. The most drastic example is perhaps the depiction of the Sri Lankan civil war, but stories such as "Nil's Wedding" also undermine smooth transitions between home and homeland. In "Nil's Wedding," a relative of Victor's family called Nil decides to marry her white boyfriend Ian although she "hate[s] so much about him" (*H*, 131). Her decision arguably stems from her fierce wish to belong to a white England.[41] Nil, who had resented wearing saris all her life "because she didn't want people thinking that she was, well, *ethnic*" (*H*, 128), perceives Ian as "a freedom, and a shutting off. He was the groundwork for everything else" (*H*, 125). Her marriage to a member of the white upper-class, whose family look "like a set of Etonesque sixth-for-

---

40 "In den Begriff der lokalen Gemeinschaft gehen nicht alle Eigenschaften der Individuen ein; es bleibt also ein Rest, der sich der Subsumtion nicht unterwirft. Umgekehrt werden andere Eigenschaften erst durch die Zugehörigkeit zur lokalen Gemeinschaft geschaffen oder hervorgetrieben. Die Subsumtion ist also nicht nur unvollständig, sondern greift machtvoll in den Bestand der zu subsumierenden Elemente ein. Und das wiederholt sich von Stufe zu Stufe. [...] Inklusion ist ein Machtfrage, und der Übertritt von einer Inklusionssphäre in eine andere findet in der Gravitation der betreffenden Machtfelder statt" (Albrecht Koschorke, *Wahrheit und Erfindung: Grundzüge einer allgemeinen Erzähltheorie* [Frankfurt a.M.: S. Fischer, 2012]: 178–179, 181, my translation). On the power politics of scales, see also Neil Smith, "Homeless/global: Scaling Places," in *Mapping the Futures: Local Cultures, Global Change*, eds. Jon Bird et al. (London, New York: Routledge, 1993): 87–119, 101: "Scale is an active progenitor of specific social processes. In a literal as much as metaphorical way, scale both *contains* social activity and at the same time provides an already partitioned geography within which social activity *takes place*. [...] It is geographical scale that defines the boundaries and bounds the identities around which control is exerted *and* contested."
41 I speak of 'white England' because Nil is drawn to and has internalized an image of England that smacks of the heritage industry: "Nil walked down the hill she had lived on since she was five. She strolled past Molly-the-widow's house, stopping to peek through the perfect round hole in the fence she had discovered as a teenager, which gave her a small view of the magnificent garden of hollyhocks and delphiniums, fuchsias and honeysuckle. This was beauty, she thought. A glorious England, a place of history" (*H*, 126). On the politics of whiteness in the heritage industry, see Sarah Mary King, *Whiteness in the English Countryside: A Case of the National Trust* [2007] (September 5, 2011), *Durham University, Durham e-Theses Online* <http://etheses.dur.ac.uk/1825/> (acc. November 28, 2013).

mers" (*H*, 123), effectively serves to 'whiten' Nil and hence points to the racial politics that inform processes of inclusion and exclusion: "Nil [...] thought about the house she would move to at the end of this week. She saw [...] the *whiteness* of the walls swallowing her up in their space, taking her into their blankness, *shaping her into something different*" (*H*, 128 [my italics]). In Nil's perception, her inclusion in the white nation requires that she sever her ties of belonging to her non-white family home (cf. *H*, 138). Her feelings of loss on her wedding day as well as her fear of 'being shaped into something different' correspond with Koschorke's description of what happens when moving up the scales of home: the persistence of an irreducible rest that defies subsumption and the 'reconfiguration of the subsumed elements' within a network of power relations.

Conclusion

Cultural ideals of home feature prominently in both Rushdie's short story and Fernando's *Homesick* as both texts associate 'home' with a sense of coherence, safety and community. The question of how such a feeling of home may be achieved in a diasporic context is addressed in both texts, albeit with very different results. As the analysis has shown, a focus on the interplay between key components of home (origins, a social unit, materiality and scale) offers a helpful grid for comparing how the diasporic home is mapped and evaluatively coded in these two texts. Rushdie concentrates on diagnosing how the notion of 'home as a place of origin' is a dangerous fiction steeped in nostalgia and an alienating material culture that invests objects with the false promise of home and wholeness. The idea of wholeness precludes tensions between different scales of home so that the meaning of 'home' may shift smoothly from a microscale (family home) to a macroscale (homeland). A restorative nostalgia together with commodity fetishism forecloses all possibility of experiencing home in the sense of communal bonding within the diasporic space of the present. Due to Rushdie's focus on home as a fetish, the story only offers hints as to how a therapeutic cure for 'homesickness' could be achieved: redefining the blessed word of home.

Fernando seems to take her cue from Rushdie by offering such a redefinition: the emphasis lies on 'doing home' through practices of intimate reciprocity, and homeland is understood in terms of 'from here-ness' and not as a place of origin. These two dimensions of home are closely intertwined because feelings and practices of intimacy or community are arguably a crucial part of home as the 'site of everyday lived experience.' By emphasizing these dimensions of home, *Homesick* rejects a form of nostalgia, "whereby spaces of home are located in the past rather than the present, in imaginative rather than material terms, and as points of imagined authenticity rather than as lived experience."[42] While this rejection of restorative nostalgia is also found in Rushdie's story, *Homesick* moves beyond Rushdie's text by showing how a diasporic home may be created in practice. Fernando hence allows for the possibility of curing homesickness, but she stops short of an idealization of the family home or community. The multiperspectival structure draws attention to how home spaces are shaped by power hierarchies and conflicts over who or what belongs to these spaces. The contested nature of home/land is illustrated by the embittered arguments between the characters over the emplotment of Sri Lankan national identity and political history. The exclusion of homosexuality in the London family home and the Sri Lankan community is but one further example of the tensions and ruptures that mark home spaces. This idea of home as a conflictual space underpins Fernando's engagement with the materiality or rather architecture of the diasporic (literary) home. By exploring the "power geometry" that traverses home spaces, Fernando's text complicates the transition between different scales of home.[43]

The literary investigation of the meanings of diasporic home in Rushdie's and Fernando's stories draws attention to home as a *"spatial imaginary:* [...] home is [...] a place/site, a set of feelings/cultural meanings, and the relations between the two."[44] Literary representations of home arguably shape this spatial imaginary by providing thick descriptions of diasporic homes, offering imaginative access to an individual's experientiality of home (or homelessness) as well as communicating alternative conceptualizations of home that work against restorative nostalgia or notions of homeland predicated on excluding all those deemed as Other. One of the key dimensions of home is the experience of community and concomitant feelings of belonging. If one adopts Gerard Delanty's definition of community as an "open-ended system of communication about belonging,"[45] then both Rushdie's and Fernando's 'fictions of home' constitute important interventions in this ongoing process of communication by rejecting the common equation of home/land with origins, thereby opening up potentialities of belonging in the diasporic space.

---

42 Alison Blunt, *Domicile and Diaspora: Anglo-Indian Women and the Spatial Politics of Home* (Oxford: Blackwell, 2005): 14.
43 Doreen Massey, *Space, Place and Gender* (Cambridge: Polity Press): 149.
44 Blunt and Dowling, *Home*, 2.
45 Gerard Delanty, *Community* (London, New York: Routledge, 2003): 187.

Narratives of Belonging:
(Hi-)stories, Boundaries, Trajectories

Ricarda Wagner

Beyond the Hall: Diasporic Constructions of Home and Belonging in *Beowulf*, *The Wanderer*, and *The Seafarer*

Abstract: This chapter examines three Old English texts, the epic *Beowulf* and the two lyric poems *The Seafarer* and *The Wanderer*, with regard to their notions of 'home,' 'exile,' and 'diaspora.' *Beowulf*, produced by a cultural community that remembered the migration of its ancestors, celebrates legendary heroic exiles in the homelike setting of the mead-hall, but ends in a diaspora. *The Wanderer* and *The Seafarer* present the voices of lonely exiles who are deprived of their halls but on their way to a heavenly home and, as such, are part of a diasporic Christian community. The chapter argues that instead of setting up a dichotomy between Christian and pagan, heroic perspectives, these three texts open a Bhabhaian Third Space that permits the negotiation of earthly existence as a hybrid between being at home and living in diaspora.

Ours is "the age of the displaced person, the refugee," Edward Said writes in his *Reflections on Exile*.[1] While this is undoubtedly true, his statement may be considered equally valid for the time of Antiquity (especially from the perspective of the Israelites) or indeed the Middle Ages, two periods in which large-scale colonialization and evangelization introduced new and conflict-laden power relations. Even though (or perhaps especially because) notions such as 'exile' and 'diaspora' must work differently before the emergence of nation states, contemporary diaspora studies should find so-called premodernity particularly worth examining.

The three texts analyzed in this paper, the epic *Beowulf* and the two lyric poems *The Seafarer* and *The Wanderer*, were all composed in or before the eleventh century. All three were written from a Christian perspective and were intended for a Christian, Anglo-Saxon audience, but are set within a pagan warrior culture whose values and preoccupations are equally prominent. An interpretation that dualistically opposes these two perspectives, as has been previously argued, does not take into account the poetic make-up of the texts beyond their vocabulary. This paper aims to further trace something like 'diasporic poetics' in *Beowulf*, *The Wanderer* and *The Seafarer* by also examining their narrative set-up and fragmented polyphony of voices. It is precisely the concept of 'diaspora' that allows both a heroic, pagan, secular and a Christian perspective to negotiate the human condition. It also makes these texts such an intriguing object for postcolonial study, particularly with regard to Homi K. Bhabha's notion

---

1 Edward Said, "The Mind of Winter: Reflections on Life in Exile," *Harper's* 269.1612 (1984): 49–55, 50.

of 'hybridity.' This paper aims to show that the diverse voices from these texts contribute to a reading of the Anglo-Saxon *conditio humana* as a hybrid between being at home and living in diaspora.

Before turning to the texts, I briefly outline definitions of 'diaspora' drawn from postcolonial studies that I will be relying on. My analysis of *Beowulf, The Wanderer* and *The Seafarer* then focuses on the following questions: Which notion of 'home' do these texts construct? Where and when is 'home' located, and in which relation to it does the displaced person find himself? Which notion of 'diaspora' do these texts sketch? I offer a synthesis of these textual observations and link them to Homi K. Bhabha's notion of 'hybridity' in order to show how these interwoven textual voices contribute to a medieval concept of 'home' and 'diaspora' that is noteworthy.

I shall use the term 'exile' for the displacement of single individuals, and 'diaspora' for the displacement of a group that identifies as a diasporic community. Nico Israel calls this self-defining aspect of diaspora "performativity."[2] The idea of diaspora as a time and place of collective performance is also emphasized by Robin Cohen, who identifies the establishment of cultural memory as an important characteristic of a prototypical diaspora.[3] By remembering a lost place of origin, a diasporic community not only works towards "the maintenance or restoration of a homeland, but its very creation."[4] This creation is achieved by means of shared narratives and retellings or reworkings thereof.

Diaspora appears to be a state of dichotomous oppositions that seem straightforward enough: homeland – hostland, native – foreign, us – them. However, as Homi K. Bhabha argues, cultures in general "are never unitary in themselves, nor simply dualistic in the relation of Self to Other."[5] The reason for this lies in the nature of communication: Whenever two different entities communicate, meaning is not simply ascribed and accepted or rejected in a unilateral way. Rather, discourse requires the two entities to open up and meet in an in-between space that both separates and unites them; Bhabha calls this "the Third Space of enunciation."[6] As a consequence, meaning is "never simply transparent or mim-

---

2 Nico Israel, *Outlandish: Writing between Exile and Diaspora* (Stanford: Stanford UP, 2000): 8.
3 Cf. Robin Cohen, *Global Diasporas: An Introduction* (London, New York: Routledge, 2008): 4.
4 Cohen, *Global Diasporas*, 6. Mayer seconds the view that diasporas are marked by their "Konstruktcharakter," and are not so much about the return home than about a common (hi)story of uprootedness. Cf. Ruth Mayer, "Diaspora," in *Metzler Lexikon Literatur- und Kulturtheorie*, ed. Ansgar Nünning (Stuttgart, Weimar: Metzler, 2008): 128–129.
5 Homi K. Bhabha, *The Location of Culture* (London, New York: Routledge, 1994): 35–36.
6 Bhabha, *Location of Culture*, 37.

etic,"[7] because it does not originate directly from one of the two entities, but is born in the Third Space between them. Critical analysis should thus not focus on multiculturalism or the diversity of cultures (which implies that there are opposing, disjunct subsets, each unitary in itself), but on their "hybridity."[8] Hybrid entities such as (sub-)cultures or even individual selves cannot be absolutely opposed to any Other, because meaning is only created in the Third Space that the two of them share. It is Bhabha's hope that, in focusing on this hybridity, "we may elude the politics of polarity and emerge as the others of our selves."[9] The following analyses of *Beowulf, The Wanderer* and *The Seafarer* examine the Third Space that these texts open up as they negotiate Old English notions of home, exile and diaspora. These analyses shall also provide the basis for a reading that demonstrates how these texts sketch a hybrid self.

While Old English provides a variety of synonyms for 'home' and 'homeland,'[10] the architectural structure central to the idea of belonging in Anglo-Saxon heroic and elegiac texts is the mead-hall, a representative place of gathering and rituals central to the community.[11] It is here that guests are received, councils held, feasts given, and songs sung about heroes both recent and ancient. It is here that social bonds are strengthened as the lord gives out rings and treasures to his favored retainers in return for their successful martial service. The mead-hall is a place shared by the community, while private homes and domestic scenes do not feature in Old English literature;[12] Howe even surmises that the mead-hall "may have functioned as a sort of surrogate home for young, unmarried warriors who shared a homosocial bond."[13] As these young, unmarried warriors are the cast for the heroes of Old English literature, it is hardly sur-

---

7 Bhabha, *Location of Culture*, 36.
8 Bhabha, *Location of Culture*, 38.
9 Bhabha, *Location of Culture*, 39.
10 Cf. the list of terms referring to home-lands, home-buildings and home-people in Anita R. Riedinger, "'Home' in Old English Poetry," *Neuphilologische Mitteilungen* 96 (1995): 51–59, 51–52.
11 Cf. Stephen Pollington, *The Mead Hall: The Feasting Tradition in Anglo-Saxon England* (Hockwold-cum-Wilton: Anglo-Saxon Books, 2003), who considers Old English literature as well as archeological findings to reconstruct the Anglo-Saxon hall culture. He emphasizes that as well as being the "nucleus of the human geography of the area" (100), halls also acted as the "interface between the community and the world at large" (101).
12 One notable exception is a passage from *Maxims I*, a collection of gnomic poetry, in which a Frisian sailor returns to his wife and is treated to domestic comforts. Cf. Nicholas Howe, "Looking for Home in Anglo-Saxon England," in *Home and Homelessness in the Medieval and Renaissance World*, ed. Nicholas Howe (Notre Dame: U of Notre Dame P, 2004): 143–163, 152–153, who discusses this passage in the light of Odysseus's homecoming to Penelope.
13 Howe, "Looking for Home," 144.

prising that the mead-hall as home is a prominent setting or point of reference in many Anglo-Saxon texts.

Appropriately, the main plotline of *Beowulf* starts with such a hall being built. King Hrothgar of the Danes

> heal-reced hātan wolde,
> medo-ærn micel men gewyrcean,
> þonne yldo bearn æfre gefrūnon,
> ond þǣr on innan eall gedǣlan
> geongum ond ealdum, swylc him God sealde
>
> [handed down orders
> for men to work on a great mead-hall
> meant to be a wonder of the world forever;
> it would be his throne-room and there he would dispense
> his God-given goods to young and old].[14]

However, "doom" (*B*, 83) would eventually bring about the end of this "hall of halls" ("heal-ǣrna mǣst" *B*, 78) named Heorot.[15] Its construction and destruction is dealt with in two successive sentences; the image of the newly created home is not allowed to stay. Indeed Heorot comes to be haunted by the man-eating monster Grendel, an exilic creature, *unheimlich* in the literal sense of the word, condemned to wander the wilderness around Heorot as one of the "banished monsters, / Cain's clan" ("fīfel-cynnes [...] Caines cynne" [*B*, 104–107]), whom God had exiled in punishment along with all his offspring. Hrothgar is powerless to defend his people against Grendel's nightly raids of the hall and must wait for the hero Beowulf, who arrives from the neighboring Geatland to kill both Grendel and the monster's mother before departing for home. After several more successful military campaigns, Beowulf himself becomes king of his people, rules for 50 suggestive years, but finds his end as he sets out to fight another monster threatening a mead-hall, a dragon that had burned down

> his sylfes hām,
> bolda sēlest [...],
> gif-stōl Gēata

---

14 Both the Old English text and the translation are taken from the edition by Seamus Heaney, *Beowulf* (London: Faber and Faber, 1999): here 68–72. Further references in the text, abbreviated as "*B*."

15 The Old English verse is "ne wæs hit lenge þā gēn, þæt", i.e., "it was not yet at hand that" disaster would come down upon the hall.

[his own home,
the best of buildings [...],
the throne-room of the Geats] (*B*, 2325–2327)

after a piece of the hoard that he had been guarding was stolen. Beowulf manages to kill the dragon before succumbing to his own wounds.

While the hall is central to the tribal communities of the Danes and the Geats, the text also makes clear that its security is very precarious. After Beowulf's death, his people articulate their worries concerning their future welfare, now that they are leaderless and defenseless against their surrounding enemies. A messenger sent to Beowulf's people to report his death prophesies:

ūs sēceað tō Swēona lēoda,
syððan hīe gefricgeað frēan ūserne
ealdor-lēasne,
[...] nalles eorl wegan
māððum tō gemyndum, nē mægð scȳne
habban on healse hring-weorðunge,
ac sceal geōmor-mōd, golde berēafod,
oft, nalles ǣne, elland tredan

[they will cross our borders
and attack in force when they find out
that Beowulf is dead.
[...] treasure no follower
will wear in his memory, nor lovely woman
link and attach as a torque around her neck –
but often, repeatedly, in the path of exile
they shall walk bereft, bowed under woe] (*B*, 3001–3, 3015–19),

Now that the power relations in the region have shifted, diaspora is imminent. Beowulf's people will be scattered and doomed to walk in "elland," i.e., "a foreign land,"[16] and will have to do so "often" and "repeatedly." Their diaspora is an enduring fate; no next or final home is envisaged. Even if a community seems firmly established in and around its hall, the difference between enjoying security at home and suffering sudden death or imminent displacement depends very much on the actions and fate of one hero. This belief is made explicit by the comments of two warriors: firstly, Hrothgar impresses upon the victorious Beowulf before his homeward departure that he will be his "people's mainstay" ("frōfre

---

16 Heaney does not translate "elland" literally but uses the "path of exile," a metaphor common in other Old English texts, among them *The Wanderer* and *The Seafarer* discussed below.

[...] lēodum þīnum" [*B*, 1707–1708]). Secondly, Wiglaf, Beowulf's companion during his last fight, complains after his leader's death that

Oft sceall eorl monig ānes willan
wrǣc ādrēogan, swā ūs geworden is

[Often when one man follows his own will
many are hurt.[17] This happened to us]. (*B*, 3077–3078)

The hall-builder king Hrothgar can no longer protect his people from a superior enemy but lets the young hero do the fighting. Beowulf, in contrast, when himself an aged king and facing the same difficult situation, confronts the monster on his own and is not only killed but also can no longer guarantee the safety of the Geats after his death. These singular men can establish or maintain a place of home, but its security may well be temporary and is easily shaken if calamity strikes.

In addition to Beowulf's entire people, many more displaced figures feature in the course of the epic. While the main plot of the text concentrates on the hero protecting hall and home, its narrative strand is repeatedly interrupted by excursive stories about warriors and peoples from the past, many of them exiles. Four are particularly noteworthy: the text opens with a reference to the great kings of old, the first of which, Scyld, forebear of the Danes, was a foundling exiled by his people for unspecified reasons and later became an exemplary king. When Beowulf arrives at Heorot, Hrothgar informs him that Beowulf's father Ecgtheow had once come there seeking and receiving shelter and fealty after he was exiled from his own people as the result of a feud. Another feuding hero is the legendary Jute Hengest, exiled in Frisia for a winter resulting in bloodshed, about whom a song is sung during the victory celebration after Grendel's death. The so-called "Last Survivor," another lonely exile wandering the world because his "own people / have been ruined in war" ("Gūð-ðēað fornam [...] lēoda mīnra" [*B*, 2249–2251]), is introduced as the narrator-poet explains the provenance of the dragon's hoard. Displaced persons and the concepts of 'exile' and 'diaspora' abound in *Beowulf* and its micronarratives. The hall/home, which has to be built in a second creation after God's,[18] is separated only by a porous and precarious border from the

---

17 The Old English "wrǣc" may generally mean any sort of "misery" or "suffering," but is also the word for "exile." Cf. the entry in *An Anglo-Saxon Dictionary*, eds. Joseph Bosworth, T. Northcote Toller (Oxford: Oxford UP, 1898): 1269.
18 Cf. Seth Lerer, "'On fagne flor': The Postcolonial *Beowulf*, from Heorot to Heaney," in *Postcolonial Approaches to the European Middle Ages: Translating Cultures*, eds. Ananya Jahanara Kabir, Deanne Williams (Cambridge: Cambridge UP, 2005): 77–102, 87 on the similarity between hall-building Hrothgar and Earth-creating God.

outside, where exile and diaspora reign as the quasi natural state into which the stories' heroes are thrown back with every turn of fate.

These displaced figures populate the cultural memory of both the Danes and the Geats in the text, as well as that of the Anglo-Saxons by and for whom the text was written. As the displacement and reintegration of legendary heroes is sung, narrated and talked about, the hall/home becomes a place for the collective performance and reception of exilic stories. The exiles of these stories do not feature as marginalized figures; rather, they are centralized, assuming the roles of foundational heroes or examples to learn from. Beowulf takes not only treasure and fame away from Heorot, but also "the gift of history"[19] in the form of stories about displaced heroes, often followed by a didactic message. At the very least, the legendary exiled heroes provide a thrilling subject-matter worthy of song. Exile is a time of trial which combines personal hardship with an impressive geographic range, connecting places like Geatland, Daneland, and Frisia to form one extended world which very few of the text's insular Anglo-Saxon listeners would have experienced as such.

This Scandinavian geography of *Beowulf* might well represent the Anglo-Saxon vision of their pagan, continental homeland that they had inhabited before their migration to Britain. Howe has even identified a "migration myth" that can be traced back to the earliest historiographical writings of Bede and Gildas, who imagined the Anglo-Saxons as another Israel crossing the sea in a diasporic exodus to reach their promised land.[20] This myth was unifying; it provided the tribal Anglo-Saxons with one common homeland to trace their origins back to, and with a common time of settlement (Bede establishes the traditional date of 449 AD) as the newly arrived strangers in a strange land. This parallel between the Israelites and the Anglo-Saxons is forced. The Anglo-Saxons arrived as conquerors and could not refer back to any attested, historical injustice done to them that had compelled them to migrate. Nevertheless, the migration myth served as a "diasporic self-fashioning"[21] that worked in favor of social unity, especially "[i]n the absence of the political cohesiveness offered by nationhood."[22]

---

19 Nicholas Howe, *Migration and Mythmaking in Anglo-Saxon England* (New Haven, London: Yale UP, 1989): 155.

20 Cf. Howe, *Migration*, 46 on Gildas and his parallelization of the Anglo-Saxons and the Israelites; 60 on Bede and the Anglo-Saxon as a chosen people; and 78 on the Old English version of *Exodus*, in which the Israelites are portrayed to resemble Anglo-Saxon warriors.

21 This term is borrowed from Israel, *Outlandish*, 16, who in turn adapted it from Stephen Greenblatt in order to relate it to twentieth-century diasporas.

22 Howe, *Migration*, 179.

How, then, does this Anglo-Saxon migration myth allow for a diasporic reading of *Beowulf*? While the exact dating of the text is still disputed and possibly irresolvable,[23] its poet does set up a clear distance between his narrating time and the time narrated: the very first verse sets the events of *Beowulf* "in days gone by" ("in gēar-dagum" [*B*, 1]). There is also a marked difference between the Christian poet and his protagonists, who, as he makes explicit (cf. *B*, 175–183), only have pagan gods to pray to. Strikingly, the text is not concerned with an Anglo-Saxon but with a Geatish hero, possibly chosen to offer "some vision of what the Anglo-Saxons might have become had they not made their exodus,"[24] namely a forcefully displaced people like Beowulf's. The epic, as the traditional genre that makes a nation,[25] provides the Anglo-Saxons with a model for diasporic self-fashioning that establishes the geography of *Beowulf* as a homeland left behind. It is an imagined place created to be both a familiar site (with a cultural memory and shared hoard of stories of legendary, exilic heroes) and an alien, pagan past in which there is little help against the cruelties of fate threatening one's home in the form of feuds and monsters. Beyond the hall, exile and diaspora are always looming.

The voice of such an exile from beyond the hall shapes the lyric poem *The Wanderer*. The speaker, homeless after the death of his lord, possibly ousted due to the change in power and now in search of a new "giver of treasure" ("sinces bryttan," 25),[26] misses exactly those communal experiences of feasting with mead and song that Beowulf and his companions enjoy. In a kenning, a creative linguistic device prominent in Old English poetry that combines two distinct lexemes into one compound, the Wanderer describes himself as "seledreorig" (*W*, 25), literally "hall-sad." Instead of taking comfort in his deserved place in a band of followers serving one lord, he is now "anhaga" (*W*, 1), which Treharne

---

23 Cf. Andy Orchard, *A Critical Companion to* Beowulf (Cambridge: D. S. Brewer, 2003): 5–6, who lists advocates for various datings between the seventh and the eleventh century.
24 Howe, *Migration*, 146.
25 As did the *Aeneid*, the *Shahnama*, and later *The Fairie Queene* or *Paradise Lost*. I use 'nation' here in the sense of Benedict Anderson's "imagined communities," meaning a socially cohesive group that identifies as such and thus has to 'imagine' its union, because no single member could possibly know every other member and survey the totality of the 'nation.' Cf. Benedict Anderson, *Imagined Communities: Reflections on the Origin and Spread of Nationalism* (London: Verso, 2006): 6–7.
26 Quotations from the Old English text and the translations are taken from *Old and Middle English Literature, c. 890 – c. 1450: An Anthology*, ed. Elaine Treharne (Chichester: Blackwell, 2010). Further references in the text, abbreviated as "*W*."

translates as "the solitary man" and Bjork as "the lone-dweller."[27] Etymology, however, suggests that the term is more complex: it is related to "haga," meaning "enclosure," which offers the literal translation "the self-enclosed one" for "anhaga."[28] Among the deprivations of his exile, the Wanderer particularly emphasizes a lack of conversation and company. His exile is a silencing; instead of exchanging thoughts with his peers he now has to "bind fast a heavy heart" ("breostcofan bindað fæste" [*W*, 18]).

The text's concept of home and hall is a longed-for time and place, but displacement, its opposite, is not just evoked as an unspecific future horror, as it is for Beowulf's people, but is described as a semantically concrete experience: the exiled speaker has to endure "the ice-cold sea" ("hrimcealde sæ" [*W*, 4]) with its "binding waves" ("waþema gebind" [*W*, 24]) and "falling frost and snow" ("hreosan hrim ond snaw" [*W*, 48]) on his wanderings. Even his state of mind merges with the exilic, icy landscape in another striking kenning, rendering him "wintersad" ("wintercearig" [*W*, 24]). Not only is his exile a very physical experience, it is also imagined as an unending passageway, rather than a single, stable, albeit unfamiliar place. Displaced "years ago" ("siþþan geara" [*W*, 22]), he is still roaming the "paths of an exile" ("wræclastas" [*W*, 5]).[29] 'Exile' in *The Wanderer* is not conceptualized as a specific, identifiable place – it is not Tomis or Elba – but rather as a thoroughfare whose end point is deferred and to be discovered by the roaming exile the text fittingly calls "the earth-stepper" ("eardstapa" [*W*, 6]).

Even the beginning of the paths of exile cannot truly provide a fixed point of reference, as the desirable images of home that the speaker evokes during his time on the paths of exile are destabilized at the turning point of the text. The Wanderer fast-forwards to the end of time and imagines the world in a post-apocalyptic setting:

Ongietan sceal gleaw hæle   hu gæstlic bið
þonne eall þisse worulde wela   weste stondeð,

---

27 Robert E. Bjork, "Sundor æt rune: The Voluntary Exile of the Wanderer," *Neophilologus* 73 (1989): 119–129, 120.
28 Proposed by Dunning and Bliss, for example, in their 1969 edition of the poem: *The Wanderer*, eds. Thomas P. Dunning, Alan J. Bliss (London: Methuen, 1973): 37–40, and re-examined and supported by Patrick Cook, "Woriað þa winsalo: The Bonds of Exile in 'The Wanderer'," *Neophilologus* 80 (1996): 127–137, 127–128.
29 Cf. Stanley B. Greenfield, "The Formulaic Expression of the Theme of 'Exile' in Anglo-Saxon Poetry," in *Hero and Exile: The Art of Old English Poetry*, ed. George H. Brown (London: Hambledon, 1989): 125–131, 129, who calls "the paths of exile" a "formula" for "the continuative motion of the exile in his state of excommunication" and discusses other instances of the same expression in Old English poetry.

swa nu missenlice   geond þisne middangeard
winde biwaune   weallas stondaþ,
hrime bihrorene,   hryðge þa ederas.
Woriað þa winsalo. [...]
Hwær cwom maþþumgyfa?
Hwær cwom symbla gesetu?   Hwær sindon seledreamas?

[The wise warrior is able to perceive how ghostly it will be
when all this world's wealth stands waste,
just as now in various places throughout this middle-earth
walls stand blown by frost, the buildings snow-swept.
The wine-halls topple. [...]
Where have the treasure-givers gone?
Where has the place of banquets gone? Where are the joys of the hall?] (*W*, 73–78, 92–93)

The instability of his concept of home is revealed in a future time in which the topography associated with home, the wine-hall buildings and places of social gatherings, looks uncannily like the exilic site of his present wanderings: frost, wintry hailstorms and silent loneliness.[30] Home and exile, the two semantic fields that were previously experienced as separate by the Wanderer (one longed for, the other suffered) now merge at an unspecified but inevitable point in the future. Consequently, no home, comfortable though it may feel for the moment, can be permanent in "this dark life" ("þis deorce lif" [*W*, 89]).

In contrast to *Beowulf*, however, which ends disconsolately with the imagined, eventual diaspora of an entire people, *The Wanderer* does offer a solution to the dilemma of longing for a home in the full knowledge that it shall ultimately turn out to be a desolate place of exile as well. While the Wanderer and anyone who "deeply meditates" ("deope geondþenceð" [*W*, 89]) deduces that all earthly existence is "transitory" ("læne" [*W*, 108]), the text concludes with "consolation from the Father in heaven, where for us all security stands" ("frofre to Fæder on heofonum, þær us eal seo fæstnung stondeð" [*W*, 115]). In addition to "security," the Old English "fæstnung" may also translate to "a strong, closed place," one that shall not be eroded by the turning of time and fate. Home in *The Wanderer*, then, is denied its comforting and durable physicality, but it is metaphorized to provide a comprehensible image of heaven. This place at the end of

---

30 Regarding the interesting intertextuality of *The Wanderer* and biblical exilic poetry, especially the exhortations to a captive Israel in Baruch 3:9–37 and Lamentations 3:19–33, cf. Muir's editorial commentary in *The Exeter Anthology of Old English Poetry: An Edition of the Exeter Dean and Chapter MS 3501*, ed. Bernard J. Muir (Exeter: U of Exeter P, 1994) 2:488. The biblical texts also offer the *ubi sunt* motif, destroyed cities, and the hope of salvation in the face of endless wanderings.

the paths of exile, the text maintains, can only be reached by him who, on the basis of his exilic experiences, "is able to know" ("Wat se þe cunnað" [*W*, 29]) and "sat apart in secret meditation" ("gesæt him sundor æt rune" [*W*, 111]).

Interestingly, this wise displaced person is not a single voice on its way home; rather, *The Wanderer* exhibits fragmentation and polyphony on the narratological level. The text is framed by two passages delivered by an impersonal, extradiegetic voice (called "the poet-philosopher" by Muir)[31] offering gnomic wisdom on divine mercy, fate and ethics, while the middle section beginning with "[o]ften, at every dawn, I alone" ("Oft Ic sceolde ana" [*W*, 8]) is spoken by the exiled Wanderer himself. His following graphic descriptions of his wintry exile are interrupted by and interlaced with different mental processes such as dreaming (of the treasure-giving ritual [cf. *W*, 41–45]), remembering (the company of kinsmen [cf. *W*, 51–53]), and imagining (a post-apocalyptic vision of the world laid waste [cf. *W*, 73–105]). However, it is not the displaced Wanderer himself who dreams, remembers, and imagines; instead, he shifts from the exiled "I alone" ("Ic [...] ana" [*W*, 8]) at the beginning of the text to the third person singular of "he who wisely reflects" ("Se [...] wise geþohte" [*W*, 88]). The Wanderer's singular experiences and insights into exile are extended to a generic 'he' who is (also) able to recognize the world's transience and to identify the place that is security and home "for us all" ("us eal" [*W*, 115]).

It is in this moment that exile becomes diaspora. In the end, the one lonely voice of the isolated "anhaga," lamenting his individual fate of displacement after having buried his lord, speaks to a community of fellow exiles; he envisages the shared diaspora of a group that is bound for the same home on the paths of a world whose transient condition is a common truth for both those still happily at home in the mead-hall and those suffering actual, physical exile. Recognizing one's true home and belonging to it, the text argues, cannot be achieved via participation in communal rituals such as treasure-giving and mead-drinking among one's kin, which would be the way of homing oneself for the individual, heroic exile. Rather, it is through solitary introspection that we understand our existence to be not only exilic but diasporic. Thus we realize we belong with a group of fellow exiles en route to an ill-defined, abstract homeland that has come into existence and is attainable for us because we conceptualized it thus. This connection of exile, insight and a diasporic conception of a heavenly home is stated even more explicitly in *The Seafarer*, the third text I consider.

---

31 Cf. Muir, *Exeter Anthology*, 2:487–488, who also offers an account of the arguments put forward by scholarship as regards the different placings of the quotation marks to indicate the speech part of the Wanderer himself.

The Seafarer's image of exile is very similar to the Wanderer's. Without any gnomic introduction to preface his personal lament, the speaker opens the texts with:

> Mæg Ic be me sylfum   soðgied wrecan,
> siþas secgan, [...]
> hu Ic, earmcearig,   iscealdne sæ
> winter wunade   wræccan lastum,
> winemægum bidroren,
> bihongen hrimgicelum;   hægl scurum fleag

> [I can narrate a true story about myself,
> speak of the journey, [...]
> how I, wretched and sad, dwelt a winter
> on the ice-cold sea on the paths of the exile,
> deprived of dear kinsmen,
> hung round with icicles; hail flew in storms] (*SF*, 1–2, 14–17).[32]

It is not entirely clear why this speaker had to flee into exile, but his concept of home, complete with "mead-drinking" ("medodrince" [*SF*, 22]) and "the joy of worldly things" ("worulde hyht" [*SF*, 45]), familiar by now after the analysis of *Beowulf* and *The Wanderer*, suggests that the Seafarer, too, is a displaced warrior beyond the hall. He imagines a generic Other, enjoying all the comforts of home, as opposed to his own exilic self at sea, suffering hardships.[33] The difference between the two is one of personal well-being, but, interestingly, also one of knowledge: "The man who lives most happily / on land does not know this" ("Þæt se mon ne wat / þe him on foldan fægrost limpeð" [*SF*, 12–13]) and "[t]his the warrior does not know, / the man blessed with luxury" ("Þæt se beorn ne wat, / esteadig secg, hwæt þa sume dreogað" [*SF*, 55–56]), the exiled speaker maintains for his counterpart. But what actually is it that the warrior at home does not

---

32 Quotations from the Old English and the translation are taken from *Old and Middle English Literature, c. 890 – c. 1450: An Anthology*, ed. Elaine Treharne (Chichester: Blackwell, 2010). Further references in the text abbreviated as "*SF*".

33 Earlier scholarship has hotly debated the question of whether *The Seafarer* is a monologue of one voice (Whitelock), or a dialogue of two voices in the first person, one from exile and another from pilgrimage (Stanley). However, I will not be using any assumed intertextual links to Horace (Osborn) or the notion of volition in other Old English texts (Greenfield) in order to resolve the issue, but aim to work with the grammatical markers of the text that distinguish the "I" from the "he" without insisting that either of these speech parts must be consistent, i.e., the I of the end may well know more than the I of the first verse because it has been interwoven by the he. Cf. Marijane Osborn, "Venturing upon Deep Waters in *The Seafarer*," *Neuphilologische Mitteilungen* 79 (1978): 1–6 for a discussion of the different positions and further references.

know? First and obviously, the Seafarer refers to the harsh, physical realities of displacement that cannot possibly be imagined unless they are experienced. In addition to this, however, exile brings with it another, deeper knowledge, an insight that comes from traveling both physically and mentally:

> Forþon nu min hyge hweorfeð   ofer hreþerlocan,
> min modsefa   mid mereflode
> ofer hwæles eþel   hweorfeð wide
>
> [now my spirit roams beyond the enclosure of the heart,
> my thought of mind, along with the sea-flood,
> travels widely over the whale's haunt]. (*SF,* 58–60)

What his wandering spirit perceives in its survey of the world is transience. Earthly happiness and secular treasures are ephemeral, and what had been the Wanderer's "dark life" becomes the Seafarer's "dead life" ("deade lif" [*SF,* 65]). The latter identifies the terrible point in time at which one's splendid place of home comes to resemble a desolate place of exile not with a remote, post-apocalyptic future (where the Wanderer had located it), but characterizes this as the state of the present. The desirable point of reference for the exile is not the present at home, but the past. "The days are gone" ("Dagas sind gewitene" [*SF,* 80]) when heroic men had lived in the glory of their feats and rewards. Those who live today are subject to a nothingness, a withering (cf. *SF,* 89) that has already begun and is an ontological state of the world everywhere, not a situational impression of one displaced man roaming unfamiliar lands. Be we exiled or at home, the life we live, paradoxically, is always already dead.

The Seafarer's solution to this disheartening insight into the present state of the world is, to borrow Homi K. Bhabha's phrase, a "gesture to the beyond."[34] At the end of the text, the speaker addresses his audience with hortatives:

> Uton we hycgan   hwær we ham agen,
> ond þonne geþencan   hu we þider cumen;
> ond we þonne eac tilien,   þæt we to moten
> in þa ecan   eadignesse,
>
> [Let us consider where we might have a home,
> and then reflect upon how we could come there
> and then we may also strive so that we should come there
> into that eternal blessedness] (*SF,* 117–120)

---

34 Bhabha, *Location of Culture,* 4; for Bhabha, it is the terms "postmodernity," "postcoloniality," and "postfeminism" that gesture to a beyond.

The text has moved from the "me sylfum" in the first verse to the "we" in this final passage.[35] The exile the Seafarer suffers on the wintry waves is not his fate alone. With our concept of home being no more than a transitory illusion, as the text maintains, we all live in an existential diaspora. Our human condition is one of displacement, which holds true both for the exiled speaker and the settled Other he invokes, as they are both still far from "that eternal blessedness," their heavenly home with God. Homing oneself, then, is an intellectual activity of "the mind's desire" ("modes lust" [*SF*, 36]) and the roaming spirit (cf. *SF*, 36–38) in meditation, which allows man in his present displaced state to "touch the future on its hither side," to adapt from Bhabha again.[36] This transcendental home has to be actively sought in the present, and the Seafarer makes more than one reference to an urging (cf. *SF*, 36 and *SF*, 50) that drives him to undertake his diasporic journey which was not, or at least not only, prompted by political necessity. His longing does not direct him back to the hall or the kin group he belongs to, but onwards into affirmative diaspora. Homing himself via the communal practices of the mead-hall is what the unwise exile would do, which would not lead him to a truly secure home in the end. Rather, the text concludes, we must understand ourselves as members of a diasporic community, each on his own, but all bound for the same homeland. In *The Seafarer*, as in *The Wanderer*, the paths of exile, paradoxically, are the way home.

I proceed to synthesize the observations on 'exile,' 'home' and 'diaspora' from the three texts and offer a concluding reading of *Beowulf*, *The Wanderer* and *The Seafarer* in light of Bhabha's 'hybridity.' With regard to notions of home and belonging, two major differences separate *Beowulf* from *The Wanderer* and *The Seafarer*. Firstly, the texts deal very differently with 'belonging' as a fluctuating feeling of allegiance and self-ascription to a group on the one hand, and 'home' as an unchanging, stable point of reference on the other. In *Beowulf*, belonging (to one's lord and kin in the mead-hall) is possible, but having a secure home is not, as it is constantly threatened by monsters or warring neighbors. Homing oneself and others is possible via the established practices of military fealty, treasure-giving, and the performance of songs in the (Geatish or Anglo-

---

35 For an analysis of all instances of the first person "Ic" and "sylf" in the first half of the text and their absence in the second half, cf. Hugh Magennis, "The Solitary Journey: Aloneness and Community in *The Seafarer*," in *Text, Image, Interpretations: Studies in Anglo-Saxon Literature and its Insular Context in Honour of Éamonn Ó Carrigáin*, eds. Alastair Minnis, Jane Roberts (Turnhout: Brepols, 2007): 303–318, 307–308. Magennis also notes an interesting intertextual link to Old English homiletic texts, whose concluding section characteristically also begins with the exhortative "uton," "let us" (Magennis, "Solitary Journey," 313–316).
36 Bhabha, *Location of Culture*, 7, when discussing postcoloniality as a "revisionary time."

Saxon) hall, but this homing is always temporary, as fate may harshly repay the efforts of the one hero on whom the safety of the hall depends.

In contrast, in *The Wanderer* and *The Seafarer*, it is belonging that is impossible: The knowing exile must be "anhaga" or "anfloga" ("the solitary flier" [*SF*, 62]) and ought not to attach himself to a specific place; to become "seledreorig" is one understandable reaction to being beyond the hall, but reflection teaches that habitations, too, topple, and that the worldly life celebrated in the hall is always already dead. While the notion of belonging is negated in the end, the idea of home is emphatically affirmed by both texts. Reaching a timeless "fæstnung" is possible for everyone who "wisely meditates," and contemplative solitude is not at all a hindrance to homing oneself. The exilic state of being one's own location and the introspection that results enable a metaphorical, intellectual way of homing oneself in the beyond.

The second difference between *Beowulf* on the one hand, and *The Wanderer* and *The Seafarer* on the other hand concerns the position of the narrator(s) with regard to exile and homeland. In *Beowulf* and all its micronarratives, the hall/home is the sphere in which the action takes place or from where it originates.[37] All the instances of heroic exile in the text are performed at home in the mead-hall. *Beowulf* is a text *about* exile; the fate of individual displaced heroes can be sung about, their stories can be presented as a complete narrative unit. Diaspora, however, is the unspeakable horror for the pagan heroes of *Beowulf*, a chaotic, aimless and open-ended scattering not of one heroic figure, but of a multitude; its occurrence after Beowulf's death dissolves the text, and final closure is awarded only to the one hero ceremoniously buried.

In *The Wanderer* and *The Seafarer*, in contrast, a diaspora is both imagined and spoken about. Exile is desirable because it is the time and place of insight into the true *conditio humana*. The two texts present voices not *about*, but directly *from* exile. The two displaced persons speaking are not identified by their legendary names from Germanic cultural memory, but rather by the generalizing and almost Homeric epithets of "earth-stepper" and "lone-flier." 'Home' for them is not a sphere of action but merely one of memory, while the experiencing 'I' portrays its own state of exile in the semantically concrete terms of a wintry wasteland. The imagined diaspora that we all find ourselves in is not the catastrophic end point of the texts, but rather the beginning of a new endeavor that starts with "Let us ponder."

---

37 Beowulf and Grendel fight on the floor of Heorot and nearly destroy it, and then Beowulf triumphantly adorns the hall with the trophy of Grendel's arm, turning the home into a battle monument of the survivors. He goes on to fight Grendel's mother and the dragon not actually in a hall, but in order to protect one.

Beowulf too, however, can be read as a diasporic construction, if one considers that it was written for and by a people that textually fixed an image of its ancestral, continental homeland. The images and settings of the texts do not merely maintain the vision of this homeland, but, in accordance with Cohen's features of a diaspora, are responsible for its very creation. There could never have been only one geographical point of reference that was 'home' to all the different Anglo-Saxon tribal groups that migrated, which explains the shifted geography in *Beowulf*; only a substrate of the text – communal life in the hall, the pagan ethic code of heroism, the micro-stories of famously named heroes of old – is 'home.' This textual creation of a shared concept of 'home' aids group identity formation as it becomes part of the self-definition of a migrated Christian people.

Interestingly, however, in contrast to other diasporic writing, the Anglo-Saxon *Beowulf*, with its author(s) and audience very much at home and settled, does not express an explicit longing for a return to that imagined pagan 'homeland' long left behind. Nevertheless, there remains a fascination with it, and the text bears witness to the effort of how to make sense of a past that was very different from one's present, be it religiously, geographically or politically.[38] It is especially the exiles of legendary status who remain part of the Anglo-Saxon cultural memory and who have a place in their hall/home, if 'only' in songs. We, as a self-fashioned diasporic people, the text suggests, 'are' their experiences; they were once scattered and, drawing on the agricultural connotation of 'diaspora,' are now engrained in what we at home cultivate as our identity.

The Wanderer and *The Seafarer*, in contrast, argue that the very concept of home needs to be destabilized if one is to correctly understand the nature of being. The two texts testify to "the migrant's double vision"[39] of being at home (in the past and possibly again in the future) and of being displaced (in the present), with the addition that both the Wanderer and the Seafarer deconstruct the former. They present their exile as an insightful experience that has enabled them to perceive any appearance of being at home in the world as an actual, existential diaspora. Their double visions are also represented narratologically in the polyphony of both texts: *The Seafarer* first sets up an opposition between the exilic, knowing 'I' and the ignorant 'he' at home, but concludes with a diasporic 'we' that includes them both. The same shift from a single, displaced 'I' to a more representative, heaven/home-bound 'he, who' occurs in *The Wanderer*. In

---

38 Despite the controversial dating of the composition, Howe finds it plausible that the *Beowulf* poet was writing "during the long and difficult transition from tribe to nation" (Howe, *Migration*, 178).

39 Bhabha, *Location of Culture*, 5, where he discusses Salman Rushdie's *The Satanic Verses*.

contrast to the legendary and very unique exilic heroes in *Beowulf*, on whose success the safety of the hall/home ultimately depends, both the Wanderer and the Seafarer, speaking of their exile, are an Everyman. Their narratological shift is generalizing; potentially, heaven/home may be reached by all those who meditate on and about the way there. The medieval diaspora in *The Wanderer* and *The Seafarer*, then, is opposed to Nico Israel's modern definition of the term with regard to one aspect: he holds that in contrast to exile, which is "the subject's melancholic refusal or inability to repudiate his or her geographico-cultural 'roots'," diaspora is responsible for "obviating the subject."[40] The Wanderer and the Seafarer, however, maintain that even for a member of a universal, diasporic group, the responsibility for homing oneself in the beyond still lies with the individual "me sylfum."

Furthermore, both *The Wanderer* and *The Seafarer* fit Cohen's notion of a diaspora that constructs rather than merely remembers a homeland. Curiously, while the secular hall/home is awarded much semantic detail, heaven/home is never defined or described more elaborately.[41] A transcendental home is created simply by calling it thus. This positing of a heavenly homeland and of a universal diasporic state shared by all Christians is advantageous for both the home-bound individual, who like the roaming, meditative Seafarer is able to expand his horizons literally and figuratively, and for the group of displaced exiles as a whole, whose shared identity is contoured by their common reference to their scattered existence.[42] Not only but particularly in these two texts, then, Christianity has bought its cohesive self-fashioning at the price of a diasporic understanding of itself. But even though they offer an absolute, transcendent answer to the destabilized concept of a hall/home, *The Wanderer* and *The Seafarer* still speak elegiacally and beautifully of the latter. The texts could have put forward their solution of a heavenly home as a straightforward and exclusive one; instead, their non-linear and polyphonic composition, which includes fond memories and dreams as well as terrifying eschatological visions of the ruined hall/home, mirrors the progress of the individual Christian to arrive at the same paradoxical conclusion that "fæstnung" is only to be found beyond the

---

40 Israel, *Outlandish*, 18.

41 Cf. Howe, "Looking for Home," 150, who finds the same lack of detail for the portrayal of heaven/home in *The Dream of the Rood*. He also notes Ezra Pound's elimination of the concluding passage on heaven from his translation of *The Seafarer*, because he felt it was a corrupting addition of a later, Christian poet.

42 For a prototypical diaspora, Cohen lists similar gains among "the positive virtues of retaining a diasporic identity," namely creativity, solidarity and transnational bonds (Cohen, *Global Diasporas*, 7).

hall.[43] Homing oneself in the beyond is an intellectual activity, an interpretation of oneself and the world to which many, sometimes conflicting voices contribute.

How, then, are the diasporic constructions of these three texts indicative of a Bhabhaian hybridity? All three texts present a diasporic self-fashioning from a Christian perspective that establishes three points of reference as Others for its dialogues on the notions of 'exile,' 'home,' 'belonging' and 'diaspora': in *Beowulf*, this reference point is the pagan, heroic past the Anglo-Saxons imagined for themselves. The Wanderer turns to "this dark life" in the future, while the Seafarer examines the present "dead life" as the Other. As a secular perspective focusing on the hall/home meets a Christian view that looks to the beyond, a Third Space opens up for the negotiation of what it means to live in exile and diaspora. The two sides cannot, then, be absolutely opposed and do not merely displace each other, as has been argued;[44] they testify not to a dualistic, but rather to a hybrid state in which the one (being at home in the present) always already contains the other (living in diaspora).

This Third Space that allows these texts to negotiate hybridity thrives on poetic ambiguity. The dialogue of the pagan, heroic and Christian perspectives does not result in a clear statement; *The Wanderer* and *The Seafarer*, for example, do not merely argue that one conception of 'home' and 'belonging' now has to make way for the other that annihilates its predecessor. This reading neglects to address the fact that these texts do not progress in a narratologically linear way but consist of fragmented pieces spoken by different voices from the hall and beyond, which produce meaning only in the communicative space between them. The message about home, diaspora and the human condition cannot be straight-

---

43 The idea of 'being with God' as 'being at home' is biblical (cf. Psalm 91:9: "tu enim es Domine spes mea Excelsum posuisti habitaculum tuum"), as is the concept of the heavenly afterlife as an eternal home (cf. Eccl. 12:5: "ibit homo in domum aeternitatis suae"). Medieval theologians take up these images and envisage heaven not only as a place of dwelling, but also as a homeland in itself. The twelve-century monk Bernard of Cluny in his poem *De Contemptu Mundi*, for example, imagines life as a journey that in the end has to cede to this heavenly homeland: "tunc patriae via [... c]edet" (I.187–189, quoted from the edition by Ronald E. Pepin, *Scorn for the World: Bernard of Cluny's* De Contemptu Mundi [East Lansing: Colleagues, 1991]). Cf. Ronald E. Pepin, "Heaven in Bernard of Cluny's *De Contemptu Mundi*," in *Imagining Heaven in the Middle Ages: A Book of Essays*, eds. Jan Swango Emerson, Hugh Feiss (New York, London: Garland, 2000): 101–117, for Bernard's conception of heaven, and Colleen McDannell and Bernhard Lang, *Heaven: A History* (New Haven, London: Yale UP, 1988): 264–273, for a discussion of the Victorian idea of heaven as a home complete with domestic detail.
44 Cf. Gwendolyn Morgan, "Essential Loss: Christianity and Alienation in the Anglo-Saxon Elegies," *In geardagum* 11 (1990): 15–33. She interprets the "destruction of the Germanic social fabric by Christianity" (15) as a process of succession gone bad because "Christianity is directly opposed to Anglo-Saxon social values" (26).

forward. Rather, homing is an intellectual endeavor for which one must listen to the *scop* performing in the halls of *Beowulf* as well as to the roaming "anhaga" and the "anfloga," and then work towards one's own interpretation. As they examine the past, the future and even the present with regard to 'home' and 'not home' and invite us to imagine, reflect, meditate, and co-negotiate, these voices transform our existence in the now "into an expanded and ex-centric site of experience and empowerment,"[45] which allows their medieval audiences and modern readers to negotiate their homelike and exilic hybridity in dialogue with the texts.

This performance is aided by the metaphoric quality of the Third Space. In order for the worldly, familiar but temporary hall/home and the otherworldly, unfamiliar but eternal heaven/hall to meet, abstraction to a *tertium comparationis* is needed. "So, homeland had become a homing desire and soon home itself became transmuted into an essentially placeless, though admittedly lyrical, space," Cohen writes of postmodern diasporic communities that come to terms with impossibility of their return,[46] which also holds true for the Christian (re-)interpretation: 'home' is turned into a metaphor for 'heavenly place in the afterlife,' which itself may then be left undefined and semantically void without losing evocative force. Using the same Old English words to refer to both homes "is to suggest the mysterious ways in which the earthly home is the necessary precondition to the heavenly and, as such, is incomplete by itself."[47] Indeed, it is as hybrid as any metaphor. Furthermore, any metaphor is always a construction, both artful and artificial, and the positing of heaven as home is as contrived as the human diasporic condition that must result. We, as the texts' audience, medieval or modern, need to understand our notions of 'exile,' 'home,' 'belonging' and 'diaspora' to be constructed, because this insight gives us the choice and the freedom to negotiate these terms instead of living in a reductively dualistic state. We – as diasporic beings – are hybrids, of heaven and the earth, at home in and belonging to both and neither.

---

45 Bhabha, *Location of Culture*, 4. This, he claims, is the role of postmodernity and postcoloniality, terms whose prefixes should not merely indicate a temporal succession to the past, but should work to reform the present.
46 Cohen, *Global Diasporas*, 9–10.
47 Howe, "Looking for Home," 149.

Vered Weiss

(Non)Autochthonous Origins and the Question of Home and Exile in Nineteenth- to Mid-Twentieth-Century English and Hebrew Literature

Abstract: From the end of the nineteenth to the mid-twentieth century, as the modern Jewish-Is-raeli nation was being formed, it required literary means to (re)construct individual and collec-tive identities. While these new identities were being (re)constructed, British identity was sub-jected to alterations and reconfigurations as the British Empire was moving from its peak to its decline. The reconsideration of both identities was based upon the relationship to land, home and exile. This paper outlines similarities in the representation of questions of identity, which are inherently intertwined with concepts of land in Mary Wollstonecraft Shelley's *Frank-enstein; Or, The Modern Prometheus* (England, 1818), Charlotte Brontë's *Jane Eyre* (England, 1847), Bram Stoker's *Dracula* (England, 1897), Daphne du Maurier's *Rebecca* (England, 1938); and *The Golem and the Wondrous Deeds of the Maharal of Prague* by Yudl Rosenberg (Poland, 1909), "Mishael" by Y. D. Berkowitz (Poland, 1910), "Avi Hashor" [Father of the Ox] (Palestine, 1945), "Tehila" (Israel, 1950), and "Ad Hennah" [Thus Far] (Israel, 1952) by Shmuel Yosef Agnon, and *Khirbet Khizeh* by S. Yizhar (Israel, 1949).

One of the most striking connections between nineteenth- to mid-twentieth-cen-tury English and Hebrew literature is the preoccupation with questions of iden-tity, and in particular with the problem of origins in relation to land.[1] As the Brit-ish were engaged with and later relinquished the imperial enterprise, they needed to reconsider their relationship to the land. In a similar manner, though from the opposite direction, the Jews too needed to reevaluate their connection to the land as they embarked upon the colonization, or mass settlement,[2] of Pal-

---

1 This essay is a part of a larger project, which compares Hebrew and English literature from the nineteenth to the mid-twentieth century in relation to states of sovereignty.
2 Both 'colonization' and 'settlement' connote the action of people moving from one place to another in order to utilize additional resources; the difference is that colonization is done under the presumption of the authority of a sovereign nation-state, and settlement is not neces-sarily conducted within such national context. Most of the Jews who came to Palestine during the massive waves of immigration of the nineteenth century were encouraged by the Zionist or-ganization to immigrate with the full intention to appropriate the land in order to establish a sovereign nation state. Throughout the following analysis I will refer to Zionist colonization and settlement in the context of the Zionist movement's conceptualizations of its credo. Specif-ically, this paper refers to Zionism as a "settler colonial" movement within the distinction be-tween "colonialism" and "settler colonialism" in relation to the situation in Palestine-Israel (S. Ilan Troen, *Imagining Zion: Dreams, Designs, and Realities in a Century of Jewish Settlement*

estine in the latter half of the nineteenth century.[3] The literature of the two cultures reflects, and contributes to, the shaping of these antithetical processes in relation to the land.[4]

This paper outlines similarities in the representation of questions of identity, which are inherently intertwined with concepts of land in Mary Wollstonecraft Shelley's *Frankenstein; Or, The Modern Prometheus*, Charlotte Brontë's *Jane Eyre*, Bram Stoker's *Dracula*, Daphne du Maurier's *Rebecca*; and *The Golem and the Wondrous Deeds of the Maharal of Prague* by Yodel Rosenberg, "Mishael" by Y. D. Berkowitz, "Avi Hashor" [Father of the Ox], "Tehila", and "Ad Hennah" [Thus Far] by Shmuel Yosef Agnon, and *Khirbet Khizeh* by S. Yizhar.[5] These texts

---

[New Haven: Yale UP, 2003]; Lorenzo Veracini, "The Other Shift: Settler Colonialism, Israel, and the Occupation," *Journal of Palestine Studies* 42.2 [2013]: 26–42, 27).

3 Although there was a continuity of Jewish presence in Palestine, primarily in Jerusalem and Zfat, the modern settlement, or *yishuv*, commenced in 1881. The first wave of Jewish immigration (1881–1904) was the result of the Zionist enterprise and included Jews from various places. Although many of the immigrants had social and political reasons to immigrate, "the return to Zion played an important role in immigration to Palestine, [and] in the creation of settler colonies" (Amir Ben-Porat, "Immigration, Proletarianization, and Deproletarianization: A Case Study of the Jewish Working Class in Palestine, 1882–1914," *Theory and Society* 20.2 [1991]: 233–258, 235). Once the new immigrants arrived, there were tensions between the 'old yishuv' and 'new yishuv', which reflected the Zionist wish to disassociate the desired image of the 'new Jew' from the rejected figure of the 'old Jew' (Yehoshua Kaniel, "The Terms 'Old Yishuv' and 'New Yishuv' in the Eyes of the Generation (1882–1914) and in the Eyes of History," *Cathedra* 6 [1977]: 3–19, 3–4).

4 Modern Jewish national identity can be perceived either as a singular phenomenon or as a part of the European post-French Revolution national revival (Anthony Smith, "The Formation of National Identity," in *Identity: Essays Based on Herbert Spencer Lectures Given in the University of Oxford*, ed. Henry Harris [Oxford: Oxford UP, 1995]: 129–153, 136–141). Additionally, modern Jewish national identity can be perceived as the product of an ethno-religious diaspora nationalism, which relies on ancient myths even as it reconfigures these narratives in order to (re)create a new identity (cf. Smith, "The Formation of National Identity," 5–9).

5 Mary Wollstonecraft Shelley, *Frankenstein: Or, the Modern Prometheus* [1818] (Berkshire: Penguin Popular Classics, 1994), further references in the text, abbreviated as "*F*"; Charlotte Brontë, *Jane Eyre* [1847] (New York: Norton, 2001); further references in the text, abbreviated as "*JE*"; Bram Stoker, *Dracula* [1898] (London: Penguin, 1994); Daphne Du Maurier, *Rebecca* [1938] (London: Virago, 2003); Yudl Rosenberg, *The Golem and the Wondrous Deeds of the Maharal of Prague* [1909], trans. and ed. Curt Levinat (New Haven: Yale UP, 2007); Yitzhak Dov Berkowitz, "Mishael," in *Sipurim Nivcharim* [Selected Stories] (Tel Aviv: Dvir P, 1926), further references in the text, abbreviated as "M"; Shmuel Yosef Agnon, "Avi Hashor," [1945] in *Ad Hennah* vol. 7 (Tel-Aviv: Schocken, 1977), further references in the text, abbreviated as "AvH"; Shmuel Yosef Agnon, "Tehila," [1950] in *Ad Hennah*, vol. 7 (Tel-Aviv: Schocken, 1977), further references in the texts, abbreviated as "T"; Shmuel Yosef Agnon, "Ad Hennah," [1952] in *Ad Hennah*,

were selected because they are canonical works of literature that exemplify and illustrate similarities in the explorations of identity in relation to the questions of home and exile, and (non)autochthonous origins.[6] Moreover, these texts were chosen because they demonstrate an inverted connection between Hebrew and English literature of the time. The texts in English appeared subversive while in fact they supported and substantiated conventions, such as moral rights to states of sovereignty, and the texts in Hebrew seemed to endorse conventional notions while subverting cultural norms.[7] While the texts in English were first rejected and only later incorporated into the canon, the texts in Hebrew were first embraced and later severely scrutinized.[8] This opposed process with regard

---

vol. 7 (Tel-Aviv: Schocken, 1977), further references in the texts, abbreviated as "AH"; S. Yizhar, *Khirbet Khizeh* [1949] in *Arbaa Sipurim* [Four Stories] (Tel Aviv: Hakibbutz Hameuchad, 1966).
6 Literary canons "represent specific cultures or social groups" (E. Dean Kolbas, *Critical Theory and the Literary Canon* [Boulder: Westview P, 2001]: 1). Canonical texts reflect their producing societies' social values and political concerns, as well as aesthetic preferences at the time of their canonization.
7 For instance, referring to *Dracula*, Ken Gelder notes that "a veritable 'academic industry' has built itself around this novel, growing exponentially in recent years and, in effect, canonizing a popular novel which might otherwise have been dismissed as merely 'sensationalist' " (Ken Gelder, *Reading the Vampire* [Routledge: London, 1994], 65). Conversely, even though *Khirbet Khizeh* appears to vehemently undermine the Zionist conquest of the land, it was incorporated into the Hebrew canon upon its publication, and only later questions regarding it rose. In 1964, *Khirbet Khizeh* was included in the Israeli high-school final exams, but in 1978, a heated public debate erupted after the film version of *Khirbet Khizeh* was broadcast on Israeli national television. Anita Shapira suggests that the 1978 debate did not produce a resolution of the issues; rather, the internal debate within Israeli society regarding the remembrance and future of the question of expulsion had increased (Anita Shapira, "Khirbet Khizah – Between Remembrance and Forgetting," *Mekhrim Be'sifrut Ivrit* 5.1 [2002]: 45–97, 93). Also, even while Agnon is renowned as the national author of the Israeli nation (Gershon Shaked, *Agnon – A Writer With a Thousand Faces* [Israel: Hakibbutz Hameuchad, 1989]: 6–7), Arye Nave reveals heretical trends in Tehila's conduct, such as seeking death in order to reunite with her lover, and the absence of God's name from the last part of the story, which support the suggestion that Tehila is, in fact, rebelling against God (Arye Nave, "Tehila – Ha'moredet Hakdosha" [Tehila – The Holy Rebel]," *Bamikhlala* 9 [1997]: 3–37, 14).
8 The texts in English are all Gothic, and were therefore first rejected and only later incorporated into the British canon. There are a couple of aspects of the Gothic that are pertinent for the following examination: First, the Gothic is considered a subversive genre, which explores social norms (Maggie Kilgour, *The Rise of the Gothic Novel* [London; New York: Routledge, 1995]: 73). The term Gothic, relating to genre or mode of writing, was transferred from architecture to political and literary discourses, and was initially attributed as a pejorative term to politics and novels that appeared to subvert in some manner the prevailing social order and its norms (Angela Wright, *Gothic Fiction: A Reader's Guide to Essential Criticism* [New York: Palgrave Macmillan, 2007]: 1–2). As a literary genre, the Gothic utilizes the setting in order to explore themes

to literary canonization operates in conjunction to the oppositional political processes the British and Jewish nations underwent during the end of the nineteenth and up to the mid twentieth century.

The various characters' relationship with the land commences with the seemingly simple question of origins, of whether or not they are from this land. The quest for a sense of belonging – the feeling that you belong to the land and vice versa – requires first the assertion or refutation of the autochthonous connection to the land. The term *autochthonous*, like the largely synonymous *indigenous*, is highly charged in the context of the study of nationalism as well as in political discourse.[9] Even though both terms have been exhausted in sociological and legal discourses, and have elicited a large body of academic debate, they cannot be avoided in the following discussion, not least because the concepts they articulate are historically contingent. I have chosen the term autochthonous because the following discussion focuses primarily on the connection between identities and the land, the soil itself. "Autochthony posits a com-

---

and propel plot: "The buildings are as important as the protagonists" (Wright, *Gothic Fiction*, 36). Second, the Gothic has been linked with the colonial enterprise and its critique, social and racial anxieties, as well as fears from the encounter with the Other that was colonized (Chris Baldick, *In Frankenstein's Shadow: Myth, Monstrosity, and Nineteenth Century Writing* [New York et al.: Oxford UP, 1987]: 1; Andrew Smith and William Hughes, *Empire and the Gothic: The Politics of Genre* [New York: Palgrave McMillian, 2003]: 1–4; John Bugg, "'Master of their Language': Education and Exile in Mary Shelley's *Frankenstein*," *Huntington Library Quarterly* 68.4 [2005]: 655–666, 656; Adriana Craciun, "Writing the Disaster: Franklin and Frankenstein," *Nineteenth-Century Literature* 65.4 [2011]: 433–480, 470; Joseph Valente, "Double Born: Bram Stoker and the Metrocolonial Gothic," *Modern Fiction Studies* 46.3 [2000]: 632–645, 632–634). The Gothic reflects fears of possible harms of colonization upon the colonizer (i.e., reverse colonization) (Stephen D. Arata, "The Occidental Tourist: Dracula and the Anxiety of Reverse Colonization," *Victorian Studies: A Journal of the Humanities, Arts and Sciences* 33.4 [1990]: 621–645, 627; Smith and Hughes, *Empire and the* Gothic, 1–2; Wright, *Gothic Fiction*, 1–2). Whereas the texts in English were labelled as Gothic, the texts in Hebrew were not, yet they contain Gothic elements. Though coming from two distinct cultural backgrounds, the texts in Hebrew and English similarly utilize Gothic tropes in their depictions of space and landscape. The importance of spatial awareness and connection to the land for the (re)construction of identity is explored using Gothic tropes because the Gothic is primarily engaged with the connection between settings and questions of identity. Though some of the texts in the Hebrew were not read previously as Gothic literature, Gothic elements in Agnon's work have been noted (Esther Fuchs, "Ironic Characterization in the Works of S. Y. Agnon," *AJS* 7/8 [1983]: 101–128, 120; Harold Fisch, "The Dreaming Narrator in S. Y. Agnon," *Novel: A Forum on Fiction* 4.1 [1970]: 49–68, 49).

9 The different definitions of authenticity in relation to colonialism have been a matter of fierce debate. For example, cf. S. James Anaya, *Indigenous Peoples in International Law* (Oxford et al.: Oxford UP, 2004): 4.

munity member's birth from the very soil he inhabits, creating a privileged connection between an individual, his community, and the land."[10] The term, which is linked to the Greek mythology of a nation born from the land,[11] draws attention precisely to the importance of the land itself in the (re)creation of individual and collective identities.[12]

The connection to the land, both figuratively and literally, is, as I would argue, at the core of the texts I examine in this paper. The literary characters reflect the problematic question of autochthonous origins, as well as the crucial impact of displacement upon the construction of identities. These aspects of identity are particularly important for British and Jewish as well as Jewish-Israeli identities. For centuries, the Jewish nation has been marked by its homelessness, and with the thrust of the Zionist enterprise in the late nineteenth century, it has begun to grapple with the new and continually forming Jewish-Israeli identities.[13] In many ways, the kernel of Jewish-Israeli identities is a multiplicity

---

10 Richard Rader, "'And Whatever It Is, It Is You': The Autochthonous Self in Aeschylus's *Seven Against Thebes*," *Arethusa* 42.1 (2009): 1–44, 2.

11 The myth is an ancient one: "According to one of its myths, Athens imagined the genesis of its forebears as an unconsummated relationship (misconsummated, we might say) between Hephaestus and Athena. Born of the very soil that received Hephaestus's seed, Erechtheus became the primordial father of the Athenians" (Rader, "And Whatever It Is, It Is You," 4). The Greek myth of autochthonous roots "entailed being born from the very earth or inhabiting it from time immemorial" (Rader, "And Whatever It Is, It Is You," 1). This myth is paradigmatic, and "has provided the model for many nations up to the current day seeking to define their identities. [...] In a way this very question informs the sometimes chilling struggles of peoples the world over that have yet to cease even today – from Ingushetia and Ossetia in the Caucasus to Israel and Palestine in the Middle East" (Rader, "And Whatever It Is, It Is You," 1). The following use of the term 'autochthonous' emphasizes the connection to the land in mythical terms, even while acknowledging its problematic employment.

12 Individual and collective identities are intricately intertwined. For the purposes of this discussion, individual identity is defined in relation to the perception of one's self as well as in relation to social affirmation of this identity (Barry R. Schlenker, *The Self and Social Life* [New York, London: McGraw-Hill, 1985]: 67). As Anthony Smith explains, "[i]dentity operates on two levels, the individual and the collective" (Smith, "The Formation of National Identity," 130). Like Smith, who suggests the discussion of multiple identities, in a similar attempt to grapple with the elusive notion of identity, Stuart Hall suggests thinking of identities "as a 'production', which is never complete, always in process, and always constituted within, not outside, representation" (Stuart Hall, "Cultural Identity and Diaspora," in *Contemporary Postcolonial Theory: A Reader*, ed. Padmini Mongia [London: Bloomsbury Academic, 1989]: 222–237, 222).

13 Throughout the ages, Hebrew culture has perceived and depicted the Land of Israel as the center, the homeland of the Jewish nation, and land had a pivotal role in the Zionist narrative (Eyal Ben-Ari and Yoram Bilu, *Grasping Land: Space and Place in Contemporary Israeli Discourse and Experience* [New York: State U of New York P, 1997]: 3–9).

that resists placement. The discourse of Jewish-Israeli identity is a reflection of and on the struggle for a coherent identity, which is "intensified by existential as well as political debates over territorialism and occupation."[14] As Barbara Mann explains, in order to depict the Jews as being at home in Palestine-Israel, "the fundamental 'unhomeliness' of European Jews in Palestine had to be overcome, or at least downplayed. What was repressed by Zionism's negation of exile surfaced within modern Hebrew culture as *das unheimliche*, 'the uncanny'."[15] Being, in fact, alien in their new homeland the Ashkenazi diaspora Jews in the early settlements in Palestine-Israel were, indeed, uncanny.[16] Similarly, the British imperial experience yielded an uncanny feeling that is reflected in English literature of the time.[17] Both the British and Jews were an uncanny presence on foreign land.

The sense of a lack of connection to the (home)land is one of the main themes explored in the texts examined here. While the Jews were trying to establish a connection to their homeland, the British were struggling with their alienation from the lands they had conquered or occupied as part of the imperialist enterprise. The years of life in the diaspora had rendered Jews a strange presence upon the Mediterranean landscape, with their European attire and customs, and they struggled to acclimatize.[18] Likewise, the British who were coming to the colonies were struggling to adapt to foreign climates and traditions. The result is

---

14 Ranen Omer-Sherman, *Israel in Exile: Jewish Writing and the Desert* (Urbana: U of Illinois P, 2006): x.

15 Barbara E. Mann, *A Place in History: Modernism, Tel Aviv, and the Creation of Jewish Urban Space* (Stanford: Stanford UP, 2006): 30, emphasis in the original.

16 While originally the term 'diaspora' meant "the threat of dispersion facing the Hebrews if they failed to obey God's will" (Stephane Dufoix, *Diasporas*, trans. William Rodamor [Berkeley: U of California P, 2008]: 4), in later Jewish tradition the term came to "designate both the scattered people and the locale of their distribution" (Dufoix, *Diasporas*, 5). The term is here used according to its later adaptation.

17 Joanna Collins explores representations of the uncanny in colonial writers, suggesting that the 'imperial uncanny' is the unresolved anxiety directed at the combination of the character of the Other and the location (Joanna Collins, "The Imperial Uncanny: Miss-oriented and Mysterious in Writings of Colonial Spaces" [unpublished dissertation, U of Kent, 2005]: 263).

18 The importance of conceptualizations of home and belonging in Hebrew literature has been explored in relation to the specific importance of 'place' for Jewish nationalism, as well as in the context of the tensions between 'home' and 'abroad' (Risa Domb, *Home Thoughts from Abroad: Distant Visions of Israel in Contemporary Hebrew Fiction* [Portland, OR: Vallentine Mitchell, 1995]: 6).

that the texts in Hebrew and English alike reveal that the land, the homeland, and the home do not offer a sense of belonging.[19]

---

19 One ought to note the subtle though important differentiation for the following analyses between 'space,' 'place,' and 'land'. Space is "the unlimited three-dimensional realm of expanse in which all material objects are located and all events occur" ("Space," in *The New Webster's Encyclopaedic Dictionary of the English Language* [New York: Gramercy Books, 1997]: 633). Foucault argues that space takes the form of relations among sites, and outlines oppositions between private and public, as well as cultural space and useful space (Michel Foucault and Jay Miskowiec, "Of Other Spaces," *Diacritics* 16.1 [1986]: 22–27, 23). Space is important in the following discussion as an active participant in the (re)creation of identities, and the relations between identities and social conventions. As Yi-Fu Tuan elucidates, "'space' is more abstract than 'place'" (Yi-Fu Tuan, *Space and Place: The Perspective of Experience* [1977] [Minneapolis: U of Minnesota P, 2001]: 6). The 'place' is the intimate known and familiar aspect of 'space'. While in English 'place' might simply be "a particular portion of space, whether of definite or indefinite extent" ("Place," in *New Webster's*, 508) in Hebrew 'place,' or more specifically 'the place,' *HaMakom*, refers to God (Mann, *A Place in History*, 4–5). Furthermore, "*Hamakom*, God is not only THE place, but place itself" (Sidra Ezrahi DeKoven, *Booking Passage: Exile and Homecoming in the Modern Jewish Imagination* [Berkeley, Los Angeles, London: U of California P, 2000]: 3–33; 12; emphasis in the original). Yet the crux of the problem of 'place' in Israeli-Jewish thought is an internal struggle over the reality and meaning of place, and Jewish-Israeli identity as natives, or the people of the place. Hence, in addition to the distinction between 'space' and 'place,' within Jewish-Israeli discourse there is a further distinction between 'place' and 'Place.' 'Place' is the notion of the Promised Land, which finds its symbolic representation represented in language, literature, and art; 'place' is the actual home and childhood landscape (Gideon Aran and Zali Gurevitch, "Al Hamakom" [Of the Place], in *On Israeli and Jewish Place* [Tel Aviv: Am Oved, 1992]: 22–74, 23–25). Land, conversely, has a clearer connotation of a solid portion of soil, or "any part of the earth's surface" ("Land," in *New Webster's*, 382). There are, of course, the differences between 'earth,' 'land,' and 'soil,' which complicate the discussion; however, for the following discussion the word 'land' refers to soil within the context of nationalist discourse. These concepts are even more complex in a literary sense, because literary space is conceptual, and "it cannot be measured, but it *can* be experienced" (Rawdon Wilson, "The Metamorphoses of Fictional Space: Magical Realism," in *Magical Realism: Theory, History, Community*, eds. Lois Parkinson Zamora, Wendy B. Faris [Durham, NC, London: Duke UP, 1995]: 209–233, 215; emphasis in the original). Therefore, "space is invariably present in literature though never precisely so" (Wilson, "The Metamorphoses of Fictional Space," 216). Rawdon Wilson proposes that "[f]ictional space invokes an experience of place (volume, distance, coordination, interiority, exteriority, and so forth) which may be both, or neither, that of the characters and that of the readers" (Wilson, "The Metamorphoses of Fictional Space," 216). Gidon Aran and Zali Gurevitch note that "place is the base of identity, because in it the individual connects to the world, and through the world to his or herself" (Aran and Gurevitch, "Al Hamakom," 24). Bearing these problems of definition in mind, spatial awareness is here formulated as the characters' comprehension of and connection to home and land, or their lack thereof.

One of the prominent nineteenth-century texts to explore themes of home-lessness is Mary Wollstonecraft Shelley's *Frankenstein; Or, The Modern Prometheus*. Indeed, the narrative of the monster composed of exhumed body parts introduces the quintessential modern monstrous Other as a rejected creature forever roaming the earth in the futile search of kinship and a home. The novel has elicited a plethora of interpretations, and it explores a number of problems and anxieties originating in the imperial enterprise,[20] the ensuing fears of the colonized Other or of a "reverse colonization,"[21] and abolitionist theories.[22] These various concerns all stem from the need for a solid grasp of the connection to the land.

The significance of the connection to the land in *Frankenstein* is evident first and foremost in the fact that the narrative is embedded within a quest for the North Pole. Also, both Walton and Frankenstein leave home and live in exile. The De Lacey family, to whose cottage the creature's hovel is attached, are French expatriates living in Switzerland, and Safie is a Turkish émigré. Dislocation is a major theme in the novel. Yet of all the characters in *Frankenstein*, the creature is most dislocated. Throughout the novel the creature searches for a home and a sense of belonging. Its physical origins are exhumed body parts from the cemetery at Ingolstadt (*F*, 52). Since the novel is written by a British subject, from a British perspective, the creature is doubly foreign and Other because the provenance of its individual components is (presumably) not British. In this respect Frankenstein's creation is alien to Britons even before it becomes a criminal. The creature lacks a fundamental connection to the British (home)land.

Like Frankenstein's creature, Count Dracula is not British, and with his criminal intentions is, perhaps, un-British. Yet, while the creature in *Frankenstein* lacks a valid and verified connection to British soil, the Count is intricately connected to a foreign land. Dracula is an aristocratic sovereign to his own land, a land that is exoticized from the British perspective. Moreover, the Count's very un-dead life depends on his ancestral land, and in order to rejuvenate after gorging on blood the Count must be interred in it for his regeneration. The vampire is thus doubly alien, due to its lack of connection to the British territory as well as its crucial reliance upon non-British soil.

On the literal level, Count Dracula comes from Transylvania to England searching for a new home – in fact, the vampire relocates in order to feed upon the British population – on a metaphorical level this has been read as a

20 Chris Baldick, *In Frankenstein's Shadow*, 1; John Bugg, "Master of their Language," 656.
21 Arata, "The Occidental Tourist," 622–624.
22 Howard L. Malchow, *Gothic Images of Race in Nineteenth-Century Britain* (Stanford: Stanford UP, 1996): 6–14.

representation of fears of an Eastern invasion.[23] The question at the heart of the novel is the importance of the connection to the land. The comfortable binary of foreign/familiar is undermined when the Count is relocated to England along with his boxes of ancestral soil, while the international team of Western men in turn ventures to the East. The Other enters the homeland while the *self* is dislocated into the foreigner's land. The narrative expresses the fears of the imperial enterprise, as the far-flung arms of British imperialism might bring back some unwanted entities onto British soil.

Likewise, Charlotte Brontë's *Jane Eyre* explores fears of the harmful effects of British imperialism, namely "reverse colonization,"[24] and the introduction of alien entities and notions into British society. Gayatri Spivak consequently reads the novel primarily as a critique of imperialism.[25] The obvious racial and national Other in the novel is Bertha Mason, Rochester's first wife, who is imprisoned in the attic. Bertha is not only mad but also not English and has neither rights nor any claim to the land. She is the embodiment of the repressed fears of reverse colonization. Interestingly, Bertha bites Rochester like a vampire (*JE*, 250), in a sense attempting to infect him with her Otherness. While Bertha has no claims to British origins, Jane Eyre is an Englishwoman; however, since Jane has been left destitute, she "no longer has the birth rights" (*JE*, 21). Thus the novel suggests that her status as a poor orphan deprives her of her entitlement to the land. The two female characters represent the two main British social concerns of the time: the fear of the racial Other from the colonies, and the concerns with regard to social mobility inside Britain. The parallels between the two female characters, outlined by Gilbert and Gubar,[26] suggest that for the British at the time, the poor female subject is nearly as horrifying as the colonized racial Other. The bildungsroman follows Jane Eyre as she (re)constructs her identity, from poor rejected orphan to land-bound married woman. The novel also outlines her constant search for a home, from Gateshead, via Lowood, through Thornfield, and Moor House, then Morton, and eventually Ferndean. Like Frankenstein and Dracula, Jane is a rejected Other searching for a home.

Published nearly a hundred years later, in 1938, du Maurier's *Rebecca* is in many ways "a rewrite of *Jane Eyre* amidst a nostalgia for the waning of the Brit-

---

23 Arata, "The Occidental Tourist," 627.
24 Arata, "The Occidental Tourist," 621.
25 Gaytari Chakravorty Spivak, "Three Woman's Texts and a Critique of Imperialism," *Critical Inquiry* 12.1 (1985): 243–261, 249–251.
26 Sandra M. Gilbert and Susan Gubar draw parallels between Jane and Bertha, suggesting the latter is the foil of the former (*The Madwoman in the Attic: The Woman Writer and the Nineteenth-Century Literary Imagination* [New Haven, London: Yale UP, 1979]: 361–362).

ish Empire and the decline of its aristocracy."[27] Yet, in *Rebecca*, the focus shifts from a representation of the British imperial enterprise and its harmful effects to a consideration of the destructive repercussions of the anticipated fall of the Empire.[28] Like Jane Eyre, the unnamed narrator is an orphan, and the novel follows her restless wanderings, from Monte Carlo, via Manderley, the South Eastern English estate, to a self-imposed exile on an unnamed sun-ridden island; like Jane Eyre, *Rebecca*'s orphaned narrator is never at home. Her persistent insistence on obtaining Manderley and becoming its mistress is the result of her subconscious awareness of the crucial deficiency in her identity as the result of the lack of authenticated origins and a connection to land.

The characters in the English novels discussed so far are restless Others. They are defined and determined by their search for a connection with the land and a home. The characters in the Hebrew texts yet to be examined similarly experience restlessness, as the narratives explore the question of home and exile, and various kinds of links to the land. This parallel is a reflection of and on the opposite political processes the British and Jewish nations were facing at the time, as one was engaged with and later abandoning the imperialist project, and the other commencing the mass colonization of Palestine.

An example of the Ashkenazi Jewish diaspora's exploration of the connection to the land is found in Yudl Rosenberg's adaptation of the legend of the golem in *The Golem and the Wondrous Deeds of the Maharal of Prague*. The narrative relates the creation of the clay golem for the protection of Jews from the blood libel.[29] The similarities between the *Golem* and *Frankenstein* invite comparison, as do the differences: while in both narratives a scholar creates a humanoid creature, one is created from exhumed body parts and the other from soil. Since the golem is made from the soil of Prague, it is autochthonous to a land foreign to the Jews and thus is paradoxically autochthonous even while alien. The golem

---

27 Alison Light, "'Returning to Manderley': Romance Fiction, Female Sexuality, and Class," *Feminist Review* 16 (1984): 7–25, 7.
28 Light, "Returning to Manderley," 7.
29 Ironically, Rosenberg locates the narrative at a time and place where blood libels were actually not prevalent. Rosenberg attributes the creation of the Golem to the Maharal of Prague. The Maharal was the head rabbi of the Jews in Prague during the latter half of the sixteenth century. (The Maharal is an acronym for 'my rabbi the rabbi Löw', also known as the Rabbi Judah Löw Bezalel). He was a well-respected scholar within both the Jewish and non-Jewish communities, a renaissance man who studied natural philosophy alongside astrology and religious studies, and was even received by Emperor Rudolph II (Hillel J. Kieval, "Pursuing the Golem of Prague: Jewish Culture and the Invention of a Tradition," *Modern Judaism* 17.1 [1997]: 1–20, 4). Under the guidance and leadership of the Maharal, Jews and non-Jews lived peacefully together in Prague at a time when, under the rule of Rudolph II, the city was a cultural centre.

is an embodiment of the dual existence of the Jews in exile; though feeling a profound connection to the land of their ancestral origins, the Jews in the Ashkenazi diaspora are by that time a part of the local scenery, and are in a sense hybrid creatures, part alien, part local.[30]

The golem is made from earth (the land) by a Jew, who has no autochthonous connection to this land, and the life it gains through the word, in some ways reflects the notion of the portable homeland as it was observed by Heinrich Heine in his *Confessions* (1854).[31] A Jewish myth suggests that "when the people of Israel went into exile, the Shekinah accompanied them as token that they were not entirely abandoned by God."[32] The Shekinah is the feminine aspect of god, manifested in the Torah. Emanuel Maier suggests that "[t]he ethological concept of 'movable territory' may be applicable to Jewish mythological symbolism collected about the Torah. Torah as movable territory developed as a symbolic substitute for the loss of territory."[33] In Rosenberg's narrative, the Maharal utilizes the power of the Torah in order to obtain command over the land of Prague. The golem is created through the employment of a speech act based upon the word of the Torah, which is the 'portable homeland' that symbolizes the Jews' lack of territorial connection. The land from which the golem was made is annexed – both figuratively and physically – to the Jews' territory as the golem becomes part of the Jewish household and community. The land is manipulated through the word of the 'portable homeland'. Thus the creation of the golem is an inversion and subversion of the Jews' lack of homeland by the employment of the portable homeland. This maneuver empowers the Jews even while they are

---

30 In postcolonial discourse, the term 'hybridity' refers to the effects of synthesis upon the identities and cultures of the colonized (Julia Kristeva, *Powers of Horror: An Essay on Abjection*, trans. Leon S. Roudiez [New York: Columbia UP, 1982]: 132; Homi K. Bhabha, *Nation and Narration* [London: Routledge, 1990]: 4). Moreover, hybridity changes the various components, making it virtually impossible to disentangle them from one another (Robert Young, *Desire: Hybridity in Theory, Culture, and Race* [London: Routledge, 1995]: 2–3, 17–19; Anthony Smith, *Myths and Memories of the Nation* [Oxford et al.: Oxford UP, 1999]: 26). Though they are dislocated, the term may be productively applied to the Jews in the Ashkenazi diaspora, and even more so to the emerging Jewish-Israeli identity.

31 Heine refers to the Jews as the long-enduring nation "who had preserved the Bible from the great conflagration of the sacred temple, and all through the middle ages carried it about with them like a portable fatherland, kept their treasure carefully concealed in their ghettos" (Heinrich Heine, "Confessions," *The Prose Writings of Heinrich Heine* [1854], ed. Havelock Ellis [September 19, 2011], *Project Gutenberg* <http://www.gutenberg.org/files/37478/37478-h/37478-h. htm> [acc. April 1, 2014]).

32 Emanuel Maier, "Torah as Movable Territory," *Annals of the Association of American Geographers* 65.1 (1975): 18–23, 21.

33 Maier, "Torah as Movable Territory," 18.

in their precarious exilic condition. Rosenberg's version of the golem narrative was published in Poland in 1909. As a product of the Ashkenazi diaspora, the *Golem* examines the Jews' relationship to the land in exile and the relationship to the Jewish and non-Jewish territories in relation to a modern Jewish Ashkenazi diaspora identity.[34]

Another text written in Poland in the following year, 1910, Y. D. Berkowitz's "Mishael" is a portrayal of Jewish exilic life that explores the problem of the Jewish and non-Jewish domains in the Ashkenazi diaspora. Like Rosenberg, Berkowitz examines the stability and sustainability of social and spatial boundaries. In the *Golem* a maneuver of spatial and linguistic appropriation leads to a tentative Jewish sovereignty in the heart of the Ashkenazi diaspora. In "Mishael" it is a rejected Jewish boy who has a strong connection to the land outside of the Jewish social jurisdiction.

The characters in this short story are all non-autochthonous. They are without exception 'displaced' Jews. Yet even in relation to this displaced community, which has no claims to the land, Mishael is an outcast. Mishael is rejected by his father, who is ashamed of his deformed and unscholarly son, and like Frankenstein who rejects his creation, and the villagers who chase Frankenstein's creature (*F*, 101), Mishael's father chases his son away with a rake ("M," 5). Interestingly, it is precisely because Mishael has a connection to the land that he is rejected. The Jews in the Ashkenazi diaspora had an ambivalent connection to their foster land because they yearned for the Holy Land, which they perceived as their origin and homeland.[35] Since Mishael is unable to study, he does not share the collective notion of the Torah as the portable homeland. Instead, Mishael develops a connection to the foster land and to the soil. Like Brontë's protagonist, who wanders in the moors, wading "knee-deep in its dark growth" (*JE*, 275), Mishael is described as coming out of the woods covered in mud ("M," 5). The only place to which Mishael feels a connection, and feels at home, is the forest, the place the people of the town, in turn, dare not enter. Like the golem, Mis-

---

34 Though Rosenberg, a Hasidic rabbi and Kabbalist, might not have been a Zionist and had no known connections to Zionism, the *Golem* may be considered to offer a supportive argument for the Zionist enterprise because it emphasizes the problems of the exilic condition in the Ashkenazi Diaspora and reiterates the legacy of the blood libel.

35 Hebrew literature can be categorized according to its articulation of the yearning for the land (Yigal Schwartz, *Do You Know the Land Where the Lemon Blooms* [Tel Aviv: Zmora-Bitan, 2007]: 19). This is partially due to the fact that Modern Hebrew literature evolved to some extent in the context of the Zionist project or its forerunners, and therefore demonstrates ideological coherence with regard to the relation of the land and the Jewish people, which is ultimately derived from the Biblical notion of the Promised Land.

hael is thus an embodiment of the complications of the Jews' (lack of) connection to the land in the Ashkenazi diaspora.

Berkowitz was not the only Jewish writer of his time to engage with these questions of identities in relation to land. In fact, his work was a part of a growing body of literature that explored these issues. One of the best known writers to address the question of modern Jewish identities was Nobel laureate Y. S. Agnon. Like the lesser-known Berkowitz, Agnon wrote extensively about the Jewish Ashkenazi diaspora.[36] He created a number of fictional characters that offer a variety of perspectives on questions such as the connection to the host land and the Holy Land. In particular the problems of the dislocated Ashkenazi diaspora's connection to the land have been addressed in several of his works. In many of Agnon's texts land carries meaning both for the individual and for national identities.[37]

In what follows, I examine three narratives that represent three main issues or conditions in relation to the (re)creation of modern Jewish-Israeli identities: in "Ad Hennah" (1952),[38] Agnon addresses the questions of the exilic condition as it was experienced by the Ashkenazi diaspora; in "Tehila" (1950), Agnon explores the ambiguous feelings of Jewish immigrants from the Ashkenazi diaspora once

---

36 Shmuel Werses, *S. Y. Agnon Literally: Studies of his Writing* (Bialik Institute: Israel, 2000); Gershon Shaked, *Shmuel Yosef Agnon: A Revolutionary Traditionalist* (New York: New York UP, 1989): 15, 18–19, and 245.

37 Agnon's personal narrative was in many ways a reflection of the national narrative of the Jewish nation (Shaked, *Shmuel Yosef Agnon*, 6–7). Referring to *Sipur Pashut* (1935), Ruhama Elbag suggests that like in many of his novels, the spatial design reflects Agnon's ambivalent attitude towards his hometown and the process of his separation from it (Ruhama Elbag, "Buczacz in *Sipur Pashut* as a Model of Agnon's Design of Space," *Criticism and Interpretation: Journal for Interdisciplinary Studies in Literature and Culture* 35/36 [2002]:167–183, 178). This ambivalence is a recurring motif in his narratives and particularly in the three Agnon texts examined here. Additionally, Elbag notes the importance of Jerusalem, Agnon's home in Palestine-Israel, in Agnon's work (Elbug, "Buczacz in *Sipur Pashut*," 178). The themes of home, homelessness, and exile are prevalent in Agnon's work. For example, as Harold Fisch notes, the two main themes in "The Last Bus" are modernity and homelessness (Harold Fisch, "The Dreaming Narrator in S. Y. Agnon," *Novel: A Forum on Fiction* 4.1 [1970]: 49–68, 62).

38 Though Hillel Halkin's translation of "Ad Hennah" is "To This Day," the title might more accurately be rendered as "Thus Far." "Thus Far" was the translation Esther Fuchs chose for her analysis of the text in 1983 (Esther Fuchs, "Ironic Characterization in the Works of S. Y. Agnon," *AJS* 7/8 [1983]: 101–128) The difference is important, because in Hebrew the words convey both a chronological and a spatial meaning which is lost in Halkin's translation. The implication of the title is then that this marks the end of the Jews' wandering, in space as well as in time.

they have settled in Palestine-Israel; and in "Avi Hashor" ("The Ox's Father," 1945), Agnon explores the moral legitimacy of the *yishuv* in Palestine-Israel.[39]

The narrator in "Ad Hennah" is a displaced figure. Born in the Ashkenazi diaspora, he emigrated to Palestine-Israel only to return to Germany and then go back to Palestine-Israel. Like Frankenstein's creature, the narrator is searching for a home. Like Jane Eyre and the narrator in *Rebecca*, he wanders between numerous locations. He travels from Palestine to Germany; from Berlin via Leipzig back to Berlin, where he continually searches for accommodation; he is in a perpetual search for a home. He says he finds being in Berlin hard, but that travelling to another town is even more difficult ("AH," 7). The crux of the narrator's dilemma is his constant displacement.

Though it was written in Israel, "Ad Hennah" explores the myth of the (Ashkenazi diaspora) Wandering Jew. The narrator is searching for a home in Germany and in a nostalgic way in Palestine-Israel, which he left because of the Great War.[40] Like in the texts in English, the reader follows the narrator in his spatial and psychological wanderings. The narrator is searching for both a real home and a conceptual one, as the narrative parallels the personal and communal search for a home. At the very end of the novella, the narrator returns to Palestine-Israel, but his identity is yet to be fully formed in the future sovereign nation-state.

The novella "Tehila" (1950) introduces the story of Tehila, whose hand was promised to Shraga, a young boy, when they were merely children. However, the groom's father appeared to be following the Chasidic movement, which at the time was considered a subversive interpretation of the Jewish religion, and therefore Tehila's father called off the marriage, did not ask for forgiveness, and Tehila

---

39 It would seem that the reverse chronology of these texts as I have outlined them here might reflect Agnon's concerns. The burning issue of the legitimatization of the yishuv at the height of the struggle for national independence during the Mandate period gave birth, with "Avi Hashor," to a short story that engages with precisely this issue. Yet only after the establishment of the Israeli nation-state did the writer engage further with issues of the Diaspora and Israeli identity in "Tehila" and "Ad Hennah."

40 Though the narrative refers to the First World War, the story has been read as a reckoning with the Second World War. Arnold Band reads the text as a narrative of constant return and dislocation (Arnold Band, *Nostalgia and Nightmare: A Study in the Fiction of S. Y. Agnon* [Berkeley, Los Angeles: U of California P, 1968]: 347–57), and as Z. J. Goodman explains, "Ad Hennah" is "not the story of the First World War, it is, rather, a transposition, as in a dream of the Second World War onto the arena of the earlier war" (Zilla Jane Goodman, "Words and their Meaning: On Linguistic and Tonal Density in Agnon's Writing," in *Agnon: Text and Context in English Translation: A Multi-Disciplinary Curriculum, Bibliographies, and Selected Syllabi*, ed. Leon I. Yudkin [New York: Marcus Wiener, 1988]: 77–105, 97).

ended up marring another man. Over the years Tehila suffers some misfortunes (two of her children die and one converts to Christianity) and she blames her calamities on her father's ill-conduct; eventually she immigrates to Jerusalem.

The novella opens with a short sentence, "There was one old woman in Jerusalem" ("T," 178), which in spite of its brevity encapsulates the crucial connection between Tehila and the Holy City. At this stage, we do not know her name or personal history, but only that the initial identification of the old woman we later get to know as Tehila is with the city. Though she was born in the Ashkenazi diaspora, and is not an autochthonous part of the Holy Land, Tehila is depicted as having strong ties to the land because of her piety and virtuous character. While Tehila embraces the Holy Land, her foil, the character of the old Rabbanit, longs for the diaspora. Though neither is native, as they both emigrated from the Ashkenazi diaspora, they have a markedly different relationship with the land. In order to emphasize the importance of a complete acceptance of Zion, Agnon juxtaposes the characters' sense of connection to the land.

The strongest connection to the land in this narrative is expressed in relation to Tehila's future burial. Tehila ensures her grave will be in the Mount of Olives, which, according to Jewish tradition, is the burial ground of the holy and righteous, and on judgment day all the saints will rise from the Mount of Olives. In a manner reminiscent of the rejuvenations of the vampire from his ancestral land Tehila dreams of a rebirth into the next world through the interment in her ancestral land. Though one character, the vampire, is the embodiment of the unholy and the other, Tehila, a righteous person, both require their ancestral land for resurrection. Both characters' identity (re)creation and existence hinges on their connection with their ancestral land.

The third Agnon text, "Avi Hashor" (1948), addresses the questions of home and exile and autochthonous origins from a perspective that seeks to affirm Jewish legal and moral rights over the land of Palestine-Israel. "Avi Hashor" is a Hebrew translation of the Arabic Abu-Tor, which is the name of a neighborhood in Jerusalem. The area has a unique history, as it is one of the first attempts at a Jewish-Arabic hybrid neighborhood in Jerusalem. During the time the story "Avi Hashor" was written, the neighborhood was literally divided between Jordan and the British Mandate for Palestine; today it is in Israel and witnesses an attempt at coexistence. One of the folk traditions related to the place suggests that when Ṣalāḥ ad-Dīn laid siege to Jerusalem, one of his officers bragged that it would be so easy to conquer Jerusalem that he would be able to do it on an ox. Agnon's narrative offers an alternative myth. In "Avi Hashor" the old man's name is *avi hashor*, 'the ox's father,' which is the name of the place; hence, in a sense, the old man *is* the land.

In addition to the linguistic appropriation of the land articulated through the name, the connection to the land in "Avi Hashor" is through the ox, which is an animal that has been a part of the local landscape for millennia. The ox has been domesticated to become a farming animal and has become a symbol of the connection to the land. In the story, the ox is a substitute for the old man's family, as he has neither children nor wife. Hence, the ox's father is perceived as autochthonous also through his familial relationship with the ox.

At the beginning of the story, the old man has a small house and field, and the ox ("AvH," 336). These will be violently taken from him, and then he will be compensated with other farm animals and many plots of land ("AvH," 442). The short story follows the old man as his beloved ox saves the town from invaders only to be slaughtered by the old man's neighbor to feed the latter's wedding guests. The ox is dismembered by the old man's neighbor, who leaves the ox's horns protruding from the ground ("AvH," 439), creating a literal connection between the ox and the land that fortifies the metaphorical link. By the end of the story, the neighbor gives many plots of land to the old man in compensation for the loss of the ox. This establishes the old man's moral and legal right to the land. Even though the old man has a home in the beginning, and the whole story is about the naming of the place after the old man and his ox, the story outlines a disturbing narrative of restlessness, and the temporary loss of the old man's home.

Whereas Agnon reinforces the Jewish connection and legitimate right to the land, Yizhar's text repudiates these claims or at least offers some possible grounds for undermining the moral validity of the Jewish-Israeli conquest of the land, and more significantly the manner by which it was conducted. *Khirbet Khizeh* (1949) presents the *sabra* male soldiers, who presumably were all born in the *yishuv* and according to this criterion would be considered natives, as invaders upon the land, misunderstanding both its simple beauty and immense grandeur.

While in "Tehila" Agnon juxtaposes the two female characters in order to explore the connection to the land, in *Khirbet Khizeh* the Arab villagers and the Jewish soldiers are contrasted. More specifically, the soldiers are destroying the fields the villagers have been cultivating for centuries and up until the commencement of the recent fighting. Gershon Shaked claims that the Arab village was a part of Yizhar's beloved landscape, part of his sense of space and location, which Modern Zionist colonization ruined, and that the land and its charms are part of an unattainable nostalgic past.[41] While the soldiers are depicted as de-

---

41 Shaked, *Agnon – A Writer With a Thousand Faces*, 12. Also, Uri Shoham suggests that the

tached from the land, as they tread upon it ruthlessly, the Arab villagers are portrayed as unable to find shelter anywhere, as if the land refused their plea for refuge. Eventually, neither the soldiers nor the villagers are harmoniously united with the land.

The conquering soldiers are, ostensibly, all *sabra*. The sabra is the Jew who was born in Palestine-Israel. One of the main symbols of the sabra is the cactus. The cactus,[42] apart from being a part of the prevalent vegetation in the region, was the way by which the Arab farmers used to mark field ownership – similar to the way hedges are used in the UK. In *Rebecca*, one finds the use of plants as signs of sovereignty, as the rhododendron that the previous Mrs de Winter planted, function as a haunting reminder of her rooted presence. Likewise, in "Ad Hennah" the cactus functions as symbol of personal and national (un-)rootedness. When the narrator comes to bid the German landlady and her two daughters farewell, he notices their pots of cacti, and says that while here (in Germany) these plants are placed in pots and cared for, in his country no one bothers with cacti except in order to pluck them out ("AH," 10). The metaphor of the sabra is subverted, as the Jew who is relocated or plucked out of the Israeli soil attempts to be planted in Germany, while the plants that represent the sabra are nourished in pots in Germany. The inversion of the location of the plant reflects the dislocation of the person. The cactus, which defined the hold of the Arabs over their land, was later appropriated by the Israelis and became the symbol of the sabra. As Daniel Lefkowitz explains,

> [t]he classic symbol for [the] image of the Israeli Self is the sabra, which refers literally to the fruit of the prickly-pear cactus, and metaphorically to native-born Israelis. The metaphorical connection highlights the centrality of emotion: the sabra fruit – like the native/ideal Israeli – is said to be soft and sweet on the inside but rough and thorny on the outside.[43]

Lefkowitz adds an important footnote to this definition, saying "[i]t should be pointed out that sabra refers most naturally to Jewish Israelis. It would be infelicitous to apply that metaphor to Palestinians, even to citizens born in Israel

---

landscape and the Arab in Yizhar's text are a complex metaphor for an emotional principle that is the nostalgic longing for a lost childhood and innocence (Uri Shoham, "Ha'arava Haptukha, Hapardes hasagur Vehakfar Haaravi" [The Open Prairie, the Closed Orchard, and the Arab Village], *Siman Kria* 3/4 [1974]: 336–346, 340).

42 The cactus itself, like the displaced Jew, is not autochthonous, as it was originally imported into the Mediterranean from South America.

43 Daniel Lefkowitz, "Negotiated and Mediated Meanings: Ethnicity and Politics in Israeli Newspapers," *Anthropological Quarterly* 74.4 (2001): 179–189, 181.

after 1948."[44] In *Khirbet Khizeh*, the soldiers arrive at a cactus hedge and wish to have a small meal but are interrupted by the commander, who provides elaborate explanations regarding the attack on the area and the village of Khirbet Khizeh specifically. At the end of the instruction the troupes receive oranges (*KH*, 7 −8). The orange is another symbol of the Jewish settlement in Palestine-Israel, and the orchard is a recurrent symbol in Yizhar's work, representing innocence.[45] The citrus is not an indigenous crop like the fig, carob, or date, but was imported by the Jews who returned during the eighteenth and nineteenth centuries from Europe to settle on the land, and this citrus fruit has also become a symbol of Israel. The juxtaposition of the sabra and the orange as symbols of the Jewish settlement in Palestine-Israel reveals the complexity of the soldiers' identity in relation to the land, as they are simultaneously invaders and natives. The plants as symbols of the problem of autochthonous origins and sovereignty reflect the connection between identity and the land.

Yizhar's lyrical depictions of the land in *Khirbet Khizeh* can be read in relation to what Karen Grumberg terms depictions of "Zionist places" in Hebrew literature. "Zionist places" are places which "provide physical and geographical expression of mainstream Zionist ideology."[46] Grumberg refers to the literary depictions of "Zionist places" as participating in the affirmation of the Zionist enterprise, and even while Yizhar might depict the setting as "Zionist places" in order to question the violence of the Zionist enterprise, he nonetheless operates within the same discourse. The soldiers trample over uncultivated land as well as land that up till recently was cultivated by the villagers alike, nullifying the villagers' labor and treating the entire land as wilderness. The soldiers' interaction with the land is depicted as a conquest of "wilderness and chaos of the 'uncivilized' space beyond."[47] Even while they are autochthonous, the soldiers in Yizhar's novel embody the Zionist endeavor to "civilize" the "wildernesses" through forceful conquest. These issues bear a striking resemblance to the problem of the British imperialist endeavor to 'enculturate the world.'

While Gideon Aran and Zali Gurevitch draw a distinction between the universal and the Jewish-Israeli question of home and belonging,[48] the comparison of the texts in Hebrew and English reveals that there are similarities in the manner by which anxieties of exile and colonialism are explored. As a result of the

---

44 Lefkowitz, "Negotiated and Mediated Meanings," 188, n. 12.
45 Shoham "Ha'arava Haptukha," 334.
46 Karen Grumberg, *Place and Identity in Contemporary Hebrew Literature* (New York: Syracuse UP, 2011): 6.
47 Grumberg, *Place and Identity*, 6.
48 Aran and Gurevitch, "Al Hamakom," 24.

importance of the sense of belonging to the land, and more specifically the ancestral land, once a character is dislocated something in their identity is undermined.

As part of the investigation of the connection to the land, the texts explore issues of exile. All the main characters in these texts are in exile at some point or from some perspective: In *Frankenstein* the creature is forever exiled, and Bram Stoker's Count attempts to go into exile. In *Jane Eyre* Bertha is in exile, and Max de Winter and his second wife end in exile in du Maurier's *Rebecca*. Berkowitz's "Mishael" is set in a typical Eastern European Jewish exilic community, and the title of *The Golem and the Wondrous Deeds of the Maharal of Prague* gives away the narrative's exilic location. In Agnon's "Ad Hennah" the narrator meanders between Palestine-Israel and Germany, and it is unclear where exile really is, and while Tehila embraces her new life in the Holy Land, the old Rabbanit misses her old home in the Ashkenazi exile. Even the stories that take place in Palestine-Israel treat issues of exile, as in "Avi Hashor" the old man experiences the loss of his home, and the Palestinian commencement of exile is explored in Yizhar's *Khirbet Khizeh*.

Moreover, the comparative analysis reveals that not only are all these texts primarily preoccupied with issues of home and exile, but that the characters are all displaced and persecuted. Both Mishael and Frankenstein's creature are rejected by their makers or parents; and while both Jane and the narrator in *Rebecca* are rejected orphans, the Golem is adopted and embraced by the Jewish community. Interestingly, because it is made of the soil of the host country by the power of the 'portable homeland,' the golem is simultaneously autochthonous and alien. Thus it shares a complicated identity with the orphan Jane and the rejected Mishael. The need for ancestral earth for rejuvenation is shared by the demonic vampire and the saintly Tehila, as the former needs the earth in order to come back to its un-dead life and the latter wishes to be resurrected on the day of doom. While both female characters in "Tehila" are not of the land, one connects to the land while the other rejects it, and though Jane and *Rebecca*'s unnamed narrator are, indeed, British, they lack agency and are alienated from the land. While the old man in 'Avi Hashor' has an intrinsic connection with the land, in Yizhar's text the autochthonous soldiers' connection and right to the land is undermined even as they conquer it. The texts all explore the connection to the land because the sense of belonging to the land – and vice versa – is so vital for the construction of individual and collective identities. Both in English and Hebrew, these narratives explore the importance of the connection to the land through the validation or refutation of autochthonous origins and the intimate connection with the land for the (re)creation of identities.

Modern British and Jewish identities share some fundamental notions, particularly with regard to issues of home and belonging. The literature of the two nations reflects these links, as well as the places where the Jewish and British cultures diverge. The analysis of literature in Hebrew and English examined here unmasked the constructed and artificial nature of the claim to autochthony, and consequently of sovereignty. It reaffirms sovereignty as "a posited law, a thesis or a prosthesis, and not a natural given."[49] In fact, this analysis revealed how sovereignty "draws all its power, all its potency, i.e. its all-powerful nature, from this simulacrum-effect, this fiction- or representation-effect that is inherent and congenital to it, as it were co-originary."[50] Literature reflects the fabricated essence of sovereignty even while it participates in its reconstitution.

---

49 Jacques Derrida, *The Beast and the Sovereign*, eds. Michael Lisse, Marie-Louise Mallet, and Ginette Michaud, trans. Geoffrey Bennington (Chicago: U of Chicago P, 2009): 77, 116.
50 Derrida, *The Beast and the Sovereign*, 289, 387.

Saskia Hertlein

Geographies of Home: Constructions of Home and Belonging in Contemporary Emerging Adult Fiction

Abstract: This chapter links the contemporary discussion about diasporas, concepts of home and belonging, and imagined diasporas with the concept of emerging adulthood, the latter stemming from the developmental sciences. Bringing this background in a dialogue with contemporary American literature can contribute to an enhanced understanding of diasporic constructions of home and belonging since, as this chapter argues, emerging adulthood is a decisive explorative, in-between phase that fosters the emancipation from previous structures and the need to create a safe space of one's own. Some contemporary examples of novels featuring emerging adults in diasporic settings through whose continuing negotiations and imaginative constructions traditional and new affiliations are explored, are briefly presented. This reflects some of the ways of representing such contemporary examples for diasporic constructions of home and belonging in fiction and therefore calls for further investigation with regard to this specific perspective.

In the context of diaspora studies, questions of underlying concepts of "home" and "belonging" have been widely discussed. However, some issues call for reconsideration and further investigation. Both notions like home and belonging and the concept of diaspora itself are used in multiple ways, and the latter concept of diaspora has become rather imprecise, as Khachig Tölölyan has argued.[1] Apart from definitions, however, further investigation into the specific circumstances as well as consequences of diasporic constructions of home and belonging is called for. This study therefore focuses on different influences on constructing a sense of home and belonging in a diasporic setting, and it connects the diasporic position in limbo with the in-between position of emerging adults in selected literary examples.

The concepts of home and belonging can be seen as temporary constructs in this context, based on imaginative efforts within and outside the community at a given time. For Avtar Brah, they can connote both security and terror at the same time, offering an ambivalent reading of both concepts.[2] Also, if home and belonging connote – seemingly contradictorily – both security and terror, Brah claims they can be "dispersals of intersectionality,"[3] with "intersectionality" re-

---

1 Khachig Tölölyan, "The Contemporary Discourse of Diaspora Studies," *Comparative Studies of South Asia, Africa and the Middle East* 27.3 (2007), 647–655.
2 Avtar Brah, Khachig Tölölyan, "Diaspora Studies in the 21st Century," Advisory Board Panel Discussion, CoHaB Conference (WWU Münster, September 22–24, 2013).
3 Brah, Tölölyan, "Diaspora Studies in the 21st Century."

ferring to Kimberlé Crenshaw's originally legal framing of this concept of interacting and intersecting factors of discrimination and oppression.[4] In addition, rather than referring to a fixed space, home and belonging could be seen as contextual and fluid concepts. In the context of diasporic constructions of home and belonging, Tölölyan reminds us of the inherent critique of the fixed and the composite term "social space" that describes a concept like home, a social space in which a person can perform any social role in a subjectively safe environment, which is encountered in some of the texts discussed below.[5] However, among the elements of the idea of a home is also the reminder that this sheltering space may be temporal and temporarily unavailable; powerful discourses may influence the sense of belonging and may call for a multilocality of this home. Generally, a home has to be claimed, which is a major task for emerging adults who are about to create their own mature sense of the self, a mature, "adult" sense of the self which is grounded in a sense of home and belonging defined by the individual. For example, in Loida Maritza Pérez's *Geographies of Home*,[6] to which the title of this chapter alludes, Jiro Adachi's *The Island of Bicycle Dancers*,[7] Monica Pradhan's *The Hindi-Bindi Club*,[8] Bich Minh Nguyen's *Short Girls*,[9] Susan Muaddi Darraj's *The Inheritance of Exile*[10] and Layla Halaby's *West of the Jordan*,[11] or Hina Haq's *Sadika's Way*,[12] it becomes apparent that imaginative efforts, both individual and collective, shape each person's perception of home and belonging. In addition, the title "geographies" in the plural already indicates a plurality of possibly cumulative or even conflicting "imagined communities," adapting Benedict Anderson's term from a different context. Joel

---

4 Kimberlé Crenshaw, "Mapping the Margins: Intersectionality, Identity Politics, and Violence against Women of Color," in *Stanford Law Review* 43.6 (1991), 1241–1299.
5 Brah, Tölölyan, "Diaspora Studies in the 21st Century."
6 Loida Maritza Pérez, *Geographies of Home. A Novel* (New York: Viking, 1999); further references in the text, abbreviated as "*GoH*."
7 Jiro Adachi, *The Island of Bicycle Dancers* (New York: Picador, St. Martin's, 2005); further references in the text, abbreviated as "*IBD*."
8 Monica Pradhan, *The Hindi-Bindi Club* (New York: Bantam, 2007); further references in the text, abbreviated as "*HBC*."
9 Bich Minh Nguyen, *Short Girls* (London: Penguin, 2010).
10 Susan Muaddi Darraj, *The Inheritance of Exile. Stories from South Philly* (Notre Dame: U of Notre Dame P, 2007); further references in the text, abbreviated as "*IoE*."
11 Laila Halaby, *West of the Jordan* (Boston: Beacon, 2003); further references in the text, abbreviated as "*WoJ*."
12 Hina Haq, *Sadika's Way. A Novel of Pakistan and America* (Chicago: Academy Chicago, 2004). The novels by Pérez, Pradhan, Nguyen, Muaddi Darraj, and Halaby are analyzed in more detail in my *Tales of Transformation. Emerging Adulthood, Migration, and Ethnicity in Contemporary American Literature* (Trier/Tempe: WVT/bilingual press, 2014).

Kuortti has linked the imaginative efforts Anderson describes with regard to communities in general with the concept of diaspora. As Kuortti remarks,

> [d]iaspora is a loaded term that brings to mind various contested ideas and images. It can be a positive site for the affirmation of an identity, or, conversely, a negative site of fears of losing that identity. Diaspora is also a popular term in current research as it captures various phenomena that are prevalent in the numerous discourses devoted to current transnational globalization.[13]

This popularity has led to a multitude of potential understandings of what constitutes a diaspora,[14] but despite these alternatives, some of the following characteristics are used as a basis for this study. For Kuortti, "[d]iaspora signals an engagement with a matrix of diversity: of cultures, languages, histories, people, places, times. [Also, in] its transformational quality, diaspora is typically a site of hybridity which questions fixed identities based on essentialisms."[15] However, "[b]eing an amalgamation of diverse cultural materials, backgrounds, and identities, it nevertheless differs from other types of heterogeneity, implying at the same time a markedly asymmetrical relationship between the different elements of a given fusion."[16] These different elements that contribute to individual fusions have been examined frequently, placing emphasis on various constellations. Nonetheless, the main focus lies on the asymmetry between the different elements.

On the other hand, a diaspora setting also includes a common ground for a group of members. In relation to the concepts of home and belonging, reference points that shape a person's perception of home and belonging include, for instance, ethnic or cultural affiliations. In addition, shared experiences can contribute to feelings of communality. These experiences may not only be based on a shared heritage, but also, for example, on the challenges faced by a particular age group. In the examples presented below, despite different socioeconomic, ethnic, cultural, linguistic, or religious backgrounds, the shared phase of find-

---

13 Joel Kuortti, *Writing Imagined Diasporas, South Asian Women Reshaping North American Identity* (Newcastle-upon-Tyne: Cambridge Scholars P, 2007): 3.
14 Khachig Tölölyan has criticized the imprecision inherent in the increased use of the term diaspora for a multitude of transnational phenomena (Tölölyan, "The Contemporary Discourse of Diaspora Studies"). In the present chapter, the difficulty of defining diasporas and of clear-cut borders between diasporas and other, similar phenomena is at issue in the choice of relevant material. Nonetheless, the qualities Kuortti identifies might provide a framework that explains the choice despite potential alternatives to defining the underlying phenomenon of diaspora settings.
15 Kuortti, *Writing Imagined Diasporas*, 3.
16 Kuortti, *Writing Imagined Diasporas*, 4.

ing a place in the world as adults continues to connect the experiences of the young adults beyond dividing factors, creating a bond of its own. One of the potential reference points for further investigation with regards to the age group could therefore be the concept of emerging adulthood proposed by Jeffrey Jensen Arnett et al., which is rooted in developmental science and developmental psychology.[17] The concept of emerging adulthood is based on shared features of contemporary legal adults' early adult years. The first studies were concerned with American citizens growing up in the USA who perceive themselves as part of a majority in US society, with all problems that such a definition entails; yet, the scope of research has been widened over the past decade, both within the US and worldwide. A shared characteristic by those to whom the concept applies is that they, as legal adults, still experience a phase "of *identity explorations*, of trying out various possibilities, especially in love and work." This phase in emerging adulthood is characterized by *"instability"* and could be regarded as "the most *self-focused* age of life," an "age of feeling *in-between*, in transition, neither adolescent not adult." At the same time, this phase is an "age of *possibilities*, when hopes flourish, when people have unparalleled opportunity to transform their lives."[18] While this basic definition has been expanded and problematized in the developmental sciences over the past decade, the literary examples discussed below suggest that this definition can also contribute to a deeper understanding of literary explorations of current concerns and challenges facing young people, beyond the previous focus on adolescent identity formation only.[19] In addition, though, besides the rather unifying social science approach which attempts to categorize larger groups of young people, the literary texts and their multilayered stories reveal the need to individualize this research in order to capture the multifaceted experiences of the emerging adults. These experiences depend on their individual matrix of diversity factors that influence their development and, thereby, their individual constructions of home and belonging. Diversity, in this definition, is understood in its broadest

---

17 Jeffrey Jensen Arnett, *Emerging Adulthood: The Winding Road from the Late Teens through the Twenties* (Oxford: Oxford UP, 2004).
18 All preceding quotations: Jensen Arnett, *Emerging Adulthood*, 8 (emphases in the original).
19 Literary forms such as coming-of-age literature, the *bildungsroman*, the story of initiation or formation, or young adult fiction have traditionally focused on adolescent heroes. Being an adolescent, however, limits the potential scope of explorations due to so-called institutional guidance, e. g., by parents or school. Therefore, their experience as well as their literary explorations differ significantly from that of emerging adults, who perceive themselves to be in a different in-between position due to other influence factors like the challenge of building their independent lives or making long-term career and relationship decisions (cf. Hertlein, *Tales of Transformation*, 36–44).

sense, covering the various influence factors that possibly influence a person's development and construction of home and belonging from their own or another's perspective, ranging from such diverse points as socioeconomic status or ethnic background to factors such as sex, gender, religion, or physical or mental health.[20] These possibly intersecting categories, following Kimberlé Crenshaw's already mentioned concept of intersectionality, influence not only a person's individual development, but, as I show from the examples of various contemporary texts, also influence their possibly diasporic constructions of home and belonging. In addition to the ideas and concepts from critical diversity studies and intersectionality, Lene Arnett Jensen connects the developmental science concept of emerging adulthood with ethnic and cultural backgrounds.[21] These ideas and concepts form the theoretical framework for the analyses in the following.

Exploring diasporic constructions of home and belonging in texts below, the focus is not only on the dispersal inherent in diasporas, but rather on creating a home and sense of belonging within the framework of influence factors on individual identity in the age group of emerging adulthood. This individual identity is shaped by various factors whose impact is not necessarily stable, which creates a creative potential of ongoing negotiations and constructions. The position in limbo, with asymmetric relationships of different influence factors, is caused both by the diasporic setting and aspects of diversity which characterize the individuals in question. However, all individual characters discussed below can be considered emerging adults, which places them in limbo between adolescence and adulthood. Therefore, this study proposes a connection between the different influence factors of being in limbo, in the sense of a mutual influence of emerging adulthood and diasporic experience on constructions of home and belonging in that particular age group. Alongside the shared experience of needing to find one's place in the world in a diasporic setting, the in-betweenness between adolescence and the perceived reaching of a 'full' adult status forms a common ground between the characters. This common ground is based on shared experiences, including an ongoing negotiation and construction of a

---

20 Melissa Steyn proposes the need for a 'critical diversity literacy' in order to understand the matrix of influence factors as well as their relationship on individuals and groups (Melissa Steyn, "Critical Diversity Literacy. Diversity Awareness in 12 South African Organisations," in *Being Different Together: Case Studies on Diversity Interventions in some South African Organisations*, ed. Melissa Steyn [EBW, 2010]: 15–42 <https://open.uct.ac.za/bitstream/handle/11427/4149/Being_different_together.pdf> [acc. April 8, 2011]).
21 Lene Arnett Jensen (ed.), *Bridging Cultural and Developmental Approaches to Psychology: New Syntheses in Theory, Research, and Policy* (Oxford: Oxford UP, 2011).

sense of home and belonging that is reflected in the contemporary literary examples for this study. In these texts, both the diasporic experience and the phase of emerging adulthood contribute to the characters' position in limbo, from which various notions of home and belonging are explored.

In the examples discussed below, the difficulty of constructing and narrating spaces as well as constructions of home and belonging is present on various levels. In addition, some of the protagonists as well as possibly some of the authors could be regarded as growing up as 'third culture kids,' following Ruth E. Van Reken's concept, which she recently expanded to that of a 'cross-culture kid'.[22] However, even though both biographies and autobiographies as well as novels of formation, coming-of-age stories, stories of initiation, or the *bildungsroman* have always been looked at with regard to identity formation and a focus on "human emergence,"[23] the texts examined here are different. They neither concern themselves with one central hero's story only, nor do they cover the developmental phase of adolescence, which has frequently been used for the depiction of the process of negotiating one's identity, as Millard's overview summarizes.[24]

Instead, the texts undermine the assumption that the characters deeply engage in the creation and construction of their individual sense of home and belonging in the explorations of emerging adulthood. In this period, external influences and structures loosen; emerging adults are less subject to institutional guidance, for example by school or parents. Therefore, for the first time (and hence: unlike in adolescence), mostly the emerging adults' individual influence factors impact their own creations of home and belonging rather than the ones provided for them by parents or other societal institutions. However, emerging

---

22 Ruth E. Van Reken, "Cross-Cultural Kids: The New Prototype," in *Writing Out of Limbo. International Childhoods, Global Nomads and Third Culture Kids*, eds. Gene H. Bell-Villada, Nina Sichel with Faith Eidse and Elaine Neil Orr (Newcastle-upon-Tyne: Cambridge Scholars P, 2011): 25–44.

23 See, for example, Mikhail Bakhtin, "The Bildungsroman and Its Significance in the History of Realism (Toward a Historical Typology of the Novel)," in *Speech Genres and Other Late Essays*, trans. Vern W. McGee, eds. Caryl Emerson, Michael Holquist (Austin: U of Texas P, 1994): 21. Bakhtin's more general sense of a novel dealing with "human emergence," in which a protagonist's unity is dynamic rather than static and in which personal development is significant for the plot (21), applies to the texts discussed here as well. However, the notion of "human emergence" is placed in a different, more fluid or instable context.

24 Kenneth Millard, for example, discusses the difficulty of applying the concept of a bildungsroman or coming-of-age story to texts covering adults: Kenneth Millard, *Coming of Age in Contemporary American Fiction* (Edinburgh: Edinburgh UP, 2007): 4–5. For further details see, e. g., Hertlein, *Tales of Transformation*, 36–44.

adulthood neither covers a clearly distinguishable age frame nor necessarily a whole age cohort, but experiencing this phenomenon depends on each individual. Young people who, by their own choice or by external forces or necessities, remain in tight structures that do not allow this time of exploration, are therefore not part of this consideration. Moreover, even if the ways in which people experience emerging adulthood differ, people navigate between various kinds of independence and interdependence, constructing their individual sense of home and belonging in their chosen or prescribed social groups with more independence than within closer-knit family or institutional structures. This ongoing negotiation and construction is an integral part of the texts used for this study as well, texts that concern themselves with constructing an individual, independent as well as interdependent sense of home and belonging in various diasporic settings. In the texts, young people as emerging adults try to construct reliable structures for themselves. Later on, as "young adults" following the phase of emerging adulthood, they move on to navigate the web or matrix that they have constructed. These constructions also entail the creation of a safe space of their own, first for themselves and possibly, in a next step, for a future family. In various contemporary literary texts, these constructions are reflected and negotiated both in form and content. These processes are explored by mirroring the ongoing constructions, for example, through multiperspectivity, fragmentation, and other narrative strategies. In addition, the experience of growing up "between worlds" or "in limbo," an experience that the protagonists share to different extents and for various reasons, contributes an additional factor in the matrix of diversity that informs their individual constructions.

Jiro Adachi's 2004 novel *The Island of Bicycle Dancers* focuses on twenty-year-old Korean-Japanese Yurika who is to practice her English by working at her Korean-American uncle's grocery store. The store is called "Lucky Market," but the name does not reflect Yurika's sense of home and belonging there. The Korean-American community as such may not be regarded as a diaspora by definitions like Tölölyan's, but through the setting in a New York City neighborhood and a store which is frequented by customers and bike messengers with diverse backgrounds, Yurika is confronted with different diasporas and links her experience to that of minor characters who are parts of diasporas. Yurika's explorations are presented to the reader mostly through an autodiegetic narrator with very few exceptions in which other characters' perspectives are included and conveyed by a different narrator. Thus, the narrative features Yurika as a possible "central hero,"[25] but the narrative places her in the context of a wider community

---

25 A single protagonist is a typical feature of novels of formation, initiation, and other novels

which introduces her and the reader to various different characters and their communities. Apart from the more obvious, external freedoms that she tries and partly succeeds to establish for herself and her identity explorations, she keeps her distance and constructs a dream-world according to her hopes as well. Even though her dreams and imaginations clash with reality more than once, as I illustrate below, they nonetheless support her breaking free from the constraints of her family's life and work that she cannot wholly identify with. In addition, the instances away from her home allow her to meet other emerging and young adults, for example in diasporic settings. Particularly the asymmetric power relations which Yurika experiences in her family provide a link to the experiences of other characters, whose constraints stem rather from their diasporic backgrounds than their families. Yurika thereby experiences some of the features that Kuortti relates to diaspora settings even though her background is not exactly diasporic.

Yurika is different and therefore distances herself from her relatives not only because of her being there only for the summer or her being a young person, but also because of her family background. When growing up in Japan, she has always been confronted with her family background of a Japanese mother and a Korean father, who, because of his different and potentially problematic heritage, had changed his name upon his arrival in Japan. Yurika, however, grew up in Japan and therefore identifies as Japanese, if with a cross-Asian background. Upon her arrival in the USA, this conflict she has become used to over the years only seems to cause difficulties with her relatives, especially her aunt. Apart from them, to Yurika's surprise, nobody seems to care (cf. *IBD*, 3–5), revealing different asymmetries of power and status in her new setting. In that instance, the role of the narration for the development of the story becomes clear as well, shifting between Yurika and her aunt as autodiegetic narrators. Other characters, such as colleagues at the grocery store or some of the bike messengers that Yurika befriends, are mainly presented through Yurika's perspective, with the exception of Yurika's closer friend Whitey. Whitey also fulfills the role of

---

featuring individual development before reaching legal adult status. *The Island of Bicycle Dancers* in part uses this feature as well, and the introduction of Yurika as a "central hero" (the term is from Bakhtin, "The Bildungsroman," 21) suggests that she lacks the freedom to explore which is an inherent part of emerging adulthood. Nonetheless, one could regard her as an emerging adult since she attempts at finding her way to explore her identity and sense of belonging (cp. Arnett's characteristics of emerging adulthood [*Emerging Adulthood*, 8]) and reaches the in-between state that links her experience to emerging adulthood. Moreover, her explorations give her the chance to learn about other communities in New York, including some diasporic communities, which is the reason for including her into this study.

guiding Yurika's first steps outside the confined space of her family's grocery store. Yurika's bike serves as her means of physically getting around, which connects her to the bike messengers whom she admires, but she equally learns more about different lifestyles and the impact of various diversity factors on individual life choices when she is able to leave the house and join other emerging adults on her bike. The importance of the bike for her explorations as an emerging adult and on her creation of a sense of home and belonging becomes clear when she decides to repair bikes for a living and to move into an apartment of her own after her friend Whitey's death. Yurika's example thereby connects an emerging adult's struggle to build one's own life and the need to create a sense of home in a position in limbo, which her friends in diasporic settings share with her transnational experience. Also, her transnational experience is equally informed by power asymmetries, even though it is not diasporic as such. Other characters in the novel, such as her host sister and cousin Suzie of a similar age, or Yurika's uncle are also represented with their own voice in the story, but they only contribute minor parts to significant aspects of this analysis.

Also, the different perspectives are integrated by Yurika as an autodiegetic narrator. The shifts between the different homodiegetic narrators are integrated into the more or less linear, chronological plot rather than presenting the perspectives in individual chapters devoted to an individual perspective. This latter strategy is used, for example, in Loida Maritza Pérez' Dominican-American novel *Geographies of Home* (1999). In this novel, the ongoing negotiations are reflected by chapters devoted to individual perspectives by different autodiegetic narrators. The reader therefore cannot rely on one perspective for plot development or characterization, but is introduced to different, sometimes contradicting viewpoints. Both the diasporic setting and questions of home and belonging are explored differently by different characters and their homodiegetic narrating voices, each reflecting their individual position among the family members and their relation to their current situation in New York City. Aurelia, the mother, for example frequently refers back to memories of her life in the Dominican Republic, integrating these memories into her constructions of her new home in the USA. These memories help her build her life despite the disappointments that she faces in New York. Contrasting her with her daughters, the impact of a stable sense of the adult self on constructing a sense of home and belonging in diasporic settings becomes visible. Her daughters struggle to find their places in the world for different reasons, but they share the insecurity of emerging adulthood. Rebecca, as the eldest of the siblings in the novel, remembers the Dominican Republic and is different from the two younger sisters whose perspectives are included in the novel. Rebecca is married with two children and has a house, but the idea of her having found her place and therefore having overcome emerging adulthood is subverted since the house is in a desolate state and her abusive husband cares more for the well-being of his chickens than for his family. Therefore, despite theoretical markers of young adulthood, Rebecca's situation can still be related to that of an emerging adult. While she tries to provide a stable home for her children, she continuously fails, which her perspective conveys through a note from her child's school in which she is asked to intensify her care for her child, or which her mother notices when her children begin to hide food as soon as they spend time at their grandparents' house. Frequently, her parents come and get her and her children, often against Rebecca's will, because they fear negative consequences if they leave the children in their run-down home. Rebecca's struggles to construct a safe home and sense of belonging for her children are expressed through the interplay of different narrating voices in the different chapters which refer to her situation – her own perception and her mother's and sisters' perspectives – and by the imagery in the text, for example the description of her house. In this novel, the house functions as a symbol for both parts of the family, which connects her experience to that of her mother and her siblings. While one might expect a house to represent a stable element in the construction of a sense of home and belonging, especially Rebecca's house but also her family's house subvert this idea in *Geographies of Home*. The insecurities connected with both houses coincide with the feeling of in-betweenness in many different respects, among others the Dominican-American heritage. In addition, however, Rebecca's abusive relationship, which places her between her chosen new home and her birth family's home, contributes to her feeling both adult and responsible and realizing the failures which, in her eyes, subvert her status as a full adult and bring her back to her birth family in the role of a child. In her case, emerging adulthood is therefore not a voluntary state.

Her two sisters who are also presented in detail in the novel, Marina and Iliana, experience different challenges in creating a sense of home and belonging in limbo. Both sisters are deeply influenced by their father's Seventh Day Adventist belief, which places the family outside the conventionally Catholic Dominican American diaspora.[26] The reactions to their father's strict interpretation of Seventh Day Adventism and its consequences on their lifestyles differ, however.

---

[26] In an interview appended to the novel and available at <http://www.penguin.com/read/book-clubs/geographies-of-home/9781440621185> (acc. March 20, 2015), Loida Maritza Pérez states that she deliberately chose Seventh Day Adventism as Papito's religion: "Because Latinos are usually portrayed as Catholic, [Pérez] wanted to delve into one of the Protestant and increasingly proselytized religions such as that of Jehovah's Witnesses, Seventh-Day Adventist, – Mormonism, Pentecostalism, or whatever. Choosing the most restrictive of these religions enabled [Pérez] to provide more of a contrast with alternate forms of spirituality and folk religions."

Rebecca seems to adhere mostly to the idea of a family and her role as a mother, but the reader learns little about her religious convictions. Similarly, her mother follows her husband's orders, but secretly resists some aspects of his strong beliefs, for example when she begins to practice supernatural powers again by communicating with her daughter Iliana, conveyed in a manner reminiscent of magical realism, and by killing her abusive son-in-law, Pasión. Marina and Iliana react in different ways to their Seventh Day Adventist upbringing. Iliana's struggles to break free from the constraints of her father's rules are conveyed throughout the novel, for example in the first chapter, when she ponders her time in college and the impact that her father's ideas still have on her when away. However, the novel begins with her returning to her family's home in order to help out with family problems, which is why she is continuously confronted with her father's worldview while at home, and she reflects on this throughout the novel. Her character shows the difficulty of finding one's own place in the world, embracing one's family background and heritage, but equally deciding on one's own way. While she does not maintain an emotional connection to the Dominican Republic in the same way as Rebecca does, Iliana nonetheless struggles to construct her sense of home and belonging in limbo. This position in limbo is due to the typical challenges of emerging adults in general, but even more due to other, intersecting diversity factors like her diasporic heritage, her family's socioeconomic status, and other family issues. One major factor that contributes to the difficulty of constructing a sense of home and belonging connected to Iliana's family home is her sister Marina's mental health issue. Due to Marina's condition, Iliana's sense of security at her family's home is challenged when Marina attacks and injures her. Marina, who has difficulties adapting to the New York setting and claims to have been raped, feels attacked at the family home during one of her bi-polar episodes and sets the house on fire, and later on, she attempts to rape Iliana. These attacks on the house as a structure and on Iliana who should feel safe inside her family's house convey an idea of instability and thereby subvert the notion of safety that might otherwise be connected to such a house (as in Tölölyan's sense of the 'safe space,' discussed above). Unlike Rebecca's children, who are safe from their abusive father at their grandparents' house, Iliana and, at least from Marina's perspective due to her mental condition, Marina are not safe in the house they consider their home. While Marina's case is solved in the novel by her receiving medical treatment away from home, Iliana could be regarded as moving forward in her pursuit of creating her sense of home and belonging. At the beginning of the novel, the autodiegetic narrator introduces her (Iliana) as having failed to create this sense of home and belonging by running away from her family's home for college, but by the end of the novel it appears as if some of her explorations and experiences have led to a new sense of home and belonging. This new sense could be regarded as a more balanced basis for her future adult life than the running away had been. Iliana and Rebecca therefore serve as examples of the interactions of different factors on creating one's sense of home and belonging, here the position in limbo due to a diasporic setting as well as other diversity factors such as emerging adulthood or socioeconomic status. Moreover, their examples show the impact of intersectionality, revealing the multiple layers of difference which add up in their impact on the character's creation of a sense of home and belonging. Here, asymmetrical relations such as the ones Kuortti refers to occur not only because of the diasporic setting, but equally because of the family's socioeconomic status. The asymmetrical relation because of the parent-children relationship, however, based on the father's idea of being the head of the house even after his children become legal adults, is reevaluated over the course of the novel. Thereby, *Geographies of Home* serves as an interesting example of different interactions in diasporic constructions of home and belonging, especially regarding emerging adults.

Monica Pradhan's Indian-American[27] novel *The Hindi-Bindi Club* (2007) uses a similar strategy, and Pradhan, like Pérez, includes a parental perspective. In *The Hindi-Bindi Club,* three mothers and their three daughters narrate individual chapters in which the autodiegetic narrator is indicated by name next to the chapter's title. This novel thereby interweaves different backgrounds based on various features since the protagonists come from different regions of India, professions, and social classes, and are linked mainly through their common challenge to build their lives in the same region in the USA at the same time. For the daughters, their parents nonetheless form a close-knit group, like an ersatz family, which explains the name *Hindi-Bindi Club,* which they attribute to their parents' friendship and which is used as the title of the novel. All three of the daughters grow up in this group, which they perceive as their Indian American diaspora. Throughout the novel, the reader begins to realize the differences between the families and the individual legacies that inform their lives. Especially the mothers' chapters provide explanations for situations, in which issues like the Indian Partition, which affected many people, and individual family issues impact the lives of the group. Since the struggles around constructing or maintaining a sense of home and belonging transcend families in this novel, the influence of one form of a diaspora on these constructions is more prominent than

---

27 It is debatable whether the Indian-American community forms a diaspora. Here, the text is included in analogy to Kuortti's *Writing Imagined Diasporas*, in which he includes Jhumpa Lahiri's Indian-American writings as well.

in the other texts in this study. The characters' position in limbo is caused by their situations in life, for example the daughters facing the challenges of emerging adulthood and trying to explore and find their place in the world. Since the daughters are already in their late twenties and early thirties, they begin to face some consequences from their first choices as emerging adults: Kiran is divorced, Rani changed her job from her training as a rocket scientist to being a freelance artist despite her unstable mental health, and seemingly 'perfect' Preity confronts her bulimia and needs to resolve an issue with her mother over a potential boyfriend of hers whom she had not even been allowed to say goodbye to since he was a Muslim. Nonetheless, their position in limbo as emerging adults has not been overcome yet, and over the course of the novel the reader learns that they need to work on their relationships with each other as well as their mothers in order to construct a more stable sense of home and belonging. This renegotiation of their relationships and, as a consequence, their sense of home and belonging happens not only individually or within the families, but it transcends family borders and relates various experiences across the different families. Issues like the inability to speak about one's fears, shame, or traumas, about health conditions, but also about diverging expectations are resolved across family and age lines, but within the Hindi-Bindi club and *The Hindi-Bindi Club*, that is, both among the characters in the close circle of friends within the text and in the novel as such. In the text, the reader sees the negotiations reflected in the structure, like the different autodiegetic narrators used in the chapters, but also in inserted emails and chat conversations and in the recipes that accompany each chapter. Both content and form thereby interact to reflect the ongoing negotiations that reveal the ongoing constructions of home and belonging in a diasporic setting, especially by the emerging adults who perceived themselves to be in limbo between their Indian and US backgrounds, their families, their own expectations, and between being their parents' child and a mature individual. In their case, the safe "social space" described by Tölölyan referring to a home becomes a shared "social space" within *The Hindi-Bindi Club*.

In the Palestinian American and Palestinian-Jordanian American[28] texts *The Inheritance of Exile* by Susan Muaddi Darraj (2007) and *West of the Jordan* by Layla Halaby (2003), similar narrative strategies are used, but without the insertion of emails, chat conversations, or recipes. Also, the mothers are either only presented from the perspective of their daughters (the autodiegetic narrators)

---

28 My use of the term 'Palestinian' is not intended to position myself in the debate over the applicability of the term, since Palestine currently does not exist as a country. This difficulty with the terminology is expressed and negotiated in the texts I discuss here and, since they use this term as a frame of reference, I also use it.

or, in some instances in *The Inheritance of Exile*, by shifts between narrators within a single chapter, which are not easily visible for the reader. Both texts, however, include soon-to-be emerging adults (in *WoJ*) and emerging adults (in *IoE*) who struggle to construct their own sense of home and belonging. All of the characters are in limbo due to the political situation in Palestine, which affects all of them regardless of their current country of residence. Most characters are based in the USA and are part of the Palestinian American diaspora, but in *West of the Jordan*, some characters maintain close relationships with Palestine and Jordan. In addition to this legacy of being in-between because of the political situation, the emerging adult protagonists struggle with other, intersecting influences on their sense of home and belonging. Similar to some examples mentioned above, Hanan (in *IoE*) breaks up with her boyfriend and becomes a single mother who has to to build a home for her son; Nadia (also in *IoE*) suffers on multiple levels ranging from her relationship to physical disabilities from the physical consequences of a car accident; and Hala (in *WoJ*) must choose between returning to Jordan and becoming a wife or continuing her education in the USA according to her dead mother's wish. All of the characters are presented as exploring their choices, and the reader is introduced to each of them and their worlds by autodiegetic narrators[29] who allow to empathize with each of them. At the same time, various intersecting challenges due to their specific circumstances influence their constructions of home and belonging. The experience of being part of a diaspora serves as an integrating factor in both texts. In *The Inheritance of Exile*, the circle of friends is formed only after schoolmates have identified all of them as coming from the Middle East, despite their different family backgrounds including different religions, as some families are Christians while others are Muslims. In the text, stereotypical images and binaries connected to the families' Middle Eastern heritage are frequently included to convey the status in limbo between their upbringing in the USA and their heritage,[30] both by

---

29 Similar to *HBC*, *Short Girls*, and *GoH*, the novel does not have one consistent narrator. Instead, narration shifts between different autodiegetic narrators in individual chapters assigned to them. However, unlike in the other novels, narration in *The Inheritance of Exile* sometimes even shifts within the chapter, for example to a parent, while none of the parents are attributed a whole chapter by themselves. These shifts are difficult to recognize at first, as they are not as clearly marked as the chapters attributed to a particular character suggest.

30 For example, all four Arab American women remember having been well integrated in their Catholic school, but when Reema's aunt, visiting from the West Bank and wearing a hijab, picks her up one day, the situation changes: "The next day in school was the first time anyone called [Reema and later Aliyah] a 'towelhead' [...] and by the end of the year, Nadia and Hanan had joined their camel jockey circle" (*IoE*, 181). In this context, Reema recalls how the four of them became friends despite their age difference and different years in school, as all four of

the narrators and characters themselves and other people referring to them. Again, the position in limbo and the struggles to create their sense of home and belonging are informed by the diasporic community and other elements such as the characters' age group, and in both cases narrative perspectives and content convey the ongoing negotiations and constructions.

The use of stereotypes alongside the literary exploration of an emerging adult's quest for their own sense of home and belonging is also part of Hina Haq's *Sadika's Way*, in which young Pakistani Sadika is sent to the USA. Sadika's story, in which the reader is introduced to both Sadika's and her mother's points of view by a heterodiegetic narrator, confronts stereotypical notions and expectations of womanhood in Pakistan and the USA. As an unwanted girl, she has been placed in limbo and therefore struggled to find her place in Pakistan and continues to do so in the USA. However, especially in the USA, Sadika uses the freedom to explore different options as an emerging adult while she tries to construct a sense of home and a safe space she had not known earlier. *Sadika's Way*, as the title suggests, focuses on Sadika as a central hero, and it traces Sadika's quest for home and belonging in the Pakistani diaspora and beyond through heterodiegetic narration. Thereby, the novel offers a different view of how diasporic settings, emerging adulthood, and other elements of diversity, here gender, interact in the construction of home and belonging.

In the Vietnamese-American novel *Short Girls* by Bich Minh Nguyen from 2010, the reader is also confronted with different autodiegetic narrators, but here restricted to chapters clearly assigned to each of the two sisters, Linh and Van. Their perspectives are presented as interwoven accounts of a short, mainly chronologically ordered plot, which is presented in clearly assigned chapters by each sister as a protagonist of the respective chapter. Through this strategy, the reader can explore the situations from two distinct perspectives, since the sisters are rather different. Both, however, struggle with their Vietnamese heritage, knowing how much their father had longed to go back while they grew up,

---

them were identified as "Arabs" by their peers. Also, as a PhD candidate, Reema is described by her friend Hanan as carrying her backpack full of books looking like a camel, but more obviously, she is constructed as the exotic other by a boyfriend who relates her and her heritage to the movie *The Sheikh* and arranges her body like a piece of art featuring Cleopatra (*IoE*, 177–178). Hanan rather uses different images to convey her position in limbo, she compares her mother's clear-cut borders between Arabs and Americans to "boxing opponents" (*IoE*, 87) while Hanan herself rather identifies with her immediate home and rejects being identified as the 'exotic other' or 'authentic expert' by others (*IoE*, 138–139). Aliyah, on the other hand, emphasizes the hyphen and the two parts of her identity as "*Arab*-American" (*IoE*, 69, emphasis in the original).

but not anymore now that he has found his place in the Vietnamese American diaspora. While Linny/Linh embraces the characteristics of an emerging adult and actively seeks to explore many options in her love and work life, Van is presented as more conservative. Nonetheless, Van is forced to explore more because of her breakup with her husband. Through this experience, Van becomes more open and realizes her need to construct her own sense of home, belonging, and self. At the same time, their father decides to become an American citizen in order to participate in a talent show for inventors. He is a contemporary version of the self-made-man, but one who heavily relies on other people for his life apart from his inventions. These other people include his children and friends from the Vietnamese American diaspora. Also, his inventions are like a bridge to the US setting for him: He always begins to invent something new in order to overcome an obstacle that Mr. Luong attributes to being Vietnamese, namely being short.[31] Van and Linny are continuously confronted with their father both withdrawing in order to work on his inventions and his claims that the inventions are his only way of earning a place in US society. The daughters, however, have found their own ways of belonging and, since they were born in the USA, experience a different feeling of being in limbo than their father. When Mr. Luong asks them to support him with his application for citizenship and the talent show, however, the sisters not only reconnect with each other and begin to get to know each other better as emerging adults rather than as rivaling children, they also confront their struggles about their sense of home and belonging in a new way. *Short Girls* thereby connects questions of the particular situation of the Vietnamese American diaspora and the situation of emerging adults trying to find their place in the world within a framework of various axes of difference. The sisters are both influenced by the legacy of having come to the USA because of the Vietnam War, living in refugee camps, or needing sponsors and slowly integrating into US society. However, each of the sisters draws her own conclusions from that experience, and as emerging adults, they begin to realize how each of them at times also misjudged the other family members and their coping strategies. Moreover, since they are presented as seemingly very different characters at first, both reader and protagonists only realize after a while that they, in some ways, are closer than one might have thought. Both the shared experience of

---

31 In one of the Linny chapters, Mr. Luong teaches his daughters that, since they as Vietnamese Americans were shorter than other Americans, they needed to be "smarter," which for him means inventing things to overcome this diversity feature (cf. *Short Girls*, 61). Unlike Linny, who simply wishes to be and look like her non-Vietnamese American peers, he thereby represents the idea of having to (re-)invent oneself and earn one's place in what he understands as "the" American society, outside his Vietnamese American diaspora.

growing up in the Vietnamese American diaspora under the given circumstances and their common experience as siblings forms a stronger bond than the sisters had imagined. This bond is conveyed as helping them through the struggles of the period covered in the novel, which includes Van's breakup with her husband, Linny's final decision for a career in favor of multiple, short-term employments, and their father's attempt at integrating into US society by participating in the talent show. The show is more relevant for the sisters than they imagine at first, because they are forced to change their typical roles in the course of events surrounding the talent show, which leads to them reconsider their relationship and their lives in general. Thereby, both sisters reconstruct their sense of home and belonging based on different features than before, drawing conclusions from this period in limbo in which they explored multiple options as emerging adults. At the same time, these explorations are always connected to their specific heritage, and their reconstructions of belonging include a new valuation and integration of the Vietnamese American diaspora as a part of their home and belonging rather than trying to distance themselves from this group of people and the heritage connected with them.

The texts discussed here offer insight into diasporic constructions of home and belonging, and they do so in a more general sense than speaking for a specific diaspora only. They transcend specific ethnic, national, or cultural ties in their depiction of emerging adults who, in different diasporic settings, perceive themselves to be in limbo and faced with the task of constructing their own sense of home and belonging. Still, the impact of particular diasporic settings and legacies should not be disregarded. As briefly indicated with some of the texts, specific circumstances such as the Vietnam War and the resulting Vietnamese American diaspora, the unresolved situation in Palestine, or the Indian Partition influence the characters and their constructions of home and belonging in different ways. At the same time, sharing a position in limbo due to being an emerging adult who needs to explore one's options in order to create an own sense of home connects the different experiences. Moreover, some literary strategies are similar even though other factors influencing the construction of home and belonging may differ. Therefore, the texts discussed here serve as examples of how novels featuring emerging adults who face in-betweenness in multiple ways can contribute to an enhanced understanding of diasporic constructions of home and belonging. These texts represent people and their experiences of trying to find their place in the world. This process of growing up and becoming an adult who has learned to navigate between independence and interdependence in an emancipated, responsible way is reflected in the texts. In this developmental phase, the characters struggle to create their own "safe space" that they can claim as a home, which is presented in various literary ways. As the examples have shown, the storytelling may reflect the negotiations, for example, through multiperspectivity. In addition, many of the examples above reject a simple dichotomy of exploring how the "exotic other" integrates into the mainstream US society or into another stereotypical social group, revealing shifting affiliations and alliances as well as mobility between margins and center. In these negotiations, uneven power structures are presented as well. The open endings, which all of the texts share, further enhance the continuing construction and the continued necessity for imaginative efforts and negotiations over affiliations, even in rather fixed settings such as marriage. Through these elements, the texts also challenge conventional stories of formation that focus on one "central hero" and a clearly distinguishable developmental phase, possibly even within fixed structures or institutions like during adolescence. Nonetheless, emerging adulthood as a transitional phase reflects more than one way of being in-between. By emphasizing a position in limbo rather than clear-cut borders between adolescence and adulthood, emerging adulthood thereby captures the level of ambiguity and of individualizing constructions of home and belonging in a specific age group. This position in limbo relates to the in-betweenness of diasporic settings, and the developmental period of emerging adulthood coincides with the first possibility independently to create one's own sense of home and belonging. Nonetheless, independence and the opportunity to explore are not unlimited, as the examples above show, especially in a setting with asymmetrical relations. Therefore, a closer examination of texts that feature this in-betweenness for many different reasons including personal development and diasporic settings could contribute important perspectives to exploring contemporary diasporic constructions of home and belonging.

Jean Amato
It All Depends on What You Mean by Home: Metaphors of Return in Chinese American Travel Memoirs from the 1980s to 2010s

Abstract: This chapter explores a diverse selection of Chinese American memoirs from the 1980s to the present by both US-born and immigrant authors that center on a 'return to the ancestral home' motif. These ancestral home narratives are inspired, continually invigorated, and revised by shifting and colliding affiliations. Despite this fluid signifying range, nostalgic ideas of an ancestral home are often constructed and ideologically solidified around very fixed representations of space and time. However, bodies, histories, and places are always in flux and refuse to be pinned down into a particular imagined geography. Of primary concern here is how each writer chooses to negotiate and represent the inevitable disparity between prior nostalgic visions of the ancestral home with their actual travel experiences in the PRC. This geographical and temporal distancing provides an imaginative gap that allows writers and/or readers to interrogate culturally specific ideologies and nostalgic constructions. As these narratives grapple with the intricate relationships between private longing and public belonging, and the fluidity of identity formation and affiliations, a key focus here is on the varied metaphoric interventions each writer draws on to address this often-uncomfortable juxtaposition in his or her work.

Ideas of home and belonging to an ancestral homeland are commonly perceived as natural givens set high in an individual's hierarchy of attachments. This association occurs on both personal and communal levels, thus generating a shared assumption that a nostalgic desire for an ancestral home and homeland – a place where one can always feel "at home" – is a given.[1] An imagined ancestral home operates as a projected site of shifting and intersecting territorial, cultural, familial, ethnic, national, and individual affiliations. Despite this fluid signifying range, nostalgic ideas of an ancestral home are often constructed and ideologically solidified around very fixed representations of space and time. In this project I reference a wide sampling of Chinese American memoirs that involve a journey to China, from the 1980s to the present to probe cultural expressions of how meanings become attached to imagined ancestral homes; whereas bodies, histories, and places are always in flux and refuse to be pinned down into a particular

---

1 Étienne Balibar, *Race, Nation, Class: Ambiguous Identities*, trans. Immanuel Maurice Wallerstein (New York: Verso, 1991): 139, 145; Emily Honig, "Native Place and the Making of Chinese Ethnicity," in *Remapping China: Fissures in Historical Terrain*, eds. Gail Hershatter et al. (Stanford: Stanford UP, 1996): 143–155; Rosemary Marangoly George, *The Politics of Home: Postcolonial Relocations and Twentieth-century Fiction* (New York: Cambridge UP, 1996): 4, 20–22.

imagined geography. I focus on a diverse range of English language memoirs from both immigrant and US-born Chinese American writers that includes: Tsai Chin's [Zhou Caiqin], *Daughter of Shanghai* (1988),[2] Pang-Mei Natasha Chang's *Bound Feet & Western Dress* (1997),[3] May-lee and Winberg Chai's *The Girl from Purple Mountain: Love, Honor, War, and One Family's Journey from China to America* (2001),[4] May-lee Chai's *Hapa Girl: A Memoir* (2007),[5] Yi-Fu Tuan's *Coming Home to China* (2007),[6] and Val Wang's, *Beijing Bastard: Into the Wilds of a Changing China* (2014).[7]

Each of these writers infuses his or her work with unique configurations of ever-evolving relationships between home, self, heritage, and nation in a diasporan context. Here, I agree with cultural geographers Alison Blunt and Robyn Dowling and their call to view ancestral homes as sites of memory that can be understood as "performative spaces within which both personal and inherited connections to other remembered or imagined homes are embodied, enacted and reworked."[8] By unpacking a diverse array of narratives that grapple with intricate relationships between private longing and public belonging, and the fluidity of identity formation and affiliations, I hope to present glimpses into the creation and reception of ancestral home return motifs with their full incongruence and complexity.

Nostalgia for the ancestral homeland is often built on a romantic myth where a pure and homogeneous idea of the home lies frozen in memory, free from change and contestation. The physical geographic space of present day People's Republic of China (PRC) often seems to challenge the imagined ideals of individual or inherited memory – in short, it functions as a necessary obstacle for nostalgia to overcome. The narration of an ancestral home is, in part, an individu-

---

2 Tsai Chin, *Daughter of Shanghai* (New York: St. Martin's P, 1988). Further references in the text, abbreviated as "*DS.*"

3 Pang-Mei Natasha Chang, *Bound Feet & Western Dress* (New York: Random House, 2007). Further references in the text, abbreviated as "*BF*".

4 May-lee Chai, Winberg Chai, *The Girl from Purple Mountain: Love, Honor, War, and One Family's Journey from China to America* (New York: Macmillan, 2001). Further references in the text, abbreviated as "*PM*".

5 May-lee Chai, *Hapa Girl: A Memoir* (Philadelphia: Temple UP, 2007). Further references in the text, abbreviated as "*HG*".

6 Yi-Fu Tuan, *Coming Home to China* (Minneapolis: U of Minnesota P, 2007). Further references in the text, abbreviated as "*CH*".

7 Val Wang, *Beijing Bastard: Into the Wilds of a Changing China.* (New York: Gotham Books, 2014). Further references in the text, abbreviated as "*BB*".

8 Alison Blunt and Robyn Dowling, *Home (Key Ideas in Geography)* (Abingdon: Routledge, 2006): 212.

alized expression of a relationship with a conceptualized and often ambivalent idea of origin, native space, and place. Rather than focusing on each writer's attachment or degree of identification with an ancestral home, my primary concern here is how each writer chooses to negotiate and represent the inevitable disparity between prior nostalgic, remembered or imagined visions of the ancestral homeland with their actual travel experiences in the PRC. I focus primarily on the varied metaphoric interventions each writer draws on to address this often-uncomfortable juxtaposition in their work. Inevitably, argues theorist Madan Sarap, "we are born into relationships that are always based in a place."[9] These memoirs can play an important role in our understanding of how desire for a sense of belonging is played out on the trope of the ancestral homeland.

In the US, with a population composed primarily of immigrants and the descendants of immigrants, terms such as 'roots,' 'ancestry,' and 'heritage' invoke personal and collective memories that imply an ethnic or ancestral homeland as a cultural and historical inheritance, imported from the country of origin, presumed as always there, waiting to be reclaimed. In his research on immigration and exile, Eric Hobsbawm asks what happens for the majority of Americans, for whom, "the country of their ancestors isn't 'home' but 'roots'."[10] He goes on to explain that for this group, their relation to their homeland is particularly complex, because, "home is not just the 'old country' but, if they are to return to it, must become in some sense a new country."[11] Despite the diversity of the Chinese diaspora, the contested legitimacy between Taiwan, the Republic of China (ROC) and People's Republic of China (PRC), the pull of US nationalism, and extended periods of broken off relations; mainland China still holds a strong command over the cultural imagination in immigrant and US-born Chinese American works as a locus of ethnic and cultural authenticity. Many Chinese American memoirs embrace or subvert a symbolic view of mainland China as the essential 'motherland' and cultural epoch of a purported 'authentic' Chineseness. If we apply Hobsbawn's argument to this return to the ancestral home motif, the physical geographic space of present day PRC, as an ever evolving "new country" may force Chinese American writers to question projections of a locatable sense of cultural belonging and 'authentic' Chineseness onto the im-

---

9 Madan Sarup, "Home and Identity," in *Traveller's Tales: Narratives of Home and Displacements*, ed. George Robertson (New York: Psychology P, 1994): 93–104, 97.
10 Eric Hobsbawm, "Introduction to 'Exile: A Keynote Address'," in *Home: A Place In the World*, ed. Arien Mack (New York: New York UP, 1993): 61–64, 64.
11 Hobsbawm, "Introduction to 'Exile: A Keynote Address'," 64.

agined space of the so-called "old country." This process, in turn, is further complicated by the complex history of the Chinese diaspora.

The perceived ancestral home is not a straightforward concept based solely on one master narrative for the Chinese diaspora. Rather, as a point of intersection it consists of the constant interweaving of multiple allegiances to nation, state, native land, sovereignty, domicile, region, clan, family, heritage, roots, and ethnic identity. Chinese immigrants to the US migrated from regions and ancestral homes permanently altered by the effects of neocolonial capitalism, cultural and economic imperialism, transnationalism, and war. Additionally, Asian immigration and East Asian transnational relations have continually shaped the national self-conception and identity of the US and its nationalisms.[12] Furthermore, many of the writers discussed in this chapter, including Pang-Mei Natasha Chang, May-lee Chai, Tsai Chin, and Yi-Fu Tuan, where influenced or raised by earlier generations who already lived cosmopolitan and transnational lives and either studied or lived as expatriates in Europe or the US before returning to China in the early 1900s. In short, the representation of the ancestral homeland is inspired, continually invigorated, and revised by shifting and colliding affiliations. In her article "Native Place and the Making of Chinese Ethnicity," Emily Honig explains "the centrality of native place [ji guan] identity to Chinese conceptions of self and community."[13] For Honig, native place is a "malleable construction" that individuals can identify with over many generations and it is "continuously in the process of being created and given new meanings."[14]

For ethnic Chinese, in both the Chinese mainland and in the Chinese diaspora, the turbulent historical events of the second half of the twentieth century included but was not limited to a series of economic, social, and political upheavals, vast migrations and emigrations, the Sino-Japanese War, the Second World War, the civil war between Nationalist and Communist forces that led to the establishment of the People's Republic of China in 1949, and the destructive legacy of the Chinese Cultural Revolution (1966–1976). Through the 1960s and early 1970s, the political oppression and ongoing debate over Chinese sovereignty between Taiwan and mainland China often foreclosed state-based Chinese nationalist or patriotic sentiments for the Chinese diaspora. All of these factors

---

12 David Leiwei Li, *Imagining the Nation: Asian American Literature and Cultural Consent* (Stanford: Stanford UP, 1997): 185–206; David Palumbo-Liu, *Asian/American: Historical Crossings of a Racial Frontier* (Stanford: Stanford UP, 1999): 1–17, 218; Rachel C. Lee, *The Americas of Asian American Literature: Gendered Fictions of Nation and Transnation* (Princeton: Princeton UP, 1999): 139–146.
13 Honig, "Native Place and the Making of Chinese Ethnicity," 144.
14 Honig, "Native Place and the Making of Chinese Ethnicity," 146.

contribute to just some of the particular challenges involved as each writer negotiates with these mingled geopolitical and historical relations involved in trying to represent an ancestral home and homeland in a memoir.

From the late 1950s to the late 1970s, internal political and social turmoil in
China, along with severed diplomatic ties between the PRC and the US, and the
larger international framework of the Cold War made almost all forms of contact
or visits to family members in mainland China untenable for Chinese Americans.
These strained conditions with very little overall formal contact lasted until 1979.
Thus, many Chinese Americans knew little about everyday life in the PRC, the
state of their ancestral homes or even the fate of their family members. As a result, they could only look to tales of an ancestral home/homeland through the
belated personal or familial legacy of memories that were embellished with
the gap of distance, loss, and nostalgia. A key point here is that the representation of an ancestral home is an imagined space for *both* immigrant and US-born
authors. While some US-born writers in this chapter seem to ask why they should
expect to feel at home in a country they have never been to, others from an immigrant generation may ask in the context of long-term exile, "what, having left
home, might it mean to return?"[15]

Once China began to open its doors after decades of political barriers that
made visits to the mainland nearly impossible for Chinese Americans, it naturally followed that more contemporary narratives from the early 1980s on would
center on a journey to the mainland in search of a remembered or imagined ancestral home. For many Chinese American writers, both US born and immigrant,
a metaphorical representation of an ancestral home, whether based on personal
or inherited memories, constitutes a discursive construction of an imagined
space defined in part by the distance and desires of its period, author, and audience. This imagined and literarily conceptualized space is also related to, but
not delimited by, the simultaneous existence of a tangible historical and geopolitical material place, namely the PRC with its own constantly evolving, ideological layers of local and global spatial relations. This geographical and temporal
distancing, which is central to this inquiry, provides an imaginative gap that allows writers and/or readers to interrogate culturally specific ideologies and constructions of belonging and nostalgia.

This chapter draws heavily on Svetlana Boym's discussion on the distinctions and interplay between what she sees as two overarching forms of nostalgia,
restorative and reflective. While by no means absolute binaries, Boym argues

---

15 Sara Ahmed, "Introduction," in *Uprootings/Regroundings: Questions of Home and Migration*,
eds. Anne-Marie Fortier et al. (Oxford: Berg, 2003): 1–20, 8.

that a more restorative impulse views itself as truth or tradition as it attempts a "transhistorical reconstruction" of a lost home rather than as nostalgia.[16] Whereas, reflective nostalgia calls into doubt any such absolutes as it embraces contradictory and ambivalent impulses as follows:

> [Restorative nostalgia] signifies a return to the original stasis [...] the past for the restorative nostalgia is a value for the present; the past is not a duration but a perfect snapshot. Moreover, the past is not supposed to reveal any signs of decay; it has to be freshly painted in its "original image" and remain eternally young. Reflective nostalgia is more concerned with historical and individual time, with the irrevocability of the past and human finitude. *Reflection* suggests new flexibility, not the reestablishment of stasis. The focus here is not on recovery of what is perceived to be an absolute truth but on the mediation on history and passage of time. [...] The two might overlap in their frames of reference, but they do not coincide in their narratives and plots of identity [...] [and they] tell different stories. [...] Reflective nostalgia does not pretend to rebuild the mythical place called home; it is enamored of distance, not of the referent itself. This type of nostalgic narrative is ironic, inconclusive and fragmentary. [It is] aware of the gap between identity and resemblance, the home is in ruins or on the contrary, has been just renovated and gentrified beyond recognition. This defamiliarization and sense of distance drives them to tell their story, to narrate the relationship between past, present and future. The past opens up a multitude of potentialities.[17]

As they each negotiate the interplay between restorative and reflective nostalgic impulses in their memoirs, a key focus in this project is on how each writer addresses and reflects on this "gap between identity and resemblance" and their own expectations, desires, and anxieties that they bring to this long awaited journey back to an ancestral home.[18]

For many of the displaced members of the elite class, who fled China during the Communist victory in 1949, the metaphoric role of a presumed, once-glorious ancestral home looms even larger in their writings. In this genre, popular in the 1980s and 1990s, Chinese American writers would often arrive to find their ancestral home and village in ruins or razed to the ground. In narratives from the late 1900s on, writers are often confronted with the dizzying speed of rapid urbanization and development, chronic demolition, the spread of global capitalism, urban and rural corruption, economic inequalities and social upheaval. In some cases, there is no trace of the dwelling that was once the ances-

---

16 Sventlana Boym, "Nostalgia" (2010), *Atlas of Transformation* <http://monumentto transformation.org/atlas-of-transformation/html/n/nostalgia/nostalgia-svetlana-boym.html> (acc. March 3, 2015).
17 Svetlana Boym, *The Future of Nostalgia* (New York: Basic Books, 2001): 49–50.
18 Boym, *The Future of Nostalgia*, 50.

tral home and no sign of its prior site. Often, even streets have new names according to political currents or entire villages are torn down.[19] Their narrative
nostalgia often laments not only a lost ancestral home/homeland, but also a
lost class and privileged way of life. The loss here appears to be not so much
about rediscovering a buried past but about an often-thwarted desire to trans-
pose a restorative nostalgic vision of the past into the present.

If we first turn to a 1997 memoir by US-born writer Pang-Mei Natasha Chang,
Bound Feet & Western Dress, we can find an example of a resilient restorative
nostalgia that refuses to be overshadowed by most of the political, material,
and economic disparities between past and present that reveal themselves in
her journey. Chang's memoir switches back and forth between her own story
and her great aunt Chang Yu-I's reminiscences of her life in a well-known and
prestigious Shanghai family in literary, banking, and political circles. In 1986,
Chang travels to Shanghai for the first time hoping for a sentimental journey
to reclaim her great aunt's history in China in the absent material locations of
the past. Chang describes her visit as she retraces the sites, buildings, streets,
and spaces where her family once worked, played, and lived. Once there, she
struggles to locate her aunt's old Shanghai home on a map. She explains that,
"all the street names were different now, and [she] sat with a map spread across
[her] knees and a bottle of whiteout in one hand, crossing out the harsh x's and
z's of pinyin romanization and Communist street names" (*BF*, 193). When she
finds her aunt's home in the former British concession it has been converted
into a rundown military hospital. Despite its poor condition, Chang describes
it as follows:

> Standing in the grounds. [...] I could still sense the grace of the past, the beckoning willow
> trees, the artistry of the landscaping. One ally that I had not counted on was the almost
> eerie timelessness of Shanghai. Somehow the ghosts of the past had not yet vanished,
> and on that morning their presence grew stronger, transporting me back several decades.
> (*BF*, 193–194)

Here Chang's narrative seems fixated on infusing the present site of the ancestral
home with an earlier 'elsewhere' that functions like a window, drawing the readers' attention back to an aggrandized domestic vision of a "long lost" Chinese
cultural past and lifestyle.

---

19 For interesting personal essays on this topic see Jianying Zha, "Beijing: A City without
Walls," *The Antioch Review* 52.3 (1994): 390–415; Margaret Y. K. Woo, "[Un]Fracturing Images:
Positioning Chinese Diaspora in Law and Culture," in *Chinese Women Traversing Diaspora: Mem-
oirs, Essays and Poetry*, ed. Sharon K. Hom (New York: Garland, 1999): 31–50, esp. 33.

In any visit to an ancestral home or homeland we are all in some fashion tourists and in our encounters with the material places from our past or our heritage we will naturally pick and choose what slices of time to focus on as belonging to us. With selective memory we decide what to emphasize, what to forget, what to see, and what not to see. As geographer Tim Cresswell explains, "place is not so much a quality of things in the world but an aspect of the way we choose to think about it – what we decide to emphasize and what we decide to designate as unimportant.[20] In *Bound Feet & Western Dress*, Chang explains that prior to her trip she longed for a sense of belonging and a deeper understanding of her origins but was also torn by an ambivalent view of her own heritage (cf. *BF*, 4). In this imagined homecoming narrative, Chang struggles to sustain an inherited and ahistorical vision of an ancestral home/homeland, possibly created out of the needs and desires that she brought with her on the journey, by emphasizing affiliations with more enduring visions of an ethnic, familial, and cultural heritage while simultaneously sidestepping complex sociopolitical and economic changes that inevitably come with the passage of time. Svetlana Boym explains that it is "the promise to rebuild the ideal home that lies at the core of many powerful ideologies of today, tempting us to relinquish critical thinking for emotional bonding" allowing us to confuse actual places with "a phantom homeland."[21] At the same time, Boym reminds us that the "sentiment itself, the mourning of displacement and temporal irreversibility is at the very core of the modern condition."[22]

For many immigrant writers, a relationship with an ancestral home/homeland that was inaccessible for decades would be radically transformed from an abstract concept when it finally became easier to go there in the 1980s and 1990s. Often these narratives reveal a pervasive sense of dread and anxiety over facing the material reminders of personal, familial, and communal uprootings and traumas of the past. In one such example, the successful actress Tsai Chin's [Zhou Caiqin] 1988 memoir *Daughter of Shanghai* reveals a bittersweet reunion with her childhood home. As a teenager in 1953, Tsai Chin left China for Great Britain and then the US in the 1970s. The daughter of possibly China's greatest Beijing Opera actor, Zhou Xin-fang, she was never able to return to the homeland to see her parents alive since they were brutally struggled against for a decade and eventually died during the Cultural Revolution. In the early 1980s, Tsai Chin was able to finally return to mainland China and visit her child-

20 Tim Cresswell, *Place: A Short Introduction* [2004] (Malden, MA: Blackwell, 2007): 11.
21 Boym, *The Future of Nostalgia*, xvi.
22 Boym, *The Future of Nostalgia*, xvi.

hood home where her parents were tortured and held under ruthless conditions of house arrest. Tsai Chin's memoir reveals a pervasive anxiety that "sooner or later" she would have to face her "ransacked" childhood home (*DS*, 225). She writes:

> I was returning to my former home which had been so full of happy memories and was now robbed of all loving people, all familiar objects. It was the visit I most dreaded. [...] The house was in a sorry state, and full of strangers. [...] I went through all the rooms, but I hardly noticed a thing. I was seized by an urge to escape, to run away from all this, from the dirty toilets and peeling walls, from the apathy bred by a repressive regime. [...] Over the years since leaving home, how many times had I walked through empty houses in my recurring dreams? The houses were never like this house, and somewhere beyond I heard the voices of my parents. Now the voices were silent. And I was the ghost, wandering through the shell of a house. [...] My sentimental journey was inevitably filled with bittersweet memories. Setting the clock back was like being Alice in Wonderland. The rooms in the house where I lived as a little girl had shrunk, which was to be expected. A nice professor now lived with his family in my old bedroom at the back. [...] He kindly invited me into his crammed room and gave me tea. (*DS*, 225–228)

In this physical encounter with the architectural and contemporary materiality of her remembered domestic past, Tsai Chin's passage is a conscious mapping of a complex and ongoing renegotiation where the ancestral home "is made and remade in the motions of continual reprocessing of what it is/was/might have been."[23] Thus, Tsai Chin's description of her belated negotiation with the "spatial imaginary" that is her ancestral home resonates powerfully as it simultaneously reveals the ghosts, injustices, traumas of her past that illuminate and inform her present.[24]

A narrative nostalgia for the ancestral home/homeland that often expresses itself as a form of family inheritance, is a reoccurring motif in many Chinese American memoirs. With a goal to uncover the "tension between remembering the past and ignoring it" (*PM*, xi–xii) in her own family, US-born writer May-lee Chai researched her 2001 memoir, *The Girl from Purple Mountain: Love, Honor, War, and One Family's Journey from China to America* for over ten years. In order to better encompass the "imperfect" and confusing way her family stories were passed from one generation to the next and show how selective memory and forgetting structured meaning over time, she decided to co-author *The Girl from Purple Mountain* with her father Winberg Chai. Thus, Chai's memoir

---

23 Anne-Marie Fortier, "Making Home: Queer Migrations and Motions of Attachment," in *Uprootings/Regroundings: Questions of Home and Migration*, eds. Anne-Marie Fortier et al. (Oxford: Berg, 2003): 115–135, 131.
24 Cf. Blunt and Dowling, *Home*, 2.

provides readers with an excellent opportunity to consider two narrative voices from the US-born and immigrant generations involved in this journey. At age sixteen her father fled China to Taiwan after the Communist victory in 1949 and a year later went to study in the US where he eventually settled permanently. Born in the US, May-lee lived in New York until age twelve when her family moved and became the only mixed-race Asian family in small town in South Dakota in the 1980s. There they were exposed to almost constant racial hatred, along with frequent violence and threats (cf. *PM* and *HG, 283*).

While both father and daughter represent travel to their ancestral homeland as a return narrative, the journey to this new place is always informed by where they are coming from, what they have left behind, and what they are looking for. Thus, in her second, 2007 memoir *Hapa Girl*, May-lee explains how their initial visit in 1985 when she was eighteen, was dramatically different for her and her father. After growing up with intense racism, May-lee refers to her experiences in China in both her memoirs as life changing and empowering. In *Hapa Girl* she explains that even though she lived in Nanjing during periods of anti-foreigner sentiment and the turbulent periods surrounding the June 4 1989 Incident (Tiananmen Massacre) she still felt at home (cf. *HG*, 193). For May-lee's father however, the shock of seeing relatives, places from his childhood, and sites of his wartime experiences for the first time in 36 years is often depicted as overwhelming. The journey to China was an "emotionally taxing experience" for Winberg, especially when he was faced with the physical embodiment of poverty and hardship that his mother's family endured during his absence as it was such a brutal point of contrast to his childhood memories (*HG*, 183). In *Hapa Girl*, May-lee explains:

> He remembered his uncles and their children as they had lived before the 1949 revolution – as wealthy physicians with refined tastes. Now they were living in a crowded Beijing apartment with bare walls, rickety wooden furniture, and a lone electric fan whirring in the corner to disperse the heat. I, however, had no memories with which to compare the present. (*HG*, 183)

In *The Girl from Purple Mountain*, Winberg also describes the huge economic disparity between a remembered past and his view of the present:

> My mother had her own school. She built our house. A huge house, brick, Western-style, indoor plumbing, central heating [...]. Our family had been rich. We had a house full of servants. Our servants dressed better than other families' servants. We were like royalty. Today everyone was dressed in the same loose cotton pants, the wrinkled cotton shirts. Everyone was poor. (*PM*, 278)

Often, a writer journeys to the mainland on a quest to retrieve the past but he or she is instead confronted with the discordant material and political realities of the present. Here a modern day Communist China disrupts the representational reality of inherited tales of an ancestral home in the narrative imagination.

Overall, in *The Girl from Purple Mountain* May-lee and her father provide a positive portrayal of their travels and experiences in China. However, when they visit her grandmother's home for the first time since her father left in 1949, they are confronted with blatant physical reminders that everything had changed. May-lee describes growing up in the US with tales of her grandmother's dream house that was abandoned in Nanjing upon her emigration. She explains that all her childhood she heard of this house and "was expecting a mansion, something exotic and spectacular" but when she finally saw it she "felt confused then disappointed" (*PM*, 290):

> A generation later in 1985, my father and I returned to Nanjing and found my grandmother's house, still standing, though the neighborhood was a bit rundown, tin-roofed shanties and squatters' shacks [lined] the twisting alley that led to the front gate. I was expecting the palace of my father's memories, but instead we found a long narrow brick house, now sooty-gray and dilapidated (*PM*, 123).

May-lee describes her father's first encounter where he "rushed through all the rooms [...] shaking his head, as if he were looking for something important, something lost (*PM*, 291). In an earlier passage she describes Winberg as follows:

> [He] shouted now into the air, 'You've ruined everything! Everything is dirt! Everything is poor! The country is poor! You've ruined China! The Communists have ruined everything!' He shouted over and over until his head turned an unhealthy crimson and his entire body was covered with sweat. Because his mother's dream house, his childhood home, had been found and was nothing like he remembered. (*PM*, 123)

When Winberg is face to face with what remains of the ancestral home, the thick depiction of its overcrowded, utilitarian, run-down, and decaying present feels like a wrenching assault against the past glory of his remembered home and his family's prior wealth and prestige (cf. *PM*, 278). This passage from *The Girl from Purple Mountain* points us back to one of Svetlana Boym's points in *The Future of Nostalgia:*

> Nostalgic love can only survive in a long distance relationship. A cinematic image of nostalgia is a double exposure, or a superimposition of two images—of home and abroad, of

past and present, of dream and everyday life. The moment we try to force it into a single image, it breaks the frame or burns the surface.[25]

Or as John Durham Peters explains, "in exile the nostalgia for the one true home can, at its worst, iconoclastically smash whatever does not measure up."[26] In ancestral return narratives, it is in these moments of discomfort where our prior visions and present experiences meet, where we can question the naturalized and taken-for-granted assumptions projected onto these highly saturated places of our shared past.

In "Places and Their Pasts," cultural geographer Doreen Massey urges us to view places as "as temporal and not just spatial: as set in time as well as space."[27] Rather than sealing "a place up into one neat and tidy envelope of space-time," Massey urges us to recognize that a place also "stretch[es] through time" and that "what has come together, in this place, now, is a conjunction of many histories and many spaces."[28] While Winberg Chai's memory of his mother's home was fixed in stasis, places and structures move on without us and have a history of their own. For example, Chai's family home was also occupied by Japanese officers during the Sino-Japanese War, temporarily turned into a Russian-run whorehouse, rented to US expatriates and eventually divided into housing for three families during the Cultural Revolution (cf. *PM*, 123; 289). Because "places are layered with competing narratives of attached meaning," Winberg cannot erase the passage of time nor evade the material markers of the past and present.[29] Since he carries (as we all do in some fashion) his own imagined "unspoilt" family vision and story of this home, Winberg cannot easily let go of the myth of the past holding the pure essence of this place in his contemporary encounter.

Turning now to a more contemporary example, Val Wang's memoir, *Beijing Bastard: Into the Wilds of a Changing China* (2014) also provides multi-generational perspectives and layered encounters with an ancestral home motif. It reveals a complex window into the ever-changing threads of personal, familial,

---

25 Boym, *The Future of Nostalgia*, xiii–xn.

26 John Durham Peters, "Nomadism, Diaspora, Exile: The Stakes of Mobility within the Western Canon," in *Home, Exile, Homeland: Film, Media, and the Politics of Place*, ed. Hamid Naficy (New York: Routledge, 1999): 17–41, 37.

27 Doreen Massey, "Places and Their Pasts," *History Workshop Journal* 39 (1995): 182–192, 186.

28 Massey, "Places and Their Pasts," 190–191.

29 David Harvey, *Justice, Nature and the Geography of Difference* (Cambridge, MA: Blackwell, 1996): 309.

economic, political, and public renegotiations with an ancestral home. Wang's memoir centers primarily on her experiences in her early twenties of living and working as a writer for an English magazine in Beijing from 1998–2003. Wang was born in the US and had never been to mainland China before this journey. She also writes about her parents' trip to visit her when they come back to Beijing for the first time since they fled China as children in 1949 to settle permanently in the US.

Wang writes of feeling little connection towards the "cookie cutter suburbs" outside of Washington, DC where she grew up, while a sense of exile left her yearning for a "place to call home" (*BB*, 73). At the same time, Wang declares herself to be adamantly anti-nostalgic towards her ancestral homeland early in her memoir. According to critic Lynn Pan, to locals in mainland China, a Chinese American who returns to rediscover his or her origins was doing a very North American thing.[30] Wang tries to refute and challenge such commonly held assumptions that locals often make by insisting that she was not simply a *meiji huaren* [US-born Chinese] but a Chinese American and that she was not coming back to China to *xun gen* [search for her roots] because she was not from there (*BB*, 61). Instead, she was simply attempting to flee her roots and family pressures and had come to China for an adventure (*BB*, 61).

Wang was initially inspired to go live in mainland China to explore her dream to become a documentary filmmaker. However, while living in Tianjin and Beijing from 1998–2003 during a period of relentless urban development, demolition and 2008 Olympic preparations, she eventually decides to write about her complex and entangled relationship with her family's ancestral properties. As she leads the reader into this and various other narrative journeys, Wang is also fully aware that her own nostalgic attachments to an ancestral home are intertwined and heavily influenced by her role as a foreigner in China and the pull of her family history (cf. *BB*, 294; 62).

As she begins to trace the history of her family's ancestral homes, she learns that their primary home was seized by the government, turned into a dormitory and eventually demolished (*BB*, 299). Her grandparent's and great aunt's ancestral homes were subdivided and given to many families of workers who lived there since the Cultural Revolution. Both structures were slated for eventual demolition to make way for developments (*BB*, 297). Due to the more recent government policy of returning previously confiscated homes, her parents have to negotiate with local cadres during their visit in a confusing series of political ma-

---

30 Lynn Pan, *Sons of the Yellow Emperor: a History of the Chinese Diaspora* (Boston: Little Brown, 1990): 295.

neuvers, *guanxi* [mutual favors] and flatteries to obtain the deed for her grand-parent's ancestral home and establish a claim for remuneration upon its demolition (*BB*, 193).

When her parents visit her grandparent's ancestral home for the first time they find a courtyard packed with makeshift sheds that were thrown together with haphazard materials leaving only a narrow and jagged passageway (cf. *BB*, 193). Wang's mother simply exclaims, "it's so broken" (*BB*, 194). Wang describes this encounter as follows:

> The layers of other people's used and unused things, piled up like a collage, made distinguishing the original layout of the house nearly impossible, and heartbreaking. There was no way to delete all that mess and rewind fifty years to when the courtyard was empty and peaceful, and my dad a little boy. (*BB*, 194)

When some of the current residents return, Wang imagines that her family must appear to them "as cartoon characters in a Communist textbook: the evil, well-fed landlords (Americans, no less) coming to survey their property and the noble workers full of dignity" (*BB*, 194). This layering of multiple perspectives on the site of the ancestral home is an important narrative technique in Wang's memoir. Further, as writer and art critic Lucy Lippard reminds us,

> Place is latitudinal and longitudinal within the map of a person's life. It is temporal and spatial, personal and political. A layered location replete with human histories and memories, place has width as well as depth. It is about connections, what surrounds it, what formed it, what happened there, what will happen there.[31]

Wang later echoes this multifaceted vision when she explains, "This trick of time is the magic of courtyard houses. They are able to conjure up the lives, so different from ours, that have been contained in their walls" (*BB*, 294).

Always attempting to unpack the push and pull of restorative and reflexive nostalgia she feels towards her family's ancestral homes, Wang confesses that despite its blatant lack of modern conveniences, an indoor bathroom and privacy, her one-week stay with relatives in her great aunt's ancestral courtyard house made her feel more a part of her family than anything else (*BB*, 301). When she later learns that it was demolished, she was close to tears while her relatives who lived there for over fifty years were resigned as they told her simply, "it's just gone" (*BB*, 31). Typical of the self-reflective tone woven throughout the memoir,

---

31 Lucy Lippard, *The Lure of the Local: Senses of Place in a Multicultural Society* (New York: New York P, 1997): 7.

Wang comments, "How very Chinese American of me to feel sappy about a past I have been told about in a fairy tale, and worse yet, to kind of enjoy the feeling" (*BB*, 58).

Living in Beijing, a city engulfed in relentless demolition, Wang is continually confronted with overt material reminders that places can never remain fixed in time, but are instead always entangled with concurrent economic, material, social, and global forces. At the same time, Wang's memoir also seems to reflect on her own tendencies to project restorative nostalgia onto domestic spaces in Beijing and make these traditional courtyard dwellings and *hutongs* [alleys around traditional courtyard homes] places that might reflect back her own ideas of belonging, family, heritage, home, and homeland. When she visits the demolition site of her great aunt's courtyard home that held such nostalgic value for her, Wang is struck by "how little space each house took up" and asks, "How could it have been enough to contain all the life that had existed here, all of the time that had passed?" (*BB*, 291). She goes on to describe how, "laying bare [their] most intimate spaces for the whole world to see," the demolition flattened the walls of the house, leaving only some scattered grey stones (*BB*, 57–58). Barely able to locate and "discern the outline of the walls, [she] rebuilt the house in [her] mind" (*BB*, 58).

After her encounter with the demolition, Wang conveys a new sense of urgency and sentimental desire to interview and document things before they disappear and clarifies her plans to write about her family's ancestral home towards the end of the memoir (cf. *BB*, 278; 290). As she begins to research this topic, Wang is still aware that she is "asking an outsider's questions and making a story out of something that was just life" (*BB*, 301). In the hopes of finding a more unbiased, local and less nostalgic view on her grandmother's ancestral home before it is demolished, she returns with the intention to interview some of the families who had been living there since the Cultural Revolution. When she asks them for stories of their home from that period, they simply respond, "What stories are there?" "They let us live here, so we live here" (*BB*, 302). They are primarily interested in complaining to her about their poor living conditions, endless repairs, and deep anxieties about how and if the government will provide them with alternative housing or remuneration (cf. *BB*, 302). Here we have another example where Wang's narrative disrupts and interrupts its own attempts at restorative nostalgia.

When Wang returns to the US, she turns to her grandmother who also emigrated there in the hopes of learning more about the history of her ancestral home. Her grandmother's response, however is surprisingly matter of fact, free of nostalgic reveries about the past and rooted firmly in the present (cf. *BB*, 326). "History?" her grandmother replies, "No history. [...] It's very terrible shape. What to say about it?" (*BB*, 326) Her grandmother then asks Wang, "You've been there. You tell me about it. What it's like now?" (*BB*, 326). She is more interested in talking to her granddaughter about its real estate value (*BB*, 326). Wang however, reveals contradictory feelings when she refers to her family's negotiations over government remuneration for the property. She asks, "what constituted enough money to compensate for the loss of your family home, the loss of your last toehold in your homeland, the loss of a life you never got to lead?" (*BB*, 302). By providing alternate commentaries on this process, Wang seems to simultaneously acknowledge, while also mourn, the effects of historical, economic, and temporal change on this place her family once called home.

In effect, Wang's memoir continually juxtaposes convergent restorative and reflective nostalgic impulses towards the ancestral home that I would argue effectively call each other into question. This points back to one of Svetlana Boym's central points in "Nostalgia and Its Discontents" that is quite applicable here,

> Nostalgia can be a poetic creation, an individual mechanism of survival, a countercultural practice, a poison, and a cure. It is up to us to take responsibility of our nostalgia and not let others 'prefabricate' it for us. The prepackaged 'usable past' may be of no use to us if we want to create our future. Perhaps dreams of imagined homelands cannot and should not come to life.[32]

By the end of the memoir Wang admits to herself that "home would never be a single place [she] could point to on a map" (*BB*, 284). She writes, "I realized China was a place I could return to, a place my parents could return to, as long as I accepted that none of it could ever be counted on to stay the same" (*BB*, 334).

What is most relevant to this chapter is how the narrative strategy in each memoir wrestles with rather than evades the often uncomfortable juxtaposition of a current geopolitical space with a previously imagined ideological space that is constructed out of individual, familial, and communal desires. As he tells the story of his travels from a simultaneously personal and theoretical view in his 2007 memoir *Coming Home to China*, Yi-Fu Tuan, one of the pioneers of humanist geography, reveals a complex ambivalence towards returning to mainland China after an absence of 64 years. As his flight circles over Beijing in 2005, at age 74, visiting the land of his birth for the first time since 1941, Tuan admits to himself that he still unrealistically expects to find "a China that [he] had left behind"

---

32 Svetlana Boym, "Nostalgia and Its Discontents" [2007], *Hedgehog Review* <http://www.iasc-culture.org/eNews/2007_10/9.2CBoym.pdf> (acc. June 3, 2013): 7–18, 18.

(*CH*, 5). *Coming Home to China* provides a fascinating glimpse into the rich and multilayered personal narrative of an important geographer who wrote over twenty books on the cultural, humanistic, and ideological constructions of home for over forty years. Known for his seamless integration of "simple and profound observations," his academic writing is preoccupied with the more personal, emotional, intimate, experiential, philosophical, spiritual, and holistic connections between people and places, culture and geography.[33]

Operating on a fascinating dual level that is both personal and theoretical in his memoir, Tuan is ever aware that he is simultaneously trying to shield the China of his distant memories from the China in front of him on this journey. For example, when he revisits his childhood middle school he writes, "I wanted to wallow in nostalgia, let memories bubble up from the deep well of my being, hold hands with my childhood self" (*CH*, 112). The administrators giving him a tour however, were focused on only showing him their new facilities as a mark of progress (cf. *CH*, 112). Tuan explains:

> Naively, I thought I would be sucked back into the past. [...] That didn't happen. I should have known that to be alive is to be disloyal to the past. As I visited my old home and walked the school grounds, ghostly presences were pushed into the background by the sights and sounds right before me, and by the nagging concerns of the moment. (*CH*, 168)

Here Tuan is mindful of how the present relentlessly intrudes on any of his attempted nostalgic reveries. Taking this further, he even avoids visiting his birthplace in Tianjin where he was born in 1930 despite its close proximity and accessibly during his trip. Tuan relates, "I think I also dreaded the thought of finding the place of my birth and young childhood totally strange, that in Tianjin I wouldn't encounter a single landmark that could resurrect a memory, that the sprawling, booming port city would wipe out what memories I do have" (*CH*, 166). Tuan's mindfulness of the simultaneous and multi-layered aspects of place and memory echoes back one of Svetlana Boym's key points about nostalgia:

> Nostalgia appears to be a longing for a place but is actually a yearning for a different time – the time of our childhood, the slower rhythms of our dreams. [...] The nostalgic desires to obliterate history and turn it into private or collective mythology, to revisit time as space, refusing to surrender to the irreversibility of time that plagues the human condition.[34]

---

33 Cf. Paul Rodaway, "Yi-Fu Tuan," in *Key Thinkers on Space and Place*, eds. Phil Hubbard, Rob Kitchin, second ed. (Los Angeles: Sage, 2011): 426–431.
34 Boym, "Nostalgia and Its Discontents," 8.

As he stood at the front door of his childhood home Tuan remarks, "I felt simultaneously and contradictorily both more unreal and more real. I was a ghost trying to relive the world of a child and an old man given a fresh burst of life by infusions of odors and tactile sensations from the past" (*CH*, 115). Even though he knows that is common for people who revisit the places they lived in as children to be shocked by how small they now seem, he is still taken aback by how small, cluttered, and dark it appears (cf. *CH*, 115). While by no means absolute binaries, Tuan's work provides rich examples of how we all wrestle with what Svetlana Boym labels as reflective and restorative nostalgia:

> If restorative nostalgia ends up reconstructing emblems and rituals of home and homeland in an attempt to conquer and spatialize time, reflective nostalgia cherishes shattered fragments of memory and temporalizes space. [...] It reveals that longing and critical thinking are not opposed to one another.[35]

With a "fresh sense of humility, openness, and wonder" much of Tuan's work centers on space and place and the emotional and material interplay of humans and their environments.[36]

As geographer Paul Rodaway explains, at the core of Tuan's academic work is "the notion that geographic discovery is also about self-discovery."[37] Despite his theoretical and academic background, Tuan realizes that he is just as susceptible to the power of nostalgia, memory, and the places of the past in this return journey. This layered awareness only serves to infuse his writing in *Coming Home to China* with a sense of reverence, openness, vulnerability, and respect rather than academic distance or cynicism. For example, when a student attending one of his lectures in China asks him "Well, what did you find when you returned home? The question took [him] by surprise" (*CH*, 122). Eventually Tuan responded with the two words that popped into his mind – "anchorage" and "tenderness" (*CH*, 122).

Tuan seems fully aware of the very fragile constructions of the imagined places of our pasts and his simultaneous desires to examine and carefully preserve them on his return journey. When he asks himself at the end of the trip, "Where do I belong? Am I a Chinese, an American-Chinese, a Chinese-American, or an American?" Tuan admits that he "remains at loose ends for an answer" (*CH*,

---

35 Svetlana Boym, "Nostalgic Memorials and Postmodern Survival in Russia," in *The Postmodern Challenge: Perspectives East and West*, ed. Bo Strath, Nina Witoszek (Amsterdam: Rodopi, 1991): 143–170, 49–50.
36 Cf. Rodaway, "Yi-Fu Tuan," 429.
37 Rodaway, "Yi-Fu Tuan," 430.

155).[38] Furthermore, at the end of his journey he acknowledges that the trip did the opposite of affirming a sense of belonging "by stirring hopes and longings that should perhaps be left in the bottom drawer of [his] psyche" (*CH*, 155). As Tuan pointed out earlier in his 1996 work, *Cosmos and Hearth: A Cosmopolite's Viewpoint:*

> A paradox peculiar to our time and to Americans especially is that 'searching for roots,' which is intended to make us (Americans) feel more rooted, can itself be uprooting, that is, done at the expense of intimate involvement with place. Rather than immersion in the locality where we now live, our minds and emotions are ever ready to shift to other localities and times, across the Atlantic or Pacific, to ancestral lands remote from direct experience. We can be dismissive of what is right before our eyes [...] in favor of some place at the other end of the globe where distant forebears lived, toiled, and danced.[39]

In the narrative of an ancestral home – *here* inevitably informs our ideas of what is *there*. The question is how to make claim for an ancestral home that does not undermine a sense of belonging for where one is located. Tuan's work beautifully embodies and embraces the unsettling and precarious aspects of identity formation and belonging. His work helps us clarify the ever-evolving range of public and private renegotiations involved in any "return" journey to an ancestral home.

While diverse in metaphorical modes and goals of representation, when viewed together, each memoir discussed in this chapter can reveal insight into the distinct, yet collectively constructed ideas of group identity and familial, national, cultural, and ethnic belonging. They ask readers to consider what an ancestral home and homeland are, where and when they begin, and if one can ever fit in or come by a sense of belonging there. Taken together, these writers address what Ian Ang refers to as the precarious and relational meaning of Chineseness and the taken-for-granted nature of ethnic identity assigned to the site of mainland China as it is negotiated via the narrative space of an ancestral home.[40]

---

38 Tuan also writes: "Where do I belong? Born in China, I became a naturalized USA citizen in 1973. In 2003, I was also granted Taiwan citizenship. Am I Chinese, American, Taiwanese, all three, or none of the above? Where does my gut loyalty lie? I am afraid to find out" (Yi-Fu Tuan, "Dear Colleague" [25 January 2005] *Online Archive Dear Colleague Letters* <http://www.yifutuan. org/archive/2005/20050125.htm> [acc. June 12, 2013]).
39 Yi-Fu Tuan, *Cosmos and Heart: A Cosmopolite's Viewpoint* (Minneapolis: U of Minnesota P, 2007): 187–188.
40 Ian Ang, "Can One Say No to Chineseness? Pushing the Limits of the Diasporic Paradigm," in *Modern Chinese Literary and Cultural Studies in the Age of Theory: Reimagining a Field*, ed. Rey Chow (London: Duke UP, 2000): 281–300, 294.

The degree with which each writer identifies with the ancestral home or the ambiguous and constructed nature of this "return" journey is not as relevant as the diversity and distinctiveness of each narrative. For each unique journey to an ancestral home is a variable construct that can be uniquely remembered, invented, and transformed by the desires and context of each writer and his or circumstances.[41] Each of these memoirs illustrate how the representation of the ancestral home is a fluid, two-way process of affiliation that is simultaneously local and global, private and public, symbolic and material, individual and communal, and in dialogue with past and present. This project explores new ways of conceiving ties to an ancestral home that can better account for the diverse manners in which these Chinese American writers imagine themselves in relation to an ancestral homeland.

Standard classifications such as nation, ethnicity, local community, religion, and citizenship all reveal insight into the power dynamics of identity formation but none of them fully acknowledge the pervasive and universal pull of the idea of ancestral home or feeling at home. This chapter offers ways of approaching ideas the ancestral home that go to the every-day micro levels of the home, family, ancestry, and territorial roots, which can be integrated into larger discussions around expanded ideas of homeland, nation, diaspora and belonging.[42] The ancestral home, in the concrete and metaphorical sense, is the site where multiple allegiances to nation, native land, borders, domicile, region, clan, family, and ethnic identity continually converge and collide. In fact, it is both the fluid and messy aspects of this motif that makes this topic so intriguing and theoretically vital. In this tangled site of contesting national discourses, affiliations, nostalgias, and ideologies we can uncover valuable insight into how we construct the story of ourselves through traveling bodies, spaces, homes, and mixed geographies.

---

41 Laura Hammond, *This Place Will Become Home: Refugee Repatriation to Ethiopia* (Ithaca, NY: Cornel UP, 2004): 10.
42 See Partha Chatterjee, *The Nation and Its Fragments. Colonial and Postcolonial Histories* (Princeton: Princeton UP, 1993); Edward Said, *The World, the Text, and the Critic* (Cambridge, MA: Harvard UP, 1993); Michael Billig, *Banal Nationalism* (London: Sage, 1995); Pyrs Gruffudd, "Nationalism," in *Introducing Human Geographies*, eds. Paul Cloke, Philip Crang, Mark Goodwin (New York: Arnold, 1999): 199–206.

Elena Igartuburu García

Too Chinese/Too Cuban: Emotional Maps and the Quest for Happiness in Cristina García's *Monkey Hunting*

Abstract: Ethnic minorities have traditionally been absent from the national imaginaries of the Caribbean. Built upon notions of mestizaje, Caribbean national identities, histories and politics tend to reproduce colonial hierarchies and discourses of inequality as they privilege certain groups as the caretakers and guides of others towards political maturity. In Cuba, the continuation of the dynamics of colonial power is established between creole and Afro-Cuban categories, while the Chinese and other ethnic minorities are completely neglected, and thus erased from the national imaginary. As it deals with the Chinese in Cuba, Cristina García's novel *Monkey Hunting* (2003) not only displays Chineseness as a category that already inhabits Cubanidad, the essence of Cuban national identity, but it also poses a challenge to reductionist definitions of these categories and spaces. The novel manages to create tension between given national and ethnic discourses while highlighting the crucial and strategic role played by emotions in processes of community making and exclusion. Impositions compelled by geographical boundaries are eluded as special relevance is placed on the disclosure of affect as performance, and alternative ways of belonging based on shared promises of happiness are championed against presumed identifications of race, ethnicity and nationality. Contrasting with traditional formations, these alternatives do not spring from ideas of a shared past or a common origin but from a collective investment in futurity which commits to the continuity of the community.[1]

The existence of Chinese immigration and the physical ubiquity of Chinatowns in the Caribbean have been widely overlooked in traditional historical and social accounts. When acknowledged, they have been generally approached in terms of alienation, so that both, community and urban structure, have been by and large described in terms of self-marginalization and disengagement from their Caribbean host societies. This approach has been broadly featured in theoretical, historical and sociological approaches, as well as in cultural and popular discourses that circulate not only in formal texts, such as historical documents or sociological studies, but also in popular media such as literature and film. Yet the presence of this image does not provide a way for Chineseness to be integrated in the fabric of Caribbean imaginaries; on the contrary, it rather establishes a hopeless distance between Chinese migrants and other social and ethnic groups as it draws neat and solid boundaries that define each of them as completely

---

1 Research for this paper was conducted within the national R&D projects *Cosmopolis. La Ciudad Fluida* (FFI2010–17296) and *Multiplicity. Encuentros incorporados y conocimientos alternativos* (FFI2013–45642-R), financed by the Spanish National R&D Programme (Ministry of Science and Innovation), whose support is gratefully acknowledged.

separate items through relations of opposition and difference. Alienation, in this context then, does not stand for an inability to become part of the dominant group, or an unrealized intent of inclusion, but it is mainly connected to the will for creating ethnically homogeneous national identities that, actually, need an Other against which they are erected. Even if the Caribbean has been generally theorized as a space of where diversity and hybridity are acknowledged and celebrated, the limits of heterogeneity are drawn in relation to an imagined rightfulness that marks the propriety of certain kinds of bodies to the property and management of the geopolitical space of the nation-state. Controlled diversity engages discourses of multiculturalism and cosmopolitanism, and more local discourses such as *mestizaje*, as it functions to distinguish different kinds of hybrid identities and evaluate them as acceptable within national populations or still outsiders. It is precisely due to this idea of uniformity and sameness even in difference that the Chinese have so far been constructed as alien within the Caribbean. Similarly, Chinatowns, which are usually understood as places which this community naturally builds and inhabits, have been represented as displaced elements within metropolitan architecture. Constrained by colonial structures of thinking, Caribbean hybrid imaginaries fail to fully contest traditional western Orientalism, and Chineseness remains, just as it is elsewhere, the utmost other: unassimilable, foreign and even menacing.

Such erasure, which was originally characteristic of discourses born at the beginning of indentured migration from China to the different islands and which avoided the inclusion of the Chinese as part of national imaginaries, remains present in literary and artistic narratives as far as the 1990s. As Anne-Marie Lee Loy has shown, the Chinese were still pictured as alien in novels such as *Guerrillas* by V.S. Naipaul, or Patricia Powell's *The Pagoda*, published in 1975 and 1999 respectively. Still, the ethical assessment of this state of alienation was not kept constant but changed over time in order to accommodate the needs of dominant discourses which still required the figure of the Other to secure their own continuity. Chinese shift from being "conceived in much more neutral and positive terms" to being perceived as a "hostile 'Other', particularly in reference to economic relationships."[2] In these works, the figure of the Chinese is not invoked in the light of identity politics, that is to say, in order to claim the historical or cultural legacy and presence of this group in Caribbean countries. It rather performs the task of reasserting the colonial imagination

---

2 Anne Marie Lee-Loy, "Neutral Aliens: A Nineteenth-Century Tradition of Chinese Representation in Twentieth-Century Caribbean Fiction," *Anthurium: A Caribbean Studies Journal* 7.1 (2010): 1–18, 1.

and, thus, those ethnic and class economies set by colonial powers. As Chineseness was staged as an unassimilable other, Caribbeanness could be defined through a relation of opposition to it and difference from it, so that a binary is established between the two terms mirroring colonial dominant apparatuses for establishing categories. Discursively speaking, Chineseness becomes a category that does not operate on its own, it is not an isolated item but is inscribed in structures of meaning-making that exceed the category. It does not spring from the idealistic imaginary of identity politics inasmuch as it is not claimed by a community in order to achieve social and/or political recognition. Rather, it serves a specific purpose not necessarily related to itself and its own construction, but for the delineation of other categories as its opposites. An empty category with a mere functional character, it was, and still mostly is, left out of the political struggle except as the recipient of blame for the country's bad economic and social situation.

Chineseness was not, and is not, at all related to an actual living community. Even if there might be a group of people that may identify as Chinese, Chinese Caribbean or Chinese Cuban, it cannot be assumed that the category comes to be due to the existence of these bodies. In fact, these bodies are labeled as such only because the category was there prior to their existence. 'Chinese' functions discursively as a tool that seeks to order reality into neat categories through which political and social discourses might be articulated. However, this more traditional and orientalizing function, which perpetuates colonial hierarchies, began to be contested in literary and artistic works produced since the beginning of the twenty-first century. Starting in the last decades of the twentieth century, the strengthening of scholarship and academic interest in discourses regarding postcoloniality and diaspora provided a new ground in which Chineseness could be appropriated for quite a different purpose. Whereas it remains connected to discourse, within the prism of this new cultural trend, it is articulated as a locus through which dominant ethnically homogeneous nationalities are questioned, hegemonic narratives of historical teleology are challenged, and more inclusive versions of hybridity and multiculturalism are both claimed as the foundations upon which Caribbean nations. Ideals such as mestizaje, which form the core of the hybrid and rhizomatic national discourse of many Latin and Caribbean nations, are problematic due to the short-sightedness of their perspective, the limited versions of hybridity that they admit. Including Chineseness into these discourses becomes an attempt to overcome their most traditional readings, as it defies the hierarchies it usually harbors. As Martha Chew points out, the rhetoric of mestizaje is similar to the rhetoric of the melting pot in that it attempts to conceal histories and practices of displacement and forced transition [which is] part of a Pan-American project, a common feature of Latin American politics of community making.[3]

In the case of Cuba, discourses of mestizaje and rhizomatic identity produce a similar effect, silencing certain presences and establishing a hierarchy among acknowledged ones that grants a system in which creoles are always in charge of the well-being of less educated and developed Afro-Cuban subjects. In the face of this perspective, the introduction of Chinese presences might be used in order to destabilize the dynamics of mestizaje as it introduces one unruly and unexpected element into the equation.

Chineseness here, then, is not regarded as a category that seeks to represent bodies, but as a discursive tool, a signifier that is not necessarily connected to reality; it does not work in the definition or the defense of an actual flesh and bone community. Its presence is purely strategic because it seeks to act as a cornerstone on which current social and political structures might be turned around and questioned. The rise of Chinese characters and themes in Caribbean literature is not concerned with contesting stereotypes or exploding preconceived images of the Chinese, nor is it concerned with claiming a political space or representation for any such category. Chineseness becomes the weak spot through which the apparatuses that construct and organize categories and the way they work are unveiled and can be contested.

Therefore, novels dealing with the Chinese in the Caribbean, written and published during the first decades of the twenty-first century are not necessarily symptomatic of a will or a need to construct a sense of community among those of Chinese descent. Whereas these works tend to focus on issues of belonging, their substance rather points towards a criticism of the ways in which ethnic affiliation is enacted, highlighting those emotional economies engrained in the tissues that form the social spectrum of Caribbean societies. In this sense, the alienation that was imposed and praised in the figure of the Chinese migrant during the nineteenth century and up to the late twentieth century is zealously challenged. In novels such as Cristina García's Monkey Hunting,[4] the sense of belonging previously denied to the Chinese in Cuban society is vindicated fiercely.

---

3 Martha Chew, "Deconstructing the Rethoric of Mestizaje through the Chinese Presence in Mexico," in Perverse Modernities: Strange Affinities. The Gender and Sexual Politics of Comparative Racialization, eds. Grace Kyungwon Hong, Roderick A. Ferguson (Durham: Duke UP, 2011): 215–240, 216.
4 Cristina García, Monkey Hunting (New York: Random House, 2003); further references in the text, abbreviated as "MH."

Although characters stand in awkward positions in which Chineseness irremediably marks them as outsiders, eventually they also become an active part of the island's cultural, political and social spheres. Nonetheless, discourses of inclusion and implication do not completely overcome dominant ones. Even if they participate in these fields, assimilation is never an actual possibility for the Chinese, whether first, second or even third generation. The burden of ethnicity always weighs heavily on their shoulders, imposing a series of stereotypes. Meanwhile, their social, political and personal engagement is continually questioned, keeping alive mainstream images of China which, like the unwanted and haunting ghosts of their ancestors, wistfully reassert the orientalist link between Chineseness and ambiguity. Ien Ang deals extensively with the curse of Chineseness in her *On Not Speaking Chinese*, where she points out that

> a dominant tendency in thinking about the Chinese diaspora[5] is to suppress what Clifford calls 'the lateral axes of diaspora', the ways in which diasporic identities are produced through creolization and hybridization, through both conflictive and collaborative co-existence and intermixture with other cultures, in favor of a hierarchical centring and a linear rerouting back to the imagined ancestral home.[6]

Such tendency leads to reductionist perspectives on Chineseness and those identified as of Chinese descent, and necessarily makes categorical adherence to this ethnic identity a burden. Even if the images of the Chinese imposed on these individuals are rid of their most negative features and entail positive connotations, as they do in *Monkey Hunting*, they are still compulsory and signify the need to fulfill a model that is always unattainable in its idealization. Through its connection to economic success in the novel, Chineseness coincides with ideas of pro-

---

5 The choice of the term 'diaspora' to refer to Chinese migration to the Caribbean attempts to dispel the connection to the homeland carried by terms formerly favored in the academic sphere, such as overseas Chinese (for further reading on the meaning and origin of the term see Jing Tsu and David Der-Wei Wang, *Introduction: Global Chinese Literature*. Leiden, Boston: Brill, 2010: 2, 66). Contemporary theoretical approaches to overseas Chinese communities and Chinese identity as a global construct tend to assimilate the language of diaspora, finding that this paradigm comprises more appropriately the experience of Chineseness as global identity and global discourse. Diaspora references, then, not only the connection to the homeland, but it takes into account that Chineseness does not spring only from China, but that it is constructed also in relation to all of the communities that identify as Chinese. The language of diaspora struggles to epitomize hybridity at the core of this category and to give voice to the global and multicultural character of Chineseness nowadays (see Rey Chow, *Writing Diaspora: Tactics of Intervention in Contemporary Cultural Studies* [Bloomington, IN: Indiana UP, 1993]; Ien Ang, *On Not Speaking Chinese: Living Between Asia and the West* [New York: Routledge, 2001]).
6 Ang, *On Not Speaking Chinese*, 45.

fessional success and social fulfillment typical in western capitalism. Notwith-standing, it is precisely the fact that this category is ingrained in hegemonic ideologies of realization and happiness which reinforces its mandatory charac-ter. The spectrum of possible ways of being is restricted, inflicting a regulation ideology that establishes dichotomies of good/bad and success/failure, and which seems to aim at subjecting individuals to the channels deemed correct by dominant powers.

Furthermore, whether the link between characters in *Monkey Hunting* and homeland China is recent or remote, whether their relation is melancholic or completely nonexistent, the imposition of a Chinese identity is somehow still linked to this idea of a common origin. This connection turns problematic as it seems to counter the novel's initial intent, which might have been that of pre-senting an alternative version of how communities might be constructed, in a way not necessarily based on traditional discourses of national togetherness. In-asmuch as it tries to undo the fabric of Cuban official historical and social tis-sues, it remains grounded, nonetheless, on discourses of nationality that restrain the potential challenge posed. The potential of this text perhaps lies precisely in the tensions it creates. As it still lingers on dominant western ideologies of a global organization constructed through well-defined geopolitical boundaries, it fails to create real hybrid identities while giving way to hybrid identifications. Unable to reverse these ideas, this text creates just one more layer of reassertion over hegemonic and patriarchal discourses of nation while it points towards al-ternative constructions of home and belonging. Ultimately, even if distinct from typical ones, these prove controversial as they relate the possibility of belonging mainly to masculinist and racist depictions of peoplehood.[7] These contradictions trigger critical approaches precisely because they wallow in the most conflictive issues of community and identification, of nation and belonging.

---

7 Peoplehood, for Étienne Balibar and Immanuel Wallerstein, is an inconstant concept that en-compasses the potential racial, socio-political and ethnic characteristics that race, nation and ethnicity tell apart. For them, "a 'people' is said to be *or* act as it does because of either its ge-netic characteristics, *or* its sociopolitical history, *or* its 'traditional' norms and values. The whole point of these categories [race, nation, ethnicity and peoplehood] seems to be to enable us to make claims based upon the past against the manipulable 'rational' processes of the present" (Étienne Balibar, Immanuel Wallerstein, *Race, Nation, Class: Ambiguous Identities*, trans. Chris Turner [London: Verso, 1991]: 79, emphasis added). Peoplehood, therefore, attempts to bridge the differences established between the three kinds of community mentioned above. It highlights that belonging to any of these is not necessarily exclusive, but that, in fact, national, racial and ethnic labels usually are interdependent. Nonetheless, this concept seems to fail to account for gendered or racist concepts of community, since although it considers the concur-rence of these labels, it does not enact a critical perspective on the way they function.

It is precisely ideas such as diaspora and peoplehood that lie at the core of the alternative ways of constructing belonging and national identity presented in works such as Cristina García's. Whereas traditional constructions of diaspora sustained that "it is the myth of the (lost or idealized) homeland, the object of both collective memory and of desire and attachment, which is constitutive to diasporas, and which ultimately confines and constrains the nomadism of the diasporic subject,"[8] this and other works on the Chinese community in the Caribbean tell a different story. *Monkey Hunting* forsakes the significance of a homeland that could never stand as ideal within western capitalist ideologies. It rather seems to re-create ideas of paradise within the newfound land. Within this frame, neither history nor origin, forcefully or solely, bring the community together. Emotions are staged as key elements which construct the borders pretending to neatly separate categories, and which arrange relations of difference, of distance and proximity, among them. Against the image of a melancholic migrant who "refuses to participate in the national game" and for whom "suffering becomes a way of holding on to a lost object,"[9] i.e., the idealized homeland, characters such as Chen Pan or Chen Fang (his granddaughter who lives in China) aspire to find a place in Cuban society. In opposition to traditional discourses of community based on blood ties and common origins, here it is the promise of happiness that Cuba embodies which stands at the center, prompting that sense of belonging. Rather than based on a shared past or a collective history, Sara Ahmed's affect theory proposes that diasporic communities are created as a resource for survival, a projection and a project that propels individuals and groups into the future. In that sense, they are linked to an idea of futurity and continuity, rather than being a product of the past. It is not the homeland anymore which is the source of both individual or collective hopes and dreams, but all of those are planted in the host country, a fresh land which is impregnated with potential and possibility. Therefore, it is Cuba itself – its physicality but also its society and its politics – which becomes central as it is presented as the source of that promise of happiness, turning into the centripetal force which constructs and spins the community around as it thrusts it into teleologies of individual and collective contingency. As Ahmed asserts in *The Promise of Happiness*,

the social bond is always sensational. If the same objects make us happy – or if we invest in the same objects as if they make us happy – then we would be directed or oriented the

---

8 Ang, *On Not Speaking Chinese*, 25.
9 Sara Ahmed, *The Promise of Happiness* (Durham: Duke UP, 2010): 142.

same way. To be affected in a good way by objects that are already evaluated as good is a way of belonging to an affective community.[10]

Cuba is turned into this happy object, into *what is good*. Meanwhile, China is stripped of any possible goodness, demonized in a signifying move that seeks to agree with western capitalist orientalizing ideologies.

In *Monkey Hunting*, it is precisely this common investment in Cuba which becomes the threat that knits together the three stories in the book. Even if the characters are related through kinship, it is the island, as an auspicious land, which brings them closer than family or ethnic ties actually do. Affective links between the characters of Chen Pan, his grandson Domingo Chen, and his granddaughter Chen Fang, are established through the idea of Cuba as a provider of happy futures, above all when taking into account their geographic, generational and communicative distance: Domingo and Chen Fang are born and raised in Cuba and China respectively, and while the former migrates to the US with his father, the latter never actually meets any member of her Cuban family. In telling the stories of three characters belonging to different generations in the same Chinese family transplanted to the Caribbean, García also intertwines the lives of characters outside this migratory flux and the Chinese community, while still bringing them together under the sun of the same Cuban dream. This way, the author leaves behind ideals of homeland, while investing in the relevant role that affect takes on shaping diasporas and nations.

Monkey Hunting features contradictions existing among and within dominant discourses and categories that govern the making of national and transnational communities. As it deals unproblematically with the construction of a wider idea of Cuban national identity understood not only as a nation-state but also as 'a people' – in Balibar and Wallerstein's terms –,[11] it acknowledges transnational ties which permeate the boundaries of such community. This recognition produces, eventually, a multifold terrain in which several ideas collide and overlay, resulting in colored and novel combinations that signify alternative conceptions of belonging. Whether the promise of happiness is fulfilled or not, as it is and is not throughout the novel, Chineseness becomes the cornerstone from which this tapestry originates. It is not an identity or a category to be explicitly or intentionally re-signified, but rather it is its mere existence which makes contingent this threading of the local and the global that undoes and reasserts both geopolitical discourses.

---

10 Ahmed, *The Promise of Happiness*, 38.
11 Balibar, Wallerstein, *Race, Nation, Class*.

The story of Chen Pan, the first of the Chen family to migrate to Cuba, begins with his arrival on the island as an indentured worker in 1857. His first impressions are key scenes already hinting at the contrast between an innovative construction and the re-assertion of dominant ideologies. As he docks in Cuba, the character reproduces traditional associations between land and femininity, as the narrator observes: "Chen Pan never understood what the sight of Havana, with its seductive curve of coast, stirred in him; only that from the moment he arrived, he knew it was where he belonged" (*MH*, 62). Even if the feminization of the island and its geography is typical of discourses of nationhood, as Agustin Lao-Montes[12] points out in his outline of decolonial theory, here it is further connected to ideas of production and reproduction. Chen Pan's affective attachment to the island is given by the promise which brought him there in the first place: that of a land of plenty where he would become rich and successful. Cuba is then infused with a productive potential. It is literally pictured as a motherland, a geographical space capable of engendering happiness, a place where opportunities for a better future ooze from every single one of the stones and sand that make it. The appeal of this newfound motherland is so strong that, even when he is treated as a slave, Chen Pan's commitment to the idea of Cuba as this promissory place does not fade out.

Far from being the stereotypical melancholic migrant, Chen Pan is temporarily presented as the image of assimilatory success. The island seems to fulfill its promise of happiness as he becomes a respected businessman owning a second-hand shop in Havana's Chinatown which turns him into one of the most famous and respected *Chinos* in the city. The existence of a specifically Chinese space within the organization of the city is both challenging and, once more, reasserting. On the one hand, the presence of a growing Chinese population disturbs dominant ideas of mestizaje. These images traditionally subscribe to a chiefly limited spectrum of Afro-Cuban diaspora and creole communities which dates back to colonial times and tends to conceal the existence of other ethnic groups. On the other hand, the fact that Chineseness is essentially confined to the rather specific borders of Chinatown seems to locate it simultaneously inside and outside the city – physically speaking inside it, but outside inasmuch as it is always set aside, somehow expendable and not at all influential, or even present, in the city's social, historical, economic or political spheres.

The recognition of Chen Pan's success seems restricted to an area specifically designated as Chinese. His determination to get involved in the country's po-

---

12 Agustin Lao-Montes, "Decolonial Moves: Trans-Locating African Diaspora," *Cultural Studies* 21.2/3 (2007): 309–338, 314.

litical struggles are pictured as rather floundered or, at least, incomplete. Such is the case of the character's attempt to contribute to the Cuban revolution, first by delivering machetes himself, during the Ten Year's War, and then by sending money to support José Martí's revolts (cf. *MH*, 86–87; 175). Although other Chinese are mentioned as war heroes, their depiction seems rather legendary, half true, half fantasy, narratively constructed as heroes just because their stories are repeated and mythicized in Chinatown. Moreover, if these heroes' contribution to the Cuban cause was their participation in actual battles, side by side with Cuban revolutionaries, Chen Pan's participation is then diminished as it is merely cooperative, in bringing supplies, but never risking his own skin as *true commitment* would require according to the masculinist standards of Cuban revolution. Not only does this reinforce the idea that the Chinese, just as Chinatown, perform a function of sheer assistance, if any, within Cuban political and social spheres, it also entails their feminization as they do not fulfill the role of sacrifice intended for authentic revolutionaries. Doubly ejected, the Chinese are useful characters to a certain extent, but never really accepted as part of the nation and always regarded with suspicion in their attempts of commitment. The lack of authenticity in their engagement connects with orientalized visions of Chineseness as essentially double, deceitful and cowardly, just as their lack of physical bravado and assistance task feminizes them also according to dominant images of the Chinese.

Even if Chineseness seems unable to have a significant impact on the Cuban national fabric, Cuba does cross the borders of Chinatown. In spite of its Chinese features, reflected in buildings, foods and smells, its streets are, nevertheless, swamped in *Cubanidad*, from language to outfits to the way the Chinos behave, everything speaks of Cuba:

> Everywhere Chen Pan went, the grumous smell of salted beef thickened the air. A Chinese peddler sauntered by with toasted peanuts: '¡Mani tosta'o caliente, pa'la vieja que no tiene dientes!' A new comer with a queue trailed after with an identical basket. '¡Lo mismo!' he shouted. 'Same for me!' Other Chinese sold vegetables from baskets hung on bamboo poles. One skin-and-bones in floppy slippers juggled dishes, his pale green pottery clattering as he walked. The ginger vendor nodded when he saw Chen Pan. Other did, too. Everyone knew him in Chinatown. His regular customers called him *un chino aplatanado*, a Chinese transplant. (*MH*, 61–6, emphasis added)

The mingling of the Cuban Spanish language and Chinese smells and groceries reflects Chen Pan's condition as an assimilated migrant. Similarly, in spite of his appropriation of a Cuban disguise, as he dresses in white linen suits and Panama hats, his face and his accent betray his origins. The contrast marks the impossibility of belonging, just as his political commitment to the island was also trivialized in the face of the national revolutionary ideal of manhood. He is, in fact, a transplant, carefully inserted in the national tree, but always carrying different fruit. Following the transplant metaphor, he is also only a small part of the nation's anatomy. Ultimately a trivial element, he does not change its outline or its essence, but it is Cuba which feeds and supports Chen Pan. As for Chinatown, it is also only a branch breeding its weird fruit but nourished by Havana's sap, which shapes it through culture and language. Although Chinatown is described as a kind of urban citadel, a self-contained space, foreign to the rest of the city, it is never self-sufficient, but dependent on Havana's socio-economic sphere. As shown in the quote above, Chinatown is far from completely severed from the city or the culture into which it integrates. Mixed smells of ginger and peanuts stand side by side with Chinese dressed in linen suits and those attired in traditional clothes and bamboo sandals. Cuba permeates its borders just as it permeates the contours of English language as the writer introduces Spanish words into the English text. The subsidiary relation that Chineseness holds towards Cuba entails a hierarchical categorization of ethnicity and culture that seems to leave the first with little room for any real possibility of destabilizing hegemonic discourses of Cubanidad. Even if emotional investment and political commitment to the host country on the part of Chinese immigrants do not manage to fully contest discourses of disengagement and alienation, it at least hints at the devaluation of Chinese culture against the appraisal of the more westernized – at least comparatively and contextually – Cuban one.

Correspondingly, the borders of Chinatown are traditionally perceived to coincide with those of the community, which is then described as a definite and homogeneous group. This idea of Chinatown and the Chinese community as definite and concurring entities springs from and contributes to absolute otherness and secures its inability to rearticulate Cuban national discourses in a way that might accommodate Chineseness. The emphasis placed on the continuity of Chinese traditions and the persistence of social and cultural systems coming from Chinese culture within Chinatown and the Chinese community seems to place them further away at a discursive level and to keep them from a contingent approximation to Cubanidad. Furthermore, the weight accumulated by this cultural commitment to Chineseness seems to obviate the mechanisms through which detachment is articulated. Alienation does not take place as an isolated phenomenon. Disengagement on the part of the Chinese community ultimately relates to discourses that create an unbridgeable difference between them and the host country. This lack of concern may indeed not be a characteristic attitude of any particular community, but rather a combination of general readings that are carried out inside and outside the group and that rely on power and affective discourses which create and strengthen the economies of fear, belonging and alienation that shape these relations. That is to say that the othering of the Chinese does not work in one direction only. It is not the community itself that sets up borders for Chinatown or delineates contours for Chineseness in an attempt of self-definition. On the contrary, difference is established in multiple ways, as we can see in the descriptions of the Chinese by members of different ethnic groups:

> He saw how the *chinos* were treated, even the respected ones like Lorenzo. When the criollos needed medical attention, they were very solicitous of his expertise – it was Doctor Chen this and Doctor Chen that. [...] But Chen Pan was immune to their flattering tongues. When times grew difficult or jobs scarce, he knew well enough that they were just *chinos de porquería*. (*MH*, 184, emphasis added)

As Étienne Balibar and Immanuel Wallerstein theorize the inevitable connection between racism and nationalism, they state that the concept of peoplehood is always constructed through national and class discourses, and in relation to racial and ethnic ones. Therefore, it entails racist exclusions and hierarchical organizations that establish abusive power relations among different social and ethnic communities. They highlight that "the privileged 'objects' of present-day racism appear as the result of colonization and decolonization."[13] Since decolonization does not entail the end of the reign of colonial ideologies or social structures, individuals and groups are objectified and subjected simultaneously to two racist apparatuses: one that gives continuity to imperialist ideologies of race and class hierarchies, while the other insists in the social and political exclusion of certain ethnic groups on the grounds of the survival of a newly independent nation. In *Monkey Hunting*, Chineseness undergoes both types of racism: colonial orientalist discourses linger, while the Chinese are kept from becoming part of Cuban society and entering the national imaginary. Differences drawn in these descriptions locate the Chinese as the antithesis – whether in positive or negative terms – of African ex-slave communities and the creole middle class, an antagonism that deems relations and coalitions among these groups almost impossible. Nonetheless, these dominant perceptions of the Chinese as inassimilable aliens, constructed through orientalist visions that place this community as an absolute Other of Cuban national identity, are contested in the text. It is precisely the representation of Chinatown that serves as a locus where the very idea of alienation is challenged. Even if the novel fails to effect a real incision in the fabric of Cuban discourses of nationhood, since the Chinese remain forever placed aside, it does challenge traditional Oriental-

---

13 Balibar, Wallerstein, *Race, Nation, Class*, 42.

ism. Chineseness, as it comes into contact with Cubanidad, is altered, not giving birth to a new and hybrid category, but rather expanding and redefining the borders of Chineseness to accommodate those Cuban transplants. *Monkey Hunting* emphasizes the permeability of categorical boundaries and their symbiotic relationships as they are redrawn as to include those individuals and groups removed from the island's physical space and of Chinatown, showing that rather than a matter of location, it is a matter of emotional economies and affective investment that brings people together. This conceptualization of Chinese diaspora in terms of affect helps to consider it through what Lao-Montes calls a "politics of translocation" which points out that ethnic categories "even though [...] connected to nationality [are] also inscribed within larger geo-historical constellations," making it possible for subjects to be considered simultaneously in national, regional and global terms.[14] Exploring the limits of ethnic categories leads to a questioning of their political possibilities. However, it also provides the grounds on which the borders of ethnicity might be redrawn. Re-signification is, in this context, directed in ways that may better acknowledge an already existing internal heterogeneity and contingency within categories, rather than just accommodating new types of subject that where originally *outside*. This vision opposes western coloniality inasmuch as it challenges the very core of essentialism which lies at the heart of the categories that build the hierarchical system that supports it.

In line with the idea of re-signification and permeability, *Monkey Hunting* features the character of Lucrecia, Chen Pan's partner. As an Afro-Cuban woman, she is at first denied the right to belong in Chinatown. It is only after she develops an emotional link with Chen Pan that she achieves a sense of belonging and is somehow accepted by the community as well. For her as an ex-slave, Cuba only becomes a livable place and her home once she has found her link to it through the space of Chinatown and the Chinese community, even if she is not completely accepted. In fact, her link to Cuba is produced precisely through her linkage to Chineseness:

> Everything she loved was in Chinatown. [...] She was a part of Chinatown now, at peace here, with the smells and sounds she'd once found so foreign. Sometimes Lucrecia questioned the origin of her birth, but she didn't question who she'd become. [...] She was Chinese in her liver, Chinese in her heart. (*MH*, 137)

Lucrecia's idea of Chineseness does not spring from hegemonic global discourses. Hers comes from everyday experience and is, in fact, the encounter

---

14 Lao-Montes, "Decolonial Moves," 317.

with a translocated Chineseness that has already been affected by Cubanidad. For Lucrecia, being Chinese is completely different from other performances of Chineseness, all of which are grounded on its dominant notions and, at the same time, construct the category. Her link to it, nonetheless, highlights the fact that identities and the categories that make them are acquired rather than essential features of individuals or communities. Furthermore, they are imbued in constant processes of becoming, subject to never-ending re-signification, expansion and contraction, and change. Still, Lucrecia's performance of Chinese identity relies not only in her own assertion of her Chineseness, but is deeply conditioned by external acceptance. Even if Lucrecia was rejected by the Chinese community at the beginning, by the end of her life, she is part of Chinatown, and she becomes literally so when she is buried in the Chinese cemetery. Categorical recognition entails, then, strengthening affective bonds as well as rethinking the boundaries of these categories in order to encompass and acknowledge the subject that already inhabits their interstitial borderlands. In fact, once the presence of alternative and challenging embodiments of Chineseness are recognized, the seizing move which seeks its inclusion within the dominant categorical imaginary is just a survival strategy which attempts to avoid the threat these subjects pose to the internal stability of the category. By encompassing what they cannot control and what questions their coherence, categories commit to futurity and invest in continuity. Since future is connected to affect and collective promises of happiness, emotional links established by border subjects to these communities install a sense of belonging as it enters a paradigm where sharing happy objects prompts a sense of common direction. In this case, Lucrecia is bound by her connection to Chen Pan, but also by her stubborn commitment to assimilation into Chinese culture, which she takes in her own terms. Thus, Havana's Chinatown is set as the place from which her happiness may emerge, just as it is pictured for the ethnic Chinese community. It is this shared investment that relocates her and re-labels her as part of the Chinese affective community.

Similarly, Chen Fang, Chen Pan's granddaughter, develops a sort of belonging to the island – and a longing for it – even when she is never physically there. Chen Fang conceives Cuba as a land of wonder and mystique in which dreams can come true. This idealization appears as a way to escape the harshness of her own story: a narrative of suffering and silencing. In her imagination, the island provides a space where she might exercise all those freedoms she is denied in China, and where all the deprivations of her life would be supplied. Her emotional link to the island is effected through letters she receives from her father, Chen Pan's son, who lives traveling between China and Cuba, but also from stories and legends that are present in Chinese popular culture and that date back to colonial discourses, such as the legends that led her grandfather away to an unknown, yet promising, land:

> The envelopes where trimmed with fancy stamps of rubied hummingbirds and skeletal palms and thickly bearded men. [...] From an early age I dreamed of running away, of joining my father in Cuba. [...] There were other tales about Cuba. How fish that rained from the sky during thunderstorms had to be shoveled off the roads before they rotted. How seeds dropped in the ground one day would shoot up green the next. How gold was so plentiful that the Cubans used it for buttons and broom handles. And when a woman fancied a man, she signaled to him with her fan. In Havana, women chose whom they would marry and when. (*MH*, 90–2)

Mirroring Lucrecia's experience, Chen Fang's Cuba is mediated through Chinese Cuban eyes but also through legend and myth. In a kind of orientalizing move, Cuba is turned into an enigmatic land. However, departing from traditional Orientalism, the island is not invested with otherness and inscrutability, but rather with an aura of possibility and potential. Cuba's allure originates precisely from its accessibility, its emotional proximity. Due to this affective bond, stands as the promise of happiness that helps Chen Fang survive even when she is in jail accused of betraying the communist regime. She thinks of those in Cuba as her only family and her only community. In fact in order to fulfill her will to escape an asphyxiating Chinese society, she forsakes her sons. Kinship – not only her offspring, but also her husband's extended family – imposes Chen Fang with social and affective obligations she struggles to avoid. In the face of this, Cuba offers Chen Fang versions of femininity that seem less oppressive than the ones imposed on her in China. It is constructed as an asset which might propel her towards futurity and which grants psychological and physical survival. Whether this image is real or not is not ultimately relevant inasmuch as it is merely the thought of it, the sheer possibility, which brings her through. Nonetheless, the fact that this suffocating femininity is connected directly not only with China but with communist regimes, while more liberating roles are connected to a Cuba already under communist rule, is nothing if not ironic. This irony of which Chen Fang is unaware pictures Cuba as an empty ideal, a false paradise, which has nothing to offer, her promise of happiness forever truncated. The play on her ignorance and the parallelism established between communist countries once again reinforces connections between Cubanidad and Chineseness in a way that demonizes their political regimes and social apparatuses. Eventually, previously appointed happy objects are vanished, while the possibility of a different society is displaced and must be re-located elsewhere, presumably, in the western capitalist world.

Finally, it is Domingo Chen, Chen Fang's brother, born and raised in Cuba, who completes the circle of displaced and translocal belongings. Having escaped the communist regime in Cuba and while proving his loyalty to the US by fighting in the Vietnam war, Domingo's thoughts do always travel back to a magical and legendary Cuba in his times of utmost struggle. His Cuba is, similar to that of Chen Fang, one filled with magical traits and legendary characters, and it stands as the only place to which he could ever really belong: "He recalled how after every rainstorm, snails had appeared like jewels in their garden in Guantánamo, snails in iridescent colors and rainbow stripes" (*MH*, 49). The myth-like qualities attached to his childhood home turn Domingo into the stereotype of the melancholic migrant, a character that is unable to assimilate and remains longing for the old homeland. In the face of his despair, Domingo's father, Lorenzo Chen, kills himself. Through this trope, Domingo's enlistment to fight in Vietnam can be read as his own suicide attempt, rather than as any sort of patriotic engagement to the US.

By the end of his life, Chen Pan wonders whether he should go back to China as many of his comrades are doing. At that point, he reflects that he is too Chinese to stay in Cuba but also too Cuban already to go back to China (cf. *MH*, 245). Going back to Ang's theorization of the situation of overseas Chinese, she states that

> 'China' is presented as the cultural/geographical core in relation to which the westernized overseas Chinese is forced to take up a humble position, even a position of shame and inadequacy over her own 'impurity'. In this situation, the overseas Chinese is in a no-win situation: she is either 'too Chinese' or 'not Chinese enough.'[15]

Chen Pan finds himself in this position regarding the two places that shape his subjectivity: China and Cuba. He is not Chinese enough anymore, but neither would he ever be Cuban enough. His stance, nonetheless, is not necessarily humble. Chen Pan inhabits a space built, precisely, upon the impossibility of authenticity. His home is a community built in and around Havana's Chinatown, a sort of third space, neither Chinese nor Cuban, but a hybrid of the two constructed through investment in ideas of happiness which are potentially feasible only within such a space.

The island becomes the center around which ideas of home are built for these four characters. Their emotional attachment is, of course, towards an idealized and mythicized version of Cuban space. Belonging is constructed through and towards Cuba only because it holds within contingent happiness, a feature

---

15 Ang, *On Not Speaking Chinese*, 32.

that is denied everywhere else. It is not towards Chineseness, or Cubanidad, or a Chinese-Cuban category that these characters drift and what they attempt to construct. They perform affective knots beyond ethnicity and nationality that permeate dominant geopolitical boundaries. Feelings of community and belonging spring, rather than from traditional ideas of nationhood and race, from a shared investment in the possibility of happiness and change the host space provides its members, whether this possibility is real or not. They transgress, therefore, not only those mainstream ideas connected to discourses of nation, ethnicity and belonging, but they go even deeper to unsettle hegemonic power at its very core as they propose alternative ways of happiness, other than those already set before them, or linger on melancholia as a way of opposing global geopolitical hierarchies.

Jaroslav Kušnír

Diasporic 'Home' and Transnational Identities in Gail Jones' *Five Bells*

Abstract: In her novel, *Five Bells* (2011), Gail Jones depicts the Australian city of Sydney as a vibrant contemporary multicultural place in which, through a depiction of the lives of four characters, she points out not only the complicated stories of these characters, but also of the city's contemporary role as both diasporic and transnational place. I analyze Jones' depiction of the city both as a diasporic home for one group of characters (diasporic in Safran's sense of the term), and as home and a site of transnational experience for another group of characters (according to Bill Ashcroft's concept of the transnation), with the main emphasis on the role of the city and Australia as a metaphorical space creating the transnational identity of the characters.

Gail Jones' novel *Five Bells* can be read not only as a tribute to Kenneth Slessor's poem "Five Bells" and the works of James Joyce (*Ulysses*, as well as "Evelyn" and other stories). It also develops themes from these authors' works, such as mourning, exile, pulsing life of (and in) the contemporary cosmopolitan city of Sydney (like Dublin in Joyce's *Ulysses*), the relation between the past and present, between physical and spiritual life, life and art. In connection with Slessor's poem, according to Robert Dixon, Jones develops a number of themes: the impact of Sydney, especially Sydney harbor as a place; its historical role as a point of arrival and departure for people whose lives are in movement around the world; and some of the core themes of social modernity, including the experience of urban life, the tidal effects of memory and mourning in relation to chronological time, and the central role of trauma in modernity, and in modern literature.[1]

As the narrator puts it, the novel is also about "death, time, recollected acts of love-making."[2] On one narrative level, *Five Bells* presents an elaborate poetic image of the vibrant life in a contemporary big city, Sydney, the city which unites the fates of several protagonists coming to or living in it for various reasons. Through walking and travelling the narrator guides the readers around the Sydney Opera House, the Rocks, the Museum of Contemporary Art, the ferries, the Sydney suburbs, all connected with a dominant image of light symbolizing the city's positive energy and possibly hope for a new life, a new beginning for most of the characters. Jones depicts the city of Sydney as connected with the

---

1 Robert Dixon, "Invitation to the Voyage: Reading Gail Jones's *Five Bells*," *Journal of the Association for the Study of Australian Literature* 12.3 (2012): 1–17, 3.
2 Gail Jones, *Five Bells* (New York: Picador, 2011): 137. Further references in the text, abbreviated as "*FB*".

personal, historical and cultural experience of characters from Australia (Ellie and James), Europe (Catherine Healey), and China (Pei Xing, her dead parents, her deceased husband, her young son Jimmy, and her former prisoner guard Dong Hua, whom she becomes reconciled with in Australia). Most of these characters are both immigrants and modern migrants and travelers displaced from their home, trying to find their personal and cultural connection with a new place, i.e., Sydney, which represents new possibilities, perhaps a new beginning and, at the same time, a reconstitution of both their personal and cultural identities in a new land. This is reminiscent of the narrative pattern of traditional diasporic texts, which are, as Françoise Kral argues, "by their very nature tales of nostalgia whose function is to re-member the fragments of motherland in a situation of either temporary displacement of permanent exile."[3] As Kral further observes,

> [d]iasporic literature is a literature of remembering, not only in the usual sense of the term
> – a literature geared towards the past, haunted by the lost country and pervaded with a
> general sense of nostalgia. It is also a literature of re-membering which unearths fragments
> of the past, pieces them together, or fails to do so, altering the perspective, exaggerating the
> importance of certain events [...].[4]

But Jones undermines this traditional narrative pattern of diasporic literature and does not depict the immigrants' nostalgia for their home country and possible return. Most of the characters' cultural experience in the new country serves as a possible stimulus for the transformation of their cultural identities connected with the new land, Australia, and its culture. This place becomes cosmopolitan and transnational, rather than a fixed and unified space. The depiction of Australia as a transnational space reflects the changes in diasporic literature in the twenty-first century that Kral has drawn attention to. As she writes,

> [t]he genre has supposedly moved away from a certain tragic mode linked to the experience
> of diaspora as loss, nostalgia and longing for the past, to embrace more alluring theme of
> positive immigration and self-invention abroad; in so doing, the diasporic experience has
> become increasingly divorced from the notion of exile and closer to that of residence in
> a foreign country.[5]

Although it would be problematic to classify Jones' novel as a traditional diasporic text depicting immigrants' nostalgia for home and a wish to return, at

---

3 Françoise Kral, *Critical Identities in Contemporary Anglophone Diasporic Literature* (Houndsmills, Basingstoke: Palgrave Macmillan, 2009): 7.

4 Kral, *Critical Identities in Contemporary Anglophone Diasporic Literature*, 75.

5 Kral, *Critical Identities in Contemporary Anglophone Diasporic Literature*, 11.

the beginning of their immigrant experience, most characters are immigrants occupying a diasporic space trying to cope with a new country and its culture. This new country becomes a place stimulating their self-invention and possible transformation of their personal and cultural identities alike. While for Ellie and James, the Australians who meet in Sydney long after their romantic teenage relationship had ended, Sydney means a possible new beginning in their professional and personal lives and careers. For the Irishwoman Catherine, as well as Pei Xing and the Chinese characters, the city of Sydney becomes a symbolic representation of their contemporary cultural identity. Despite their strong emotional connection with the past in their former home countries, they decide to live in the vibrant, cosmopolitan modern city offering not only physical, but also cultural space integrating different nations and individuals' cultural identities while retaining the specificity and diversity of each culture. The city of Sydney also serves as a symbolic place of comparison between these characters' past belonging to their former home countries and a new cultural space forming their new cultural identity. In the case of Irish and Chinese characters mentioned above, their home countries represent negative experience partly connected with their cultures (e. g., the religious bigotry of Catherine's Ireland). On the other hand, the city of Sydney and Australia at large, where they decide to live, represent a new cosmopolitan and multicultural space offering the freedom, religious and cultural tolerance that these characters miss in their former home countries. For example, Catherine' Ireland is not connected only with religious conservativism and even bigotry, but also with religious intolerance and violence, which are not typically national characteristics. Similarly, Pei Xing's past life in China is not depicted as negative because of cultural characteristics of this country, but because of the authoritarian political regime's violence in the past. What these characters seek seems to be a value of personal, political and cultural freedom, that is, the universal values they cannot find in their former home countries. They do find them in Sydney's religious, cultural and political tolerance. What for these characters symbolizes freedom in their former home countries is the power of imagination represented by literature, books and art. Both Catherine and her brother highly value Irish literature, and Pei Xing and her father Russian literature, and they do so not primarily for nationalistic reasons. The freedom offered by literature, however, can be realized only through the personal escape to the imaginary world of art, while the freedom in the external world is inaccessible for these characters in their former homelands.

The characters' identity oscillates between the immigrant, diasporic but also transnational modern identities as defined by Bill Ashcroft.[6] It is also close to Kral's understanding of contemporary diasporic identity. She argues that the diasporic

> constitutes a unique locus from which to observe the predicament of identity construction at the turn of the twenty-first century, in a context where traditional definitions of identity inherited from the nation state are being challenged by the ever-growing fluxes of diasporic populations worldwide.[7]

Kral's understanding of what she calls the diasporic is close to both cosmopolitan and Bill Ashcroft's understanding of transnation. Bill Ashcroft, however ambiguously, identifies cosmopolitan people at present with the people of the transnation. In his view,

> cosmopolitans are not defined by a particular subject position but by an orientation to the Other and to diversity. Cosmopolitans, although they tend to be footloose, are not *necessarily* immigrants, travellers, expatriates or exiles; they are not necessarily diasporic subjects, they almost certainly aren't refugees or labour migrants [...]. Yet these are the people who inhabit the transnation.[8]

Both Bill Ashcroft and Simon Gikandi associate cosmopolitanism with the contemporary metropolis. As Gikandi argues, "a discourse of cosmopolitanism remains incomplete unless we read the redemptive narrative of being global in a contrapuntal relationship with the narrative of statelessness and, by reproduction, of locality, where we least expect it – in the metropolis."[9] And, as Ashcroft further observes, "[t]he transnation, by seeing the 'movement' of peoples in globalization as a fundamental feature of spatiality, accentuates the 'circulation' of the local in the global."[10] Similarly, Arjun Appadurai speaks about the global cultural economy which, in his view, "has to be seen as a complex, overlapping, disjunctive order, which cannot any longer be understood in terms of existing

---

6 Bill Ashcroft, " Transnation," in *Rerouting the Postcolonial: New Directions for the New Millennium*, eds. Janet Wilson, Cristina Sandru, Sarah Lawson Welsh (London: Routledge, 2010): 72–85, 81.
7 Kral, *Critical Identities in Contemporary Anglophone Diasporic Literature*, 15.
8 Ashcroft, "Transnation," 77.
9 Simon Gikandi, " Between Roots and Routes: Cosmopolitanism and the Claims of Locality," in *Rerouting the Postcolonial: New Directions for the New Millennium*, eds. Janet Wilson, Cristina Sandru, Sarah Lawson Welsh (London: Routledge, 2010): 22–35, 26.
10 Ashcroft, "Transnation," 81.

center-periphery models [...]."[11] He further identifies "five dimensions of global cultural flow" – ethnoscapes, mediascapes, technoscapes, financescapes, and ideoscapes – which represent, in his view, the complexity of the current global economy.[12] Although Appadurai is rather interested in the relation between culture and economy, his understanding of the ethnoscape in particular is close to the cultural spaces characters such as Catherine and Pei Xing occupy by living in Sydney. Appadurai defines ethnospace as "the landscape of persons who constitute the shifting world in which we live: tourists, immigrants, refugees, exiles, guestworkers and other moving groups and persons constitute an essential feature of the world and appear to affect the politics of (and between) nations to a hitherto unprecedented degree."[13] Although Appadurai does not deny these communities' various affiliations with their former homelands, he emphasizes the movement of these communities not necessarily directed to their former homelands as their central characteristic.[14]

I believe that Gail Jones constructs Sydney as a place and space beyond state and national boundaries similar to Appadurai's ethnospace, Bill Ashcroft's transnation and Kral's understanding of contemporary diasporic identities which, through the immigrant protagonists' relations with it, also creates their cultural identity. Place, home, displacement and identity are frequent themes not only of post-colonial literatures, but also of postcolonial theories. As early as in the 1980s, in their seminal work, *The Empire Writes Back*, Bill Ashcroft, Gareth Griffiths and Helen Tiffin argued that

> [a] major feature of post-colonial literatures is the concern with place and displacement. It is here that the special post-colonial crisis of identity comes into being, the concern with the development or recovery of an effective identifying relationship between self and place.[15]

Jones' characters, Catherine from Ireland and Pei Xing, a Chinese woman, are at the beginning diasporic characters, immigrants trying to find a new home in Australia after leaving behind a tragic past in their home countries. They might be seen as typical diasporics in William Safran's understanding of 'dia-

---

11 Arjun Appadurai, "Disjuncture and Difference in the Global Cultural Economy," in *Colonial Discourse and Post-Colonial Theory: A Reader*, eds. Patrick Williams, Laura Chrisman (New York et al.: Harvester Wheatsheaf, 1994): 324–339, 328.
12 Appadurai, "Disjuncture and Difference in the Global Cultural Economy," 328.
13 Appadurai, "Disjuncture and Difference in the Global Cultural Economy," 329.
14 Appadurai, "Disjuncture and Difference in the Global Cultural Economy," 329.
15 Bill Ashcroft, Gareth Griffiths, Helen Tiffin, *The Empire Writes Back: Theory and Practice in Post-colonial Literatures*, second ed. (London: Routledge, 2002): 8.

spora,' retaining the memories of their old country and keeping up their relationship with the imaginary homeland in a new land.[16] Their connection with their
home country is not only physical, through various forms of interaction with it,
but also metaphorical and imaginary. According to Hui-Ching Chang,

> [w]ith the traumatic memory, diasporic people develop a strong sense of 'imagined com-
> munity' to which they are faithful. [...] The relationship of the diasporic group to its home-
> land is not exclusively physical but, for most diasporas, metaphorical.[17]

However nostalgic the reminiscences of most characters are, especially about
their childhood, a new land and culture to them represents a place of self-invention or a reconsideration of their cultural identity, which can now be associated
with a new cultural space. For Catherine, her home country Ireland is a country
suffering from the effects of nationalism and religious bigotry, which she ironizes
in recollections of her past, as can be seen from the comments on her mother
after her husband's (Catherine and Brendan's father's) death: "Mam believed:
she led a little prayer. They all crossed themselves [...] and consoled her in
this way. Pretending. Performing. In this gorgeous mad fuck-up" (*FB*, 88). But
for Catherine, Ireland is also the country of her family's tragic fate (her brother
Brendan's death in a car accident). For her, Australia becomes a country where
she wants to heal the wound of her family tragedy, and which becomes a possible place of new beginning, just as for James Joyce's Evelyne (in his eponymous
short story), although Evelyne still considers Ireland her home, a place she could
possibly return to. Catherine in Jones' novel also often thinks of returning home:
"Catherine realised that she was missing her home. Even though she had been
living in London since she was twenty-two, Dublin, which she visited annually,
was still her default comparison" (*FB*, 52). The idea of a possible return is one of
the major features of diasporic people according to Safran, and it manifests
much more explicitly in Jones' depiction of the oldest generation of diasporic
characters, i.e., James's Italian parents, especially his mother, and Pei Xing, a
woman who escaped to Australia after her imprisonment and family tragedy during the cultural revolution in China. Despite their tragic backgrounds, these characters still consider their home countries, Italy (James's parents) and China (Pei
Xing) to be their home countries at the beginning. They cannot identify with Aus-

---

16 William Safran, "Diasporas in Modern Societies: Myths of Homeland and Return," *Diaspora.
A Journal of Transnational Studies* 1.1 (1991): 83–99.
17 Hui-ching Chang, *The Diasporic Experience: Home and Identity in V. S. Naipaul's* A Bend in
the River (MA thesis, National Chengchi U, 2006): 23 <http://nccur.lib.nccu.edu.tw/bitstream/
140.119/33343/6/51011406.pdf> (acc. March 27, 2015).

tralia as a new country and feel alienated there, they even refuse to learn English as a medium of integration and the key to a successful life in Australia. This finally leads to their alienation, which represents another important feature of Safran's, albeit perhaps rigorous, definition of diaspora. In Australia, James's mother "spoke to herself in Italian, further marking her foreign state, announcing to everyone that she had returned to the country of her birth and was immured there, alone, tethered elsewhere by words [...] as if in resistance to migrancy, Giovanna learned almost no English and maintained a prideful and fierce isolation" (*FB*, 27; 34). Despite her tragic experience in China, her home country, and despite being of the same generation as James' mother, Pei Xing expresses a similar resistance to migrancy, the new country and her personal position. She refuses to learn English, isolates herself from the locals and lives only for her young son Jimmy. This diasporic and almost unified attitude of these characters to immigration, to integration in a new country, and such resistance not only to the past but also to the present tends, according to Jones' narrator, to lead not only to cultural but also to social isolation, and finally it results in tragedy. This tendency manifests itself in the depiction of several characters in Jones' novel. The failure of James' mother's marriage, for example, is a result of her not only personal, social, but also cultural isolation, which finally leads to her death, and Pei Xing's isolation finally leads to loneliness and despair. Most of the characters finally understand that cultural isolation can lead to personal isolation and even to tragedy. Just as the unity of love cannot necessarily be maintained through marriage, as Jones seems to imply, the unity of an imagined diasporic community cannot necessarily be preserved through a nostalgic construction of unitary cultural identity connected with the old home country. This symbolically manifests itself in Jones' depiction of James' parents' marriage in which, by contrast to James' mother, his father understands the necessity of communication as the key to social integration and success in the new country. James' father Matheus "joined his paisano for drinks and local advice. He worked hard, learnt English, took his wife to the south-west following an Italian building team" (*FB*, 34). Although he finally "demolished himself in physical labour" (*FB*, 34) and eventually abandons the family, and although he represents one of the tragic examples of immigration, he also symbolically represents an attempt to overcome the kind of diasporic identity typified by his wife. His attempt to overcome his diasporic identity and build a relationship with the new cultural space also symbolically develops through the character of Pei Xing. She is of almost the same generation as Matheus and finally breaks away from her imagined Chinese diasporic identity, her cultural and thus also personal isolation and alienation, through her reconciliation with the tragic past in the new country, and through her gradual understanding of the impossibility of cultural isolation in the contemporary globalized world, which, as she comes to understand, can lead to personal and social isolation. The connection with her past representing her previous life in China and symbolizing tragedy and evil is impossible to translocate to a new country characterized by different cultural, social and historical conditions. It is symbolically broken by Pei Xing's forgiveness for her former cruel and aggressive Communist prison guard, Dong Hua, in China during Mao's cultural revolution, whom she meets again by chance in Australia and whom she eventually takes care of after his physical and mental deterioration. Dong Hua's decline not only represents the symbolic destruction of evil (the totalitarian régime in China), but also the impossibility of transferring the past into the contemporary globalized cultural situation. Dong Hua's death, finally, represents not only the idea of forgetting but also the possibility of stopping the tragic past in a new country, an idea which is further developed through Jones' depiction of Pei Xing herself, who is strongly affected by her Chinese experience and thinks, "I can never escape this, never; it has followed me to Australia. I am Australian now, and it still it is here. Still it is here" (*FB*, 115). Her understanding of cultural isolation leads to social isolation in the new country, in which she feels the necessity of communication with her Arab neighbors, that is, people who are in no way responsible for either her past or her present condition:

> In the shopping centre there were dozens of small businesses with signs above the doorways in Vietnamese and Arabic: these Pei Xing found particularly enchanting. She loved to look directly into the faces of people on the street. [...] Then there were Vietnamese at the fishmongers on the corner. [...] This version of Australia was Asian and Arab. These people moved in an aura of their own, not afraid to claim space: and among them were other populations, migrant as she, each pulled from another history and cast up at the bottom of the world. (*FB*, 42)

As can be seen from this passage, Pei Xing does not only represent a character realizing the necessity of communication and breaking with the past as a path to acquiring a new identity in a new country, but she also symbolically represents the transition from a typically diasporic to a contemporary cosmopolitan subject. This process is finally symbolically completed by her son Jimmy's acquisition of a new cosmopolitan identity through the friendship with his Chinese-Australian peers. Starting her life in Australia, Pei Xing is, like James's mother, a culturally isolated and typically diasporic character, but her decision to finally speak English makes her rather a cosmopolitan and transnational. The process of a transition from a typically diasporic to a cosmopolitan subject in a new country is eventually completed by Pei Xing's and Dong Hua's sons' friendship. They are both children of initially diasporic characters whose life was heavily influenced by negative experience in their former homeland under Mao's authoritarian regime, during which they stood on opposite sides. These children, however, are connected by a friendship which does not take their parents' relationship in the old country as a source of conflict in the new land. The children are already born there and have acquired a cultural identity understood rather as transnational, cosmopolitan and occupying what Appadurai calls ethnospace, which is further, in the novel, strongly connected to what Appadurai calls mediascapes that

> refer both to the distribution of the electronic capabilities to produce and disseminate information (newspapers, magazines, television stations and film production studios), which are now available to a growing number of private and public interests throughout the world, and to the images of the world created by these media. [...] Mediascapes, whether produced by private or state interests, tend to be image-centered, narrative-based accounts of strips of reality, and what they offer to those who experience and transform them is a series of elements (such as characters, plots and textual forms) out of which scripts can be formed of imagined lives, their own as well as those of others living in other places.[18]

The mediascape is another space which contributes to the creation of a cosmopolitan identity in the novel by influencing the characters' construction of the world based on the accessibility of media to most of them. For example, for Catherine, media and pop star Bono a symbol of suppressed sexual desires, and her brother Brendan fantasizes about the exoticism of China. As the narrator comments on that, "Bono was so televisually distraught every young woman in Ireland wanted to comfort him" (*FB*, 91), and based on seeing the Chinese pandas at the Dublin Zoo and TV programs on them, Brendan creates an exotic image of China and fantasizes about visiting it. His construction of the image of China is a combination of typical tourist images of the country based on which he appreciates the country: "In a single sentence Brendan produced both this wild ambition for both of them and presented his sister with wanderlust associations: the Great Wall, cups of tea, bamboo brushes, twirly noodles. China was a machine of formula images and folkloristic associations" (*FB*, 86). While characters such as Pei Xing and Catherine have come through a process of transition leading towards transnational and cosmopolitan identity, Dong Hua's and Pei Xing's sons are already accommodated to this new cultural identity. This can be seen in the following passage in which Jimmy, Pei Xing's son, introduces his best friend, Lin, who turns out to be Dong Hua's son:

---

18 Appadurai, "Disjuncture and Difference in the Global Cultural Economy," 330–331.

> One day in Sydney's Chinatown Jimmy had introduced a new friend, Lin, a young man in a leather jacket and with hair gelled into a high dark helmet. Pei Xing thought he looked like a gangster from a Hong Kong movie; she imagined black dollars, heroin, bad luck, spilt blood. His family, said Jimmy, was also from Shanghai. (*FB*, 114)

As can be seen from this description of Lin, Pei Xing does not associate him with the diasporic character connected with Chinese culture, but as a modern transcultural subject influenced by contemporary popular and mass culture represented by his dress. Catherine, too, after nostalgic thoughts of Ireland and after thinking of a possible return to her home country, finally realizes that Australia can represent a possible new personal beginning, as well as feeling a certain cultural identification with the land, as can be seen in the following passage:

> In the centre of the city you couldn't really see the stars. But she knew they were there. They were new stars, new, southern hemisphere stars. There must have been convicts who looked upwards in the early nights and felt entirely confounded. They must have felt that the very heavens had changed, that the all-mothering and humbling darkness had let them fall away, had released them into disaster. Mere perforations of a night curtain that had fallen over their heads. Poor buggers. Stranded. No direction home. (*FB*, 169)

In this passage, Catherine not only realizes her loneliness by imagining the fate of the convicts brought to Australia in the past. She also understands the necessity of adapting to life and cultural conditions in a new country, just as the convicts had to do, and at the same time this enables her to understand one aspect of Australian cultural identity, that is isolation, which turns out to be also a necessary condition of living. On the other hand, Jones does not idealize Australia as a moral and cultural paradise, but through a depiction of Irish and Chinese characters draws a parallel between negative aspects of these countries' and Australia's past connected with the racial oppression of the Aborigines. This is represented through Ellie's and James' recollections of their childhood, racism and nationalistic propaganda connected with the celebrations of Australia Day.

However, Elen Sideri, for example, understands diasporics as transnationals and sees in them an undermining potential towards the unitary concept of the nation and to nationalism. In her view, diasporas form a reaction to the described political and cultural hegemony. On the other hand, they often construct relations to transnational movements (political, cultural, religious) that try to overcome the obstacles of national boundaries and territoriality.[19]

These ideas are even more radically developed by Chang. As Chang observes,

> multiple belongings and dual loyalties undermine the demarcated parameters of nation-states and nationalism as discrete categories of identification and political constitution. [...] Essentially speaking, the boundaries of a unified and coherent nation are established by the territories demarcated by expelling and excluding those who are constructed as outsiders and aliens. Among them are diasporans whose living within the margins of the nation-space and in the boundaries of in-betweenness make them an easy target for nations. They are strangers among nations.[20]

Bill Ashcroft uses the concept of the transnation to refer to people who live in a contemporary cosmopolitan world and, in his view, their position undermines the traditional concept of the nation: "Whereas, in the old global order, the nation was the reality and category that enabled the socialization of subjects, and hence the structuring of cultures, in today's globalized world, the nation has become a near-absent structure."[21] In his view, in the twenty-first century the concept of a nation should be reconsidered, especially because of the influence of two megacultures, China and India. Ashcroft argues:

> [T]he phenomenon of their emergence may also force us to reconsider the importance of the nation as a cultural phenomenon, a horizontal reality distinct from the vertical reality of the state. In this horizontal reality culture still escapes the bounded 'national' society, 'exceeding' the boundaries of the nation state and operating beyond its political strictures through the medium of the local. This excess is the transnation. [...] Transnation is the fluid, migrating 'outside' of the state that begins 'within' the nation. This 'outside' is geographical, cultural and conceptual. [...] The idea of a 'transnation' disrupts and scatters the construct of centre and periphery [...], a space in which national and cultural affiliations are superseded, in which binaries of centre and periphery, national self and other are dissolved.[22]

This concept of the transnation is close to the cultural condition experienced by Pei Xing's son, Jimmy, and his friends living in Australia. Their home and cultural identity should, by their parents' expectations, be Chinese, but they have fully

---

19 Elen Sideri, "The Diaspora of the Term Diaspora: A Working-Paper of a Definition," *Transtext(e)s Transcultures* 4 (2008): 32–47, 35.
20 Chang, *The Diasporic Experience*, 28.
21 Ashcroft, "Transnation," 72.
22 Ashcroft, "Transnation," 73.

adapted to the new culture and thus acquire a new, cosmopolitan and transnational identity close to Bill Ashcroft's understanding. This condition experienced in modern Australian society is not necessarily negative and creates a cultural identity similar to Hector St. John de Crèvecoeur's idea of a melting pot of nations and cultures. An example of this is the following passage from *Five Bells*, which almost literally copies Crèvecoeur's *Letters to an American Farmer:*

> There were Turks selling Gozlemes; they had turned off their hotplates and were scraping leftover tabouli into plastic containers. There was an African man wrapping wooden statues, elongated human figures and animals with horns; there was a Hungarian baker, over-supplied with poppyseed cakes, and a Thai woman who sold jewelry made from sea shells. Merchants of many parts of the world were here, in a hippy leftover rehearsal of united nations. (*FB*, 204–205)

This passage creates a culture which brings a vital energy undermining both the essentialist concept of identity and the diasporic identity of the older generation of immigrants. Crèvecoeur characterizes the creation of a new man, a new American in a new land, as follows:

> What attachment can a poor European emigrant have for a country where he had nothing? The knowledge of the language, the love of a few kindred as poor as himself, were the only cords that tied him; his country is now that which gives him land, bread, protection, and consequence; *Ubi panis ibi patria* is the motto of all emigrants. What then, is the American, this new man? He is either an European or the descendant of an European; hence that strange mixture of blood, which you will find in no other country. I could point out to you a family whose grandfather was an Englishman, whose wife was Dutch, whose son married a French woman, and whose present four sons have now four wives of different nations. He is an American, who, leaving behind him all his ancient prejudices and manners, receives new ones from the new mode of life he has embraced, the new government he obeys, and the new rank he holds. He becomes an American by being received in the broad lap of our great Alma Mater. Here individuals of all nations are melted into a new race of men [...].[23]

Crèvecoeur thus understands America as a melting pot of races, nations and cultures creating a new multicultural society which, by absorbing different cultures creates a new cultural situation and identity of the people living there. The new land accommodates the cultural potential of the immigrants and uses it for a creation of a new, specific, cosmopolitan culture which is similar to Jones' depiction of Sydney and Australia as such a place. This condition, now in a contemporary

---

23 J. Hector St. John de Crèvecoeur, *Letters from an American Farmer and Sketches of Eighteenth-century America* [1782] (Harmondsworth: Penguin, 1986): 69–70.

multicultural and globalized world, is observed by James, Ellie's ex-lover with a tragic past:

> Worlds were converging, he thought. Australia was Asian. He saw how various it all was, the zeal of many nations, the emporia of many merchants, the international energy that pulsed between languages and countries. The translations were less of words than of these perplexing combinations: shops, peoples, signs and wonders. (*FB*, 38)

This is the world of a new generation of the descendants of immigrants influenced by this cosmopolitanism, popular culture and media, whose belonging to their parents' culture is symbolic rather than real. This generation of young Chinese, but also of other nations living in a modern country like Australia, is influenced by cosmopolitan cultural conditions, and their cultural identity is shaped not only by the varied experience of living in a big city, but also by popular culture and media affecting their behavior and their relation to their parents' home country. This cosmopolitanism is closely connected with Ashcroft's concept of the transnation. In the case of these characters, the connection with their parents' home country is rather symbolic and they hardly intend to return there, rejecting the traditional and unitary concept of both nation and diaspora. This in-betweenness straddling cultures enables them to acquire the transnational status and identity Bill Ashcroft describes.

In her novel, through her depiction of the destinies of various immigrants meeting randomly in a modern city loaded and pulsing with energy, Gail Jones constructs the cultural identity of her characters as being shaped by the cosmopolitan force of a big city. The city represents a place of belonging and a possible beginning for a new transnational cultural identity, which some of the central characters acquire after realizing what isolation and alienation will follow if they stick to their diasporic identity, understood as a nostalgic recuperation of their tragic past, and after realizing the impossibility of returning to their former home country. This gradual transition from the diasporic to the transnational is represented by several characters showing various stages of this self-realization. James' mother's death symbolically represents the death of the traditional understanding of diasporic identity, because she is unwilling and unable to communicate with the new culture and adapt her cultural identity to the new cultural space. Her husband, on the other hand, represents at least an attempt to overcome this condition by means of economic improvement, and the symbolism continues through Pei Xing, who finally understands her changed cultural identity in a new country as cosmopolitan. This develops into the fully transnational through Jones' depiction of Pei Xing's son and his contemporaries living in a modern cosmopolitan Australian city.

Verena von Eicken

German-Turkish Identity in Fatih Akin's *Head-On:* Transgressing Gender Boundaries, Redefining Home and Belonging

Abstract: Fatih Akin's internationally acclaimed film *Gegen die Wand/Head-On* (2004), one of the key works of contemporary Turkish-German cinema, interrogates and complicates conceptions of homeland, ethnicity and gender. *Head-on* shows that our sense of home is shaped as much by cultural customs as by the place we live in. Its lead character Sibel (Sibel Kekilli) rejects the home her parents are offering because she finds its religious and cultural customs oppressive and irreconcilable with the liberties she enjoyed growing up in Germany. She moves to Istanbul, where she experiences complete freedom, but also complete isolation and alienation, failing to belong. This chapter analyzes the film's poignant take on the experiences of young Turkish-German women forced to negotiate conflicting feelings of home and belonging. It argues that at the end of the film, Sibel achieves a self-chosen identity by defining herself not against her family background, but independently from it, and that she does so through role-play and a performance of gender, of different versions of both femininity and masculinity. Furthermore, it demonstrates how the Istanbul location is used in the film to explore the protagonist's complex relationship with her country of origin, and to illustrate Sibel's journey towards independence.

Head-On (in German *Gegen die Wand*, literally 'Against the wall'), directed by acclaimed Turkish-German filmmaker Fatih Akin, was the first German film in eighteen years to win the Golden Bear for Best Film at the 2004 Berlin International Film Festival, and was named 'Best Film' at the 2004 European Film Awards. Its success is representative of a development which has seen films by directors with a Turkish background, such as Thomas Arslan or Yüksel Yavuz, gain a firm place in German cinema.

It is perhaps no coincidence that some of the first and most influential films addressing the situation of Turkish immigrants in Germany also dealt with a woman's fate: *40 m² Deutschland/40 Square Meters of Germany* (1986, dir. Tevfik Başer) tells the story of Turna, a young woman, who, after her arrival in Hamburg from Turkey, is imprisoned in her own apartment by her husband. *Yasemin* (1988, dir. Hark Bohm), on the other hand, has its heroine achieve independence and liberation from her despotic father by escaping with her German boyfriend and severing all ties with her family. The filmmakers who addressed the experiences of Turkish immigrants in the 1970s and 1980s often focused on Turkish-German girls and women at the center of the conflict between their families' allegedly archaic and oppressively patriarchal structures as well as on the more liberal German society in which they lived. Rob Burns used the term 'cinema of the affected' to describe these films,[1] since they often took a patronizing stance towards immigrant cultures, portraying them as backward, narrow-minded and cruel towards their inferior female members and provided "narratives of rescue, liberation and Westernization."[2]

Head-On offers an infinitely more complex portrait of its young Turkish-German heroine, who is very strong-willed and actively shapes the course of her own life, despite encountering various obstacles. Unlike the characters associated with the 'cinema of the affected,' *Head-On*, as Stephen Brockmann explains, "treat[s] its protagonists as self-directed individuals trying to negotiate their own personal and social problems."[3] Set in Hamburg, the film tells the story of Sibel (played by Sibel Kekilli), a woman in her twenties and a daughter of Turkish immigrants. Unable to endure her life being controlled by her strict and overbearing father, she attempts suicide. In a psychiatric clinic, she meets 44-year-old Cahit (Birol Ünel), who also sought to end his life. Sibel convinces him to marry her, since his Turkish background would satisfy her parents, yet give her independence. Despite it being a marriage of convenience, the couple initially finds comfort in each other's company. However, their fiery temperaments and self-destructive tendencies ultimately lead to their separation and at the end of the film, both start new lives in Turkey.

Head-On offers a fresh perspective on the Turkish diaspora that constitutes the biggest group of what German policy makers have labeled 'people with a migration background.' There are about 2.5 million people of Turkish origin living in Germany, constituting around three percent of the country's total population.[4] In her review of *Head-On* for the weekly newspaper *Die Zeit*, Katja Nicodemus observes that the film offers an accurate picture of this contemporary nation of which German-Turks are an integral part:

> This Germany, for which [...] directors like Fatih Akin [...] and actresses like Sibel Kekilli stand, does not need to be constructed by the cinema anymore. One might ignore it, but

1 Rob Burns, "Turkish-German Cinema: From Cultural Resistance to Transnational Cinema?", in *German Cinema After Unification*, ed. David Clarke (London, New York: Continuum, 2006): 127–149, 148.

2 Deniz Göktürk, "Turkish Women on German Streets: Closure and Exposure in Transnational Cinema," in *Spaces in European Cinema*, ed. Myrto Konstantarakos (Exeter: Intellect, 2000): 64–76, 66.

3 Stephen Brockmann, *A Critical History of German Film* (Rochester: Camden House, 2010): 480.

4 Jan Hanrath, "Vielfalt der türkeistämmigen Bevölkerung in Deutschland. 50 Jahre Abwerbeabkommen mit der Türkei," *Aus Politik und Zeitgeschichte* 43 (2011): 16–21, 16.

one might equally ignore Cologne Cathedral or the *Siegessäule*. This Germany is there, it is the only possible one.[5]

The film's matter-of-fact portrayal of Turkish-Germans in Hamburg prompts Nicodemus to suggest that in *Head-On*, "the balancing act between familial constraint and urban socialization [...] has moved into the background."[6] However, this is an assessment with which I do not fully agree, because the pressure and ultimately, complete rejection Sibel experiences for not meeting her family's expectation to be obedient and docile is the reason for her extreme distress and rebellion, and it is central to the formation of her identity, which is at the heart of the film.

The origins of the first generation of the so-called guest workers still contribute to the illiberal outlook of some Turkish-German families today. 2011 marked the fiftieth anniversary of migration from Turkey to Germany, which began in 1961, when the German government signed labor recruitment agreements with Turkey. Many of the men recruited were unskilled workers, since the jobs they were hired for, such as operating machines, assembly line work and other factory jobs, did not require specific skills.[7] Psychologist Ferah Aksoy points out that "most families who came in the sixties came from traditionally conservative rural regions,"[8] and her conversations with young Muslim women in Germany suggest that "many have hardly budged from their values" until the present day.[9] They live in communities that consider the family to be the most important social unit, its honor and reputation being central. Controlling and violent behavior of Turkish-German men towards their wives, daughters and sisters often harks back to a code of honor originating from Turkish villages that demands

---

5 "Natürlich muss jenes Deutschland, für das nicht nur Regisseure wie Fatih Akin, Thomas Arslan und Schauspielerinnen wie Sibel Kekilli stehen, vom Kino nicht mehr gemacht werden. Man kann sich weigern, es zur Kenntnis zu nehmen, doch genauso könnte man den Kölner Dom oder die Siegessäule ignorieren. Dieses Deutschland ist da, es ist das einzig mögliche" (Katja Nicodemus, "Ankunft in der Wirklichkeit" [February 19, 2004], *Die Zeit* <http://www.zeit.de/2004/09/Berlinale-Abschluss> [acc. September 4, 2013]. Unless otherwise noted, all translations are my own.

6 "Der Spagat zwischen familiärer Eingebundenheit und Großstadtsozialisation [...] rückt [ ] allerdings in den Hintergrund" (Nicodemus, "Ankunft in der Wirklichkeit").

7 Deniz Göktürk, David Gramling, Anton Kaes, *Germany in Transit: Nation and Migration, 1955–2005* (Berkeley: U of California P, 2007): 9.

8 Qtd. in Göktürk, Gramling, Kaes, *Germany in Transit*, 172.

9 Qtd. in Göktürk, Gramling, Kaes, *Germany in Transit*, 172.

the man to act if the woman's honor is compromised.[10] In order to safeguard the woman's honor, her virginity needs to be protected, which requires women to dress appropriately and, in some cases, limit their contact to men outside the family circle. If she fails to adhere to these principles, the woman risks not only damaging her honor, but also that of the family. As Angelika Königseder and Birgit Schulze explain,

> the first generation of labor migrants, whose stay in Germany was supposed to be temporary, clung to this value system. Opening up to German society seemed unnecessary and was also difficult, because the majority of migrants did not come from big cities with a strong western influence, but mostly from rural Anatolia, where old traditions had remained valid for centuries.[11]

It is the persistence of these traditions and family structures that Sibel suffers from in *Head-On*. However, as I mentioned earlier, throughout the film she is portrayed as proactive and in charge of her own life, despite the strictures and the denigration she experiences at the hands of her brother and father.

Therefore, I want to argue that *Head-On* offers a progressive and empowering representation of a young Turkish-German woman. I will demonstrate how, through a painful and complex process of personal development, Sibel achieves independence and a self-chosen identity, which she does through role-play and a performance of gender, namely of femininity as well as of masculinity. Sibel's experimentation with gender roles is a reflection of the conflicting social mores and views on female equality held by her conservative, religious parents and the more permissive German society in which she grew up. While her parents and the Turkish-German community they belong to are part of a Turkish diaspora that can be defined as "a migrant group[] who ha[s] left [its] homeland but who continue[s] to share a religious, ethno-national, or national identity"[12]

---

10 Angelika Königseder, Birgit Schulze, "Türkische Minderheit in Deutschland," in *Vorurteile. Information zur politischen Bildung 271* (2006), *Bundeszentrale für politische Bildung* <http://www.bpb.de/izpb/9698/tuerkische-minderheit-in-deutschland?p=all> (acc. September 4, 2013).

11 "Die erste Generation der Arbeitsmigranten, deren Aufenthalt in Deutschland nicht auf Dauer angelegt war, hielt an diesem Wertesystem fest. Eine Annäherung an die deutsche Gesellschaft schien nicht erforderlich und war zudem schwierig, weil ein Großteil der Zuwanderer nicht aus den westlich orientierten türkischen Großstädten kam, sondern meist aus dem ländlich geprägten Anatolien, wo die jahrhundertealten Traditionen weiterhin ihre Gültigkeit behielten" (Königseder, Schulze, "Türkische Minderheit in Deutschland").

12 Girish Daswani, "The Anthropology of Transnationalism and Diaspora," in *A Companion to Diaspora and Transnationalism*, eds. Ato Quayson, Girish Daswani (2013): 29–53, 36 <http://onlinelibrary.wiley.com/book/10.1002/9781118320792> (acc. February 13, 2015).

which markedly differs from that of the host nation, Sibel's cultural and personal identity is still in flux. *Head-On* illustrates her process of constructing a home and sense of belonging for herself that takes into account both her experience of living in Germany with migrant parents and her return to her parents' homeland, which initially is anything but a home to her. The cities of Hamburg and Istanbul function as sites of Sibel's identity formation, both corresponding to a definition of the diasporic location by Jopi Nyman, who observes that

> [t]he diasporic location [...] can be seen as a liminal space of identity, as a space where various [...] forces, both global and local, remould identity. In this sense, diasporic identity can be addressed as a form of hybridized identity, as it is in this space of in betweenness where the diasporic subject reconstructs itself, problematizing the issues of home [and] belonging.[13]

The negotiation of conceptions of 'home' and 'belonging' is evident in Akin's representation of Turkey in *Head-On*, which, as this chapter will demonstrate, refuses to idealize the country as a lost homeland in a way that is typical of recent narratives of migrant experiences: "[T]he notion of home is rearticulated in post-colonial narratives of diaspora and migration, and its link with some mythical geographical homeland is severed."[14] Instead, the film uses the Istanbul location both as a manifestation of the protagonists' fraught relationship with their country of origin, and as the site of Sibel's experience of a newly and independently defined home, corresponding to an understanding of home common to diasporic fiction, whose "meaning [...] is [...] found in the future-oriented project[ ] of constructing a sense of belonging in a context of change and displacement."[15]

Turkish-German Femininity in *Head-On:* Transgressing Cultural and Gender Boundaries

We first encounter Sibel in a sexually suggestive pose (00:06).[16] Wearing a tight red top, black eyeliner and red lipstick, she sits with her elbows resting on her knees, showing her cleavage, and confidently reciprocates Cahit's gaze with a

---

13 Jopi Nyman, *Home, Identity, and Mobility in Contemporary Diasporic Fiction* (Amsterdam: Rodopi, 2009): 22.
14 Nyman, *Home, Identity, and Mobility*, 25.
15 Nikos Papastergiadis, *Dialogues in the Diasporas: Essays and Conversations on Cultural Identity* (London: Rivers Oram, 1998): 9.
16 *Head-On* (2004, dir. Fatih Akin, Soda Pictures, DVD 2010). Numbers in parentheses indicate the running time (hh:mm).

knowing half-smile. A close shot of her bandaged wrists testifies to her attempted suicide that stands in stark contrast to the vivacity and strength communicated by her look and pose. But this is not a serious decision to end her life: As Jana
Burgerová points out, Sibel's "suicide attempt in its ambivalence must be seen
as an outcry against the strictures imposed by her father and brother, as well
as an attempt to communicate to her family the strong attachment especially
to her mother" (played by Aysel Iscan),[17] the only family member sympathetic
to her plight. Sibel finds it unbearable to be controlled and policed for doing
what would be completely acceptable for the German girls whose company
she grew up in. Yet she must suffer brutal chastisement, explaining to Cahit
that when her brother (Cem Akin) caught her holding hands with a boy, he
broke her nose (00:13).

Rather than wanting to die, Sibel is keen to live life to the fullest. In one of
the most frequently quoted lines from the film, she states: "I want to live, Cahit.
To live and to dance and to fuck! And not just with one guy" (00:13).[18] She openly
pursues sexual adventures and uses a rough, vulgar language that degrades
women. "In her gender-specific disorientation, she acts like a man," as Burgerová observes.[19] Sibel assumes an identity and demeanor that negate her experiences as a woman and verbally perpetuate the abusive mindset of the men
around her. At the same time, Sibel opts for a markedly feminine appearance
in order to attract men. At this point in the film, she is unable to develop a conception of self, for example, based on her abilities or the achievement of economic independence. Instead, Sibel takes on an identity based on rejecting
and rebelling against everything her parents and her culture are demanding of
her. Polona Petek points out that "Sibel's desire for freedom from the constraints
and expectations of her atavistic family appears to be directed towards a singular
goal – unbridled promiscuity rather than emancipation or acquisition of social,

---

17 "Ihr Selbsttötungsversuch ist in seiner Ambivalenz sowohl ein Aufschrei gegen die erlebten
Einschränkungen, zugemutet durch Vater und Bruder, als auch ein Versuch, dem Elternhaus ihre
Verbundenheit insbesondere mit ihrer Mutter laut mitzuteilen" (Jana Burgerová, "Gegen die
Wand. Migration im Film," *Forum der Psychoanalyse* 24 [2008]: 96–103, 97).
18 "Ich will leben, Cahit. Ich will leben, ich will tanzen, ich will ficken! Und nich' nur mit einem
Typen." All quotations from the film are taken from the English subtitles (*Head-On* [2004, dir.
Fatih Akin, Soda Pictures, DVD 2010]). The German original is provided in the footnotes, based
on the subtitles of the German DVD release (*Gegen die Wand* [2004], dir. Fatih Akin, Arthaus,
DVD 2009).
19 "In ihrer geschlechtsspezifischen Orientierungslosigkeit gebärdet sie sich wie ein Mann"
(Burgerová, "Gegen die Wand. Migration im Film," 97).

economic and/or cultural capital."[20] Her fake marriage to Cahit gives Sibel the freedom she longed for, and in the following months, she and Cahit enjoy a life of partying, drugs and sex with different partners.

Sibel's libidinous lifestyle in this part of the film is offset, however, by a scene in which she prepares a traditional Turkish meal for Cahit. Sibel's process of self-discovery and of finding her own identity is informed both by her Turkish background and the German surroundings. Maha El Hissy notes that "the crossing of boundaries in *Head-On* is characterized by role play and the oscillation between conformist and non-conformist identities."[21] For Sibel, trying out different identities through masquerade and role play is a means of negotiating between the identity her parents assigned to her, that of the dutiful daughter and future housewife, and the life she wants to live, emotionally and sexually independent. This process of role playing and the oscillation between expected and rebellious behavior is epitomized by the dinner scene. In a montage sequence accompanied by Turkish vocal music, Sibel buys food and drinks, and we see her preparing stuffed peppers (00:52). There are close shots of her hands cutting vegetables, stuffing the peppers, preparing a red sauce and laying out a colorful tablecloth with Cahit's help. The strong colors of the food – greens, reds and oranges – and the fact that we see Sibel blending the filling with her hands make the sequence a very visceral experience to the viewer, and one that is very positively coded. The preparation of food that we see has a life-affirming quality, conveying a warmth and comfort that contrasts with the images of squalor in Cahit's apartment, the grimy interiors of the bars and pubs the two frequent, and the cold, clinical environment of the psychiatric clinic. It suggests that the characters do not experience Turkish traditions and customs solely as restrictive and stifling, but that they also function to provide a sense of home and belonging. Petek comments on this scene by saying that "Cahit and Sibel [...] develop a genuine, and not disabling, appreciation for their culture of descent. It is an appreciation [...] encapsulated in culinary delights."[22]

---

20 Polona Petek, "Enabling Collisions: Re-thinking Multiculturalism through Fatih Akin's *Gegen die Wand/Head On*," *Studies in European Cinema* 4.3 (2007): 177–186, 181.

21 "Kennzeichnend für die Grenzüberschreitung in *Gegen die Wand* sind das Rollenspiel und das Wechseln zwischen konformen und nonkonformen Identitäten" (Maha El Hissy,"Transnationaler Grenzverkehr in Fatih Akins *Gegen die Wand* und *Auf der anderen Seite*", in *Von der nationalen zur internationalen Literatur. Transkulturelle deutschsprachige Literatur und Kultur im Zeitalter globaler Migration*, ed. Helmut Schmitz [Amsterdam, New York: Rodopi]: 169–186, 173–174).

22 Petek, "Enabling Collisions," 183.

The montage also contains a shot of Cahit approvingly watching Sibel's efforts. It captures the moment in which his affection for her, which we saw growing in previous scenes, is cemented. Yet by the end of the scene, Cahit will be storming out of the apartment in anger. It is worth considering what exactly happens between these two moments. Significantly, Cahit's feelings for Sibel culminate in a moment in which she assumes the role of a Turkish housewife, emulating a traditional way of life that Cahit has so far vehemently rejected. Now he praises Sibel's cooking and her performance of the 'wife' role by saying that "marrying you wasn't such a bad idea" (00:53).[23] Sibel declares that she learned the recipe from her mother (00:53), which further underlines that in cooking this meal, she conforms to the behavior expected of a Turkish woman, continuing a family custom that is passed on from generation to the next. She then goes on to say that her mother asked her about children, to which Cahit, in his enthusiasm, responds: "Let's make some [babies]" (00:53).[24] At this point, Sibel abruptly breaks with the housewife role and reasserts her desire for absolute independence by bluntly rejecting this proposition (00:53). She explains that should her mother get too insistent, she could always say that Cahit was impotent, which would also be a good reason for a divorce. She then insults Cahit's feelings further by asking if they will go to their local club that night, implying that there she will meet someone for casual sex, which we have seen her do before. This sequence illustrates how Sibel temporarily assumes an identity and behavior that she has learned from her family, but only as long as this does not conflict with her demand for complete personal and sexual independence that is key to her new, chosen identity. Her changeful behavior suggests that, rather than being clear about who she is and how she wants to live, she is very much in a state of transition. El Hissy calls this state of transition a 'liminal phase' and points out that it is "marked by a certain ambiguity and shows how the character[] exhibit[s] characteristics of the old, as well as the new phase."[25] Sibel willfully ignores Cahit's feelings for her and hurts him by making clear that she prefers the company of other men to his. Her defensiveness suggests the fragility of the new identity that she has chosen for herself, and that she feels is endangered even by committing to a caring partner who has proven that he will not curtail her freedom.

---

23 "[W]ar keine schlechte Idee dich zu heiraten."
24 "Lass uns doch welche machen."
25 "Diese liminale Phase ist [...] durch eine gewisse Ambiguität gekennzeichnet und zeigt, wie die Charaktere Züge der abgeschlossenen, aber auch der neuen Phase in sich vereinen" (El Hissy, "Transnationaler Grenzverkehr," 173).

The pair's shared life ends abruptly when Cahit smashes one of Sibel's lovers over the head with an ashtray, killing him (01:06). Having fallen in love with Sibel, Cahit could not contain his jealousy when being provoked by the rival. As a consequence, Sibel is cut off from her family and lives in fear of them avenging what they see as her guilt and shameful behavior. The following morning, Sibel spots her brother in the street and runs away from him as soon as their eyes meet, narrowly escaping him as he follows her (01:10). He had threatened her already in the beginning of the film after her suicide attempt, saying that "if anything happens to [their father because of his grief and worry over Sibel], you will be dead meat" (00:10).[26] The murder Cahit commits places Sibel in a situation where she is not only deprived of any support or comfort from her family, but also has to expect physical violence or worse from her own brother. The identity of the dutiful Turkish daughter, which she performed in front of her parents in marrying Cahit, and which she re-enacted in the dinner scene, is now irredeemably lost to her.

Sibel takes up her cousin Selma's (Meltem Cumbul) offer to live with her in Istanbul. Once there, Sibel abandons her markedly feminine appearance from the Hamburg scenes, in which she had long hair and wore either short skirts or tight jeans that highlighted her female curves. She now looks very masculine, having her hair cut short and wearing baggy trousers and a pilot's jacket (01:15). In a voiceover, Sibel explicitly states that she is not living, but merely surviving in Istanbul, and likens her life to Cahit's experiences in prison: "you pulled the short straw, but jail is the only thing I can compare my life to here" (01:21).[27] The depiction of the city in the early Istanbul scenes underscores Sibel's feelings of alienation and isolation. Most of these scenes take place at night, and show Sibel moving either through empty streets or walking past other people who take no notice of her and whom she does not interact with. Akin here repeatedly uses wide, high-angle shots, which show Sibel in a crowd of people, making her look small and forlorn. The depiction of Istanbul as anonymous and of Sibel as isolated demonstrate that "she [...] is [...] an 'exile' — banished from her diasporic home as well as from her ethnic homeland,"[28] as Petek rightly observes. She is often pictured walking alone in dark back alleys of Istanbul, which are portrayed in the film as a male-dominated territory in which women are vulnerable to sexual assaults. These back streets provide the setting for one the most striking scenes of the film, in which Sibel gets into a fight with a group of

---

26 "Wenn dem Alten was passiert, wisch ich dich weg."
27 "Du hast das härtere Los gezogen, doch Gefängnis is' das einzige, was mir einfällt, wenn ich an mein Leben hier denke."
28 Petek, "Enabling Collisions," 183.

men. Müller-Richter comments on this scene by saying that "it is particularly noticeable that Akin opts to have scenes of excessive violence always set in [...] so-called *backstages*, and also in moments that primarily concern the breach of spatial boundaries or the breach of [...] masculine territoriality."[29] Sibel finds herself in a liminal space populated by hotel and service staff as they leave work through the back door, but also by thugs and drug dealers. It is a liminal space also in the sense that here she undergoes a temporary transformation from a feminine' to a 'masculine' persona, in order to be able to meet the men she encounters as an equal.

The previous scenes have shown Sibel taking opium with a bartender, who rapes her after she has passed out (01:25). When Sibel leaves the bar and encounters a group of men in a back alley who proposition her, her reaction is somewhat unexpected. In an outburst of rage that seems disproportionate to the provocation, she stops, turns around and shouts at one of the men: "Why don't you go fuck your mothers?" (01:26).[30] She then runs towards him, knees him in the groin and kicks him as he lies on the ground. The other two men rally to his defense, beating and kicking Sibel to the ground. The men then walk away, but Sibel gets up and shouts more insults at them, upon which the man she first attacked walks towards her again. She attacks him a second time, and is again beaten up by his friends. Although she is now severely injured, her face covered in blood, her eyes swollen and her nose broken, Sibel gets up and provokes the men a third time, only for one of them to stab her with a knife (01:28).

Being easily provoked and answering a verbal provocation with physical violence, Sibel emulates a "domineering form[] of masculinity characterized by physical control, aggression, conquering and competition."[31] Her body language – she first reacts to the men's calls by smashing her sports bag on the ground and turning around with her fists clenched and her shoulders rounded like a wrestler – and her ruthless fighting style, is stereotypically masculine rather than feminine. As Burgerová observes, Sibel "denies [...] her own female boun-

---

29 "Es ist überaus auffällig, dass Akin Szenen exzessiver Gewalt stets in [...] so genannten *backstages* spielen lässt; in Moment, in denen es vorrangig um die Verletzung von Raumgrenzen oder um Verletzungen [...] maskuliner Territorialität geht" (Klaus Müller-Richter, "Phantasmagorien der Rückkehr aus der Migration – Fatih Akins kinematographische Konstruktion und Inszenierung von Heimaträumen," in *Imaginäre Topographien: Migration und Verortung*, eds. Klaus Müller-Richter, Ramona M. Uritescu-Lombard [Bielefeld: transcript, 2007]: 177–194, 186 [emphasis in original]).
30 "Niye defolup ananızı sikmiyorsunuz?" [trans. Beyza Ates].
31 Niall Hanlon, *Masculinities, Care and Equality: Identity and Nurture in Men's Lives* (Basingstoke: Palgrave Macmillan, 2012): 61.

daries and fragility in a subconscious suicidal drive."[32] However, explaining her behavior as merely self-destructive or suicidal does not do justice to Sibel's motives in this scene. First and foremost she seeks to avenge the violence and humiliation she suffered at the hands of men; her unbridled rage and defiance exemplified by her overreaction to being provoked and her repeated taunting of the men. Even though she is acting irrationally and self-destructively, as viewers we are struck by Sibel's extraordinary courage and resilience.

Sibel's "gender-crossing masquerade"[33] corresponds to an understanding of gender as performative as contended by queer theory. Judith Butler has argued that the gender categories of 'male' and 'female' are socially learned rather than innate. Butler states that "there is no gender identity behind the expressions of gender; [...] identity is performatively constituted by the very 'expressions' that are said to be its results."[34] Thus, in Butler's view, it is our acquired and internalized behavior and appearance that codes us as distinctly male or female:

> a sedimentation of gender norms produces the peculiar phenomenon of a 'natural sex' or a 'real woman' [and] this is a sedimentation that over time has produced a set of corporeal styles which [...] appear as the natural configuration of bodies into sexes existing in a binary relation to one another.[35]

Sibel's performance of masculinity draws attention to the constructedness of gender by breaking up this male-female binary. Her gender identity in this scene is ambiguous: She fully inhabits a male demeanor and appearance, but her opponents are well aware that she is a woman. The confrontation is started by a man who addresses her by saying "Hey baby? What are you doing out so late? [...] You need a man?" (01:26).[36] Later, the men call her a "fucking slut"[37]

---

32 "Sie [...] leugnet in unbewusster suizidaler Absicht [...] die eigene weibliche Grenze und Fragilität" (Burgerová, "*Gegen die Wand*. Migration im Film," 101).

33 For the term "Gender-Crossing-Maskerade," see Ortrud Gutjahr, "Migration in die Ungleichzeitigkeit: Fatih Akins *Gegen die Wand* und die Wende im deutsch-türkischen Film," in *Krisenkino. Filmanalyse als Kulturanalyse: Zur Konstruktion von Normalität und Abweichung im Spielfilm*, eds. Waltraud Wende, Lars Koch (Bielefeld: transcript, 2010): 225–249, 245.

34 Judith Butler, *Gender Trouble: Feminism and the Subversion of Identity* (New York: Routledge, 1990): 25.

35 Butler, *Gender Trouble*, 240.

36 "Güzelim, yavrum sen n'apıyorsun gecenin bu saatinde sokaklarda ha? [...] Canım, güzelim erkek mi istiyorsun ha?" [trans. Beyza Ates].

37 "Pis orospu!" [trans. Beyza Ates].

and tell her: "Watch your mouth, girl" (01:27).[38] At the same time, Sibel's appro-priation of a typically masculine brand of verbal and physical aggression prompts the men to treat her as they would treat a male adversary. Their reaction suggests that our perception of gender is influenced as much by a person's be-havior as it is by their biological make-up.

Butler proposes to consider gender as an "'act', as it were, which is both in-tentional and performative, where 'performative' suggests a dramatic and contin-gent construction of meaning."[39] As Gutjahr notes, the violent confrontation be-tween Sibel and the men is a re-enactment of the abominable physical violations such as the rape that immediately preceded it, but also of Sibel's mistreatment through her male relatives back in Hamburg.[40] Sibel's performance of masculin-ity has the purpose of holding up a mirror to these abusive forms of hyper-mas-culinity she has encountered. Gutjahr comments on her verbal provocations, which are less pronounced in the finished film than in the script (which has her say "I fuck your mothers, I fuck your fathers, I fuck your children, I fuck your families"),[41] by saying that "through her provocations, Sibel reenacts [...] her [...] rebellion against traditional gender roles and ways of life."[42] Behaving like a man herself allows Sibel to create a new identity as she refuses to be do-minated, ordered about, and humiliated by men any longer. Although severely injured, she survives and starts a new life, thus ultimately emerging triumphant.

When Cahit comes to meet Sibel in Istanbul after having served his sentence, he finds her transformed. In Berghahn's words, "Sibel has traded the role of femme fatale for that of mother."[43] She has renounced the excessive and promis-cuous lifestyle that she practiced in Hamburg for a more secure, conventional life with a boyfriend and daughter. Although they spend a few days and nights together (01:43–01:47), Cahit cannot convince Sibel to stay with him, so he em-barks on the journey to Mersin alone (01:49). Cahit's plan to relocate to his birth-place Mersin, motivated by nostalgic memories, and Sibel's decision not to join

---

38 "Ya kızım, gitsene sen işine ya!" [trans. Beyza Ates].

39 Butler, *Gender Trouble*, 139.

40 Gutjahr, "Migration in die Ungleichzeitigkeit," 246.

41 "Ich fick' eure Mütter, ich fick' eure Väter, ich fick' eure Kinder, ich fick' eure Sippen" (Fatih Akin, Gegen die Wand. *Das Buch zum Film mit Dokumenten, Materialien, Interviews* [Cologne: Kiepenheuer und Witsch, 2004]: 156).

42 "Sibel reinszeniert mit ihren Provokationen [...] ihre [...] Auflehnung gegen tradierte Ges-chlechtervorstellungen und Lebensprinzipien" (Gutjahr, "Migration in die Ungleichzeitigkeit," 246).

43 Daniela Berghahn, "'Seeing everything with different eyes': The Diasporic Optic in the Films of Fatih Akin", in *New Directions in German Cinema*, eds. Paul Cooke, Chris Homewood (London: I. B. Tauris, 2011): 235–252, 247.

him are indicative of the ways in which *Head-On* interrogates the concept of homeland by juxtaposing the different ways in which first and second generation immigrants relate to the place of their ethnic origin.

Complicating Conceptions of Home and Belonging: The Representation of Istanbul in *Head-On*

Throughout the film, Akin complicates the concept of homeland or *Heimat*, which is a central theme not only in *Head-On*, but in several of his other films such as *Solino* (2002) and *Auf der anderen Seite/The Edge of Heaven* (2007), which also feature home-seeking journeys.[44] It is noteworthy that Akin indirectly addresses the idea of *Heimat*, since, as Daniela Berghahn notes, "*Heimat* is a quintessentially German theme,"[45] which gained prominence in German cinema during the 1950s with the proliferation of the *Heimatfilm*. The concept of *Heimat*, which resists any simple definition, involves a deep feeling of belonging to one's place of origin and its community that is often tinged with nostalgic longing, because one has left it behind or because it has been transformed in some process of modernization. The work of exilic filmmakers often contains a similarly idealized vision of the lost homeland. In his analysis of exilic and diasporic cinema, Naficy uses the concept of the 'chronotopes': "cinematic chronotopes are specific temporal and spatial settings in which stories unfold,"[46] and which are used to depict the homeland and the place of exile. While the homeland is typically presented as a utopian idyll and is associated with open spaces, boundlessness and timelessness, life in exile has a contemporary setting that is presented as a dystopian, claustrophobic, and closed space.[47] The depiction of the lost "homeland is cathected by means of fetishization and nostalgic longing for [its] natural landscape."[48] *Head-On* refuses to simply reproduce such an idyllic rendering

---

44 Daniela Berghahn, "No Place like Home? Or Impossible Homecomings in the Films of Fatih Akin," *New Cinemas: Journal of Contemporary Film* 4.3 (2006): 141–157, 145 (emphasis in the original).
45 Berghahn, "No Place like Home?", 144.
46 Hamid Naficy, *An Accented Cinema: Exilic and Diasporic Filmmaking* (Princeton, Oxford: Princeton UP, 2001): 152.
47 Naficy, *An Accented Cinema*, 5, 152–153.
48 Naficy, *An Accented Cinema*, 5.

of the lost homeland, which is evidenced by the depiction of the urban space of Istanbul in the film.

The only idealizing visual representation of Istanbul in the film occurs in the six musical interludes, which show actress Idil Üner in a long red dress, singing melancholic songs about unrequited love (00:00; 00:15; 00:45; 01:15; 01:29, 01:50). These inserts frame and interrupt the narrative flow and comment on the protagonists' feelings via the melodramatic lyrics: "Have all those who love and who have lost their lovers lost their senses like me? [...] / I lost my mind / May the mountains rejoice in my stead" (01:50).[49] Akin states that he chose the songs to demonstrate how classical Turkish music addresses heartbreak and excessive passion in a similar way to the western punk music used elsewhere in the film.[50] Üner is accompanied by the Roma clarinetist Selim Sesler and his ensemble; the ground they stand on is covered with Oriental rugs, the majestic Süleymaniye Mosque and the Golden Horn towering in the background. This panorama is the only setting in *Head-On* that reproduces the open chronotopes of the homeland, its idyllic scenery and landmarks, which Naficy associates with exilic and diasporic filmmaking.[51] However, it does so in a knowing and distancing way. As Landwehr comments, the musical interludes constitute a postmodern rendering of Turkish history that reduces it to stereotypical images: the Istanbul "tableau can be regarded as a self-referential statement on the role of the media, especially film, to alter or even create the images by which people remember a specific time and place."[52] The static shots of the musicians and the mosque quote other idealized depictions of the city, namely those directed at tourists. Akin himself states that this representation "was a way to break the Western, realistic look of the film with a kitschy postcard element."[53] Thus, Akin uses the musical interludes to expose idealized depictions of Turkey, while at the same time they demonstrate the filmmaker's tendency to merge elements of eastern and western culture.

---

49 "Herkes sevdiğine böyle mi yanar? [...] / Ben perişan oldum, efendim, aman/Dağlar şen olsun" [trans. Beyza Ates].
50 Fatih Akin, Wendy Mitchell, "Going to Extremes: Fatih Akin on His Turkish-German Love Story *Head-On*," *indiewire* (2005) <http://www.indiewire.com/article/going_to_extremes_fatih_akin_on_his_turkish-german_love_story_head-on> (acc. September 13, 2013).
51 Naficy, *An Accented Cinema*, 153.
52 Margarete Landwehr, "Liminal Spaces in Fatih Akin's *Gegen die Wand/Head-On*: Orientalism vs Globalisation," in *Performing Difference: Representations of 'The Other' in Film and Theatre*, ed. Jonathan C. Friedman (Lanham: UP of America, 2009): 76–88, 84.
53 Akin, Mitchell, "Going to Extremes," 2005.

The multifaceted and changing representations of Istanbul throughout *Head-On* reflect Akin's status as a second-generation immigrant who is influenced by both German and Turkish culture. Born in Germany in 1973 to Turkish parents, Akin is not an exilic or diasporic filmmaker; instead he fits Naficy's category of 'postcolonial ethnic and identity filmmaker.' Naficy writes that "ethnic identity films [...] deal with [...] the conflict between descent relations, emphasizing [...] ethnicity, and consent relations, stressing self-made, contractual affiliations. [...] [They are] concerned with becoming,"[54] that is, the individual's identity formation in their new country. *Head-On* blurs the boundaries between home and host country – neither Germany nor Turkey are clearly one or the other – but at the same time it emphasizes Sibel's self-chosen affiliation with Istanbul, her new home: she initially feels like a stranger in the city, but by the end of the film, she is settled there.

This process is reflected in the changing representation of Istanbul in the film. During Sibel's initial 'exile,' that is, from the time she is taken in by Selma until she is found by a taxi driver after the climactic fight with the three men, the city is portrayed as anonymous, dark and hostile. But the scenes showing Sibel and Cahit in Istanbul after he has served his sentence portray the city in a much friendlier light. The characters often enjoy panoramic views of Istanbul from a comfortable distance: when Cahit meets Selma at one of the top floors of the Marmara Hotel to enquire after Sibel, his gaze shifts to the windows overlooking the Bosporus (01:37). Later, Selma, Sibel and her baby are pictured in a brightly lit, spacious flat overlooking the city (01:42), and Sibel and Cahit are seen sitting on a balcony on a sunny afternoon, looking at buildings and the sea below (01:45). The fact that the protagonists are frequently shown looking down on the city visualizes the degree of mastery over their own lives that they have achieved. Cahit has overcome his alcoholism, which played a part in the murder he committed, and he seems much calmer, even if he is still in search of a place to settle down in. Sibel's situation is mirrored in the two opposing representations of Istanbul in the middle and end sections of the film. She is no longer at risk of being swallowed by its dark streets, but is able to look back at her former, self-destructive actions from a spatial and emotional distance. *Head-On* thus renounces any simplistic rendering of Turkey as an idyllic homeland. Instead, it uses Istanbul locations to mirror the characters' conflicted and changing feelings, or to knowingly comment on romanticized or clichéd representations of (life in) Turkey.

---

54 Naficy, *An Accented Cinema*, 15.

At the same time, the fact that both protagonists settle down in Turkey at the end of the film is highly unusual for second-generation migrants naturalized in Germany, as Petek points out:[55] Both Cahit and Sibel are German citizens who had lived in the country for decades. However, the film's ending questions whether Germany ever became a home for its protagonists by suggesting that while Sibel was unable to achieve a fulfilling life in Hamburg, she does so in Istanbul. Indeed Sibel's relationship to Turkey and Istanbul is marked by contradictions that the film never fully resolves. On the one hand, she moved to Istanbul to escape her family, initially has little connection to the city and is very isolated there. On the other hand, Istanbul is the place where Sibel's identity formation culminates after her fight with the men: "Sibel's symbolic 'death', the beating, and her daughter's birth can be perceived as the death of Sibel's old persona and the birth of a new self."[56] While the Istanbul setting of these climactic scenes point to the redemptive qualities of Sibel's ethnic homeland Turkey, one might conversely argue that she could lead a life very similar to that in Istanbul in Germany or any other country once she is no longer being controlled by her male relatives and has found a partner who offers her both independence and support.

Akin himself strongly opposes a reading of the ending as an endorsement of Turkey as a lost homeland where German-Turks may find redemption. He states that

> what interests me is not the place [Sibel lives at the end of the film], but the situation. She has a man and she has a child. But she is not happy with that. I think [...] [that] all my characters are searching for something. Searching for a better life. [...] [But] whether they find it remains unclear. And in their country of origin they look for redemption. But they do not find redemption.[57]

Thus, for Akin, the return to the country of origin alone does not provide a simple solution to his protagonists' problems. This is exemplified by the ending of *Head-On*, which sees Sibel forced to choose between freedom and security. As

---

55 Petek, "Enabling Collisions," 180.

56 Landwehr, "Liminal Spaces in Fatih Akin's *Gegen die Wand/Head-On*," 81.

57 "[M]ich interessiert nicht der Ort, sondern der Zustand: Sie hat 'nen Typen und sie hat ein Kind. Sie ist aber nicht glücklich damit. Ich denke [dass] alle meine Figuren [...] auf der Suche [sind]. Auf der Suche nach einem besseren Leben. [...] [Aber] es bleibt offen, ob sie das bessere Leben finden. Und im Ursprungsland suchen sie Erlösung. Aber die Erlösung finden sie nicht" (Fatih Akin, Rüdiger Suchsland, "Ich bin wirklich davon ausgegangen: Ok, das könnte mein letzter Film sein..." [March 11, 2004], *artechock* <www.artechock.de/film/text/interview/a/akin_2004.htm> [acc. September 4, 2013]).

Margarete Landwehr points out, "Sibel realizes at the film's conclusion [that] complete freedom doesn't exist as she must choose between her child and her lover."[58] She has to decide whether to stay with her partner or follow Cahit to Mersin.

It is notable that *Head-On* does not judge Sibel's nights with Cahit in Istanbul in any way or condemn them as morally reprehensible. We do not see her having to answer to her boyfriend about where she is going; not even her cousin Selma, whom she leaves her daughter with, reprimands her for what she is about to do. In fact, Selma gives Sibel her blessing, telling her "I wish you all the best" as Sibel leaves (01:43).[59] Rather, the film stresses Sibel's decision-making process. When she is with Cahit, we see her looking out of the window several times, deep in thought, while back home, we see her packing her suitcase and then having second thoughts as she hears her boyfriend and daughter playing next door (01:48). The question, then, is how to evaluate Sibel's decision to stay.

In the later Istanbul scenes, Kekilli's enunciation and body language indicate that Sibel has changed. She appears more serene in the presence of her daughter and Selma (01:42), suggesting that she has achieved a degree of stability and contentment that she was lacking earlier in the film, when she was compulsively striving to live in a way that contradicted everything demanded by her parents and their cultural tradition. *Head-On* depicts Sibel's struggle not only to liberate herself from her oppressive family but also to relinquish the reckless and self-destructive lifestyle she had adopted as a result of this oppression. By the end of the film, she is able to define herself not against her family background, but independently from it, having started a family of her own: one scene shows Sibel in her apartment with her daughter Pamuk. Sibel casts the child an affectionate look (01:42), suggesting that Pamuk gives her happiness and a new responsibility to care not only for herself, but for the child that depends on her.

Scholars differ in their opinions on the degree of fulfillment Sibel has achieved. Brockmann reads the ending as follows: "Sibel [has] trie[d], [...] unsuccessfully, to emancipate herself from the patriarchal power of Turkish traditionalism,"[60] since her life is now defined by precisely the role of housewife and mother that her parents would have envisioned for her. Similarly, Berghahn notes that in renouncing the relationship with Cahit, which we know would be more fiery and volatile, "Sibel forsakes her sensuality and egocentric pursuit of pleasure for the kind of stable and conventional life she abhorred."[61] However,

---

58 Landwehr, "Liminal Spaces in Fatih Akin's *Gegen die Wand/Head-On*," 86.
59 "Hayırlısı olsun" [trans. Beyza Ates].
60 Brockmann, *A Critical History of German Film*, 486.
61 Berghahn, "No Place like Home?", 155.

as Berghahn goes on to stress, "the mediocrity of Sibel's new life back in Turkey provides the structure and stability that will keep her alive. And in this sense her homecoming [also] brings about her redemption."[62] Similarly, El Hissy argues that "her decision is not to be understood as a sign of her imprisonment, but as a commitment to a civil and familial life and her obligations in Istanbul."[63] I agree with these latter readings, firstly because Sibel is given the opportunity to decide freely and independently whether to go or to stay (a choice she did not have when escaping from her family), and secondly since she appears to be much more settled in and in control of her life even before making this decision. Therefore, I would argue that the film is more optimistic about Sibel's situation than Akin is ready to admit.

Conclusion

Head-On offers an intriguing and complex account of the identity formation of its Turkish-German heroine. At times consciously, and at times without knowing, Sibel adopts stereotypical feminine and masculine roles such as the seductive femme fatale, the caring housewife or the rough young man, which she uses as blueprints for behavior and appearance. The ability to try out and then cast off these roles helps her in the process of finding an identity that is not shaped by her family's expectations. In her attempt to distance herself from them, Sibel deliberately violates the rules of what is acceptable for a young Turkish woman, according to her strict family, by rejecting the role of 'woman' altogether and acting like a man. Her performance of masculinity in the fighting scene is particularly fascinating in that Sibel is fully able to match her opponents in their gestures, aggression and fighting skills and thus completely inhabits features commonly associated with masculinity rather than femininity, thereby underscoring Butler's observation that gender identity is fluid and performative.

Sibel takes on this excessive identity defined by promiscuity, rebellion and a body that is able to endure extreme pain inflicted upon it by herself and others in order to counteract her experiences of suppression and confinement. Her decision in favor of a more conventional life at the end of the film suggests that this extreme lifestyle has become redundant as she has managed to construct

---

62 Berghahn, "No Place like Home?", 155.
63 "[Ih]re Entscheidung ist [...] nicht als Ausdruck der Gefangenschaft zu verstehen, sondern als Bekenntnis zu ihrem bürgerlichen und familiären Leben und ihren Verpflichtungen in Istanbul" (El Hissy, "Transnationaler Grenzverkehr," 179).

new familial relationships based on trust, commitment and affection rather than oppression and fear.

Moreover, *Head-On*'s representation of Istanbul largely eschews an idealized representation of Turkey. Akin complicates the portrayal of his country of origin, which in the work of diasporic filmmakers analyzed by Naficy is frequently rendered as a mythic, primordial homeland. The visual representation of Istanbul exposes clichéd images of the city as an oriental paradise by arranging the group of musicians in front of a picture postcard view of its largest mosque. More importantly, the depiction of Istanbul is used to illustrate Sibel's personal development. Initially Istanbul is a locus of anonymity and hostility that functions to demonstrate Sibel's lack of connection with her ethnic homeland and her feelings of loneliness and despair. At the end of the film, the images of Sibel looking down onto a sunny and friendly Istanbul visualize the control over her life she has achieved. Sibel experiences both her darkest hours and her greatest contentment in Istanbul, which suggests that the journey to Turkey has redemptive qualities that Akin himself is unwilling to admit. At the same time, Sibel's process of self-discovery begins already in Hamburg and her move to Istanbul is coincidental rather than intentional.

Although both protagonists ultimately choose to live in Turkey rather than Germany, *Head-On* does not so much proclaim the failure of migration as portray the challenges and opportunities faced by people growing up or living with both Turkish and German culture. It shows how experiencing the western lifestyle with all its merits and pitfalls has shaped the characters' identities and affected their perception of their ethnic homeland. While Cahit as a first-generation immigrant retains a romantic image of his birthplace, Sibel has no strong ties to Turkey. She only knows the customs and family structures belonging to a specific time and place in Turkey (the city of Zonguldak her parents left presumably in the 1960s or 1970s) that her family continues to practice in Germany. Through her character, *Head-On* problematizes the persistence of archaic family structures in Turkish-German families that have lived in Germany for decades but which, in an effort to preserve their cultural integrity, have ignored the liberalization of German society and female emancipation and are therefore more conservative than many families that live in Turkey. The confrontation of her family's oppressive patriarchal outlook with the female equality Sibel experiences in Germany is the basis for her rebellion against her father and brother. By the end of the film, Sibel has both liberated herself from this familial oppression, and achieved a sense of belonging, having built a new life in Istanbul. Thus, with its affirmative ending, *Head-On* is a poignant tale of empowerment of its heroine that portrays her throughout as a self-directed person rather than a mere victim, without denying the problem of lingering patriarchal structures within German-Turkish communities.

Chantal Zabus
Shared Pleasures and Strange Elisions: Three Types of Queer Ambiguity and 'Return-Migration' in Afrosporic Fiction

Abstract: In light of the emergence of African texts addressing same-sex desire as of the late 1970s, I examine three types of queer Afrosporic women's writing, i.e., *Sky-High Flames* (2005) by Nigerian, US-based Unoma Azuah; *Cracks* (1999) by South African, US-based Sheila Kohler; and *The World Unseen* (2001) by Shamim Sarif, born in the United Kingdom of African and Indian descent. These authors' characters are doubly diasporic on account of their queerness, complicated by two imaginative renditions of "return" – "return migration" and "ethnic return migration." Even if the passage from the sending society to the host society and the relocation in a Western country was voluntary, all three writers' imaginative return-migration involves some significant tension between the source and the target cultures, which is also verifiable in the authors' shuttling back and forth between sending and host society and in the canonical source subtexts that all three authors target to revisit or subvert. In examining how these authors' diasporicity impacted upon the representations of queer encounters, I also aim to show how this empowering representation of queer subjectivity and desire is fraught with elisions, which I deem strange given the authors' supposedly enabling displacement and relocation in the diasporic space.

In the wake of the emergence of African texts addressing same-sex desire as of the late 1970s, African diasporic or Afrosporic fiction started outlining a subtle move away from earlier concerns with establishing homosexuality as a lived experience contributing to shaping identity towards increased reciprocity in same-sex relationships. Unlike early anthropological discourse, which tried to establish exclusive links between homosexuality and initiation rites, and unlike colonial discourse, which often documented unequal relations between partners (differences in age, social status, and pecuniary means), a growing number of Afrosporic literary texts project what Plutarch called *charis*. The term could be translated as what Michel Foucault called "la grâce,"[1] referring to the love of boys, or, in English, "obligingness" or "gracious reciprocity" and, in a more recent legal discourse imbued with Human Rights vocabulary, as "consent."

My main focus is here on three types of queer Afrosporic women's writing: one that elides the desire; one that demonizes it; and one that represents it more directly and positively. The first of these is the Nigerian, US-based Unoma Azuah; the second, the South African, US-based Sheila Kohler; and, last, Shamim Sarif, born in the United Kingdom of South African and South Asian descent. Despite their elected exile and positioning, all three women writ-

---

1 Michel Foucault, *Histoire de la sexualité: Le souci de soi* (Paris: Gallimard, 1984): 242.

ers have set their work in a resolutely African environment, in which homosexuality is criminalized and perceived gender dissidents are at risk of harassment, blackmail, extortion and even death. Even though African legislators and ordinary citizens continue to portray same-sex relationships as un-African and therefore inauthentic, the African continent is currently hosting a proliferation of nonconforming performances of gender and is ancestrally receptive to queer relational nexuses such as "female husbandry" or woman-woman marriages, even though none of the above writers acknowledge their existence.[2]

All three women writers – Azuah, Kohler, Sarif – have experienced displacement. Azuah left Nigeria for a combination of reasons, as she herself acknowledges, "because of the pressures of patriarchy as well as for a desire to further [her] studies abroad"; indeed, when she left in the mid-1990s, "the Nigerian educational system was in shambles due to constant closures of Universities due to political upheavals."[3] We might add the adverse reactions to lesbian fiction such as that of Nigerian critic Oladele Taiwo, who famously proclaimed that "if tenable in Europe [lesbianism] has no chance of succeeding in Africa."[4] South African Sheila Kohler also elected to go and live in the United States after studying in France while Shamim Sarif, although born in the United Kingdom, deals with diasporic subjects in her fiction.

Few scholars have studied how certain diasporic peoples have also been returning to their ethnic homelands. In his introduction to an edited book, *Diasporic Homecomings: Ethnic Return Migration in Comparative Perspective* (2009), Takeyuki Tsuda distinguishes between two types of diasporic return:

> The first is the return migration of first-generation diasporic peoples who move back to their homeland (country of birth). The second is ethnic return migration, which refers to

---

2 See, among others, Joseph M. Carrier and Stephen O. Murray, "Woman-Woman Marriage in Africa," in *Boy-Wives and Female Husbands: Studies in African Homosexualities*, ed. Stephen O. Murray and William Roscoe (New York: Palgrave, 1998): 254–266; Denise O'Brien, "Female Husbands in Southern Bantu Societies," in *Sexual Stratification: A Cross-Cultural View*, ed. Alice Schlegel (New York: Columbia UP, 1977): 109–126. "Female husbands" are widows without a male offspring, who take on "wives" to produce heirs for their husbands' lineages. The "wives" then take on male lovers and have children who are in turn handed over to the "female husbands." The first study to show awareness of gender bending in Nigerian female husbandry was British anthropologist Sylvia Leith-Ross, *African Women: A Study of the Ibo of Nigeria* (London: Faber & Faber, 1939). Leith-Ross was, however, unfairly dismissed as a "racist" by Nigerian anthropologist Ifi Amadiume in *Male Daughters, Female Husbands: Gender and Sex in an African Society* (London, New Jersey: Zed Books, 1987).
3 Unoma Azuah, personal communication by email, 25 May 2010.
4 Oladele Taiwo, *Female Novelists of Modern Africa* (London: Macmillan, 1984): 24.

later-generation descendants of diasporic peoples who "return" to their countries of ancestral origin after living outside their ethnic homelands for generations.[5]

To these two types of "return" – "return migration" and "ethnic return migration," also called "ethnic affinity migration" – , one could add the imaginative and imaginary return to the homeland, e.g., Nigeria in the case of Unoma Azuah and South Africa in the case of Sheila Kohler or Shamim Sarif. They have, in a sense, "return-migrated" through literature, which does not exclude the return to the migrant-sending society or the physical shuttling back and forth between the migrant-receiving country and the migrant-sending country, for instance, in Unoma Azuah's case, her going back and forth between the United States and Nigeria.

Unoma Azuah is one of the most vocal of West-African-born lesbian-identified authors. In a 2005 contribution, Azuah theorized her work for the first time and presented it as part of a Nigerian lesbian continuum that comprises her Nigerian "sisters" back home like Promise Okekwe and Temilola Abioye.[6] She has focused on desiring women in her debut novel *Sky-High Flames* (2005) but more resolutely in her poetry as in the collection *Night Songs* (2001), in which a new brand of Afrosporic feminism is making room for the material and discursive factors that act together to define what it is to be a lesbian.[7]

---

5 Takeyuki Tsuda, "Introduction: Diasporic Return and Migration Studies," in *Diasporic Homecomings: Ethnic Return Migration in Comparative Perspective*, ed. Takeyuki Tsuda (Stanford: Stanford UP, 2009): 1–21, 1.
6 Unoma Azuah, "The Emerging Lesbian Voice in Nigerian Feminist Literature," in *Body, Sexuality, and Gender: Versions and Subversions in African Literatures*, eds. Flora Veit-Wild, Dirk Naguschewski (Amsterdam, New York: Rodopi, 2005): 129–142, 130. In Promise Okekwe's novel *Women from the Crystal Deep* (2002), Rebecca's lesbian leanings are stigmatized as being unnatural and evil desires, and in Temilola Abioye's story "Taboo," Oyinkan daringly suggests in the midst of a conversation with four women: "Why don't we all take a shower and go down on each other. It wouldn't be copulating, it would be a lot of petting, smooching and caring" (qtd. in Azuah, "The Emerging Lesbian Voice," 130). Azuah also discusses her own short story, "The Rebel," in which a woman suffers because of her sexual orientation and ultimately loses her lover to a monastery, as well as her own poem "Onishe," named after the Nigerian feminine deity revered in her novel *Sky-High Flames*.
7 As Azuah herself admitted in an interview, fiction is her "wife" and poetry her "mistress" (in Azuonye Nnorom, "Interview with Unoma Azuah," *Sentinel Poetry Quarterly* 4 [2005], n.p.). The somewhat illicit status of poetry as a "mistress" rather than a "wife" has enabled Azuah to provide what I call the "stuff of desire" by celebrating lesbian bonding. It is thus the form that dictated her approach in sketching same-sex love between Nigerian women. I discuss Azuah's poetry in relation to her prose narratives in my *Out in Africa: Same-Sex Desire in Sub-Saharan*

Set in Igboland in the 1970s, *Sky-High Flames* chronicles the life of Ofunne, who overcomes "sky-high flames," fanned mostly by aggressive men, before attaining self-realization. The first daughter of an Igbo polygamous household, Ofunne queers the general distribution of sex roles. Such initial transgressions are later comforted through what I have called furtive, flash-like "moments of intimacy," after Virginia Woolf's "moments of being,"[8] with women such as her childhood friend and the European Reverend Sister at the Teachers' Training College. Such moments of intimacy are imbued with "the beauty and libidinality of transgression," as South African exile Bloke Modisane eloquently put it in another context.[9] Nevertheless, what may be argued is "missing" in the novel set in an exclusive girls' school where girls sleep in communal dormitories and are expected to take baths in "an open wide bathroom"[10] is homosociality and sexuality, as if desire had been excised from the narrative. The boarding schoolgirls are, however, not completely unaware of the fluidity of shifting performance. Physical intimacy between young and older women is discursively confined to the flogging that teachers inflict upon students but without any mention of the psychological consequences of corporal punishment, let alone the girls' recuperation of flogging in sadomasochistic or fetishistic terms.

The confessional scenario by proxy (Azuah providing a first-person narrative with Ofunne as main narrator while telling the story of her real-life aunt 'Asua) suggests, as I have argued elsewhere,[11] an allegory of sexual self-discovery, which deviates into fiction, as indeed all sexuality does, since it inevitably rests on unconscious, infantile-determined scenarios of fulfillment. Azuah is in the same position as John in J. M. Coetzee's *Youth* (2003), confronted with the violence of the archive of her (and her aunt's) past; in order to bring off the narrative, she "will need to know less than [she] knows now, and [she] will need to forget things."[12]

The boarding school, seething as it does with pubescent sexuality, can easily conjure up the idea of "situational homosexuality." This has been applied by

Literatures and Cultures (Woodbridge, Suffolk; Rochester, NY: Boydell and Brewer/James Currey, 2013): 147–149.

8 Cf. Virginia Woolf, *Moments of Being: Unpublished Autobiographical Writings*, ed. Jeanne Schulkind (London: Chatto and Windus, 1976): 221.

9 Bloke Modisane, *Blame Me on History* [1963] (New York: Simon and Shuster, 1990): 299.

10 Unoma Azuah, *Sky-High Flames* (Baltimore: PublishAmerica, 2005): 39. Further references in the text, abbreviated as "*SHF.*"

11 Chantal Zabus, "Of Female Husbands and Boarding School Girls: Gender Bending in Unoma Azuah's Fiction," *Research in African Literatures* 39.1 (2008): 93–107.

12 J. M. Coetzee, *Youth* (London: Vintage, 2003): 138–139.

Robert Aldrich in *Colonialism and Homosexuality* (2003) to unequal power relations between colonials and natives, and by T. Dunbar Moodie to South African "mine-marriages," that is, initiatory and intergenerational relations between "hubbies" (*indunas*) and "boy-wives" (*tinkonkana, skesanas*) in Bantu-speaking, all-male, mining complexes.[13] Yet, the notion of circumstantial homosexuality in a West African context does not do justice to, for instance, *supis* in Ghanaian boarding schools, that is, girls who participate in sexual activities with their girl partners in secrecy (it is called a *pash*) until one party denounces the other.[14] Most *pashes* are, however, over before reaching even "this innocent stage" and suggest that the schoolgirl's "crush" is a necessary prelude to the "serious business" of adult heterosexuality.

American girls' comic and teenage magazines as well as girls' boarding school stories host a similar script of sexual self-discovery in both homosexual girls and heterosexual girls, who experienced the same "lesbian" feelings but never questioned their status as heterosexual. Same-sex attraction among girls therefore materializes as "lesbianism" when sexual identity develops from a "pre-given state, waiting to be discovered or expressed."[15] The boarding-school situation therefore provides the matrix where that "pre-given state" may be "expressed" and that expression is made flesh in "doing lesbian," which is, according to Jane M. Ussher, "something that women *do*, rather than something they *are*."[16] Similarly, *female husbands* and their women mates may find an expression of their mutual attraction within the institution of female husbandry but this does not mean that all *female husbands* are lesbians and "doing lesbian."

What is adumbrated in Azuah's narrative is the shifting of the various subject positions of being, doing, resisting or subverting "girl" by being a "tomboy," as in the scene in which Ofunne takes up the virile role by protecting her (female) childhood friend from boys' intimidations in the River Niger (*SHF,*

---

13 Robert Aldrich, *Colonialism and Homosexuality* (London, New York: Routledge, 2003); and T. Dunbar Moodie, "Migrancy and Male Sexuality on the South African Gold Mines" in *Hidden from History: Reclaiming the Gay and Lesbian Past*, eds. Martin Duberman, Martha Vicinus and George Chauncey (New York: Meridian, 1989): 411–425.

14 Angela Lambert, *No Talking After Lights* (London: Penguin, 1991): 99. Lambert mentions that, in British boarding schools, a "pash" can indeed develop "between a pretty junior and a receptive senior [that] might lead to a secret meeting in the long grass at the end of the games field."

15 Jane M. Ussher, "Framing the Sexual 'Other': The Regulation of Lesbian and Gay Sexuality," in *Body Talk. The Material and Discursive Regulation of Sexuality, Madness and Reproduction*, ed. Jane M. Ussher (London, New York: Routledge, 1997): 131–158, 149. See also Jane M. Ussher, *Fantasies of Femininity: Reframing the Boundaries of Sex* (London: Penguin, 1997).

16 Ussher, "Framing the Sexual 'Other'," 150.

26—27). But Azuah has chosen not to give narrative space to the boarding school-girls' "doing lesbian" and has thus been resistant to allow their sexuality to develop as a set of repeated performances in a Butlerian sense.[17] Desire is here carefully sanitized, leaving one to wonder why Azuah allowed the potential feminine *amitiés particulières* to be dulled by the college's monotonous routine of meals, siestas, afternoon preps and prayers. The novel seems to endorse the stereotype that if lesbianism exists, it is just a "passing thing." However, since Azuah is writing about her aunt or, rather, is writing her own story by proxy, this debut novel may be considered as being traversed by the partially told story of Azuah's aunt and the as yet untold story of Azuah growing up as a lesbian girl-child in Nigeria.

Elsewhere, on the West African scene, both Ghanaian writer Ama Ata Aidoo in *Our Sister Killjoy* (1977) and Nigerian Lola Shoneyin in her short story "Woman in Her Season" (1997) deal with interracial lesbian relations: between a Ghanaian woman and a German one, and between a Nigerian woman and a Swiss one. They can, however, only imagine lesbian love between a black and a white woman in Europe, as if the lesbian partner could only be a (Northern) European and never a consenting Nigerian (or African) woman.[18] But Aidoo, who is not lesbian-identified and has denied dealing with a lesbian theme in *Our Sister Killjoy*,[19] and Shoneyin, who is lesbian-identified, are both writing from their African platform, where queer practices are generally construed as a deviant import from the West, or psychological aberrations that would require a cure and, in some cases, rehabilitation in a camp.[20] In any case, it is vociferously criminalized. As a case in point, Nigerian President Goodluck Jonathan has in January 2014

---

17 I am here referring to Judith Butler's Foucauldian analysis of performativity in her *Gender Trouble: Feminism and the Subversion of Identity* (New York, London: Routledge, 1999): 171–190.

18 Same-sex sexuality between African women has, however, been documented, even in the distant past. The seventeenth-century (1672) Ethiopian book *The Life and Struggles of Our Mother Wälättä Peggle* (*Gädlä Wälättä Peothe* in the Gləʿnəz language) features a life-long partnership between two Ethiopian women and the depiction of same-sex sexuality among nuns.

19 "All I have to say is that I have not dealt with lesbianism at all on a conscious level though I know it is in the story. I know that in certain girls' schools there is something there, but in the Ghanaian society everybody comes out of the boarding schools and he or she is a properly heterosexual being. [...] Everybody comes out and is a very respectful heterosexual being: we marry, we have children, we carry on with our lives" (in Maria Frías, "An Interview with Ama Ata Aidoo: 'I learnt my First Feminist Lessons in Africa'," *Revistas Estudios Ingleses* 16 [2003]: 6–53, 38–39).

20 This is the case of a Mozambican woman, qtd. in Adrienne Rich's seminal essay, "Compulsory Heterosexuality and Lesbian Existence," in *The Lesbian and Gay Studies Reader*, eds. Henry Abelove, Michele Aina Barale and David Halperin (London: Routledge, 1993): 227–254, 240.

signed a bill outlawing same-sex relationships and sentencing sexual dissidents to imprisonment for up to fourteen years.[21]

By contrast, *Cracks* (1999) by American-based, South African Sheila Kohler goes to the opposite extreme of Azuah's *Sky-High Flames* in making the headmistress Miss G the abusive lover of one of her wards and in entrenching the idea that lesbianism is a ritualistic phase before accessing early adulthood. *Cracks*, which was made into a movie (2009), is an anxiety-ridden autobiography-cum-thriller which ghosts apartheid policies as twelve adults, who spent their formative years at an English school in the South African *veld*, hold a school reunion in the post-apartheid era under the aegis of the former school Principal. "Sheila" is one of the thirteen girls on Miss G's swimming team and has the same name as the author; yet the author, Sheila Kohler, has never acknowledged that her fiction is infused with autobiographical material,[22] even though she openly admits on her personal website that her sister's violent death during apartheid in circumstances that are not revealed to the reader haunts all of her writing.[23] Overall, the novel reads like the confession of a collective secret guilt concerning the thirteenth girl who joined Miss G's swimming set, Fiamma Coronna, the Roman Catholic "Crowned Flame" or "crush" from Italy.

Kohler's novel title is explained in an early subchapter's question – "What are Cracks?" – to which the omniscient narrator's answer is "Miss G was our crack" (*C*, 26) while conjuring up the colloquial term for vagina. But the "cracks" are also the narrative cracks and crannies of which the reader gets voyeuristic glimpses, as through a confessional's grille. The world of "cracks" is the impressionable, highly emotive sphere of budding adolescent sexuality, which is here exacerbated by the girls' forced separation from their English mothers. Kohler

---

21 Felix Onuah, "Nigerian Leader Signs Anti-Gay Law, Drawing U.S. Fire" (January 13, 2014), *Reuters* <http://www.reuters.com/article/2014/01/13/us-nigeria-gay-idUS BREA0C10820140113> (acc. February 28, 2014).

22 There is one passing reference to the character Sheila Kohler's early thwarted ambitions "to be a writer like Alan Paton [...] but she has only written thrillers, all of them about murdered girls" (Sheila Kohler, *Cracks* [1999] [London: Bloomsbury, 2002]: 98; further references in the text, abbreviated as "*C*").

23 "When my sister died a violent death thirty years ago in apartheid South Africa, my writing took a new turn. I was driven to explore the reasons for violence within intimate relationships, in particular, the abuse of power and privilege. Since then I have published nine novels, three collections of short stories, and several others not yet collected, all of which focus in some way on this theme. They represent my attempt to delve into the mysteries of hate and anger, and of love and compassion, as well. I am hoping that you will share them with me" (Sheila Kohler, qtd. on "Welcome to the Official Site for Sheila Kohler" [2009–2014] *Sheila Kohler* <http://www.shei lakohler.com> [acc. March 1, 2014]).

ingeniously orchestrates Miss G's decline, as the iconoclastic swim teacher, smitten with Fiamma, becomes distracted and loses weight. Her neglected girls consequently ask Fiamma to "be sweeter to Miss G" and "sacrifice [herself] for the common good" (C, 93) to appease the female horde; but this culminates in her murder. During one outing in the veld under the supervision of Miss G, the girls frantically insert sticks into the asthmatic child's orifices and gag her until she dies of asphyxia. They subsequently lay down Fiamma's corpse along the Boer War hero Sir George's remains inside his tomb, burying their secret until the time of the school reunion several decades later, in post-apartheid Africa.

The role of Miss G in this act of teenage tribalism, which recalls William Golding's Lord of the Flies, is not at all clear, but she seems not to have known about Fiamma's ultimate fate.[24] Yet, she remains a facilitator of sorts, for she seals a butch pact with an older girl, Di Radfield, who ends up being the vengeful murderer of Miss G's femme by proxy. Short of writing out of homophobia, Kohler's incomplete sketch of the consensual relation between Miss G and Di Radfield finds a disturbing corollary in her eliding of race — there are no Black or Coloured characters in the text. Such an elision, which seems logical given the context of an all-white school in the apartheid era, is unsettling when one considers the almost intangible presence of one Black helper in the boarding school as a form of tokenism and of gesturing towards race as a displacement for the white woman's burden of general guilt. Kohler's fictional surrogate, "Sheila," acknowledges her role in Fiamma's death but it is somewhat played down and shrouded in her love of fiction, the constant pull of which continuously deters the reader from reading Cracks as a repentant autobiography delivered to the readership of a fictive South African Truth and Reconciliation Commission.

Kohler's relocation in France in 1958 and then in the United States in 1981 has not helped shed such psychological hang-ups but has instead vitiated memorial rehearsals of her return to the native land, thereby leaving wounds to fes-

---

24 I here differ from Cheryl Stobie's reading in "Between the Arches of Queer Desire and Race: Representing Bisexual Bodies in the Rainbow Nation," in Body, Sexuality, and Gender: Versions and Subversions in African Literatures, eds. Flora Veit-Wild, Dirk Naguschewski (Amsterdam, New York: Rodopi, 2005): 66–87. Taking her cue from Marjorie Garber (in Vice Versa [London: Penguin, 2007]), Cheryl Stobie applies a bisexual epistemology to post-apartheid novels in the South African "Rainbow Nation" and casts Miss G as a bisexual individual whose paedophile abuse and rape of Fiamma helps demonize her boundary-crossing. Such a reading indeed occludes the fact that Miss G is primarily a lesbian rather than a bisexual individual and, beyond bisexuality, the novel leaves little room for "wasbians," "maybians," and other interstitial ways of being sexual.

ter as in the unclaimed experience of trauma. Moreover, the older women's act of ritual cleansing in the post-apartheid plot of the novel – swimming, naked, down the river – may alleviate their guilt, but Fiamma's ritual murder is left unpunished. Even though Kohler may be said to have "gather[ed] the past in a ritual of revival," as Homi K. Bhabha put it in another context,[25] the healing ritual remains Kohler's surrogate's private exorcism. "Sheila" is thus stuck between an impasse and melancholia, blockage and mourning, two opposite stances limned in postcolonial and diaspora theory.[26] Kohler's stance as well as the persistent haunting memory of her sister's death also illustrate the grief and pain of living in diaspora, which Ahmad Aijaz and Benita Parry have emphasized in an effort to balance out the somewhat optimistic celebration of exile by Salman Rushdie or Edward Said.[27]

Significantly, *Cracks* was published in the aftermath of the new South African Constitution and the implementation of its 1996 Bill of Rights including its 9:3 clause granting people "the right to equality before the law and freedom from discrimination. Prohibited grounds of discrimination include race, gender, sex, pregnancy, marital status, ethnic or social origin, colour, sexual orientation, age, disability, religion, conscience, belief, culture, language and birth."[28] But the South Africa Kohler revisits in *Cracks* is not the Rainbow nation or the first country in the world to constitutionally prohibit discrimination based on sexual orientation but rather apartheid South Africa, shortly after the official beginning of the infamous regime in 1948, with its Immorality or Sexual Offences Acts, which were obsessively repealed and renamed.

The return of the repressed – race – occurs in Shamim Sarif's *The World Unseen* (2001). The novel breaks new ground in depicting an interracial same-sex attraction in South Africa in the 1950s, the same time period as in *Cracks*. The novel is definitely set in a queer place and time, to borrow Judith (Jack) Halberstam's book title,[29] as it is set against the tormented canvas of the 1946 Indian

---

25 Homi K. Bhabha, *The Location of Culture* (London: Routledge, 1994): 139.

26 Cf. Eleanor Byrne, "Diasporic Literature and Theory, Where Now? Passing Through the Impasse," in *Diasporic Literature and Theory – Where Now?*, ed. Mark Shackleton (Newcastle-upon-Tyne: Cambridge Scholars P, 2008): 18–34.

27 Cf., for instance, Ahmad Aijaz, *In Theory: Classes, Nation, Literature* [1992] (New Delhi: Oxford UP, 2001); and Laura Chrisman and Benita Parry (eds.), *Postcolonial Theory and Criticism* (London: D. S. Brewer, 2002).

28 Constitution of the Republic of South Africa (1996), s. 9(3), see <http://www.gov.za/sites/www.gov.za/files/images/a108-96.pdf> (acc. March 10, 2015).

29 Judith Halberstam, *In a Queer Time and Place: Transgender Bodies, Subcultural Lives* (New York, London: New York UP, 2005).

Congress protests against the Ghetto Bill, the 1949 Mixed Marriages Act, and the Group Areas Act.

The World Unseen, which novelist and film director Sarif made into a movie in 2007, sketches a relationship between two women, Amina, a lesbian-identified local girl, and Miriam, raised in Bombay and trapped in a loveless marriage of convenience in forlorn Delhof, South Africa. Against a background of miscegenation, bi-racial rape, and unresolved tensions, the growing intimacy between the two women is sealed in Miriam's garden, a prelapsarian space where genesis can start all over again. After a scene of sweaty eroticism "in the rising heat,"[30] Sarif benevolently follows Miriam's gradual shedding of all past relics before she propels her into her diasporic and disjunctive present. There is a faint hint at the novel's closure that Miriam and Amina will "do lesbian" and continue some sort of relationship, yet suspended, queer.

Shamim Sarif takes the romance to its sulfurous conclusion in her third, semi-autobiographical novel, *I Can't Think Straight* (2007), which she also brought to the screen, and in which a young Palestinian Christian bride, Leïla, patterned after Sarif's partner Hanan Kattan, falls in love with Sarif's alter ego, Tala, a young British Muslim woman of Indian descent. The happy ending is, of course, possible and more plausible in London, where the two young women can enact their mutual attraction, than in Pretoria in the 1950s, where the bi-racial lesbian affair is doomed to failure or at any rate secrecy. Amina and Miriam's relationship in *The World Unseen* will indeed thrive in secret; yet it is, paradoxically, apartheid South Africa which provides Amina, a diasporic subject, with insights into her queer desire. Likewise, Miss G, who is the one truly diasporic queer subject in *Cracks*, comes from Wales and flees to South Africa under mysterious circumstances, which Kohler does not explore. It is, however, intimated that she can enact her queerness in that particular enclave in the South African *veld* until she is betrayed by her own and, as a result, loses her job, goes derelict, and is sacrificed for a common good that is ultimately obscure.

The South African context, especially under the post-apartheid Constitution, with its debates on Human Rights, sexuality and accountability, offers an excellent terrain for testing queer theory. Retrospectively, the apartheid period also provides such a theoretical testing ground, precisely because homosexual bonding, like interracial love, let alone interracial queer relations, was criminalized and the African National Congress's developments toward democratization

---

30 Shamim Sarif, *The World Unseen* (London: Women's P, 2001): 118. Further references in the text, abbreviated "*WU*."

had not yet helped create new spaces of queer visibility.[31] The "world" of desiring women was, in Sarif's words, "unseen," but by documenting highly charged, volitional same-sex relationships, both her novel and her movie help excavate one more layer of lesbian history from what Ann Cvetkovitch has called an "ephemeral transnational archive."[32]

Besides pulling the trigger of queer visibility, Sarif also connects two women, one Indian and one South African of Indian and African descent, in an attempt to make sense out of her own double belonging through her parents' background. Even though Amina has black blood from her grandmother's rape by her husband's African employee back in 1892, she is construed as Indian and Coloured under apartheid. Like West African writers Ama Ata Aidoo and Lola Shoneyin, who could not or would not imagine a lesbian affair between two African women, Sarif did not imagine or did not dare imagine a relationship between an Indian-born woman and a Black South African woman, let alone between a Coloured and a Black woman under apartheid. This relative elision, validated by the novel's semi-autobiographical vestment and evened off by Amina's touch of the tar brush, entails that the Afrosporic novel practices its own politics of inclusion and exclusion, which reflects in turn other exclusions in diaspora theory.[33]

All three women writers – Unoma Azuah, Sheila Kohler, Shamim Sarif – have experienced exile but a chosen exile, which may at first disqualify them from being described as truly diasporic. In the theoretical conjectures on diaspora of e.g., Robin Cohen, William Safran, Khachig Tölölyan, and Nicholas Van Hear, diaspora is often assimilated to the territorial dispersal of ethnic groups across different nations because of ethnopolitical or economic reasons. Such groups, always conceived in their plural form, retain a sense of attachment to the "ethnic homeland" of origin.[34] This definition of diaspora is, however, based on the notion of exile since for the diasporic individuals, the ethnic homeland "remains a distant place of nostalgic longing to which they cannot re-

31 I discuss "Interracial Queer Relations" at more length in my *Out in Africa*, 207–216.
32 Ann Cvetkovitch, *An Archive of Feelings. Trauma, Sexuality and Lesbian Public Cultures* (Durham, NC: Duke UP, 2003): 1.
33 Cf. Swaraj Raj, "Problematics of Theorizing Diaspora and Situating Diaspora Literature," in *Contemporary Diasporic Literature: Writing History, Culture, Self*, ed. Manjit Inder Singh (Delhi: Pencraft International, 2007): 49–60, 49.
34 See Robin Cohen, *Global Diasporas: An Introduction* (Seattle: U of Washington P, 1997); William Safran, "Diasporas in Modern Societies: Myths of Homeland and Return," *Diaspora: A Journal of Transnational Studies* 1.1 (1991): 83–99; Khachig Tölölyan, "Rethinking Diaspora(s): Stateless Power in the Transnational Moment," *Diaspora: A Journal of Transnational Studies* 5.1 (1996): 3–36; Nicholas Van Hear, *New Diasporas: The Mass Exodus, Dispersal, and Regrouping of Migrant Communities* (Seattle: U of Washington P, 1998).

turn."[35] Exile and diaspora therefore overlap. A case in point is Bessie Head, who, presumably because of her pan-African political activities, never envisaged returning to the South African homeland that she deliberately left to relocate in Botswana. In her autobiographical *A Woman Alone,* she describes her *exile* in Botswana from 1964 to 1979, after which date she became a full-fledged citizen,[36] whereas Lloyd Wesley Brown lists Head under "Diaspora" in his *Women Writers in Black Africa* (1981).[37] For her part, as already argued, Sheila Kohler elected exile in the United States but frequently returns to South Africa; and Shamim Sarif, although born in the United Kingdom, deals with diasporic subjects in her fiction and in her movies. Yet, these authors write from the perspective of a (post)colonial position rather than from a victim or economic diasporic position.

All three writers do not wish to "return" to the ethnic homeland, the way first-generation diasporic peoples move back to their country of birth after experiencing migration. As a second-generation descendant of South African diasporic parents, Shamim Sarif has not expressed the desire to "return-migrate" to the birth country of her Indian (grand-)parents; in other words, there is no "ethnic return migration" or "ethnic affinity migration," in the sense in which Takeyudi Tsuda has envisaged the different types of diasporic homecoming. The "return" to the homeland is imaginative and is enacted through literature. Instead of conceiving of the diasporic individual as moving from a migrant-sending society to a migrant-receiving country like England or the United States in a unipolar or one-way process, it is more fruitful to envisage a bipolar or even a multipolar flow or migratory dispersal. The works of such women writers allow for at least the bipolar flow of literature.

In their elected dispersal, these authors' characters inhabit the uneasy "cracks" of the hosting cultures – between India and South Africa, between the United States and South Africa, between South Africa, India, and the United Kingdom. But the characters are also doubly diasporic on account of their queerness, which is to heterosexuality what the diasporic state is to the notion of "home." At the same time, these characters' desire is, with a cautionary tale attached to Kohler's fictional surrogate, forward-looking and proves Gayatri Gopi-

---

35 James Clifford, "Diasporas," *Cultural Anthropology* 9.3 (1994): 302–338, 304.
36 Bessie Head, *A Woman Alone: Autobiographical Writings*, ed. Craig McKenzie (London: Heinemann, 1990): 11.
37 Lloyd Wesley Brown, *Women Writers in Black Africa* (Westport, CT: Greenwood P, 1981): 158–179.

nath right when she holds that "queer desire reorients the traditionally back-ward-looking glance of diaspora."[38]

Even if the passage from the sending society to the host society and the re-location in a Western country was voluntary, all three writers' "return" or "pas-sage," here understood in a loosely psychological sense, involved "some signifi-cant tension between the source and the target cultures."[39] Tellingly, the authors' shuttling back and forth between sending and host society or target and source cultures is also verifiable in the canonical source subtexts that all three authors target to revisit or subvert. Each text under scrutiny contains in filigree referen-ces, embedded allusions to, and at times extensive rewritings of, mainstream, first-world texts, *Jane Eyre* being among the favorites, which is confirmed by Sheila Kohler's 2009 eponymous novel *Becoming Jane Eyre*.

Miss G's name in *Cracks* conjures up the unconventional Miss Jean Brodie in Muriel Spark's 1961 novel. There is more to it than mere homonymy since, upon the publication of *Cracks*, *Books Magazine* called Kohler's novel "[m]ore sinister and sexual than *The Prime of Miss Jean Brodie*."[40] Miss G follows the same tra-jectory as Miss Brodie but her queerness is moved several notches higher. Her shady Welsh past, her dark-eyed slim athletic appearance and dark hair, "as glossy as a gypsy's" (*C*, 31) recalls the dubious origins and swarthy looks of Heathcliff. Significantly, the Brontë subtext, specifically that of *Jane Eyre* and of *Wuthering Heights,* is queered in the process, for Heathcliff is revisited as butch and Jane Eyre is imagined as having an affair with Miss Temple through the subdued relationship between Miss G and her pupil "Reckless [Di] Radfield" to whom, however, Miss G recommends reading "not *The Tempest* or *Jane Eyre*" but D. H. Lawrence (*C*, 34). In Shamim Sarif's *The World Unseen*, among the fif-teen books stored in her cellar since her departure from Bombay, Miriam singles out "[Thomas Hardy's] *Far from the Madding Crowd* and *Jane Eyre*" (*WU*, 222) but settles finally on Louisa May Alcott's *Little Women*, for she had, as a girl, "always imagined herself as the fiery, independent character Jo March, but when she thought about it now, it was someone else that she pictured in that role" (*WU*, 225). The tomboy Jo March in Alcott's novel also reflects on the male "switch" character, Laurie, in the plot development. Laurie is the next-door neighbor who has spent years wooing Jo March and, who, after she rebuffed him, simply married Jo's kid sister, Amy, on the rebound. In a chiasm of sorts, Miriam reluc-tantly contracts a marriage of convenience in India to then embark, once in

38 Gayatri Gopinath, *Impossible Desires: Queer Diasporas and South Asian Public Cultures* (Dur-ham, London: Duke UP, 2005): 3.
39 Makarand Paranjape, *In Diaspora* (New Delhi: Indialog, 2001): 6.
40 Kohler, *Cracks*, backcover blurb.

South Africa, on a loving relationship with the tomboy Jo March-like Amina, whom she had first identified with.

Even though they have markedly different agendas, both Kohler and Sarif inflect and queer the canonical texts to suit their characters' sexual dissidence and, in destabilizing the source-target cathexis, they help shift and reshuffle priorities in the circulation of knowledge. Also, in staging a growing sense of reciprocity and relationality and in covering a spectrum of marginal sexualities and of ethnic minorities (Black, Coloured, Indian) under apartheid, Afrosporic women writers have contributed to locating "queer times and places," that is, queer temporal and spatial niches in repressive systems. In so doing, Afrosporic women writers share a larger diasporic space, which can host female queerness while they point to aporias and exclusions. I deem these elisions "strange," given the authors' supposedly enabling displacement and relocation in the diasporic space.

Such exclusions therefore reveal the continued inadequacy of contemporary diaspora theory while pointing to what we hope will be curious and curiouser attempts to portray shared pleasures and *charis* between African women at "home." Kagure Mugo, a UK-trained Kikuyu young woman studying at the University of Cape Town and a member of HOLAA!, a pan-African site publishing the work of queer women, seems to show the way. In a letter to her parents in her native Kenya, she writes:

> Replace the spectrum of
> Everything I was and replace it
> with a single identity.
> Gay.[41]

"A Little Longer," is, however, written from a diasporic location, post-apartheid South Africa, and is a plea for the revelation of her "gayness" to her parents to be postponed while she waits "a little longer." It remains to be seen whether the African "home" rather than its diasporic counterpart can truly host same-sex desire for both men and women in African nation-states.

---

41 Kagure Mugo, "A Little Longer: A Plea for Full Existence," *Q-Zine* 6 (2013): 76–81, 76. Accessible via ISSUU <http://issuu.com/q-zine/docs/qz6e> (acc. March 2, 2014).

List of Contributors

Holding a PhD in Comparative Literature, **Jean Amato** has studied and conducted graduate research in Mainland China and Taiwan for over six years. Working in Chinese and English, her research centers on theories of gender and nationalism and the ancestral home and homeland in twentieth century Chinese, diasporic and Chinese American literature and film. An Associate Professor in the English Department at the Fashion Institute of Technology, State University of New York (SUNY), her publications include "Ideological Mappings of Gendered Bodies, Nations and Spaces in Louis Chu's 1961 Chinatown Novel, *Eat a Bowl of Tea*," in *Ecologies of Seeing*, eds. Asbjørn Gronstad, Mark Ledbetter (Newcastle: Cambridge Scholar's Press, forthcoming); "*Oxhide II* [牛皮二] (2009), Chinese Filmmaker Liu Jiayin's New Geography of the Home," in *Spaces of the Cinematic House: Behind the Screen Door*, eds. Fran Pheasant-Kelly, Stella Hockenhull and Eleanor Andrews (New York: Routledge Taylor and Francis, 2015): 106–120; "Relocating Notions of National and Ethnic Authenticity in Chinese American and Chinese Literary Theory through Nieh Hualing's Overseas Chinese Novel, *Mulberry and Peach*," *Pacific Coast Philology* 34.1 (1999): 32–52; as well as entries in *Asian American Novelists: A Bio-bibliographical Critical Sourcebook*, ed. Emmanuel S. Nelson (Connecticut, Greenwood Press, 2000) and *Asian American Autobiographers: A Bio-bibliographical Critical Sourcebook*, ed. Guiyou Huang (Connecticut: Greenwood Press, 2001).

Annika Bauer received her M.A. in English Literatures at Chemnitz University of Technology in 2011. Her thesis, entitled *German Preschool Children Encountering Postcolonial Picture Books in English*, focuses on Indian and African children's literature and was published by Social Softwork, Wettingen in 2012. She has been a research assistant since 2012 and since 2013, a PhD candidate at the Chair of English Literatures at Chemnitz University of Technology. In her dissertation project, she concentrates on literary representations of postcolonial metropolises. More specifically, she researches constructions of living spaces and their social, political and architectural structures in Mumbai, Delhi and Kolkata in Indian English fiction. She is co-editor of and contributor to the essay collection *Stadt der Moderne* (City of Modernity) published by WVT, Trier in 2013.

Homi K. Bhabha is Anne F. Rothenberg Professor of the Humanities at Harvard University. He holds a BA from the University of Bombay and an MPhil and a DPhil from the University of Oxford.

Gesa Bierwerth is a PhD candidate in Ethnology and Cultural Heritage at Laval University, Quebec City, Canada. She holds a master's degree from the same university. Gesa Bierwerth investigates tourism practices of displaced people and is particularly interested in personal heritage tourism. More specifically, she focuses on questions of longing and belonging amongst German expellees from East Prussia. She conducts fieldwork in the former German Eastern territories.

Stella Butter is Teaching Centre Coordinator at the International Graduate Centre for the Study of Culture (Justus Liebig University Gießen, Germany). She teaches and writes on cultural functions of literature and is interested in how processes of modernization are depicted and shaped by literature and the media. Her current research project deals with the interplay of home and subjectivity in contemporary British and Anglophone literature. Recent publications include a book on contingency and literature (*Kontingenz und Literatur im Prozess der Modernisierung*, 2013) and an article on transnational fictions of home in Lloyd Jones's *Mister Pip*, published in the *Anthropological Journal of European Studies* (2014). She also co-edited the special issue of *Anglistik* on "Community in British and Irish Cultural Production" (2015). In 2007, she received her PhD from Gießen University and was awarded her postdoctoral degree by the University of Mannheim in 2012.

Rasha Chatta is a final year PhD candidate at the Centre for Cultural, Literary and Postcolonial Studies (CCLPS) at SOAS, University of London. Her research project, entitled "Marginality and Individuation in Literary Discourse: Theorising Contemporary Migrant Literature through the example of Arab Migrant Writing," deals with the theoretical issues arising from the problematic field of Migrant Literature, through the specific practices peculiar to the contemporary novel written by Arab migrant writers. Her research explores possibilities for a theoretical delineation of Migrant Literature through notions of identity, individuation and marginality beyond national parameters. She is currently preparing contributions to special issues in the journals *Middle Eastern Literatures* (Routledge) and *Transantlatic Studies* (Routledge), and she has also been a teaching assistant in the department of the Near and Middle East at SOAS since 2011.

Sonja Fielitz is Professor of English Literature at the University of Marburg (Germany). She studied English, Latin and German at the University of Munich and received her PhD in 1992 with a study on Shakespeare's *Timon of Athens* and its possible relatedness to a hitherto unedited comedy by the German Jesuit Jakob Gretser. Her post-doctoral thesis, published in 2000, examines the status of Ovid's *Metamorphoses* within the various theoretical and critical discourses in

England between 1660 and 1800. She is the editor of two (German-language) series of books and has furthermore edited six collections of essays in English on various topics. Her main field of expertise in research and teaching is the early modern period with a focus on religious discourses such as the early Jesuit mission, as well as Shakespeare and his contemporaries. Her most recent publications include a student book on the *Analysis of Drama* (2011) and an *Introduction to the Study of Shakespeare* (2013). She has also published a book-length study of Shakespeare's *Othello*, and about forty-five articles on the early modern period, the long eighteenth century, children's literature, school- and university novels and (post)modern drama with particular reference to performance criticism.

Jaqueline Flack received her M. A. in sociology, German and comparative literature at Eberhard Karls University Tübingen. She currently works at the International Centre for Ethics in the Sciences and Humanities (IZEW) in Tübingen and is a doctoral candidate at the European University Viadrina Frankfurt (Oder). In her dissertation she focuses on the cultural practices of identity construction processes of the East German "Wendegeneration" after 1989. She has published on the East German "Wendegeneration" and on cultural memory.

Nina Gren holds a PhD in Social Anthropology from the University of Gothenburg and is currently employed at the Centre for Middle Eastern Studies, Lund University as a researcher and teacher. Her ongoing research focuses on encounters between staff at Swedish authorities and newly-arrived Palestinian refugees. For more than a decade, Gren has carried out extensive field studies among Palestinian refugees in the occupied territories as well as in Scandinavia. Her main work is published in a monograph, *Occupied Lives: Maintaining Integrity in a Palestinian Refugee Camp in the West Bank* (American University Press in Cairo, 2015). Gren's research interests include transnational migration, diasporic practices, resilience when facing political violence, morality, memory and gender.

Ihab Hassan was Vilas Research Professor of English and Comparative Literature at the University of Wisconsin-Milwaukee until his retirement in 1999. He holds degrees in literature from the University of Pennsylvania and has held visiting professorships at Yale, Trinity College Dublin, and the University of Washington. He has taught in Sweden, Japan, Germany, France, Austria, as well as in the US.

Saskia Hertlein studied English, History, and Social Sciences with a special focus on the Americas and Northern Cultures at the universities of Eichstätt, Germany and Oulu, Finland. Currently, she works as assistant professor in American

Studies at the University of Duisburg-Essen. She recently completed her doctorate with a dissertation on *Tales of Transformation. Emerging Adulthood, Migration, and Ethnicity in Contemporary American Fiction,* and has published on contemporary American multiethnic literature as well as various issues of diversity. With Hermann Josef Schnackertz, she edited a volume on *The Culture of Catholicism in the United States,* and with Josef Raab she is currently editing a volume on *Spaces – Communities – Discourses: Charting Identity and Belonging in the Americas.*

Elena Igartuburu García holds a degree in English Studies and a Master's Degree in Gender Studies (Máster en Género, Identidad y Ciudadanía), both from the University of Cádiz. Currently, she is writing her PhD dissertation and enjoys a FPI grant through which she participates in the research project *Cosmopolis. The Fluid City: Literary Representations of the Transnational City* (FFI2010 – 17296) and *Multiplicity. Embodied Encounters and Alternative Knowledge* (FFI2013 – 45642-R) led by Professor Isabel Carrera at the University of Oviedo (Spain). Her interests include gender studies and queer theory, as well as Caribbean and Asian studies.

Frank Jacob is Assistant Professor of World History (tenure track) at the City University of New York (QCC). He received his MA in Modern History and Japanese Studies from the University of Würzburg in 2010, and his PhD in Japanese Studies from the University of Erlangen in 2012. Dr. Jacob is the editor of three academic journals, including *ChiMoKoJa. Histories of China, Mongolia, Korea, and Japan,* three academic series, including *War (Hi)Stories,* and the author of numerous books and articles focusing on German, Japanese, and Global History.

Maria Jakob studied Political Science, International Relations and Cultural Studies ("Kulturwissenschaften") in Leipzig and Warsaw from 2005 to 2011. From 2011 until 2014 she was a member of the Graduate Class "Secularities: Configurations and Development Paths" at Leipzig University's Research Academy. Since 2014 she has been a research assistant at the Institute for the Study of Culture, University of Leipzig. Her research interests include qualitative methodology, migration, integration and cultural sociology.

Anita Janassary graduated in political science at Freie Universität Berlin and works as Junior Researcher at the Centre for Area Studies at the University of Leipzig. Previously, she was assigned project manager at the German Center for International Peace Operations (ZIF) and implemented human resources related projects funded by the German Foreign Office as well as the German Development Agency (GIZ). She is co-author of the practitioners handbook "Roster management handbook" (2011, available online https://www.civcap.info/fileadmin/user_upload/Research_Reports/roster_management_handbook.pdf). Currently, she is working on her dissertation project dealing with the impact of direct diaspora involvement as staff members in peace building measures in the Western Balkans. The publication of her work is expected in 2016.

Annette Kern-Stähler is Chair of Medieval Studies at the University of Bern and Honorary Professor of the School of English at the University of Kent at Canterbury. She was *professeur invitée* at the École Normale de Supérieure de Lyon and has held a number of fellowhips, among them an Andrew Mellon Fellowship at the Harry Ransom Center of the University of Texas at Austin and a Christopher Isherwood Fellowship at the Huntington Library. She has published widely on medieval, Victorian and contemporary British literature, more specifically on interrelations between medicine, ethics and literature, concepts of authorship and British-German relations after the Second World War. She is the author of a monograph and several articles on the uses and transformations of space in late medieval England. She is currently working on a project on the five senses in medieval literature and completing a monograph on British writers in occupied Germany for Northwestern University Press.

Florian Kläger is assistant professor of British Studies at the University of Münster, where he also co-heads a research group on literary constructions of Europe and co-coordinates the Marie Curie Initial Training Network "Diasporic Constructions of Home and Belonging" (CoHaB). He has published on the novel in English as well as on Irish drama and on early modern cultural identities.

Jaroslav Kušnír is Professor of American, British and Australian literature at the University of Prešov, Slovakia, where he teaches courses on American, British and Australian literature, as well as on literary theory and criticism. His research interests include American postmodern and contemporary fiction, Australian postmodern fiction, and the critical reception of American, British and Australian literature in Slovakia. He is the author of *Poetika americkej postmodernej prózy (Richard Brautigan a Donald Barthelme)* [Poetics of American Postmodern Fiction: Richard Brautigan and Donald Barthelme] (Prešov, Slovakia: Impreso, 2001); *American Fiction: Modernism-Postmodernism, Popular Culture, and Metafiction* (Stuttgart, Germany: Ibidem, 2005); and *Australian Literature in Contexts* (Banská Bystrica, Slovakia: Trian, 2003).

Qianqian Li was born in Beijing, China. Since 2007 she has been studying at the Philipps University of Marburg. She obtained her BA degree in Media Studies in 2010 with her final thesis on "The Renaissance of the Cinema of Attraction." In 2012, she obtained her MA degree in North American Studies with a thesis entitled "The Role of Mass Media in American Democracy." As a Chinese national in Germany, Li feels that the topics of diaspora and immigration relate to her own background, so she chose these topics as her research fields. Now she is working on her doctoral thesis, "Settling Down in a Foreign Country: A Comparison between the US and German Immigration Policies and Their Consequences." Her focus is on the cultural aspect of immigration policies.

Andreas Niehaus studied Japanese language and culture, English and German literature at Cologne University, where he also received his PhD. His dissertation focused on the life and work of the Japanese educator Kanô Jigorô. In 2004, he was appointed professor and head of the Institute for Japanese Language and Culture at Ghent University, and in 2011, he additionally became adjunct professor for Japanese at the University of Eastern Finland. Since 2012, he has held the position as head of the Department of Languages and Cultures at Ghent University. His main research interest is Japanese sport history, sport sociology, and body culture. In 2011, he received funding from the Japan Foundation for a joint project with Düsseldorf University in order to conduct research concerning the impact of the Triple Disaster in 2011 on the Japanese diaspora worldwide.

Anke Patzelt is currently enrolled in the PhD program for Sociology at the University of Ottawa (Canada) and is a recipient of the Ontario Trillium Scholarship. Previously, she graduated from Malmö University (Sweden) with a Master of Arts degree in International Migration and Ethnic Relations in August 2013. Her master thesis, entitled *Of 'Modern Immigrants' and 'German Bread': A Case Study of Ethnic Identity Construction Amongst Contemporary German Immigrants in the City of Ottawa, Canada*, investigates the migration experience and ethnic identity construction of contemporary German immigrants in Canada and was awarded the German-Canadian Studies Master's thesis Prize of the University of Winnipeg (Canada) in 2014. She obtained her Bachelor of Arts degree in Anthropology and Scandinavian Studies from WWU Münster (Germany), with an exchange semester at Umeå University (Sweden). Her current research interests include international migration, concepts of identity construction, home, and belonging, aging migrants, and German immigrants in Canada.

Annegret Pelz is professor of Modern German Literature and co-initiator of the trans-disciplinary research platform "Mobile Cultures and Societies. Interdisciplinary Studies on Transnational Formations" at the University of Vienna. Her research focuses on questions emerging in the field of Cultural Studies, Media and Literature Theory. She is especially interested in forms of staging the act of writing, the materiality of notebooks, albums, portfolios and cultural transformations of spaces and objects. In 2013, she edited *Album. Organisationsform narrativer Kohärenz*, together with Anke Kramer, available online at <http://germa nistik.univie.ac.at/fileadmin/user_upload/inst_germanistik/Album_Einleitung_. pdf>.

Klaus Stierstorfer is Chair of British Studies at the University of Münster. He holds a DPhil from the University of Oxford and has published widely on literary and cultural theory. He has worked in and managed a number of research projects on diaspora studies and constructions of home, and he is the co-ordinator of the Marie Curie Initial Training Network "Diasporic Constructions of Home and Belonging" (CoHaB, see <itn-cohab.eu>). He has been a corresponding fellow of the English Association since 2011.

Milena Uhlmann graduated from University of Potsdam in political science and worked as a Research Associate at the Institute for European Politics in Berlin before focusing on fieldwork for her doctorate on "Conversions to Islam in Western Europe." During her PhD research, she was a guest scholar at the International Policy Institute for Counter-Terrorism at the Interdisciplinary Center Herzliya, the International Centre for the Study of Radicalisation and Political Violence (ICSR) London, City University London, the Institute for Political Science Paris (SciencesPo), and the National Center of Scientific Research (CNRS) in Paris. She currently works as a freelance consultant and researcher with a focus on Muslim converts and counter-radicalization issues.

Verena von Eicken recently completed her PhD at the University of York's Department of Theatre, Film and Television. Her PhD research focused on contemporary German film (2000–2015 and ongoing), specifically on a new generation of actresses within the renascent German cinema of the last decade, investigating their performance style in relation to female performers in the history of German cinema, as well as analyzing their films with respect to their representations of national identity and the position of women in post-reunification Germany. Her research interests include contemporary German cinema, gender and film, representations of the past in film and television and the figure of the film actor as both performer and star.

Ricarda Wagner studied English, German, and Classics at the Universities of Heidelberg and Cambridge, UK. She is currently a junior lecturer at the German Department of the University of Heidelberg, where she teaches Medieval German Language and Literature. She is also working on her PhD thesis that examines instances and poetics of 'exile' in medieval literature, drawing on a corpus of texts ranging from Germanic heroic epics and courtly romances to Dante. In addition, she is involved in a project on "Emotions in Literature" (funded by the Robert Bosch Stiftung) that aims to bring medieval literature to high school classrooms and high school students to universities.

Tine Walravens received her MA in Chinese Studies (Ghent University, Belgium; Xiamen University, China), finished a second bachelor in Japanese studies (Ghent University, Belgium; Nagasaki University, Japan), and gathered additional education and experience on European integration (University of Agder, Norway; EU-Japan Centre for Industrial Cooperation, Japan; European Commission, DG Trade, Belgium). Since 2012, she has been employed as an assistant lecturer in the Department of Japanese Language and Culture at Ghent University. Her current research includes food safety issues in Sino-Japanese relations, and EU-Japan relations. She has also been involved in a project financed by Japan Foundation focusing on the reaction of the Japanese diaspora in Belgium to the Triple Disaster of March 11, 2011.

Vered Weiss is Assistant Lecturer in Comparative Literature at the University of Kent, Canterbury. After earning her BA in Comparative and English Literature at Tel Aviv University (Israel), Vered completed her MA in Comparative and World Literature at San Francisco State University. Her main research interests include nineteenth- and twentieth-century literature in English, Hebrew, and Spanish; literature and nationalism; postcolonial literature and theory; gender studies; and critical theory. She recently completed her doctoral research, which examines (re)construction of individual and collective identities in relation to spatial awareness in nineteenth- to mid-twentieth-century English and Hebrew literature. Specifically, she considers the manner in which the location of the monstrous Other is indicative of the relationship of the respective 'imagined community' and sovereignty.

Pnina Werbner is Professor Emerita of Social Anthropology, Keele University, and author of 'The Manchester Migration Trilogy', including *The Migration Process* (1990/2002), *Imagined Diasporas among Manchester Muslims* (2002) and *Pilgrims of Love: the Anthropology of a Global Sufi Cult* (2003). In 2008 she edited *Anthropology and the New Cosmopolitanism: Rooted, Feminist and Vernacular Perspec-*

tives, and is the editor of several theoretical collections on hybridity, multiculturalism, migration and citizenship. She has researched in Britain, Pakistan, and Botswana, and has directed major research projects on the Muslim South Asian, Filipino and African diasporas. Her most recent books are *The Making of an African Working Class: Law, Politics and Cultural Protest* (Pluto 2014) and she co-edited *The Political Aesthetics of Global Revolt: Beyond the Arab Spring* (Edinburgh 2014).

Wim Weymans holds degrees in history (MA), philosophy (PhD) and political theory (MPhil) from the universities of Cambridge and Leuven, Belgium. He is currently a Guest Professor at the Law Faculty of the University of Antwerp (UA). Before that he was a Visiting Scholar at the Minda de Gunzburg Center for European Studies (CES) (Harvard University), *Chercheur Invité* at Sciences Po (Paris), Postdoctoral Fellow at The Research Foundation – Flanders (FWO), Fulbright scholar at UC Berkeley and Visiting Scholar at NYU's Remarque Institute. From 2008 to 2009 he was an Adjunct Assistant Professor at Columbia University, teaching courses in the human rights program. He is chiefly interested in French social, historical and political thought post-1968. He has published on the crisis of political representation, on republicanism and political freedom and on ways to redefine the university "beyond the market and tradition." He has also published on concrete attempts to turn internationalist ideals (such as human rights or the creation of a European Research Area) into reality.

Marianne Windsperger holds an MA in Comparative Literature and Romance Languages. She currently works as a pre-doc assistant at the Department of German Language Studies at the University of Vienna. In her dissertation project, she examines the multiple ways in which contemporary Jewish-American authors refer to their family's ancestral homeland in Eastern Europe. As a junior researcher she is involved in the trans-disciplinary research platform "Mobile Cultures and Societies. Interdisciplinary Studies on Transnational Formations" at the University of Vienna. Her dissertation research has been funded so far by the FWF Austrian Science Fonds (2010–2013), the University of Vienna (2011, 2014), and the Austrian Ministry of Science and Research (Marietta-Blau-Fellowship, 2012).

Chantal Zabus holds the "Institut universitaire de France" (IUF) Chair of Comparative Postcolonial Literatures and Gender Studies at the University Paris 13-Sorbonne-Paris-Cité, France. She is the author of *Out in Africa: Same-Sex Desire in Sub-Saharan Literatures and Cultures* (Boydell & Brewer / James Currey, 2013); *Between Rites and Rights: Excision in Women's Experiential Texts and Human*

Contexts (Stanford UP, 2007); *The African Palimpsest* (Rodopi, 1991; rpt. 2007); and *Tempests after Shakespeare* (Palgrave, 2002). She has also edited *Le Secret: Motif et moteur de la littérature* (with Jacques Derrida, Louvain, 1999); *Changements au féminin en Afrique noire: Littérature et Anthropologie* (L'Harmattan, 2000; Italian transl. 2003); *Fearful Symmetries: Essays and Testimonies on Excision and Circumcision* (Rodopi, 2009); *Colonization or Globalization? Postcolonial Explorations of Imperial Expansion* (with Silvia Nagy-Zekmi) (Lexington Books, 2010); *Perennial Empires: Postcolonial, Transnational and Literary Perspectives*, also co-edited with Silvia Nagy-Zekmi (Cambria Press, NY, 2011); and *Transgender Experience: Place, Ethnicity and Visibility* (with David Coad) (Routledge, 2014). Her edited volume *The Future of Postcolonial studies* was released by Routledge in 2015. She is the Editor-in-Chief of *Postcolonial Text* (www.postcolonial.org); her personal website can be accessed at <www.zabus.eu>.

Index

www.ingramcontent.com/pod-product-compliance
Lightning Source LLC
Chambersburg PA
CBHW051946270326
41929CB00015B/2548

* 9 7 8 3 1 1 0 5 7 7 8 1 5 *